# An Introduction to Behavioral Economics

# Praise for the third edition of *An Introduction to Behavioral Economics*

'With new material on neuroeconomics, as well as applications to current political and economic develop-ments such as Brexit in the UK and polarization in the US, the third edition of *An Introduction to Behavioral Economics* expands, and brings up to date, this superb introduction to the field of behavioral economics. With their unique and interesting perspective, and engaging writing, the authors help readers share in the excitement of those currently working in the field.' – **George Loewenstein**, *Carnegie Mellon University, USA*

'*An Introduction to Behavioral Economics,* by Nick Wilkinson and Matthias Klaes, is an excellent introduction to behavioural economics from the perspective of economic psychology and the deter-minants of choice behaviour, building on the tradition established by Daniel Kahneman and Amos Tversky. Moreover, Wilkinson and Klaes present behavioural economics in the context of economic theory thereby linking behavioural economic insights with contemporary economic theory. They also pay some attention to the sociology of choice which further enriches their presentation and insights. This is definitely a book that should be read by anyone interested in behavioural economics.' – **Morris Altman**, *The University of Newcastle, Australia*

'A thoroughly updated third edition of this popular textbook which covers cutting-edge behavioral econom-ics in a pleasingly engaging style. Students will appreciate the structure of chapters: after the Introduction to the field section, including the nature of behavioural economics and methodology, the Foundations section provides the fundamental groundwork, followed by Intertemporal Choice, and then Strategic Interaction, including game theory and social preferences, before the Conclusion ties everything together and considers the future of the field. Mathematics is used sparingly, and there are thoughtful pedagogic features that will aid learning. The breadth of coverage is impressive, ranging from evolutionary approaches, biology and neu-roeconomics, to recent political events in the UK (Brexit) and elsewhere (e.g., the election of Donald Trump in the USA). This excellent textbook should inform and inspire students.' – **Philip J. Corr**, *City, University of London, UK*

'The third edition provides a superbly accessible introduction to behavioural economics, whilst ensuring a detailed examination of the theories and research studies underpinning them. The text remains at the forefront of theoretical development, whilst providing topical and engaging applications to hold students' attention.' – **Piers Thompson**, *Nottingham Trent University, UK*

'This new edition of Wilkinson and Klaes' excellent text is most welcome given my students' very positive appraisal of the previous edition. The book's strengths are its comprehensiveness, open approach to the issues behavioral economics raise, and methodology emphasis. Strongly recommended for advanced under-graduate and beginning graduate students.' – **John B. Davis**, *Marquette University, USA, and University of Amsterdam, The Netherlands*

'By now *An Introduction to Behavioral Economics* is firmly established in the field of behavioral economics. It continues to be a premier textbook despite the recent appearance of several competitors. The academic rigor and depth of coverage are unmatched. It is also an invaluable reference for which you will reach again and again. The reader will particularly appreciate the discussions of the bridges between behavioral economics, experimental economics, neuroeconomics, and psychology. Concise and comprehensive, a must-have for any behavioral economics scholar.' – **Natalia V. Czap**, *University of Michigan-Dearborn, USA*

Nick Wilkinson **and Matthias Klaes**

# An Introduction to Behavioral Economics

**THIRD EDITION**

First edition published 2007
Second edition published 2012
This edition published 2018 by
RED GLOBE PRESS

Red Globe Press in the UK is an imprint of Springer Nature Limited,
registered in England, company number 785998, of 4 Crinan Street,
London, N1 9XW.

Red Globe Press® is a registered trademark in the United States,
the United Kingdom, Europe and other countries.

ISBN 978–1–137–52412–6 paperback

A catalogue record for this book is available from the British Library.

A catalog record for this book is available from the Library of Congress.

# Brief Contents

# Detailed Table of Contents

# PART V  CONCLUSION

# List of Figures

# List of Tables

# Preface

The first two editions of this book started out by saying that there should not really need to be a book entitled 'Behavioral Economics'. The same still applies some ten years later. All  economics is behavioral in the sense of examining how people choose to act and allocate resources in different types of situation. However, over the last three decades the standard model of economic rationality, based largely on the assumption of expected utility maximization, has come under increasing criticism from both outside and inside the economics profession. The global financial crisis of 2008–2010 exacerbated this situation. It prominently drew attention to a large number of empirical anomalies that the standard model fails to explain; the timing of the second edition was such that these could be examined, and the third edition continues that examination in more detail. However, the political events of 2016, specifically the Trump victory in the USA and Brexit in the UK, may offer us an even greater source of anomalies than the financial crisis. Certainly the majority of experts found themselves left footed by either political event, showing a significant misunderstanding of voters' behavior in terms of their values and beliefs. In this edition therefore, we will extend our discussions and examples to these political events too, in the light of behavioral economics.

Behavioral economics, as we understand it, attempts to answer many of the criticisms of the mainstream of economic thought by taking a broader approach to studying economic phenomena. It is behavioral in the sense that it combines the approaches of all the behavioral sciences, in particular economics, psychology, sociology and biology. This is currently not easy to do, since these disciplines have traditionally adopted different and in many ways conflicting approaches. It is the essential philosophy of our book that economics is 'at its best' when it takes a cross-disciplinary approach.

However, behavioral economics and 'mainstream economics' have both moved on over the last ten years. In previous editions the recurrent theme in the text was to draw comparisons between theories and predictions in behavioral economics with those of a 'standard economic model' or SEM. This has now become both misleading and impractical, since the latter model is continuously changing and has now incorporated some of the concepts that have been previously regarded as 'behavioral'. Therefore, rather than comparing the current state of behavioral economics with an ambiguous and moving target, we have now found a different approach preferable, that proceeds from comparison with what we introduce as the neoclassical model (NM). While outdated in many respects, the NM has the virtue of being a static benchmark. Not only does this add methodological consistency to our discussion, it also achieves greater pedagogical clarity by offering the student of behavioral economics a set of coordinates within which to locate the increasing range of models and frameworks that can now found across the economic mainstream and the various behavioral approaches.

We discuss these changing terms of reference in detail in the first chapter. Looking forward, there may come a time in the not-too-distant future when all behavioral aspects are incorporated into a new 'standard model', in which case 'the field of behavioral economics will disappear', as Thaler (2015) states in the last paragraph of his book *Misbehaving*.

Many undergraduate students are now starting to study aspects of behavioral economics. This book is particularly appropriate for students in the third or fourth years of undergraduate study, or in a postgraduate program, once they have become familiar with the standard economics curriculum, its assumptions and methods, and to some extent its limitations. For postgraduate students in particular the text should serve as a foundation of linked themes and materials, providing a jumping-off point for further reading of the original papers on which the book is based.

The objectives of the text remain essentially the same as with the first two editions, but are somewhat modified in terms of the replacement of the term 'standard model' with 'neoclassical model' that we have already mentioned:

1   Present the principles and methods of behavioral economics in a logical and amenable manner, comparing and contrasting them with those of the NM.
2   Illustrate how behavioral models represent an improved modification and refinement of the NM in terms of power of explanation and prediction, using a wide variety of empirical examples from both observational and experimental studies.
3   Provide a critical examination of the rapidly growing literature in behavioral economics.
4   Explain the policy implications of behavioral economics, particularly when these differ from those of the NM.
5   Provide a coherent psychological framework underpinning the findings of behavioral economics.
6   Indicate the way forward for the subject, in terms of future challenges and areas meriting further research.

It should not be inferred from this that there is a single behavioral model that has universal acceptance. Within particular areas, like intertemporal choice and social preferences, there is often a profusion of models. Indeed, one main criticism of behavioral economics has been that there is an excessive number of different models, many of which may apply in a given situation. However, this issue also arises in different guises with 'mainstream' approaches as well, notably in the context of solution concepts in game theory, or more generally in response to 'ad hoc' model specifications in applied areas such as industrial organization or the theory of the firm. Economics has a common analytical language but it has certainly moved away from grand unifying frameworks of analysis such as general equilibrium theory once promised to offer.

As stated above, the central theme of the book is that it is intended to be highly cross-disciplinary in nature. Any book on behavioral aspects must of course involve psychology, but it is important to consider other areas too, notably evolutionary psychology and neuroscience, social psychology and sociology.

Many economists and psychologists reject the theories of evolutionary psychology as being largely speculative. They are frequently dismissed in the social sciences as being 'just-so' stories, meaning that they are not true scientific theories in terms of proposing testable hypotheses. This view is caused by two main factors: (1) it is impossible by definition to perform experiments on the past; and (2) the past record of facts is highly incomplete. But on a closer look, there is considerable evidence in support of key tenets of evolutionary psychology. Furthermore, the tendency of many economists to limit explanations to economic phenomena is even more unsatisfactory as far as 'just-so' stories are concerned. For example, many readers would not be satisfied with the explanations that people tend to succumb to temptation because they have short time horizons in decision-making, and that they make bad decisions when they are angry. These can also be regarded as 'just-so' stories because they both beg the questions regarding *why* people have short time horizons, and *why* we have seemingly harmful emotional responses like anger.

The fast-developing area of neuroscience can also be of great benefit to economics. The conjunction of the two disciplines has led to the birth of neuroeconomics. Economists have traditionally relied on 'revealed preference', meaning choice, in market behavior to develop their theories, but this approach has significant limitations. We will examine situations where choice and preference do not coincide, and where intertemporal choice and framing effects cause preference reversals. These anomalies have important welfare implications. Cognitive neuroscience is offering fresh insights into the neurological basis of individual behavior. We now know, for example, that different types of cost and benefit are processed in different areas of the brain, and that both altruistic and spiteful behavior, in the form of punishment, give pleasure, in spite of what the doer might say about their motivation. Current research in neuroscience is now connecting to economic decision making more than in the past, and although neuroeconomics, like evolutionary psychology, has attracted some strong criticism from within the economics profession, it is a fast expanding field. We feel that students of behavioral economics will benefit from studying the underlying debates to sharpen their understanding of the evidence base and methodological basis of behavioral frameworks of analysis.

This edition of the text has considerably expanded the second edition, with some 35,000 words of new material. Most of the chapters have undergone detailed revision, although the structure of the text and the chapter titles are largely unchanged. The only chapter title to have changed is Chapter 4, which was titled 'Beliefs, heuristics and biases', and is now titled 'Beliefs and expectations'. The reason for the change is that heuristics and biases are also covered in Chapter 3, in the context of values, preferences and choices. The expansion of the text has been caused by several factors: (1) there has been a large amount of relevant research over the last five years, presenting new models to be tested; (2) there has also been much research and testing of earlier models with new evidence; and (3) new and important global issues have arisen where behavioral economics can shed much light.

In summary, the intention is to provide a book which is comprehensive, rigorous and up to date in terms of reviewing the latest developments in the field of behavioral economics; cross-disciplinary in approach; and user-friendly in terms of exposition, discussing a large number of examples and case studies to which the average reader can relate. Typically three case studies are included at the end of each chapter, with questions reviewing the relevant material.

It is also appropriate here to give a note of apology: readers may find some repetitiveness in the materials in the various chapters. We offer the following excuses. Some readers or instructors may wish to skip certain chapters, like the more technical chapter on game theory. Also, many of the themes in different chapters are linked, with the features of prospect theory and mental accounting in particular applying in many different areas. As a final point, it seems appropriate to hammer home certain points of behavioral analysis, especially when these are at variance with other commonly held theories or beliefs.

Lastly, some words of thanks are in order regarding several people who have helped to improve this edition of the book. Matthew Rablen, from Brunel University, invited the first author to share the teaching of a course in behavioral economics, and discussions with him have aided various aspects, notably the mathematical exposition in the text. The students there, and at other institutions, have also made various suggestions and contributions. This third edition has also benefited greatly from feedback by colleagues who have used the book in class. In particular, we would like to thank Bertie du Plessis, who invited the first author to present some workshops on the theme 'What's with the human animal?' in Cape Town, South Africa, in October 2015. This led to the sharpening and refinement of various ideas relating to preferences and attitudes to risk. Finally, we would like to thank our anonymous reviewers for their comments and suggestions, which have allowed us to improve the text in many respects. Of course, any remaining inaccuracies and oversights are the sole responsibility of the authors.

# Acknowledgments

The following rights holders kindly granted permission to reprint the material that appears in the book:

## Scientific American

For Figure 4.1. From: Asch, S.E. (1955). Opinions and Social Pressure. *Scientific American*, November, 193(5).

## Cambridge University Press

For Table 5.1. From: Camerer, C.F. (2000). "Prospect theory in the wild: Evidence from the field". In D. Kahneman and A. Tversky (Eds), *Choices, Values, and Frames*.

## Springer

For the lottery examples on p.158 and p.199. From Tversky A. and Kahneman D. (1989). "Rational Choice and the Framing of Decisions". In: Karpak, B. and Zionts, S. (eds) Multiple Criteria Decision Making and Risk Analysis Using Microcomputers. NATO ASI Series (Series F: Computer and Systems Sciences) vol. 56.

## Elsevier

For Table 5.8. From: Birnbaum, M.H. (2004). "Causes of Allais common consequence paradoxes: An experimental dissection", *Journal of Mathematical Psychology*, 48(2).

## The American Economic Association

For Table 7.1. From: Frederick, S., Loewenstein, G. and O'Donoghue, T. (2002). "Time discounting and time preference: A critical review". *Journal of Economic Literature*, XL, June.

For Figure 10.7. From: Fehr, E., and Gächter, S. (2001). "Fairness and retaliation: The Economics of Reciprocity". *Journal of Economic Perspectives*, 14(3).

## Princeton University Press

For Table 9.10. From: Camerer, C.F. (2003). *Behavioral Game Theory*.

We should also like to thank the following authors for granting personal permission to reproduce their work: Ernst Fehr, Shane Frederick, Simon Gächter, George Loewenstein and Ted O'Donoghue.

# PART · I

# Introduction

# CHAPTER · 1

## Nature of Behavioral Economics

2016 was a calamitous year for experts and their opinions. Two events happened that defied these opinions and have caused chaos and volatility in various markets all over the world. In June the Brexit referendum in the UK caught most experts, including economists, by surprise. Many of them had publicly expressed views that, in their assessment of evidence, lent support to a Remain position. The chairman of the Bank of England, Mark Carney, was one of many to have done this, in terms of forecasting the effects on the UK economy of leaving the EU. Various other institutions, including the International Monetary Fund and the European Central Bank, had made similar statements, thereby supporting the stance of the UK prime minister and chancellor. Michael Gove, a prominent supporter of Brexit, responded by saying 'We have had enough of experts'.

Donald Trump's victory in the US election in November came as even more of a surprise to many. At the beginning of the year he was not even expected to feature well in the election primaries, let alone be a viable candidate for president. In the run-up to the election and during the pre-election debates he stumbled repeatedly, continually making factual errors and gaffes. Not least, he received highly unfavorable publicity regarding his attitudes and behavior towards women. At the date of the election he had 75 lawsuits outstanding against him and his business concerns. Trump garnered many votes from immigrants, Muslims and other minorities, women, and unionized workers, in spite of the fact that in previous months he had behaved or advocated policies against their interests. One commentator likened the situation to turkeys voting for Christmas.

Following these two history-changing events, the political climate in Europe is undergoing significant change. Some of the underlying developments were evident before 2016, such as the rise of xenophobic far-right, or alt-right, parties, but this trend has gathered considerable momentum since then. For many years, questions of European integration seemed to turn on economic issues: trade liberalization, convergence to common standards, and monetary union, to name just some of the more prominent ones. What we are seeing since 2016, however, is the return of fundamental political concerns regarding the European Union, with many expecting significant changes in the political and economic map of Europe over the coming years.

The issues raised by Brexit and the Trump victory reach beyond the traditional domain of economics, certainly if seen through the eyes of the economic mainstream. And yet, many of the concerns that people were voting on were economic in nature: trade, jobs and social policy, and increasing income inequalities in particular. At the heart of all this lies a fundamental question which mainstream economics struggles to answer:

> Why did voters behave the way they did in both the US and the UK, seeming to vote against their own interests?

We will argue that this question can only be answered by applying the principles of behavioral economics, which involves an interdisciplinary approach. Economists have spent too much time focusing on what people do and trying to understand empirical patterns of behavior through analyses that, at their heart, lack a behavioral approach, making implicit assumptions related to rationality. In doing so, they have avoided examining why people do what they do. Only by considering the 'why' question, which means incorporating psychology and related disciplines, can we develop a deeper understanding of economic behavior that at first sight appears irrational and beyond the remit of economic analysis. As we will see, much of our day-to-day behavior proceeds along lines quite different from those of a putative *homo oeconomicus*. It is only through an appreciation of this richer perspective on economic behavior that we can hope to arrive at better predictions.

## 1.1   Behavioral economics and the standard model

*What is behavioral economics?*

Economic phenomena relate to any aspect of human behavior that involves the allocation of scarce resources; thus economics is very wide-ranging in its subject area. For example, all of the following can be described as economic phenomena, although they may also of course involve other disciplines of study: searching for a future spouse on the internet, watching a documentary on television, making a charitable donation, giving a lift to one's neighbor in order to make it easier to ask them for a favor later, deciding to take a nap rather than mow the lawn, teaching one's child to play tennis, and going to church.

Economics, like any other social science, is concerned with developing theories whose ultimate aim it is to help us better understand the world we live in. Economic theories attempt to describe and explain relationships between economic phenomena. In order to do this they need to proceed on the basis of a number of assumptions or premises. Sometimes these assumptions are made explicit, but in many cases they are implicit, and it is often important to tease out these implicit assumptions: if a theory proves to be inaccurate in its empirical implications this tells us that if we have deduced these implications correctly from the underlying assumptions of the theory, we should query those themselves.

This is where behavioral economics is relevant. As Camerer and Loewenstein (2004, p. 3) succinctly put it:

> Behavioral economics increases the explanatory power of economics by providing it with more realistic psychological foundations.

Hence, behavioral economics is not seeking to replace the standard framework of analysis. It seeks to add to this framework:

> It is important to emphasize that the behavioral economics approach *extends* rational choice and equilibrium models; it does not advocate abandoning these models entirely. (Ho, Lim and Camerer, 2006, p. 308)

In order to understand these claims, and also to understand various critiques of behavioral economics, we must examine the major assumptions underlying the standard model that Ho, Lim and Camerer allude to in the quotation above, and then consider various important and widespread phenomena where this model has run into some difficulty to explain – which are frequently referred to as anomalies.

We will also see that unrealistic assumptions as such may still yield useful empirical insights. It is difficult to conceive of economic theories that are not built on some kind of abstraction from the rich complexity of economic phenomena. This means that there will always be a trade-off situation between highly abstract but general behavioral assumptions, such as they can be found in the standard model, and empirically better grounded yet often quite context-specific assumptions as we find them in behavioral economics, an issue that was recognized as far back as 1991:

> It is in the nature of economic anomalies that they violate standard theory.
> The next question is what to do about it. In many cases there is no obvious way to amend the theory to fit the facts, either because too little is known, or because the changes would greatly increase the complexity of the theory and reduce its predictive yield. (Kahneman et al., 1991, p. 205)

## *Standard models and economics*

The term 'standard model' has been used in the previous two paragraphs to indicate a contrast between behavioral economics and what might be called 'mainstream' economics. However, as mentioned in the preface, this distinction has been losing its validity over recent years, particularly since the financial crisis in 2007. In order to understand this dynamic it is really necessary to consider 'standard models' in other areas of science. Perhaps the most fundamental, at least in a reductionist sense, is the standard model of particle physics, which seeks to describe and explain the elementary particles and forces in the universe. This theory coalesced in the 1970s and has had great success in predicting the existence of new particles, notably the Higgs boson in 2012. However, it is acknowledged that the theory is incomplete, since it does not give an account of gravity, nor does it account for either dark matter or dark energy, which cosmologists estimate constitute about 96% of the mass-energy in the universe. As a result, some might say this means that the 'standard' theory is highly incomplete. Cosmologists have developed the model further in the 1990s, referring to a lambda-CDM model, which does take into account dark matter and dark energy, but this is also incomplete and is more speculative.

Both of the above models have certain aspects in common with what has been called the standard economic model, but there are some differences also. Both have coalesced into a generally accepted standard model much more recently, and for that reason can be claimed to have fewer anomalies. As a consequence scientists expect further observations to result in minor modifications of the models rather than a drastic overhaul. However, caution is needed here, since physicists had the same attitude at the end of the nineteenth century, believing classical physics was more or less complete, and then came the revolutions of quantum mechanics and general relativity which dramatically altered the previous 'standard model'.

Perhaps the 'standard model' closest to economics is in evolutionary biology, with the neo-Darwinian synthesis. As in economics, the main foundation was laid in the nineteenth century, but fundamental modifications to the model were made in the twentieth century to take into account discoveries in genetics, and then molecular biology. It wasn't until the discovery of DNA in 1953 that this model moved close to being regarded complete. It can be claimed that the 'modern synthesis' has fewer anomalies than most other standard models in the sciences, and again biologists expect future observations to only yield minor modifications. Nevertheless, alternative models, most recently emerging from the so-called Evo-Devo literature in evolutionary biology, for example, out of attempts to better account for the morphogenetic development of organisms, proceed from different assumptions and the underlying debates are far from resolved. This aspect of theory development is discussed further in the next chapter.

Where does this all leave us as far as any standard model in economics is concerned? As we will see in the following section, the standard model in economics has its intellectual origins in the neoclassical tradition of economic thought, and is therefore more appropriately referred to as the neoclassical model (NM). By the end of the 1970s it was clear that there were numerous fundamental anomalies in this model, and these accounted for the emergence of behavioral economics. For some decades there was an uneasy tension in the economics discipline, with behavioral economics being regarded as an unruly offshoot from the mainstream, consisting of a number of often conflicting and ad hoc hypotheses, with no coherent body of theory. This situation has gradually changed since the millennium, with more behavioral aspects becoming incorporated into the mainstream of the discipline. As mentioned in the preface, this may ultimately lead to the death of behavioral economics, in terms of its current status as a collection of separate approaches: if its main precepts all become absorbed into a revised standard model that is commonly accepted then the distinction will cease to be meaningful. For this reason we regard it now preferable to benchmark behavioral economics against a static 'neoclassical model' rather than against a dynamic, constantly changing 'standard model'.

In many ways, debates in economics on the strengths and weaknesses of a standard model are debates on useful and less useful ways of arriving at economic concepts and theories through abstraction from concrete phenomena. Methodological considerations are thus at the heart of many debates in behavioral economics, and the best starting point for understanding these debates is to look at some of the methodological foundations of economic rationality and how it has been captured with the NM.

## *Economic rationality*

The standard model of rationality in the neoclassical tradition of economics is essentially a decision-making model, which claims to be both **descriptive** and **normative**. This means that the model is supposed to both accurately describe how people behave, and to prescribe how they should behave to achieve a certain given objective.

Unfortunately the term normative is used in two main different senses by economists, causing confusion. Sometimes it is used in the sense of being opposite to positive. **Positive statements** relate to descriptions involving factual information. Such statements can be judged to be correct or incorrect, often with a margin of error, based on empirical observation. **Normative statements** in this context relate to value judgments, which are necessarily subjective, and cannot be judged to be correct or incorrect empirically. An example is Statement 1:

**Statement 1**    It is not fair that Firm A pays its workers such a low wage.

Such statements often include the words 'ought' or 'should'; for example, we might modify the above statement by saying:

**Statement 2**    Firm A ought to pay its workers a higher wage.

However, care must be exercised here, because statements including these words are not always normative in the sense of involving a value judgment. An example is:

**Statement 3**    Firm A ought to pay its workers a higher wage if it wants to maximize profit.

Statement 3 does not involve a value judgment, and can be evaluated empirically. Of course one can question the social value of profit, but that is a separate issue.

Confusion can arise because the last type of statement is also often referred to as normative. In this context the term normative is interpreted as a statement that refers to behavior *as it should be* if it were to accomplish goals in an optimal way, in contrast to a descriptive statement that describes behavior *as it actually is*.

It is perhaps preferable to label it as prescriptive, as opposed to descriptive. **Prescriptive statements** can be considered as policy implications, for individuals, firms or governments, in terms of being guides to behavior, *assuming* a particular objective or set of values. Thus such statements, or 'normative theories' as they are often referred to, tend to involve some kind of optimization. A fundamental example is the theory of expected utility maximization. Prescriptive statements in the above sense always follow logically from descriptive statements; for example, Statement 3 can be restated as follows:

**Statement 4**    In Firm A's situation a higher wage will maximize profit.

A more precise prescription would determine the specific level of wage that would maximize profit. Thus such prescriptive statements can also always be evaluated empirically.

Normative, in the sense of prescriptive, statements have various sources of appeal to social scientists (Niv and Montague, 2008):

- Throughout evolutionary history animal behavior has been shaped and constrained by its influence on fitness, so a reasonable starting point for theory or model development is to view a particular behavior as an optimal or near-optimal adaptation to some set of problems (Kacelnik, 1997).
- Discrepancies between observed behavior and the predictions of normative models are often illuminating. They can shed light on the neural and informational constraints under which animals make decisions, relating to Simon's concept of bounded rationality, leading to heuristics and biases. Alternatively, they may suggest that animals are in fact optimizing something other than what the model assumed.
- Treating behavior as optimal allows for the generation of computationally explicit hypotheses that are directly testable. A simple example is the marginal cost equals marginal revenue rule for profit maximization.

When referring to normative statements as value judgments, it should be noted that sciences in general, including social sciences like economics, are not in any privileged position in terms of making such statements. The privilege which scientists enjoy is that they are better able to understand the factual implications of value judgments. Thus while an economist may not have any superior 'moral authority' in judging whether Firm A is acting fairly, she may be able to point out that its existing low-wage strategy is likely to cause more labor unrest, higher labor turnover, and higher recruiting and training costs.

As far as this book is concerned our interest is not the validity of normative statements as value judgments but the question *why* people make certain value judgments; this is a psychological issue that has important policy implications in the prescriptive sense. We will also see that the standard model is essentially a normative model in this prescriptive sense, while behavioral approaches are largely based on descriptive models. Indeed, Tversky and Kahneman (1986) claim that no theory of choice can be both normatively adequate and descriptively accurate.

Take the example of a game of tic-tac-toe ('noughts and crosses'), where two players compete on a 3-by-3 grid to first succeed in placing three of their own marks in a straight line. As is well known, in this game best play from each player results in a draw. In other words, there exists a strategy for each player that ensures that they will not lose regardless of how their opponent plays (and if their opponent makes a mistake it will allow them to win). Call this their rational strategy. It is clear that if they seek to win they should adopt this strategy. Likewise, assuming that they know this and behave accordingly, this strategy will accurately account for their moves in the game.

Most situations faced by economic actors are more complex than a game of tic-tac-toe. A purely rational decision model will not account for how most individuals react in a large range of situations. If we still want to understand and explain their choices, what we need is not a model that is able to explain moves along the best-response strategy path but along the actual-response strategy path which in many instances could be bettered. In this sense, individuals appear to act irrationally to the extent that they deviate from the best-response path.

But what do we mean by 'rational' here? The terms 'rationality', and its opposite, 'irrationality', are used extensively in economics, and particularly in connection with behavioral economics. It is in many ways a fundamental assumption underlying the whole of the discipline. Indeed many people think of behavioral economics as being an approach to understanding why people act irrationally. Dan Ariely for example has written extensively in this way about the subject in his popular books *Predictably Irrational* (2008) and *The Upside of Irrationality* (2010). In the context of our game of tic-tac-toe, players knowingly deciding against the adoption of the best-response strategy would act irrationally in the sense that they would not choose the means best suited to further their end of seeking to win the game. But this approach to economic behavior is still limited by reducing behavior that appears unrecognizable within the confines of strict economic rationality to an aberration from the standards of rational choice, rather than approaching it as valid phenomena in its own right.

It is important to understand that the term 'rationality' is used in many different senses, depending on the discipline of the user of the term; even within the discipline of economics there are different meanings. When we refer to people acting rationally in the everyday sense we usually mean that they are using reason. This kind of action is often contrasted with people being prompted either by emotional factors or by unconscious instinct. However, economists have tended to regard this interpretation of rationality as too broad and imprecise.

Instead, they have started out from a tightly specified means-end framework of rational decision making, as a particular interpretation of instrumental rationality. In that framework, individuals are assumed to entertain preferences over a set of available courses of action and act such as to realize their most preferred outcome. At the heart of this version of the NM lie several basic assumptions regarding the nature of these preferences:

**Completeness**    Individuals entertain a preference ordering across all alternative courses of action that they face.

**Transitivity**    Individuals make consistent choices, in the sense that if A is preferred to B, and B is preferred to C, then a rational individual will prefer A to C.

These two axioms together ensure that individuals will be able to pick at least one most preferred course of action out of the various alternatives they face. Both axioms may be relaxed in certain ways while it will still be possible to meaningfully talk of instrumentally rational choice. But for the most part, economists have added stronger assumptions in addition to these rationality axioms, either to simplify technical treatment, or sometimes just out of tradition. Two important additional assumptions, sometimes referred to as the 'economic' assumptions that are added to the two rationality axioms above, are that more of an economic good is preferred to less of it ('monotonicity'), and that averages are preferred to extremes ('convexity').

However, this simple model of economic rationality is only applicable to decisions under certainty, such that outcomes are unambiguously tied to actions. As soon as one allows for uncertain outcomes, more complex frameworks of analysis become necessary, based on mathematical theories of uncertainty such as probability theory. The standard NM for these contexts is usually augmented by the twin assumptions of expected utility maximization and Bayesian probability estimation. Further assumptions are necessary to adapt the model to decision-making stretching over a period of time into the future, notably assumptions regarding time preference and discounting of future horizons.

But even this framework is not yet sufficiently general for all decision contexts studied by economists. Uncertainty may not just be an exogenous factor, in the sense of being given independently of the decision taken. You may for example decide to act on a weather forecast predicting sunshine with 90% probability by leaving your umbrella at home. Unless you are subject to superstitious beliefs, you would not accept that this decision has any effect on whether it will actually rain in the end or not.

Many economic problems are subject to a different kind of uncertainty still that is endogenous to the situation studied. This is behavioral uncertainty that arises from the mutual dependencies involved in the strategic interaction of two or more individuals. Assume you are walking down a narrow lane and find yourself walking towards another individual heading into the opposite direction. Whether or not you will brush coats with that individual will not just depend on your own actions but also on how the other side behaves. Economists have used a strong assumption known as the common knowledge assumption, as a further augmentation of the standard model. This is a stricter assumption, whereby it is not sufficient for each person or player to be rational, they must also know that all other players are rational, and that all other players know that all other players are rational … ad infinitum.

Finally, some economists hold the view that the rationality of individual behavior should be judged not on the level of the individual but on the level of systemic outcomes. This tends to be the view of Vernon Smith, who has been particularly concerned with examining the predictions of economic rationality in terms of long-run market equilibria. Smith does not accept the norms of the standard model in terms of individual behavior, and believes that individuals can violate these norms and still act rationally according to his view of rationality. This view equates rationality with the end results of the decision-making process as far as market efficiency is concerned. For Smith, if markets are efficient, for example in terms of market clearing, then this is evidence that individuals are rational.

On the other hand, by other definitions of rationality, people may act rationally and the predictions of the standard model may prove incorrect; this tends to be the view of Kahneman and Tversky, whose approach is discussed in detail in Chapter 5. Unlike Smith, Kahneman and Tversky do accept the norms of the NM as a benchmark for judging rationality. By these standards they claim that individuals frequently act irrationally. However, they also argue that the systematic errors and biases that they find in their empirical studies do not necessarily constitute irrational behavior. We see here a theme emerging that will run through the other chapters of this book, by which the NM of economic rationality, under which a considerable amount of frequently observable behavior would have to be classed as irrational, gives way to alternative conceptions of rationality that more properly account for observed behavior.

At one extreme we have a view, which was perhaps first formulated by Ludwig von Mises (1949), that any action must by definition be rational. This approach essentially defines rationality in terms of revealed preference. If we perform a certain act it must be because we have a preference for doing so; if we did not have such a preference then we would not perform the act. Associated with this approach is the view that 'a pronouncement of irrational choice might seem to imply nothing more than our ignorance about another's private hedonic priorities … individual tastes are not a matter for dispute, nor can they be deemed rational or irrational' (Berridge, 2001, p. 17). The problem with such an approach is that it obscures the important factors involved in terms of the determination of revealed preference, and therefore, while it is a coherent view, it is not very useful in terms of aiding analysis and understanding since it remains consistent at the price of becoming a tautology.

Similar to the above view is the argument that evolution has necessarily produced organisms that form true beliefs and that reason rationally (Fodor, 1975; Dennett, 1984). However, this view has been much criticized as misunderstanding the role of natural selection in the evolutionary process. Most evolutionary biologists agree that natural selection does not guarantee that rational beings will evolve, or even intelligent beings for that matter. Indeed, one of the ironies of many studies carried out with animals is that their behavior is often more 'rational' according to the criteria of the NM than human behavior. Thus woodpeckers, ducks, pigeons and rats tend to behave in a manner predicted by expected utility theory, while chimpanzees behave more rationally in ultimatum games than humans (Jensen, Call and Tomasello, 2007).

*Behavioral perspectives on economic rationality*

Psychologists tend to take a different approach to rationality. For example, according to Baumeister (2001): 'A rational being should *pursue enlightened self-interest*.' This definition draws attention to three crucial concepts: 'pursue', 'enlightened' and 'self-interest'. However, it is only a starting point, since all of these concepts need further examination.

First, the description 'enlightened' implies that an individual has perfect knowledge, something that is obviously not realistic. Sometimes the term 'long-run self-interest' is employed, which is definitely more useful, since we will observe many instances of conflicts between short-run and long-run considerations. However, an even more useful qualification in this context is the term 'perceived self-interest'. Many behavioral economists take the view that if we misjudge what is in our self-interest then this is not a failure of rationality; it may not even be a failure of 'bounded rationality', as we will explain in the next section. There may be many reasons why we fail to judge what is in our 'self-interest' (leaving until later a discussion of how this term can or should be interpreted). We may have incomplete knowledge, or we may have cognitive failures in terms of the processing of information within given time constraints. These failures are often ascribed to 'bounded rationality', and behavior that fails to achieve self-interest because of bounded rationality is therefore not irrational according to this criterion.

We now need to focus on a second concept: is pursuing the same as maximizing? The NM is a normative model in the prescriptive sense of achieving optimality because it equates pursuing perceived self-interest with maximizing expected utility. Again the constraints of bounded rationality are relevant. The work of Kahneman and Tversky in particular concludes that people tend to take a **heuristic** approach to decision-making. The term 'heuristic' means that people use simple 'rules-of-thumb', often unconsciously, in order to make decisions when there is a lot of information involved, much uncertainty and a realistic time constraint. Thus we may have a personal rule always to pay by cash for purchases of less than $100, even if we have a credit card handy. Sometimes this can result in inconsistent or incoherent behavior, and may not maximize expected utility, at least in the short run, since it will lead to more time wasted going to ATMs to withdraw cash. What can be said at this stage is that bounded rationality is not concerned with optimality, or even suboptimality; the heuristics involved in the decision-making processes of bounded rationality are more related to '**satisficing**'.

What about cases where we misjudge what is in our self-interest even according to the more forgiving criterion of bounded rationality? Such instances tend to relate to the influence of 'self-serving' biases, discussed in Chapter 4. An often-quoted example of **self-serving bias** is the 'above average' effect: well over half of survey respondents typically rate themselves in the top 50% of drivers (Svenson, 1981), ethics (Baumhart, 1968), managerial prowess (Larwood and Whittaker, 1977), productivity (Cross, 1997) and health (Weinstein, 1980). Some economists and psychologists would claim that such acts are irrational.

We can now move on to the third concept; the term 'self-interest' also lends itself to different interpretations. Economists have traditionally measured this concept in terms of utility, where utility is a measure of subjective value. With the formalization of rational choice theory in economics, it assumed a technical shorthand for underlying preference orderings that obey the rationality axioms. The concept of self-interest causes confusion because it is often assumed that this excludes consideration of the interests or utilities of others. However, one does not have to be altruistic (another term that can be defined in many ways) to realize that a total lack of consideration of others is unlikely to further one's own interests in a social environment requiring cooperation. Thus behavioral economics often distinguishes between 'self-regarding' preferences and 'other-regarding' preferences; acting in one's self-interest involves a consideration of both types of preference, which can be combined in a single utility function for an individual agent.

There is another aspect that merits discussion in the context of rationality. Arguably, actions where no deliberation is involved, sometimes called instinctive, are neither rational nor irrational. These actions tend to occur on the spur of the moment, like ducking a flying object likely to cause harm. Such actions are sometimes referred to as **arational**. It has been argued that maybe 90% of our daily activities, like driving to work, doing housework, watching TV or going for a walk, are governed by subconscious brain processes. Even when we do sense that we are 'willing' an action this may be an incorrect assessment. Of particular relevance here are experiments carried out by Libet (et al. 1983, 1985, 1993). These showed that brain electrical activity occurred at a significant interval (about 300 milliseconds) before conscious willing of finger movements. There has been much speculation and criticism regarding Libet's research findings and their interpretation, in particular regarding the suggestion that our sensation of conscious will as a cause of action is an illusion (Wegner, 2002). Wegner and others hold the view that the sensation of will is not the real cause of our actions, but is merely an accompanying or following phenomenon, or **epiphenomenon** in philosophical terms.

The implication of this would be that many or indeed all of our actions may be arational in terms of not being caused by any kind of conscious deliberation. This is not to assert that conscious deliberation does not take place in many cases, but raises the possibility that, contrary to our intuitions, such deliberation merely accompanies events rather than causes them. Wilson, Lindsay and Schooler (2000) have proposed that we may have dual attitudes toward many things in our lives, one a rapid response and the other a more studied reaction that takes into account the context and our personal theory of what we ought to be feeling. Wegner (2002, p. 58) adds: 'The conscious attitude will only govern our responses when we have had time to consider the situation and get past the automatic reaction.'

The preceding discussion introduces another factor into the discussion of rationality: does rationality relate just to decision-making, involving choice and actions, or does it relate to attitudes and beliefs? In general, economists have tended to concentrate on decision-making and actions, while psychologists have often taken the view that, while decision-making involves deliberate choice, the formation of attitudes and beliefs may be beyond our conscious control, and therefore outside a discussion of rationality. If, as evidence like Libet's experiments suggests, our decisions involving action are also outside conscious control, then attitude and belief formation can be claimed to be arational in the same way.

This leads us to one other view of rationality that can be considered at this point. Sen (1990, p. 200) is perhaps the best-known proponent of this view, stating:

> Rationality may be seen as demanding something other than just consistency
> of choices between different subsets. It must, at least, demand cogent relations
> between aims and objectives actually entertained by the person and the choices
> that the person makes.

It may appear that this focus on the correlation between objectives and choices has the advantage that it no longer makes any assumptions regarding the nature of the objectives; these are simply taken as given. Sen thus considers the nature of our objectives to be outside the realm of rationality, on the grounds that people are concerned with more than well-being and happiness. The weakness in this view is that it takes an excessively narrow view of well-being. Our well-being does not just include material factors, it includes psychological aspects that relate to our emotions. Furthermore, these aspects are becoming easier to identify and measure using neural imaging. Neuroscience is now frequently able to tell us more about what 'makes us tick' than psychological introspection. In particular it reveals that many of the motives for our actions are permanently hidden from ourselves, because the neural processes involved are inaccessible to the parts of our brain that are responsible for conscious processing.

*Nature of the neoclassical model*

Economists generally try to eliminate the many ambiguities surrounding the notion of 'pursuing enlightened self-interest' by using the more precise and formal model of rational behavior described in the (augmented) NM. Although it may seem daunting at first, it will facilitate the exposition of the material throughout the book if we now consider a stylized version of the standard model, modified from Rabin (2002a), proceeding from the three components of rationality psychologically defined as above, and being covered in the rest of the book as described.

The reader should not be intimidated by the mathematical language of this model; it is designed to make it easier to understand, not more difficult. The expression of the NM in mathematical terms enables us to achieve three important objectives:

1    A concise description of the relevant factors affecting decision-making.
2    An illustration of the various components of the model that will be examined in the following chapters.
3    A general consideration of the assumptions underlying the model in terms of how they relate to the various components.

The model can be stated in the following terms:

**Individual $i$ at time $t = 0$ maximizes expected utility subject to a probability distribution $p(s)$ of the states of the world $s \in S$:**

$$\max_{x_i^t \in X_i} \quad \sum_{t=0}^{\infty} \delta^t \quad \sum_{s_t \in S_t} p(s_t)\, U(x_i^t \mid s_t). \tag{1.1}$$

The utility function $U(x \mid s)$ is defined over the payoff $x_i^t$ of individual $i$ and future utility is discounted with a (time-consistent) discount factor $\delta$.

We can now disaggregate equation (1.1) into four main components as follows:

$$\textbf{(1)} \quad \max_{x_i^t \in X_i} \qquad \textbf{(2)} \quad \sum_{t=0}^{\infty} \delta^t \qquad \textbf{(3)} \quad \sum_{s_t \in S_t} p(s_t) \qquad \textbf{(4)} \quad U(x_i^t \mid s_t).$$

The main assumptions underlying the NM can now be stated in terms of how they relate to these components:

• Economic agents are rational (1), (2), (3) and (4).
• Economic agents are motivated by expected utility maximization (1), (3) and (4).
• An agent's utility is governed by purely selfish concerns, in the narrow sense that it does not take into consideration the utility of others (4).
• Agents are Bayesian probability operators (3).
• Agents have consistent time preferences according to the discounted utility model (2).
• All income and assets are completely fungible (4).

We will examine the meaning and implications of these assumptions in detail in the relevant chapters, since in some cases this will merit a considerable amount of discussion. The various components of the NM, along with the chapters where each aspect is discussed, are outlined below:

1    Value formation (4) and choice (1): Chapters 3 and 10.
2    Belief formation (3): Chapter 4.

**3** Expected utility theory (EUT) (1), (3) and (4): Chapter 5.

**4** Discounting (2): Chapters 7 and 8.

At this point, in view of the abstract nature of the exposition of the NM above, it is useful to provide a simple example that will illustrate some of the above points, in particular the first, third and fourth components of the model. You are a new student of behavioral economics and you are considering what to drink before going to class. The canteen offers only coffee and beer. There are also two 'states of the world' as far as the class is concerned: it could be interesting or it could be boring. You believe from what you have heard that there is a probability of 0.8 that the class will be interesting and a probability of 0.2 that it will be boring (these are subjective 'Bayesian priors'). Table 1.1 shows the payoffs that result from either drink in either state of the world.

**Table 1.1** Decision-making in the neoclassical model (NM)

| Decision | State of the world | Probability | Payoff |
|----------|-------------------|-------------|--------|
| Coffee | interesting | 0.8 | 10 |
| | boring | 0.2 | 2 |
| Beer | interesting | 0.8 | 6 |
| | boring | 0.2 | 4 |

If the class is interesting it is a good idea to drink coffee beforehand in order to get the most benefit. However, if the lecture is boring, drinking beer is better than drinking coffee (it is assumed here), because then it allows the student to drift off to sleep which is better than staying awake and not getting any benefit from listening to the class. Therefore the optimal decision, which maximizes expected utility, depends on the probability estimates of the states of the world. The student should verify that the expected payoff or utility of drinking coffee is 8.4, while the expected utility of drinking beer is 5.6. Thus the best decision in this situation is to drink coffee. However, if the probabilities were reversed, so that it was estimated that the probability of an interesting class was only 0.2, then the optimal decision would be to drink beer. We can see from this example that the estimation of Bayesian prior probabilities has an important effect on decision-making. The rational person will update these in the light of new information, so that if the class turns out to be boring this will reduce the estimated probability of the next class being interesting, and may affect the student's drink decision next time round.

### Applicability of the neoclassical model

Since the 1980s behavioral economists have drawn increasing attention to various limitations in the NM. Consider the following questions:

- Why is the return on stocks so much higher on average than the return on bonds?
- Why do sellers often value their goods or assets much higher than buyers?
- Why are people willing to drive across town to save $5 to purchase a $15 calculator but not to purchase a $125 jacket?
- Why are the fresh fruit and vegetables usually found at the entrance of the supermarket when they are easily damaged in the shopping trolley?
- Why are people delighted to hear they are going to get a 10% raise in salary, and then furious to find out that a colleague is going to get 15%?
- Why do people forever make resolutions to go on a diet or stop smoking, only to give in later?

- Why do people go to the ATM and withdraw a measly $50?
- Why do people prefer to postpone a treat like a luxury dinner rather than have it sooner?
- Why is someone unwilling to pay $500 for a product, but then delighted when their spouse buys them the same product for the same price using their joint bank account?
- Why is someone willing to drive through a blizzard to go to see a ball game when they have paid for the ticket, but not when they have been given the ticket for free?
- Why are people willing to bet long odds on the last race of the day, but not on previous races?

None of these questions are readily answerable using the NM, because of the restrictive nature of the assumptions involved. In some cases there are anomalies, meaning that the NM makes inaccurate predictions; in other cases the NM is incomplete or silent, meaning that it cannot make predictions at all. Both aspects together have been key drivers in the rapid development of behavioral economics as an emerging sub-discipline of economics. It should be noted in this context that the limitations of the NM have led to a broadening of economic theory more generally towards analysis of the range of 'imperfections' that arise once one leaves the narrow confines of the NM behind (e.g. Klaes, 2015a) and the rise of behavioral economics should thus be regarded as part of a wider trend of how economics has developed over the past three decades.

The relationship between the NM and behavioral economics in the light of those limitations may be described as follows. Every model has a **domain of application** which comprises those phenomena that it seeks to explain. There is also a **domain of validity**, the range of phenomena for which the model offers a valid account or explanation. The traditional domain of the NM, ranging over all economic decision-making, is vast. The limitations listed here all indicate that its domain of validity may be much smaller than its traditional domain of application, and the dynamics that arise from extending this domain through conceptual innovation are an important driving force of scientific progress in economics (Klaes, 2003). Whether and to what extent alternative models from behavioral economics are able to offer complementary and even competing accounts of decision-making, depending on whether their domain of validity overlaps with or extends the original domain of the NM is one of the most hotly debated questions in economics today and it has, as we shall see, a long and distinguished trajectory in the history of the discipline.

## 1.2  History and evolution of behavioral economics

As we will see, behavioral economics finds its twentieth-century origins in various empirical critiques of the standard NM of economic decision-making. That model itself only came to dominate the discipline as economics gradually severed its traditional ties to psychological, sociological and historical inquiry. An instrumental factor in this shift has been the so-called formalist revolution in economics during the immediate post-World War II era (Blaug, 2001). But in order to appreciate the emergence and position of behavioral economics within the wider context of the development of economic thought, one needs to bear in mind that prior to the twentieth century much of economic thought has evolved in close proximity to psychological reasoning (Drakopoulos and Katselidis, 2017).

*The classical and neoclassical approaches*

There tends to be a widespread belief that the economists of the eighteenth and nineteenth centuries who pioneered the discipline had no time for psychology. The neoclassicists in particular are often portrayed as systematizers who wanted to bring mathematical rigor to their subject by imposing some simplifying assumptions regarding motivation. A good example is the work of Daniel Bernoulli (1954 [1738]), who might be regarded as the originator of the theory of choice under risk, explaining risk-aversion in terms of the diminishing marginal utility of money.

However, the portrayal of the classical and early neoclassical schools as economic schools of thought that developed in disregard of psychological and sociological insight gives a misleading impression. Although Adam Smith is best known for his *Wealth of Nations*, in 1776, he was also the author of a less well-known work, *The Theory of Moral Sentiments*, in 1759. The latter contains several vital psychological insights and foreshadows many more recent developments in behavioral economics, particularly relating to the role of emotions in decision-making.

Similarly, Jeremy Bentham, best known for introducing the concept of utility, had much to say about the underlying psychology of consumers (Quinn, 2016). Francis Edgeworth wrote *The Theory of Mathematical Psychics* in 1881, the title indicating his concern with psychology; this is reflected in the well-known 'Edgeworth Box' diagram, named after him, which relates to two-person bargaining situations and involves a simple model of social utility. However, psychology was in its infancy at this time as an academic discipline, and many economists wanted the also-new science of economics (then still largely referred to as political economy) to aspire to a more rigorous grounding, comparable to that of the natural sciences. Hence the birth of the concept of *homo oeconomicus*, that embodiment of economic rationality as self-interested utility maximization (Coats, 1976).

## Post-war economic approaches

In the first half of the twentieth century there were still economists who considered and discussed psychological factors in their work, for example Irving Fisher, Vilfredo Pareto and John Maynard Keynes. The latter famously speculated, both figuratively and literally, on the stock market, with notable success. However, the general trend during this time was to ignore psychology, and by World War II psychologists were *personae non gratae* in economists' circles. Psychological reasoning continued, at best, to maintain some currency at the fringes of the discipline (Earl, 1990).

This trend continued after the war, aided in many ways by the advent of better computational methods. As computers became more powerful it became possible to build and estimate mathematical models of both markets and the economic system as a whole. The sub-discipline of econometrics became a vital tool for economists as a means of both developing and testing theories. Economists became obsessed with mensuration, meaning the measurement of variables, and the estimation of economic parameters using mathematical equations and econometric methods. Much progress was made in terms of theoretical development, and the emphasis on mathematical treatment led to greater rigor and more precise, if not accurate, results.

Some economists realized that the behavioral assumptions underlying their models were unrealistic, but there has been a methodological approach, typified by Milton Friedman, that economic theory had little to do with the accuracy of these behavioral assumptions, or with understanding why individuals behave as they do. This approach is discussed in the next chapter.

## The resurgence of behaviorism in economics

Some heretics, like Herbert Simon, viewed the standard approach as somewhat blinkered. He was not prepared to accept the host of ready excuses that were offered when predictions went astray: temporary 'blips', the introduction of new and unpredictable factors, measurement discrepancies and so on. He believed it important to understand the underlying motivation behind the behavior of economic agents in order to improve existing theories and make more accurate predictions. Simon (1955) introduced the term 'bounded rationality' to refer to the cognitive limitations facing decision-makers in terms of acquiring and processing information.

There were several seminal papers written in the 1950s and 1960s which complemented the work of Simon (Klaes and Sent, 2005). These papers all pointed to various anomalies in individual decision-making if seen through the lens of the NM, and suggested theoretical improvements. Notable contributions included those by Markowitz (1952), Allais (1953), Strotz (1955), Schelling (1960) and Ellsberg (1961).

During the 1970s there were important developments in the field of psychology that heralded some important foundations of behavioral economics. Most notable of these was the 'heuristics and biases' program of Daniel Kahneman and Amos Tversky. However, it was really at the end of the 1970s that behavioral economics was born. Two papers were largely responsible for this. The first, in 1979, was entitled 'Prospect theory: Decision making under risk', written by Kahneman and Tversky, and published in the prestigious and technical economic journal *Econometrica*. Prospect theory built on their earlier work on heuristics and biases, but also introduced several new and fundamental concepts relating to reference points, loss-aversion, utility measurement and subjective probability judgments (for a good overview of these developments, see Heukelom 2014).

The second paper, 'Toward a theory of consumer choice', was published by the economist Richard Thaler in 1980. In particular he introduced the concept of 'mental accounting', closely related to the concepts of Kahneman and Tversky, and this is discussed at length in Chapter 6.

Since 1980 the field of behavioral economics has become a burgeoning one, as both economists and psychologists have expanded and developed the work of the pioneers mentioned above. As more success has been achieved in explaining the anomalies of the NM and in developing a more complete body of theory the field has now become a more respectable one, with a variety of journals publishing relevant research.

However, it should be made clear that behavioral economists do not conform to a uniform school of thought. Although they all are concerned with the psychological foundations of economic behavior, they may have quite conflicting beliefs regarding fundamental aspects. For example, we will see that the views of Kahneman and Tversky, Vernon Smith, and Gigerenzer, all differ substantially regarding the role and nature of assumptions, appropriate methods of investigation, the value of various kinds of empirical evidence, and conclusions regarding such issues as rationality, efficiency and optimization.

## 1.3  Relationship with other disciplines

One of the main criticisms of behavioral economics that has been leveled at it ever since its inception has been that it is essentially an *ad hoc* collection of observations relating to behavioral biases that has no underlying uniform theoretical foundation. At first sight this criticism may seem to have some justification, in that over the last three decades many biases have been discovered that present themselves as anomalies within the confines of the NM, some working in opposite directions from each other, and many researchers have been content to record and model these in a narrow behavioral context. However, it is a fundamental objective of this book to examine not only how people behave in 'idiosyncratic' ways, but also why they behave in these ways. This approach is discussed in more detail in the next chapter, but at this point it is sufficient to propose the idea that our behavior is determined by a mixture of biological and environmental factors, sometimes inextricably blended together. This acknowledgement stands in a long tradition in economics to incorporate findings from allied disciplines, notwithstanding its more recent curtailment as a result of the formalist narrowing of the core of the discipline around the NM (Arena, Dow and Klaes, 2009). It is therefore necessary to have a basic understanding of some of the fundamental concepts related to biology, psychology and sociology.

## Evolutionary biology

Theodosius Dobzhanksy, a field naturalist and evolutionary biologist, once famously said "Nothing in biology makes sense except in the light of evolution" (Dobzhansky, 1973). Scientists in this field have for several decades reached a general consensus regarding evolutionary theory, sometimes referred to as 'the modern synthesis' or the 'neo-Darwinian synthesis'. There are four main features of this synthesis:

1   Inheritance – genes are the unit of inheritance, and are transferred from parents to offspring.
2   Variation – there is a diversity of genes in any population, sometimes referred to as the 'gene pool'.
3   Change – the mixing of genes from parents (recombination), and mutation from one generation to another, result in offspring having different genes from parents.
4   Natural selection – the genes of those members of a population best able to survive and reproduce tend to spread and predominate over time, leading to adaptations to the environment.

The last feature has tended to be the most controversial among biologists, and is what distinguishes the general theory of evolution from the more specific 'Darwinian' theory, although these terms are often used interchangeably. While no serious scientist doubts the process of evolution, some have questioned the relative importance of natural selection in relation to other factors that cause intergenerational change, such as 'genetic drift'.

## Evolutionary psychology

Closely related to the discipline of evolutionary biology is evolutionary psychology. Evolutionary psychology is a relatively new discipline, and it is fundamentally an offshoot of evolutionary biology. While it may be hazardous to try and condense all psychological explanations into a universal protocol, we believe that evolutionary psychology can be a significant aid in understanding and relating many of the different findings from empirical studies. The foundation of this area of science is that, just as our anatomical and physiological systems evolved over millions of years in the crucible of natural selection, so did the anatomy and physiology of our brains, resulting in evolved psychological mechanisms (EPMs) which are essentially mental adaptations. Our beliefs, preferences and decision-making processes are therefore heavily shaped by our evolutionary past. One important implication of this, which will be explored in various aspects of the book, is that some of our EPMs may be obsolete, and even harmful in our current vastly changed social and natural environment; an often-quoted example is our nearly universal desire for sweet and fatty food. This may indeed have aided the survival of our Pleistocene ancestors, but when food is plentiful it causes obesity and disease. Readers who are interested in learning about evolutionary psychology in more detail should peruse one of the many good texts on the subject, for example that by Buss (2008). The more casual reader can be referred to *Mean Genes*, an eminently readable bedside book, written by Burnham and Phelan (2001), who combine the disciplines of economist and biologist.

Now it should be made clear from the start that it is certainly not proposed that every psychological mechanism determining behavior is of genetic origin resulting from natural selection. This caricature of evolutionary psychology, combined with the misleading label of genetic determinism, is one that is unfortunately both pervasive and pernicious in many social sciences. There are many differences between individuals, groups and societies that have obviously arisen for cultural reasons, and no evolutionary psychologist denies this. However, what is also striking in many of the empirical studies that will be examined throughout this book is that there are certain universal features of human, and even primate, psychology, which lend themselves to an evolutionary explanation. Such explanations will not be attempted here in terms of argument; suggestions will be made, but it is not appropriate to delve at length into the various factors that relate to whether psychological mechanisms are likely to be evolutionary or cultural. However, one particular area of behavior can be mentioned here as an example of this approach, and this is the evolution of time preference. There have been several papers in the *American Economic Review* on this topic (Robson and Szentes, 2008; Netzer, 2009; Robson and Samuelson, 2009); these have discussed the role of intergenerational transfers of wealth, uncertainty concerning survival rates, and the conflict between short-term and long-term interests. The implications of this research will be considered in Chapter 8.

Many economists and psychologists reject the theories of evolutionary psychology as being largely speculative. They are frequently dismissed in the social sciences as being 'just-so' stories, meaning that they are not true scientific theories in terms of proposing testable hypotheses. This view is caused by two main factors: (1) it is impossible by definition to perform experiments on the past, and (2) the past record of facts is highly incomplete. We will show that this dismissal is largely unjustified, and that evolutionary psychology can indeed produce testable hypotheses, many of which have been confirmed by substantial empirical evidence. Furthermore, the tendency of many economists to limit explanations to economic phenomena is even more unsatisfactory as far as 'just-so' stories are concerned. For example, many readers would not be satisfied with the explanations that people tend to succumb to temptation because they have short time horizons in decision-making, and that they make bad decisions when they are angry. These are also fundamentally 'just-so' stories because they both beg the questions regarding *why* people have short time horizons, and *why* we have seemingly harmful emotional responses like anger.

As mentioned above, a caricature of evolutionary psychology has persisted among some people, relating to the claim that this new science can explain all human cognitive, affective, and moral capacities. However, most evolutionary psychologists would instead support a model of **gene-culture coevolution**. This model takes the view that these capacities are the product of an evolutionary dynamic involving the interaction of genes and culture (Cavalli-Sforza and Feldman, 1982). For most of the evolutionary history of living species information has been passed on from one organism to another purely by genetic means. The genetic code incorporates instructions for building a new organism, and for making decisions based on sensory inputs. Because learning is costly and prone to mistakes, it is efficient for the genome to encode all aspects of the environment that are constant or changing only slowly, so that decisions can be easily and automatically made in familiar circumstances. When environmental conditions vary considerably or change rapidly, organisms need to have more flexible responses, which means they need to be genetically programmed to be able to learn in order to deal with less familiar circumstances. In relatively recent times on an evolutionary scale, meaning over the last 7 million years or so, a different method of information transmission has assumed increasing importance, labeled epigenetic. This non-genetic mechanism for transferring intergenerational information is cultural in nature. It can be vertical (from parents to children), horizontal (peer to peer), oblique (older to younger), or can take other directions, such as from higher status to lower status. Dawkins (1976) has proposed that the method of transmission of cultural information is broadly analogous to that involved with genetic transmission, introducing the term '**meme**' as a unit of information. Thus memes are replicated from one person to another, but imperfectly, in that they mutate, just as in a game of 'Chinese Whispers' or 'Telephone'. Furthermore, a process of selection operates so that those memes that enhance the fitness of their carriers tend to survive and be passed on more frequently and faithfully. Memes can be as simple as the opening four notes of Beethoven's Fifth Symphony, or highly complex, like a religious dogma. This large variability in nature has led to some criticism of the gene-meme analogy, but, as Gintis (2009) has pointed out, modern research has shown that genes also often have ill-defined and overlapping boundaries.

The interaction of genes and culture has been of vital importance in providing the foundation for the rapid evolution of human traits, for example the development of speech and language, and the development of morality and sophisticated social emotions such as jealousy, shame, pride, envy, empathy and guilt. The capacities for these traits are ultimately determined genetically since they depend on neurological development, but their survival value depends on the culture in the relevant environment.

The importance of this concept of gene-culture coevolution is explored in more detail in the next chapter, since it represents a worldview that is not incorporated in all the different behavioral sciences. As a result, it has been claimed to be a fundamental component of the framework for unifying these sciences (Gintis, 2009), an approach sometimes referred to as **consilience**.

## *Evolutionary economics*

Just as evolutionary psychology is an offshoot of evolutionary biology, so evolutionary economics is often understood nowadays as an offshoot of evolutionary psychology. Read in this way, it proposes that given the way our brains evolved, they are not well adapted to the grasping of certain key concepts in economics because our ancestral environment was radically different. Economic activities during most of our past have not involved trade, division of labor, and the use of capital equipment in particular. Thus it has been argued that this makes it difficult for modern humans to understand the benefits of free trade. Also it may make them prone to the 'lump of labor' fallacy, whereby new jobs can only be created at the expense of old ones. More controversially perhaps, we may have evolved with a tendency to believe in the labor theory of value, and support a minimum wage, and might underestimate the advantages of technological progress, or believe that income and wealth inequalities are caused by exploitation rather than by differences in productivity. When we consider these factors in the light of Brexit and the Trump victory, perhaps they are not without some validity. Deriving and testing concrete hypotheses based on them is a more difficult task.

More generally, evolutionary economics has developed as a largely separate school of thought in economics over the past 100 years or so (see Klaes, 2004). It was put on the map by Veblen's (1898) *Quarterly Journal of Economics* article that asked his fellow economists why economics had fallen behind modern science through adherence to the immutable logic of the rational choice paradigm, instead of seeking to address economic phenomena on the basis of a causal inquiry into how individuals engage in economic decisions, and how in doing so they interact within groups and institutions. Some of the seminal thinkers of the neoclassical school, like Alfred Marshall, displayed important features of such an alternative approach in their work (Raffaelli, 2003). The NM, however, came to epitomize the formalization of the rational choice model in economics, rather than its opening up towards more empirically oriented approaches to understanding economic behavior.

Evolutionary economics narrowly conceived, as a behavioral economics grounded in evolutionary psychology, is offering important insight into the limitations and constraints inherent in how we make choices between given alternatives. But such an approach will have less to say on the motivational dimensions of economic behavior that open up once preferences are no longer assumed as given (Witt, 2011). At the group level, questions relating to how preferences are learned through reinforcement patterns give way to how institutions and, arguably even more importantly, processes of economic innovation shape and are shaped by acquired wants that cannot be fully reduced to biological needs. Much attention in evolutionary economics more generally understood as an institutional economics has therefore focused on the role of such innovation in the economy and its implication for economic development and growth (Hodgson, 1998).

### Cognitive neuroscience

This is another relatively new discipline, taking off in the 1980s, and it essentially forms the nexus of evolutionary biology and evolutionary psychology. Cognitive neuroscience seeks to relate neural states in the brain to mental states, and to events in the world external to the organism under study. In many ways thus, cognitive neuroscience studies behavior, and decision-making in particular, in ways that are relevant for the attempts of economists to understand the material basis of decision-making. This had led to the formation of the new field of neuroeconomics, which refers to the use of empirical evidence relating to brain activity in order to come to conclusions relating to economic behavior.

Cognitive neuroscience has seen significant empirical advances made possible by several recent technological developments, particularly in terms of brain scanning and imaging techniques such as positron emission tomography (PET), functional magnetic resonance imaging (fMRI), electroencephalography (EEG), regional cerebral blood flow (rCBF) and transcranial magnetic stimulation (TMS). These methods detect (or in the case of TMS, block) brain activity in particular areas in terms of electrical activity or increased blood flow, and this has been used to shed light on various topics of interest in behavioral economics. Relevant results have been influential in the area of decision-making heuristics, learning processes and the role of the emotions.

Perhaps the most fundamental discovery in neuroscience has been the concept of **brain modularity**. This means that different types of thinking or mental process are performed in different parts of the brain, indicating the importance of brain structure or anatomy, and it is attributed to evolutionary processes, whereby new parts of the brain have been successively added to older more primitive parts, and have become more developed over time. One of the most profound consequences of modularity, certainly as far as behavioral economics is concerned, is that humans have different decision-making systems that operate in different circumstances. The most obvious illustration of this is that we have a 'cold' rational system for reasoning through some problems, like doing a crossword puzzle, and a 'hot' system involving emotions, that tends to operate for example when somebody cuts in front of us in a traffic jam. We also find that we tend to perform some processes automatically, like a skilled musician playing the piano, without conscious thought about what keys to play, whereas other actions require conscious decisions, for example where a beginner is attempting to play the same piece. The reason why this aspect of brain modularity is significant for behavioral economics is that there are often conflicts between different systems, and these can cause phenomena such as preference reversals and time-inconsistent preferences, that are frequently observed anomalies in the NM. There are executive control systems that mediate these different systems, and these are necessary in order to bring into effect some action when there are internal conflicts. However, it is important that we do not think of these control systems as being the 'self', or the 'I' that decides. This would amount to Cartesian Dualism, or a belief in what the philosopher Gilbert Ryle has termed 'the ghost in the machine' (Ryle, 1949). Executive control systems may indeed operate subconsciously, for example when we run from a wasp flying toward us.

Another important discovery in neuroeconomics is that different chemicals, neurotransmitters and hormones, such as dopamine, serotonin, adrenalin, cortisol, testosterone and oxytocin, have a significant influence on behavior. This should not be surprising given the effects that these substances have on our brains and therefore our emotions. This issue is discussed in the context of reductionism in the next chapter. Given these developments, various examples of neuroeconomic studies will be given throughout the book. It is important to realize, however, that the relevance and application of neuroeconomics has remained a controversial issue in the discipline. Many mainstream economists argue that it is not a discipline that is relevant to understanding economics or applying economic principles. This argument is developed further, along with counterarguments, in the next chapter.

## 1.4  Objectives, scope and structure

*Objectives*

In view of the foregoing discussion, this book has the following major objectives:

1  Present the principles and methods of behavioral economics in a logical and amenable manner, comparing and contrasting them with those of the neoclassical model (NM).

2  Illustrate how behavioral models represent an improved modification and refinement of the NM in terms of power of explanation and prediction, using a wide variety of empirical examples from both observational and experimental studies.

3  Provide a critical examination of the existing literature relating to behavioral economics.

4  Explain the policy implications of behavioral economics, particularly when these differ from those of the NM.

5  Provide a coherent psychological framework underpinning the findings of behavioral economics.

6  Indicate the way forward for the subject, in terms of future challenges and areas meriting further research.

*Structure*

In order to achieve the objectives described at the beginning of the section the book is divided into five parts. Following the introductory two chapters there is a part on the foundations of behavioral economics, in which the fundamental concepts of preferences, beliefs, decision-making under risk and uncertainty and mental accounting are discussed. This relates to the first, third and fourth components of the model in equation (1.1). The third part of the book examines intertemporal decision-making, where costs and benefits of decisions are incurred in different time periods. This relates to the second component of the model in equation (1.1). The fourth part examines strategic interaction and the applications of game theory, which relates to aspects of the third and fourth components not discussed earlier. The final part represents a conclusion. We are concerned here with summarizing the various aspects of behavioral economics and presenting an integrated view of rationality; this part also relates to the sixth objective stated above, looking at the future of the discipline. In terms of overall structure this text is compatible to the introductory text by Angner (2016), which places focus on a somewhat more technical treatment of the NM and may thus act as complementary reading in teaching contexts where closer integration of our treatment and approach into the core economics curriculum is desirable.

   Within each chapter there is also frequently a typical structure. The principles and assumptions of the relevant aspects of the NM are examined first, with a description of shortcomings or anomalies. Various behavioral models are then introduced, and these are evaluated in the light of the empirical evidence available, with comparisons being made between different models. Normative or policy implications are also discussed. Finally, some important applications of behavioral economics are examined in more detail in case studies at the end of each chapter.

## 1.5  Summary

*   Behavioral economics is concerned with improving the explanatory power of economic theories by giving them a sounder psychological basis.
*   Behavioral economics relaxes key assumptions of the NM, in order to explain a wide variety of anomalies in that model.
*   Behavioral economics is a relatively new discipline, becoming recognized around 1980; before that time psychology had largely been ignored by economists for many decades.
*   Behavioral economists use a variety of methods or approaches, based on both traditional economics and psychology, and also borrowing from those commonly used in other sciences as well. Thus both observational and experimental studies are used, and sometimes computer simulations and brain scans. This relates to the concept of consilience.
*   There are various methodological issues related to the behavioral approach, and in particular to the application of related disciplines such as evolutionary psychology and cognitive neuroscience to economics.
*   Evolutionary biology and psychology are best viewed in terms of the broader concept of gene-culture coevolution.
*   Evolutionary economics may help us understand why certain economic principles are difficult to grasp, because they did not apply in our ancestral environment. More generally, it points us to institutional analysis in economics and to the significance of motivational issues and the role of innovation.
*   Rationality can be defined in several ways. In economics, a standard model of economic rationality is used but is subject to considerable variation depending on context and sub-discipline.

## 1.6  Review questions

1   What is behavioral economics?
2   Summarize the assumptions of the NM.
3   Give four examples of phenomena that cannot be explained by the NM.
4   Explain what is meant by evolutionary psychology and why it is related to behavioral economics.
5   Explain the difference between a descriptive and a normative theory.

## 1.7  Applications

Three situations where the behavioral economics model (BEM) can be usefully applied are now presented. In each case it is not appropriate at this stage to engage in a detailed discussion of the issues involved, since these are examined in the remainder of the book; instead a summary of the important relevant behavioral issues is given in outline form. However, these applications should serve to give the reader a flavor of what behavioral economics is about in general terms.

## **Case 1.1** Loss-aversion in monkeys

When humans display behavior that departs from rationality as defined in the NM, there is often an issue regarding whether such a departure is culturally determined or whether there is a more fundamental evolutionary cause. One method that is often used to distinguish between these two hypotheses is to conduct experiments with primates and monkeys to see if they display similar departures to those observed in humans. Capuchin monkeys are frequently used in such experiments, since they have relatively large brains, live in social groups, and can easily learn to trade tokens for food. One of the most interesting experiments performed in this regard was carried out by Chen and colleagues (2006), and consisted of three main stages, which are described below.

The first stage involved a standard test of rationality, investigating whether the monkeys would respond to a 'price change' by reallocating their budget towards the 'cheaper' item. When the monkeys were allocated a budget of tokens to spend on either jello cubes or apple slices, it was found that a halving of the price of apple slices, achieved by offering two slices instead of one for every token, and reducing the budget accordingly to maintain the same purchasing power, resulted in an increase in the number of apple slices consumed. In this respect the monkeys behaved like rational consumers in the NM.

Then the experimenters wanted to examine whether the monkeys displayed two common behavioral features that are anomalies in the NM. This involved testing for reference dependence, to see whether monkeys viewed outcomes in terms of a previous reference point. In this protocol one experimenter always held up one apple slice to signal a willingness to trade, but when the monkey offered a token in exchange the experimenter offered one slice half the time and two slices half the time, with an average outcome of 1.5. The second experimenter always held up two apple slices initially, but again was equally likely to offer one or two slices in trade, with the same expected outcome of 1.5. Expected utility theory in the NM predicts equal preferences for equal outcomes, but it was found that 71% of the monkeys traded with the first experimenter, indicating the importance of reference dependence. Monkeys trading with the first experimenter would experience a gain compared the reference point of one slice, while those trading with the second experimenter would experience a loss compared with the reference point of two slices.

To confirm this finding suggesting loss-aversion, a second protocol was implemented. The first experimenter always initially offered two slices of apple, but only traded one slice after receiving a token; the second experimenter always initially offered one slice, but again always traded one slice. Thus again outcomes were the same for both experimenters, and the NM predicts indifference between them. In actuality nearly 80% of the monkeys revealed a preference for the second experimenter.

Thus these experiments not only provide evidence for two of the key elements of prospect theory, the foundation of behavioral economics, but also indicate that these elements have an evolutionary origin. Capuchin monkeys diverged from the evolutionary line that led to humans about 35 million years ago.

However, both of the above conclusions have been questioned by a later study by Silberberg and colleagues (2008). The first ground of criticism is that the Chen study does not properly take into account the reversed-contingency effect, where subjects are repeatedly shown a larger reward but offered a smaller one, and vice versa. Humans can grasp this

▶

process after repeated trials, but Silberberg and colleagues (2008) show that capuchins are incapable of doing this over 500 trials. The second ground of criticism is that the delay involved in reducing a reward compared with paying the reward initially offered introduces a discounting factor, in that subjects should prefer an immediate reward to a delayed one if the rewards are identical in amount.

It is important to note that Silberberg and colleagues (2008) do not claim that this new evidence contradicts the conclusions of the original study, it simply means that the original evidence has an alternative explanation. The study therefore involves a confound. Further experimental studies need to be performed in order to confirm the conclusions of the Chen and colleagues study, where the methodology eliminates any alternative explanations.

### Issues

This ingenious experimental study illustrates three particularly important aspects of behavioral economics:

**1** *Methods*
  The experimental approach, traditionally followed by psychologists, is used here in order to achieve a degree of control that would be impossible to gain through mere observation. Different trading regimes are used to compare responses and test the basic hypothesis of loss-aversion. Note the use of deception, although it is unlikely in this case to cause a general increase in cynicism among the population of capuchin monkeys available as subjects.

**2** *Evolutionary psychology*
  The purpose of the experiment is not just to test whether capuchin monkeys have loss-aversion, but more importantly to test whether the widely observed loss-aversion in humans is likely to have an evolutionary explanation. The fact that loss-aversion has been observed in many different countries and societies constitutes evidence of an evolutionary origin, but the observation of the same characteristic in a fairly closely related species is even stronger evidence. This is a typical type of experiment carried out by evolutionary psychologists to test their hypotheses. It is also notable that the issue regarding why loss-aversion should be an evolved psychological mechanism or adaptation is also raised. This issue will be discussed in more detail in Chapter 5 on prospect theory.

**3** *Rationality*
  We have seen that the concept of rationality is a highly ambiguous term, which can be used in many different senses. However, in the current context, a 'rational' individual behaving according to the NM should have no preference between the two experimenters in the two trading regimes, since the outcomes from each are ultimately identical. The 'irrationality' observed in the monkeys is explained by the concepts of reference points and loss-aversion, important aspects of prospect theory. Thus the BEM is better able than the NM to explain the behavior observed in the experiments.

**4** *Confounds*
  Confounds arise when an outcome has more than one possible explanation, but it is difficult or impossible to determine which explanation is appropriate. These are a very common problem in all areas of economics, and are discussed in detail in the next chapter, since careful methodology can often eliminate them.

## Case 1.2  Money illusion

The issue of money illusion is one that has been much discussed by economists, since the days of Irving Fisher (1928). It has been defined in various ways, which has been the cause of some confusion, but a brief and useful interpretation has been given by Shafir, Diamond and Tversky (1997) in a classic article:

> A bias in the assessment of the real value of transactions, induced by their nominal representation.

It should be noted that such an interpretation does not limit money illusion to the effects of inflation, as will be seen.

Economists have tended to take an attitude to the assumption of money illusion that Howitt describes in the *New Palgrave Dictionary of Economics* (1987, p. 3) as 'equivocal'. At one extreme there is the damning quotation by Tobin (1972): 'An economic theorist can, of course, commit no greater crime than to assume money illusion.' The reason for this view is that money illusion is basically incompatible with the assumption of rationality in the SEM. Thus a rational individual should be indifferent between the following two options:

**Option A**    Receiving a 2% yearly pay increase after a year when there has been inflation of 4%

**Option B**    Receiving a pay cut of 2% after a year when there has been zero inflation

In each case the individual suffers a decrease in pay in real terms of 2%. However, some empirical studies indicate that people do not show preferences that are consistent with rationality in the traditional sense, and that money illusion is widespread.

Perhaps the best-known study of this type is the one quoted earlier by Shafir, Diamond and Tversky (SDT). This used a questionnaire method, asking people questions about a number of issues related to earnings, transactions, contracts, investments, mental accounting, and fairness and morale. We will concern ourselves here with questions related to earnings and contracts, since these will illustrate the main findings.

An earnings-related situation was presented as follows:

Consider two individuals, Ann and Barbara, who graduated from the same college a year apart. Upon graduation, both took similar jobs with publishing firms. Ann started with a yearly salary of $30,000. During her first year on the job there was not inflation, and in her second year Ann received a 2% ($600) raise in salary. Barbara also started with a yearly salary of $30,000. During her first year on the job there was a 4% inflation, and in her second year Barbara received a 5% ($1,500) increase in salary.

The respondents were then asked three questions relating to economic terms, happiness and job attractiveness:

1   As they entered the second year on the job, who was doing better in economic terms?

2   As they entered the second year on the job, who do you think was happier?

3   As they entered the second year on the job, each received a job offer from another firm. Who do you think was more likely to leave her present position for another job?

▶

71% of the respondents thought that Ann was better off, while 29% thought that Barbara was better off. However, only 36% thought Ann was happier, while 64% thought that Barbara was happier. In the same vein, 65% thought that Ann was more likely to leave her job, with only 35% thinking Barbara was more likely to leave.

A contracts-related question was designed to test people's preferences for indexing contracts for future payment to inflation. From a seller's viewpoint this would be preferred by decision-makers who were risk-averse in real terms, while those who were risk-averse in nominal terms would prefer to fix the price now. The situation featured computer systems currently priced at $1,000; sellers could either fix the price in two years at $1,200, or link the price to inflation, which was expected to amount to 20% over the two years. The options were framed first of all in real terms (based on 1991 as the current year) as follows:

**Contract A**   You agree to sell the computer systems (in 1993) at $1,200 a piece, no matter what the price of computer systems is at that time. Thus, if inflation is below 20% you will be getting more than the 1993 price; whereas, if inflation exceeds 20% you will be getting less than the 1993 price. Because you have agreed on a fixed price your profit level will depend on the rate of inflation.

**Contract B**   You agree to sell the computer systems at the 1993 price. Thus if inflation exceeds 20% you will be paid more than $1,200, and if inflation is below 20%, you will be paid less than $,1200. Because both production costs and prices are tied to the rate of inflation, your 'real' profit will remain essentially the same regardless of the rate of inflation.

When the options of fixing the nominal price and index-linking were framed as above in real terms a large majority of the respondents (81%) favored the option of index-linking, indicating risk-aversion in real terms. However, when the equivalent options were framed in nominal terms, as shown below, a different result was obtained:

**Contract C**   You agree to sell the computer systems (in 1993) at $1200 a piece, no matter what the price of computer systems is at the time.

**Contract D**   You agree to sell the computer systems at 1993's price. Thus instead of selling at $1200 for sure, you will be paid more if inflation exceeds 20%, and less of inflation is below 20%.

In this case a much smaller majority (51%) favored the index-linking option, which now seemed more risky.

When the contract situation was reversed, so that respondents were now in a buying situation, it was also found that the framing of the options affected the responses. Once again respondents were risk-averse in nominal terms when the options were framed in nominal terms and risk-averse in real terms when the options were framed in real terms.

### Issues

The discussion of money illusion raises a number of important issues in behavioral economics. Some of these are similar to the previous case:

1   *Methods*
    Economists have criticized the validity of the SDT results on two main grounds. First, they have doubts about the questionnaire methodology, suspecting that there may be

considerable differences between what people say they might do in a hypothetical situation and what they would actually do in the real world when motivated by economic incentives. Second, they point out that it is not sufficient to show money illusion at the level of individual behavior; it must also be present at the aggregate level in order to have real economic significance. Individual differences may cancel each other out, thus resulting in no overall economic effect.

**2** *Rationality*

It is usually argued that money illusion is not rational at the level of the individual. However, it is notable from the SDT study that the majority of the respondents realized that Ann was better off in economic terms, even though a majority thought that Barbara was happier. This perceived decoupling of absolute economic welfare from happiness is not necessarily irrational, and will be discussed further in Chapter 3. Furthermore, it may well happen that a majority of individuals do not themselves suffer from money illusion at the individual level, but may believe that others do. Therefore, in order to understand the existence of money illusion at the aggregate level, it is necessary to examine the strategic interaction of individuals in the economy.

**3** *Mental accounting*

It is notable that the SDT study not only attempts to test for money illusion in a descriptive sense, it also goes some way towards trying to explain its existence in psychological terms. This involves in general aspects of mental accounting, more specifically the theory of multiple representations. These aspects are discussed in detail in Chapter 6, but at this stage we can outline the theory by saying that it proposes that people tend to form not just a single mental or cognitive representation of information, but several simultaneously. Thus we may form both a nominal and a real mental representation of different options, but, depending on how they are framed, one or other may be salient. Thus the concepts of framing effects and saliency are important. The SDT study maintains that normally the nominal representation tends to be salient, since it is cognitively easier to handle, demanding less information. This therefore tends to give rise to money illusion. In Chapter 5, in the discussion of reference points, we will see that there are similarities here with types of optical illusion.

**4** *Strategic interaction*

As already stated, it is important to consider strategic interaction in order to understand money illusion at the aggregate level. If some economic agents act irrationally, for example by raising prices without any inflationary cause, then it may be optimal for other agents who are rational to react in the same way and 'follow the crowd'. This effect is of vital importance in stock markets, as noted by many researchers in behavioral finance, particularly in relation to the financial crisis that began in 2007. Strategic interaction also has to take into account the possible existence of 'super-rationality', as discussed by Fehr and Tyran (2003). These aspects are all examined in Chapter 9.

# CHAPTER·2

## Methodology

Imagine being encased in a large and noisy machine, lying on your back in claustrophobic conditions. A barrage of questions related to economics is now fired at you, while your responses are monitored by the machine. Reponses in this case relate to increased blood flow in particular brain areas. This is how functional magnetic resonance imaging (fMRI) works, one of the most common techniques in neuroscience and its application within behavioral economics.

Is there a case for studying 'mindless' economics? That is, does it help us to know what is going on in the brains of individuals when developing and testing economic theories? This is a highly contested topic in behavioral economics at present. Less controversial by now are experiments, which are still a relatively recent methodological tool employed by economists. Do findings in experiments act as a useful guide to how people will behave in real life?

Questions like these lead economists into the terrain of methodological considerations and debate. Adopting and applying a particular research method is one thing, reflecting on it in comparison to alternative approaches quite another. On the face of it, it seems that economists should employ whatever method yields the best results. But this is less straightforward than it may appear. For example, what counts as a result in this context, and what criteria should we apply to this question? Is a theory that is pretty general in scope but only allows us to arrive at relatively weak conclusions preferable or not to a highly domain specific theory that, within that domain, comes to quite detailed and strong conclusions?

## 2.1  Theories

*Theories and assumptions*

The objective of all sciences is to develop theories. Theories consist of abstract statements that relate a set of fundamental concepts or entities to a domain of application in a way that allows us to identify systematic relationships between the phenomena we observe in that domain. A key ingredient of theories are general statements that enable us to formulate hypotheses about these empirical relationships. Take the law of demand for example, or the proposition that postulates that economic agents act such as to maximize their utility over attainable outcomes. Initial conditions, together with a general proposition of this kind, allow the formation of a hypothesis or prediction as to how prices, or individuals, will relate to those conditions and any ensuing changes in them.

In modern economics, theory is usually expressed in terms of a collection of models. Take game theory for example, or principal agent theory, or the theory of the firm. In each case, we have a collection of standard models that together seek to address key features of their domain of application. The theory of the firm combines models addressing various aspects of corporate governance and internal organization. Game theory combines a family of models studying strategic interaction. Principal agent theory seeks to explain basic contracting relationships between two parties. Note from these examples that theories may be nested to a certain degree. For example, both principal agent theory and non-cooperative game theory can be regarded as building blocks of the modern theory of the firm.

If well specified, models allow the formulation of testable hypotheses; for example, in the most general case, a simple model in demand theory predicts that if the price of a good rises, the quantity demanded will fall, other things being equal. Any hypothesis of this kind is based on certain assumptions or premises, although these are sometimes implicit in the formulation of the model or theory, rather than explicit. The nature, role and interpretation of these assumptions often leads to controversy, in particular if more than one prima facie plausible model is conceivable. At this stage, methodological considerations enter the picture and may tip the balance in favor of one alternative over the other. In economics, this has traditionally been discussed as part of a general debate on the role of assumptions in economic theorizing.

In a highly influential article Friedman (1953) claimed that the scientific worth of a theory is determined purely in terms of the predictive power of the hypothesis that can be generated from it. According to Friedman, the issue is thus not primarily one of identifying realistic assumptions as the primary building blocks of a theory, but to judge the value of the particular assumptions chosen in the light of how well the theory, or a particular model formulated within that theory, is able to account for the phenomena under study, and how they change. Simply querying the descriptive accuracy of assumptions in isolation would be:

> fundamentally wrong and productive of much mischief … [I]t only confuses the issue, promotes misunderstanding about the significance of empirical evidence for economic theory, produces a misdirection of much intellectual effort … [T]he relevant question to ask about the "assumptions" of a theory is not whether they are descriptively "realistic," for they never are, but whether they are sufficiently good approximations for the purpose at hand. (Friedman, 1953, pp. 14–15)

According to this view, a theory that makes accurate predictions is valuable even if the assumptions on which it is based are descriptively inaccurate. Under such a theory, individuals may be regarded as behaving 'as if' they follow the (inaccurate) behavioral assumptions. While Friedman's argument has been controversially discussed for many years (Mäki, 2009), most economists, including critics of the neoclassical model (NM), agree regarding this aspect of the role of assumptions. To achieve any level of generality, assumptions will have to be inaccurate at some level of abstraction. This means that economic theories cannot be rejected on the basis of their assumptions alone, however unrealistic these may appear to be. Additional considerations are involved, such as their inability to make accurate predictions, as Friedman would have it.

However, a factor that confuses this issue is that behavioral economics often proposes **'process' models** as opposed to **'as-if' models**. Whereas 'as-if' models aim at predicting overt choices, process models – based on psychology – aim at predicting choices, while also modeling and predicting the processes that produce them. Some researchers believe that progress in modeling can only be made by using process models (for recent examples of such an approach, see Glimcher, 2009; Johnson, Schulte-Mecklenbeck, and Willemsen, 2008; Brandstätter, Gigerenzer, and Hertwig, 2008). It is not always clear to which class a model belongs (see Brandstätter, Gigerenzer, and Hertwig, 2008). With a process model it can be claimed that if it fails to predict a particular process, such a process is factually falsified. Since this process may be an assumption in another model, it may be possible for a study examining a process model to prompt the rejection of an assumption in a different theory. However, it may be claimed that economic 'as-if' models are immune to this problem, since, even if a process is falsified, the underlying assumption is only that people behave *as if* the process operated. The litmus test relates to the ability of a model to explain and predict.

Some economists, notably Gul and Pesendorfer (2008), have argued that the assumptions described above are not to be treated as **axioms** or fundamental premises that are 'self-evident'. They claim instead that, as far as the rationality of agents is concerned, this is not an assumption in economics but a **methodological stance**. Their paper also implies that at least some of the other 'assumptions' need to be treated in a similar manner. Expanding this claim they state:

> This stance reflects economists' decision to view the individual as the unit of agency and investigate the interaction of the purposeful behaviors of different individuals within various economic institutions. One can question the usefulness of this methodological stance by challenging individual economic models or the combined output of economics but one cannot disprove it. (Gul and Pesendorfer, 2008, p. 38)

However, we must take issue with Gul and Pesendorfer when they compare the situation of critics of the rationality assumption with the situation of critics of experimental economics. In this context they claim that: 'a critic cannot expect to disprove the usefulness of experimental methods for understanding choice behavior' (p. 38).

In principle it is possible to demonstrate the *usefulness* or lack of usefulness of experimental methods. If various types of experiment fail to predict behavior in the real world, then it could be claimed that such methods are not useful. The important point here is that, although theories cannot be falsified simply on the basis of their assumptions, these assumptions, or methodological stance, may be shown not to be useful, at least in certain circumstances. We will see numerous examples of this throughout the remaining chapters, but a simple one will suffice here for illustration. It is generally assumed in the standard model of economic decision making that people use exponential discounting when evaluating future preferences. This results in the normatively desirable behavior of having time-consistent preferences. However, empirical evidence shows that people frequently display inconsistent preferences, for example by overestimating future utilities. Thus gym members often overestimate future usage when they join a club; gyms are aware of this and structure their membership fees accordingly, with high start-up costs or initiation fees and low per-use charges. In this situation, discussed in more detail in Chapter 8, the assumption of exponential discounting in the standard model is not *useful*, since it cannot explain the behavior of either consumers or producers.

Before moving on to discuss and compare the methods used in economics and neighboring disciplines such as psychology, it is necessary to examine issues relating to the evaluation of theories and relationships between theories in different disciplines, in order to gain a better understanding of the advantages and disadvantages of different approaches and models.

## Evaluating theories

What constitutes a 'good' theory? There are various criteria that scientists in general propose as being relevant in terms of evaluating theories. For example, Stigler (1950, pp. 392–396) proposes three essential criteria for judging economic theories: congruence with reality, generality, and tractability. The evolutionary biologist E. O. Wilson adds a further criterion, parsimony, which ironically is particularly pertinent for the standard model of economic rationality. These criteria are now discussed in more detail.

**1**  *Congruence with reality*

  This factor is generally recognized as being the most important for any scientific theory. Good theories are able both to explain or fit existing observations, and to make testable predictions that later prove to be correct. In this respect Newton's laws of motion represent a good theory, but not as good as Einstein's theory of relativity, since they do not fit reality as well on a cosmic scale. It is notable that such theories are sometimes referred to as 'laws', in the sense that they represent regularities; this is particularly applicable when such 'laws' involve general principles with widespread application, which is the subject of the second criterion.

Before moving on to this, there is a complication here, explored in more detail in later chapters: explanation, meaning fitting existing data, and prediction are not the same thing. Models can be made to fit data better by adding more adjustable parameters, but by explaining more they lose predictive power. For example, in astronomy Ptolemy's geocentric system with epicycles, proposing that all the planets and the sun move around the earth in complicated orbits, fitted existing observations better than Copernicus's later heliocentric theory. However, the latter theory, particularly when modified by Kepler, allowed more accurate prediction, which is, in the words of Binmore and Shaked (2010a), the 'scientific gold standard' of a theory.

The relationship between fitting and predicting has aroused considerable controversy in experimental economics. In particular, fitting parameters to the same data that one aims to explain is an inadequate test of models (Brandstätter, Gigerenzer, and Hertwig, 2008). Furthermore, a model's predictions should always be tested with new data that was not used to estimate the model originally (Binmore and Shaked, 2010a).

Another issue that has caused considerable controversy in recent years regarding congruence with reality is the replicability of empirical studies. This issue has actually been even more problematical in other sciences, with a meta-analysis by Camerer and colleagues (2016) reporting 61% of a sample of 16 economic studies having their findings replicated. A good example in behavioral economics where replicability has been a problem is with the so-called anchoring effect, discussed in the next chapter. Maniadis, Tufano, and List (2014) suggest that there are several factors that cause this problem, including the nature of the statistical analysis used, research priors, and number of investigators in the study. The result of this problem is that the findings of many studies may have very limited application in real life and this issue is discussed further in the next subsection.

However, another recent paper by Smaldino and McElreath (2016) suggests that the problem is more serious and fundamental than simply replication. The authors state that 'many prominent researchers believe that as much as half of the scientific literature – not only in medicine, by also in psychology and other fields – may be wrong'. It is claimed that the core of the problem lies in incentivization, meaning that researchers and labs are judged more on the quantity of research published than quality, and are thus tempted to take shortcuts, which in particular result in a tendency to report false positives. Smaldino and McElreath implement an evolutionary model based on natural selection in order to test their hypothesis regarding this systemic tendency to produce inaccurate and distorted results, and found that, even with the incorporation of a penalty for failure to replicate results built into the model, the studies that are likely to survive and be published are those which take shortcuts. In this situation pressure to replicate results will not be able to eliminate the consequent publication bias. A failure to report unfavorable results, combined with a cherry-picking of favorable supporting evidence, may be common in many sciences.

At this stage it may be worth giving an example of this problem, in order to alert the reader to its gravity and nature. A classic case is a study by Ancel Keys (1957), which has become known as the Seven Countries Study. It established what became known as the diet-heart hypothesis (DHH) in medicine, which then became mainstream for many decades and is still widely accepted by many medical authorities, for reasons discussed in Chapter 4. Many current researchers (Weinberg, 2004; Kendrick, 2007; Colpo, 2008; Ramsden et al., 2016) have found conflicting evidence, and some have suggested the DHH has caused enormous harm because of its ill-advised dietary recommendations, increasing the incidence of heart disease, obesity, and diabetes rather than reducing it. There were many flaws in the study, but one prime one is cherry-picking seven countries which supported a positive correlation between saturated-fat intake and heart disease. These seven countries were: Italy, Greece, former Yugoslavia, Holland, Finland, the USA, and Japan. The study never justified the use of these particular countries, since reliable data relating to other countries was available. Kendrick (2007) has shown that if a different sample had been used, namely Finland, Israel, Holland, Germany, Switzerland, France, and Sweden, an exactly opposite result, showing negative correlation, would have occurred. Not only was the original study flawed, but once the DHH became accepted other studies with conflicting results were ignored or not published. The main example of this was the Minnesota Coronary Experiment (MCE), which was a double-blind randomized controlled trial, the gold standard in experimental studies. It also involved a large sample of over 9,000 subjects over a prolonged period (1968–1973). The MCE indicated that there were no differences in cardiovascular events, cardiovascular deaths or overall mortality between an intervention group consuming 9 grams of saturated fat daily and a control group consuming twice this amount. This study is discussed further in Chapter 4 in the context of belief formation and maintenance.

2    *Generality*

Good theories apply to a wide selection of phenomena. Once more, Newton's and Einstein's theories qualify. Einstein's may be preferable in terms of applying to a larger range of situations but this comes at the expense of giving up the comparative simplicity of classical mechanics which for many situations involving macroscopic objects travelling well below the speed of light remains adequate. Theories of quantum mechanics and evolution by natural selection are further examples of general theories. Examples from economics are standard consumer theory and the law of demand, the theory of comparative advantage, general equilibrium theory, or principal-agent theory.

3    *Tractability*

This criterion refers to how easy it is to apply theoretical models to different situations in terms of making testable predictions. In practice this relates in particular to the complexity of the theory involved. More complex theories take into account more parameters (usually by making fewer assumptions) and are therefore more difficult to represent as models. In many sciences, including economics, these models are often best represented in mathematical form. There are two reasons for this: first, mathematics allows the theory to be represented most concisely and unambiguously, including the assumptions involved; second, it allows manipulation to be performed, resulting in precise predictions for given values of the parameters involved in the model. However, highly complex theories may prove to be somewhat intractable if the resulting mathematical analysis becomes unmanageable. In practice there is often a trade-off between tractability and the final criterion, parsimony.

4    *Parsimony*

This criterion refers to the principle of Occam's razor, named after the philosopher William of Occam, and first expressed in the 1320s. He said: 'What can be done with fewer assumptions is done in vain with more.' In the words of E. O. Wilson (1998, p. 57):

> Scientists attempt to abstract the information into the form that is the simplest and aesthetically the most pleasing – the combination called elegance – while yielding the largest amount of information with the least amount of effort.

The astronomical example described earlier also relates to the characteristic of parsimony. The Copernican theory was more simple or parsimonious than the epicycle theory. However, there may be another trade-off here: if a theory is too parsimonious it may not satisfy the first criterion so well, since it may make too many assumptions to apply to real-world situations. The original Copernican theory was not much better at prediction than the Ptolemaic theory with epicycles. It was not until Kepler introduced two modifications (elliptical instead of circular orbits, and off-center orbits with the sun at one focus), making the theory less parsimonious, that more accurate predictions were possible.

The criterion of parsimony is particularly relevant as far as the NM in economics is concerned, since parsimony is one of its great virtues. By assuming that economic agents are selfish utility maximizers the NM is able to derive a large number of predictions regarding the behavior of individuals and firms. However, behavioral economists accuse the NM of being too parsimonious, since it cannot explain the anomalies described earlier, or indeed many others.

The behavioral economists Ho, Lim, and Camerer (2006) propose a somewhat different list of desirable properties of theories. They include generality and congruence with reality (they refer to this as 'empirical accuracy'), but they add the features of **precision** and **psychological plausibility**. Precision refers to the ability to give exact numerical predictions about behavior, and they give the example of Nash equilibrium analysis in game theory, which is discussed in Chapter 9. Ho and colleagues also argue that generality and precision are particularly important in economic models, while empirical accuracy and psychological plausibility have been given more importance in psychology. The authors then claim that the goal in behavioral economics is to have all four properties. As we have already argued, psychological plausibility is likely to lead to more accurate and useful models, albeit more complex ones. Numerous examples will be given of such models in the remainder of the book.

## *Theory development*

An important issue in science in general, which has particular import for behavioral economics, concerns the basis on which theories become accepted, rejected, or modified.

In economics, the Popperian approach is widely mentioned in this context. Also sometimes known as 'critical rationalism', it has two main aspects: theories must be able to produce testable predictions (although not necessarily with current technology, as in astrophysics), thus being falsifiable; and while they can be proven false, they can never empirically shown to be correct. The example of white swans is sometimes given here. One can develop a theory that all swans are white, based on observing a thousand white swans, but no number of observed white swans can rule out the possibility that there may be some swans that are in fact black. What is more, it only takes an observation of a single black swan to disprove the theory.

While the above approach is seemingly straightforward in principle, in practice it faces a number of difficulties. To begin with, it is not fully clear whether critical rationalism should be understood positively, as a depiction of how science works, or normatively as a model for what would constitute good science. At any rate, certainly in economics, commentators such as Blaug (1992, p. 241) have often noted that economists are very good at paying lip service to the scientific method as described by Popper but in practice behave quite differently in their own work, in that they limit themselves to showing how the real world conforms to the implications of their models rather than engaging in sustained attempts to falsify predictions derived from them.

Conceptually too there are problems with falsification. We limit ourselves here to a discussion of a particularly vexing issue, which is that a hypothesis can never be tested in isolation, since it will always involve a bundle of assumptions, both fundamental ones and auxiliary ones which may be implicit. This problem is known as the Duhem-Quine thesis (DQT). Thus if a hypothesis makes an incorrect prediction it may be that the central hypothesis is incorrect, that some auxiliary assumption underlying the hypothesis is incorrect, or that the methodology underlying the testing of the hypothesis was faulty. We can use the DHH described earlier as an example. When this fails to predict coronary heart disease it may be because there is no link between intake of saturated fats and blood cholesterol, or that there is no link between blood cholesterol and heart disease, or that any link depends on what countries are included in the empirical evidence used.

The DQT has posed particular problems for behavioral economics, since many studies rejecting mainstream theories have been criticized on the grounds that they are methodologically flawed, and that the underlying theory can still therefore stand. These criticisms relate particularly to experimental studies and some of the problems are described in a later section in the chapter. An extreme example of this accusation of flawed methodology is the hypotheses suggested by Galileo's telescopic observations regarding the structure of the solar system. The philosopher Cremonini refused to look through Galileo's telescope, blaming the instrument for producing false evidence.

This example also illustrates another phenomenon regarding theory development. Theories sometimes become 'sacred' over time, particularly in the minds of their inventors, and it becomes difficult to challenge them, either because of behavioral factors such as cognitive dissonance, conformity bias, and confirmation bias (discussed in Chapter 4), or because it is professionally unwise in terms of difficulty in achieving publication. Thus a considerable intellectual force, usually exerted by several authorities, is necessary to 'shift the paradigm', as Kuhn (1970) has observed.

## Reductionism

Reduction is traditionally regarded as a methodological strategy in support of the unification of the sciences. A radical reductionist would accept that all theories about the material world, including its organisms and their interactions, can ultimately be reduced to the level of physics. This claim is highly controversial even in the sciences, let alone the social sciences. It is important to examine the nature of reductionism in order to understand the relationship between theories in different disciplines, since behavioral economics involves methods and concepts from not just economics and psychology but also other social sciences, biology, and neuroscience.

Ernest Rutherford is famously reported to have said: 'All science is either physics or stamp-collecting' (quoted in Birks 1962, p. 108). This statement pithily summarizes a reductionist approach to science. However, the term reductionism has come to take on many different interpretations over the years; thus we have for example ontological reductionism, explanatory reductionism, eliminative reductionism, classical reductionism, derivational reductionism, hierarchical reductionism, precipice reductionism, and 'greedy' reductionism.

The type of reductionism that is espoused in this book, and for pedagogical reasons in the first instance, can be labeled as explanatory and hierarchical. This version proposes that complex entities and concepts are best explained in terms of entities and concepts only one level down the hierarchy; these in turn may be explained in terms related to one level further down, and so on. This approach involves making distinctions between **proximate**, or immediate, causes, and **ultimate** causes. An example from economics will aid an understanding of this approach, in particular what is meant by the term hierarchy in this context. We may seek an explanation for the poor level of economic performance of a country. The proximate cause may be the low level of productivity. We then ask why productivity is low; maybe the reason is a lack of investment. In turn, the main reason (there may be multiple causal factors here) for the lack of investment may be poor managerial practices.

So far the explanations have related to phenomena at the economic level of hierarchy. When we ask why managerial practices have been poor, the explanation is likely to lie in social, political, or institutional factors, which are at a lower level of the hierarchy. These in turn may need to be explained in terms of social psychology; then explanations may become biological, then chemical, and finally we get down to physics at the bottom of the hierarchy, where ultimate causes are to be found. Actually there is a problem at this level, because in quantum physics there may be no causation as we generally understand the concept. However, by reducing things one level at a time we can obtain explanations for phenomena at the appropriate level. Similarly, if someone wants an explanation for how an internal combustion engine works, normally they are looking for an explanation at the mechanical level, not one in terms of chemistry or particle physics.

This hierarchical approach has proved extremely successful in the physical sciences. For example the phenomenon of light can now be explained in terms of electromagnetic radiation, and the outstanding achievement of Maxwell was in providing a unified explanation for visible light, heat, x-rays, ultraviolet rays, and radio waves.

Some social or behavioral scientists have welcomed this hierarchical approach, for example the polymath Jared Diamond, who is a professor of both geography and physiology, and Diamond has emphasized the importance of the distinction between proximate causes and ultimate causes in his work (Diamond, 1991, 1997, 2005). However, on the whole, behavioral scientists have been more reluctant than natural scientists to accept reductionism, perhaps fearing encroachment on their specialist areas by outsiders who show a cavalier disrespect for the formalities of the subject. This issue has become particularly relevant in the discipline of behavioral economics, in terms of the role of neuroeconomics and evolutionary biology and psychology; many economists and psychologists have opposed cognitive neuroscience, for different reasons, but often claiming that neuroeconomic studies have no relevance to their discipline. Two areas where the reductionist program has been particularly controversial in behavioral economics are discussed below.

1    *'Just-so stories'*

It is often claimed that evolutionary psychology is not a 'true' science in terms of producing testable hypotheses, but is rather a series of 'just-so stories'. Behavioral economics has attracted the same criticism from some mainstream economists. However, to others it is unsatisfactory to be told that, for example, procrastination is just a human psychological failure, without asking why procrastination should be such a widespread phenomenon. In view of this problem behavioral economists are sometimes accused of ignoring the psychological underpinnings of their findings and presenting their accounts of people's behavior as 'just-so stories'. In other cases, when they do venture psychological explanations for different aspects of economic behavior, the explanations seem to be of an ad hoc nature, with no coherent universal framework that can embrace the different psychological phenomena.

2    *Constraints on theorizing*

Scientists in disciplines 'lower down' the reductive tree tend to claim that their findings act as constraints on theories in disciplines higher up. Thus Rangel (2009), who is actually a social scientist, argues that 'a central goal of neuroeconomics is to construct theories or value-based decision-making that are neurobiologically grounded'. Glimcher (2009), a neuroscientist, takes this argument still further: 'the explicit ties to neurobiological data will reveal that only a tiny space of economic theory can be viewed as compatible with human neuroarchitecture.' A moderate version of this stance can be found in Gallistel (2009, p. 421):

> I believe that any study of successful physical reductionism – that is any study of the establishment of hypotheses such as that the action potential is the physical realization of the nerve impulse, or that the base-pair sequences in DNA are the physical realizations of genes – will show that the reductionist program only succeeds when the variable whose physical identity is sought is already well defined and understood in its own terms, at its own level of analysis, within a theoretical framework that rests on observations at that level.

While this statement obviously makes fewer claims in the cause of reductionism, its implications for the sciences are still far-reaching. A prominent example here is the philosophical concept of free will, which depends on mental causation. While philosophers have traditionally claimed that this concept is not constrained by any theory of science, and have assumed that the mind can cause physical phenomena, many physicists claim that the concept of mental causation is as outdated as the concept of the ether, in that it contradicts a basic theory in physics, in this case the universally accepted first law of thermodynamics relating to the conservation of energy.

Philosophers and social scientists often defend their disciplines against reductionism by endorsing the doctrine of **emergentism**. This school of thought proposes that (1) complex systems possess properties that are not possessed by the more simple systems of which they are composed, and that (2) these properties cannot be analytically derived from those of the simple systems, even in principle. Consciousness and free will are often quoted as examples. The first part of this claim is uncontroversial: living cells have properties of replication that their component atoms and molecules do not; human brains can 'think', but the neurons from which they are composed cannot; social systems have features, such as culture and social norms, that an individual in isolation cannot have. The second part of the claim is highly contentious and can be difficult to support empirically. However, the emergence of different properties at higher levels of complexity is what makes different branches of science necessary; otherwise we would only need to have particle physics. Thus psychologists would consider the question 'Why are you reading this book?' in terms of motivation theory, not usually in terms of neurons, and still less in terms of atoms and quarks. In general, behavioral economists regard neuroscientific causes of behavior as proximate, or mechanistic, while ultimate causes of behavior relate to evolutionary biology and the effects of natural selection. Thus any underlying science relating to physics is ignored in this perspective of causation.

On the philosophical level, reductionism has been most hotly contested in the philosophy of the mind. It is an open question for example in neuroscience how biological processes in the brain relate to mental entities in any general sense. Neuroscientists have to infer mental constructs as mediators between the neural level within the brain and the manifest behavior of the individual. This is a highly relevant issue when it comes to questions of causality and freedom of the will, which are beyond the scope of this book. Basically, the question is how consciousness, as a psychological phenomenon, relates to the neural level. On the neurological level, the behavior of the human organism should be fully determined in principle. And yet, we experience that our actions are not determined, in a sufficient sense, through psychologically causal conditions. In other words, it is still an open question, both in philosophy and neuroscience, whether the experience of free will is neurobiologically real.

## 2.2  Evidence

Traditionally there has been a contrast between the empirical methods used by economists and those used by psychologists, and it is important for students of behavioral economics to be familiar with the historical differences between the two disciplines and their implications if they are to understand the critical attitudes that are sometimes expressed by the different camps. Much of the difference has stemmed from the fact that the two disciplines have tended to use different types of empirical study in their investigations. More recently, we have experienced a marked shift towards applied analysis and empiricism in most fields of economics (Backhouse and Klaes, 2009), and the range of empirical methods used by economists has seen significant expansion.

### Types of empirical study

There are two main types of study in general terms that can be conducted. One type of study is a **field study**, and the other type is an **experimental study**. Before discussing each of these in detail it should also be mentioned that either type of study can be between-subjects or within-subjects. A **between-subjects** study examines differences between two or more groups of people, each of which is given a different task or series of tasks. For example one group may be asked to state preferences relating to rewards a week from now, while another group is asked to state preferences relating to rewards a month from now. A **within-subjects** study examines different responses from the same subjects, which necessitates each subject performing a series of at least two tasks. For example, subjects may be asked to state preferences relating to rewards both one week from now and one month from now. As will become evident from the following discussion, in some circumstances the first type of study is preferable or is the only practical possibility, while in other circumstances the second type of study is preferred.

Although both branches of social science make use of empirical studies in order to test their theories, economists have tended to rely more on field studies while psychologists have relied largely on experimental studies. There have been three main reasons for this.

1   Economists are primarily concerned with studying behavior, what people do; this is shown by their revealed preference in terms of what products they buy. Psychologists are primarily concerned with studying motivation, why they behave as they do.

2   For a long time, the prevalent view in economics has been that it is impossible or impractical to use experiments in economic situations, for the researcher may lack the relevant control. Even when such control is possible, as when an economic adviser can influence or determine government policy, experimentation may have damaging or unethical consequences. Governments may be unwilling to experiment with tax levels (for example based on the infamous Laffer curve), or with using different policies for different groups (for example by giving educational vouchers to one group and general subsidies to another). Although observational studies do not allow the kind of manipulation of relevant variables that is possible in experimental studies, economists have often been able to overcome the resulting problems by using sophisticated statistical or econometric techniques that enable them to isolate the effects of specific variables.

3   Economists have also been more concerned with studying the behavior of groups of agents, in particular markets, rather than single individuals.

## Field studies

These studies involve observing real decisions that people make in their lives. The following are examples of situations involving such types of study:

- Choices involving buying different electrical appliances, where some are more expensive, but save electricity and reduce costs during their lifetime
- Life-cycle saving behavior
- Choices of betting in horse races
- Investment choices, involving buying and selling stocks and bonds
- Choices of smokers and drug addicts which involve trade-offs between current benefits and long-term costs
- Shopping choices where consumers respond to different promotional offers

The advantage of field studies compared with experimental studies is their high level of **ecological validity**. This means that there is no concern that the results do not apply in reality, for the simple reason that the results are, by necessity, real. However, this does not mean that the results are **conceptually valid**, meaning that they actually succeed in measuring what they are supposed to measure. This is because field studies (and experimental studies also to a lesser extent) may be subject to a number of **confounds**. A confound occurs when a result or reported value is a conflation of two or more effects which are not, or cannot be, isolated from each other. The problem of confounds is very common in economics, and makes it difficult to choose between different competing theories or explanations where they are both supported by the same facts.

We shall encounter numerous examples of confounds in the following chapters, but at this stage it will suffice to give one example, involving inter-temporal choice. When people buy inefficient but cheaper electrical appliances this may not be because they discount future cost savings at a high rate. Various other factors may be relevant: (1) people may be ignorant of the future cost savings; (2) people may be informed about future cost savings but disbelieve them or regard them with a large amount of uncertainty; (3) people may have cash constraints that do not permit a higher current expenditure; (4) there may be hidden costs related to buying more efficient appliances, in terms of greater maintenance or reduced reliability; and (5) people may be incapable of translating the relevant monetary information into a basis for decision-making and simply make a random choice, or choose out of habit or current convenience.

As a result of their preference for using field studies, economists tend to shrug off critics who claim that their experiments show that individuals do not act according to the standard assumptions of economic analysis. Economists have various counter-arguments:

1   The assumptions are merely a methodological stance; the standard model makes no claim to say anything about the underlying psychological processes of agents. This argument was discussed earlier.
2   Markets average out individual deviations in behavior; individuals who deviate will tend to be eliminated from the market by competitive forces similar to natural selection.
3   The experiments of psychologists tend to be flawed. This last accusation is discussed in the next section.

The result of these differences in approach has been a significant parting of the ways between economics and psychology for much of the twentieth century. Only in the last 25 years or so has some degree of *rapprochement* been achieved.

To an important extent, this has been the result of the impact of the work of psychologists who had turned their attention to economic decision-making in the new field of economic psychology, while at the same time economists developed an interest in experiments, following in the footsteps of Kahneman and Tversky. Peer-reviewed articles using the methodology of experimental economics only reached 50 per year by 1982, but by 1998 the number of experimental papers published had exceeded 200 (Holt, 2006). Indeed, **experimental economics** is now recognized as a sub-discipline in its own right within economics. The field of experimental economics was largely pioneered by Vernon Smith, who believed that economics could be enriched by experimental methods that would not only lend insight into psychological processes but would also enable a tighter control over the relevant variables in order to come to more specific and reliable conclusions than is often possible with conventional observational studies. This experimental approach has important implications regarding research design and interpretation of results.

### Experimental studies

These studies involve asking subjects to evaluate either real or hypothetical prospects that are manipulated by the investigator. The experimental approach traditionally used by psychology has significant advantages over the observational approach in terms of control over the relevant variables, allowing investigators to manipulate them in order to determine their influence directly. For example, one group of subjects may play a game of chance against a player who is shabbily dressed and deliberately acts diffidently, while another group may play the same game against a professionally dressed and confident opponent. Evidence indicates that subjects bet more against the first type of player, even though the outcome of the game is entirely governed by chance.

In experimental studies either real or hypothetical rewards and costs can be used. These do not have to be monetary in nature, but may relate to health or levels of comfort and discomfort. The obvious advantage of using real rewards is that subjects are more motivated to act in ways that correspond closely to their behavior in real life, and such studies are therefore more likely to yield accurate predictions. However, there is also an advantage of using hypothetical outcomes in terms of flexibility; it is possible to use both large rewards and losses in this case, as well as using longer time delays in intertemporal studies. For example, a study by Kirby and Marakovic (1995) compared discounting under both kinds of situation, using 30 permutations of five different rewards (between $14.75 and $28.50) and six different delays (between 3 and 29 days). The conclusion was that discount rates were lower for hypothetical rewards, and this was also the conclusion of Coller and Williams (1999) in a different type of study, although in this case the results were more ambiguous.

It is thus possible to design experiments and divide subjects into different groups to reveal a large amount of information regarding the influences of different factors that would be impossible or impractical to achieve in observational studies. However, the design and interpretation of such experiments, including those performed under the rubric of behavioral economics, are often viewed by economists as being flawed, for a variety of reasons. We now need to discuss the methodological issues related to behavioral economics in general terms.

There are three main issues that have been raised relating to the experimental methods used in behavioral economics specifically, although further issues are raised regarding neuroeconomics that will be discussed in the next section. The first issue follows on from the discussion above, that mainstream economists often view the design of behavioral experiments as flawed. A second related issue involves the interpretation of results, and the third concerns the treatment of assumptions.

1   *Experimental design*

There are three main issues here. These relate to the use of financial incentives, the use of deception, and lack of control.

a)   *The use of financial incentives*

These incentives are used in order to motivate participants. They are widely used in economic experiments, but not in psychological ones. Economists tend to believe that financial incentives are vital in order to ensure that subjects behave in the same manner that they would in the real world and that they invest appropriate cognitive attention to the demands of the experiment. Psychologists frequently counter that such incentives may distort the results, by vitiating the intrinsic interest that subjects may have in participating in the experiment. Evidence is mixed here, but let us give one example that will illustrate the importance of the issue. A study by Hoffman and colleagues (1996), using unearned rewards, found that people acted more generously in dictator games than the NM predicts, sharing on average 40% of their wealth when acting in complete anonymity. However, a later study by Cherry and colleagues (2002) found that when subjects earned rewards, as opposed to receiving them 'as manna from heaven', the majority of them behaved in a significantly different way, acting as pure self-interested agents as the NM would predict. In this case 95% of them shared none of their wealth with their partners under conditions of complete anonymity. These experiments, and the nature of dictator games, are discussed in more detail in Chapter 10, in terms of their implications for the concept of fairness.

b)   *The use of deception*

Another criticism of many psychological experiments is that the necessary manipulation involves a deception of at least some of the subjects. Several studies, in particular by Hertwig and Ortmann (2001), have indicated the widespread use of deception in experimental studies, with between 30% and 50% of studies published in leading journals such as the *Journal of Personality and Social Psychology* and the *Journal of Experimental Social Psychology* using deception.

Deception is often justified by practitioners on two grounds. First, it allows investigators to create situations that they would not otherwise be able to observe under normal circumstances, such as how people react in emergencies. Second and more important, it enables the investigator to camouflage the real purpose of the experiment from the subjects, in order to prevent them reacting strategically and producing a misleading result. This is particularly important when researching people's behavior and attitudes on sensitive social issues. For example, a study involving racial prejudice may need to be disguised in order to prevent people realizing the purpose of the experiment and reacting with a political correctness that they might not otherwise observe.

The main problem arising from the widespread use of deception is that it becomes common knowledge that psychologists use such methods, and this also influences the behavior of subjects, who tend to react cynically in the knowledge that they may be being deceived. Psychologists are then forced to continually search for new and naïve pools of subjects in order to obtain reliable results from their experiments. The studies of Hertwig and Ortmann indicate the increasing use of freshman students for such experiments.

c)   *Lack of control*

A final problem relating to experimental design is that economists often criticize experiments performed by behaviorists for their lack of control, resulting in a misinterpretation or confounding of effects. This is particularly important when the objective is the elicitation of subjects' preferences. A good illustration of this relates to the endowment effect, discussed in Chapter 5. We will see that some studies show a strong endowment effect, with sellers demanding twice the price that buyers are willing to pay, while other studies with different experimental protocols show no endowment effect at all. Another example concerns the issue of discounting, discussed in Chapters 7 and 8. Many studies show that people discount heavily over the short-term time frame compared with the long term, but this effect may arise because of greater transactions costs for delayed payments compared with immediate payments. The higher short-term discount rate may therefore be a result of confounding two different effects, 'pure' time preference and transactions costs. We will see that this problem can be eliminated by greater experimental control, involving the comparison of two delayed payments.

2    *Interpretation of experimental results*

One problem here relates to the concept of ecological validity mentioned earlier. Can insights gained in the lab be extrapolated to the world beyond? If results cannot be generalized in this way they are of very limited value as far as forming the basis for a good theory, as we have seen in the section on evaluation of theories. In the physical sciences extrapolation is not usually such a problem, since the physical laws of nature are the same everywhere, but the study of humans (and animals) presents problems. Levitt and List (2007) examine five factors, apart from the monetary factors mentioned above, that systematically influence behavior in the lab, causing it to differ from behavior in the field. These factors include: (1) the presence of moral and ethical considerations; (2) the nature and extent of scrutiny of one's actions by others; (3) the context in which the decision is embedded; (4) self-selection of the individuals making the decisions; and (5) the stakes of the game. Levitt and List do not regard these biases as being an insuperable blow to the experimental approach, but rather make various recommendations to allow for such biases in terms of experimental design and interpretation. We will examine the effect of such biases and ways of allowing for them in individual situations throughout the remaining chapters.

Another criticism of experimental economics is that there has been a tendency to be overzealous in 'making far-reaching claims … extrapolated from very slender data' (Binmore and Shaked, 2010a, p. 87). This claim has been fiercely resisted by some leading researchers in the discipline, notably Fehr and Schmidt (2010) and Eckels and Gintis (2010). Binmore and Shaked also make more specific criticisms directed at Fehr and Schmidt's model of inequality-aversion, and these are discussed in Chapter 10. We will examine various claims by experimentalists throughout the remainder of the book, along with the relevant evidence, so readers can decide for themselves whether Binmore and Shaked's claim is well-supported or otherwise.

A further criticism raised by Binmore and Shaked concerns the 'cherrypicking' of results. They claim that there is a tendency for experimental economists to (1) use data sets which support their theories, ignoring other data; (2) report conclusions where data supports their theoretical predictions without reporting conclusions where the data is inconsistent with their theories; and (3) fail to compare these predictions with those of other theories which predict just as well if not better. Some of these criticisms are again leveled at the work of Fehr and Schmidt in particular, and will be discussed in more detail in Chapter 10.

3    *A set of assumptions needs to be evaluated as a whole*

This is a recommendation of Fudenberg (2006) in his article 'Advancing beyond "Advances in Behavioral Economics"'. He observes that the normal approach in developing theories in behavioral economics has been to modify one or two assumptions in the NM in the direction of greater psychological realism. Fudenberg points to the dangers of this step-by-step approach, particularly in the analysis of equilibrium and strategic interaction, and in self-control theories. Relaxing one assumption may have a 'knock-on' effect on other assumptions, making the new set inconsistent, and this needs to be taken into consideration. Therefore modelers need to take all the assumptions as a set and see how many need to be modified in order to end up with a new set that is self-consistent.

By way of conclusion, it is important to note that the purpose of the study is relevant in choosing whether to conduct a field study or an experimental study (Plott and Zeiler, 2007). In general there may be two main purposes: parameter estimation and theory testing. If the purpose is parameter estimation, for example estimating the price elasticity of demand for a good, then a field study may be more appropriate, with the main advantage being the achievement of ecological validity. On the other hand, if the purpose of the study is to test a particular theory, it is necessary to clearly separate the predictions of competing theories to reliably identify the theory that best explains the observed results. Experimental studies are best suited to this task, since they allow the use of controls, replication, and manipulation to facilitate the comparison of different theories.

### Extra-laboratory experiments

Although the discussion above treats field and experimental studies as being dichotomous, it has recently been proposed that empirical studies should be reclassified to introduce a third category of study, extra-laboratory experiments (Charness, Gneezy, and Kuhn, 2013). These are essentially a hybrid between field and experimental studies, whose purpose is to gain some of the advantages of each type of study. Such studies would be performed in the field, without the subjects being aware that they are under observation, thus achieving ecological validity, but at the same time various factors affecting the subjects would be controlled, allowing for the investigation of the effects of a single variable. It is proposed that these studies can also be used as a follow-up to laboratory experiments, since they allow larger subject pools and variations in location. For example, Eckel, El-Gamal, and Wilson (2009) were able to use such a method to investigate risk-taking behavior after Hurricane Katrina, and how this declined over time. Charness, Gneezy, and Kuhn (2013) suggest that extra-laboratory experiments are particularly useful when it is desired to test the effectiveness of a policy intervention. A recent example of such a study concerns the introduction of a 'stand-your-ground' gun law in Florida in 2005, where it has been shown that this resulted in an increase in both total homicides and homicides by firearm among young males (Humphreys, Gasparrini, and Wiebe, 2017), suggesting that this intervention had the opposite effect to that intended.

### Neuroeconomics

Alongside field studies and experiments, there is a third source of evidence that has begun informing behavioral economists. Neuroeconomics has been defined as 'an interdisciplinary line of investigation that combines research from neuroscience, neurobiology, and economics' (Brocas and Carillo, 2008a). Clithero, Tankersley, and Huettel (2008) define neuroeconomics as 'the convergence of the neural and social sciences, applied to the understanding and prediction of decisions about rewards'. A somewhat narrower definition, but what is most important about both these statements, and other similar definitions, is that they involve terms such as 'interdisciplinary' or 'convergence'. There has been a great expansion in the number of neuroeconomic studies performed in the last ten years, as technology has improved and more economists have been persuaded of their value.

Neuroeconomic investigations rely particularly on brain scanning and imaging techniques such as positron emission tomography (PET), fMRI, and regional cerebral blood flow (rCBF). These methods detect brain activity in particular areas in terms of increased blood flow. Other related techniques involve electrophysiology, which measures the electrical activity of the central nervous system (electroencephalography, or EEG, and transcranial magnetic stimulation, or TMS), the peripheral somatic nervous system (electromyography, or EMG), and the peripheral autonomic nervous system (electrodermal activity, or EDA). The last method involves changes in skin conductance caused by various emotional stimuli, and is a common (but not perfectly reliable) basis for lie detection.

The use of fMRI is particularly popular; this involves using an MRI scan to detect increased blood flows in particular regions of the brain (a baseline level of blood flow must be established in a neutral environment for the purposes of comparison), while asking the subject questions related to economics (the functional component). Thus it can be seen which areas of the brain 'light up' in response to various stimuli. The method is not without its problems though; for one thing it is a coarse technique in that there is a low level of resolution, so the responding brain areas can only be determined approximately, whereas many brain interactions occur over very short distances at the neuronal level, requiring a high level of resolution in order to pinpoint.

Neuroscientists can achieve much higher levels of resolution, even to the point of identifying individual neurons activated, but this involves using invasive techniques like inserting needles into the brain, and to this point these techniques have only been used with monkeys. Neuroscientists hope that with the aid of ever-improving technology new techniques will be developed over the next few years that will improve the level of resolution without endangering the safety of the subject.

In addition to, and in combination with, the above techniques, neuroscientists also research how stimuli affect various neurotransmitters and hormones. These include dopamine, serotonin, oxytocin, adrenalin, testosterone, and cortisol. Much is now known regarding the effects of these chemicals, both in terms of what events stimulate their increase or decrease and the effects of these changes on the brain and behavior.

However, while there is general agreement relating to the nature of neuroeconomics in terms of the kind of data and variables that it uses, there is much controversy relating to its objectives, scope, interpretation, and its general role in informing and testing economic hypotheses. Many of these issues relate to the concept of reductionism, discussed in general terms in the first section of the chapter.

There appear to be five main issues related to the incorporation of neuroeconomics into the discipline of economics, all of which have implications for behavioral economics: (1) neuroeconomic studies are irrelevant to economics; (2) neuroeconomics is not relevant in discussions of economic welfare; (3) neuroeconomics is essentially concerned with correlation not causation, leading to invalid conclusions; (4) the 'Emergent Phenomenon' argument, related to ecological validity; and (5) the use of inappropriate statistical analysis.

It goes beyond the scope of this book to discuss these objections in detail, but it is important for any student of behavioral economics to have a flavor of the issues involved, and the reader can examine the studies referred to in the discussion below for further details.

**1**    *Neuroeconomic studies are irrelevant to economics*

Supporters of neuroeconomics sometimes claim that the discipline opens up the 'black box' of the mind in decision-making, in the same way that the theory of the firm opened up the black box of decision-making in the firm. Bernheim (2009) counters this claim in two ways. First, the theory of the firm may have opened the black box of the firm, but it still examined decision-making, at the level of the individual. The same cannot be said for neuroeconomics. Second, neuroeconomics may open a black box, but in reality there is a series of black boxes here, like Russian dolls. As Bernheim puts it: 'Do we really believe that good economics requires a command of string theory?' This is a reductionist problem, and it follows from what has been said before in this context that it is only worth opening the black box of the mind under certain circumstances. We will return to this question in the concluding section of the chapter, on consilience.

Gul and Pesendorfer (2008) are perhaps the most forceful advocates of the irrelevance of neuroeconomics argument, sometimes referred to as the 'Behavioral Sufficiency' argument (Clithero, Tankersley, and Huettel, 2008). They take issue in particular with the approach of Camerer, Loewenstein, and Prelec (2005), expressed as follows:

> First, we show that neuroscience findings raise questions about the usefulness of some of the most common constructs that economists commonly use, such as risk aversion, time preference, and altruism. (Gul and Pesendorfer, 2008, pp. 31–32)

Gul and Pesendorfer go on to state: 'The argument that evidence from brain science can falsify economic theories is … absurd.' The basis for their view is that economics makes no claims regarding the psychological or neurological processes involved in making choice decisions. They draw an analogy, by considering the reverse situation, concluding that an economic study cannot invalidate a theory relating to neuroscience, on the similar grounds that neuroscience takes no position regarding economic axioms such as revealed preference.

A second related argument put forward by Gul and Pesendorfer is that if two different economic models make different predictions regarding decisions then they can be evaluated by examining standard choice data; if the two models make the same predictions, then economists will not be interested in distinguishing between them.

There appears to be some misunderstanding here regarding the claims of the behaviorists. Gul and Pesendorfer are correct in saying that economics makes no claims regarding psychological processes and also that evidence from brain science cannot falsify economic theories. Models related to the NM tend to involve 'as if' statements, meaning that agents behave as if a particular mental calculus was being performed. Gul and Pesendorfer explain that this is 'an expositional device not meant to be taken literally'. They then give an example relating to consumer behavior, where it is predicted that consumers will buy the amount of a good which equates the marginal utility of the last dollar spent with the marginal utility of the last dollar spent on other goods. This does not imply that consumers actually perform the mental processes involved, but it does make the implicit assumption that consumers aim to maximize their total utility. Again, we will return to this issue in the final section on consilience.

It is notable that there is less resistance to neuroscience in psychology than in economics. This should not be surprising, since there is a more direct and closer relationship between neural activity and psychological states than there is between neural activity and decision-making. There are several cases where neuroscientific studies have aided the development of psychological theories. One example is the phenomenon of placebo analgesia, where the mere belief that one is receiving an effective treatment reduces the emotional experience of pain. For a long time this was attributed to response bias, with no real reduction in pain. This theory was contradicted by Wager and colleagues (2004), who provided evidence from observations of changes in neural activity that placebos do reduce the actual experience of pain.

**2    *Neuroeconomics is not relevant in discussions of economic welfare***

Gul and Pesendorfer argue that behaviorists not only make invalid claims of a positive nature regarding the value of neuroscientific studies, but make invalid normative claims, in particular that the economic choices people make do not maximize their happiness. In particular they dispute the claim by Kahneman (1994) that 'the term "utility" can be anchored in the hedonic experience of outcomes, or in the preference or desire for that outcome'. They also challenge the following claim by Camerer, Loewenstein, and Prelec (2005, p. 36):

> If likes and wants diverge, this would pose a fundamental challenge to welfare economics.

Behaviorists therefore tend to form conclusions regarding rationality based on this divergence, and these are discussed in detail in the next two chapters.

Gul and Pesendorfer respond by saying:

> Welfare in economics is a *definition* and *not a theory* (of happiness). Therefore, the divergence between "liking and wanting" does not pose any challenge to the standard definition of welfare, no matter how the former is defined.

This may be true, but it is also a source of confusion, since in a different article Gul and Pesendorfer (2007, p. 471), in referring to happiness as a problem in moral philosophy, argue that:

> Any faith in economists' (behavioral or otherwise) abilities to resolve such problems in moral philosophy cannot be based in the past accomplishments of welfare economics, and the best way to understand welfare economics is to view it as a part of positive economics.

In this context the term 'welfare economics' is being referred to as a body of theory, rather than a definition. Gul and Pesendorfer also question the ability of developments in neuroscience to resolve 'age-old problems in moral philosophy about what constitutes true happiness'.

Behaviorists tend to take a paternalistic approach to welfare policy, according to Gul and Pesendorfer, since people need to be 'prodded' in order to take actions that will make them happier. This paternalistic approach is described and supported by Thaler and Sunstein (2009) in their recent book entitled *Nudge*; it may be noticed that Thaler and Sunstein did not use the title *'Prod'*. Differences between prodding and nudging and various issues related to this approach will be discussed at various points in the book in the context of policy implications.

**3**   *Neuroeconomics is essentially concerned with correlation not causation, leading to invalid conclusions*

The standard approach in neuroeconomics has been to make inferences from behavior to brain, observing how different aspects of behavior are correlated with activity in particular brain regions. For example, ultimatum game rejections are correlated with high activation of the anterior insula relative to the dorsolateral prefrontal cortex (dlPFC) (Sanfey et al., 2003). But, as any scientist will remind us, this does not prove causation. However, causation in neuroeconomics can be established by various experimental protocols. In the above example it has been shown that disruption of dlPFC function by repetitive transcranial magnetic stimulation (rTMS) leads to increased acceptance of low offers, indicating a causal relationship between dlPFC activity and rejection of low offers. Likewise, administration of an amygdala inhibitor, benzodiazepine, has also been found to lead to a lower rejection of low offers, indicating the importance of amygdala activation in rejection.

A main area of controversy in the causation issue concerns what is known as 'reverse inference', which is claimed to be invalid, rendering studies relying on it inconclusive. Reverse inference involves observing neural states and drawing conclusions regarding emotional or cognitive states or probable behavior. Several economists, including neuroeconomists, have issued cautions relating to this approach. Poldrack (2006) has shown that its usefulness is limited by the selectivity of the activation in question. This means that if a specific brain region only activates for a particular emotional/cognitive state then reverse inference may be valid and useful. However, Fox and Poldrack (2009) claim that there is little evidence for strong selectivity in current neuroimaging studies and urge caution in using reverse inference. They give the example of activity in the ventral striatum; this can mean the subject is experiencing reward, but activity in this region can also be associated with aversive stimuli, or with novel non-rewarding stimuli. Fehr (2009) suggests that in these situations where multiple causes are possible, additional data, such as other physiological responses or self-report measures, should be sought before drawing conclusions regarding mental states.

There are many problems involved in applying and interpreting brain scans, even though the level of technology is continually improving. A further problem, related to the one above, and described by Fudenberg (2006), concerns another complication regarding the relationship between behavior and neural correlates. Because there is a high level of interactivity between different brain areas, it is difficult to unravel cause from effect in terms of neural processes and functions. Correlation does not imply causation. Therefore, just because there is activity in a certain part of the brain, this does not mean that this part of the brain is initiating the activity; there may be an underlying cause elsewhere, involving 'upstream' neurons. Thus it is difficult to draw conclusions regarding the neural causes of behavior. It is sometimes possible to surmount this problem using studies with lesion patients; in these cases it is known that there is a certain area of the brain which is damaged, so that any deviant behavior observed can usually be concluded to be an effect of this neural deficit.

**4    *The 'Emergent Phenomenon' argument***

This argument is essentially the same as the one described earlier in terms of issues in behavioral economics regarding the use of experimental studies and their ecological validity. It applies even more strongly to neuroeconomics, since by its very nature this discipline is constrained to using experimental studies, usually with very small samples. Thus it may be invalid or misleading to extrapolate findings in the laboratory to behavior, or even neural states, in the real world. Neuroscientific experiments may be conducted under highly artificial conditions, and therefore may not translate well into out-of-sample situations.

**5    *The use of inappropriate statistical analysis***

An important recent study has cast serious doubt on the findings of many neuroeconomics studies involving fMRI (Eklund et al., 2016). This study used various standard software packages commonly used to analyze fMRI scans and applied them to a large set of data relating to resting-state control subjects, comparing different random samples. According to standard assumptions parametric analysis would predict no difference between such random samples, with a 5% error rate in terms of finding false positives. Instead the authors of the study found a false positive rate as high as 70%, shedding doubt on the validity of as many as 40,000 past neuroeconomic studies using fMRI analysis.

There is a broader lesson to be learned from this study in terms of methodology, which applies to all economics, not just neuroeconomics. Analysis and predictions are only as good as the assumptions on which they are based. Parametric statistical analysis is based on the assumption of underlying distributions having a 'normal' or Gaussian curve. Many variables do not have distributions conforming to this shape, notably in the financial markets, leading to what have been referred to as 'black swans' (Taleb, 2007). This can have disastrous consequences in terms of false predictions, and this aspect is discussed in a case study later in the text, relating to the global financial crisis of 2007.

## 2.3  Consilience

The behavioral sciences in general include economics, psychology, sociology, political science, anthropology, and those aspects of biology that deal with human and animal behavior. However, over the last century these disciplines have become highly fragmented and isolated from each other. Gintis (2009) claims that there are currently four different, and incompatible, models of decision-making and strategic interaction being used in these disciplines: economic, psychological, sociological, and biological. He makes a plea for unification of the behavioral sciences so that each can learn best practice from the others. There is some further discussion of Gintis's recommendations later in the section, but before entering this discussion it is useful to consider the position of behavioral economics specifically. In many ways, behavioral economics may be regarded as being at the forefront of this movement towards unification.

From the birth of behavioral economics the methods used by researchers in the area have tended to combine the traditional methods used by economists with those more commonly used by psychologists. In particular experiments have become more popular, and this has led to the development of the field of experimental economics discussed earlier. The advantages of control are clear compared with the ambiguity often resulting from observational studies. A good example is the study of bargaining situations that often result in deadlock or impasses, such as the failure of legal cases to settle before trial and labor strikes, where the concept of fairness is relevant. Mere observation of such situations in the real world often cannot lead to definite conclusions. Failure to reach agreement could be caused by agency problems, reputation-building effects in repeated negotiations, or simply by a lack of cognitive understanding by the participants. However, by modeling the negotiation process into an ultimatum bargaining game experiment (discussed at length in Part 3), it is possible to eliminate the last three possibilities and test in isolation the nature of people's concept of fairness.

So what does consilience mean, and why is it relevant? First it is necessary to explain the origin of this term. It is perhaps best known as the title of a book by the sociobiologist E. O. Wilson, although he borrowed it from the philosopher of science Whewell, who in 1840 defined consilience as follows:

> The Consilience of Inductions takes place when an Induction, obtained from one class of facts, coincides with an Induction, obtained from another different class. This Consilience is a test of the truth of the Theory in which it occurs. (quoted in Wilson, 1998, pp. 6–7)

Consilience thus involves both horizontal and vertical integration between disciplines, and it can relate not only to the sciences, both natural and behavioral, but also to philosophy and the humanities in general. A couple of examples will aid an understanding of its practical application.

An example illustrated by Wilson himself concerns the problem of regulating forest reserves. Many different disciplines can provide input as far as solving this problem: ecology, economics, biology, geography, history, ethics, sociology, and ethics can all aid an informed environmental policy. If any one of these disciplines is ignored the policy is likely to prove less than optimal. Of course, given an issue of such worldwide scale, one can question the use of the term 'optimal', and its meaning must be clarified in this context.

A different kind of example, more in keeping with Whewell's definition, and more relevant in terms of the traditional conflict between economics and psychology, is provided by research into the role of the emotions in human decision-making. The majority of philosophers in the past, notably Kant, have held that the emotions should be kept out of decision-making, as being an enemy of reason. However, recent empirical evidence from different disciplines questions this assertion. Frank (1988), an economist, has used an essentially game-theoretic approach to conclude that emotions are a valuable aid in making optimal decisions, because they provide credible commitments. Similar conclusions have been reached independently by the economists Schelling (1960) and Hirshleifer (1987). The evolutionary biologist Trivers (1971, 1985) and the evolutionary psychologists Daly and Wilson (1988) and Pinker (1997) have arrived at the same conclusion in terms of emotions having evolved as adaptive psychological mechanisms. Damasio (1994, 2009), a neuroscientist, has again arrived at the same conclusion regarding the value of the emotions in decision-making, by studying patients with brain damage and developing a 'somatic marker' hypothesis. These different kinds of approach, all making use of independent facts and methodologies, provide strong evidence against the traditional Kantian model.

A further example of consilience is in the field of evolutionary biology, which underlies much of behavioral economics in the reductionist approach. Developments in the late twentieth century synthesized and amalgamated a lot of research findings in diverse fields, which until then could not be connected to each other or even seemed contradictory. These fields include genetics, cytology, systematics, morphology, ecology, botany, and paleontology.

The examples above indicate first that the disciplines of economics and psychology can complement each other, as the pioneering studies of Kahneman and Tversky, and Thaler, have demonstrated, along with many more recent studies in behavioral economics. They also indicate that both disciplines can be further enriched by research from other new disciplines, notably evolutionary psychology and neuroscience. It is important to stress that the relationship is one of *complementarity* here, not *substitution*. Gintis (2009) has argued persuasively that the unification of the behavioral sciences requires not just borrowing from research findings but also borrowing of methodologies, since at present these are conflicting in the different sciences. He proposes that there are five conceptual units where a more uniform approach would benefit all the sciences: (1) gene-culture coevolution; (2) the sociopsychological theory of norms; (3) game theory; (4) the rational actor model; and (5) complexity theory. All of these elements are explained and discussed in more detail elsewhere in the text: gene-culture coevolution was discussed in the first chapter; social norms are discussed in Chapter 10; game theory is discussed later in this section and also in more detail in Chapter 9; the rational actor model is the basis of expected utility theory, discussed in Chapter 5; and complexity theory, related to the complexity of social systems involving multiple human interactions, is involved in the behavioral aspects of all the topics in the text. Therefore at this point a broad summary of the different approaches in the behavioral sciences will suffice:

- Economics focuses on the rational actor model and classical game theory.
- Psychology focuses on norms and complexity theory, sometimes incorporating gene-culture coevolution.
- Sociology focuses on norms and complexity theory, but tends to stress cultural evolution at the expense of the genetic component.
- Biology focuses on the genetic component of evolution, at the expense of the cultural component, and also on aspects of the rational actor model and evolutionary game theory.

Gintis is essentially suggesting that consilience is only likely to be achieved to any significant extent when the different sciences borrow from methods used in other sciences and take a less blinkered approach. This is where we need to return to some of the issues described earlier related to neuroeconomics.

*Behavioral sufficiency*

Gul and Pesendorfer (2008) state that 'different objectives demand different abstractions'. They claim that economics and psychology have different rather than similar objectives, and that therefore they use different concepts and different methods. We are in agreement with this, because we do not believe it detracts from the complementarity of the different disciplines. Gul and Pesendorfer rightly claim that brain scans are not a substitute for studies involving revealed preference or actual behavior, but the latter cannot substitute for brain scans either in terms of the information revealed. This is not to say that brain scans are some panacea for understanding human behavior, for we have seen that their interpretation is problematic.

Most behaviorists agree that it is legitimate for economists to proceed with 'as if' models *provided that* they make accurate predictions. However, behaviorists do not generally claim that evidence from brain science can falsify economic theories. Instead the behaviorist claim is that economic theories are often falsified by empirical studies involving economic data relating to revealed preference; in other words they are falsified on their own terms. Where studies in brain science are useful is in understanding *why* the theories are falsified, in terms of the underlying psychological or neurological processes. These studies may then indicate that certain implicit assumptions in the 'as if' statements of the standard model may be bad assumptions to make because they lead to false predictions.

A good illustration of this issue concerns credit card spending. People spend more on credit cards than if they pay cash, contradicting the NM. Evidence falsifying the model comes from economic data. However, brain studies, like those conducted by Knutson and colleagues (2007), can help us to understand why people act in this way. There is also evidence from neuroeconomic studies that neural imaging data can be used to predict future behavior. For example, the Knutson and colleagues study shows that brain activity in different regions can predict purchasing behavior above and beyond self-report variables. Relationships between consumer preferences, prices, spending, and brain activation are discussed in more detail in Chapter 6, in connection with mental accounting.

Further evidence of the ability of neural imaging to predict economic behavior comes from a study by de Quervain and colleagues (2004). This indicated that activation of a particular neuron during one game was correlated with punishment in a different game. The de Quervain and colleagues study is discussed in more detail in Chapter 10 in relation to fairness. The finding here may have large implications for economics, since it indicates that data relating to neural states can be a better predictor of behavior than other aspects of subjects' behavior.

Therefore, although Gul and Pesendorfer (2008) maintain that brain scans are not economic phenomena and are therefore not relevant to economic theory, it seems fair to say that if they can be used to predict economic phenomena better than existing economic models, then they may suggest how to construct better economic models.

As mentioned earlier, Gul and Pesendorfer have also argued that if the same economic or behavioral data can be explained by two different economic theories, then economists are not concerned with distinguishing between the two theories. An example is the level of health insurance cover that people have, which is generally agreed to be too low, but which can be explained by two different theories: (1) people have carefully weighed up the costs and benefits of health insurance and decided that cover is too expensive to buy; or (2) people have not attended to the issue of cover and therefore have not taken any action to obtain it. Although the two theories make the same prediction, that people will not take out sufficient health insurance, the policy implications are quite different. In the first case government may want to examine the costs of cover to see if these are excessive and what can be done to reduce them, but in the second case some kind of 'nudge' policy may be appropriate in order to encourage people to act in their own best interests. As we will see in Chapter 8, Section 8.7, this may be as simple as changing the default option in people's employment contracts. Thus it is important to distinguish between the two theories from a policy-making viewpoint. The task of the economic researcher therefore is to conduct a further field study or experiment designed to eliminate the confounds.

A related issue, again involving the claim of behavioral sufficiency, returns to the concept of reductionism. Let us consider the remark by Bernheim regarding economists understanding string theory. This would be a case of 'precipice reductionism', where we seek for an understanding of some phenomenon by reducing the explanation to the lowest possible level, which is particle physics. The approach and many behavioral economists recommend is hierarchical reductionism where the explanation sought is at only one level lower. Of course this does not eliminate the need for further explanations lower down the chain, and Bernheim's analogy with the Russian dolls is quite correct, but such explanations are regarded as being beyond the scope of economics, and unhelpful in understanding economic relationships.

## Happiness

Gul and Pesendorfer are correct in saying that the NM has nothing to say about happiness, and that it makes no normative or 'therapeutic' claims in terms of helping decision-makers to make choices that will make them happier. However, contrary to their claim, neuro-economics does not try to improve an individual's objectives. It can clarify the different implications of pursuing different objectives, for example happiness and welfare, but it does not as a science propose any moral philosophy regarding what people 'should' do. Individual behaviorists may of course make normative statements, as do other economists, but this is not an element of neuroeconomics per se.

Furthermore, defining welfare purely in terms of revealed preferences does narrow the scope of economic analysis. We will see examples in later chapters of situations where the difference between liking and wanting is significant, and where preference and choice are not identical. There are important policy implications here. It is not just a matter of people making 'mistakes', in terms of bad judgments based on bounded rationality, for example looking the wrong way when crossing the road in a foreign country. There are other reasons why individuals may take actions that they regret afterwards in terms of not maximizing their welfare. Decisions involving intertemporal choice frequently involve this situation, for example experimenting with drugs and then becoming an addict, or choosing a lump sum pension instead of an annuity. If we can analyze the reasons for these non-optimal decisions this can help both the individuals involved and policy-makers. Some may still regard this as being beyond the scope of economics, but, if we are concerned with the study and achievement of the optimal allocation of resources, it seems curious not to extend the NM in ways that may better enable us to attain this end.

## Constraints on economic theory

This is the area in which consilience is hardest to achieve. As we have said before in connection with reductionism, scientists tend to be defensive when specialists in other disciplines start to tell them that they can only develop theories within certain constraints determined outside their discipline. These 'external' constraints apply in particular to theories in evolutionary biology and neuroeconomics. Obviously this is a highly contentious area. We believe that the best approach here is to review basic neuroscientific premises and then take some examples which illustrate the principle of biological plausibility, advocated by Clithero, Tankersley and Huettel (2008).

Perhaps the most basic premise underlying neuroeconomics is that there are multiple brain systems, involving modularity (Brocas and Carrillo, 2008a); this is supported by evidence from evolutionary biology, suggesting that multiple systems are the result of an evolutionary process whenever an adaptation that serves one function cannot, because of its specialization, serve other functions. However, there is no rigid one-to-one mapping of system to function, which is why reverse inference presents problems. Furthermore, there is evidence for 'strategic interaction' between different systems, with different brain systems performing different and sometimes incompatible functions. As a result, the brain may have to select among competing options.

Now we can consider some examples which illustrate how the decision-making process is shaped by these fundamental premises, and why biological plausibility is a relevant principle. All the examples involve behavior that cannot be explained by the standard economic model. Psychologists, in particular evolutionary psychologists, often refer to the brain having a dual system for decision-making. One system is quick, automatic, and is sometimes referred to as 'hot', because it can rely on emotional responses; we sometimes refer to 'acting on instinct' when this system is used, liking it to ducking when an object comes flying at our head. The other system, much more recently evolved, is a 'cold' analytical one, which takes longer to implement; we tend to use this when deciding whether or not to take up a job offer, or what savings policy to invest in. Although this second system, unlike the first, involves conscious thought, it does not necessarily result in better decisions (Damasio, 1994); however, the existence of the two systems can lead to conflicts like preference reversals and decision biases, which will be discussed in the following chapters. Methodologically, it is important to note that dual-systems models relying on neurobiological data can be tested empirically in terms of developing hypotheses regarding the nature and timing of interactions between different brain systems. If such models are supported by evidence from their own discipline, they can be useful in guiding economic models that will explain behavioral phenomena better.

A similar example applies to intertemporal decision-making, where we will see that the standard economic model of exponential discounting does not explain behavior nearly as well as a hyperbolic or quasi-hyperbolic model in a number of situations. Neuroscientific evidence suggests that people use different reward valuation systems for immediate reward versus future reward (Bechara, 2005), and this would explain why the standard model frequently does not fit behavioral data – it is not biologically plausible. Dual-system models like the 'planner-doer' model discussed in Chapter 8 may be more plausible.

We will give one more example at this stage. There is much neuroscientific evidence that there is a dopamine-mediated reward prediction error, where the neurotransmitter dopamine records the difference between how good an event is and how good it was expected to be (Caplin and Dean, 2008; Bernheim and Rangel, 2004). This effect would translate into decision-making behavior that would contradict the expected utility maximization theory (EUT) in the NM. Furthermore, it can be used to develop competing predictions of behavior to be compared with the NM. Since empirical evidence of behavior tends not to support NM in many instances, this again suggests that EUT is not biologically plausible.

### Game theory

There are many different, and confusing, terms used to describe different aspects of, or approaches to, game theory: standard game theory, classical game theory, analytical game theory, epistemic game theory, behavioral game theory, psychological game theory, and evolutionary game theory.

It is useful at this point to clarify these terms and see how the different aspects of game theory relate to each other. Essentially it is possible to distinguish between three main branches of game theory: (1) standard game theory; (2) behavioral game theory; and

(3) evolutionary game theory. Since different disciplines vary in their use of these three different branches of game theory, and since there appear, at least superficially, to be certain conflicts between the branches, some consilience between the branches is necessary.

Standard game theory is also referred to as classical game theory, and analytical game theory (which is confusing, since all game theory is analytical). This type of game theory is what might be called 'mainstream' in economics. Behavioral game theory incorporates additional elements, and also includes epistemic and psychological game theory. Both of these approaches involve the analysis of how people reason about other people's actions, and how they form beliefs, including beliefs about the beliefs of others.

The NM incorporates classical game theory, but makes more basic assumptions than those generally involved in behavioral game theory. However, a discussion of the differences between the two approaches can be postponed until Chapter 9, because both of them treat the players as thinking agents (not necessarily rational) interacting with each other. Players can consider the outcomes of their actions in the future, even if these outcomes are uncertain because of incomplete information. These interactions need to be examined before considering social preferences and fairness in Chapter 10.

Evolutionary game theory is different from either of the other branches, because it does not treat agents as being 'thinking'. The evolutionary process is generally considered as a principal-agent situation with 'Nature' being the principal and the individual being the agent (although the individual might be a tree for example). In this context we can examine how our evolutionary history has shaped our preferences, beliefs, and attitudes to risk, all of which are discussed in Chapters 3 to 8; therefore a brief explanation regarding the nature of this theory is required at this stage.

The most fundamental point to observe here is that evolutionary game theory is best understood by anthropomorphizing the principal and agent, that is, considering them as thinking beings. Thus it may seem strange to say that Nature 'wishes' individuals to maximize their biological fitness, but this is really a shorthand way of saying that individuals who maximize fitness will ultimately dominate the population through the process of natural selection. Similarly, we may say that trees in a jungle will 'strive' to be taller and taller, meaning that taller trees gain more sunlight and are more likely to survive and reproduce than shorter trees, again leading to taller trees dominating the tree population. In the context of the human population, an example is that people with a preference for salty, sugary, and fatty foods would have survived and reproduced better than others, thus coming to dominate the population, *without these people ever consciously making the relevant judgments and deliberately adopting a strategy for finding these foods*. The phrase in italics is important because it stresses the fact that evolutionary game theory can be applied to 'non-thinking' situations.

## 2.4  Summary

- Theories are statements that describe or explain relationships between phenomena we observe.
- Theories should not be evaluated on the basis of their assumptions.
- There are four main criteria for evaluating and comparing theories: congruence with reality, generality, tractability, and parsimony.
- Reductionism is a vital key to success in developing science, in spite of its bad press. It is a means of relating explanations at different levels of science to each other and integrating them into a whole.
- Economics has traditionally relied on using field studies to test theories empirically, whereas behavioral economics follows psychology in using experimental studies to a greater degree.

- Issues raised in behavioral economics include experimental design, the interpretation of experimental results, and the need to evaluate assumptions as a set.
- Neuroeconomic theory can be defined as an interdisciplinary line of investigation that combines research from neuroscience, neurobiology, and economics.
- Issues raised in neuroeconomics are its relevance to economic theory, its relevance to economic welfare, its tendency to use reverse inference and its ecological validity.
- Consilience refers to a horizontal and vertical integration of disciplines in terms of synthesizing their theories and empirical findings in a complementary manner.
- Consilience may furthermore involve a unification of methodology, since at present the various behavioral sciences tend to utilize different and incompatible approaches to developing theories.
- The most contentious aspect of neuroeconomics, causing a significant problem for consilience, lies in its claims to constrain economic theory; it is suggested that the concept of biological plausibility is relevant here as a guiding principle for theory development.

## 2.5  Review questions

1  Explain why theories should not be evaluated on the basis of their assumptions.
2  Explain the meaning of reductionism as it is used in the chapter, giving an example.
3  Describe the differences between a within-subjects study and a between-subjects study, giving examples of each.
4  Describe the advantage and disadvantages of an experimental study compared with a field study.
5  Explain three issues that have been raised with the methods used in behavioral economics.
6  Explain what is meant by neuroeconomics and describe four issues that have been raised by its use.
7  Explain what is meant by 'reverse inference' and why it is problematical in terms of analysis.
8  Explain what is meant by the term consilience, giving an example.
9  Explain the 'behavioral sufficiency' argument.
10  Explain what is meant by neuroeconomics imposing constraints on economic theory, giving an example of how this might happen.

## 2.6  Applications

### Case 2.1  Altruism and the brain

Economists have frequently been accused of having physics-envy. This is because the subject has traditionally been regarded as a 'soft science', lacking the rigorous methodology, objectivity, and explanatory precision of the 'hard sciences'. However, with the increasing application of neuroscience in economics, the new discipline of neuroeconomics has developed considerably in the last 15 years or so, and this has enabled the discipline of economics to improve its credentials as a hard science. In the early years of neuroeconomics, studies concentrated on using fMRI scans to identify different parts of the brain which

▶

appeared to 'light up' in terms of increased blood flow under different types of stimulus. These studies, while certainly useful, have been limited in scope and explanatory power. More recently a second generation of more sophisticated studies has been performed, often using a combination of techniques, and these have produced more precise and robust results, along with some interesting testable predictions. A good example of this progress is in the area of altruistic behavior. This is an aspect of behavior where self-report is notoriously unreliable, with people being reluctant to reveal their real motives, in order to preserve their image, or indeed being unaware of their real motives, since these are subconscious. Thus studies of brain activity are particularly revealing here.

Altruism is usually defined as behavior involving costs to the self with no corresponding material benefit. This aspect of behavior has always posed problems for the NM of economic behavior which proposes that all behavior is selfish, and for many people this has been a fundamental criticism of economics as a science. Neuroeconomic studies have now shown that it is relatively easy, at least in principle, to modify the NM to take altruistic behavior into account. The key to this lies in the word 'material'; neuroeconomics has shown that the benefit is psychic. Thus people can be simultaneously altruistic and selfish, in the sense that their behavior, outwardly appearing to benefit others, is actually performed in order to make us feel better. Moll and colleagues (2006) use fMRI scans to investigate giving to charity and report that this behavior activates the same mesolimbic reward system that is involved when we receive monetary benefits.

Later studies have increased our understanding of altruism and the empathy that may underlie it. Marsh and colleagues (2008) find using fMRI scanning that subjects with lower empathy and more antisocial traits tend to have less activity in the amygdala. Marsh and colleagues (2014) furthermore find that, when subjects are exposed to facial expressions showing fear, prosocial individuals, who are more likely to display altruism, tend to have more activity in the right amygdala. They also tend to have a larger right amygdala, which may suggest that this aspect of empathy is genetic.

One of the most advanced studies of the neural processes underlying altruism has been performed by Hein and colleagues (2016). This study examines the different motives behind altruism by investigating not just the parts of the brain that are involved but also the way they interact with one another. By doing this they can examine a particular behavior, and determine whether it is motivated by empathy or by reciprocity. This behavior related to donating in a dictator game, where a subject must decide how to share a given pot of money with a partner, with no obligation. In their experiments they induce empathy in some subjects by requiring them to observe a partner (collaborating with the investigators) in pain from an electric shock; they also induce reciprocity in other subjects by requiring them to observe a partner donating money to prevent the observer suffering a shock, thus making the subject feel obligated to the partner. Using fMRI combined with dynamic causal modeling they find that different motives for the same altruistic behavior activate different neural pathways. For empathy-induced altruism there is positive connectivity between the anterior cingulate cortex and the anterior insula, while for reciprocity-induced altruism there is positive connectivity between the anterior insula and the ventral striatum. Having established a measure of degree of selfishness/prosociality based on giving in a dictator game, the study also performs a further experiment and finds a difference in motivation between selfish and prosocial people: inducing empathy increased altruism in selfish people but not in prosocial people, while inducing reciprocity increased altruism in prosocial people but had no effect on selfish people.

▶

There are a number of interesting issues raised in these studies:

1   *The nature of economic behavior*
    Economic behavior is not just about monetary transactions. 'Altruistic' acts and spiteful acts also are relevant. We need to understand the basis of such acts in order to explain and predict human behavior in a wide variety of different situations, such as donating to charity, labor strikes, lending the neighbor one's car, and remonstrating with people who litter the streets.

2   *Fairness and social preferences*
    This aspect is closely related to the first one. We need to understand the importance of inequality-aversion, the perceived kindness of others, reciprocity, and the intentions of others if we are to predict behavior in social situations when strategic interaction is important. This area is covered in Chapter 10.

3   *The role of neuroscience*
    The study described above demonstrates clearly how useful neuroscience can be in explaining behavior that cannot easily be explained by the standard economic model. In particular it shows that 'self-interest' needs to be understood in a broad context. Charitable acts are thus self-interested acts because they make us feel good, contrary to the common narrow understanding of self-interested acts. It is important to realize that only by performing neuroscientific studies involving techniques such as fMRI can we establish firm evidence regarding the real motivations behind 'altruistic' and spiteful acts, since people often deny these motivations, and even 'honest' introspection may not reveal them. We can also see here the importance of the concept of consilience, with the disciplines of economics, psychology, and neuroscience complementing each other.

4   *Policy implications*
    The NM is only concerned with behavior, not with the motives underlying this behavior. Economists may justify this if their models can correctly predict behavior, but if the same behavior can have different underlying motivations with different people then there may be important policy implications. For example, a charity may need to know the psychological attributes of its target audience to successfully persuade them to donate money, food, or other goods, while governments may also need to know these attributes to persuade people to donate blood or refrain from littering the streets.

## Case 2.2  Riots in the UK

On August 6, 2011 and for the following four days riots spread throughout several cities in the UK. They started in the Tottenham area of London, sparked off by the shooting of a suspect by the police, and then spread to other parts of London, and to other major cities, including Birmingham, Liverpool, and Manchester. Cars, businesses, and houses were set alight, shops looted, and the police and other emergency services were attacked with bricks, petrol bombs, and even guns. Like other riots in various countries over the last few years, BlackBerries and Facebook were commonly used by rioters as a means of communication in order to coordinate quick mass movements and outmaneuver the police. However, these riots were unlike any others in recent times for several reasons. First, they were not primarily politically or ideologically motivated, unlike the 'Arab Spring'. There was

▶

▼

no broad issue involved, such as antiglobalization or the poll tax, in the case of the majority of the participants. Second, the riots were not race riots. Although the original incident involved a black man being shot by the police, the participants in the rioting were both black and white. The common features were that the rioters tended to be young, poor, and were often gang members or operated in gangs.

So why are these events of particular relevance as far as the methodology of behavioral economics is concerned? Because they have come as a vast shock to most of the British public, in terms of their violence and novelty, the riots have initiated a wide variety of theories attempting to explain their causes. It is not intended here to judge or evaluate these theories; however, it will illustrate many of the concepts and issues of the chapter if we examine three main issues: (1) the relationships between the various theories; (2) the type of evidence that is relevant in evaluating the theories; and (3) the policy implications.

The differences between theories are largely related to the political persuasions of those holding the theories. Those on the left have blamed the frustrations of young and often low-skilled people, increasingly marginalized in society because of joblessness or working in dead-end jobs with no prospects. Increasing cuts in public services, such as the closing of youth centers, have aggravated their situation, and frustrations are also increased when these cuts are blamed on the recent financial crisis, which in turn is blamed on the greed of bankers who are seen as profiting enormously at the expense of ordinary working people. The French press in particular has blamed Anglo-Saxon capitalism for increasing inequality to intolerable levels.

Commentators on the right often blame the strategy of the police in attempting to maintain order. They claim the police have been hindered in their willingness and ability to take control of the situation by fears of human rights activists who view any police action as a violation of human rights, particularly if minorities are involved. The police therefore took a very defensive stance during the rioting and looting, not even attempting to maintain public order in many places, let alone prevent criminality. These commentators claim that this 'do nothing' strategy encouraged people to participate in riots, in terms of both violent actions against persons and property, and simple opportunistic theft. Other theories from the political right, as voiced by David Cameron, the former British prime minister, blame outright criminality and a 'sick' element in society.

These have been the two main camps of theory thus far. A further twist has been added by certain commentators both in the UK and abroad, who blame the unregulated and uncensored social media. The main point to make in terms of relationships between theories is that the different theories are not necessarily mutually exclusive. Different theories relate to different levels of explanation. Criminality and 'sickness' in society are superficial explanations, since they beg the question regarding what has caused these to the very wide extent that has been witnessed. It may be true that more active or 'robust' policing would have contained the rioting much more effectively, but such actions would do nothing to reduce the frustrations of many participants that caused them to riot in the first place. Such frustrations may be regarded as an underlying cause at a psychological and sociological level. Cultural factors are also relevant here, with some commentators blaming the gang culture common among the poorer youth for instilling a violent element into the fragile social environment. However, even these factors can often be explained at a lower level: economists generally view the increasing income inequality in developed countries

▶

▼

as being caused by changes in technology and globalization. Low-skilled workers in developed countries lack the ability to take advantage of improvements in technology and cannot compete with low-wage workers in developing countries. As for unregulated media, again these can only be relevant if underlying social and economic factors are present.

Thus we first have to realize that theories are not necessarily mutually exclusive, even if they at first appear very different and coming from opposite camps in the political divide. Then we have to consider evidence. Ultimately, as we have seen, good theories should be judged on their ability to make accurate predictions, but a first step in evaluation concerns their ability to account for existing evidence. The nature of the relevant evidence depends on the nature of the theory. We have seen above that some commentators have explained the riots in terms of poverty and inequality. In this case the demographic characteristics of the rioters are relevant. First, are the rioters invariably from the lower echelons of society in terms of income, employment, and social standing? Even if this is shown to be the case (and there are certainly some glaring exceptions observed), it does not show that poverty and inequality were the cause of the riots: correlation does not prove causation. It may be that poverty and inequality are associated with certain cultural factors, and these cultural factors were a causative factor behind the riots. The untangling of these kinds of relationships often makes it difficult to evaluate this kind of theory.

When it comes to the effectiveness of different methods or approaches to policing a totally different kind of evidence is appropriate. It is necessary here to examine cross-sectional studies of different countries and communities where different methods have been used. The main problem here is the existence of confounds: other factors, such as social, legal, and institutional factors, will almost certainly vary when we compare different countries, and these make it very difficult to make valid comparisons. For example, we have to consider whether 'community policing' has been practiced in the different areas, and whether this has operated along similar lines.

In evaluating all the different causative theories, it must be realized that it is most unlikely that there is a single underlying cause involved. There are probably a variety of contributory causes, all of which were necessary, but none of which may have been sufficient individually to bring about all the events that occurred.

Why is it important to identify and establish these causative factors and their relative importance? Different causes have different policy implications. In the case of the recent UK riots these policy implications are both profound and wide-ranging. The aspect that has been most controversial in the immediate aftermath of the riots has been the issue of appropriate punishment. The initial punishments handed down by the courts were often criticized as overly harsh by a number of social commentators, and also as being inconsistent with previous practice. Such comments have come particularly from the Liberal Democrat faction within the previous government, opposing the 'get tough' approach of the former prime minister. Yet surveys of the general public have shown that more people regard the sentences handed down as being too soft rather than too hard. Some criminologists, such as Roger Graef, commented that harsh sentences merely alienate criminals further, and that the only way to rehabilitate violent offenders back into society is to force them to interact with those in the community whom they have harmed, thus inculcating empathy and remorse rather than increasing hostility. Other commentators have pointed out that sentences have always tended to be harsher for offences when there is general

▶

disorder, because the offences are more threatening in these circumstances. Thus we can see that there is wide disagreement about appropriate punishment.

However, punishment is by no means the only policy issue involved, although it may be the most important in the short run. In the long run policies regarding welfare and education and training are also important. In some cases these policies overlap in their implications. For example, there has been substantial support for punishing offenders by removing their entitlement to welfare benefits, including subsidized council housing. This has the effect of increasing poverty and inequality, as well as punishing the families of offenders who themselves may be innocent of any crime. However, those who support policies designed to reduce inequality through income redistribution need to be aware that in a number of developed countries, including the UK and the USA, recent studies have shown that such policies seem not to be supported by the general public (Kuziemko et al., 2014). This, perhaps surprising, finding is related to the phenomenon of reference points, discussed in more detail in the next chapter: people on low incomes may not want those who have still lower incomes, and are on the bottom of the income ladder, to become better off, since this would reduce the gap between them.

The education and training of the youth is also a vital issue here, particularly since it affects the economic prospects of the whole country in the long term. The achievement of appropriate skills and experience is essential in order to have promising career potential, and the motivation to achieve these is also vital. This involves a huge network of social interactions, involving parenting, schooling, the availability and effectiveness of youth clubs, the availability and effectiveness of training schemes, the welfare and housing systems, and the university system and relevant financing, to name some of the most important. Within each of these broad areas there are many components. For example, within schooling there is type and variety of school available, the nature of the curriculum, type of exam system, school leaving age, the training of teachers, the evaluation of individual schools, and so on. All of these factors may play a role in determining whether a person becomes a committed member of society, and makes a significant economic contribution – or becomes a dropout destined to become a parasite on society, committing violent offences against people and property.

## Questions

1 Explain what is meant by mutually exclusive and complementary theories.

2 What kind of evidence is relevant in evaluating arguments that poverty and inequality caused the riots? What problems exist in evaluating this evidence?

3 Explain how the policy implications of the riots depend on the evaluation of theories, giving examples.

# PART · II

# Foundations

# CHAPTER 3

# Values, Preferences and Choices

What can star tennis players teach us about economics? Yes, top players make a lot of money, but that option is not open to the vast majority of us. However, some famous multi-grandslam winners over the years have made some remarks that give us some important insights into what makes them tick, and how other people are likely to tick too. Consider the following quotes:

'The older I get, the better I used to be.'
**John McEnroe**

'I hate to lose more than I love to win.'
**Jimmy Connors**

'I don't remember the games I won, I only remember the games I lost.'
**Boris Becker**

'Victory is fleeting. Losing is forever.'
**Billie Jean King**

'What makes something special is not just what you have to gain, but what you feel there is to lose.'
**Andre Agassi**

The key concepts that come across in these comments are reference dependence and loss-aversion. These are the determining components of the 'three-act tragedy' of happiness described in the chapter as a fundamental area where the standard model has nothing to say.

---

## 3.1  The neoclassical model

*The decision-making process*

We need to begin our analysis of decision-making by examining the process involved in most decisions. Of course, some 'decisions' do not really appear to be decisions at all because we act on instinct, without conscious thought. This is often because there is no time for using the 'cold' analytical cognitive system described in the previous chapter as one component of our dual system; instead we rely on the 'hot' affective system, which is often dependent on instantaneous emotional or visceral responses to a situation. Hence we may duck an object flying at our head, or lash out in anger, physically or verbally, at someone who has offended us. However, even in cases where this 'hot' system is used, and we are not aware of making a conscious decision, there is still a situation where some kind of stimulus results in an action. Whenever this situation arises we deem that a decision-making process is involved. What is needed therefore is a general model of the decision-making process that applies to automatically reaching for the Oreo cookies at the supermarket, deciding where to buy a lottery ticket, investing in a particular stock, or choosing a particular medical treatment. Obviously these decisions are very different in nature and involve different factors and even decision systems, but there are certain elements in common.

In general there are three fundamental characteristics of decision-making; these are described below, along with their corresponding components in the neoclassical model (NM) as expressed in equation (1.1), which is repeated here for ease of reference:

$$\textbf{(1)} \quad \max_{x_i^t \in X_i} \quad \textbf{(2)} \quad \sum_{t=0}^{\infty} \delta^t \quad \textbf{(3)} \quad \sum_{s_t \in S_t} p(s_t) \quad \textbf{(4)} \quad U(x_i^t \mid s_t). \quad \text{(1.1) repeated}$$

1   Preferences – these are the rankings people have over a set of options or gambles that are based on attitudes and values related to the outcomes of these options (4).

2   Beliefs – these relate to the probabilities with which people think various outcomes will occur, conditional on available information (3).

3   Rationality – this involves all four components of the standard model, referring to the ways in which people:
   •   determine preferences based on attitudes and values (4)
   •   appropriately modify their beliefs in the light of new information (3)
   •   discount values of future outcomes (2)
   •   succeed in choosing optimal actions given their preferences and beliefs (1)

In a comprehensive survey of empirical findings in the field related to behavioral economics, DellaVigna (2009) examines deviations from the NM according to the above classification; he refers to these deviations as non-standard preferences, non-standard beliefs, and non-standard decision-making. Many of the examples he gives are discussed in this chapter and the following chapters. The first of these deviations is examined in this chapter, while the second deviation is examined in the next chapter. It should be noted that there is significant interdependence and overlap between these three categories: beliefs affect preferences, and both of these affect choices as reflected in decision-making. Furthermore, rationality involves both beliefs and preferences; thus aspects of rationality are discussed in both chapters, as well as in later chapters in the book. There is also a final discussion of rationality in the concluding chapter, after the topics of risk and uncertainty, intertemporal preferences, and social preferences, have been discussed. Nevertheless, we shall see that the beliefs–preferences–rationality classification is useful, in that the factors within each category are involved at different stages of the decision-making process.

### Consumer behavior

We have already seen how the NM can be described in mathematical terms in expression (1.1). This can be translated into a NM of consumer behavior very simply. As Varian (2006) expresses it: 'people choose the best things they can afford' (p. 33). This is essentially a constrained optimization problem. The objects of consumer choice are referred to as consumption bundles, and these relate to a complete list of the goods and services that are involved in the particular choice problem being considered. In a generalized situation we also need a description of when, where, and under what circumstances these goods would become available. People care not only about what goods are available now but about what will be available at a later date; they also care more for a bottle of water if they are in the middle of a desert than if they are in the Antarctic. Any bundle of goods can be described in the simplest terms as $(x_1, x_2)$ or just $X$, where $x_1$ denotes the amount of one good and $x_2$ the amount of another good, or the amount of all other goods. By limiting the number of parameters to just two it is possible to use a graphical method of representation and analysis.

### Preferences

In the NM it is assumed that consumers can rank bundles according to their desirability. If a consumer definitely wants an $x$-bundle rather than a $y$-bundle then it is said that he or she **strictly prefers** the x-bundle to the y-bundle. This can be written as follows: $(x_1, x_2)$ > $(y_1, y_2)$. Alternatively, if a consumer is **indifferent** between the two bundles this means that they have no preference for either bundle over the other. This relationship is usually described by the expression: $(x_1, x_2) \sim (y_1, y_2)$. Finally, if a consumer prefers or is indifferent between the two bundles we say that he or she **weakly prefers** $(x_1, x_2)$ to $(y_1, y_2)$ and this is written: $(x_1, x_2) \geq (y_1, y_2)$.

Preference relations are meant to be operational notions. Thus it is also assumed in the NM that choice is determined by preference; this is important since it is choice that is directly observable, not preference. If a consumer chooses a particular bundle, it is assumed that this bundle is preferred to another bundle if that other bundle was both available and affordable. This is what is meant by the concept of **revealed preference**.

*Indifference curves*

The theory of consumer choice is often illustrated using a graphical approach involving indifference curves. An indifference curve represents different combinations of two goods between which the consumer is indifferent, that is, which yield the same total utility. Figure 3.1 is an indifference map, showing a number of indifference curves, with curves further away from the origin representing bundles involving greater quantities of goods; these bundles are therefore preferred to those on lower indifference curves. Thus any combination of goods on curve $I_2$ is preferred to any combination on curve $I_1$. However, nothing is specified regarding how much more these goods are preferred; thus we can say nothing regarding the relative sizes of the difference between $I_2$ and the difference between $I_3$ and $I_2$. Indifference curves are normally drawn as downward-sloping and with convex to the origin; this is because of certain assumptions that are described in the next section.

**FIGURE 3.1**   Indifference curve map

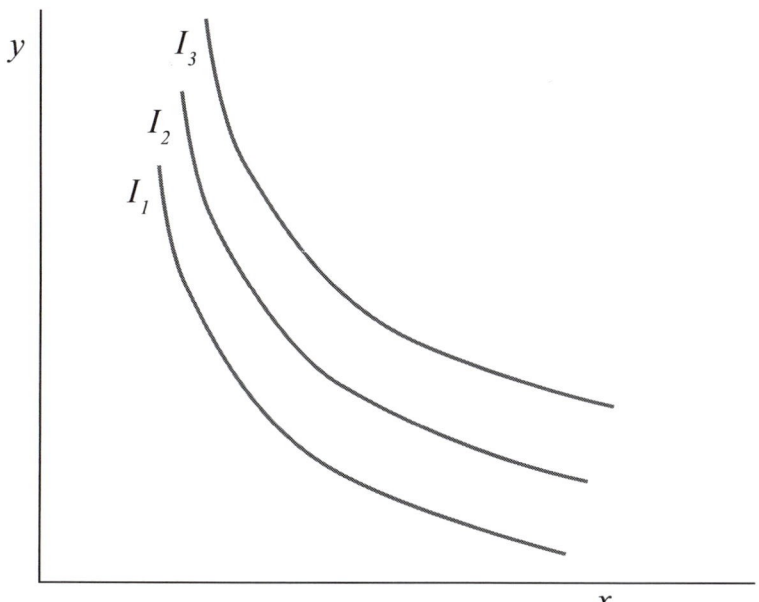

### Equilibrium

Indifference curve maps can be used to illustrate the notion of consumer equilibrium. It is assumed that consumers have a **budget constraint** relating to the amount of money that they have available to spend on the relevant consumption bundles. This budget constraint can be represented in terms of the following inequality:

$$p_x x + p_y y \leq m$$

where $m$ is the available budget. The budget constraint is shown in Figure 3.2 as the line going through points A, C and B. Although the budget is sufficient to buy combinations A and B, these are not optimal combinations since they are not on the highest indifference curve that can be reached. Combination C is the optimal combination, where the consumer purchases the bundle $(x_1, y_1)$. This situation can be generalized: any optimal point of consumption will occur at a point of tangency between an indifference curve and a budget constraint line. Setting the slopes of these two curves equal gives the condition that the consumer should spend so that the marginal utility of the last dollar spent on each good is the same. This condition can be further generalized to apply to any number of goods in a consumption bundle.

The exposition of consumer equilibrium in the NM often uses the term 'marginal utility', but in fact this is not essential. The slope of an indifference curve can also be expressed in terms of the **marginal rate of substitution** (MRS) of one good for another. The $MRS_{xy}$ represents the amount of $y$ that a consumer is prepared to give up in order to get one more unit of $x$. Thus the equilibrium condition amounts to consuming a combination such that the MRS is equal to the ratio of the prices: $MRS_{xy} = p_x/p_y$. The advantage of this form of exposition is that it avoids the thorny concept of utility. A detailed discussion of utility is deferred until a Section 3.7. Applications of indifference curve analysis related to behavioral anomalies are discussed in Angner (2016, ch. 3).

**Figure 3.2    Indifference curves and consumer equilibrium**

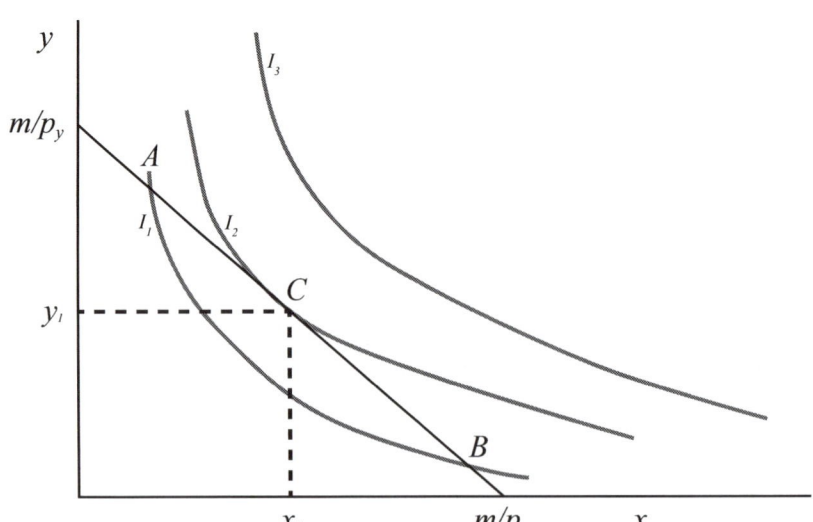

## 3.2  Axioms, assumptions and definitions

*Axioms*

In discussing the foundation of the NM, in particular in terms of how it relates to consumer preference, it is essential to distinguish between the basic axioms of the model and other auxiliary assumptions that often accompany it. While the former are fundamental to the model, the latter are somewhat flexible and are varied in different circumstances. This distinction is relevant in discussing the weaknesses of the NM in the following section, and relates to the Duhem-Quine thesis discussed in the previous chapter. We will also see that there is a distinction between descriptive and normative axioms. This aspect is discussed in Chapter 5 in the context of risk and uncertainty.

There are four main axioms relating to consumer preference:

1   **Completeness.** A person can compare any two consumer bundles, $X$ and $Y$. Such a comparison must lead to one of three possible mutually exclusive outcomes:

   a)   Basket $X$ is preferred to basket $Y$; we have seen that this can be written: $(x_1, x_2) > (y_1, y_2)$.

   b)   Basket $Y$ is preferred to basket $X$; we have seen that this can be written: $(y_1, y_2) > (x_1, x_2)$.

   c)   The consumer is indifferent between the two baskets; we have seen that this can be written: $(x_1, x_2) \sim (y_1, y_2)$.

   This is referred to as the completeness principle because the preferences cover all possible outcomes.

2   **Transitivity.** If three different baskets, $X$, $Y$ and $Z$, are considered, a consumer who prefers basket $X$ to basket $Y$, and who prefers basket $Y$ to basket $Z$, must also prefer basket $X$ to basket $Z$. This can expressed as:

   if $(x_1, x_2) > (y_1, y_2)$ and $(y_1, y_2) > (z_1, z_2)$, then $(x_1, x_2) > (z_1, z_2)$.

   Similarly, if a consumer is indifferent between basket $X$ and basket $Y$, and who is also indifferent between basket $Y$ and basket $Z$, must also be indifferent between basket $X$ and basket $Z$.

3   **Reflexivity**. Any bundle is at least as good as itself: $(x_1, x_2) \geq (x_1, x_2)$. This axiom is generally regarded as being trivial.

4   **Revealed preference**. This axiom can come in either weak or strong forms:

   If $(x_1, x_2)$ is revealed directly/indirectly preferred to $(y_1, y_2)$, and the two bundles are not the same, then it cannot happen that $(y_1, y_2)$ is revealed directly/indirectly preferred to $(x_1, x_2)$.

*Assumptions*

In addition to the above axioms there are four other main assumptions, often referred to as principles, which frequently accompany the NM. These assumptions are particularly relevant in situations where there is uncertainty; they are therefore discussed in more detail in Chapter 5 in relation to expected utility theory (EUT), which is the aspect of the NM that is relevant in such situations. We will also see that EUT involves certain additional assumptions, apart from the ones discussed below. Tversky and Kahneman (1986) claim that the following substantive assumptions can be ordered in terms of a hierarchy of increasing importance as far as their normative appeal is concerned. Thus the cancellation condition has been challenged by many theories, but the invariance condition is absolutely necessary for any normative theory.

1   **Cancellation.** This is the principle that any state of the world that results in the same outcome regardless of one's choice can be cancelled or ignored. It is sometimes referred to as a minimal approach to decision-making, as opposed to a topical or comprehensive approach (discussed in Chapter 5). Thus, if $X$ is preferred to $Y$, then the prospect of winning $X$ if it rains tomorrow (and nothing otherwise) should be preferred to the prospect of winning $Y$ if it rains tomorrow, because the two prospects both result in the same outcome (nothing) if there is no rain tomorrow. This assumption is also consistent generally with the marginalist approach of the neoclassical economists.

2   **Dominance.** This condition is simpler and stronger than the first one, and therefore is more fundamental to the standard model. It states that if option $X$ is better than option $Y$ in one state and at least as good in all other states, then option $X$ is dominant over option $Y$ and should be chosen. This is related to the reflexivity axiom discussed earlier, but is not as strong a condition.

3   **Extensionality.** The NM generally assumes that people have the same attitude to a particular object and attribute the same value to it, however that object is described, given a certain level of information about that object. Thus people should have the same attitude to a particular kind of packaged meat, whether it is described as 5% fat or as 95% fat-free. This is again related to the reflexivity axiom.

4   **Invariance.** This condition is essential for any normative theory. It states that different representations of the same choice problem should yield the same preference. This therefore rules out 'framing effects', discussed at length in the next few chapters. It states that the relation of preference should not depend on the description of the options (**description invariance**) or on the method of elicitation (**procedure invariance**). Without stability across equivalent descriptions and equivalent elicitation procedures, a person's preferences cannot be represented as utility maximization in the standard EUT.

There is also the assumption in the standard model that consumers maximize utilities. This is usually taken as both a descriptive and a normative statement: people *do* behave in this way, and *ought* to behave in this way to maximize their welfare. This normative aspect is related to the concept of rationality.

Certain other assumptions are invoked in particular situations; these are discussed in the relevant context in the remaining sections and chapters. However, we need to be aware of the differing status of these assumptions; some are really not a necessary component of the NM and can easily be relaxed without compromising the model. For example, the NM is sometimes said to involve assumptions regarding three characteristics of indifference curves. The first of these has already been stated as an axiom, involving transitivity of preferences. The second characteristic is that the curves are downward-sloping; this implies that more of a good is always preferred to less of a good. This principle is referred to as the **monotonicity** of preferences, and can be expressed in technical terms thus: if $(x_1, x_2)$ is a bundle of goods and $(y_1, y_2)$ is a bundle of goods with at least as much of both goods and more of one, then $(y_1, y_2) > (x_1, x_2)$. This assumption follows directly from the definition of a **good**, that it is commodity where more of it is preferred to less. Some commodities, like pollution and garbage, are referred to as '**bads**'. The assumption of monotonicity is not essential to the standard model; for example, when people reach satiation the principle no longer applies. The third characteristic of indifference curves is that they are convex to the origin. This is sometimes referred to as the assumption of **convexity** of preferences, but it is not really an essential assumption either, since it follows from the **law of diminishing marginal utility**. This law states that, as more of a good is consumed within a certain time period, additional units of consumption will eventually yield less marginal utility. The law is in the nature of an empirical regularity rather than being an assumption in analysis. It is this characteristic of convexity which determines the inverse relationship between price and quantity demanded in the conventional demand curve, although such a relationship can also be derived by other means (Becker, 1976).

## Definitions

Before discussing the weaknesses of the standard model in terms of consumer preference, it will help to clarify the situation if we give definitions of four terms that are involved in the decision-making process: attitude, value, preference and choice. It should be stated at the start that the definitions that follow are not universally agreed upon or followed by either economists or psychologists, but they are widely shared.

1   *Attitude* – This has been usefully defined as 'a psychological tendency that is expressed by evaluating a particular entity with some degree of favor or disfavor' (Eagly and Chaiken, 1996). This concept has a broader range of application than the concept of preference, as will be seen shortly. Attitudes relate to any entity that people can like or dislike. Entities include physical objects, living beings and abstract concepts, involving anything that can elicit an affective response. It is important to realize that objects of attitudes are **mental representations**, not objective states of affairs. This means that attitudes are based on beliefs, discussed in the next chapter. Realizing this helps us to understand the violations of the invariance and extension principles discussed above. People have a different mental representation of meat with 5% fat compared with meat that is 95% fat-free.

A related characteristic of attitudes is that they tend to involve **judgment by proto-type**. This refers to the phenomenon that global judgment of a category is determined primarily by the relevant properties of a prototype, and is based on the older concept of a **representativeness heuristic** (Kahneman and Tversky, 1972, 1973; Tversky and Kahneman, 1971, 1983). This heuristic is explained in the next chapter, and leads to various kinds of extension bias. An example, discussed in more detail in the next section, involves **duration neglect**: people tend to recall past experiences in terms of a prototypical moment, rather than as the total experience. Thus they may ignore the length of an unpleasant experience like a colonoscopy, recalling instead the moment of most intensive pain.

2   *Value* – This is a problematical term, for it is widely used in two different senses. In one sense our values determine our attitudes, while in the other sense our attitudes determine our values. In the first sense values refer to tastes or likes/dislikes: we may have a taste for cauliflower, a taste for roller coasters, or a taste for making charitable donations. Thus values in this sense include moral values. One can of course take the question further back, following a reductionist theme, and ask what determines a person's values; however, important as this issue is, it goes beyond the scope of this book and into the details of evolutionary psychology.

The second sense of the term value refers to the quantitative evaluation that results from an attitude. The determination of value involves judgment. This sense of the term value is what economists conventionally mean by the term utility, whether referring to experienced or decision utility. These terms will be discussed in more detail in the following sections.

3   *Preference* – As we have already discussed, economists are conventionally more concerned with preferences, in particular so-called 'revealed preferences', while psychologists may be more concerned with attitudes. In the NM it is assumed that attitudes determine preferences, but that is not necessarily true.

4    *Choice* – This involves an action on the part of the subject/consumer, involving some kind of decision. The standard model generally assumes that choice is simply revealed preference. We will see however that preferences and choices are not necessarily identical and that choices need not be a reflection of attitudes and judgments (Tversky, Sattath and Slovic, 1988; Tversky and Griffin, 2000).

There are other terms related to these that also need to be clarified, such as pleasure, happiness and well-being. In order to shed further light on them, and on the four terms above, we need to examine the foundations of utility in evolutionary biology. Only then can we understand why the goods we consume give us utility at all.

## 3.3   The evolutionary biology of utility

*Nature and functions of utility*

As explained earlier, it is necessary is to take a reductionist approach in order to understand the ultimate causes of human behavior. The brain did not evolve in order to maximize utility, well-being or hedonic pleasure. The forces of natural selection have caused the brain to be designed as a system that maximizes **biological fitness**. This term can be understood as meaning our ability to survive and reproduce. Evolutionary biologists also use the term inclusive fitness, where the ability extends to our kin, since that increases the overall likelihood of 'spreading our genes'. It is important to realize that this driving force behind evolution operates at the genetic level strictly speaking, not at the level of the individual. One main strength of neuroeconomic analysis is that it recognizes this biological basis of behavior, not just for humans but for all animals.

Historically speaking, biological fitness is therefore closely linked to the number of offspring, and this allows the construction of testable models of economic behavior, as we shall see in following chapters. In particular these models involve the application of evolutionary game theory, involving a principal-agent situation where Nature is the principal and the individual is the agent. The objective of the principal is to maximize biological fitness, which entails maximizing the number of viable offspring, meaning offspring who are in turn likely to be able to reproduce successfully. This is achieved through the competitive forces of natural selection. In terms of economics, however, there are two fundamental and linked questions, posed by Robson (2002): (1) Why is there utility at all? (2) Why is it defined on **intermediate goods** rather than on offspring?

The first question is easier to answer. Utility exists as the criterion that humans, and other animals, use when selecting actions in response to the variety of environmental situations they encounter. As Robson (2002) states: 'animals with the best repertoire of instinctive and learned procedures for making these choices would be favored by evolution.' Thus fear and pain engender negative utility, urging animals to avoid actions that cause these aversive sensations; animals with effective fear and pain disutility signals are likely to have greater biological fitness. Likewise, nutritious foods engender high utility signals, so that animals with effective food signals will again have greater biological fitness.

The second question involves a more complex answer. Nature imbues rankings or preferences over consumption goods, which are really intermediate goods as far as the ultimate goal of producing offspring is concerned. Why? Robson (2002) suggests that a strategy whereby people or animals determine their consumption habits according to personal experience or direct observation of the number of offspring of others would not be effective, mainly because of the problem of the small sample involved. People would only be able to observe a few relatives or friends, and maybe one or more of these has an unhealthy diet but has a lot of offspring, while another or others may have a healthy diet but no offspring. The observer might then conclude on the basis of this small sample that an unhealthy diet was best. A more effective strategy for Nature to achieve biological fitness would be to imbue animals with preferences over consumption bundles, in order to avoid this small sample error. Furthermore, it is more efficient for individuals to have a utility function that applies to all bundles rather than to determine consumption by comparing each pair of possible bundles. When there is a very large number of possible pairs to be compared it would require a larger brain to process and analyze the relevant information, and therefore greater metabolic energy resources to build and maintain this organ. This would in turn detract resources from other productive uses, like building the body, which may be more effective at improving biological fitness. A utility function allows a more efficient process of simply selecting the bundle with the highest utility rather than making myriad comparisons.

We can therefore state that the individual is prompted to maximize hedonic pleasure as a means to the ultimate end of maximizing biological fitness. Actions that result in hedonic pleasure have in the past generally improved biological fitness, while actions causing displeasure or pain have been an indication that our biological fitness is threatened. Furthermore, it is important to understand that this hedonic pleasure relates not only to conventional goods but also to what we can call moral sentiments, using the terminology of Adam Smith [1759] (2000), the first economist to inquire into their nature. Thus we tend to take actions that make us feel proud or increase our self-esteem, while avoiding those that cause us to feel guilt or shame. If we do not recognize that moral sentiments also involve hedonic pleasure or pain we will become entangled in the problem of dualism, which, as we will see in Chapter 11, still bedevils the thinking of some neuroscientists, as well as economists and philosophers.

## Types of selection process

The mechanism of natural selection is responsible for producing adaptations over time, to both bodies and brains, which ensure the maintenance of biological fitness of a species in a particular environment. However, there are various aspects of the environment that are relevant. We operate not only in a physical environment, but also in a social environment. Therefore there are other aspects to the selection process that are also important in understanding the nature of utility. One aspect is referred to as **sexual selection**, and involves the selection of individuals within a species who are most successful in finding and retaining mates who will produce the most viable and healthy offspring. Since there is sexual specialization as far as rearing offspring is concerned, in both humans and many other animal species, the different sexes have different characteristics that are particularly desirable to the opposite sex. Human males tend to be attracted to females who are fertile and healthy-looking, while females tend to be attracted to males who promise to be good providers. **Signaling** is of great importance in this selection process. Women often want to signal youth and beauty, thus the great demand in the cosmetics industry, mainly (although certainly not exclusively) from women. For men, conspicuous consumption is a vital signal, and this can be displayed by buying designer clothing, accessories like watches and jewelry, luxury cars and the like.

A further aspect of the selection process is referred to as **group selection**. Instead of operating at the level of the gene, or the individual, group selection acts at the level of a group of individuals. The relative importance in evolution of these three different levels of selection is still a highly controversial issue in biology and sociology; it is not intended to enter this debate in this book, merely to describe the process of group selection that has been proposed, and its relevance in understanding utility. The theory of group selection essentially proposes that if a group within a population possesses certain characteristics that enable that group to reproduce faster than other groups, and that group is isolated reproductively from other groups for substantial periods, then these characteristics may be able to spread within a population, even if individuals possessing them are at a disadvantage within a particular group. The main examples that are often given here relate to the characteristics of empathy and cooperation, which can operate in many different ways. These characteristics relate to social preferences; for example, an inequality in the distribution of payoffs among a group may give a person disutility. This aspect will be discussed in more detail in Chapter 10. This does not mean that the existence of social preferences relies on the process of group selection, merely that group selection may have shaped our social preferences in our evolutionary past.

### Evolution and optimization

A common misconception regarding the neo-Darwinian synthesis (NDS) is that 'survival of the fittest', as natural selection is often called, leads ultimately to optimization of design as far as species are concerned. This is very far from the truth. As Richard Dawkins (1986) has explained, the evolutionary process resembles a 'Blind Watchmaker', and has no ultimate aim or objective. In philosophical terms it is a mechanistic rather than a teleological process. Furthermore, the process can only build on biological structures that already exist; thus our bodies and even our brains often appear as components that have been cobbled together, in a similar fashion to kludges in computer science and engineering.

As far as the nature of utility is concerned, there are two essential problems caused by the mechanistic nature of the evolutionary process, causing our hedonic systems to be easily hijacked:

1  *Time lags*. Lags exist between the optimal design and the demands of the current environment. A good example is our liking for sugary and fatty foods, which improved our biological fitness in the past, but is now a serious threat given their easy availability and the sedentary nature of many of our lives.

2  *Use of heuristics*. These rules are useful shortcuts that simplify the decision-making process, particularly given time constraints and bounded rationality, but they are prone to error. For example, we may be trying to choose a car to buy. Heuristics that could be used here might be: only buy a make you have bought before; buy a domestic make; buy the safest model within certain price bracket; buy the model with the best fuel economy. These heuristics have again been shaped by the evolutionary process, as adaptations, related in the above examples to different aspects of risk-aversion. However, they are unlikely to maximize utility because each of them ignores many relevant factors.

After this summary of the underlying evolutionary aspects of utility, we can now turn our attention to its neuroscientific basis, and this will then allow a further discussion of rationality and how this relates to the predictions of the standard model. This will in turn enable us to identify various different types of utility.

## 3.4  The neuroscientific basis of utility

### Techniques and comparisons

Over the last 25 years, and particularly in the last 15, there have been many neuroeconomic studies relating to utility, in terms of how it is correlated with neural activity. These studies have important implications for economic theory. Positron emission tomography (PET) can detect changes in neurotransmitter release, and although there are some technical problems here, these studies can detect which areas of the brain are activated. The main advantage of PET studies is that they can be used to detect neurochemical changes related to neurotransmitters like dopamine. The other main analytical technique, functional magnetic resonance imaging (fMRI), is not able to do this, but fMRI is superior to PET in terms of providing greater temporal and spatial resolution. This means that fMRI can pinpoint more precisely when a neural change occurs in time, and where in the brain it occurs. The use of both techniques in a complementary manner helps to confirm neuroeconomic hypotheses.

Other neural studies examine the effects of lesions or disruption of neural activity using transcranial magnetic stimulation (TMS). Such studies are useful in identifying the necessary (but not sufficient) conditions for a particular psychological effect or economic behavior to occur. The main advantage here is the higher degree of certainty with which these studies can draw conclusions compared with other studies, but the main drawback concerns the limited nature of their conclusions.

The other main type of study that has been used relating to the concept of utility involves single neuron studies. These are extremely accurate in pinpointing brain areas involved in different functions, but their highly invasive nature currently restricts their use to non-human primates.

The major neuroscientific findings related to utility that need to be discussed at this stage relate to (1) the nature of utility and reference dependence; (2) loss-aversion; (3) measurement of utility; and (4) the difference between reflective and reflexive brain modes. Some conclusions relating to neuroeconomic evidence are then drawn.

## Nature of utility and reference dependence

Animal studies have for a long time indicated that reward was associated with dopamine release, which creates a hedonic 'high'. A major development was a study by Schultz, Apicella, and Ljungberg (1993), later supported by many other studies, that it was not consumption itself that stimulated dopamine release, but the expectation of consumption. For example, when monkeys learned that the tone of a bell was likely to be followed by a reward of juice, there was a release of dopamine at the tone but not at the later point of consumption. Thus only unanticipated consumption led to dopamine release. These studies led to the development of the '**dopaminergic reward prediction error**' (DRPE or just RPE) hypothesis concerning the encoding of utility in the brain. This hypothesis proposed that it was the difference between how 'rewarding' an event is and how rewarding it was expected to be that determined dopamine release and therefore utility (in the hedonic sense). If the utility from consumption is fully anticipated, then there is no prediction error and no dopamine release. The key point here is that utility is reference-dependent.

Although the RPE hypothesis is not universally accepted within the neuroscience community, other theories relating to dopamine are fairly similar in terms of also being reference-dependent, for example Zink, Pagnoni and Martin (2003). Another example of a reference-dependent theory proposes that dopamine encodes 'incentive salience', which differentiates between how much something is wanted and how much it is liked (Berridge and Robinson, 1998). Caplin and Dean (2009) claim that various more recent experiments support the basic RPE model compared with its rivals, but identify areas for further development and expansion of the model.

Although fMRI studies cannot test the RPE model directly, they have been able to provide indirect evidence that at least is consistent with it. Various studies have now shown that anticipated gain causes increased blood flow in the nucleus accumbens (NAcc), whereas actual gain outcomes cause increased blood flow in the medial caudate, MPFC, and posterior cingulate regions (Knutson et al., 2001a, 2001b, 2003). This finding is what might be expected if utility is reference-dependent, being determined by the difference between what is expected and what is actually obtained.

There is another important implication of these studies. The fact that actual gains activate different brain areas from expected gains suggests that those areas, like the medial prefrontal cortex (mPFC), that are activated by actual gains serve as a control center, checking to see if outcomes turned out as expected. Evidence indicates that if the mPFC is damaged people are unable to learn from mistakes, for example in the Iowa gambling task.

Another aspect of outcomes and reference points concerns opportunity cost and regret. Regret entails recognition that an alternative, or counterfactual, action would have produced a more valued outcome than the one achieved. In humans, the orbito-frontal cortex (OFC) is active during expressions of regret, and humans with damage to the OFC do not express regret. In rats and non-human primates, both the OFC and the ventral striatum have been implicated in reward computations, and Steiner and Redish (2014) have performed experiments to induce sensations of regret in rats.

Some fMRI studies have also examined the prediction of choice. Knutson, Rick and Wimmer (2007) claim that ventral striatal activation not only correlates with preference while viewing products, but also predicts the choices of subjects better than self-reported preference. Of course, traditional economists might not be too impressed with this finding, believing that self-reports are unreliable anyway, and that economists should only be concerned with revealed preference or actual purchase decisions and behavior.

Single neuron studies also support the principle of reference dependence, by indicating that multiple representations of value exist in the primate brain (Platt and Padoa-Schioppa, 2009). More specifically, representations of value in the OFC are absolute (rewards from a particular good do not depend on the alternatives available), whereas representations of value in the parietal cortex are relative.

### Loss-aversion

The main finding here is that gains and losses appear to activate or deactivate different areas in the brain. For example, O'Doherty and colleagues (2001) reports that gains and losses activate different areas of the ventromedial prefrontal cortex (vmPFC). Another finding of importance, from PET studies, is that it appears that there is no detectable change in dopamine release following unexpected loss, at least in the ventral striatum, which is the brain area most affected by unexpected gain. This suggests that losses are encoded in a different brain area, utilizing a different neural pathway. Even within the striatum, the evidence for responsiveness to losses is weaker in the ventral striatum than in the dorsal striatum (Knutson, Delgado and Phillips, 2009). Several studies, using fMRI, implicate the insula as being involved in encoding losses, although other areas such as the amygdala may also be involved. The significance of both PET and fMRI studies is that their findings provide a neurological basis for the economic phenomenon of loss-aversion.

### Measurement of utility

The studies discussed so far have been mainly concerned with the nature of utility and how and where it is encoded in the brain. Other studies have examined the measurement of utility. A number of these have shown that the OFC and dorso-lateral prefrontal cortex (DLPFC) are important here. Plassman, O'Doherty and Rangel (2007) performed an experiment with hungry subjects viewing snacks and the bids they made for them afterwards. They found that these bids correlated positively with activation in the OFC. Other studies have shown that lesions or disruptions to the OFC or DLPFC interfere with the ability to compute values and make consistent choices.

Glimcher (2009) has a particularly ambitious neuroeconomic program. The key concept in his analytical approach is '**subjective value**', which is defined in neural terms rather than in psychological terms, as is the case with utility. The distinction is a crucial one, since subjective value obeys different axioms to expected utility. Glimcher proposes that existing studies support the hypothesis that subjective values 'are equal to (or better yet defined as) the mean firing rates of specific populations of neurons' and 'subjective values are linearly proportional to the blood oxygen level dependent (BOLD) signal of fMRI as measured in these same populations.' He also proposes that subjective values defined in this way have a reference-dependent anchoring point, called the baseline firing rate. RPE is defined in terms of the difference between forecast and experienced subjective value. The main implications of this approach are that subjective value can be measured in cardinal terms (not just in terms of an ordinal ranking of preferences as with some approaches to utility), and that subjective values are always consistent with choice on a stochastic basis, again unlike expected utility. The stochastic basis is necessary because in the Glimcher model of subjective value there is a noise term or random element in terms of how we measure value. This is consistent with the approach in terms of economic theory of Butler and Loomes (2007), who emphasize the role of imprecision in causing preference reversal.

It is important to note that Glimcher does not reject outright the expected utility model of traditional economic theory; he agrees that it can be a very useful predictor of choice in many situations. Instead, his approach claims that neuroeconomic insights can guide the development of economic models of choice that are better predictors in situations where EUT produces anomalies. Glimcher is also aware of the limitations of his subjective value model. It is essentially a model of choice, not of well-being. Although subjective value is related to well-being, the two concepts are not identical; thus maximizing well-being is not just a matter of maximizing subjective value. For example, drug addicts could claim to be maximizing subjective value at any point in time, but the concept of well-being involves a longer-term state. Neuroscientists know much less about the neural systems related to well-being compared to choice, but it appears that subjective value is mediated by these other systems in order to determine well-being.

## Reflective and reflexive brain modes

There has been a large number of neuroscientific studies performed that have indicated that the human brain has two main modes of operation: a reflective mode for making cold, rational decisions like accepting a job offer or buying a house, and a reflexive mode for making quick decisions based on instinctive, emotional or visceral impulses, like the 'fight or flight' reflex. This dichotomy is discussed at length in Kahneman's book *Thinking, Fast and Slow* (2012). Stress plays an important part in flipping the brain from reflective to reflexive mode. It causes a release of the neurotransmitter catecholamine, which reduces the rate of neuron firing in the prefrontal cortex (PFC), the most recently evolved brain area, responsible for higher cognitive functions. Simultaneously, the primary sensory cortices, the amygdala and striatum are stimulated, leading to reflexive action. From an evolutionary perspective such a switch is certainly valuable as a survival aid, but it has been shown that excessive stress over a prolonged period can lead to impaired functioning of the PFC, in turn causing a deterioration in decision-making (Arnsten, 2015).

## Conclusions

Various conclusions can be drawn regarding the neural process of valuation, particularly from the research conducted since 2000:

1   There are multiple brain components and systems involved, which interact with each other in a complex and dynamic way.

2   Different stages in this process recruit different striatal components.

3   The brain responds differently during anticipation of incentives than in response to incentive outcomes, an indication of reference dependence.

4   Processing of gains does not appear to be the opposite of processing of losses.

However, even the most ambitious researchers are generally agreed that, in spite of substantial recent progress, much more work needs to be done in order to clarify the neural anatomy and physiology involved in the functions of value measurement.

Further aspects of neuroeconomic studies of utility as far as they relate to risk and uncertainty, intertemporal preferences, and social preferences, will be examined in later chapters. It will also be seen in these later chapters that a vital aspect of understanding neuroeconomic processes relates to the fact that they have evolved over millions of years and are therefore largely shaped by the forces of natural selection as they have operated in an environment very different from the one in which most humans now function.

## 3.5   Broadening rationality

*Criteria for rationality*

Now that the basic parameters of the standard model have been described, and evolutionary and neuroscientific factors discussed, it is possible to consider criteria for rationality. In the light of the discussion of rationality in Chapter 1 and at the beginning of this chapter, a particularly useful view of rationality involves the following four criteria:

1   Attitudes and preferences should adhere to the basic rules of **logic and probability theory**.

2   Attitudes and preferences should be **coherent**.

3   Attitudes and preferences should not be formed or changed based on **immaterial or irrelevant factors**.

4   Attitudes and beliefs should not be **incompatible with empirical observations** known to the individual, including their own conscious actions.

The first three of these criteria have been outlined and utilized by Shafir and LeBoeuf (2002), and in conjunction with the fourth one they are useful in discussing the different types of irrational behavior that are then described. Before moving on to this, however, it is useful to note various similarities between these criteria and the axioms of consumer preference described earlier in the chapter. In particular the first three criteria above relate closely to completeness, transitivity, independence, monotonicity (or dominance) and invariance.

The one exception is the final criterion for rationality, relating to compatibility with empirical observations. This is not explicitly covered by either EUT or the scheme of Tversky and Kahneman (1986) relating to cancellation, transitivity, dominance and invariance. It has to be said that this is a controversial addition. For example, it does not coincide with Baumeister's description of irrational behavior as being self-defeating. People could violate this fourth criterion, but still not necessarily engage in behavior that was self-defeating. This aspect is further discussed in the next chapter, in the context of causes of irrational behavior, in relation to cognitive dissonance.

However, the inclusion of the fourth criterion can be justified by comparing it with the second one. The second criterion for judging attitudes and beliefs is whether they are **coherent**, in the sense of being consistent with each other. This criterion can be regarded as relating to internal consistency. The last criterion for judging the rationality of beliefs relates to external consistency, meaning whether they are supported by empirical evidence known by that individual. An individual may hold a set of beliefs that are mutually consistent, but are contrary to known empirical evidence. In this case it may be claimed that the person is acting irrationally by clinging on to such beliefs. This aspect of rationality is the one involved in the commonly used economic concept of '**rational expectations**', and it was also implied in Alan Greenspan's often-quoted expression 'irrational exuberance', in referring to the stock market boom in 1996. It is relevant that the empirical evidence must be known by the individual, for otherwise the fault is ignorance, not irrationality. However, it is not relevant that a person may not have any 'free will' in choosing what to believe; such a choice can still be regarded as a decision-making action. Of course this kind of phenomenon, which we will see may be extremely widespread, raises the issue of why people would cling on to their beliefs in the face of contrary empirical evidence. This aspect is again discussed in the next chapter.

We can now discuss aspects of attitudes, values, choices and preferences that deviate from these criteria. This entails a consideration of both anomalies and incompleteness in the standard model. As explained in the first chapter, it is important to distinguish between these two problems. The first relates to deviations, or situations where the standard model makes inaccurate predictions, while the second relates to situations where the standard model has nothing to say, making no predictions at all. As far as the first area is concerned, DellaVigna (2009) describes three main types of deviation related to: self-control; reference dependence; and social preferences. However, many of these deviations involve factors discussed in later chapters. Self-control aspects are mainly discussed in terms of intertemporal choice in Chapters 7 and 8; many aspects of reference dependence involve risk and uncertainty and are discussed in Chapters 5 and 6; and social preferences are discussed in Chapter 10.

The second area of alleged weakness is more controversial, since some economists argue that these areas of 'silence' do not represent a weakness at all; as we have also seen in the previous chapter, it is claimed that economics has no interest in such areas. This issue is not a matter of testing a theory by empirical evidence; it involves a subjective value judgment regarding what economics *should* be concerned about. The first area discussed below involves one such area.

## Happiness is a three-act tragedy

Perhaps the most obvious weakness in terms of omission concerns the nature of happiness. It might be intuitively surmised that the objective of expected utility maximization would involve the concept of happiness, although, as we shall see later in the chapter, there are complications here in terms of reasons why happiness might not correspond to utility (Clark, Frijters and Shields, 2008). The evolutionary psychologist and psycholinguist Steven Pinker (1996) has described happiness as a three-act tragedy. This claim has the following elements:

1   Happiness involves an interpersonal comparison of one's perceived well-being, or subjective well-being (SWB) with that of others. Although self-reported happiness appears to increase sharply with income at any point in time (Easterlin, 2001), studies in the USA (Myers and Diener, 1995), Japan (Easterlin, 1995) and Eastern Europe (Easterlin, 2009) indicate that self-reported happiness in general has not increased over several decades, in spite of a several-fold increase in real income in some cases. It also appears that similar relationships between material wealth and life satisfaction occur with children, but only for young males not females (Hudson, 2013); boys reported greater life satisfaction with more wealth, but less satisfaction with more peer wealth. A recent German study examined how household consumption was affected by the consumption of households perceived to be richer than that household

(Drechsel-Grau and Schmid, 2014). It was found that a 1% increase in consumption of households perceived to be richer was associated with a 0.3% increase in a household's consumption. This observation therefore invokes the notion of a **reference point**, a key element of prospect theory that is discussed in detail in Chapter 5. Pinker quotes the words of Gore Vidal: 'It is not enough to succeed. Others must fail.'

2    Happiness also involves an intrapersonal comparison of one's perceived well-being with one's previous well-being. This again involves reference dependence, but in this case the reference point is related to a previous self-state rather than a current other-state, as in the previous case. A frequently quoted study regarding this issue is that of Brickman, Coates and Janoff-Bulman (1978), which found that, after a period of adjustment, lottery winners were not much happier than a control group, and paraplegics not much unhappier.

3    Happiness and unhappiness are not symmetrical reflections of gain and loss. The impact of losses is greater than equivalent gains. This observation invokes the concept of **loss-aversion**, another key element of prospect theory. Pinker quotes the tennis star Jimmy Connors: 'I hate to lose more than I like to win.'

As discussed in Chapter 2, this weakness does not represent an anomaly of the NM, since economists generally issue disclaimers as far as the concept of happiness is concerned, only being concerned with a particular definition of welfare.

In the NM there is much consideration of **Pareto efficiency**. This measure of efficiency is normally expressed that nobody can be made better off without making anyone else worse off. However, it is normally assumed in the NM that **Pareto efficiency** is a desirable goal. As Varian (2006) states:

> If there is some way to make some group of people better off without hurting
> other people, why not do it? (p. 613)

The second act of the happiness tragedy indicates why we might not want to do it. Making some people better off will automatically make others worse off in terms of happiness, if not in terms of welfare in the narrow sense. This has very important political implications as far as government policy is concerned. The growing gap between the pay of bosses and workers in the USA is a case in point. In general the economic welfare of workers has not suffered over the last 20 years but they feel worse off knowing that their bosses are so much better off than they are. Although the disparity is largest in the USA, resentment at 'fat cat' CEO pay has been expressed in many other countries also.

### Stable, well-formed preferences

It is a fundamental tenet of both the NM and the everyday notion of rationality that people have stable, well-formed preferences, according to the second criterion related to coherence described earlier. Without such preferences it would not be possible to make normative statements in economics since there would be no meaningful concept for people to optimize. However, going back to the 1970s, several researchers have found that significant anomalies occur in this respect. Much of this research centered on experiments involving what are called P-bets and $-bets. A P-bet offers a near sure thing, meaning a relatively large probability of a modest sum of money. A $-bet is a riskier gamble, offering a smaller probability of a considerably bigger prize and a larger chance of zero. Respondents are asked first to state a preference between the two bets, and most people choose the P-bet since they prefer a nearly sure thing. However, when respondents are told that they own the bet and are asked to state the lowest price at which they are prepared to sell it, the majority value the $-bet more than the P-bet (Lichtenstein and Slovic, 1973; Grether and Plott, 1979). Grether and Plott initially attributed this anomaly to the fact that the studies were laboratory experiments, lacking in real-world application, mainly because with no stakes there was a lack of incentives. This is a common criticism of behavioral studies which contradict standard theories. Yet both the studies mentioned above replicated their findings using real money, the Lichtenstein and Slovic study using a Las Vegas casino, so the anomaly cannot be explained by a lack of incentives.

A recent study by Isoni and colleagues (2016) attempts to isolate the effects of endogenous and exogenous price cues on shaping preferences from the effects of market discipline on revealed preferences by designing an experiment to 'switch off' the effects of market discipline. They find that market discipline does cause shaping to be reduced, but that substantial shaping effects remain, indicating that market discipline does not cause preferences to be revealed in an unbiased way, as predicted in the NM.

## *Desire for consistency*

More recent research on stable preferences has revealed some even more startling findings. A study by Johansson and colleagues (2013) has found that not only do people often fail to notice mismatches between their decisions and the outcome of their choice but they also, in addition, endorse the opposite of their chosen alternative. Subjects were given the task of choosing which of a pair of faces they found most attractive. Unknown to them, the experimenters sometimes used a card trick to exchange one face for the other. The standard model, and indeed our intuition, predicts that most people would easily notice such a radical change in the outcome of a choice. But that was not the case: no more than a third of the exchanges were detected by the participants. The study also included a second round of choices using the same face pairs, and two stages of post-choice attractiveness ratings of the faces. This enabled the study to measure preference strength both as choice consistency and by looking at measures of rating differences between chosen and rejected options. It was found that the initially rejected faces were chosen more frequently in the second choice, and the perceived attractiveness of these faces was increased even in uncoupled individual ratings at the end of the experiment. This finding reveals another important factor underlying consumer preferences: the desire for consistency.

This desire for consistency means that a previous choice frequently leads to the same or similar choice in a later situation, in spite of the first choice being arbitrary, trivial, or non-optimal. The phenomenon can manifest itself in many different situations. Cialdini (1984) discusses a number of cases, which vary considerably in context. Examples include: American POWs writing down tenets of Chinese communism and then sympathizing with the communist ideology; painful hazing initiation ceremonies increasing the loyalty of members of a group; and California home-owners signing a petition to keep their state beautiful and then later allowing big and ugly 'drive carefully' signs to be erected on their lawns.

Another aspect of the desire for consistency involves cognitive ease, a recurring psychological theme in behavioral economics. It simply requires less cognitive effort to repeat a previous decision, like ordering the same meal from a restaurant menu as before. This results in **status quo bias**. However, there is something of a confound with this effect: the repeating of a previous choice may confer more utility, but it also may be a result of estimating that the probability of a previous choice being a good one is higher than if selecting a previously untried option. The existence of status quo bias has important policy implications related to sales strategy and also government intervention, as discussed in a later section. Other examples of the desire for consistency involve confirmation bias, the resolution of cognitive dissonance, commitment to a future action, or the establishment of social status, and these aspects are discussed in later chapters.

*Anchoring effects*

In one respect these have a common factor with both of the phenomena described above. They relate to the effects of prior events which result in unstable preferences. However, in this case these events do not necessarily relate to actions taken by an agent, since they can involve any environmental factor. More specifically, anchoring effects occur when people's responses are 'anchored' to other phenomena in their consciousness, however irrelevant these might appear to be. An interesting example is given in *Nudge*, the book by Thaler and Sunstein (2009): the urinals at Amsterdam airport have houseflies etched into them. This 'anchor' has apparently had the effect of reducing spillage by 80%. Several studies have also found some apparently very strange results here, in particular two papers by Ariely, Loewenstein and Prelec (ALP) in 2003 and 2006. For example, in one experiment a group of students was asked as a preliminary question to write down the last two digits of their social security number (essentially a random number between 00 and 99). They were then asked to value half a dozen different products, including a box of chocolates, two different bottles of wine, a cordless trackball, a cordless keyboard and a design book. The results showed remarkable consistency in the sense that the students with higher-ending social security digits valued all the products more highly. Those in the top 20% (from 80 to 99) bid highest, and the difference between their bids and those of the lowest 20% (from 00 to 99) varied between 216% and 346%!

Ariely, Loewenstein and Prelec (2003) have explained this phenomenon in terms of a theory of **arbitrary coherence**. This is described as follows: 'valuations of goods and experiences have a large arbitrary component, yet, after one valuation has been made, people provide subsequent valuations that are coherent in the sense that they are scaled appropriately relative to the first.' The coherence aspect can be explained in terms of another experiment which was conducted in the same study. In this case the students were divided into two groups, one of which was initially asked if they were prepared to pay $2 to listen to a poetry recital, while the other group was asked if they were prepared to accept $2 to listen to the poetry recital. Only 3% were prepared to pay, while 59% were willing to be paid the $2. However, when both groups were asked if they would listen for free the proportion of the first group rose to 35%, while for the second group the proportion fell to 8%. This demonstrates the anchoring effect of the first question. It also illustrates two other factors. First, it demonstrates an expectations effect, whereby people expect more value or utility when they are cued with a question involving willingness to pay, whereas they expect disutility if they are cued with a question involving willingness to accept. Second, it demonstrates that both groups are displaying a normal downward-sloping demand curve, as expected by standard economic theory. The coherence aspect is demonstrated further by responses to another question in the experiment, which asked how much each group was willing to pay/be paid to listen for different periods, of one minute, three minutes, and six minutes. The responses were consistent again with economic theory, in that they showed that the paying group were willing to pay more to listen for longer periods, while the paid group wanted to be paid more to listen for longer periods. The conclusion of the study regarding coherence was that in spite of the arbitrariness of the initial anchor, demand curves would still be the normal downward-sloping shape and stable.

A number of other empirical studies have found evidence of anchoring effects in various different contexts. For example, a study by Guéguen and Jacob (2013) found that handling money at an ATM had the effect of causing people to be less helpful to others immediately afterwards, either in terms of participating in surveys or prompting them to pick up an item that they appeared to have accidentally dropped. Another study found that the anchoring effect was context-dependent (Dogerlioglu-Demir and Kocas, 2014). This applied to anchor numbers which can be interpreted in different units depending on the context. For example, '99' can be perceived as $.99 in the context of a hamburger price (cheap), or as $99 in the context of a meal (expensive). Thus different anchors may be more or less successful in increasing sales depending on context.

Many recent researchers have endorsed the conclusions of the above studies regarding the importance of anchoring effects as an anomaly in the standard model of EUT (Kahneman and Sugden, 2005; Bernheim and Rangel, 2007, 2009; Beshears et al., 2008; Fehr and Hoff, 2011), suggesting necessary modifications. However, as discussed in the previous chapter, there has been some criticism of the anchoring studies in terms of their conclusions regarding the importance of the anchoring effect. Maniadis, Tufano and List (2014) were unable to replicate the findings of ALP in some of their experiments using the same protocol. These authors suggest a number of possible reasons for this, and caution that the anchoring effect, while still real, may not be as prominent or ubiquitous as some researchers have suggested.

## Framing effects

These effects, which are discussed further in the next two chapters, are one of the most important phenomena in behavioral economics, violating the invariance principle. Numerous studies have found that people's responses, in terms of values, attitudes and preferences, depend on the contexts and procedures involved in eliciting these responses. For example, when subjects have been asked to rate their overall level of happiness, their responses have been influenced by a prior question regarding the number of dates they have had in a recent time period. While this can be seen as an example of an anchoring effect, it might be considered that the prior question in this case is relevant to the second; however, if the first question influences the answer to the second, it is an example of procedural invariance, and therefore a violation of the standard model of EUT.

Framing effects are particularly important since they account for a high incidence of **preference reversal** (Slovic and Lichtenstein, 1983; Tversky, Slovic and Kahneman, 1990). This phenomenon relates to situations where people favor option A when a question or problem is posed or framed in one way but favor option B when the same problem is posed in a different way. Evidence from both the field and from experiments suggests that framing effects are widespread, occurring in many different situations. For example, there is evidence that products are evaluated more favorably, and chosen more frequently, when the surrounding environment contains more perceptually or conceptually related cues (Berger and Fitzsimons, 2008). There is much evidence that people's eating habits, especially the quantity consumed, can be influenced by the size of plates, packages or serving bowls used (Wansink, Just and Payne, 2009), even though people deny this (Wansink and Cheney, 2005). Large sizes can increase the amount served and consumed by 15% to 45% (Wansink, 2006). This principle appears to operate even when cues are not intrinsically related to the product. An interesting example is that when NASA landed the Pathfinder spacecraft on Mars in 1997, there was an increase in sales of Mars Bars, even though the Mars Bar takes its name from its company founder, not the planet. There is also evidence that framing effects even extend to experimental economists themselves, at least at a junior level (Gächter et al., 2009). Framing effects relate to the social and institutional context of choice too in many instances, but theories of social framing are still at a relatively early stage of development in behavioral economics and sit uneasily with the individualist psychological focus that dominates the field (see Klaes, 2002, 2008).

## Menu effects

There is another type of framing effect that is sometimes referred to as a 'menu effect', since it refers to how people choose from several options on a menu, rather than how each option is described. There are a number of different types of menu effect, which all involve different choice heuristics; seven are discussed here and another two will be discussed in Chapter 6 on mental accounting, since they involve aspects of risk and uncertainty or ambiguity.

**1**  *The 'attraction effect'*

This is a prominent example of a menu effect, and involves the principle of reference dependence mentioned earlier (Huber and Puto, 1983). Ariely (2008) refers to the effect as a '**decoy effect**', since it has become a much-used marketing practice. He opens his first chapter of Predictably Irrational with an example relating to subscriptions to the *Economist* magazine. There are three options on the menu:

(1)  1-year online subscription for $59

(2)  1-year print subscription for $125

(3)  1-year online and print subscription for $125

Ariely suggests that the second option is offered merely as a decoy. The underlying psychology is that when offered only options 1 and 3, consumers are not sure which one to choose, because there is a trade-off between price and quality, and they may prefer the cheaper and less profitable option 1. In Ariely's survey of MIT MBA students 68% chose this option. However, when all three options are presented, options 2 and 3 are more easily comparable because they are the same price, and only differ on quality. Since option 3 offers more in quality, it is said to dominate option 2; thus it is a 'no-brainer' that most people will prefer option 3 to 2, and this comparison will tend to cause them to prefer this over the first option as well. Thus he found that when presented with all three options 84% of the students chose option 3, another example of preference reversal.

These effects have significant marketing implications. The 'decoy effect' or attraction effect is a widespread practice in marketing strategy, offering consumers decoys that firms do not really want them to buy. We can generalize about the practice by saying that if a firm has two main offerings on the menu, A and B, but A is more profitable, the firm can encourage consumers to buy A by extending its offerings to include a decoy, which we can label A– (following Ariely, 2008). A– is obviously inferior to A, in terms of being a dominated choice.

Hedgcock and Rao (2009) have proposed that the underlying psychological explanation for the attraction effect involves trade-off aversion, and they have conducted a neuroeconomic study to test this theory. The fMRI technique was used, and this detected a number of differences in brain activation when subjects faced a three-item menu with a decoy compared with a two-item menu. In particular these included a decreased activation in the amygdala, an area of the brain associated with negative emotion, and an increased activation of the DLPFC, an area of the brain associated with the use of decision rules. The authors of the study are cautious in interpreting these results, bearing in mind the problems of reverse inference discussed in Chapter 2, but suggest that the introduction of a dominated option in the three-item menu allows people to avoid a stressful evaluation of a trade-off and instead apply the simple heuristic of choosing the dominating option.

There is evidence that firms are becoming more conscious of different types of menu effect in their marketing practices. Not surprisingly, fast-food chains are among the foremost to take an interest. Domino's Pizza announced that it has asked its media agency, Arena Media, to integrate behavioral economics into its planning process (*Marketing Magazine*, 2011). This actually involves much broader aspects of marketing than simply menu effects, as will be seen later. Many fast-food chains are coming under pressure from government agencies to become more socially responsible and try to encourage people, particularly children, to eat healthier foods. This is a very challenging task, given people's propensity to like starchy, fatty and sugary foods. Simply adding healthier options to the menu will not necessarily be effective, especially given the vicarious consumption effect discussed later in this subsection.

Some more recent studies have suggested that the attraction effect is not as important or widespread as claimed in earlier studies (Frederick, Lee and Baskin, 2014; Yang and Lynn, 2014), in particular only applying to situations where all the relevant variables can be described quantitatively. These studies suggest that most comparisons involve non-quantitative factors, like quality of hotel bedrooms or restaurant food, and the Yang and Lynn study was unable to detect attraction effects in more than 11 cases out of 91 attempts. On the other hand Huber and colleagues (2014) maintain that the attraction effect is still robust, since it can be replicated under similar experimental conditions.

**2**  *Preference for the salient*

Evidence suggests that people simplify complex decisions by choosing a salient option. This may apply to supermarket shoppers, for example when faced with a large shelf filled with different brands, although the factor of limited attention (discussed in the next section) is also important here. In the case of financial markets, Barber and Odean (2008) show that investors prefer to buy stocks of companies that are currently in the news, even if the news is bad. Being first on a list of options is often a considerable advantage. In 1981 American Airlines found that travel agents booked the first flight that appeared on their computer screen 53% of the time, and a flight that appeared somewhere on the first screen almost 92% of the time. This caused the airline to manipulate the order of flights as they appeared in the booking system in order to increase profits, and this ultimately led to complaints from other airlines and intervention from federal government. This 'first on the list' heuristic also applies in voting in the political arena. Ho and Imai (2008) conducted a study in California, where the order of candidates on the ballot is randomized, and found that there was a significant advantage for a candidate in being first on the list. The advantage was greater for minor party candidates compared with those from major parties, suggesting that voters use irrelevant information when they lack other informational cues.

The order of items on a list can be relevant in more complex ways. For example, Suk, Lee and Lichtenstein (2012) report that when differing brand options are listed in descending price order, people tend to choose higher-priced items, while when options are listed in ascending price order people tend to choose lower-priced items. The authors suggest that the reason for this phenomenon lies in the association between price and perceived quality for branded products combined with reference dependence, where consumers compare items with others earlier on the list.

**3**  *The compromise effect*

This effect refers to the finding that people frequently choose intermediate options in terms of price. This finding has been reported in a number of different settings, such as contributing to savings plans. A recent study by Pinger, Ruhmer-Krell and Schumacher (2016) indicates that in a restaurant setting this phenomenon appears to be quite robust, and persists in the presence of many other influencing factors, such as size of choice set and opportunity to choose familiar options.

**4**  *Choice avoidance*

This is another counterintuitive finding, sometimes referred to as the **paradox of choice**. Marketing managers may feel that they are both maximizing profits and benefiting consumers by offering them a greater range of choices, but the end result may be that consumers avoid the choice altogether, which often means not purchasing any item in the range. For example, Iyengar and Lepper (2000) compare the behavior of consumers who were offered the opportunity to taste 6 jams (the simple-choice treatment) with consumers who were offered the opportunity to taste 24 jams (the difficult-choice treatment). They find that, although more consumers stop to sample jams when there is more choice, substantially fewer actually buy jams (4 compared with 31 customers). Choi, Laibson and Madrian (2009b) report the same paradox in financial decision making, in that a smaller number of investment options increases participation in a 401(k) plan. Beshears and colleagues (2013) find that offering a binary choice, with a pre-set contribution level and asset allocation versus the status quo, increased enrollment in retirement savings plans by 10–20%. Kida, Moreno and Smith (2010) find a similar effect for inexperienced investors, but the opposite effect for experienced investors, who were actually less likely to invest when faced with a limited choice set.

What could explain the psychology underlying the paradox of choice? Evidence suggests that making complex decisions is stressful and people may try to avoid this stress. Sagi and Friedland (2007) propose a theory that post-decisional regret is related to the comparison between the alternative chosen and the union of the positive attributes of the alternatives rejected. This of course contradicts the standard model's view of opportunity cost, which considers only the positive attributes of the next best alternative rejected. However, the Sagi–Friedland theory does explain the paradox of choice, since a greater number of alternatives would increase post-decision regret, and the authors find that their theory was supported by four experiments.

A flip side to the above situation, which again represents a paradox, is that people are averse to single-option offers. Mochon (2013) finds that the choice share of an option increases (relative to deferral) when a competing attractive option is added to the menu. When only a single option is offered, DVD players in this study, people are more inclined to defer purchase. This may occur because people are more likely to consider a larger set of alternatives, with more positive attributes, when a single option is presented, whereas the addition of a single competing option may serve to limit the alternatives and attributes considered.

5   *The momentum effect*

This effect occurs when an initial purchase provides a psychological impulse that enhances the purchase of a second, unrelated product (Dhar, Huber and Khan, 2007). These authors report experimental evidence that the purchase likelihood for a second 'target' item (a key chain) increases with the purchase incidence of an initial, unrelated 'driver' item (an educational CD). This increased likelihood was not caused either by complementarity between the two items or by a consequent reduction in transaction costs. It was proposed that the effect is explained by Gollwitzer's (1990) theory of implementation and deliberation mindsets, where an initial purchase moves the consumer from a deliberative to an implemental mindset, thus driving subsequent purchases. The existence of this effect has important marketing implications, for example related to the use of loss leaders to get people into stores.

6   *The vicarious consumption effect*

A study related to choice of food items has shown that adding a healthy item to the list of available options has the perverse effect of causing people to choose less healthy food items than otherwise (Wilcox et al., 2009). Apparently 'the mere presence of the healthy food option vicariously fulfills nutrition-related goals and provides consumers with a license to indulge'. It would be interesting to follow up this research and observe if supermarkets that display fruit and vegetables near the entrance actually sell more of these items.

7   *Confusion*

A final behavioral deviation noted by DellaVigna (2009) concerns confusion. This does not reflect a preference, but is really an effect of cognitive failure. Examples include mistaken trades of stocks (confusing MCI with MCIC), reported by Rashes (2001), and mistaken voting in elections, where votes are placed for candidates whose names are adjacent to the intended candidate on the ballot, reported by Shue and Luttmer (2009).

## *Discrepancies between objective causes and subjective effects*

There appear to be discrepancies between objective measures of sources of comfort/ discomfort and reported measures of subjective feelings. Again, many defenders of the NM would argue that reported measures of subjective feelings are not economic phenomena, and that therefore they are of no concern to economists (Gul and Pesendorfer, 2007). However, when such feelings do or can affect later decisions, this is of relevance to economics. A study by Redelmeier and Kahneman (1996) of patients undergoing colonoscopies illustrates this phenomenon well. The patients were asked to report the intensity of current pain on a scale of 0 to 10 at minute intervals over a period up to 69 minutes. However, those patients who suffered more pain for longer periods did not necessarily have a worse recollection of the experience as a whole. Instead it seemed that the most important determinant of post-experience evaluation was a combination of the maximum pain suffered at any point and the mean pain suffered during the last three minutes. This finding has become known as the **peak-end rule**. It has been confirmed by later studies on the basis of evidence from a range of different areas, in the context of both negative and positive experiences, and also extending to the experience of material goods (Do, Rupert and Wolford, 2008).

More recent research has indicated that the peak-end rule is not just confined to humans. Egan Brad and colleagues (2016) have conducted experiments involving capuchin monkeys as well as humans where subjects could select the sequence of food intake, finding that capuchins also experience peak-end effects. The authors of the study derive two important conclusions from their experiments. First, the fact that the peak-end effect is found in a species that diverged from the human one 35 million years ago is an indicator that this effect, and many other decision-making biases discussed in behavioral economics, 'do not necessarily emerge as a result of specific cultural experiences and human-specific selective pressures—instead, our human biases might be the result of evolved cognitive strategies or the result of shared cognitive limitations, ones present in our primate lineage for considerable phylogenetic time.'

The second main conclusion of the study relates to policy implications, and involves a further anomaly as far as the standard economic model of rationality is concerned: both capuchin monkeys and humans seem incapable of learning how to implement the peak-end rule to maximize hedonic payoffs. This issue is discussed further in the section on policy implications, in terms of saving the best to last.

## *Expectations effects*

Another problem with the NM concerns the effect of expectations. There is some evidence that high expectations of happiness can lead to disappointment. This emerges in particular from the study by Schooler, Ariely and Loewenstein (2003) regarding people's plans for the millennium celebration of 2000. Those people who spent the most time, effort and money tended to be the least satisfied. It seems that the reference point phenomenon is again relevant here. Of course in this case it can be argued that the disappointment, or lower utility, after the event may be more than offset by the higher utility associated with the anticipation of the event. This leads to a consideration of a further related omission from the NM, relating to **anticipatory utility**. This issue is discussed further in the next section, but the essential point is that anticipation of pleasure can itself be pleasurable, with the result that people may defer the pleasurable experience in order to prolong the anticipatory utility. A study by Richins (2013) entitled 'When wanting is better than having' finds that materialistic people experience a hedonic high before purchase, due to the expectation that a particular product will transform their lives in some significant manner, and after purchase there is a hedonic decline. Such a pattern in utility was not found to occur with people low in materialism. It is this anticipatory factor that may at least partly explain the saying that revenge is a dish that is better served cold (it is also better for being planned rather than hastily delivered in an emotional state, as will be explained shortly).

There is another aspect of expectations effects, which is described well in Ariely's book *Predictably Irrational (2008)* with the Chapter 9 subtitle 'Why the mind gets what it expects'. The examples he reports all show that the utility that we derive from activities or consumption depends on our expectations, as does our behavior in general. It is worth considering three examples here to give a flavor of the phenomenon involved. Bargh, Chen and Burrows (1996) performed an experiment which showed that after a group of subjects were given a word-unscrambling task involving words related to the concept of the elderly, like 'Florida', 'bingo' and 'ancient', their walking speed was substantially slower than a control group that had not been primed with such words. This experiment therefore indicates the importance of subliminal messages in prompting expectations, as well as the effect of expectations on behavior. We shall return to this at the end of the chapter in the discussion of policy implications.

A second example of expectations effects also has important policy implications, related to pricing. A study by Waber and colleagues (2008) involved using a placebo for reducing pain. Subjects were administered electric shocks in two consecutive treatments, but given a 'drug' purported to be a painkiller before the second treatment. Sure enough, the subjects reported less pain in the second treatment compared to the first, even though the 'drug' was actually a vitamin C capsule. The interesting point was that in a following test the subjects reported a very different response according to the advertised price of the pill; at a price of $2.50 almost all the subjects experienced pain relief, but at a discounted price of 10 cents only half of them did.

Whereas the study described above involved examining self-reports of pain, a subjective measure, another study by Shiv, Carmon and Ariely (2005) examined the behavioral effect of different prices in an objective way. This study involved the use of an energy drink, SoBe Adrenaline Rush, in order to see if the price paid had an effect on actual performance. Performance in this case was measured in terms of the ability to solve anagram word puzzles. It was found that not only did the student subjects drinking the regular-priced beverage report less fatigue subjectively, they were also able to perform significantly better on the word puzzles than a group who drank the same beverage discounted to only about a third of the regular price (although no better than a control group who did not consume the drink). Again, the policy implications of these findings will be discussed later.

Another area where expectations effects are important is with the performance of branded products. There are conflicting findings here. A study by Garvey, Germann and Bolton (2015) concludes that the use of status brands improves performance by consumers, as might be expected from the findings of the studies described above. There was a twist to this outcome: the consumers took the credit for the improved performance themselves; this is an interesting example of overconfidence, a phenomenon discussed in more detail in the next chapter. The authors speculate that the psychology underlying this effect is that the status of the brand improves self-esteem, which in turn reduces task-induced stress, which then leads to an improvement in the performance of many consumers. However, the findings of this study conflict with those of another study by Gosline, Banker and Lee (2013). This study finds that, although consumers may rate branded products more highly and be prepared to pay more for them, their performance may be lower. In this case the authors speculate that consumers rate their performance relative to other users, and that using the abilities of high-status brand consumers as a reference point can lead to low expectations regarding one's own abilities. The jury is therefore still out regarding the effect of status brands on performance, and there appear to be a number of mitigating factors involved, in particular the preexisting beliefs of the consumer regarding self-efficacy in the relevant domain.

### Addiction and abstention

In the conventional model it is assumed that more consumption of a good gives more total utility. The NM does take into account 'bads', like garbage or pollution, where more consumption decreases total utility, but these are phenomena where increasing consumption is monotonically bad, meaning increasingly bad throughout the range of consumption. For some people, however, there are goods that give *too much* pleasure, and *excessive* consumption is associated with various problems in terms of health, and time and money spent. Addiction is a major factor in this context. The phenomenon of addiction can cover a wide range of goods: alcohol, tobacco and other recreational drugs are the most commonly cited examples, but one can also include food in general (or particular types of food like junk food), gambling, sex, computer games and indeed any activity involving a significant degree of excitement.

The psychological and physiological mechanisms relating to enjoyment of these goods are complex, being of a double-edged nature. However, one factor that deserves mention at this point is the concept of **diagnostic utility**. A number of studies have found that people infer their happiness from their actions in a **self-signaling** manner (Campbell and Sawden, 1985; Elster 1985a, 1989; Bodner and Prelec, 1997, 2001). The last study quotes as an example a person who takes a daily jog in spite of the rain, who may view that activity as a gratifying signal of willpower, dedication or future well-being. Bodner and Prelec continue: 'For someone uncertain about where he or she stands with respect to these dispositions, each new choice can provide a bit of good or bad "news".' One implication of this concept is that people who fear that they may be, or may become, addicted to a good may be better off, and feel themselves better off, abstaining from consumption completely. To indulge even slightly may reveal themselves to indeed have an addictive personality, and the acknowledgment of such weakness may make it impossible to break the addiction. These concepts of diagnostic utility and self-signaling may well help to explain the unfortunate and all-too-common phenomenon of 'falling off the wagon', with its vicious circle of low self-esteem and compensatory indulgence. The issue is discussed in more detail in Case 3.2.

### Endowment effects

These effects are discussed in more detail in Chapter 5, but the essence of the phenomenon is that utility is not independent of possession. Those people who have acquired a good in some way, through either purchase or gift, tend to value it more highly than others. Some researchers, notably Plott and Zeiler (2007), object to the use of the term 'endowment effect' since it suggests a particular theory for the phenomenon to be explained, and prefer to use the term '**exchange asymmetry**' for the phenomenon itself; this is an important distinction, since we shall see that there is some controversy regarding theories underlying the effect.

The effect was first noted in a study by Knetsch (1989). He performed an experiment which divided subjects randomly into three groups: one group was endowed with a mug, another with a candy bar and the final group was not endowed with either.

The first two groups were allowed to trade their good for the other one, while the third group was offered the choice of either good. If preferences were independent of endowment one would expect the proportions favoring one good over the other to be the same for each group. However, while 56% of the third, non-endowed, group favored the mug over the candy bar, 89% of the mug-endowed group preferred the mug, being unwilling to trade, and only 10% of the candy-endowed group preferred the mug, wanting to trade.

The main psychological factor underlying endowment effects was originally claimed to be **loss-aversion**, discussed in Chapter 5 in the context of prospect theory. More recent explanations examine the role of the possession-self link (Dommer and Swaminathan, 2013) and self-threat involved with sale (Chatterjee, Irmak and Rose, 2013). We will also see that the evidence regarding endowment effects is mixed (List, 2004; Plott and Zeiler, 2005, 2007; Knetsch and Wong, 2009).

*Attention*

We have already encountered the concept of bounded rationality in the previous chapter, seeing that people tend to simplify complex decisions by using heuristics; one implication is that they process only a subset of the information available. The size and type of this subset depends on the importance of the decision, the salience of signals relating to the decision, and the number of competing signals. There is evidence of inattention in several field studies in different situations. DellaVigna (2009) states that limited attention helps explain neglect of (1) shipping costs in eBay auctions; (2) non-transparent taxes, like indirect state taxes not included in the price; (3) complex information in rankings, like those of hospitals and colleges; and (4) earnings news, especially before weekends, on days with more competing news, news related to linked companies, or news related to events several years in the future. Related to evidence of limited attention is the finding by Frederick and colleagues (2009) that consumers often do not consider alternative purchases and the opportunity costs involved in purchase. Malmendier and Lee (2011) find dramatic evidence of this in online auctions, where for a particular item (a board game) auction prices exceeded the fixed price for the same item on the same web page over 40% of the time.

Paradoxically, there appears to be another effect related to attention that acts in an opposite manner to the one described above. There is some evidence that suggests that excessive attention, in terms of deliberating over a choice, can result in a poorer decision; for example, preference consistency has been found to be reduced (Nordgren and Dijksterhuis, 2009). This may be caused by the confusion factor described above.

## 3.6  Visceral factors

*Nature*

There is a general consensus among behavioral scientists that emotions are evolved tools for dealing with the challenges of human life. The term 'emotion' refers to 'some change in subjective experience, autonomic responses (e.g. heart rate, respiration, electrodermal activity), physical action (or an increased likelihood to perform an action, such as facial muscle movements, skeletal muscle movements), as well as some perception, thought, or judgment of the surrounding world' (Lindquist et al., 2013). Thus emotions involve both a psychological dimension and an underlying physiological state. There is much evidence that emotions like anger, fear, joy, surprise, anxiety, envy and pity affect our behavior in significant ways. We have already seen that 'drives', like hunger, thirst and sex, as well as cravings and pain, affect behavior. Psychologists tend to use the term 'visceral factors' to refer to the combination of all of these feelings. At sufficient levels of intensity, these feelings tend to cause people to behave in ways contrary to their long-run self-interest, often with the full awareness that they are doing so. This behavior violates various aspects of the standard model: (1) people do not maximize any kind of function; (2) people miscalculate probabilities; (3) people do not discount exponentially, at a constant rate; (4) people measure utilities inconsistently. In this chapter we are primarily concerned with the first and fourth aspects, while the other aspects are discussed in later chapters.

## Salience

Visceral factors like drives tend to be recurring states, which increase in intensity until they are assuaged, when they temporarily fall to a low level before rising again. This inevitable roller-coaster ride has a number of important implications for decision-making. First of all, as they increase in intensity, they narrow our attention onto the satisfaction of the drive, making it salient. Starving people become obsessed with food, prison inmates become obsessed with sex, drug addicts become obsessed with getting a 'fix'; all other desires fade into obscurity. In economic terms the MRS between the desired object and other goods approaches zero.

Furthermore, the increase in intensity also focuses attention on the present at the expense of the future, causing a lapse in self-regulation, at least as far as that particular visceral factor is concerned. Short-sighted decisions tend to occur in such circumstances as future consequences are ignored. These aspects are examined in Chapter 8, related to hyperbolic discounting and modifying instantaneous utility.

Another kind of narrowing of attention occurs as individuals experiencing intense levels of visceral factors tend to become more selfish. They are less likely to cooperate with others, unless they see that such cooperation is likely to achieve the satisfaction of their needs. We have already discussed a relatively mild example of this in the context of anchoring effects: simply handling money, as in visiting an ATM, has the immediate effect of reducing cooperation, in terms of not being willing to participate in a brief survey, or failing to prompt others to pick up an item that they appeared to have accidentally dropped. The other side of this coin is that people are also more likely to 'defect', in game-theoretic terms. For example, under duress like interrogation they are more likely to betray friends and family.

In moderation visceral factors tend to prompt us to take sensible actions, but as they increase in intensity and narrow our attention excessively they tend to cause us to make self-defeating choices, as Loewenstein (1996) has noted. Thus extreme fear may produce a panic that causes people to 'freeze' rather than adopting a more healthy 'fight or flight' reaction (Janis, 1967). Likewise, extreme anger can result in impulsive and destructive behavior that is regretted soon afterwards.

Sometimes even moderate anxiety may cause us to make irrational decisions, by focusing our attention unduly on certain factors. For example, it has been observed that earthquake insurance purchases rise after earthquakes, when the objective probability is probably at a low-point (Palm et al., 1990). Similarly, purchases of flood and earthquake insurance are influenced more by whether friends have experienced the event than by the experience of one's immediate neighbors, even though the experience of neighbors should provide a better guide to the probability of experiencing flood or earthquake (Kunreuther et al., 1978). We tend to give friends more attention than neighbors. Thus the problems relating to salience involve both the estimation of utility, or disutility, and to the calculation of subjective probabilities, an issue discussed in the next two chapters.

## Consciousness

Visceral factors, particularly when they are intense, tend to affect behavior directly, without any **conscious** deliberation process (Bolles, 1975). Brain centers are activated, either chemically or electrically, which often bypass conscious or cognitive mediation, and action results. This mechanistic language indicates once again the irrelevance of volition as far as at least some behavior is concerned. An extreme example is people falling asleep at the wheel; nobody makes a conscious decision to do this, but an intense desire for sleep can override the instinct for survival in this case. The extreme sensitivity of the brain's pleasure centers to stimulation is a vital factor in understanding drug addiction. It has long been known that laboratory animals will continue to administer electrical stimulation to pleasure centers, in preference to food, water and sex until the point of collapse and even death (Olds and Milner, 1954).

This does not imply that we are not conscious of the operation of visceral factors, or that we are not able to regulate them in terms of their effects. Regulation is particularly important when the visceral factor changes in intensity gradually, like the onset of hunger, and this has important policy implications in terms of well-being that are considered later in the chapter.

## Impulsivity

Visceral factors also play an important role in influencing **impulsivity**. In general terms we tend to think of impulsivity as relating to situations where people depart from prior decision plans. Usually the departure is prompted by some trigger factor, and this has an immediate effect. Impulsivity is often explained in terms of non-constant discounting, discussed in Chapter 8, but there are certain aspects that cannot be easily explained in such terms. These aspects relate particularly to the effects of visceral or emotional states such as hunger, sexual desire, anger or fear, which are frequent causes of impulsive behavior. We will see that modification of the instantaneous utility function may be necessary in order to account for such factors.

We can also consider impulsivity in terms of the distinction drawn by Loewenstein (1996) between **actual** and **desired** value, which parallels the distinction of Kahneman, Wakker and Sarin (1997) between predicted and decision utility discussed in the next section. As the intensity of the relevant visceral factor increases, this increases the desired value (or decision utility), and thus the discrepancy between actual and desired value, increasing the probability of impulsive behavior. Another way of describing the situation is that we want something more than we expect to like it. This distinction between wanting and liking is important in a number of different contexts. For example, a smoker may want to give up, meaning he has the motivation to give up, but does not like giving up, because he gains no hedonic pleasure from giving up. It has been found that depressive people want self-esteem, but do not like pursuing it; similarly, they have been found to want, but not like, alcohol and friendship (Bushman et al., 2012). The implications of this in terms of different types of utility are further discussed in the next section.

## Effects of environmental factors

The intensity of visceral factors, and the resulting impulsivity, are also strongly influenced by situational factors. Temporal or physical proximity, or sensory contact (sight, sound, touch or smell), can elicit visceral cravings. In a series of experiments carried out by Mischel (1974) and Mischel, Shoda and Rodriguez (1992) children were placed in a room by themselves and taught they that they could summon the experimenter by ringing a bell. They would then be shown a superior and inferior prize and told that they would receive the superior prize if they could wait successfully for the experimenter to return. One main finding was that the children found it harder to wait for a delayed reward if they were made to wait in the presence of either one of the immediate or delayed reward objects. This finding is particularly important since it provides evidence for the visceral factor theory as against the non-constant discounting theory. According to the latter children should be more willing to wait in the presence of the superior delayed reward.

Visceral cravings may even be relevant in decision-making situations where the relevant drive or emotion may not be directly related to the decision. For example, people showing their homes to prospective buyers may do well to bake bread or cakes beforehand to create a more 'homely' environment, even though buying a home is not normally considered to be an impulsive purchase. There is substantial evidence that environmental factors like the above can significantly affect mood and thus behavior, representing another type of anchoring effect. The weather is a good example. People tip more at restaurants on sunny days (Rind, 1996). There tends to be a negative relationship between cloud cover and aggregate stock returns (Saunders, 1993; Hirshleifer and Shumway, 2003). International soccer matches also adversely impact daily stock returns for the losing country (Edmans, Garcia and Norli, 2007). Simonsohn (2010) found that students were more likely to enrol at colleges known for their academic rigor when they visited on cloudy, rather than sunny, days. The author suggested that this was because on sunny days the opportunity cost of studying was more salient, since other outdoor activities were more likely to be considered. Likewise, temperature also has significant effects on emotional response. Bruno, Melnyk and Völckner (2017) conducted an experiment that found that physical coldness enhances consumers' attitudes towards emotionally warm ads, while physical warmth decreases consumers' responses to emotionally warm ads and instead enhances attitudes towards emotionally cold ads. This finding has policy implications for advertising themes being linked to seasonal and geographical factors.

In some cases the environmental factors that affect behavior are very general. For example, it has been shown that investor sentiment is reflected in the tenor of status updates on Facebook, so that daily stock returns are correlated with the Facebook Gross National Happiness Index (FGNHI). Using data from millions of such status updates on an international basis, Siganos, Vagenas-Nanos and Verwijmeren (2014) were able to show a positive causal relationship, with returns following upticks in sentiment in the short term, but then reversing and returning to normal in the long term. This trend essentially is the same as predicted by De Long and colleagues (1991), when financial markets have a large population of 'noise' traders. It is also noteworthy that the effects of these environmental factors tend to be reduced when people's attention is drawn to them.

## *Affective forecasting*

We tend to be poor at predicting visceral states. For example, we tend to overestimate how long our current emotional state, whether happy or sad, angry or fearful, will last. This also applies to hunger; hence the advice: don't go to the supermarket when you are hungry. Furthermore, when the visceral drive has been satisfied, we tend to underestimate its strength in the future; for example, we think we will be able to control our hunger pangs and not eat all the junk food we just bought in a big binge. Meyvis, Ratner, and Levav (2010) report five studies that indicate that we tend to mispredict our emotional states, and then misremember them; these errors and biased recall involve events such as a Superbowl loss, a presidential election and an important purchase. The investigators propose that the biased recall is caused by an anchoring effect related to the subject's current emotional state. However, the consequence of this is that we fail to learn from past mispredictions, and there is a compounding of errors over time.

## Theoretical foundations

Some psychologists have proposed general theories relating to the relationships between emotions and decision-making. A prominent recent example is the Appraisal-Tendency Framework (ATF) of Han, Lerner and Keltner (2007). This theory addresses how and why specific emotions carry over from past situations to influence future judgments and choices. It differs from previous theories using a valence-based approach, which assumed that positive moods had typical effects on judgment and decision-making, which contrasted with the typical effects of negative moods. Han, Lerner, and Keltner, following Lerner and Keltner (2001), demonstrated that two mood states such as fear and anger can lead to different judgmental effects, even though both have negative valence. They also find that other negative emotions do not have identical effects on decision-making. Disgust reduces buying prices or willingness to pay (WTP) whereas sadness increases them. The effect is reversed for selling prices, or willingness to accept (WTA).

Construal level theory (CLT) has also been frequently applied to explain different emotional responses. CLT proposes that people think about objects and events on a dimension of concreteness or abstractness according to their psychological distance. This distance can be temporal, spatial or social. Anger, for example, tends to be directed towards specific targets, and therefore involves a more concrete construal level compared with shame, which is a more general attitude, and therefore more abstract. The significance of this distinction is that, while anger and shame are both negative emotions, angry people are more likely to hold on to prior preferences, while shameful people are more accepting of new information and prone to change (Han, Duhachek and Agrawal, 2014). Similarly, sad people, having a more concrete construal level, tend to be more inclined to choose high-risk/high-reward options, while anxious people, with a more abstract construal level, tend to choose low-risk/low-reward options.

A strong negative emotion that has already been mentioned earlier in the context of different responses is fear. People commonly try to use fear as a means of persuading others to take specific actions because of its intensity. However, this strategy can easily backfire. For example, anti-smoking campaigns often make use of cancer statistics or even shocking pictures and photos, as in Australia. There is much controversy regarding whether government policy has been effective here, but research has shown that people tend to erect strong psychological defences when presented with disturbing and disgusting information and images. The emotion of disgust tends to lead to avoidance for sound evolutionary reasons. This issue is discussed further in the next chapter in the context of the theory of cognitive dissonance. However, one further research finding is relevant here. It has been found that mixing humor with fear can be effective in advertising, since humor can reduce the fear tension, preventing consumers from building defences against the advertising message (Mukherjee and Dubé, 2012).

Regret can also be considered as a visceral factor and regret theory has an important role in consumer choice. This is discussed in more detail in Chapter 5, but one aspect can be touched on here, relating to the opportunity cost of choice and counterfactuals. If we decide to buy an item, we may later suffer regret in the form of buyer's remorse. On the other hand, if we decide not to buy than we may also suffer from regret, this time in the form of missing an opportunity. One study has suggested that when people buy a material good the first type of regret (from action) is more important, while when people buy an experience then the second type of regret (from inaction) is more relevant (Rosenzweig and Gilovic, 2012). The authors contend that not only do people tend to get more lasting satisfaction when they buy experiences rather than material goods, but also they suffer less from regret. This is because there are more obvious substitutes for material goods, whereas experiences tend to be more unique, making comparisons more difficult, and the opportunity cost is less salient.

Conflict can also cause negative emotions, such as depression and anxiety. Some past research has indicated that these emotions result in poorer decision-making (Shah and Kruglanski, 2002) or choice deferral (Iyengar and Lepper, 2000). Anxiety may cause us to ignore certain new information, or not seek it; for example, we may choose not to visit a doctor when we have a significant medical symptom. This may increase our short-term utility, but cause us to misestimate probabilities. However, a recent study has suggested that conflict can aid decision-making, since a conflict mindset can lead to more systematic processing using more available information (Savary et al., 2015).

The flip side of the above situation is that a state of happiness may cause decision-making to become more difficult. When choosing between various options the tendency is to focus on differences or unique qualities. A positive mood tends to increase this focus, making the choice more difficult (Pocheptsova et al., 2015).

Positive emotions like pride and compassion also have different effects on consumption when bandwagon effects are involved. This has policy implications, since undesirable social tendencies like teenage binge drinking may be reduced by appealing to people's pride, or desire to be different.

## 3.7  Types of utility

In order to shed light on the different aspects of judgment and decision-making described above we now need to examine more closely the concept of utility. This involves a discussion of the concept's evolution over time, the issue of measurement, and the different types of utility that are relevant in decision-making.

### Historical evolution

The concept of utility is one of the most basic building blocks in economic theory. In particular it underlies the theory of consumer choice. In this chapter, however, we will only be concerned with riskless choice; the effects of risk and uncertainty will be discussed in the next two chapters.

The assumption that the objective of consumers is expected utility maximization is the most fundamental single component of the NM, dating back to Jeremy Bentham [1789](1948). It should be noted that, strictly speaking, the term 'expected' implies an element of risk or uncertainty, the discussion of which is deferred until the next two chapters. In Bentham's original usage of the term utility referred to the experiences of pleasure and pain, which 'point out what we ought to do, as well as what we shall do.' Thus utility has a **hedonic** characteristic, which later researchers, notably Kahneman (2000), refer to as **experienced utility**. We shall see later in this section that the meaning of the term utility has changed since Bentham's time, and is now regarded as outmoded by many economists, who tend to favor the concept of **decision utility**. As discussed in more detail in Chapter 5, this meaning of utility refers to the weight assigned to an outcome in a decision, and is revealed by people's choices. It is this revealed preference meaning of utility that is generally used in the NM.

This modern concept of utility appears to have two obvious advantages over Bentham's concept. First, it is easier to measure, since decision utility can be inferred from the choices and actions that people take. Second, it no longer implies a commitment to a hedonistic philosophy. Sen (1987) in particular has been at pains (excuse the hedonistic pun!) to point out that the maximization of experienced utility is not always what people are trying to achieve, and his opinion is shared by many economists and psychologists. Indeed, some economists would go further and say that the study of people's objectives is outside the realm of economics and belongs in psychology or even philosophy. As stated in the introductory chapter, this is not a view that we share, since it is not consistent with our reductionist approach, which advocates consilience between different disciplines.

So where does this leave us as far as the concept of utility is concerned? The main point is that Bentham's hedonistic concept of utility may well still be appropriate in terms of determining our choices and actions, as well as conferring the additional advantage of allowing a more parsimonious model of behavior. This argument will become clearer as we examine the various types of utility later in the section.

### Cardinal and ordinal utility

Early economists believed that utility could be measured quantitatively, in terms of an arbitrary unit called 'utils', using a ratio scale with a zero point. Thus if consumption of basket A yielded 10 utils and basket B yielded 20 utils, then it could be said that basket B yielded twice as much utility as basket A. Some economists even considered that utility could be added interpersonally, meaning that a utility for John of 10 utils could be added to a utility for Jane of 20 utils, yielding a total utility of 30 utils.

Some economists tend to disfavor any **cardinal** measure of utility, meaning a measure involving an interval scale. Instead they favor an **ordinal** measure, where baskets of commodities are simply ranked according to preference. This view implies that statements like 'basket A has twice as much utility as basket B' are meaningless, and certainly interpersonal additions of utility are invalid. The use of an ordinal measure as opposed to a cardinal measure has the advantage of involving fewer assumptions regarding the nature of utility. We have already seen that the equilibrium condition relating to the behavior of consumers in terms of utility maximization can be expressed in terms of ordinal utility using the concept of the MRS. The law of diminishing marginal utility can also be expressed in ordinal terms. However, the NM as it has been stated in this text does use a cardinal measure of utility, since this has the advantage of being far more tractable mathematically than any model expressed in ordinal terms. Furthermore, we will see that neuroeconomic evidence supports the existence of a cardinal utility function.

We will now see that the concept of utility is a complex one, having many differentiated meanings and determinants. By examining these we will attain a much greater understanding of observed behavior, and in particular the types of judgment and choice described in the previous section.

### Decision utility

This is the type of utility usually discussed by economists, since it is easiest to measure in terms of revealed preference. It is important to note that decision utility does not therefore necessarily reflect attitudes or judgments. A study by Tversky and Griffin (2000) illustrates this point. Sixty-six undergraduate students were presented with the following information:

Imagine that you have just completed a graduate degree in communications and you are considering one-year jobs at two different magazines.

(A)   At Magazine A, you are offered a job paying $35,000. However, the other workers who have the same training and experience as you do are making $38,000.

(B)   At Magazine B, you are offered a job paying $33,000. However, the other workers who have the same training and experience as you do are making $30,000.

Approximately half the students were asked which job they would choose, while the other half were asked which job would make them happier. The first question relates to decision utility while the second relates to hedonic, or experienced utility. In this case the experienced utility is expected in the future, and it appears that people try to imagine what it would feel like to experience those states, involving the formation of an attitude. However, when people are asked to make a choice or decision, they tend to search for reasons or arguments to justify their choice. This difference was reflected in the survey results: 84% of the subjects chose (A), the job with the higher absolute salary and lower relative position, but 62% of the subjects thought that (B), the job with the lower absolute salary and higher relative position, would make them happier. In this sense then it could be claimed that people preferred (B), thus indicating a distinction between choice or revealed preference on the one hand and actual preference in terms of happiness on the other. A more recent study by Comerford and Ubel (2013) reports a similar discrepancy between preference and choice when it comes to effortful jobs. They find that people express a preference for jobs requiring more effort, but choose jobs that involve less effort. In a laboratory experiment where subjects were assigned to work at a job based on the wage they set themselves, they also find that those whose wage demands led them to be assigned to the effortless job experienced lower enjoyment than those who were assigned to the effortful job. Thus we observe a discrepancy between preference and choice, and also between decision utility and experienced utility. Why do people choose an option that they think will make them less happy? There are various possible reasons that we will have to explore.

Another discrepancy between choice (decision utility) and attitude (experienced utility) arises when the object of choice/attitude has many attributes. For example, the consideration of a car may involve the attributes of safety, fuel economy, size, durability and performance (to name just a few). The standard decision-making approach involves two steps: (1) determine values for each attribute, using some kind of scale, and (2) determine weights for each attribute, in order to compare them. For example, a loss of one mile to the gallon in terms of fuel economy may be equivalent to two cubic feet of boot space. There may also be certain minimum requirements for each attribute. However, it has been shown, for example by Tversky, Sattath and Slovic (1988), that this procedure is more relevant in determining attitudes or judgments; when it comes to preference the most important attribute is weighted more heavily, presumably because it is a more convenient rationale for choice (Tversky and Kahneman 1973). This bias is sometimes referred to as the **prominence effect**.

This effect may also be explained by the **Somatic-Marker Hypothesis (SMH)**, proposed by the neuroscientist Damasio (1994). He points out the problems involved in the conventional utility maximization model, both in terms of the amount of time involved and the other cognitive difficulties described by Tversky and Kahneman, and concludes that people can still make good, and quick, decisions based on 'gut feeling'. In essence Damasio is referring to the existence of visceral factors discussed in the previous section, but in this case proposing that they can lead to better rather than worse decisions. His SMH proposes that these factors create a 'somatic marker', an unpleasant gut feeling when a bad outcome connected with a given response option comes to mind. The somatic marker:

> forces attention on the negative outcome to which a given action may lead, and functions as an automated alarm signal which says: Beware of danger ahead if you choose the option which leads to this outcome. The signal may lead you to reject, *immediately*, the negative course of action and thus make you choose among other alternatives. The automated signal protects you against future losses, without further ado, and then allows you *to choose from among fewer alternatives*. (Damasio, 1994, p. 173; emphasis in original)

Thus this mechanism is a first stage in the decision-making process, which Damasio believes probably increases both the accuracy and efficiency of the process. He has observed that patients with damage to the PFC of the brain, where this process appears to occur, tend to be handicapped in many real-life decisions, for example the choice of who to befriend, who to have as a marriage or business partner, and what to pursue as a career. By using only 'pure reason' as opposed to 'practical reason' they take too long to make many decisions, and end up making many mistakes that ultimately reduce their well-being.

In conclusion it can be said that sometimes decision utility, as illustrated by revealed preference, will cause us to make bad decisions in terms of our happiness. However, in other circumstances, taking into account the SMH, and indeed any subconscious factors involved in decision-making, people may make good decisions even though utility maximization may not be involved as a conscious mental process at all. Of course this particular phenomenon does not contradict the NM; people may be performing in an 'as if' manner.

### Experienced utility

So far experienced utility has been described as a unified concept. However, Kahneman (2000) draws a useful distinction between **remembered utility**, after the experience, and **real-time utility**, during the experience. These are measured in different ways, and are relevant for different purposes.

1   Remembered utility is measured using a **memory-based approach**; this involves a retrospective evaluation of past experience. The concept is therefore subject to bias, in particular the application of the Peak-End rule. It has been observed in colonoscopy studies by Redelmeier and Kahneman (1996) that a prolongation of the duration of pain at a lower level of intensity can lead to a more favorable evaluation, violating the principle of dominance. This can also be relevant in decision-making, if people base decisions on remembered past utility, or disutility. Cowley (2008) refers to this process as **retrospective hedonic editing**, and draws attention to its dangers in terms of decision-making. In particular it can result in the justification of past indulgences, like gambling or over-eating, thus leading to a continuation of self-harming behavior. This phenomenon is related to cognitive dissonance, discussed in the next chapter, where people adjust their attitudes to be consistent with their behavior.

2   Real-time utility is measured using a **moment-based approach**; this is a more difficult procedure to implement, since it involves a continuous monitoring of the subjects. For example, in the colonoscopy studies the subjects were asked to rate their pain on a scale of 0 (no pain at all) to 10 (intolerable pain) every 60 seconds. An example relating to two patients is given in Figure 3.3. This moment-based approach can also be used to derive what Kahneman refers to as **total utility**, which in turn can be used as a measure of 'objective happiness', under certain assumptions, as will be discussed in the next section.

There is another aspect of lack of unity as far as the concept of experienced utility is concerned, and this concerns the distinction between 'wanting' and 'liking' (Berridge, 2007). 'Wanting' is associated with the motivation aspects of reward, which can be dissociated from 'liking', which is concerned with the hedonic aspects of reward. Thus we can want not to like something, like smoking. There is neuroeconomic evidence for this distinction in terms of different neural systems being involved; it appears that dopamine is associated with the motivation aspects of reward, and disruption of the dopamine system does not impair the hedonic aspects, which appear to be mediated by opioid systems in the ventral striatum and palladium (Fox and Poldrack, 2008). We shall examine the neuroeconomic aspects of utility in more detail in the next section.

**Figure 3.3**   Moment utility of two colonoscopies

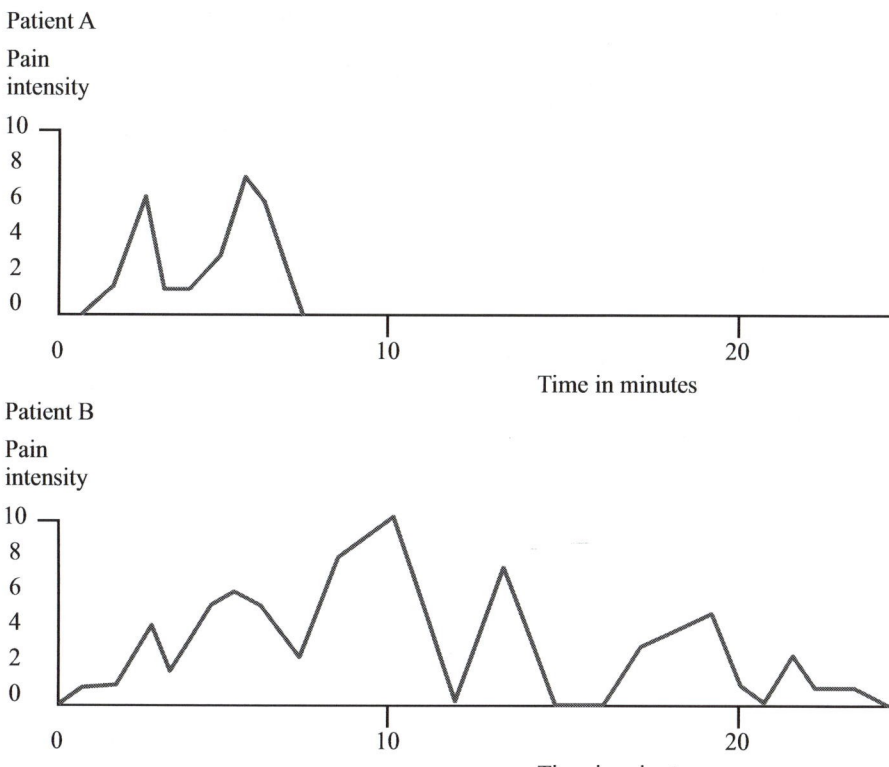

## Endowment and contrast effects

An important theory regarding happiness and well-being (not necessarily the same thing as we will see) is that people judge their level of these based on the concepts of **endowment** and **contrast** effects (Tversky and Griffin, 2000). It should be noted that the endowment effect in this context is not the same kind of endowment effect referred to earlier, where the acquisition of goods causes the acquirer to value the goods more highly than expected. In the words of Tversky and Griffin:

> The endowment effect of an event represents its direct contribution to one's happiness or satisfaction. Good news and positive experiences enrich our lives and make us happier; bad news and hard times diminish our well-being. (p. 709)

The contrast effect is an indirect effect that works in the opposite direction:

> A positive experience makes us happy, but it also renders similar experiences less exciting. A negative experience makes us unhappy, but it also helps us appreciate subsequent experiences that are less bad. (p. 709)

Contrast effects are particularly important in societies where people are generally becoming more affluent over time, and in this context are often referred to as **treadmill effects**. They are responsible for the second act of Pinker's three-act tragedy, described earlier.

There are two main theories explaining the existence of treadmill effects. The oldest theory explains them in terms of **adaptation** (Helson, 1964; Brickman and Campbell, 1971). This is a hedonic response, which can be most easily seen in physiological terms. When subjects immerse one hand in cold water and the other in hot water for a period of time, and then immerse both hands in the same container of lukewarm water, they experience the strange sensation of one hand feeling warm (the one that was previously in cold water) and the other hand feeling cold (the one that was previously in hot water). This theory has been used to explain why both lottery winners and paraplegics appear to adjust rapidly to their changes in circumstances.

However, not everyone is convinced by the adaptation theory as far as such explanations are concerned. Frederick and Loewenstein (1999) have proposed a number of reasons why reported happiness may not be reliably measured on the scales used. Kahneman (2000) proposes a different mechanism by which treadmill effects can be explained, using the term '**satisfaction treadmill**'. This explains the phenomenon in terms of an **aspiration effect**. Kahneman explains this effect by using an example of a graduate student who is constrained by her income to eating mediocre dishes when she goes to a restaurant. When she takes a lucrative job she can afford to consume food of a higher quality, and her overall utility increases for a time. However, after a transition period, we observe that her satisfaction returns to its previous level. Her aspiration level has increased, and her utility is influenced by her aspiration level; other things being equal, the higher the aspiration level, the lower the utility. Alternatively, we can say that there is no longer a contrast between the dishes she is consuming now and the ones that she was consuming a while ago, just after her income had increased.

Two points should be noted regarding this aspiration effect. Kahneman refers to the satisfaction treadmill as being distinct from the hedonic treadmill. However, while the mechanism involved is different, it can also be claimed that the aspiration effect is still hedonic in nature. The second point is that the aspiration effect may involve a **ratchet effect**. Further research needs to be done in this area, but it may be that people find it easier to adjust their aspirations upwards rather than downwards. The concept of loss-aversion is relevant here.

The endowment and contrast theory (ECT) has some interesting applications. For example, room surroundings have been found to affect people's general satisfaction and their satisfaction with their current housing situation in a way that is incompatible with conventional theory but compatible with the ECT (Schwarz et al., 1987). Subjects were required to spend an hour either in an extremely pleasant room (spacious, nicely furnished and decorated with posters and flowers) or in an extremely unpleasant room (small, dirty, smelly, noisy and overheated). Subjects who were placed in the pleasant room reported higher overall life satisfaction than those in the unpleasant room, showing the dominance of the endowment effect as far as general satisfaction or well-being is concerned. However, subjects placed in the unpleasant room reported higher satisfaction with their housing than those in the pleasant room, showing the dominance of the contrast effect in the context of a relevant standard of comparison. Thus Tversky and Griffin (2000) conclude:

> A specific event, therefore, is likely to have a significant contrast effect in the domain to which it belongs, and little or no contrast effect in others. (p. 719)

### Anticipatory utility

As mentioned earlier, people gain hedonic utility from the anticipation of events in the future, for example by looking forward to a holiday or dreading a visit to the dentist. This anticipatory utility is based on a person's expected or **predicted utility**, meaning their belief about the future experienced utility of an event. Again endowment and contrast effects are relevant. Playing the lottery presents an interesting application, since this type of behavior is not readily explained by EUT, as discussed in more detail in the next two chapters. Unrealized hopes and fears can give rise to positive or negative endowment in terms of anticipatory utility. The probability of winning a lottery is very low, which means that the failure to win does not cause much disappointment. Therefore, as Tversky and Griffin (2000) state, 'the dream of becoming an overnight millionaire could produce enough pleasure to offset the mild disappointment of not winning the lottery'. When the positive endowment effect outweighs the negative contrast effect people can enjoy playing the lottery even when they do not win. Evidence regarding this anticipatory utility comes from a study by Kocher, Krawczyk and van Winden (2014), who conduct an experiment with real lottery tickets and find that a substantial minority of subjects prefer delayed resolution of risk, meaning they prefer to wait longer before finding out the result. They also preferred to spread outcomes, in terms of preferring two tickets in separate draws rather than in the same draw, thus prolonging the period of anticipation.

It should be noted that the contrast effect appears to be highly sensitive to the probability of winning or losing. As the probability of winning increases, the costs of the disappointment of losing (the contrast effect) appear to increase more quickly than the benefits of hope of winning (the endowment effect). The implication of this is that, for a given expected value, people should tend to prefer long-odds situations rather than short-odds – they have sweeter dreams and milder disappointment. Another possible explanation of people playing the lottery is given in Chapter 5, in terms of probabilities and decision-weighting.

## Residual utility

Whereas anticipatory utility looks forward to future events, residual utility relates to pleasure or pain felt at later periods of time in separate episodes. This phenomenon arises because utility profiles may be concatenated or disjunctive. For example, a person may gain anticipatory utility regarding going on holiday in Hawaii for a month before the actual event, then enjoy the holiday for a week, and then maybe suffer a contrast effect when they return to work. In addition, maybe a month later, they may feel another 'utility boost' related to the same holiday experience, when they reminisce with friends. These later episodes may be repeated at various intervals after the original experience to which they relate. Residual utility can also be negative if someone dwells on a bad experience in the past, for example thinking about the time when they had a match point in a tennis championship but then went on to lose the match.

## Diagnostic utility

This aspect of utility has already been mentioned as an anomaly in the NM. Diagnostic utility refers to the situation where people infer their utility from their actions. It was seen that the phenomenon that is relevant here is the process of self-signaling, which is particularly important for people who are uncertain where they stand in terms of certain personal attributes, for example the possession of strong willpower. Thus when we consider the situation of someone deciding whether they should have an alcoholic drink, we should not just consider the experienced or hedonic utility of the good consumed, we should also consider the utility to be inferred from the action of consumption, in terms of signaling the vice of a weak will or the virtue of a strong will. It may be that the negative diagnostic utility of an action may outweigh the positive expected experienced utility related to the good consumed. In this case the person will abstain from consumption. The significance of this is that temptation should not just be seen as a cost; it can also bring a benefit (Dhar and Wertenbroch, 2012). Thus a dieting person may experience hunger as disutility, but simultaneously gain the benefit of positive diagnostic utility in terms of improved self-esteem if they refrain from eating. If the dieter feels no hunger, for example if they have had gastric band surgery, they will not gain such diagnostic utility. It will be seen in the first case study at the end of the chapter that this concept of diagnostic utility has widespread applications.

*Transaction utility*

The NM frames the net value of the purchase in terms of benefit minus cost. In reality the phenomenon of loss-aversion makes this coding of the purchase hedonically inefficient. Both Kahneman and Tversky (1984) and Thaler (1985) therefore reject the idea that costs are necessarily viewed as losses. Thaler proposes instead that there are two types of utility that consumers gain from a transaction:

1  **Acquisition utility** – this represents the value of the good obtained relative to its price, equivalent to the concept of consumer surplus.

2  **Transaction utility** – this corresponds to the perceived value of the 'deal', in other words the difference between the reference price and the price paid.

The reference price may often be the price that the consumer expected to pay for the good. Thaler notes two important implications of the transaction utility component. The first is that people are often tempted to buy 'deals', where transaction utility dominates acquisition utility; we then often find that these items are seldom used. Marketing strategies skillfully manipulate the framing of offers, using reference prices and emphasizing savings ('silver linings'). Examples of such goods are clothing, household gadgets and health club memberships (Wilkinson, 1996, 2003). In the last case self-control factors are also relevant, and these will be discussed in the next section. The other implication relates to the opposite situation, where people forgo goods that have the potential to benefit the consumer in terms of acquisition utility, but are rejected because of a high perceived transaction disutility. Thaler gives the example of a thirsty beer drinker who will pay $4 for a beer from an expensive resort, but refuse to pay $2.50 for the same beer from a grocery, on the grounds that he has a reference price of only $2 in the latter case. We will see later, in Chapter 10, that there is an additional dimension that may also be involved in these sorts of decisions: our notion of fairness may be violated.

More recent research has added some nuances to the concept of transaction utility. For example, it has been reported that consumers perceive the deal to be better if they believe that the offer is more valuable than the marketer intended (Sela, Simonson and Kivetz, 2013). The flip side of this phenomenon is that customized offers that are tailor-made for particular consumers may be perceived as less valuable. The authors of the study concluded that competitive consumers gain utility if they believe they are outsmarting the market. This has important counter-intuitive policy implications for marketers in terms of targeting promotions, a strategy normally regarded as desirable.

## 3.8  Policy implications

As we have already seen, the factors discussed in this chapter have a number of implications for managerial and public policy, which may not be intuitive, and often contradict current practices and government policies in many countries. Some examples have already been mentioned, for example menu effects and the paradox of thrift; other examples that have been investigated by empirical studies are discussed below, and some are discussed in more detail in the case studies. The first four situations refer to managerial implications, the next two to personal implications, and the last three to government policy.

*The desire for consistency and commitment*

There is a sales tactic referred to as 'lowballing', where a salesperson offers a customer a deal at a particularly low price, but the deal is not genuine, since the dealer never intends it to go through. It is commonly used by car dealerships, the purpose being to cause a customer to make a buying decision for a certain car. Once the decision has been made, various activities ensue that are designed to cement a sense of commitment to the purchase item. For example, forms may be filled out, the customer's credentials checked, finance terms arranged, and the customer may be encouraged to use the item on a trial basis for a certain time (preferably in public). During this time the dealer knows that the customer will develop a number of new reasons for buying the product. Once these props are in place, the original trigger for buying the product is then removed by the dealer. This is frequently done by detecting some kind of 'error'; maybe the salesperson overlooked the pricing of some option on the car, or, better, some external agent like the finance company may have discovered the 'error', thus shifting the blame. The customer then faces the original price, or a price not too much higher than the lowball, and at this point is inclined to take the new offer. Sometimes the lowball is applied to the price offered for a trade-in, in this case an excessively generous offer. Again this offer is later withdrawn, after the 'error' has been spotted. In both kinds of lowball the psychology involves creating a sense of commitment by the buyer, so that even when the original trigger is removed, the additional reasons for buying the product that the consumer has developed in pursuit of consistency drive the purchase (Cialdini, 1984).

Companies can also take advantage of customer loyalty and status quo bias. Whereas many companies reward regular customers for their loyalty, for example airlines and coffee shops, others take the opposite strategy, increasing their rates and relying on customers renewing existing contracts. This applies to utility and insurance companies in particular. In 2016 the Competition and Markets Authority (CMA), Britain's antitrust agency, concluded that 70% of customers of the Big Six energy suppliers—Centrica, SSE, Scottish Power, Npower, E.ON and EDF—had failed to switch from the highest standard variable tariffs (SVTs). On average, in 2011–15 they paid 11% more for their electricity than those on other tariffs. Essentially, the suppliers boosted their profitability by taking advantage of inactive customers, who tend to be poor, under-educated and elderly. The CMA found no evidence of collusion between the Big Six, and concluded that price-rigging would not be beneficial since it would stifle competition and reduce incentives for consumers to switch suppliers. However, in April 2017 the Conservative government ignored this advice and decided to incorporate a price cap policy on the Big Six in their election manifesto for the upcoming election in June, following the Labour Party's pledge to do the same thing. A nudge policy aimed at increasing the availability of relevant information for both suppliers and customers may actually be more beneficial here.

Another tactic, also aimed at establishing consistency and creating commitment, but less questionable from an ethical viewpoint, is sometimes used in hotels that want to reduce their laundry expenses, and at the same time be environmentally friendly. This specifically targets towel use, and asks guests to hang towels for reuse. One experiment, reported by Baca-Motes and colleagues (2013), involved a hotel requesting guests to wear a lapel pin signaling their commitment to be environmentally friendly by reducing towel usage. The authors find that this had the effect of increasing the number of towels hung by over 40%. There is another interesting finding in this experiment, relating to the desire for conformity, which will be described in the next chapter.

## Deterring unhealthy behavior

Governments frequently want to deter behavior which is unhealthy, both for the individuals involved and for others, for example smoking, eating junk food, and driving under the influence of drugs. Usually a combination of approaches is used. Australia is perhaps a leading example as far as deterring smoking is concerned. The government has set a target of reducing the proportion of adults who are daily smokers to 10% by 2018. In order to achieve this the following measures have been implemented:

- A regime of large yearly tax increases, 12.5% per year, to reach a price of AUD$40 by 2020.
- Plain packaging rules, implemented since 2012, with no branding or logos. These require 75% of the front of the cigarette pack to be covered by a health warning, and 90% of the back.
- Graphic health warnings with a strong visceral impact, showing images of throat cancer and other physiological harm. Rousu and colleagues (2014) find evidence that this policy is more effective than a text-only health warning in reducing purchase behavior. Although some smokers use an avoidance strategy, it has been found that such smokers are more likely to quit later.
- Restrictions on locations where smoking is allowed. This includes many public places, like bars and restaurants, and also places where people tend to congregate, like bus stops, taxi ranks and train platforms. Smoking is also prohibited within 10 meters of playgrounds and in vehicles if children are present. Heavy fines, up to AUD$2,000 can be levied.

The Australian government has reported that the prevalence of smoking has fallen by 0.55% since 2012. Encouraged by this fall, the UK government has also adopted some of the above policies, for example the requirement for all cigarettes to be sold in plain packaging with large and graphic health warnings. One important aspect of these policies is that a social norm is developing whereby smokers are becoming marginalized. This is created in particular by the restrictions on locations, so that smokers have to seek places to smoke that are generally undesirable, inconvenient or uncomfortable. Further examples of government policy and deterrence are illustrated in the case study on obesity in Chapter 10, since this also involves social norms.

### The pricing of medicines

Superficially it might appear that the demand for medicines obeys the general law of demand that more is bought at lower prices. However, this superficial finding for most medicines obscures an interesting socio-psychological phenomenon. Samper and Schwartz (2013) have found that the price of a medication influences consumers' beliefs about their own disease risk. This is because they believe that government policy generally favors access to goods that are necessities; therefore they perceive a low price as a signal that a medicine must be an essential lifesaving product. This in turn causes consumers to perceive a greater threat to their health if they do not buy the product, thus leading to greater consumption. The opposite effect occurs with higher prices. However, this phenomenon only appears to apply to situations where the health threat is perceived is to be relevant to the individual, and indicates that consumers make inconsistent assumptions about risk and need. The conclusion is that greater price transparency for medications may not necessarily lead to better choices; lower prices may encourage unnecessary consumption, a serious problem in the case of antibiotics, while higher prices may discourage the use of highly beneficial products.

### Using framing effects to increase sales

Many empirical studies discuss the policy implications of framing effects in different contexts. For example, many firms use non-rounded numbers when it comes to pricing, in particular odd numbers such as $19.95 as opposed to $20, and much evidence suggests that this tactic is successful in increasing sales. However, a study by Wadhwa and Zhang (2015) suggests that the success of this tactic depends on the nature of the purchase decision. They provide evidence that non-rounded prices may be more attractive for purchasers driven by cognition, since they require more mental processing; however, for purchasers driven by feelings or visceral factors, rounded prices may be more attractive since they involve less mental processing.

A different, and counter-intuitive, policy implication arises when consumers who perceive eating healthy food as mandatory sampled a food framed as healthy and later reported being hungrier and consumed more food than those who sampled the same item framed as tasty or those who did not eat at all (Finkelstein and Fishbach, 2010). The authors of this study suggest that the psychology here is that eating the healthy food signals that the health goal was sufficiently met, and thus it increases the strength of the conflicting motive to fulfill one's appetite. This kind of signaling, which can even be achieved through vicarious consumption, has been found to occur in other situations regarding the consumption of healthy items, as is seen in Case 3.3.

Another framing effect related to increasing sales involves the use of alliteration. A study by Davis, Bagchi and Block (2012) theorizes that alliterative offers increase sales because the repetition of phonological units in alliterative prices 'sounds' better, which in turn influences perceptions of the deal presented. For example, the offer '9 for $.90'sounds better than '9 for $.88', and '3 Threybles $30' sounds better than '3 Fables $30'. The authors provide evidence from several studies that supports this contention.

Sometimes consumers make decisions through inaction rather than action. This distinction can be important in the context of choice options where the difference in utility is large or small. A study by Evangelidis and Levav (2013) suggests that when the options involve a large difference in utility consumers prefer to make an active choice. However, if the difference in utility is small, meaning there is considerable uncertainty regarding the optimal outcome, consumers may prefer an inaction frame, using some kind of default mechanism as a tie-breaker.

Framing effects are examined in more detail in Case 3.3, where the psychology of supermarket shoppers is considered.

## Use of default options

Firms can also use default options as a means of manipulating consumer choices. The default option may be chosen for various reasons, including cognitive ease, an implication that it is the norm or that it is recommended. Sometimes firms may actually have the best interests of their consumers at heart, for example when the default option on a restaurant menu is a healthy one, like salad instead of chips as a side dish, to encourage customers to eat more healthily. Colby, Li and Chapman (2014) show that this may not always achieve the desired results. Although customers may be more likely to choose the healthy dish if it is a default, they may also be less likely to return to the restaurant. This latter effect may be caused by the finding that people feel less virtuous when they choose the healthy dish as a default than when they choose it when it is not the default. This is a good example of a framing effect, once again violating the invariance principle of EUT.

## Bonus packs and discounts

Both bonus packs and discounts are common sales promotion techniques in marketing. The issue that many firms face is to determine which method is most effective in particular circumstances. Mishra and Mishra (2011) propose that the relevant factor here is whether the product is regarded as a '**virtuous good**' or a '**vice good**'. Most goods are virtuous goods, being good for us in the long run, and in this case Mishra and Mishra conclude that bonus packs are the more effective method for promoting additional sales. The reason is that price discounts can be harmful to brand image if they are used on a regular basis. However, for vice goods the conclusion is that price discounts may be a better method. The reasoning here relates to post-purchase guilt. Consumers may find it difficult to justify to themselves buying additional amounts of goods that are bad for them in the long run, so bonus packs may not be an effective promotional tool in this case. With a price discount the consumer may end up buying more of a good than otherwise over a particular time period, but the salience of this is not so great as when they buy a bonus pack. There are additional behavioral factors that are relevant in this context, as we shall see in later chapters, for example consumer reactions to product bundling, and whether consumers are naïve or sophisticated.

### Saving the best to last

As seen earlier, peak-end effects have been observed not only in humans but also in capuchin monkeys (Egan Brad et al., 2016), suggesting that they are not simply a cultural artifact but represent an evolved psychological adaptation. However, this study also found that both humans and capuchins were unable to construct optimal sequences of consumption that apply the peak-end rule. An optimal sequence involves leaving the best until last. This presents something of a puzzle, since, in the context of food consumption, adult humans and capuchins are able to delay gratification in order to gain greater future rewards, and humans at least are able to select sequences of rewards, for example income profiles, that implement the peak-end rule in laboratory experiments. The authors suggest that the reason for the human (and capuchin) failure to implement the peak-end rule in real-life situations is that when it comes to constructing sequences, as opposed to choosing among preselected sequences, the salience of visceral factors causes people to act impulsively and consume the best first. Once again, in spite of millions of years of evolutionary development of the PFC, we seem to lack the insight to appreciate and apply a rule that maximizes hedonic well-being. There is perhaps an evolutionary reason for this, however: in real-life situations animals are often under pressure to eat quickly, either because of competition from other members of their own species or to avoid predators. In this situation it may be optimal to eat the best parts first.

### Regulating the emotions

As with the phenomenon above, the regulation of emotions relates to an area of behavior where individuals often do not act in optimal ways, and in this case are also frequently aware of this after the fact. The situation becomes even more problematical when the relevant behavior is repeated over and over again, with the individual failing to learn from experience. An example of this is where a person tends to become aggressive and abusive after consuming alcohol, comes to realize this, but fails to alter their behavior, either in terms of the aggression or the drinking.

Research indicates that the regulation of emotional arousal depends on the innate qualities of a person and on the strategies, conscious or unconscious used by the individual. Gross and John (2003) have identified two main strategies that are relevant here, reappraisal and suppression, which tend to have very different outcomes in terms of optimality. The reappraisal strategy demands a certain amount of self-awareness, so that the person can implement it as the emotion starts to develop. Reappraisal refers to cognitively changing a situation's meaning in a way that alters its emotional impact. Using reappraisal strategy has shown to efficiently alter the entire subsequent emotion trajectory, especially when down-regulating negative emotion (Hariharan et al., 2015). This may well involve thinking about the positive side of a negative incident or putting it into the broader context. For example, if we are beaten in a competitive game we may reassure ourselves that the winner was a highly rated opponent and that the game served as a useful learning experience. Thus the negative emotions related to loss of self-esteem and disappointment may be softened. Reappraisal might therefore be an adaptive strategy.

In contrast, suppression comes relatively late in the process of emotion development, and modifies the behavioral aspect of emotion response tendencies, referred to as a response focused strategy (Gross, 1998). Suppression refers to influencing physiological, experiential or behavioral responding as directly as possible, and may involve efforts to hide what one is feeling, or attempts to inhibit what one is feeling (Hariharan et al., 2015). In the previous example of being beaten in a competitive game it may involve dwelling on defeat but trying to hide the loss of self-esteem by an outward display of bravado. Use of suppression has been shown to be correlated with increased negative affect, poorer recovery from changes in negative affect, and decreased self-efficacy for managing future emotions (Gross, 2002).

## Jury awards of punitive damages

The psychology underlying these awards was investigated by Kahneman, Schkade and Sunstein (1998). Three main questions were asked about scenarios relating to compensatory damages in product liability cases:

1   How outrageous was the defendant's behavior?
2   How severely should the defendant be punished?
3   How much should the defendant be required to pay in punitive damages?

The first two questions required a rating on a seven-point scale, while the third question required a dollar amount to be stated. It is notable that correlations between the evaluations are high, always at least 0.80. Since the outrage rating appears to be a direct measure of the affect evoked by cases of personal injury, the implication is that the amount of punitive damages awarded is determined largely by the outrage factor, determined by attitude rather than economic preference.

In addition to this general finding, the same authors found that respondents experienced a degree of outrage that was independent of the amount of harm caused. Thus it seems that we judge behavior in terms of outrageousness regardless of its consequences. However, when it comes to judging punitive intent and assessing damages, the second and third questions, the consequences of the behavior are of great importance. This finding does seem intuitive, since punishment contains a retributive element based on the harm caused. A further finding of the study was that the defendant's ability to pay was relevant as far as the third question is concerned. Large firms with more resources were penalized more heavily in terms of damages, although size of the firm had no effect on evaluations of outrageousness or punitive intent. This finding again seems plausible, since a $10 million payment represents a large amount for a small firm whereas it is small change for a large firm.

A further finding illustrates the importance of **context-dependence,** which can cause preference reversals. It is commonly observed that there is a high correlation between punitive awards and compensatory damages awarded. When there is a large amount of financial harm compensatory damages tend to be high, leading to high punitive damages. This is likely to be caused by the anchoring effect of the high compensatory damages. On the other hand, in cases of personal injury punitive damages tend to be low, since compensatory damages are also low. It should be noted that in real life these cases are determined in isolation, by different juries. However, it is very probable that outrage is higher in cases of personal injury (such as a child being burned by a faulty product) than in cases of business fraud. This presents a possibility for testing the theory that degree of outrage is relevant in evaluating the size of punitive award. An experiment by Kahneman, Schkade and Sunstein (1998) placed subjects in the position of having to judge two cases together as well as independently; in both situations compensatory damages had already been awarded, $500,000 for the personal injury case and $10 million for the financial harm. As predicted, subjects who only judged one case awarded more punitive damages in the financial case (median = $5 million) than in the personal injury case (median = $2 million). However, a large majority (75%) of the respondents who judged the two cases together assessed larger awards in the personal injury case, resulting in a significant preference reversal (median of $2.5 million for personal injury, $0.5 million for the financial harm). This result confirms two important theories in behavioral economics: the existence of context-dependence and anchoring effects, and the influence of affect on attitudes and evaluations.

In response to these anomalies, Sunstein, Kahneman and Schkade (1998, p. 2079) have proposed certain reforms which 'would require jurors to do what they can do well, not what they can do poorly'. Their conclusion was that jurors are good at combining normative evaluations with empirical facts, meaning that they have sound intuitions about the appropriate severity of punishment. However, their ability to translate these intuitions into dollars appears to be weak; therefore the authors proposed that the jury make graded recommendations relating to the severity of punishment to the judge, who would then perform the task of translating this intent into a dollar amount.

## The contingent valuation method and public goods

The **contingent valuation method (CVM)** is often used as a means of eliciting the value the people place on public goods, including non-use goods such as the continued existence of rare species. The valuation produced is then used as a basis for public policy decisions. CVM sometimes relies on asking people to report their **stated willingness to pay (SWTP)** to achieve various results, although more recently superior indirect techniques of valuation have been used, which may reduce some of the problems discussed below. Although asking people to value public goods, like cleaning up a lake, may superficially seem quite dissimilar to asking jurors to estimate punitive damages, there are important similarities and problems.

Studies have shown similar results in terms of high correlations between various evaluation methods when attitudes towards protecting the environment are involved (Kahneman and Ritov, 1994; Payne et al., 2000). For example, Kahneman and Ritov (1994) used four different measures to evaluate an intervention to protect the peregrine falcon from pollution:

1   Stated willingness to pay (SWTP) for the intervention
2   Degree of political support for the intervention
3   Personal satisfaction expected from making a voluntary contribution
4   Importance of the problem as a public issue

The last three measures were all based on a rating scale. As with the punitive damages situation, the high correlations between the different measures suggest that the measures are all a reflection of an underlying attitude or affect. There are two important implications of this relating to the use of SWTP in terms of obtaining biased and unreliable results:

1   *Anchoring effects*. As we have already seen, these are prominent in several situations, for example the estimation of punitive damages. A further example is given in Case 3.3 involving environmental protection.

**2** *Insensitivity to scope*. This is a form of extension bias. Kahneman (1986) found that Toronto residents were willing to pay only a little more to clean up all the polluted lakes in Ontario than to clean up polluted lakes in a particular region of Ontario. Jones-Lee, Loomes and Philips (1995) found that the SWTP of UK respondents to a programme to reduce the risk of non-fatal head injuries increased by only 29% when the number of prevented injuries was increased by 200%. Further examples relating to environmental protection are again given in Case 3.3.

An important consequence of this bias is that when CVM uses the technique of asking for people's SWTP it is highly misleading to use the **add-up principle**, whereby the values of different results are simply added together. For example, one cannot reliably conclude that the value of saving two species, A and B, from extinction is the value of saving species A plus the value of saving species B, even in the situation where the two events may seem quite independent from each other (the species being unrelated).

Some improvements to the SWTP technique of CVM have been proposed, notably the **referendum protocol**. This involves asking people simply to vote on an issue; the wording of the question for a particular respondent would therefore only quote a single value, for example: 'Would you vote for a proposition requiring you to pay $20 to clean up Lake Ontario?' Different groups of respondents are given different values to respond to, and the responses allow a distribution of WTP to be estimated. However, although this survey protocol may alleviate the problem of anchoring effects, the general problems of framing effects, extension bias and insensitivity to scope remain. When values are based on attitudes, the standard rules of economic theory regarding preference no longer apply. Kahneman, Ritov and Schadke (2000) propose a somewhat similar solution in general terms to the problem of CVM to the solution proposed for jury awards: elicit and measure public opinion regarding their attitudes to the relevant issue using psychometric criteria, and then use expert opinion to convert these judgments into monetary terms.

## Placebo effects

We have seen a number of examples of 'the mind getting what it expects', for example with aspirin and energy drinks. There are some far-reaching policy implications of this, which Ariely (2008) points out. These relate in particular to government policy regarding health. Many governments have been trying to reform their health policies, which are often seen as inadequate, inefficient and excessively costly. The USA currently spends a greater proportion of GDP on health care than any other Western nation, though much of this is accounted for by the private sector, whereas in Europe medicine tends to be more 'socialized', with state provision being more prominent. Since 2008 state provision in particular has been threatened by recession and government cutbacks forced by the need for deficit reduction (large deficits themselves largely being caused by recession and financial bailouts). Expensive drugs for diseases like cancer and AIDS have to be rationed and are often not available via state systems. Many people are scandalised by this, particularly since there is a fairness issue involved; drugs may be provided in some areas or regions but not others.

Ariely poses the question: 'How do we deal with the fact that expensive medicine (the 50-cent aspirin) may make people feel better than cheaper medicine (the penny aspirin)?' In view of the psychological effects involved this is not an easy issue to address. We can indulge in people's irrationality, raising the costs of health care, or we can insist that people get the cheapest generic drugs, which are in objective terms identical to the more expensive ones, but in practical terms are less effective. Of course, these are stark alternatives; there may be variations of both that are judged to be preferable.

Other ethical issues arise with respect to placebo effects. It is illegal in many countries to hype products with false claims on labels or in advertising. Yet it has been found that such claims can actually increase the perceived quality of the product, and even the effectiveness of the product in objective terms. For example, when it was (falsely) claimed that there was evidence from 50 scientific studies that the SoBe energy drink increased mental functioning, the subjects who were notified of this claim did significantly improve their scores on the anagram word puzzle test compared to those who were not notified of the claim. So was the false message hype after all?

## 3.9  Summary

- Decision-making involves three characteristics: preference formation, belief formation and rationality.
- The standard model relating to consumer preferences uses the analytical framework of indifference curves and budget constraints.
- The standard model is based on axioms related to completeness, transitivity, reflexivity and revealed preference.
- In addition to the above axioms, the assumptions of cancellation, dominance, extension and invariance are frequently made, in a hierarchical order of importance.
- There are many deviations from the predictions of the standard model as it relates to consumer preferences, indicating that the nature of utility is much more complex than the model supposes.
- The standard model is silent about the concept of happiness, concentrating instead on welfare.
- Anomalies in the standard model include the neglect of reference dependence, loss-aversion, the lack of stable, well-formed preferences, the desire for consistency, discrepancies between objective causes and subjective effects, expectations effects, addiction, endowment effects, framing effects, menu effects and inappropriate attention.
- Visceral factors, meaning drives and emotions, have an important role in affecting attitudes, preferences and choices.
- There are many different concepts of utility, all of which have developed from the original hedonic concept of Bentham.
- There are six types of utility that can be distinguished: decision utility, experienced utility, anticipatory utility, residual utility, transaction utility and diagnostic utility.
- Endowment and contrast effects are important in determining utility.
- Objective happiness can be measured in terms of total utility, which involves a moment-based measurement approach.
- There are different dimensions of utility: it is not just the valence that is relevant but also the level of arousal. Experiences can thus be represented on an affect grid.
- Neuroeconomic studies have important implications in terms of guiding utility theory. In particular they support the principles of reference dependence and loss-aversion.
- There are a number of policy implications of the behavioral aspects discussed in the chapter. Examples are: jury awards of punitive damages, the CVM approach to valuation, deterring unhealthy behavior, the decoy effect and placebo effects.

## 3.10  Review questions

1  Give an example of an experiment where neuroeconomics has been helpful in explaining people's behavior.
2  Explain the neuroeconomic basis of loss-aversion.

3   Explain the term RPE, and its implications for utility theory.

4   Explain what is meant by the 'peak-end' rule and its implications as an anomaly in the standard model.

5   Give an example showing the difference between preference and choice; what may account for this difference?

6   Explain the significance of the difference between decision utility and experienced utility.

7   Why are wanting and liking different?

8   Explain what is meant by a framing effect and give an example.

9   Explain what is meant by arbitrary coherence, giving an example.

10  Explain what is meant by the paradox of choice.

11  Give an example of a decoy effect, and explain how it can be used in marketing.

12  Explain what is meant by salience in the context of anomalies in the standard model.

13  When is hype not hype?

## 3.11  Applications

### Case 3.1 Drug addiction

Drugs can take many forms. They may bring to mind immediately substances like cocaine, heroin, marijuana and ecstasy, but they also include alcohol, tobacco, caffeine products; performance-enhancing substances like anabolic steroids, growth hormone, erythropoi-etin and amphetamines; and medicines like beta blockers, analgesics, corticosteroids, antibiotics and tamoxifen. Not all of these substances are addictive, and some are much more addictive than others; similarly, there may be other products, not classed as drugs, which may have addictive properties, like chocolate. Our concern here is with the concept of addiction rather than with the product.

Addiction involves cravings, which may be either psychological, physiological or both. How-ever, recent medical research indicates that all kinds of craving are ultimately physiological in nature, by having some effect on neural processes. These cravings are of a visceral nature, and for the regular user tend to be predictable, in the sense that the intensity of the cravings tends to increase steadily after each 'fix', until the next one. The cravings also tend to increase according to the duration of usage, largely because users tend to increase their dosages over time.

The phenomenon of increasing dosages has been explained by Solomon (1980) in terms of an *opponent process theory*. This essentially involves an allostasis mechanism, whereby physical events that cause extreme affective responses trigger an opponent process that produces the opposite affective response, to avoid prolonged, extreme reactions. For example, when people take cocaine, the extreme emotional high that is caused in turn is followed by an opponent process that neutralizes the reaction, as physiological processes take place to remove the chemicals from the brain. This process is initially weak, but is strengthened with repeated usage, thus explaining habituation and the need for ever-higher doses. Similar effects are known to occur with anabolic steroids, as muscle cell receptor sites become saturated, reducing the effectiveness of given dosages. In addition,

▶

▼

the body's endogenous production of testosterone is shut down, offsetting the effect of the exogenous testosterone being administered.

Furthermore, the opponent process continues to occur after usage of the drug has ceased. This explains withdrawal symptoms, as the cocaine addict no longer obtains a pleasure-inducing response, but still suffers from the opponent pleasure-reducing response. The steroid user who comes off anabolics suffers a similar fate: there is no longer any exogenous testosterone, but it takes time for the body's endogenous production to kick back in. In the meantime they shrink in size and strength and lose their libido.

The hardships of withdrawal make it hard for addicts to abstain from usage. Visceral factors are intense, making it easy to relapse, particularly if situational factors are unfavorable. Even if addicts do manage to abstain for some time, two factors go against them. First, the longer they abstain, the weaker the memory of the negative consequences of addiction. Second, they fail to anticipate the strength of the future visceral states that will occur if they relapse. These two effects are neatly summarized by the organization Alcoholics Anonymous in the saying: 'the further away one is from one's last drink, the closer one is to the next one.' When addicts abstain for a while, they may then revert to a low level of consumption, believing that they can maintain this. However, they tend to underestimate the strength of the cravings produced by even small levels of consumption, and frequently rapidly resume their previous addictive pattern of consumption (Stewart and Wise, 1992).

### Questions

1  What are the implications for an organization like Alcoholics Anonymous in terms of strategies they can adopt to counter addiction?

2  How applicable is the above analysis to other 'addictions' like food, sex and gambling?

3  How applicable is the opponent process theory in dealing with psychological responses to emotional events like winning the lottery or losing a loved one?

## Case 3.2 When abstention is better than moderate consumption

Addictive behavior is of great interest to anyone studying utility. Of particular relevance here are the concepts of self-signaling and diagnostic utility. The psychology involved goes back to the James-Lange theory of emotions, where people infer their own states from their behavior.

According to Bodner and Prelec (1997) there are many situations where it is useful to consider both the outcome utility and the diagnostic utility of a decision, with the total utility being a combination of the two types. For example, a person may have the preferred disposition of not being addicted to a particular 'vice'; the list of such vices could be extensive: alcohol, cigarettes, recreational drugs, eating unhealthy foods, gambling, hiring prostitutes are some of the more obvious examples. People have only a limited knowledge of this disposition; it is largely unknown and inferred from behavior. Therefore a person may refrain from indulging in such a vice if the payoff in terms of diagnostic utility (having higher self-esteem) exceeds the loss of outcome utility in terms of immediate pleasure. Alternatively,

▶

they may reduce their indulgence below the 'natural consumption level', which relates to the level of activity when only outcome utility is considered.

However, Bodner and Prelec (1997) point out that the above conclusion is only a 'face-value' interpretation. If we are to achieve a more realistic explanation and prediction of behavior we have to consider the 'true' interpretation of such situations, where the subject is more sophisticated. In their words:

> In the true interpretations case, the signalling value of good actions is discounted for the diagnostic motive, which creates an escalating pressure for behavioural per-fection. The generic result is that either diagnostic utility wins, and the person does the same 'perfect' thing irrespective of disposition, or natural impulses win, and the person simply ignores the diagnostic component of the utility structure. (p. 113)

We will consider the implications of face-value interpretations first, using an example where a person may have three different natural dispositions – 'low', 'moderate' and 'high' – and each is assumed to be equally likely. It is also assumed that even with a low disposition there is a tendency to consume a light amount rather than abstain completely. This situation is illustrated in Figure 3.4. The first set of arrows indicates the optimal actions for each disposition, which can be derived mathematically from certain basic assumptions; the second set of arrows indicates the corresponding face-value interpretations. Two conclusions can be drawn here:

1  In equilibrium a person cuts back on the vice by one step from the natural level.
2  Face-value interpretations induce a self-image that is too good by one step, except for the best disposition, which is correctly diagnosed.

The face-value interpretations ignore the diagnostic motive for reducing consumption. However, the true interpretations show that the consumption levels shown in Figure 3.4 will not be optimal, or in equilibrium, since the true interpretations do not match the actual disposition. Therefore we now need to complicate the situation by determining the consumption levels that would be consistent with true interpretations.

There are three possibilities here, depending on the strength of the diagnostic utility. When this is zero or weak consumption will be at natural levels. People with high dispositions to

**Figure 3.4**   Equilibrium with face-value interpretation

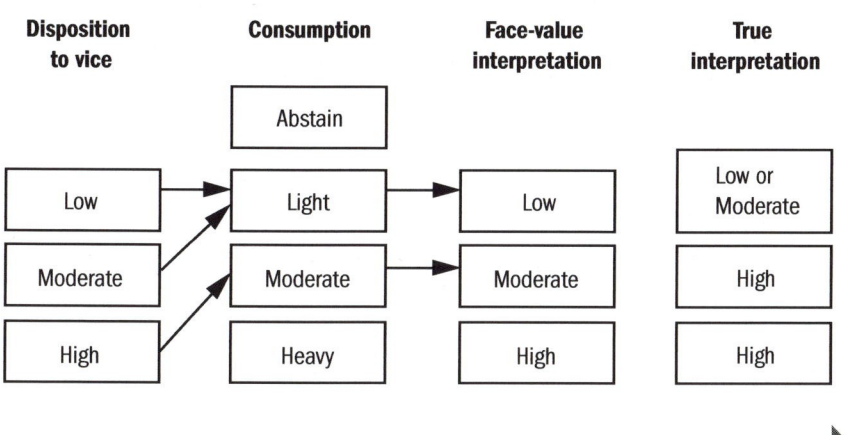

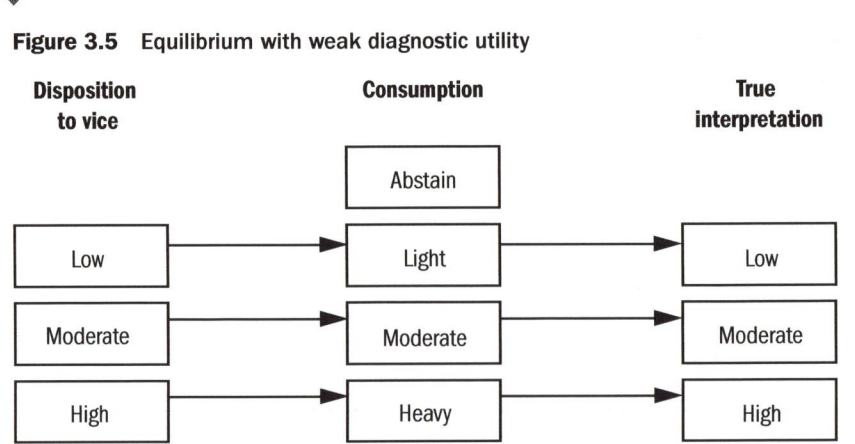

**Figure 3.5**   Equilibrium with weak diagnostic utility

the vice will not be persuaded to reduce consumption to moderate levels since this will not convince them that their disposition is only moderate. The situation is shown in Figure 3.5.

As diagnostic utility becomes stronger, a different equilibrium emerges, in which consumption falls to zero (abstention) for the two better dispositions, but remains heavy for those with a high or unfavorable disposition. This is referred to as a partially separating equilibrium, and is shown in Figure 3.6. It should be noted that abstention does not maximize outcome utility for any of the dispositions (under our assumptions), but it emerges as an optimal outcome when diagnostic utility becomes sufficiently high. This is an example of 'excessive virtue', caused by the harsh interpretation of even a light level of consumption. Bodner and Prelec (1997) express the reasoning as follows, in terms of gambling:

> A person who is concerned about his inclination to gamble, and who has, as a result, never ventured into a casino, would treat even one lapse as evidence of a strong gambling urge. The person might say – 'given how much I care not to discover that I have a taste for gambling, then I must indeed have a strong taste for it if I succumb on this occasion!' Moderation is not an option. (p. 115)

Finally, when diagnostic utility is sufficiently strong, even people with a high disposition will abstain. The result is a pooling equilibrium, shown in Figure 3.7.

**Figure 3.6**   Equilibrium with moderate diagnostic utility

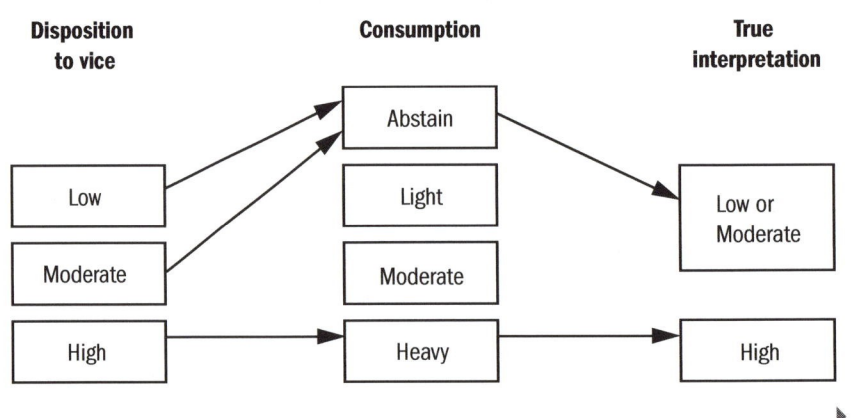

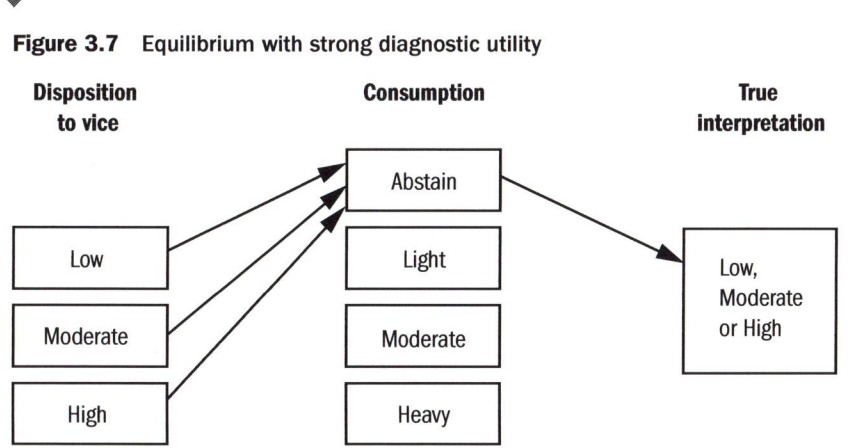

**Figure 3.7**   Equilibrium with strong diagnostic utility

It is interesting that in this situation when everyone abstains, the abstention provides no information about a person's underlying disposition. The conclusion here is somewhat paradoxical: the fact that the abstention rule is not informative actually enforces the rule. If a person could be sure that their disposition was perfect they could afford to relax and consume a light amount, for example gamble occasionally.

As Bodner and Prelec are at pains to point out, even though the true-interpretation situations may be more 'realistic', this does not mean that they provide the best empirical model of how people actually behave. As we saw in the previous chapter, self-deception is common, and in particular many people have a misplaced confidence in their own abilities. Bodner and Prelec make the following comment relating to the study by Quattrone and Tversky (1984), involving the use of a cold-pressor test to diagnose heart function:

> The subject population apparently divided into a self-satisfied, face-value interpretations majority, and a pessimistic, true-interpretations minority. (Bodner and Prelec, 1997, p. 114)

### Questions

1   Explain why there may be another good reason for abstention from a 'vice', in terms of 'enforced ignorance'.

2   Explain why, when diagnostic utility is strong, it is not possible to have an equilibrium that pools on Light or Moderate consumption. Consider in particular the likely behavior of those with the best disposition.

3   Explain why it can be best to follow a rule even if that rule is not informative.

## Case 3.3 The psychology of supermarket selling

Supermarket shopping is a chore for most people, a time-consuming necessity but not usually a very rewarding experience. It is actually ceasing to be a necessity for many, as they are increasingly shopping online. Ocado, launched in 2000, has had a phone app for online

▶

sales since 2009, and now has over £1 billion in sales revenue on 45,000 different products. Cognitive and physical effort can be significantly reduced, as well as travel costs and time.

However, for many shoppers there is still no complete substitute for visiting a supermarket chain. It is obvious to shoppers that these outlets are remarkably similar in layout and design, and this is no coincidence. The operating companies have studied various aspects of consumer psychology in order to prompt and trigger sales.

The entrance is often regarded as a 'decompression zone', designed to slow people down and adjust to their new environment. Walmart has traditionally operated a system of 'greeters' in this part of their stores. The system was temporarily changed to move such staff to other parts of the store, but was reintroduced in 2016, with such staff now being referred to as 'customer hosts'. Their tasks are varied, and include not just greeting shoppers, but dealing with customer problems and general PR, as well as checking receipts. 'Shrinkage', meaning losses through error, shoplifting and employee theft, is a particular problem at Walmart, amounting to $300 million a year. Employee theft has been discouraged by improving pay and other conditions for workers, but 'greeters' serve the purpose of discouraging shoplifting. This is done both by checking receipts and by relying on the psychology that it is less tempting to steal from nice people.

Once through the entrance shoppers normally enter the fresh fruit and vegetables area. For shoppers, this may seem an anomaly. Fruit and vegetables can be easily damaged, so it is better to put them in your cart and the end of a shopping trip. Psychology is again relevant here: selecting good wholesome fresh food improves shoppers' mood, sending an encouraging signal of diagnostic utility; it also gives them a license to buy junk food later on, which they otherwise might not buy because of guilt-aversion.

Everyday items, like milk, eggs and bread, are usually located at the rear of the store, so shoppers have to walk the length of the aisles to reach them. However, since supermarkets know that shoppers know this, they deliberately place some everyday items halfway down the aisles, to slow shoppers down as they look for them. The longer people are in the store, the more they spend generally.

Usually prepared food, involving the fishmonger, the butcher and the deli, are also at or near the rear of the store. This is also true of the in-store bakery, which can be smelt before it is seen. Even small supermarkets now use in-store bakeries. These bake mainly pre-prepared items and frozen dough, and they have boomed even though central bakeries that deliver to several stores are much more efficient. The reason here is related to visceral factors: the smell of freshly baked bread, which makes people hungry and thus encourages people to buy not just bread but also other food, including frozen stuff. Odor is important for other items too; for example, laundry detergent triggers a sense of cleanliness, which is relevant in aisles selling many domestic items.

Other visceral factors are also relevant to shoppers' mood. Sounds, like rustling sheets, may trigger detergent sales, and music is certainly important. Romantic cues are often used by sellers to encourage purchases. One study by Yang and colleagues (2014) suggests that the use of conceptual metaphor, in this case romance, can have different effects according to the romantic status of the consumer. They find that romantic stimuli affect consumers who are not romantically involved in terms of making them more likely to choose sweeter foods (an assimilation effect), while leading consumers who are romantically involved to be more likely to choose less-sweet foods (a contrast effect).

Retailers have long known that product positioning within either the store or on a menu has significant effects on purchasing behavior. For example, end-of-aisle displays may be effective in catching attention, while the positioning of impulse-purchase items, such as magazines and chewing gum, near the checkout is also commonplace. Items with higher profit margin, such as prestigious brands, are usually placed at eye-level or just above. Location on the right-hand side of an eye-level selection is often considered the very best place, because most people are right-handed and thus most consumers scan items from left to right. Some of these framing effects can therefore be quite subtle: a recent study by Romero and Biswas (2016) suggests that the placing of healthier foods on the left of less healthy ones rather than on the right tends to increase purchases.

Shoppers spend different lengths of time purchasing different items. For example, people normally spend little time purchasing beer, indicating that they have already decided on a brand before entering the store. In the case of fruit juice, however, they spend much more time looking at labels, and often not buying. This indicates that shoppers are interested in buying fruit juice as a healthier alternative to carbonated drinks, but are unsure which one to buy. One implication is that clearer labeling and categorization of products may encourage sales, along with reducing choice. This counter-intuitive aspect was discussed earlier in the chapter in connection with the study by Iyengar and Lepper (2000) concerning jams.

Stores can attempt to find out why customers are not buying by carrying out surveys. Many customers report that not being able to decide what to buy is more relevant than regarding the price as being too high. Other reasons for not buying may be that the product is out of stock, the customer cannot find it on the shelves, or that service is poor. However, new technology may prove even more reliable than surveys in this respect. Surveys rely on self-report, and sometimes shoppers are simply unaware of their reasons for not buying, since these factors lie in the subconscious. An example of this may be disgust, when certain items like cooking oils or cat litter are located close to other food items; this aspect is discussed further in the next chapter in the context of contagion. New technology involving brain scanning may be able to detect these hidden visceral factors. At present such scanners are large immobile machines, but in the future VR-type headsets may be able to record visceral factors in terms of increased blood flow in different brain regions. Consumers will have to be willing to buy in to such technology, since this degree of invasion of privacy may be resented. However, they are already willing to accept companies keeping track of their purchases, and using such information to suggest further purchases, so consumers may be ready to accept scanning technology in the future. Even using this on a sample of consumers may yield some important results and policy implications which could be of benefit to both sellers and buyers.

## Questions

1  Explain what is meant by 'greeters' and why they are used.

2  Why is milk often located at the back of the store?

3  Why do small supermarkets often have in-store bakeries when it is more efficient to use larger central bakeries?

4  Why are fruit and vegetables located at the front of supermarkets?

5  Name four factors that may discourage consumers from buying items.

6  Why might brain scanning be useful in the context of supermarket shopping?

# CHAPTER 4

# Beliefs and Expectations

Why would anyone pay $959,500 for a used guitar?

Because it was owned by Eric Clapton is the simple answer. Similar reasoning explains why someone would pay $48,875 for a tape measure that had belonged to Jackie Kennedy or $3,300 for Bernie Madoff's footstool. However, behavioral economists are curious as to why celebrity ownership should inflate values so highly, a phenomenon known as 'positive contagion'.

## 4.1  The neoclassical model

*Assumptions*

In the previous chapter we have examined how people form attitudes, values, preferences, and finally make choices. In terms of the standard model described in equation (1.1), these aspects are largely related to component (4), involving utilities, and, when it comes to choices, component (1) involving maximization. However, various assumptions were made at that stage regarding the options and outcomes of these options in the decision-making process. The factor we want to focus on in this chapter is the certainty of these outcomes. Therefore the component we now need to examine is (3), related to probabilities or beliefs. As far as beliefs are concerned, the main assumptions in the neoclassical model (NM) are that decision-makers have perfect as opposed to bounded rationality, and that they are Bayesian probability estimators. Let us explain each in turn:

1   *Perfect rationality*

This means that people not only have all the relevant information pertaining to a decision, but have the cognitive resources to process it instantly, accurately and costlessly. If this is not the case, and it is obviously unlikely in most real-life situations, then we can say that there is **bounded rationality**. This term was introduced by Simon (1955), who was the first researcher to emphasize its implications for decision-making. The most general implication is that we tend to use **heuristics** in many decision-making situations; these are 'methods for arriving at satisfactory solutions with modest amounts of computation' (Simon, 1990). The term heuristic was originally introduced in psychology to refer to simple processes that replace complex algorithms (Newell and Simon, 1972), and has become extended now to include any decision rules that we implement as shortcuts to simplify and or accelerate the decision-making process. A good example is to never order the lowest-price or highest-price items on the menu in a restaurant. This might imply that the decision-maker believes that neither of these items represents good value. As we shall see, there are a large number of heuristics described in the behavioral literature, and indeed some have proposed that there are too many. Shah and Oppenheimer (2008) propose that there is much redundancy in the field of heuristics, with different names for similar and overlapping concepts, too much domain-specificity, and insufficient attention paid to the overriding principle that heuristics are effort-reducing mechanisms. We shall return to these issues at various points throughout the following chapters.

The most significant implication of using heuristics is that they often result in **biases**, meaning systematic errors. In terms of beliefs these errors are factual; biases can also occur in terms of preferences, where the errors may result in non-optimal choice.

**2**   *Bayesian probability estimation*

This means that people are able to estimate probabilities correctly, given the relevant information, and in particular are able to update them correctly given a sequence of prior outcomes. The interpretation and significance of this will be examined in the section on the law of small numbers, along with deviations in estimation or biases, but a simple example will suffice at this stage. When a coin is tossed several times and comes up heads each time, a correct Bayesian updater will still estimate the probability of heads on the next coin toss as being 0.5, since the prior outcomes have no effect on the next outcome in this situation. However, many people tend to incorrectly assume that the prior outcomes do affect the probability of the next outcome here (as it would in other situations), and estimate the probability of the next outcome being a head as less than 0.5. This is an example of a 'mean-reverting' regime resulting in the 'gambler's fallacy'. Both of these terms are explained in the third section related to the law of small numbers.

The Bayes formula in general terms is as follows:

$$P(A|B) = \frac{P(B|A)\,P(A)}{P(B)} \qquad\qquad (4.1)$$

This formula can be used to estimate probabilities of the truth or falsehood of events that are not random, but where the truth is unknown, such as when a die has been thrown within a cup – there is a definite outcome, but until the cup is removed we do not know what it is.

**Bayes' theorem** updates or modifies probabilities, given new pieces of evidence, in the following way:

$$P(H|E) = \frac{P(E|H)\,P(H)}{P(E)}$$

where

- $H$ represents a specific hypothesis, which may or may not be some **null hypothesis**.
- $E$ represents the evidence that has been observed.
- $P(H)$ is called the **prior probability** of $H$ that was inferred before new evidence became available.
- $P(E|H)$ is called the **conditional probability** of seeing the evidence $E$ if the hypothesis $H$ happens to be true. It is also called a **likelihood function** when it is considered as a function of $H$ for fixed $E$.
- $P(E)$ is called the **marginal probability** of $E$: the a priori probability of witnessing the new evidence $E$ under all possible hypotheses. It can be calculated as the sum of the product of all probabilities of any complete set of mutually exclusive hypotheses and corresponding conditional probabilities:

    $$P(E) = \Sigma\, P(E|H_i)\,P(H_i)$$

- $P(H|E)$ is called the **posterior probability** of $H$ given $E$ and is the new estimate of the probability that the hypothesis $H$ is true, taking the evidence $E$ into account.

The factor $P(E|H) / P(E)$ represents the impact that the evidence has on the belief in the hypothesis. The interpretation of this factor, and an example of an application of all of the above concepts, is given in the discussion of base rate bias in the next section.

## 4.2  Probability estimation

The types of deviation described in this section relate to rational Bayesian updating. There are various aspects of bias here. Before discussing these, there is a general point to be clarified. It is often assumed by researchers that a bias implies faulty reasoning. This is not necessarily true, since systematic errors in probability estimation can occur because of random noise interfering with information processing (Costello and Watts, 2014). However, many researchers support the existence of dual process theories popularized by Kahneman and Frederick (2002, 2005), where cognitive processes involve two separate systems, frequently referred to as system 1 and system 2 (Evans 2011; Evans and Stanovich, 2013). System 1 relates to intuitive aspects, dominated by perception, where beliefs and judgments are formed quickly, on the basis of **heuristics**. It is useful to think of these as being shortcuts to decision-making, often based on rules-of-thumb. System 2 relates to reasoning, a slower, more conscious and calculating process. The main consequence of this duality is that system 1 can lead to biases in judgment, which system 2 fails to correct in many cases. As an example, consider the following problem: a bat and a ball together cost £11, and the bat costs £10 more than the ball. How much does the ball cost? A majority of people quickly answer £1. This is an incorrect answer, which system 2 frequently fails to adjust. We will now consider a number of common heuristics and their consequent biases.

*The availability heuristic*

People are often lousy at estimating probabilities of events occurring, especially rare ones. They overestimate the probability of dying in plane crashes, or in pregnancy, or suffering from violent crime. An often-quoted example of overestimating low probabilities concerns playing the lottery. The California lottery, one of the biggest in the world, requires matching six numbers between 1 and 51 in order to win the main prize. The odds against doing this are over 18 million to one. In other words, if one played this lottery twice a week, one could expect to win about every 175,000 years. It was found by Kahneman, Slovic and Tversky (1982) that people overestimated the odds of winning by over 1,000%.

In many of their papers Kahneman and Tversky have suggested that people use an availability heuristic when estimating probabilities. This means that people believe that events are more frequent or more probable if examples of it are easier to remember. In general, this heuristic works reasonably well because it is easier to recall examples of events that happen more frequently. A type of availability bias occurs when people judge the probability of a category in a population occurring. Research has found that a category size bias exists in which 'consumers perceive an outcome as more likely to occur when it is categorized with many rather than few alternative possibilities, even when the grouping criterion is irrelevant and the objective probability of each outcome is identical' (Isaac and Brough, 2014). For example, participants in one study irrationally predicted being more likely to win a lottery if their ticket color matched many (vs. few) of the other gamblers' tickets, and wagered nearly 25% more as a result.

The main source of error with the availability heuristic is **salience**; this factor features in other types of bias also, but the main effect here is that events that have been well publicized or are prominent in people's memories tend to be estimated as having exaggerated probabilities. Thus it has been found that there is an increased purchase of earthquake insurance following a recent quake, in spite of the fact that such events will be less likely to recur in the short-term future. This error may be compounded by the effect proposed by Vosgerau (2010), related to misattribution due to arousal, sometimes referred to as the affect heuristic (Pachur, Hertwig and Steinmann, 2012).

Both of these heuristics may be relevant in decision-making when high stakes are involved compared with low stakes. One would expect rational decision-makers to use more system 2 processes and rely less on heuristics when stakes are higher. However, a study by Freling, Saini and Yang (2012) has found contrary evidence. They propose that when stakes are higher people rely more on anecdotal evidence than objective statistical information, since it tends to have more emotional impact and salience, and also tends to be easier cognitively in terms of processing.

The combination of the availability and affect heuristics can have serious impacts on government policy, so that governments may devote too few resources to big problems and too many to small problems (Sunstein, 2002). Thus a government may engage in a knee-jerk reaction in response to public fears relating to a contagious disease or terrorism threat, but spend insufficient funds on key infrastructure or disease prevention.

## The representativeness heuristic

In general the representativeness heuristic refers to the phenomenon that global judgment of a category is determined primarily by the relevant properties of a prototype (Kahneman and Tversky, 1972, 1973; Tversky and Kahneman, 1971, 1983). This means that people have the tendency to evaluate the likelihood that a subject belongs to a certain category based on the degree to which the subject resembles a typical item in the category. Although this strategy may be effective in certain circumstances, the basic principles of probability and set theory are often ignored by people in making judgments involving representativeness. An illustration of this phenomenon is where respondents are given a description of a personality of a woman, Linda, who has the characteristics of a typical feminist. The majority of respondents rank the statement 'Linda is a bank teller' as less likely than the conjunctive statement 'Linda is a bank teller and an active member of the feminist movement' (Tversky and Kahneman, 1983). In this case the strong representativeness of feminism overcomes the basic probability rule that P(A and B) can never be higher than P(A). The difficulties that people have in reasoning related to connectives and conditionals has been observed in several studies (Johnson-Laird et al., 1992, 2000).

A different example of the representation heuristic, which is applicable to financial markets, concerns investor behavior and reactions to new information. According to a model developed by Gennaioli, Shleifer and Vishny (2015) 'investors overreact to a series of good news, because such a series is representative of a good state. A few bad news do not change investor minds because the good state is still representative, but enough bad news leads to a radical change in beliefs and a financial crisis.' At this point the bad state then becomes the norm, and a few good news may be ignored. The authors claim that this model generates 'debt over-issuance, "this time is different" beliefs, neglect of tail risks, under- and overreaction to information, boom-bust cycles, and excess volatility of prices in a unified psychological model of expectations.' Essentially, the model adds a behavioral component to the Minsky hypothesis regarding the relationship between debt and financial crises.

It is helpful to give a further example here, since it illustrates not only the representation heuristic but also the base rate bias, discussed further below. A woman, Jane, is described as having the following characteristics: she likes aromatherapy, new age music, reads her horoscope regularly and belongs to a spirituality group. When people are asked whether they think Jane is more likely to be a holistic healer or a schoolteacher, they regularly answer that she is more likely to be a holistic healer, since her personal characteristics more closely match those of a holistic healer than a schoolteacher.

*Base rate bias*

The reason the response above is incorrect is that it ignores the fact that the proportion of holistic healers in the population is much smaller than the proportion of schoolteachers. This is an example of base rate bias, a common phenomenon again resulting from salience. In general terms base rate bias means ignoring general information relating to a population and focusing on specific information which is more salient.

A more complex example involving conditional probabilities is given by Casscells, Schoenberger and Graboys (1978), and relates to the problem of 'false positives'. This involves a situation where a person takes a medical test, maybe for a disease like HIV, where there is a very low probability (in most circumstances) of having the disease, say one in a thousand. However, there is a chance of a false prediction; the test may only be 95% accurate. Under these circumstances people tend to ignore the rarity of the phenomenon (disease) in the population, referred to as the base rate, and wildly overestimate the probability of actually being sick. Even the majority of Harvard Medical School doctors failed to get the right answer. For every 1,000 patients tested, one will be actually sick while there will be 50 false positives. Thus there is only a 1 in 51 chance of a positive result meaning that the patient is actually sick.

This example can be explained in more detail using Bayes' theorem. For simplicity, it is assumed initially that if the patient has the disease the test returns a positive result 100% of the time, meaning that there are no false negatives.

Let $A$ represent the condition in which the patient has the disease, and $B$ represent the evidence of a positive test result. Then, the probability that the patient actually has the disease given the positive test result is

$$P(A|B) = \frac{P(B|A)P(A)}{P(B|A)P(A) + P(B|\text{not }A)P(\text{not }A)}$$

$$= \frac{1 \times 0.001}{1 \times 0.001 + 0.05 \times 0.999} = 0.0196$$

This means that the probability that a positive result is a false positive is about $1 - 0.0196 = 0.98$, or 98%. If, more realistically, there is also a chance of the test returning a false negative, this would mean that $P(B|A) < 1$, and this would modify the result slightly. The difference would be small, assuming that the chance of a false negative is low; for example, if the probability of a negative result given the person has the disease is 0.99, then $P(A|B) = 0.0194$.

In general terms, if it is likely that the evidence $E$ (a positive test) would be observed when the hypothesis under consideration (the person is sick) is true, but, when no hypothesis is assumed, it is inherently unlikely that $E$ would have been the outcome of the observation, then the factor $P(E|H) / P(E)$ will be large. Multiplying the prior probability of the hypothesis, $P(H)$, by this factor would result in a larger posterior probability of the hypothesis given the evidence. However, if $P(H)$, the base rate, is very low, the posterior probability will still tend to be low. Thus the consequence of base rate bias, meaning ignoring the base rate, is that we tend to overestimate the probability of being sick, given a positive test.

Conversely, if it is unlikely that the evidence $E$ would be observed if the hypothesis under consideration is true, but a priori likely that $E$ would be observed, then the factor would reduce the posterior probability for $H$. Under Bayesian inference, Bayes' theorem therefore measures how much new evidence should modify a belief in a hypothesis.

## The 'law of small numbers'

The main error here is when people apply principles that apply to infinite populations to small samples. We will examine the model described by Rabin (2002b). This model examines the situation where people are observing a sequence of signals from a process that involves independent and identically distributed (iid) random variables. This means that each random variable has the same **probability distribution** as the others and all are mutually **independent**. A simple example is a sequence of coin tosses, where the probability distribution is 0.5 for a head and 0.5 for a tail for each toss, and the outcome of each toss has no effect on the outcome of any other toss. The model assumes that people believe, incorrectly, that the signals are drawn from an urn of finite size without replacement, whereas the correct assumption in this case is that there is replacement after each draw from the urn. We now need to examine the consequences of this incorrect assumption.

**1**    *The 'gambler's fallacy' effect*

This effect derives its name from the observation that gamblers frequently expect a certain slot machine or a number that has not won in a while to be 'due' to win. We find that that the effect occurs when the distribution of signals is known, as it is with the coin toss situation. If an urn contains ten balls, five representing Up and five representing Down, and one ball is drawn at a time with replacement, this experiment is identical to tossing a coin. Thus if three successive draws all result in an Up outcome (equivalent to three heads in a row), then the rational person will estimate the probability of an Up on the next draw as 0.5. However, if the person believes that the balls are not being replaced, this means that there is only two Up balls left in the urn out of seven balls in total, so they will estimate the probability of the next draw being Up as only 2/7 or about 0.286, with the probability of Down being 0.714. This is an example of the representativeness heuristic, in that the sequence Up, Up, Up, Down is judged as being more representative of the population than the sequence Up, Up, Up, Up. We shall encounter other examples of this heuristic in the following chapters. The 'gambler's fallacy' is sometimes referred to as the '**law of averages**', in this case meaning that the number of Ups should on average be the same as the number of Downs, given there is a 50% chance of each event occurring.

There is a variety of empirical evidence supporting the existence of the 'gambler's fallacy' effect. For example, New Jersey's pick-three-numbers game is a **pari-mutuel** betting system; this means that the fewer people bet on a number, the higher is the expected payout. It has been found that the amount of money bet on a particular number falls sharply after the number is drawn, and only gradually returns to normal after several months (Clotfelter and Cook, 1993; Terrell, 1994).

There is an interesting explanation for this apparently irrational phenomenon in terms of evolutionary psychology (Pinker, 1997). It is proposed that in our past evolutionary environment there was often good reason to believe that a series of common outcomes would be likely to be broken at some point. This was particularly true for meteorological events, like rain or sunshine. Of course the expected length of the series would depend on the circumstances, but, just as a cloud eventually blows past the sun, at some point the probability becomes higher that in the next time period the sun will come out again. We shall see that many of the biases that people have are based on evolutionary adaptations or factors in our past.

In the examples people are incorrectly inferring from a sequence of identical signals, like three Ups, that the next signal or outcome will be of a different type. However, there are many situations where people make exactly the opposite inference, that the sequence will continue. This contradictory finding is now described and explained.

**2**    *The 'hot hand' effect*

This effect derives its name from the mistaken belief among basketball players and fans that a player's chance of hitting a shot is greater following a hit than following a miss on the previous shot (Gilovich, Vallone and Tversky, 1985). Although it appears that this 'overinference' is the opposite of the 'gambler's fallacy', it is actually a complementary effect, again involving a misapplication of the assumption of non-replacement.

The effect arises when there is uncertainty regarding the distribution of signals, for example whether a stock price will go up or down in any particular time period. It is instructive here to follow the example given by DellaVigna (2009), involving a mutual fund with a manager of uncertain ability. This time the situation involves two urns, each with ten balls; the well-managed fund has seven Up balls and three Down balls, meaning the fund goes up in value seven times out of ten, while the poorly managed fund has three Up balls and seven Down balls, meaning it only goes up three times out of ten. There is a prior probability of 0.5 that the fund is well managed and a probability of 0.5 that the fund is poorly managed, so that before we observe any draw of a ball from an urn it is equally probable that the fund is well or poorly managed. Balls are then drawn in sequence from an urn, but the investor does not know which urn they are drawn from. After observing a sequence of three Up balls the investor has to compute the probability that the urn drawn from was the one with seven Up and three Down balls, which is equivalent to estimating the probability that the fund is well managed after it has gone up three times in succession.

The rational investor will implement Bayes' theorem to solve the problem, on the assumption that the balls are replaced after each draw. Repeating the Bayes formula in Equation (4.1):

$$P(A|B) = \frac{P(B|A)\,P(A)}{P(B)}$$

Thus the rational investor computes the probability that the mutual fund is well managed as:

$$P(Well|UUU) = \frac{P(UUU|Well) \times .5}{[P(UUU|Well) \times .5 + P(UUU|Poor) \times .5]}$$

This equals $0.7^3/(0.7^3 + 0.3^3) = 0.927$.

However, if the investor behaves according to the law of small numbers and assumes that there is no replacement after each draw, the Bayesian expression becomes:

$$P(Well|UUU) = (7/10 \times 6/9 \times 5/8)/[(7/10 \times 6/9 \times 5/8) + (3/10 \times 2/9 \times 1/8)] = 0.972.$$

Thus we can see that this type of investor will overinfer about the ability of the mutual fund manager after three good performances. When the rational investor forecasts the performance of the fund in the next period, they will calculate the probability of an Up performance as $0.927 \times 0.7 + (1 - 0.927) \times 0.3 = 0.671$. On the other hand, the law-of-small-numbers investor, assuming they believe that the urn is replenished after three periods, estimates the probability of an Up performance as $0.972 \times 0.7 + (1 - 0.972) \times 0.3 = 0.689$, representing a perceived more probable outcome.

There are various studies relating to financial markets which provide evidence for the 'hot hand' effect. Benartzi (2001) found that the degree to which employees invest in their own firm's stock depends strongly on the past performance of the stock. In companies in the lowest 20% of performance in the past ten years, 10.4% of employee savings were allocated to the same firm's stock, compared to 39.7% for firms in the top 20%. Overinference in stock holdings can cause predictability in returns, since investors will tend to overinvest in stocks with high past returns, making them overpriced and reducing their later returns, as demonstrated by De Bondt and Thaler (1985).

**3    *Synthesis***

At this point it might appear that the contradictory effects of the 'gambler's fallacy' and the hot hand are difficult to reconcile with each other. Indeed, there appear to be some cases of situations where different people can experience both effects. The lottery is one of these; most players exhibit the 'gambler's fallacy' in selecting numbers, like avoiding recent winners, but one recent Chinese study finds the opposite, where players chase winners, even bearing a cost to do so (Yuan, Sun and Siu, 2014).

A study by Shleifer and Vishny (1998) illustrates this phenomenon in a different environment, again demonstrating that the law of small numbers can lead to both effects, causing both underreaction and overreaction to market signals. In the short term investors follow the 'gambler's fallacy', believing that a series of identical signals, like the stock price rising, will be followed by a fall (a **'mean-reverting' regime**). Thus they do not invest in the stock (underreact), causing it to be underpriced, and returns will continue to be high over a short period of time, demonstrating positive correlation or momentum. However, after a longer sequence, the investors overinfer, and expect a **'trending' regime**, whereby the stock is now expected to continue to rise. This 'hot hand' effect causes overreaction, as investors now overinvest, making the stock overpriced, and reducing returns, this time demonstrating negative correlation of returns in the long term.

There are other applications of the law of small numbers that help to solve the apparent contradictions between the 'gambler's fallacy' effect and the 'hot hand' effect. One of these again relates to the purchase of lottery tickets. As we have seen, people often avoid betting on numbers in a lottery if they have recently won, demonstrating a 'gambler's fallacy' effect'. Yet there is evidence that people also have an increased probability of buying their tickets from stores that sold winning tickets the previous week; winning stores experience a 12–38% relative sales increase in the week following the sale of a large-prize winning ticket. Guryan and Kearney (2008) have investigated this 'hot hand' effect and propose an explanation for the paradoxical combination of the two effects in lottery betting. They suggest that:

> A belief in the hot hand comes not from the signals produced by the
> data-generating process – as the representativeness explanation would require –
> but rather from the characteristics of the data-generating process itself, namely
> whether the data-generating process is perceived as having an animate or an intentional element.

Research in psychology provides some support for this hypothesis (Ayton and Fischer, 2004; Caruso, Waytz and Epley, 2010). The result of this is that the hot hand may actually be real in certain situations. For example, Raab, Gula and Gigerenzer (2012) found that in volleyball the hot hand existed for half of the players in their study. Furthermore, this had policy implications for the other team players in terms of allocation; it was beneficial to pass the ball to players perceived to have the hot hand, and this increased their team's winning chances. There have also been two recent studies of professional sports that have confirmed the 'hot hand' effect. In an analysis of results in tennis tournaments, Jetter and Walker (2015) find that an additional win in the most recent ten matches raises the likelihood of winning by 3.2–3.4 percentage points. In a study of professional golfers Rosenqvist and Skans (2015) find that those 'making the cut' in top tournaments had a substantially better performance record afterwards than players just failing to make the cut.

In terms of a lottery situation, Guryan and Kearney suggest that the selection of the balls does seem to involve a random process, without any intentional element, and therefore the law of small numbers would cause people to exhibit a 'gambler's fallacy' effect as they expect a small sample to resemble the underlying population; thus winning numbers are not expected to occur again in the near future. However, with stores there could be a human element in how winning stores are selected, leading to a 'hot hand'. How this human element operates in this case is open to speculation: it might be that the store is chosen deliberately by the person buying the winning ticket; or the location of the winning ticket could be attributable to a corrupt lottery commissioner, bearing in mind that the winning store owner receives 1% of the prize and thus has an incentive for bribery.

Guryan and Kearney also note that the 'lucky store' effect is larger in areas with more high-school drop-outs, more people living in poverty and more elderly. They suggest that this may be caused by cognitive biases.

### Conformity bias

This phenomenon occurs when people tend to 'follow the crowd' in deciding how to behave, rather than think independently. Thus their judgment of probabilities depends on the behavior of others in a non-Bayesian manner. The first research relating to this was by Asch (1951), and he published a number of other studies in the 1950s elaborating on this. In the initial study groups of eight students were shown two cards, the first showing a single line, and the second showing three lines, where one matched the line on the first card in length, while the other two lines were clearly shorter or longer. This is illustrated in Figure 4.1. The students were then asked in turn to state aloud which line on the second card matched the line on the first card. Seven of the students, however, were 'confederates' of the investigator and briefed to give an identical answer, which would sometimes be incorrect. The other non-confederate student was always asked to give his answer last. In control groups, with no confederate pressure, the error rate was very low, less than 1%. Under confederate pressure the average error rate rose to 37%, with 5% of subjects always conforming, and 75% making at least one error on the 12 critical trials. After various criticisms of the methodology Asch refined this experiment, but the conformity bias remained. Other evidence supporting this bias was provided by

**Figure 4.1**  Asch experiment

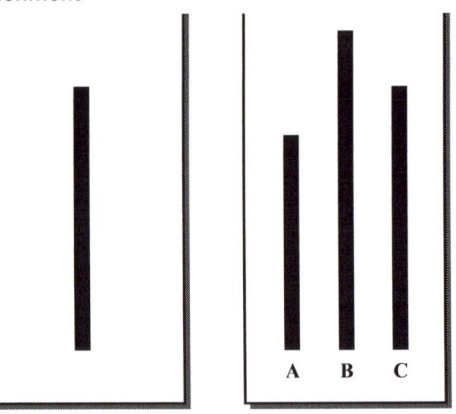

the notorious Milgram and Stanford Prison experiments (Milgram, 1963; Zimbardo, 1972), where subjects were willing to impose pain on others, under the auspices of obedience to authority.

Since this early work there has been much other evidence, both in experiments and in the field, where people have displayed a herd mentality in following the behavior of others. The phenomenon of conformity bias also has policy implications, for individuals, firms and governments, and we will give an example here relating to an experiment described in the previous chapter involving hotels desiring to reduce towel usage (Baca-Motes et al., 2013). As well as finding that wearing a lapel pin established consistency and increased commitment among guests, it was also found that a notice in rooms stating that the majority of guests reused towels had the same effect of increasing the number of towels hung, even if the statement was actually untrue.

In a rational analysis of conformity and how to determine beliefs or probabilities according to the beliefs of others, rational Bayesian updaters should imitate others to some extent, but should also realize that this will result in a correlation of beliefs. This should in turn cause them to 'anti-imitate' the behavior of others. Eyster and Rabin (2014) show that any learning rule in which people regularly imitate more than one person without anti-imitating others will lead to a positive probability of people converging to confident and wrong long-run beliefs.

Although at times it appears irrational, there are two sound bases for conformity bias. The first lies in evolutionary psychology, which suggests that following the crowd is an adaptive behavior since it aids survival in many situations, like fleeing from a fire, a phenomenon frequently seen in various animal species. In terms of human behavior, a very important example relates to investor behavior in financial markets. Herding behavior is frequently observed here, both in booms and in crashes. Conformity bias is a major cause of this, and there are two reasons. First, we may simply assume that others know something that we don't and therefore it is a good idea to follow them; and second, since most large-scale investments are carried out by professional fund managers who are responsible to their clients for making a good return, it is better to be wrong with the crowd than to risk being right but in the minority. The safer strategy for keeping clients happy and keeping one's job is to follow the crowd. Another similar example concerns research and academia. In all sciences there tend to be dominant models which are currently favored by the mainstream, sometimes referred to as the current paradigm (Kuhn, 1970). Since the status of scientists depends on publications, it is safer to keep within the broad confines of the existing paradigm when trying to achieve publication. As time goes on, this envelope becomes stretched as existing models struggle to explain new anomalies. At some point one or a few bold researchers will introduce a new model, significantly different from the previous one, and a new paradigm may become established as further researchers find support for the new model. In the early twentieth century this happened in physics, where 'classical physics' was overturned by quantum mechanics and relativity theory.

The second basis for herding is that it means we do not have to use cognitive effort. Instead of fully evaluating a list of options we use the simple heuristic of doing what others do, like going to the same restaurant, buying the same sunshades or watching the same movies. It should be noted that this behavior can have two possible interpretations: (1) it implies a belief that the crowd has good reasons for its behavior, and that if we follow it there is a greater probability of maximizing utility or at least increasing it in terms of making a better decision; and (2) people get to like things that other people like, thus receiving an 'other-conferred' utility. Therefore conformity bias is relevant both for values, preferences and choices as well as beliefs and expectations. Further discussion of this issue is given in Chapter 10 in the context of social preferences and neuroscientific evidence.

*Roundness*

Some research has shown that in certain circumstances consumers may have a preference for either odd or round numbers. Round numbers may be preferred for simplicity, but in lottery situations odd numbers may be perceived as more likely to occur, since they may be seen as more concrete and realistic (Dehaene and Mehler, 1992; Sevilla and Bagchi, 2014).

## 4.3  Self-evaluation bias

This factor is sometimes described in terms of overconfidence, but we shall see that, while overconfidence is an important aspect, there are other aspects, including its opposite, underconfidence. In addition there is self-serving bias, which while it often involves over-confidence, can relate to other aspects of belief. We shall see that visceral factors are relevant here also. Thus we use the term self-evaluation bias as a general all-embracing term that includes all aspects of beliefs where some kind of evaluation of the role of the self relative to a situation is involved.

*Overconfidence*

It has been claimed that 'No problem in judgment and decision making is more preva-lent and more potentially catastrophic than overconfidence' (Plous, 1993). It is useful to distinguish between three different kinds of overconfidence, since this helps to explain apparent inconsistencies in empirical findings, and we will follow the classification proposed by Moore and Healy (2008). This involves the concepts of **overestimation**, **over-placement** and **overprecision**.

1   *Overestimation*

This relates to overestimation of one's actual ability, performance, level of control or chance of success. Empirical evidence suggests that this is a widespread phenomenon extending to many situations. People overestimate their abilities to perform various tasks, overestimate how quickly they can finish a project (which seems to be happen-ing with this book!) and overestimate their faculty for future self-control (examined in Chapter 8). Studies have documented this overestimation of abilities in a wide vari-ety of different professional fields: team managers choosing players in the NFL pick (Thaler, 2016); political experts (Tetlock, 1999 and 2005); financial consultants (Hoelzl and Rustichini, 2005); investors (Kadous et al., 2014); and CEOs (Malmendier and Tate, 2005, 2008). People can also become overconfident in their abilities after viewing the performance of a skillful master, for example in sports (Scopelliti, Botti and Donato, 2013) and they can be unrealistically optimistic about their future pros-pects (Buehler, Griffin and Ross, 1994; MacDonald and Ross, 1999).

Some researchers have attempted to explain the results of studies indicating the existence of overconfidence in other ways, in particular in terms of it being a statisti-cal artifact caused by regression to the mean (see Kahneman, 2012), but the majority suggest that it is caused by underlying psychological factors. We shall also see that in some cases people underestimate their abilities and are overly pessimistic. This will explained in the section relating to underconfidence. The existence of both overcon-fidence and underconfidence represents something of a puzzle. The reason for the puzzle is that it is obviously beneficial for individuals to be able to gauge their abilities accurately from the biological viewpoint of survival and reproduction. This issue is discussed further later in the section.

**2    Overplacement**

This aspect of overconfidence is sometimes referred to as the 'better-than-average' (BTA) effect, since it relates to estimating one's abilities relative to others rather than in absolute terms. Again, this phenomenon has been documented by a large number of studies in different areas of behavior. Respondents typically rate themselves in the top 50% regarding driving ability (Svenson, 1981); ethics (Baumhart, 1968); managerial prowess (Larwood and Whittaker, 1977); productivity (Cross, 1997); health (Weinstein, 1980); skill in solving puzzles (Camerer and Lovallo, 1999); social skills (Swann and Gill, 1997); and physical abilities (Dunning, Meyerowitz and Holzberg, 1989). A somewhat different example of overplacement has been observed where people overestimate the amounts others are willing to pay for things compared with oneself, with such varied items as chocolate truffles, books, teddy bears, smoked salmon, sporting equipment, iPhones, artwork, gift certificates, gambles, a trip to the moon, and a magic pill that confers the ability to speak French (Frederick, 2012).

As with overestimation, some researchers have tried to explain these findings in terms of regression to the mean, a lack of financial incentives, or people not caring about their reporting, but in general the findings appear to be quite robust, presenting the same puzzle as mentioned above.

**3    Overprecision**

This refers to excessive certainty regarding the accuracy of one's beliefs. Studies frequently ask their participants questions with numerical answers (e.g. 'How long is the Nile River?') and then have participants estimate confidence intervals for their answers. Results show that these confidence intervals are too narrow, suggesting that people are too sure they know the correct answer. For example, Alpert and Raiffa (1982) found that a group of MBA students who were asked for 98% confidence intervals stated intervals that only contained the correct answer 57% of the time instead of the expected 98%. Similar results have been found in experimental studies by Klayman and colleagues (1999) and Soll and Klayman (2004), and have been duplicated in the field in the case of trading by individual investors (Odean, 1999; Barber and Odean, 2001). In this last case investors overestimated the precision of their information about individual companies, with the result that they traded too much. Barber and Odean further found that men were more overconfident in this respect than women.

The phenomenon of overprecision has also been found in the field of voters' political beliefs. One study indicated that a number of voter characteristics were associated with this kind of bias, in particular ideological extremeness, voter turnout, and partisan identification (Ortoleva and Snowberg, 2015).

Kahneman (2011) reports that experts in various professional fields are particularly prone to overprecision. One example relates to CFOs of large organizations forecasting returns on the Standard and Poor index; when asked to give 80% confidence intervals for their forecasts these turned out to be only a quarter of the correct size, which was between $-10\%$ and $+30\%$. Another example concerns doctors, where autopsy results showed that in cases where they had been 'completely certain' of their antemortem diagnosis they were actually wrong 40% of the time. Once again we have a puzzle, in the sense that on the face of things it would seem that experts who are proved wrong should not prosper. This issue is addressed in the synthesis at the end of the section.

## Underconfidence

Empirical studies have sometimes found conflicting results, in that sometimes people underestimate their abilities, control, and also underplace their performance relative to others (Kirchler and Maciejovsky, 2002; Burson, Larrick and Klayman, 2005; Fu et al.,

2005). Some studies have reported overconfidence when the tasks were easy (like driving), or success likely, and underconfidence when tasks were difficult (like playing the piano), or success unlikely. This phenomenon is referred to as the **'hard-easy' effect** (Lichtenstein and Fischoff, 1977).

There has also been conflict in that other studies have reported underconfidence with easy tasks and where success is likely. Moore and Healy (2008) suggest that this conflict is caused by the confound between overconfidence and overplacement. They have proposed a theory that can explain these empirical anomalies and resolve the apparent conflicts. This is described as follows:

> People often have imperfect information about their own performances, abilities, or chance of success. However, they often have even worse information about others. As a result, people's estimates of themselves are regressive, and their estimates of others are even more regressive. Consequently, when performance is high, people will underestimate their own performances, underestimate others even more so, and thus believe that they are better than others. When performance is low, people will overestimate themselves, overestimate others even more so, and thus believe that they are worse than others. (p. 503)

Thus according to this theory it is possible, and indeed likely that people will combine overestimation with underplacement and vice versa. Moore and Healy conducted an experiment involving students performing trivia quizzes, and the results supported their theory.

There is one other factor that has been suggested as playing a role as far as excessive optimism and pessimism is concerned. This is the role of arousal, sometimes referred to as visceral influences. Thus this phenomenon is sometimes referred to as the affect heuristic, as mentioned earlier. Vosgerau (2010) has proposed that people judge the likelihood of desirable and undesirable events to be higher than similar neutral events because they misattribute the arousal caused by those events to their greater perceived likelihood. Thus we may overestimate the likelihood of a terrorist attack or getting cancer; similarly we may overestimate the likelihood of our country winning the World Cup in soccer. Vosgerau finds evidence of this misattribution phenomenon in four studies.

The misattribution effect above may also explain another curious aspect of behavior: people's reluctance to exchange lottery tickets (Risen and Gilovich, 2007). Miller and Taylor (1995) have pointed out that precisely because undesirable outcomes that result from actions taken are more painful than identical outcomes that result from actions foregone, instances in which one has been punished for acting are likely to be overrepresented in the memory. The aversion caused by this anticipated regret from switching would then be mistaken for the increased probability of the event occurring. Thus we may be reluctant to exchange lottery tickets; similarly, we may be disinclined to switch lines at the supermarket checkout when our line appears to be going slowly and the line next to us is speeding along. There may be another aspect to this behavior that we will discuss later, in connection with 'tempting fate'.

### Self-serving bias

This term refers to any cognitive process that is distorted by the need to maintain and enhance self-esteem, and has been used to describe a number of belief biases that are different in nature. For example, it has been used to refer to the asymmetry whereby people ascribe their successes to their own ability or skill, but ascribe failures to situational factors, the actions of other people, or bad luck (Zuckerman, 1979). People also tend to overestimate their contribution to joint or team projects (Ross and Sicoly, 1979). These are aspects of overconfidence, and conform to the findings of much social cognitive research, which suggests that people shape their beliefs and judgments of the social world to maintain sacrosanct beliefs of the self as a capable, lovable, and moral individual (for a recent survey, see Dunning, 2007). This kind of self-serving bias is consistent with the observation by Glaeser (2004):

> Mistaken beliefs will be more common when errors increase the current flow of utility. Thus, if people enjoy anticipating a rosy future, they should believe stories that make them overly optimistic and in particular, they should happily accept stories about a life after death. (p. 4)

A further aspect of this general phenomenon is that self-serving bias relates not just to individuals' evaluations of themselves, but also to groups with which they are affiliated. Observe any team game with partisan spectators; the different fans will interpret the play, and in particular aspects involving foul play or penalties, quite differently. A study of investor behavior also demonstrates how self-serving bias relates to how beliefs relate to the beliefs of others (Egan, Merkle and Weber, 2014). They find that investors are positively influenced by the optimistic beliefs of other investors in terms of investing in stocks, which is an example of conformity bias, but they also find two other biases which are self-serving: (1) investors tend to believe that their own opinion is relatively more common among the population (false consensus); and (2) others who hold divergent beliefs are considered to be biased (bias blind spot).

There is some evidence for both psychological and neurological mechanisms related to this overoptimism. It has been reported that depressed subjects make more accurate assessments, and so are more realistic than normal subjects; this phenomenon has been labeled **depressive realism** (Abramson, Metalsky and Alloy, 1979). It has also been suggested that the phenomenon of **Pavlovian withdrawal** associated with predictions of negative outcomes is an important route to the overoptimism of normal subjects, and that one of the underlying neural malfunctions associated with depression is associated with a weakening of this withdrawal, thereby leading to more accurate, but more pessimistic, evaluations (Huys and Dayan, 2008). This means that when normal people contemplate the future, any thought leading towards a negative outcome will engender a Pavlovian withdrawal response, which may lead to the thought being terminated. There are similarities here with Damasio's somatic market hypothesis. It has been suggested that this withdrawal is mediated by the neurotransmitter 5-HT, which opposes dopamine (Daw et al., 2002), and that depressives have low effective 5-HT levels (Graeff et al., 1996), resulting in their withdrawal mechanism being impaired.

There is also evidence of another type of self-serving bias, relating to a non-conscious desire for autonomy. People generally consider themselves better decision-makers than others and devalue the thoughts and feelings others use to make decisions (Pronin and Kugler, 2007; Pronin, 2008). As a result they may resist communications from external sources that are designed to be persuasive, and endorse their original beliefs even more strongly (Brehm, 1966; Stein, Ackerman and Bargh, 2012). The Remain campaign discovered this effect to their cost in the UK Brexit referendum in 2016. It should be noted that the effect here operates in the opposite direction to conformity bias described earlier. This issue is discussed later in Chapter 10, in the context of nudging strategies.

## Confirmation bias

Confirmation bias is a major type of self-serving bias, and refers to the tendency to search for, process, interpret and recall information in a way that confirms one's prior beliefs, while also having the tendency to discount information that is inconsistent with one's prior beliefs (DellaVigna, 2009). Thus it has some factors in common with the desire for autonomy described above. For example, in financial markets, as traders receive additional private information, in the short term they interpret the information that confirms their existing beliefs as being more informative, rejecting non-confirming information, and this causes them to become more overconfident and trade excessively. As we have already seen, this phenomenon can also be caused by the representation heuristic, since recent information is often regarded as the norm. The main implication of this is that it leads to **momentum**, meaning that there is positive correlation of returns in the short term, so that a stock that goes up in value in one day or over a few days may well continue to go up in the next short time period. In the long term prior beliefs are adjusted in line with the additional information and valuation returns to fundamentals. These effects may operate in the opposite direction to the effects of the law of small numbers, but if they are strong enough they may contribute to bubbles in asset markets. Confirmation bias may also explain why people like to invest in their own company's stock, if they are overconfident about own company performance. Furthermore, it may help to explain why they prefer to invest in national companies rather than foreign companies for a similar reason.

Another type of confirmation bias exists in the sciences and academia. Once a researcher has developed a certain theory, and particularly when it has become published and related to their reputation, the originator becomes emotionally and professionally attached to that theory. This can cause the person to carry out biased research, by cherry-picking data and ignoring inconvenient conflicting evidence, as we have seen in Chapter 2 with the diet-heart hypothesis. It can also lead to distorted, imbalanced and misleading conclusions. Again this occurred with the Minnesota Coronary Experiment described in Chapter 2. The results were not published until 1989, 16 years after the end of the experiment, and the conclusions suggested that the diet-heart hypothesis may have been confirmed if the experiment had lasted longer, and that 'there was a favorable trend' for younger patients. This is an extremely charitable view of the results, considering that the average duration for subjects on the experiment was over a year, and that the results showed that there was an *inverse* rather than the hypothesized positive relationship between blood-cholesterol levels and coronary deaths, particularly for older patients. A similar distorted conclusion was found in the follow-up to the long-standing Framingham study (Dawber, Moore and Mann, 1957, 2015), often quoted as being a major supporter of the DHH. In the follow-up study it was found that, for subjects over 50, those with falling cholesterol levels experienced an *increase* in both CHD and overall mortality, a similar finding to the MCE. The authors suggested that after age 50 years there was a possible confounding effect because people with low cholesterol may be suffering from diseases predisposing to death.

There is a substantial literature in psychology relating to confirmation bias, with recent surveys conducted by Lord and Taylor (2009) and Mercier and Sperber (2011). It has also been modeled by Rabin and Schrag (1999), who propose that people use modified Bayesian probabilities involving non-zero probabilities of misperceiving signals. Thus they may misperceive a signal as confirming hypothesis A when hypothesis B is correct.

### Cognitive dissonance

These examples of confirmation bias demonstrate the existence of an important psychological phenomenon related to self-serving bias known as **cognitive dissonance** (Festinger, 1957). This theory proposes that people suffer mental discomfort when they simultaneously hold conflicting attitudes, beliefs or ideas, and that they try to reconcile these by changing them to achieve consistency. As we have seen in the previous chapter, the **desire for consistency**, in both beliefs and behavior, is a basic psychological phenomenon. As a result people are prone to self-deception; people may '**confabulate**' their intentions, meaning that they invent them after they have taken some action, The situation is demonstrated by Aesop's fable of the fox and the sour grapes. The fox wanted the grapes, but when she found she couldn't reach them she decided that they were probably sour, so she revised her original intention and believed that she never really wanted the grapes in the first place. The phenomenon of cognitive dissonance has been claimed to have played an important role in recent political campaigning, both in the Brexit referendum in the UK and in the Trump campaign in the USA. This political aspect is discussed further in Case 4.3.

There is also evidence of cognitive dissonance in the financial markets. A study by Chang and colleagues (2016) indicates that it is an important factor underlying the disposition effect, discussed in more detail in Chapter 6. Investors may be more willing to sell stocks that have risen in value since purchase than stocks that have fallen because to do the latter may be seen as an admission that they may have made an error of judgment. The evidence suggesting this comes from the fact that when investors delegate the decisions to money fund managers the disposition effect disappears and is replaced by an opposite effect. Furthermore, increasing the salience of the delegation was found to increase the extent of the reverse-disposition effect. Thus cognitive dissonance theory can explain contrary aspects of investor behavior, where investors in individual stocks show a disposition effect but managers investing in mutual funds exhibit the reverse effect.

Perhaps the most extreme cases of mass cognitive dissonance have occurred with the millennium religious movements over the centuries, usually predicting a cataclysmic end of the world. However, when such prophecies fail, 'rather than disbanding in disillusion, the cultists often become strengthened in their convictions' (Cialdini, 1984). Cialdini then identifies several such cults where this has happened: Montanists of second-century Turkey, Anabaptists in sixteenth-century Holland, Sabbataists of seventeenth-century Izmir, and Millerites in nineteenth-century America. A more recent case of the same phenomenon has been described by Festinger, Riecken and Schacter (1956), who were able to observe the behavior of a similar cult in detail by posing as insiders. They were able to witness the astonishing conclusion of the prophesy failure: 'the little group, sitting alone all night long, had spread so much light that God had saved the world from destruction.' One cannot wish for a clearer example of cognitive dissonance.

The tendency of people to strengthen their views after the appearance of evidence refuting them has been documented on a number of occasions, causing the phenomenon to be labeled the 'backfire effect' by Nyhan and Reifler (2010). These authors found a similar effect in an experimental study examining the political beliefs of liberals and conservatives towards the Iraq War in 2003.

Once again this phenomenon presents a puzzle, since it would not appear at first sight that self-deception would serve a useful purpose in terms of biological fitness.

## Visceral fit

The phenomenon of cognitive dissonance involves visceral factors, since we tend to be emotionally attached to our beliefs. Recent research has also pointed to a similar phenomenon, in that when there is a fit or match between our current visceral state and the visceral state associated with an outcome we are judging, we tend to increase our estimate of the likelihood of this outcome occurring (Risen and Critcher, 2011). For example, if we are in a visceral state of being warm, this tends to increase our belief in the reality of global warming. Of course, if this experiment is performed naturally, as when we ask people about their beliefs in the probability of global warming on a hot day, then the resulting bias could be explained by the law of small numbers. In this case people would be using the current warm temperature as a diagnostic device for estimating the probability of warm temperature in the future. However, Risen and Critcher found that their subjects expressed a stronger belief in global warming even when the experiment was performed in a warm room. They therefore eliminated the explanation that temperature was being used as a diagnostic, and instead propose a **simulational fluency** explanation. This means that people construct mental images of hot outdoor scenes more clearly when they are in a hot room than when they are in a normal room, suggesting that, when warm, participants had a more fluent or clear representation of heat-relevant stimuli.

The above research concentrates mainly on the effect of heat as a visceral factor. However, there may be wider implications of the concept of visceral fit to other visceral states. For example, a possible change in government policy, like higher taxes, may make us angry; if we are currently in an angry state, would this make us believe such a change in policy is more likely? Further research is needed in this area to clarify the effects of visceral fit in different situations.

### Projection bias

Another kind of bias where people have systematically incorrect beliefs is that they expect their future preferences to be too close to their present ones. This kind of misestimation of probabilities can also be regarded as a kind of self-evaluation bias, in that we tend to make incorrect judgments of our future selves. For example, it is generally not a good idea to go to the supermarket when we are hungry – we tend to buy all kinds of junk that we don't normally eat or want to eat, and not only is our bill higher than normal, but we end up with stuff we don't consume or don't want to consume. This happens because at the time of shopping we incorrectly anticipate that our future hunger will be as great as it is now. The term 'projection bias' was introduced by Loewenstein, O'Donoghue and Rabin (2003) to describe this phenomenon. They proposed a simple model as follows: assume that utility $u$ is a function of consumption $c$ and of state variable $s$ (which incorporates tastes or preferences), so that:

$$u = u(c, s)$$

The current state is $s'$ and the (unknown) future state is $s$. Then, when predicting the future utility $\hat{u}(c,s)$, and person with projection bias expects utility:

$$\hat{u}(c, s) = (1 - \alpha)u(c, s) + \alpha u(c, s') \tag{4.2}$$

whereas the person without projection bias (who has complete knowledge about the future state $s$) has expected utility $\hat{u}(c, s) = u(c, s)$. The parameter $\alpha$ (which must be between 0 and 1) measures the extent of projection bias, so that if $\alpha = 0$ there is no projection bias, and if $\alpha = 0$ there is full projection bias.

Read and van Leeuwen (1998) confirmed this effect in a study of office workers. These workers were asked to select a healthy snack or an unhealthy snack to be delivered a week later (in the late afternoon). One group of workers was asked the question at a time when they may have been hungry, in the late afternoon, and 78% chose an unhealthy snack. The other group was asked the same question after lunch, when they were probably satiated, and only 42% chose the unhealthy snack.

Evidence of projection bias has also been provided in the field; an example is a study by Conlin, O'Donoghue, and Vogelsang (2007). They examined the effect of weather at the time of purchase on the return of cold-weather apparel items that had been ordered. The NM predicts that there should be no relationship here, or a negative one if colder weather at time of purchase is correlated with colder weather later, making people less likely to return the item. The projection bias hypothesis predicts the opposite effect, with people overestimating their later use and being more likely to return the item. The authors of study did indeed find the opposite effect, estimating that a reduction in the order-date temperature of 30°F (17°C) increases the average return rate of a cold-weather item by nearly 4%. In this case the model (4.2) above estimates the value of $\alpha$ to be about 0.5, indicating that consumers predict future tastes roughly half-way between present tastes and actual future tastes.

Further evidence of projection bias in the field, again related to weather, relates to car purchases. Busse and colleagues (2015) examined 40 million vehicle transactions, finding that the choice to purchase a convertible or a four-wheel-drive is highly dependent on the weather at the time of purchase in a way that is inconsistent with neoclassical utility theory.

An associated kind of bias is **hindsight bias**, which could be considered to be a retrospective projection bias. This means that events seem more predictable in retrospect than in prospect, as in 'we knew it all along'. There is again evidence for this phenomenon both from experiments and in the field. For example, a study by Biais and Weber (2009) conducted an experiment with 85 investment bankers in London and Frankfurt and found not only evidence of hindsight bias among some subjects, but also that the biased agents have lower performance.

## Synthesis

During the discussions in this section we have seen that there are various puzzles as far as explaining the existence of various types of overconfidence. These puzzles are all related to the concept of biological fitness and adaptation. None of the types of overconfidence described appear to improve biological fitness, and therefore one might expect such disadvantageous psychological traits to have been weeded out by Darwinian natural selection. For example, as argued by Anderson and colleagues (2012), recognizing one's limitations would help people set more realistic goals (Ehrlinger and Dunning, 2003), avoid contests one will lose (Camerer and Lovallo, 1999), and select strategies that facilitate success (Neale and Bazerman, 1985).

It is therefore useful at this point to try to synthesize the various types of overconfidence by discussing some of the psychological explanations that have been offered. Three different types of causal factor have been identified (Kahneman, 2011; Anderson et al., 2012), all of which may endow overconfidence with some advantages; these are emotional factors, cognitive factors, and social factors. The emotional factors relate to self-esteem and self-aggrandizement. Overconfidence, by improving self-esteem, may improve mental health, and reduce stress and the incidence of depression. It may also encourage people to persist in tasks that they would otherwise give up on.

Cognitive factors include what Kahneman refers to as the WYSIATI syndrome, meaning 'what you see is all there is'. This is a blinkered perspective where we can see our own efforts but ignore the efforts, or even existence of others, in an extreme case of salience. Thus this phenomenon is also referred to as the competition neglect bias, and it can affect both individuals and groups, for example companies. Kahneman suggests that it can cause overplacement bias in particular, since we tend to underrate the performance of others. In this case this is not because of self-aggrandizement, but because we do not perceive the behavior of others. Another cognitive factor that is relevant here is that some people may be too incompetent to appreciate their own incompetence (Kruger and Dunning, 1999). Williams, Dunning and Kruger (2013, p. 2) report that 'incompetent performers display little insight into just how poorly they perform. On average, the bottom 25% of performers on some task, such as logical reasoning, grammar, or taking a classroom exam, think their performance lies above the 60th percentile, overestimating their raw score by as much as 50%.' The authors go on to suggest that the cognitive problem here may be due to the consistent application of inappropriate algorithms for solving problems.

Social factors are also important in explaining various types of overconfidence, in particular overprecision, self-serving bias and self-deception. Kahneman (2011) suggests that experts who make precise predictions appear more knowledgeable and therefore have more market value; on the other hand, experts who make much vaguer but more realistic predictions are likely to appear clueless and provoke disparagement. The explanation of self-deception is more complex. Evolutionary psychologist Steven Pinker has speculated that self-deception has evolved as a form of commitment (Pinker, 1997). The nature and purpose of commitment is discussed in more detail in Chapter 8 in relation to intertemporal decision-making, but at this stage we can simply say that Pinker's theory involves the concept of an evolutionary arms race in psychological terms. Our emotions are a form of commitment, so for example people may be less inclined to harm us if they know it will make us angry and retaliate. However, anger can be faked to have the same effect. To be credible, commitments like the facility for anger have to be hard to fake. Smiling is notoriously hard to fake, since voluntary or deliberate smiling involves different muscles and parts of the brain (the cerebral cortex) compared to involuntary or genuine smiling, controlled by the limbic system. Taking the arms race one step further, in order to 'fake' emotions that are hard to fake, Pinker proposes that the best solution is to genuinely feel emotions like anger, fear, shame, guilt, sympathy and gratitude, that is, believe in false feelings and intentions that one does not really have. Trivers (2013) takes this explanation further, suggesting that genuine-seeming expressions of overconfidence are more likely to convince others, and therefore improve the social status of those who are better able to deceive themselves. This would apply in particular to supposed experts. Since high social status has important implications in terms of control over resources and thus biological fitness, self-deception may paradoxically be adaptive after all.

## 4.4  Magical beliefs

This title is a general term for certain irrational beliefs that violate the assumptions of the NM, but do not fit it any of the above three categories. They are often termed 'superstitions' in folk psychology. Superstitions are another example of situations where according to dual process models system 1 dominates our thinking and the resulting errors are not corrected by system 2. Two main categories are important to discuss here.

*Tempting fate*

This phenomenon has been touched on earlier in connection with arousal and misattribution of probability. We have seen for example that people can be reluctant to switch lines at supermarket checkouts or exchange lottery tickets. There are widespread instances or applications of this: if you don't take your umbrella to work, it's bound to rain; if you don't do your homework reading, the teacher is bound to pick on you in class to answer questions on it. There are various factors involved here: we have seen that the misattribution effect states that undesirable outcomes resulting from actions taken are more painful than identical outcomes that result from actions foregone, and the aversion caused by this anticipated regret from switching would then be mistaken for the increased probability of the event occurring. We shall also see in the next chapter that loss-aversion is an important factor governing decision-making in risky or uncertain situations.

It is interesting to note that this superstition is a cultural universal. In some cultures people explicitly believe in fate or some supernatural being or force which can act with discretion in the relevant circumstances, but even in cultures where there is no explicit belief in the intervention of some supernatural agent, the superstition exists at an intuitive level that we should not tempt fate. A further point here is superstitions frequently persist even when we know that they are errors (Risen, 2016). The implication is that the processes of error detection and correction are disconnected. Thus system 2 can detect an error but still fail to correct it. Although further research is needed in this area, it may be that cognitive dissonance theory is relevant here, meaning that the correction of the error involves an emotional loss or threat which an individual may prefer to avoid.

It is also important to realize that superstitions, however irrational they may appear to be, can have significant physiological effects on their holders. A dramatic example of this concerns the superstition in China and Japan concerning the number four. The reason for this is that in Mandarin, Cantonese and Japanese, the words 'four' and 'death' are pronounced nearly identically. As a result the number four evokes discomfort and stress in many Chinese and Japanese people, and this number is avoided in various circumstances, for example floor and room numbers and some phone numbers. A large-scale study by Phillips and colleagues (2001) examined over 47 million deaths in the USA from 1973 to 1998 and found that cardiac deaths peak on the fourth of the month for Americans of Chinese and Japanese descent, but this pattern is not seen among whites.

## Contagion

Disgust is a strong aversive emotion or visceral factor. It has been described as 'a revulsion at the prospect of (oral) incorporation of an offensive substance' (Rozin and Fallon, 1987). However, we can note that disgust can also be prompted by touch or even proximity, not just ingestion. Disgust causes certain unique responses as an emotion: a distinct facial expression with closed nostrils, an attempt to get away from the disgusting object, and a physiological response of nausea, as well as an emotional state of revulsion. These responses are different from those related to anger or fear, although there may be some similarities.

It might be initially thought that disgust is not that important in terms of having a frequent and significant effect on behavior. Evidence suggests otherwise, for two reasons:

1  A large number of everyday objects can cause disgust – A survey by Morales and Fitsimons (2007) found that six of the top-ten-selling non-food supermarket items elicit feelings of disgust, including trash bags, cat litter and diapers. Many food or ingested items also elicit disgust, such as cigarettes, mayonnaise, oils and lard. Therefore consumers are likely to experience some degree of disgust routinely on shopping trips.

2  The property of contagion means that other products coming into contact with a disgusting object are contaminated – this process is described by a phenomenon referred to by anthropologists as 'sympathetic magic'. This is not just a belief system found in primitive cultures; it exists in the same general forms in all cultures, although in developed countries people are often reluctant to admit such beliefs for fear of appearing foolish. One of the fundamental laws of sympathetic magic is the 'law of contagion'. This law states that objects or people can affect each other by merely touching, that some or all of the properties of the disgusting object or person or transferred, and that this transfer is permanent. Thus the law is sometimes referred to as 'once in contact, always in contact'.

The ramifications of the two factors described above are widespread as far as consumer behavior is concerned, but before discussing these it is appropriate to give some explanation as to why the 'law of contagion' is a universal phenomenon, given its sometimes strange effects. For example, Rozin, Millman and Nemeroff (1986) found that a drink touched briefly by a sterilized cockroach became undesirable, as did a laundered shirt previously worn by a disliked person, although subjects were often not able to verbalize or acknowledge their contagion belief. Sometimes people are not even conscious of their emotional disgust, but it is reflected in lower evaluations of products. We really need to consider the evolutionary psychology involved here: a product contagion heuristic really follows on from a general 'contact causing' inference. For example, if people eat a lot of fat, they tend to get fat; eating a lot of garlic leads to a garlic odor on the breath and the body. Furthermore, biologically speaking, it would have been a useful adaptation in human history to avoid situations where contamination was possible. Cockroaches can cause contamination of food through microbial infection, as can contact with raw meat, dirt or feces. Thus contamination has historically speaking been a significant and dangerous problem in terms of human survival; we seem as a species to err on the cautious side and misapply the concept in situations where science now informs us it is not relevant.

It should be noted at this point that the phenomenon of contagion involves two aspects from an economic viewpoint: it affects values, preferences and choices, in particular through visceral factors; and it affects beliefs and the estimation of probabilities, discussed in this chapter. Also, particularly important from the viewpoint of behavioral economics, contagion and disgust can activate different parts of our dual-sensory systems, meaning the fast-thinking and slow-thinking systems in the terms of Kahneman (2011). This dual processing aspect has been illustrated in a study by Schulze, Maertens and Wansink (2013), where consumers were required to consider both sandwiches containing (healthy) dogfood and fat-free ice cream. The experiment involved manipulation of cognitive load, so that in its absence consumers were able to implement slow-thinking cognitive processes in evaluating the health benefits of dog food, which would otherwise evoke the fast-thinking emotion of disgust.

What are the consumer behavior ramifications of these findings? Morales and Fitsimons (2007) found that direct physical contact itself was not necessary for a contagion effect to occur, merely a perception of contact was sufficient. Thus raw meat, or drinks in transparent containers, was more likely to cause a perception of contamination than if packaged in opaque containers. In the supermarket situation contamination can occur in terms of either proximity of items on the shelves or proximity in the shopping cart. Thus when lard is positioned on shelves near other baking products, pans and utensils, as is commonly found, these other products are likely to receive a lower evaluation from consumers.

There are obviously implications here in terms of managerial policy. Managers need to take care in determining shelf location for products to minimize the effects of lower evaluations. Even though they cannot control proximity in the shopping cart, they can allow consumers to take avoidance measures. Opaque and substantial packaging may be important for some products. Some supermarkets are now providing facilities for double-wrapping meat. Governments also need to be aware that there can be consumer panics in response to food health scares, involving overreactions caused by visceral factors; reassurance may be necessary in these circumstances.

There is one final point that is worth raising here in terms of disgust. We have concentrated so far on situations where the disgust is purely physical; people can also feel moral disgust. An outstanding example can be seen in the BP oil spill in the Gulf of Mexico. In this case the discussion may combine elements of physical and moral disgust; people do not like to see birds coated in oil, but they have also been revulsed by the seeming negligence and reactions of BP management, and the ramifications of this have been huge. Not only has BP been treated as a pariah by press and public internationally, but other oil companies have suffered also, as has the US president. Evidence also exists of increased anti-British sentiment in the USA as a result of the disaster. The plunge in the BP share price, arguably not justified by economic fundamentals, has important implications for UK pension funds (and ultimately pension investors) that have invested heavily in BP stock. A more recent example of this phenomenon relates to an incident on a United Airlines flight in April 2017, where a passenger was involuntarily dragged from the plane by security. The already troubled airline has faced huge criticism in the press and social media, and the affair has been badly handled by the CEO. It is too early at this stage to see if the company's stock price will suffer accordingly.

So far we have examined only the negative aspects of contagion. As was indicated in the introduction to the chapter, contagion can have positive aspects also. It can vastly inflate the values of objects, such as 'Blackie', a guitar once owned and played by Eric Clapton, which sold for $959,500 in 2004. According to Paul Bloom, a psychologist from a team at Yale University who looked into this phenomenon a bit more closely, when interviewed on his research by the *New York Times* (Tierney, 2011, p. A16):

> Our results suggest that physical contact with a celebrity boosts the value of an object, so people will pay extra for a guitar that Eric Clapton played, or even held in his hands.

This is the same kind of thinking that makes people reluctant to wear the sweater of a murderer. Bloom and colleagues find that people value highly the possessions of celebrities even if they despise them, since they expect the possessions of notorious celebrities, or even pariahs like Saddam Hussein, to be valued by others (Newman, Diesendruck and Bloom, 2011). Furthermore, the values of these possessions are significantly reduced if they are washed or in some way sterilized.

A similar psychology applies even with replicas of objects owned by celebrities. In this case the phenomenon is known as 'imitative magic', meaning that things that look alike are alike. Thus a replica of 'Blackie', perfect down to the cigarette burns and belt buckle scratches fetched $30,500 in auction in March 2011. Less perfect replicas sell for lower prices, but are still valued highly. The replica fetish is important in the musical business, extending not only to guitars and strings but also to amplifiers, microphones and other instruments.

Fernandez and Lastovicka (2011) have studied the phenomenon of consumption fetishes and their connection to magical beliefs extensively in modern mass consumer culture. Ultimately, they consider that the foundations for these magical beliefs are to be found in evolutionary biology, as explained by John Lastovicka in the same *New York Times* article:

> Beliefs about contagion, and especially biological contagion, by our ancestors are one of the reasons why we are here today. Those who did not stay away from those who died from the plague in the Dark Ages also died of the plague; those who died of the plague in the Dark Ages likely have few, if any, descendants today. So in our modern and scientific world, these manners of magical thinking still persist.

The subject of magical beliefs and contagion is examined in more detail in Case 4.2.

## 4.5   Causes of irrationality

We have now surveyed a variety of situations where people exhibit a formation or holding of beliefs that violates the kind of rationality proposed in standard economics. It is therefore worthwhile at this stage to discuss the causes of the underlying phenomena.

Baumeister (2001) has identified five different causes of irrational, or what he terms self-defeating, behavior. We can really equate self-defeating behavior with behavior that is not in a person's long-run self-interest. One can of course question whether it is legitimate to equate irrational behavior with self-defeating behavior, and this aspect will be discussed further in the final subsection. However, what is important here is the usefulness of the categories that he proposes in terms of analysis. These categories are: emotional distress, threatened egotism, self-regulation failure, rejection and belongingness, and decision fatigue. The first of these categories involves a variety of factors, and it is helpful to discuss memory and cognitive dissonance as separate categories.

## Emotional distress

The general impact of emotions on preferences and choices has been discussed in the previous section. We now need to explain how and why these effects occur, recognizing that this remains a highly controversial area in psychology.

There has been a lot of research into the effects of emotions on decision-making. The conventional attitude taken by economists, and also by philosophers in the Kantian tradition, is that emotions tend to cloud good judgment, resulting in 'irrational' decisions or self-defeating behavior. However, this raises the issue mentioned in the previous section in relation to evolutionary psychology: how can emotions serve as an adaptive evolved psychological mechanism? If they were a maladaptation, people with genes for emotional behavior would not have passed them on to succeeding generations, and we would now be living in a world full of unemotional people, like Doctor Spock from Star Trek; this is clearly not the case. In the late 1980s the economist Robert Frank proposed a theory that emotions served as a commitment mechanism, and thus were a useful adaptation. Frank's theory was supported by independent research by Jack Hirshleifer. The neuroscientist Damasio (1994) also researched the role of the emotions in decision-making, by examining patients with brain damage, again concluding that emotions could be an aid as well as a hindrance. These theories are discussed in more detail later in this section. At this stage we can summarize the situation by saying that emotions can lead to either better or worse decisions, depending on the circumstances.

While the effects may be unpleasant and destructive, the evolutionary advantages of such changes in behavior are obvious. The need to satisfy or reduce basic drives is fundamental to survival and reproduction. This also applies to the sensation of pain; its unpleasantness is a signal that something is wrong with the biological system, and we should be doing something to remedy the situation (get out of the heat/cold, rest an injured limb, defend ourselves against the person attacking us).

The theory of emotions as an evolved psychological mechanism or mental adaptation was described by Frank (1988) in the seminal work *Passions within Reason*. According to Frank our emotions serve as **commitment** devices, meaning that they commit us to perform certain actions at a later time if other people behave in certain ways. The nature of commitment in general is considered in Chapter 8 in relation to intertemporal decision-making, and it is also relevant in game theory. Frank's insight was to see the role of emotions in prompting us to perform actions that we would not carry out if we were acting on purely 'rational' grounds. A simple example can illustrate the situation. Imagine that we make an agreement with another person such that we perform some work for them now in exchange for being paid afterward. Such 'delayed exchange' contracts have been extremely common in human history, on both a formal and informal basis. The person doing the work first is always subject to a '**holdup**' problem (unless the details are formalized in a written contract), in that the other party can renege on the deal. Without any formal contract the cheated party has no comeback, and a 'rational' person may simply write off the loss, and put it down to experience. An 'emotional' person on the other hand would be angry with the cheat and take steps to gain revenge, at risk and cost to himself, which the 'rational' person would be unwilling to take. However, the knowledge that an emotional person may react in this way might well be enough to prevent the other party from cheating in the first place. This is an example of what is called a '**reputation effect**'; emotional people may gain a reputation for not standing for any nonsense or backsliding in their dealings, thus encouraging others to be straight with them.

This example illustrates how our emotions can serve our long-run self-interest, but Pinker (1997) has gone a step further, showing how our emotions can backfire on us, referring to them as '**doomsday devices**', after the movie *Doctor Strangelove*. The problem with doomsday devices is that they cannot be disarmed, even if they are activated by mistake, and will explode regardless of the consequences. Thus they may lead to futile and self-destructive reactions; a well-known example is the successive rounds of retaliation that occur with feuds between gangs or clans. It is possible that the reaction to social rejection, discussed in more detail later, is of this type. Emotions are indeed a two-edged sword.

One aspect of emotional distress where research has indicated a bad effect on decisions is the role of anger on risk-taking. Leith and Baumeister (1996) found that people who were upset were more inclined to take foolish risks, like betting on long shots in a lottery. There were various possible explanations for this; for example, people who were already upset had less to lose by taking a long shot and more to gain, while people who were in a good or neutral mood had more to lose by taking a long shot. However, Leith and Baumeister were able to eliminate this explanation by further experimentation, requiring respondents to reflect on their decisions for about a minute before choosing. Although the respondents were still angry when they made their decision they now became more risk-averse. Thus it seems that emotional upset does indeed cloud judgment of risk, and that when upset people are forced to think about things they make better decisions.

Fear is another negative emotion that can result in adverse or self-defeating consequences rather than favorable ones. The traditional response is a fight-or-flight reaction, which is generally a useful adaptation. However, as some governments have found, trying to invoke excessive amounts of fear in a population may backfire. This has been true of some anti-smoking campaigns. Sometimes, when people are faced with information they really do not want to have to process in terms of its unfavorable consequences, they are inclined to filter it out and ignore it. The research findings here are somewhat conflicting. Some research has shown that a message where fear is combined with disgust can be more compelling (Morales, Wu and Fitzsimons, 2012), but as discussed earlier, disgust can also be aversive, causing people to ignore the message.

A less extreme but more chronic negative emotion is anxiety, which can also cause self-defeating responses. In this case it appears that it affects the ability of people to process new information about a situation, resulting in a failure to implement Bayesian updating and leading to poor decision-making (Browning et al., 2015).

## *Memory*

As far as our emotional states over time are concerned there are two important factors that need to be discussed, in terms of both their causes and their implications:

1    People tend to revert to a 'normal emotional state' after any kind of emotional experience, whether it be pleasant or unpleasant.
2    People tend to overestimate the length of time that it will take to revert to this normal state.

The first aspect of human nature has long been known. According to Adam Smith in *The Theory of Moral Sentiments* of 1759:

> The mind of every man, in a longer or shorter time, returns to its natural and usual state of tranquillity. In prosperity, after a certain time, it falls back to that state; in adversity, after a certain time, it rises up to it. (p. 172)

This 'certain time' turns out to be a shorter rather than a longer time in general. There is now a substantial body of research showing that emotional reactions to life-changing events are surprisingly short-lived (Suh, Diener and Fujita, 1996; Frederick and Loewenstein, 1999). When people win large amounts of money in a lottery, they do not remain happy for very long (Brickman, Coates and Janoff-Bulman, 1978; Kaplan, 1978). In the opposite direction, the majority of bereaved spouses reported themselves to be doing well two years after the death (Lund et al., 1989; Wortman, Silver and Kessler, 1993).

Similarly, people who have suffered serious injury confining them to a wheelchair have recovered equanimity within a period of a year.

The second aspect of human nature is less well known. However, experiments have been performed that measure people's forecasts of emotional events and compare these with their actual duration, and there is evidence of a consistent **durability bias** in both directions. Thus there is a tendency for people to overestimate the duration of their reactions to both positive and negative emotional events (Gilbert et al., 1998; Wilson et al., 2000).

Several theories have been proposed to explain both of the above factors. These are discussed further in the final chapter in relation to happiness.

## Cognitive dissonance

Self-deception is an important category of irrational behavior, as we have seen. It can be the result of a type of emotional distress discussed earlier. The most important psychological theory that is relevant here is that of **cognitive dissonance**, originated by Festinger (1957), and discussed in an earlier section. This theory states that people are motivated to avoid having their attitudes and beliefs in a dissonant or conflicting relationship, and they feel uncomfortable when dissonance occurs. This discomfort can cause people to do many things that could be classed as irrational. Thus cognitive dissonance generally involves people justifying their actions by changing their beliefs. This is because it is often easier to change one's beliefs than to change actions that have already been taken. However, cognitive dissonance may also involve situations where beliefs are held steadfastly in spite of contrary evidence. This is the kind of situation where the fourth criterion for rationality is relevant. These violations of rationality occur when it is harder to change an ingrained belief system than to change one's interpretation of empirical evidence. There may be a variety of ways to explain away uncomfortable empirical findings, as many smokers can attest.

We can of course ask the question why such behavior, or the mental processes leading to such behavior, can have evolved as an adaptive response. It might initially seem that such processes would be maladaptive, obscuring the realities of situations and leading to bad decisions. While self-deception may certainly lead to bad decisions, as we will see in more detail in some case studies, it may also be advantageous in other respects. In particular it may bolster confidence and self-esteem, increasing one's sense of well-being, and, if one can also deceive others, it may have the effect of increasing one's status in society. The evolutionary psychologist Pinker (1997) has gone so far as to claim that self-deception can be adaptive because it makes it easier to deceive others. If we really believe that we are the best person to do a certain job, in spite of our lack of ability, then we are more likely to convince others and be offered the job.

## Threat to self-esteem

There is considerable evidence that concern with self-esteem can affect the quality of decision-making. In particular there appears to be a relationship between low self-esteem and self-defeating behavior such as self-handicapping, binge eating and alcohol abuse. These consequences are discussed later in the section. However, research also indicates that the relationship is not a straightforward one. People with high, but misplaced, self-esteem may also indulge in alcohol and drug abuse, believing that they are strong enough to withstand the harmful physical effects and the tendency to addiction. This can be referred to as the '**peacock's tail**' syndrome, after the theory of the evolutionary biologist Zahavi (1975), that the seemingly useless and wasteful peacock's tail evolved as a sign of health for its owner, who was strong enough to withstand the waste of resources.

Baumeister, Heatherton and Tice (1993) also found evidence of a more complicated relationship between self-esteem and quality of decision-making. In general they found that people with high self-esteem made better decisions in risk-taking experiments, in terms of judging their own performance better than people with low self-esteem, and gambling in an appropriate manner. However, when people with high self-esteem received a blow to their pride they started to make bad decisions, worse even than those with low self-esteem, by making large bets that were not justified by their own performance. They seemed to be anxious to wipe out the loss of face involved.

## Failure of self-regulation

**Self-regulation** in the current context refers to the need for individuals to reflect on advantages and disadvantages before making decisions rather than acting impulsively. One aspect of this has already been described, in connection with emotional distress. Another aspect of self-regulation involves the weighing of long-run costs against short-run benefits of decisions. This aspect is often referred to as intertemporal decision-making, and is discussed in Chapters 7 and 8. Self-regulation in this situation involves the delay of gratification. The ability for self-regulation is obviously a useful adaptation, enabling our ancestors to withstand temptations that would have resulted in early death, and encouraging them to make long-run investments in the health of themselves and their families.

There may be different reasons why self-regulation breaks down, as we have seen in various contexts. One factor that can be repeated at this stage is that the capacity for self-regulation is an exhaustible resource, much like physical strength (Muraven and Baumeister, 2000; Muraven, Tice and Baumeister, 1998). When this capacity is reduced the phenomenon is sometimes referred to as **ego depletion**, and is discussed further in Chapter 8. For example, a study by Shiv and Fedorikhin (1999) showed that cognitive load reduced self-control, as people who had to remember longer numbers were more likely to eat chocolate cake than fruit salad. Other studies have shown that the depletion effect can be eliminated by replenishing the self-regulation resources, for example by consuming glucose (Gailliot et al., 2007; Vohs et al., 2008), suggesting that brain blood glucose is the relevant resource.

However, there are some conflicting findings regarding failure of self-regulation and ego depletion. Later studies have found that a placebo can serve equally well to eliminate the depletion effect (Molden et al., 2012; Sanders et al., 2012). Furthermore, the effect can also be offset by motivational factors, including positive mood induction (Tice et al., 2007), explicit feedback on task performance (Wan and Sternthal, 2008), motivational incentives (Muraven and Slessareva, 2003; Muraven, Shmueli and Burkley, 2006), the belief that willpower is unlimited (Job, Dweck and Walton, 2010), personal prayer (Friese and Wänke, 2014) and feelings of autonomy support (Muraven, 2008).

Another complication is that the similarity between the capacity for self-regulation and physical strength is two-fold. First, as we have seen, it is easily depleted in the short run, so that people cannot continue to resist temptation indefinitely; also as they have to deal with more stress in one situation, they tend to lose control in other situations, for example by smoking, drinking or eating more. But there is also a second similarity: the capacity for self-regulation appears to be something that can be increased in the long run, just as a muscle adapts to physical exercise by becoming stronger in the long run. For example, Muraven, Baumeister and Tice (1999) found that repeated exercises in self-control, such as trying to improve posture, over a period of two weeks led to improvements in self-control in laboratory tasks relative to people who did not exercise. Similarly, when subjects are assigned two consecutive tasks to perform which require similar control processes, the previous use of self-control can enhance the subsequent self-control performance (Dewitte, Bruyneel and Geyskens, 2009).

### Decision fatigue

It seems that people not only tire when it comes to self-control, they also tire of making decisions in general. This may well be the main reason that people are creatures of habit; having a routine avoids the need to expend scarce resources by making choices. A good illustration of this phenomenon is provided by the research of Vohs and colleagues (2008). They found that a group of respondents who had to make a series of product choices had a reduced capacity for self-regulation compared with a control group. The capacity for self-regulation was measured by asking the respondents to drink as much as they could of an unpleasant, bitter tasting beverage. This finding suggests that people tire of making decisions, and when they do so it is possible that any further decisions that are forced on them before they have had time to recover may result in a fall in quality. Military psychologists have found a similar tendency with commanders in battle (Dixon, 1976).

### Interpersonal rejection

Humans have a strong innate desire to belong to a social group that is virtually universal. The evolutionary advantages of this are obvious, which is why this desire tends to be even greater and more fundamental than the desire for self-esteem. However, if people feel rejected socially, this appears to be such a psychological blow that they cease to function effectively in a number of ways. Experimental research indicates that they make poorer decisions, making more unhealthy choices, gambling foolishly and also becoming more aggressive and less cooperative. Even performance on intelligence tests is adversely affected. The reasons for this general loss of effective function are not clear at present; further research needs to be performed in this area, most likely of a neuroscientific nature. It is likely that rejection causes a change in the body's output of hormones and neurotransmitters. Research has already established for example that winning teams and their supporters both enjoy an increase in testosterone output following victory, while losers and their supporters suffer from a drop in testosterone.

### Foundations in evolutionary neurobiology

We now need to say something in general about all the above causes of irrationality. Our starting point is to take a reductionist approach. We must examine how the human organism, and in particular the brain, evolved if we are to gain a real understanding of behavior. The human organism did not evolve in order to be a rational decision-making system, or to maximize utility, well-being or hedonic pleasure. The forces of natural selection have caused us to be designed as a *system that maximizes biological fitness*. **Biological fitness** relates not only to our own individual survival and reproduction, but also in broader terms to the survival of our relatives who share the same genes. Those of our ancestors who were most successful in achieving biological fitness were most able to spread their genes, ensuring the survival of more people with the same genetic abilities. In order to achieve this end, however, the brain and other body mechanisms must have a signaling system to guide the brain to make the correct decisions. This is where pain and pleasure enter the picture. Pain generally can tell us we have made a bad decision as far as biological fitness is concerned, whereas pleasure can tell us we have made a good decision. Thus we can say that the individual is prompted to maximize hedonic pleasure as a means to the ultimate end of maximizing biological fitness. It is largely the indirect nature of this mechanism that leads to the objection described earlier that inappropriate norms are used to judge rationality.

Furthermore, it should be recognized that this hedonic pleasure relates not only to conventional goods but also to what we call moral sentiments. This point has been made earlier, in Chapter 3, but it is important to realize that talk about 'life being about more than happiness' misunderstands this crucial insight. Although morality has been heavily influenced by cultural factors over the last few thousand years, it originally evolved for the same reason as our physical organs, to maximize biological fitness. Ultimately this involves the same signaling system in terms of pain and pleasure. If we feel the pain of guilt this may be a signal that we have made a bad decision; others may punish us if they discover our actions. Likewise the pleasure, in terms of 'warm glow' or pride, in performing a virtuous action or 'doing our duty' may signal a good decision; others may reward us.

The essential problem with this mechanism is that our hedonic system can be easily hijacked. One main reason for this is that there is always a time lag between the optimal design and the demands of the current environment. Just as the military are often accused of preparing to fight the last war, our brains and physiological systems are geared to dealing with the demands of a past environment. Thus we have cravings for salt and sugar, which in the past were vital nutrients necessary for survival, but which now cause all kinds of health problems when consumed in excess. Our endorphin receptors in the brain can be fooled into craving opiates as a source of pleasure, getting us addicted to hard drugs. It can also be argued that our hedonic system may be hijacked in the case of our moral sentiments as well; for example, a bad or brutal environment may eliminate feelings of guilt for performing antisocial actions.

Another reason why our hedonic systems can be hijacked is that they use **heuristic devices** to achieve their ends. Natural selection is a 'blind watchmaker', as Dawkins (1986) has elegantly described it, and is a **mechanistic** rather than a **teleological** process. This means that it has no 'purpose'; it builds on what has developed from the past, rather than by looking ahead to the future and setting a goal. The implications of this mechanistic process are often misunderstood even by educated and intelligent commentators, so it is worthwhile expanding on this aspect. The maximization of biological fitness, or **'selfish gene' theory** as it is sometimes described in reductionist terms (Dawkins, 1976), is sometimes rejected out of hand on the basis that it cannot explain why we use contraceptive devices and other non-reproductive sexual practices. The response to this is that our brains are not designed to further reproduction *directly*. This would involve fantastically complicated neural machinery, which may well not adapt well to changes in the environment, and which would use great resources of precious energy. Instead, our brains operate using basic heuristic processes, so that sexual activity in general gives pleasure, regardless of whether it results in reproduction. The association of sexual activity with pleasure is generally sufficient to promote reproduction, and certainly has been throughout evolutionary history until very recently.

On this foundation of neurobiology, Zak has argued that people are neither rational nor irrational; rather, people are 'rationally rational' (Zak, 2011):

> The rational rationality model predicts that people will invest scarce cognitive resources in solving a decision problem only when the expected payoff is sufficiently large. Otherwise, human beings will expend the minimum resources needed to achieve a "good enough" outcome. "Good enough" means that there is a wide range of acceptable choices. Rational rationality is similar to Herbert Simon's notion of satisficing (Simon, 1991), but clearly identifies when people will satisfice and when they will not. Rational rationality occurs because cognitive resources are constrained and the brain evolved to conserve energy and deploy these resources only as needed. The neuroscience behind rational rationality requires that any economic model identify why individuals would expend scarce brain resources when making a decision rather than rely on previously learned heuristics. (p. 55)

Thus, as we have already seen, it may make sense to formulate **dual-process models** of reasoning and judgment, which involve the operation of different decision-making systems in different situations (Epstein, 1994; Osherson, 1995; Evans and Over, 1996; Sloman, 1996; Stanovich, 1999). The essence of such models is that in certain situations people use analytical, logical, rule-based systems with a relatively high computational burden, while in other situations people use various types of heuristic procedures. The use of heuristics can be viewed as a shortcut; frequently it results in an efficient use of personal resources, leading if not to optimization at least to satisficing. However, like many shortcuts, the use of heuristics can also lead to many bad decisions in situations where a more cognitive, analytical approach is desirable. Thus heuristics are both a good and a bad method of decision-making, depending on the circumstances.

If we accept the abundant evidence of the mechanistic nature of evolution and the way it builds structures without purpose, the implication of the use of heuristic devices is that they provide simple rules for appropriate action in a given situation, but they tend to be highly fallible. Many of the anomalies that we have now observed with the standard model are a result of this factor. Therefore, because of the way in which our brains and minds have evolved, we may be bad at performing what may seem simple abstract tasks, using inappropriate heuristic devices. However, these are tasks that have never been required in our ancestral past. On the other hand, human beings are extremely good at performing complex tasks that we take for granted, like visually following an object, changing focus and perceptions of color, speed and distance as it moves, and making the necessary biomechanical adjustments involved in catching a ball. Even the most advanced artificial intelligence systems designed cannot rival this performance. The moral appears to be that we are good at what we need to be good at, or, more correctly, we are good at what we needed to be good at in our evolutionary past. This kind of behavior may then not be so 'irrational' after all; this raises the issue of appropriate norms, which is discussed further in the final chapter.

At the psychological level, the kind of 'irrationality' that we observe in human belief systems may not really be irrational in evolutionary terms either, in spite of initial appearances. Hood (2010) has claimed that the human mind has adapted to reason intuitively, in order to develop theories about how the world works even when mechanisms cannot be seen or easily deduced. This adaptation has had huge benefits in terms of the development of scientific theories related to invisible forces like gravity and electromagnetism. However, according to Hood, it also results in people being prone to making irrational errors, in particular relating to superstition and religion. This is because in our evolutionary past it has been more advantageous from a survival viewpoint to believe in a cause-and-effect relationship that does not exist (for example, God punishing people with bad weather) than not to believe in a cause-and-effect relationship that does exist (for example, the growl behind the nearby bush being caused by a lurking predator). Thus people tend to be overly fond of positing cause-and-effect relationships, even when none exists. Hood claims that it is therefore unlikely that we will evolve a rational mind, and that religion and superstition are here to stay.

## 4.6 Summary

- The neoclassical model (NM) assumes that people are perfectly rational, and that they are Bayesian probability estimators.
- There are three main sources of deviations from the standard model: incorrect probability estimation, self-evaluation bias and magical beliefs.
- Incorrect probability estimation has several sources: salience, the representativeness heuristic, base rate bias, the 'law of small numbers' and conformity bias.
- Conformity bias refers to the desire to follow the beliefs and behavior of others and affects both preferences and the estimation of probabilities.

- Self-evaluation bias involves overconfidence, underconfidence, self-serving bias, confirmation bias and cognitive dissonance.
- Confirmation bias is the tendency to discount information that is inconsistent with one's prior beliefs.
- Cognitive dissonance refers to a conflict of beliefs within a person, causing a feeling of discomfort, which often leads to confabulation.
- Confabulation involves self-deception where a person makes up a story that they then believe.
- Overconfidence has three aspects: overestimation, overplacement and overprecision.
- The 'gambler's fallacy' effect is that people expect a particular sequence of identical signals to be reversed, due to mean reversion.
- The 'hot hand' effect is that people expect a particular sequence of identical signals to continue, with a 'trending' effect.
- Projection bias means that people expect their future preferences to be too close to the present ones.
- Hindsight bias means that events seem more predictable in retrospect than in prospect.
- Magical beliefs are general non-rational superstitions that tend to be universal, although in developed countries people are often unwilling to admit to them for fear of seeming foolish. They include 'tempting fate' and contagion.

There are many causes of irrational beliefs and behavior: emotional distress; memory; cognitive dissonance; threat to self-esteem; failure of self-regulation; decision fatigue; and interpersonal rejection.

## 4.7  Review questions

1   Explain the difference between overestimation and overplacement, and why this distinction is important.
2   Explain the 'hard-easy' phenomenon and why it occurs.
3   Explain what is meant by the representativeness heuristic, giving an example.
4   Explain what is meant by base rate bias, giving an example.
5   Explain what is meant by 'the law of small numbers'.
6   Explain why people tend to avoid betting on numbers that have recently won in a lottery, but also may want to buy their tickets from a store where a big-winning ticket has recently been sold.
7   Give an example of a situation where projection bias can result in a bad decision.
8   Explain why people may be reluctant to 'tempt fate'.
9   Explain why contagion is relevant in supermarket shopping; give two examples of how the concept of contagion can affect people's shopping habits.
10  Give two examples of how managers can reduce the effects of contagion.

## 4.8  Review problems

1   **Gambler's fallacy**
    A coin is tossed 12 times; on the first 3 tosses it lands up heads.
    a)   What would be the rational gambler's estimate of the probability of the fourth toss resulting in a tail, assuming the coin is unbiased?

b) What would be the gambler's estimate of the probability of the fourth toss resulting in a tail, if he believes in the gambler's fallacy?

**2  'Hot hand' effect**

A manager of unknown ability is managing an investment fund. Well-managed funds rise in value in 60% of time periods, while badly managed funds only rise in value 40% of the time. It is observed that a particular fund rises in value on four consecutive occasions. Assuming that there is a prior probability of 0.5 that the fund is well managed:

a) What would be the rational investor's estimate of the probability of the fund being well managed, after observing four consecutive rises?

b) What would be investor's estimate of the probability of the fund being well managed, if she believes in the 'hot hand' effect?


## 4.9  Applications

### Case 4.1 Trading on testosterone

Financial traders take a lot of risk, but often make high rewards. Until recently the role of the endocrine system in a trader's success or failure had not been investigated. We now know that a high level of testosterone is a good predictor of daily trading profitability, while a high level of cortisol is associated with a high variance in a trader's profit and with market volatility. This was established by a study by Coates and Herbert in 2008, who examined 17 male traders in the City of London over a period of 8 days, recording testosterone and cortisol levels at 11 a.m. and 4 p.m., coinciding generally with the start and end of the main trading of the day. These findings are important in understanding not just the underlying psychology behind bubbles and crashes in financial markets, but also the physiology. A high level of testosterone tends to lead to high confidence and increased risk-taking (Apicella et al., 2008; Garbarino, Slonim and Sydnor). In a bull or rising market this will tend to lead to greater profits, which may engender more confidence and risk-taking in the future. Cortisol is a stress hormone. When markets are falling or when they are highly volatile this increases stress, which in turn tends to cause not only caution, but a reluctance to transact altogether. The psychology of the market is driven by an underlying physiology. Furthermore, this system is a circular one. High levels of testosterone are associated with a greater degree of risk-taking, while successful outcomes increase testosterone levels. Unsuccessful outcomes decrease testosterone and increase cortisol levels. However, it has also been shown in laboratory experiments and through the analysis of real traders that gains and losses from financial trading lead to greater variance in male hormone levels and risk preferences than is observed in females (Dreber and Hoffman, 2010). Since these effects have become known, there has been pressure on policy-makers to increase the proportion of female traders in financial markets in order to reduce volatility and the likelihood of bubbles and crashes.

A recent study by Bose, Ladley and Li (2016) has investigated the validity of this policy implication. They model the trading situation essentially along the lines of De Long and colleagues (1991), with heterogeneous beliefs among informed investors and positive feedback investors. However, they also incorporate two additional elements: time-varying endogenous risk preferences, to allow for hormonal effects; and heterogeneity between

▶

male and female investors in terms of these risk preferences. Their main findings are as follows:

1  An increased proportion of female traders increases volatility in asset prices.

2  An increased proportion of female traders decreases the likelihood of extreme events.

3  Female traders on average earn more than males, but the best and worst performers tend to be male.

In view of these findings the authors report that, in spite of female earnings on average being higher, it is not surprising that financial markets are dominated by males, given hormone and reward systems. They recommend that, if policy-makers wish to increase the proportion of females in the financial markets, then it is necessary to 'fundamentally change the bonus culture of investing'.

**Questions**

1  Explain how overconfidence and underconfidence are related to hormones.

2  Explain one main implication of this study as far as trends in financial markets are concerned.

3  How is the above case related to the concept of reductionism described in the previous chapter?

4  Explain the implications of the study by Bose, Ladley and Li (2016) for policy-makers.

---

## Case 4.2  Celebrity contagion and imitative magic

When Eric Clapton's Fender Stratocaster guitar 'Blackie' sold for $959,500 in 2004, this set a record price for a guitar sold in auction. A replica of Blackie, complete with every single nick and scratch, including the wear pattern from Mr. Clapton's belt buckle and the burn mark from his cigarettes, fetched $30,500 at auction in March 2011. Some psychologists believe they have developed a theory that explains these enormous values. After conducting experiments and interviewing guitar players and collectors, they have published papers analyzing 'celebrity contagion' and 'imitative magic'. One of their conclusions is that the seemingly irrational desire for a Clapton relic, even an imitation of a relic, stems from an instinct crucial to surviving disasters like the Black Death: the belief that certain properties are contagious, either in a good or a bad way. Another conclusion is that the magical thinking chronicled in primitive tribes affects bids for memorabilia in auctions.

Some bidders might rationalize their purchases as good investments, or as objects that are worth having just because they provide pleasant memories and mental associations of someone they admire. But those do not seem to be the chief reasons for buying celebrity memorabilia, according to Newman, Diesendruck and Bloom (2011). The researchers asked people how much they would like to buy objects that had been owned by different celebrities, including popular ones like George Clooney and outcasts like Saddam Hussein. People's affection for the celebrity did not predict how much value they assigned to the memorabilia—apparently they were not buying it primarily for the pleasant associations.

Nor were they chiefly motivated by the prospect of a profit, as the researchers discovered when they tested people's eagerness to acquire a celebrity possession that could not be resold. That restriction made people less interested in items owned by villains, but it did not seriously dampen their enthusiasm for relics from their idols.

The most important factor seemed to be the degree of 'celebrity contagion'. The study found that a sweater owned by a popular celebrity became more valuable to people if they learned it had actually been worn by their idol. But if the sweater had subsequently been cleaned and sterilized, it seemed less valuable to the fans, apparently because the celebrity's essence had somehow been removed.

'Our results suggest that physical contact with a celebrity boosts the value of an object, so people will pay extra for a guitar that Eric Clapton played, or even held in his hands,' is the opinion of Paul Bloom (quoted in the *New York Times*, March 8, 2011). This sort of direct physical contact helps explains why the original Blackie guitar sold for nearly $1 million—Mr. Clapton had played it extensively for more than a decade. But why build an exact replica of the guitar and all its nicks and scratches?

The replica's appeal is related to another form of thinking called the law of similarity, according to George Newman. That is a belief in what is called 'imitative magic'; this proposes that things that resemble each other have similar powers:

> Cultural practices such as burning voodoo dolls to harm one's enemies are consistent with a belief in the law of similarity. An identical Clapton guitar replica with all of the dents and scratches may serve as such a close proxy to Clapton's original guitar that it is in some way confused for the real thing. Of course, the replica is worth far less than the actual guitar that he played, but it still appears to be getting a significant amount of value for its similarity.

Even a mass-produced replica guitar without the nicks and scratches can become magical, according to another study by Fernandez and Lastovicka (2011). The researchers conducted in-depth interviews with 16 men who owned more than one guitar and resided either in New Zealand or the USA, including one who had spent hundreds of thousands of dollars on replicas of Beatles gear. They found that many participants believed in the idea of 'contagious magic' (the idea that two entities that touch can influence each other). For example, many fans want to have rock stars sign their instruments, and one established performer explained how he used another rock star's discarded guitar strings. The research also revealed that replica guitars appeal to participants' belief in imitative magic:

> They often bought the best possible copy they could attain, and then if needed, made further changes to it so that it resembled the desired object even more closely.

The authors go on to explain that, for example, some consumers switch out knobs on their guitars to more closely resemble the instruments of the artists they admired. These consumers did not conform to the theory described in existing academic literature that a mass-produced object could never acquire the aura of a fetish, the anthropological term for an object believed to have supernatural powers. The guitar collectors insisted that even a factory-made replica of a famous musician's guitar had a certain something that enabled them to play better music. According to Fernandez and Lastovicka:

> Consumers use contagious and imitative magic to imbue replica instruments with power. Semiotically signified magical thinking causes replicas to radiate aura and thus transforms them into fetishes.

Of course, the collectors still preferred a beat-up guitar used by a star to a brand-new replica of it. One of them told the researchers how he had improved his own guitar playing by using old guitar strings that had been discarded by Duane Allman. This belief in contagious magic may sound irrational, but it makes a certain evolutionary sense.

### Questions

1   Explain why magical beliefs are related to probabilities as well as utilities.

2   Explain why a belief in contagious magic makes a certain evolutionary sense.

3   Why would sterilizing an object have an effect on its value?

4   What is the connection in the case with voodoo dolls?

5   Explain whether the theory described in the case applies to objects like Jackie Kennedy's tape measure and Bernie Madoff's footstool.

## Case 4.3 Trump, Brexit and post-truth politics

Politicians have never been known to place great importance on the truth. The nature of their trade is to lie, evade unwelcome questions or to be 'economical with the truth' as the delightful euphemism goes. So what is different about post-truth politics compared with earlier times?

The term 'post-truth politics' (PTP) was originally coined by David Roberts (2010) in a blog relating to environmental issues as 'a political culture in which politics (public opinion and media narratives) have become almost entirely disconnected from policy (the substance of legislation)'. The defining feature of PTP is that exponents repeat their claims even when they are found to be untrue by the media or independent experts.

Although the term 'post-truth politics' is a relatively new one, it can be claimed that the phenomenon it describes has a long history. It has been traced back to pamphleteering in the seventeenth century, where pamphlets written in exaggerated and emotional terms went into widespread circulation espousing certain political ideas, and often slandering opponents. It was also commonplace in the first half of the twentieth century, when extreme political movements like Nazism were popular. However, in the second half of the twentieth century political discourse was generally toned down in democratic countries, with certain exceptions like the McCarthy 'witch-hunt' in the USA in the 1950s. When political leaders made claims they were usually careful to be able to back them up with facts or statistics when challenged. This 'backing up' may have involved distortions of the facts and cherry-picking, but there was usually a general expectation among the voting public that the factual statements made by politicians, media and experts were at least worthy of consideration, even if their arguments based on these facts were ultimately rejected.

It is claimed that the crucial difference with PTP is that facts are now ignored. 'Facts are negative. Facts are pessimistic. Facts are unpatriotic,' states a sketch in the British *Daily Telegraph* newspaper (Deacon, 2016). Instead of an emphasis on facts PTP plays on the emotions. The sketch also notes how Arron Banks, unofficial founder of the Leave.EU campaign, summarized the recipe for the campaign's success: 'Facts don't work [...]

You've got to connect with people emotionally. It's the Trump success.' It also appears that it was the Cameron failure. Ironically, having established a Behavioural Insights Team to advise his government on behavioral issues, British Prime Minister David Cameron did not take on board some important behavioral factors in the Brexit referendum. He relied on voters being rational and being able to judge their own best interests if they were given the relevant factual information. He underestimated the emotional factor, and that many voters felt a large amount of resentment as far as the European Union (EU) was concerned, related to the size of financial contributions and in particular to immigration and loss of sovereignty ('being told what to do'). The Leave campaign played on these factors, and also gave a large amount of publicity to a particular 'fact', alleging that the UK was spending £350 million per week on remaining in the EU, and that this money could be spent instead on the NHS. The salience of this 'fact' (it was visible on posters and the sides of buses everywhere) did seem to have an impact on voters, in particular the mention of the alternative, since the NHS is often regarded with an almost sacred reverence in the UK. Challenges given to the £350 million figure, showing that it was at best a distorted and misleading statistic, seem to have had little effect on voters.

Although there have been many examples of PTP in recent years, the Trump phenomenon stands out, not just in terms of the frequency of false claims, but the brazenness with which they are made. Thus in 2016 we have heard that not only is Obama the founder of IS, but also he is not an American; Hillary Clinton is also responsible for IS, has had many people murdered and wants to tax small firms out of business; US veterans are often treated worse than immigrants; Mexicans are bringing drugs, crime and rapists into the USA; crime is reaching record levels in US cities; and youth unemployment is 'through the roof'.

The big question at this point concerns the causes of the perceived changes relating to PTP. Some publications have claimed that there are two main factors here: distrust in institutions and changes in the media (Economist, 2016b; Drezner, 2016). The Brexit vote certainly defied the opinions of institutions like the IMF, the OECD, the EU and the Bank of England, all of which predicted serious economic consequences for the UK. Michael Gove, a prominent leader of the Leave camp, was famously quoted as saying that the people in the country 'have had enough of experts'. However, taking a reductionist approach, one has to ask why this distrust of institutions and experts has arisen. The immediate response to this involves resentment. The resentment is not specifically aimed at the institutions and experts necessarily, but many people in both the USA and UK feel that their lot in life has deteriorated in recent years, as their living standards have declined, certainly relative to others who have prospered. Increased immigration is often blamed for this. However, the increased inequalities that have undoubtedly occurred over the last 20 years or so are really due to two main phenomena: increased globalization and improvements in technology. Increased globalization has resulted in a greater degree of competitiveness between both countries and individuals on a worldwide basis, so that unskilled workers in the USA have to compete for jobs with unskilled workers in developing countries, thus depressing their wages. Improvements in technology have left many of these unskilled workers behind, so that skills which they do have are no longer in demand, while workers who have skills based on new technology, in particular IT, are able to command high incomes.

Changes in the media have also been claimed to have led to PTP, but they are also an underlying factor behind the distrust discussed above. The amount of information available to people on a 24/7 basis has increased exponentially in recent years mainly due to increasing access to the internet. Faced with this barrage of information people tend to raise their filters, and the result is a phenomenon known as 'homophilous sorting'. This means that people only view the information that appeals to them, typically blogs and talk shows, and automatically become divided into like-minded groups who may have little in common (Sunstein, 2002; Farrell, 2012). Although there are many fact-checking sites available, people tend not to use them because there is such a plethora of information, and also the sorting process causes people to distrust information from unfamiliar sources, which may become accused of bias. This distrust relates both to national and supranational political and economic institutions and to major media like Fox News. Of course some of the media have behaved in ways which encourage the bias accusation.

This trend is exacerbated by the social media, as the communication or transaction costs of using like-minded groups to share information become negligible. The result is the decentralization of the communications process, which ceases to be hierarchical and becomes splintered into separate streams catering to partisan factions who share information with each other within groups. This can have advantages, for example by helping to topple dictators in the Arab Spring, but it also causes, or at least exacerbates, a dangerous polarization. Another phenomenon which reinforces this relates to search technology. Algorithms aid people to find those sites they are likely to prefer based on their past click history, and this causes a 'filter bubble' where people become separated from information that disagrees with their views, and isolates them in their particular ideological group. Twitter retweets and hashtags can further aid this process. Sunstein (2002) suggests that these various factors result in increasing polarization, as like-minded groups only share information between themselves, thus reinforcing their original beliefs. This can lead to an increasing prevalence of conspiracy theories, for example about 9/11, the CIA masterminding a recent attempted coup in Turkey and evolution being a scientific hoax.

In spite of all the challenges, the disbelief of opponents in both the Democrat and the Republican camp, a frequently chaotic and unorthodox campaign, various damaging personal revelations, and a gaffing, stumbling performance in the presidential debates, Trump ultimately stormed to victory in the election. Ironically, he gained the support of various groups who should have been alienated by his policies, for example unionized workers and many minorities. Trump also had a winning conspiracy theory in his presidential campaign: the election is likely to be rigged. If he had lost the election, he would have said: 'I told you so.'

However, for no-Trumpers there is also some irony in the final revelation of his medical records in September 2016: according to his doctor he is in 'impeccable' health and has no history of heart problems, yet he is taking a statin medication. A considerable body of evidence, for example the IDEAL, EXCEL, PROSPER and ALLHAT studies, suggests that statins have no effect on improving mortality for men without a heart disease history, while incurring the possibility of various undesirable side-effects including muscle pain and weakness, kidney and liver problems, increased risk of diabetes and cognitive impairment. Maybe this time Trump is the victim of a conspiracy, originated by post-truth medicine.

## Questions

1  Explain why message repetition is important in post-truth politics.
2  What factors in behavioral economics underlie Trump's political success?
3  'David Cameron paid the price for his overconfidence in the Brexit referendum'. Discuss.
4  Explain the role of cognitive dissonance in post-truth politics.

# CHAPTER 5

## Decision-making under Risk and Uncertainty

What do most people see as the most important characteristic of the credit crunch of 2008? Interest rates were at a historical low, but banks were not willing to lend. In particular, not so obvious to the general public, banks were not even willing to lend to each other. The Federal Reserve reduced their target federal funds rate (the rate at which banks lend to each other) to 0–0.5%, but still the interbank market for three-month loans virtually dried up, and when banks did lend to each other, actual rates were much higher than the Fed's target rate. Furthermore, banks were no longer willing to trade financial instruments, particularly the notorious collateralized debt obligations (CDOs), a complex form of derivative. This put an enormous strain on the whole financial system. Liquidity problems, meaning shortage of cash, turned into solvency problems, as the value of assets on banks' balance sheets plummeted, in many cases to zero. Many banks, including the largest mega-banks, tottered on the brink of bankruptcy. Of the five big investment banks in the USA, Bear Stearns and Merrill Lynch were taken over by JP Morgan Chase and Bank of America respectively, Lehmans famously went bust, and Morgan Stanley and Goldman Sachs both changed their corporate charters. The two largest commercial banks, Citigroup and Bank of America, both faced huge multibillion dollar losses.

The causes of the financial crisis and the associated credit crunch are highly complex, and indeed controversial, but undoubtedly one factor played a big part: ambiguity aversion. People, and institutions, do not like situations where outcomes are uncertain and they cannot estimate probabilities of these outcomes. The state of the financial system and credit crunch was such an unprecedented event in recent times that people had no past history on which to draw in order to estimate Bayesian probabilities. Their reaction was to refuse to lend to borrowers whose ability to repay was uncertain, and refuse to buy securities whose value was uncertain.

## 5.1 Background

*Expected utility theory*

The neoclassical model (NM) of decision-making under risk is expected utility theory (EUT). This has been widely accepted and applied as both a descriptive model of economic behavior and as a normative model of rational choice; this means that it assumes that rational people would want to obey the axioms of the theory, and that they do actually obey them in general. The basic EUT model was described in mathematical terms in expression 1.1 in the first chapter. In disaggregated form it is repeated here:

$$\textbf{(1)} \quad \max_{x_i^t \in Xi} \quad \textbf{(2)} \quad \sum_{t=0}^{\infty} \delta^t \quad \textbf{(3)} \quad \sum_{s_t \in S_t} p(s_t) \quad \textbf{(4)} \quad U(x_i^t \mid s_t).$$

We are now concerned with examining (1), (3), and (4), omitting a discussion of (2) until Chapter 7.

The concept of utility was discussed in Chapter 3, and we have seen that we can think of it in terms of subjective value. In this case we are using the term in a psychological sense, although we have also seen that it can be used in a more technical neurological sense. Decision-making under risk can be considered as a process of choosing between different **prospects** or gambles. A prospect consists of a number of possible outcomes along with their associated probabilities. Thus any theory of decision-making under risk will take into account both the consequences of choices and their associated probabilities. In keeping with the rest of this text, situations will often be explained in words or in terms of examples first, before using mathematical notation, even though the latter is often both more concise and more precise, in terms of avoiding ambiguity. As explained in the preface, this sequence should help the reader to relate abstract terms to real concepts more easily. This is particularly important in the initial stages of analysis, until the reader becomes familiar with mathematical notation. A simple example of a situation involving decision-making under risk is given below, where an individual is required to choose between two alternative courses of action, resulting in two prospects:

**Prospect A:**     50% chance to win 100     50% chance to win nothing
**Prospect B:**     Certainty of winning 45

It will be convenient to denote prospects with bold case letters. In general terms a prospect can be described mathematically as follows:

$q = (x_1, p_1; \ldots; x_n, p_n)$   where $x_i$ represents outcomes and $p_i$ represents associated probabilities. Riskless prospects yielding a certain outcome $x$ are denoted by $(x)$. Thus prospect A above can be expressed: $q = (100, 0.5; 0, 0.5)$, but for simplicity null outcomes can be omitted, thus reducing prospect A to $(100, 0.5)$. Prospect B can be expressed: $r = (45)$.

The axioms underlying EUT were originally developed by von Neumann and Morgenstern (1947), and are related to the axioms of preference described in Chapter 3:

**1**   *Completeness*

This requires that for all $q, r$:

Either $q \geq r$ or $r \geq q$ or both.

**2**   *Transitivity*

If we take any three prospects, $q, r, s$:

if $q \geq r$ and $r \geq s$, then $q \geq s$

Sometimes the two above axioms are combined together and referred to as the **ordering** axiom.

**3**   *Continuity*

This principle guarantees that preferences can be represented by some function that attaches a real value to every prospect. In formal terms this can be expressed as follows:

For all prospects, $q, r, s$ where $q \geq r$ and $r \geq s$, there exists some probability $p$ such that there is indifference between the middle-ranked prospect $r$ and the prospect $(q, p; s, 1-p)$. The latter is referred to as a **compound prospect**, since its component outcomes $q$ and $s$ are themselves prospects. We will see that such prospects are important in experimental studies, since they often lead to violations of EUT.

The majority of economists have assumed that the existence of some preference function involving the above axioms is the starting point for constructing any satisfactory model of decision-making under risk. Essentially the assumption amounts to consumers having well-defined preferences, while imposing minimal restrictions on the precise form of those preferences.

A further axiom of EUT is the independence axiom; this imposes quite strong restrictions on the precise form of preferences. It is described below, and examples will be given in the following subsection related to anomalies in EUT.

**4**   *Independence*

This axiom relates to the cancellation principle described in Chapter 3, that any state of the world that results in the same outcome regardless of one's choice can be cancelled or ignored. Kahneman and Tversky refer to this axiom as the **substitution axiom** in their 1979 paper. Let us illustrate the independence axiom with a simple numerical example first, before giving the formal representation. If prospect $q$ = ($3,000) is preferred to prospect $r$ = ($4,000, 0.8), then prospect $q'$ = ($3,000, 0.25) is preferred to prospect $r'$ = ($4,000, 0.2). The reader should note that the last two prospects have 25% of the probabilities of the first two prospects. The independence axiom can be generalized in the following formal representation:

For all prospects, $q, r, s$:

$$\text{if } q \geq r \text{ then } (q, p; s, 1-p) \geq (r, p; s, 1-p), \text{ for all } p. \tag{5.1}$$

It can be seen that there is a common component of the compound prospects, $(s, 1-p)$; according to the cancellation principle this component can be ignored in the comparison. In the example above $s = 0$ and $p = .25$.

EUT provides a simple model for combining probabilities and consequences into a single measure of value that has various appealing qualities. One particularly important property is commonly referred to as the **monotonicity** principle. Although we have discussed monotonicity earlier, in the context of indifference curves, in EUT the term implies that objective improvements to a prospect, meaning increasing some of its payoffs while holding others constant, should make it at least as attractive if not more so than before. It is thus related to the principle of dominance described in the last chapter, but in this situation we say that the dominance is **stochastic** since we are comparing not just outcomes but also probabilities. Again an example will aid understanding before giving a formal representation; this one comes from Tversky and Kahneman (1986):

Consider the following pair of lotteries, described by the percentage of marbles of different colors in each box and the amount of money you win or lose depending on the color of a randomly drawn marble. Which lottery do you prefer?

**Option A**

| 90% white | 6% red   | 1% green  | 1% blue    | 2% yellow  |
|-----------|----------|-----------|------------|------------|
| $0        | win $45  | win $30   | lose $15   | lose $15   |

**Option B**

| 90% white | 6% red   | 1% green  | 1% blue    | 2% yellow  |
|-----------|----------|-----------|------------|------------|
| *$0*      | *win $45*| *win $45* | *lose $10* | *lose $15* |

Source: Tversky A., Kahneman D. (1989). Rational Choice and the Framing of Decisions, p.102. In: Karpak B., Zionts S. (eds) Multiple Criteria Decision Making and Risk Analysis Using Microcomputers. NATO ASI Series (Series F: Computer and Systems Sciences) vol. 56. Springer, Berlin, Heidelberg.

The reader can verify that option B will be preferred to option A because it **stochastically dominates** it. For white, red and yellow marbles the situation is the same, but for both green and blue marbles the outcomes are more favorable, with the probabilities remaining the same.

It has been generally held by economists that the monotonicity principle is fundamental to any satisfactory theory of consumer preference, both descriptive and normative. Therefore its formal representation as an axiom is necessary:

**5**   *Monotonicity*

Let $x_1, x_2, .., x_n$ be outcomes ordered from worst $(x_1)$ to best $(x_n)$. A prospect $q = (p_{q1}, ... p_{qn})$ stochastically dominates another prospect $r = (p_{r1}, ... p_{rn})$ if for all $i = 1, ..., n$:

$$\sum_{j=i}^{n} p_{qj} \geq \sum_{j=i}^{n} p_{rj} \tag{5.2}$$

with a strict inequality for at least one *i*.

EUT also is based on the **Expectation principle**, that the overall utility of a prospect is the expected utility of its outcomes. In mathematical notation:

$$U(x_1, p_{1;} \ldots; x_n, p_n) = p_1 u(x_1) + \ldots + p_n u(x_n)$$

Based on the five axioms above, and the expectation principle, EUT states that consumers will behave in such a way that they will maximize the following preference function:

$$V(q) = \Sigma \, p_i \cdot u(x_i) \tag{5.3}$$

Where *q* is any prospect, and *u*(.) is a utility function defined on the set of consequences $(x_1, x_2, \ldots x_n)$. We have seen a simple example of this in Chapter 1, where a student is deciding whether to drink coffee or beer before attending a lecture. However, in that example we ignored two factors that now need to be discussed. These concerned asset integration (since we only considered gains) and the nature of the utility function (we measured all gains in terms of utility rather than money, so no conversion was necessary). Thus, in addition to the five axioms above, two further assumptions are commonly made in EUT:

(i) **Asset integration**: a prospect is acceptable if and only if the utility resulting from integrating the prospect with one's assets exceeds the utility of those assets alone. Thus it is final states that matter, not gains or losses. In mathematical notation:

$(x_1, p_{1;} \ldots; x_n, p_n)$ is acceptable at asset position *w iff*
$U(w + x_1, p_{1;} \ldots; w + x_n, p_n) > u(w)$

(ii) **Risk-aversion**: a person is said to be risk averse if he prefers the certain prospect (*x*) to any risky prospect with expected value *x*. In EUT risk-aversion is caused by the concavity of the utility function. This characteristic is in turn caused by the law of diminishing marginal utility. Concavity and risk-aversion are best explained by means of a graphical example. A graph of the EUT utility function is shown in Figure 5.1.

If a person starts at any point of wealth $x_1$ then any gain in wealth will produce a relatively small gain in utility $(u_2 - u_1)$ compared with the loss of utility $(u_1 - u_3)$ associated with an

**Figure 5.1**   Expected utility theory utility function

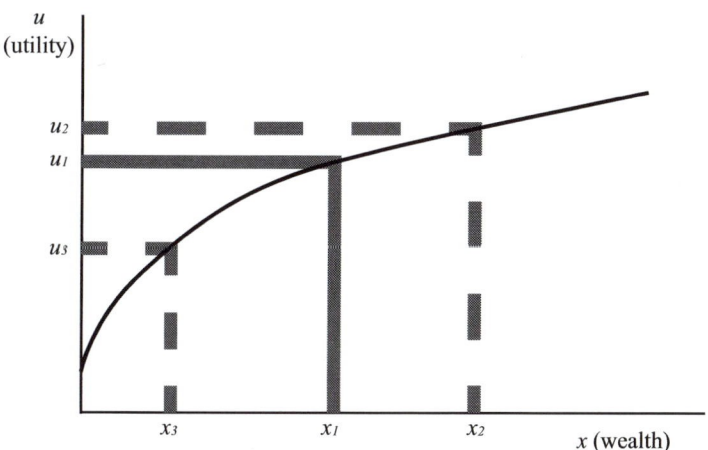

equal loss in wealth. Nobody would ever want to make a fair bet, meaning one where the expected value of the prospect is zero, for example betting on the toss of a coin.

It can be seen in Figure 5.1 that this utility function is monotonically increasing, meaning that $u$ is increasing throughout the range of $x$; in mathematical terms: $du/dx$ or $u' > 0$. However, the slope of the utility function decreases, meaning that the second derivative of $u$ with respect to $x$ is negative. In mathematical notation: $u'' < 0$. The most common type of mathematical function that conforms to these characteristics of risk-aversion is a power function of the form $u = x^b$, where $b < 1$. With this type of function risk-seeking occurs if $b > 1$, and the utility function is convex. When $b = 1$, the power function becomes a linear function, implying risk neutrality.

### Evolutionary foundation

What can we say about EUT in terms of its foundations in evolutionary biology? At first sight it might seem that there was a sound evolutionary foundation for EUT. If individuals have to choose among a number of prospects related to expected offspring, evolution through natural selection would favor the choice of the prospect that leads to the highest expected offspring, *assuming that the economic and biological risk is independent across all individuals*. If, as discussed in the previous chapter, expected offspring translates into expected utility, then evolutionary theory would support EUT.

However, as Robson (2002) argues, this foundation is heavily dependent on the underlying assumption that all risks are independent, and this assumption is not reasonable in an evolutionary setting. In this setting there is an important difference between **idiosyncratic risk** and **aggregate risk**. Idiosyncratic risk refers to situations where decisions have purely selfish effects, such as the risk of heart disease or driving a car. Aggregate risk refers to situations where outcomes are shared by others, like the risk of catching 'mad cow' disease or being involved in a plane crash. Other things being equal, gambles involving idiosyncratic risk are preferable from an evolutionary standpoint to gambles involving aggregate risk. This may explain why people tend to be averse to the aggregate risk, for example regarding air travel as more dangerous than travel by car.

There is a very important implication of this evolutionary distinction between idiosyncratic risk and aggregate risk that has already been mentioned in Chapter 3 and will be further explored in this chapter: what matters biologically is not *absolute* success in producing offspring, but success *relative* to other types (Robson, 2002). Translated into economic terms, this means that utility is reference-dependent. Thus by relaxing the assumption relating to all risks being independent, we can understand why evolutionary theory can explain anomalies in EUT. We now need to examine the nature of these anomalies in more detail.

### Anomalies in expected utility theory

A number of anomalies have been observed relating to the axioms and assumptions of EUT, arising both from laboratory experiments and from field data. Some of these observations predate Kahneman and Tversky's classic paper on prospect theory (PT) of 1979, some relate specifically to the paper, and others have come to light since then. At this point we will move on to discuss the last category of observations first; this will give the reader a general feel for the problems of EUT, since all the observations come from field data. We will then examine two examples predating PT; both date back to Allais (1953), although both are also discussed in the 1979 PT paper. Finally, the specific results from Kahneman and Tversky (KT) and other studies are discussed in more detail in later sections, examining the components of PT and adopting a more rigorous analysis.

Many of these anomalies have been described, categorized and analyzed by Camerer (2000). A useful summary is given in Table 5.1, which is adapted from Camerer. This table names and describes the phenomena involved, classifies the anomalies according to domain, and indicates which elements of PT are relevant in terms of explaining the anomalies. These

**Table 5.1**  Phenomena inconsistent with expected utility theory

| Phenomenon | Domain | Description | Elements in PT |
|---|---|---|---|
| **Equity premium** | Stock market | Stock returns are too high relative to bond returns | Loss-aversion |
| **Disposition effect** | Stock market | Hold losing stocks too long, sell winners too early | Loss-aversion Reference points |
| **Downward-sloping labor supply** | Labor economics | New York City cab drivers quit around daily income target | Loss-aversion |
| **Asymmetric price elasticities** | Consumer goods | Purchases more sensitive to price increases than to price cuts | Loss-aversion |
| **Insensitivity to bad income news** | Macroeconomics | Consumers do not cut consumption after bad income news | Loss-aversion reference points |
| **Status quo bias Default bias** | Consumer choice | Consumers do not switch health plans; choose default insurance | Loss-aversion |
| **Favorite-long-shot bias** | Horserace betting | Favorites are underbet, long shots are overbet | Decision-weighting (overweighting low probabilities) |
| **End-of-the-day effect** | Horserace betting | Shift to long shots at the end of the day | Reference points Diminishing marginal sensitivity |
| **Buying phone wire insurance** | Insurance | Consumers buy overpriced insurance | Decision-weighting (overweighting low probabilities) |
| **Demand for Lotto** | Lottery betting | More tickets sold as top prize rises | Decision-weighting (overweighting low probabilities) |

*Source: Camerer, C.F. (2000). Copyright © Cambridge University Press. Prospect theory in the wild: Evidence from the field. In D. Kahneman and A. Tversky (Eds), Choices, Values, and Frames, Table 16.1, p. 289.*

anomalies are discussed in more detail in later sections of the chapter, and also in the following chapter on mental accounting, after the elements of PT have been explained.

It should be noted that the above table does not imply that all anomalies in EUT can be explained in terms of PT. Ariely (2013) gives a good example in his book *The (Honest) Truth about Dishonesty* which he refers to as the Simple Model of Rational Crime, or SMORC. According to EUT there are only three factors which affect our propensity to commit a crime: (1) the perceived benefit, (2) the perceived risk of being caught, and (3) the cost of being caught. In practice Ariely suggests that there are emotional or visceral factors that are very important, which affect our perceived risk of being caught and the cost we may incur in terms of guilt or self-esteem, regardless of whether we are caught or not. Furthermore, according to Ariely, the guilt feeling from cheating to obtain a money reward depends on how far removed the monetary benefit is from the activity required to obtain it. The more steps involved in the separation, the less guilt is felt regarding the crime and the greater the tendency to cheat. Thus in the recent LIBOR scandal, bankers may manipulate the benchmark interest rate, which in turn affects the price on their trades, which then increases their profit, which may finally affect their bonus. Such a long chain of connection may mean that this kind of activity is not really regarded as cheating at all. Factors like guilt and separation of reward are discussed in more detail in Chapter 10 in the context of social preferences.

Let us now examine a more detailed example of an anomaly in EUT, this time from experimental data. This is sometimes referred to as the **Allais paradox**, and dates back to 1953. This is illustrated in the payoff matrix in Table 5.2. Each row represents an act involving a prospect, while each column represents a 'state of the world', with the associated probabilities at the top of each column. The values in the matrix represent payoffs to each act (in $ for example) given a certain state of the world. Subjects are first presented with a choice between options A and B. The independence axiom implies that since these two acts have the same consequence (a payoff of $500) in the third state of the world, the third state should be irrelevant to that choice. The same argument applies when subjects are then presented with a choice between options C and D (the common consequence being a payoff of 0). It should now be seen that, when the third state of the world is ignored, the choice between A and B is identical to the choice between C and D, that is a choice between (500, 0.11) and (2,500, 0.1). Therefore, according to the independence axiom, if A is preferred to B, C should be preferred to D, and vice versa. However, there is evidence from numerous studies that many people faced with similar pairs of choices choose A over B, but D over C, violating the independence axiom. This phenomenon is an example of what is called the **common consequence effect**.

**Table 5.2**  The Allais paradox

|          | Option | 0.1   | 0.01 | 0.89 |
|----------|--------|-------|------|------|
| Choice 1 | A      | 500   | 500  | 500  |
|          | B      | 2,500 | 0    | 500  |
| Choice 2 | C      | 500   | 500  | 0    |
|          | D      | 2,500 | 0    | 0    |

Another anomaly in EUT is described in the KT paper, again relating to the independence or substitution axiom. This situation is shown in the payoff matrix in Table 5.3. It can be seen that the choices between A and B and between C and D involve the same payoffs, and also the same relative probabilities, with the probability of the lower payoff being twice the probability of the higher payoff. Once again the independence axiom implies that if A is preferred to B then C should be preferred to D, and vice versa. The KT paper found a very contrasting result, with only 14% of their subjects preferring A to B, but 73% preferring C to D. This is an example of a phenomenon called the **common ratio effect**, since the ratio of the probabilities in each option is the same in both choices.

**Table 5.3**  Same payoffs but different probabilities of winning

|          |   |                  |
|----------|---|------------------|
| Choice 1 | A | (6,000, 0.45)    |
|          | B | (3,000, 0.90)    |
| Choice 2 | C | (6,000, 0.001)   |
|          | D | (3,000, 0.002)   |

These preliminary examples should give the reader a flavor of the anomalies related to EUT. Furthermore, the observed departures from the theory were **systematic**, meaning that they were in a predictable direction, rather than being random errors. Now we can turn our attention to various attempts that have been made since the late 1970s to account for these violations of EUT in terms of proposing a more satisfactory theory.

It is useful here to use the broad classification proposed by Starmer (2000), who distinguishes between **conventional** and **non-conventional** theories. The former accepted the first three axioms of completeness, transitivity and continuity, but were prepared to allow violations of the independence axiom, since these violations had been widely observed since the work of Allais. However, these conventional theories proposed that preferences should still be '**well-behaved**'; in particular this characteristic involves maintaining monotonicity or dominance, and also the principle of invariance described in Chapter 3. Non-conventional theories do not insist on preferences being well-behaved in these ways. We will consider the conventional theories first, since these represent both the earlier departure and the least modification of EUT.

## 5.2  Conventional approaches to modifying expected utility theory

There are a large number of different theories that have been proposed in this category, and it is not intended to review all of them here. Instead the leading contenders are described in terms of their main features, advantages and disadvantages. It is not possible to conduct such a review on an entirely chronological basis, since many theories have been developed over some period of time by several writers. Instead, theories are presented largely in the order that corresponds to the extent of their departure from EUT, with those theories that depart least being presented first.

### Weighted utility theory

One of the earliest extensions of EUT was termed weighted utility theory (Chew and MacCrimmon, 1979). The preference function is represented as:

$$V(q) = [\Sigma\, p_i \cdot g(x_i) \cdot u(x_i)] / [\Sigma\, p_i \cdot g(x_i)] \tag{5.4}$$

Where $u(.)$ and $g(.)$ are two different functions assigning non-zero weights to all outcomes. This model incorporates EUT as a special case when the weights assigned by $g(.)$ are identical for every outcome. The model has been axiomatized by various economists, including Chew and MacCrimmon (1979), Chew (1983), and Fishburn (1983). These all involve a weaker form of the independence axiom, for example:

if $q > r$ then for each $p_q$ there exists a corresponding $p_r$ such that
$(q, p_q; s, 1 - p_q) > (r, p_r; s, 1 - p_r)$, for all $s$.

A similar model, which generalized this approach, was proposed by Machina (1982). In behavioral terms these theories proposed that people became more risk averse as the prospects they face improve. The main advantage of such theories was that they explained the violations of independence in the common consequence and common ratio cases, but they lacked intuitive appeal because there was no psychological foundation. They were empirically rather than theoretically grounded.

### Disappointment theory

Later theories had a better psychological foundation. An example is the disappointment theory developed by Bell (1985) and Loomes and Sugden (1986). In the latter version the preference function is represented as follows:

$$V(q) = \Sigma\, p_i \cdot [u(x_i) + D(u(x_i) - \underline{U})] \tag{5.5}$$

where $u(x_i)$ refers to a measure of 'basic' utility, meaning the utility of $x_i$ considered in isolation from the other outcomes of $q$, and $\underline{U}$ is a measure of the prior expectation of the utility of the prospect. It is assumed in the model that if the outcome of a prospect is worse than expected, meaning if $u(x_i) < \underline{U}$, a sense of disappointment or regret will be experienced. On the other hand, if an outcome is better than expected, there will be a sense of elation. When $D(.) = 0$, the model reduces to EUT. However, the extension to the EUT model is intended to capture the psychological intuition that people are disappointment averse; this entails the disappointment function $D(.)$ being concave in the negative region and convex in the positive region. Disappointment theory is closely related to regret theory; in this case the decision-maker is trying to minimize a regret function, which represents the difference between the outcome yielded by a given choice and the best outcome that could have been achieved in that state of nature.

### Betweenness models

Theories of this type have been proposed by Gul (1991) and Neilson (1992). Again they involve a weakened form of independence. Betweenness can be described as follows:

if $q > r$ then $q > (q, p; r, 1 - p) > r$ for all $p < 1$.

In behavioral terms this implies that any probability mixture of two lotteries will be ranked between them in terms of preference and, given continuity, an individual will be indifferent to randomization among equally valued prospects.

### Non-betweenness models

Other models do not impose restrictions as strong as betweenness. **Quadratic utility theory**, proposed by Chew, Epstein and Segal (1991) is based on a weakened form of betweenness called **mixture symmetry**. This can be represented as follows:

If $q \sim r$ then $(q, p; r, 1 - p) \sim (q, 1 - p; r, p)$

The lottery-dependent utility model of Becker and Sarin (1987) has even weaker restrictions, assuming nothing regarding independence (although still assuming completeness, transitivity, continuity and monotonicity).

### Decision-weighting theories

All the theories described so far assign *subjective* weights, or utilities, to outcomes. The value of any prospect is then determined by a function that combines these subjective weights with *objective* probabilities. Decision-weighting theories involve the use of probability transformation functions which convert objective probabilities into subjective decision weights. Betweenness does not generally hold in these cases.

These theories are empirically grounded in that there is much evidence that people tend to systematically underestimate probability in some situations and overestimate in others. For example, Pidgeon and colleagues (1992) found that people underestimate the probability of dying from common causes, like heart disease and cancer, and overestimate the probability of dying from rare causes, like in an airline accident. This evidence is reviewed in more detail in the next section on PT. The effects of this phenomenon can be captured by incorporating decision weights in the preference function. An early version of this kind of model was proposed by Edwards (1954, 1955, 1961, 1962), being called a **subjectively weighted utility (SWU)** model. This model used subjective probabilities but objective outcomes, meaning that outcomes were entered into the model in a 'raw' form with $u(x_i) = x_i$. The resulting preference function is given by:

$$V(q) = \Sigma\, w_i.x_i \tag{5.6}$$

A similar model, better known as the **subjective expected value** (SEU) model, was axiomatized by Savage in 1954. This model proposed that people used Bayesian methods in estimating subjective probabilities.

A later version, developed by Handa (1977), employed a probability weighting function $\pi(p_i)$ which transforms the individual probabilities of outcomes into weights. $\pi(.)$ is assumed to be increasing with $\pi(0) = 0$ and $\pi(1) = 1$. Variations of this model were proposed that allowed non-linear transformations of both probabilities and outcomes; both probabilities and outcomes are measured subjectively. Starmer (2000) refers to such forms as **simple decision-weighted utility** models, and they are also sometimes referred to as '**stripped prospect theory**', since they essentially use the second stage of the PT process, but omit the editing rules of the first stage (explained in the next section).

The corresponding preference function is shown below:

$$V(q) = \Sigma \, \pi(p_i) . u(x_i) \tag{5.7}$$

Since non-linear transformations of probabilities did not satisfy the monotonicity principle as far as preferences were concerned these models were generally not taken seriously by most economists. For example, Machina (1983) argued that any such theory will be: 'in the author's view at least, unacceptable as a descriptive or analytical model of behavior' (p. 97).

## Rank-dependent expected utility theory

Rank-dependent utility (RDU) models, were first developed by Quiggin (1982, 1993) in response to the problem described above. They proposed decision-weighting with more sophisticated probability transformations designed to ensure monotonicity in the preference function. In this type of model the weight attached to outcomes depends not only on the true probability of the outcome but also on its ranking relative to the other outcomes of the prospect. It is more complex to describe mathematically than previous models, but the starting point is to rank the outcomes $x_1, x_2..,x_n$ from worst $(x_1)$ to best $(x_n)$. The model then proposes the preference function:

$$V(q) = \Sigma \, w_i . u(x_i) \tag{5.8}$$

where the weights are given by the weighting function:

$$w_i = \pi(p_i + ... + p_n) - \pi(p_{i+1} + ... + p_n)$$

The interpretation of this function is that $\pi(p_i + ... + p_n)$ is a subjective weight attached to the probability of getting an outcome of $x_i$ *or better*, while $\pi(p_{i+1} + ... + p_n)$ is a weight attached to the probability of getting an outcome of *better than* $x_i$. In this theory therefore $\pi(.)$ is a transformation on **cumulative probabilities**. A variation on this model is the rank-and-sign dependent utility (RSDU) model of Luce and Fishburn (1991, 1995), which involves an asymmetric utility function to take account of loss-aversion.

Rank-dependent models have become popular among economists because they have both empirical and theoretical appeal. Empirically they take into account the psychological tendency to overestimate and underestimate probabilities related to particularly good or bad outcomes. Theoretically the appeal has been the preservation of monotonicity.

The form of $\pi(.)$ is critical in determining the predictions of the model. For example, convexity of $\pi(.)$ implies a pessimistic outlook, in that it attaches relatively high weights to lower ranking outcomes compared with higher ranking ones. A favorite form, employed by Quiggin (1982), involves a more complex inverted S-shape, illustrated in Figure 5.2.

This function has $\pi(p) = p$ when $p = p^*$; it is concave below $p^*$ and convex above it. These forms of weighting function can be obtained using a variety of mathematical forms,

**Figure 5.2** Rank-dependent probability weighting function with inverted S-shape

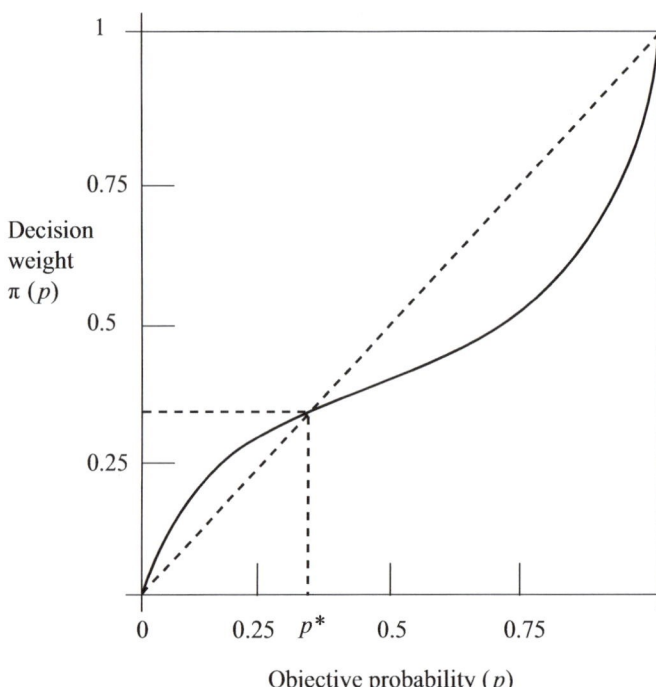

some using one parameter and some using two. It goes beyond the scope of this book to discuss these in detail, but the single-parameter model of Tversky and Kahneman (1992) is described in the next section.

As with other conventional extensions of EUT, rank-dependent EUT relies on a weakened form of the independence axiom called **co-monotonic independence**. This imposes the restriction that preferences between prospects will be unaffected by substitution of common consequences so long as these substitutions do not affect the rank order of the outcomes in either prospect. Other variations of the rank-dependent model have proposed similar axioms, like **ordinal independence** (Green and Jullien, 1988).

## Conclusions

These more complex extensions to EUT have without doubt explained some of the observed violations, in particular those relating to independence. Over the last 50 years a very large body of studies has built up evidence that can discriminate between the theories described above in terms of their predictive ability. In particular, studies by Conlisk (1989), Camerer (1992), Harless (1992), Gigliotti and Sopher (1993) and Wu and Gonzalez (1996) tend to support the decision-weighting models in favor of other conventional models. Furthermore, those models involving an inverted S-shaped weighting function tend to have better empirical fit than those using other functional forms of the weighting function (Lattimore, Baker and Witte, 1992; Tversky and Kahneman, 1992; Camerer and Ho, 1994; Abdellaoui, 2000; Gonzalez and Wu, 1999). These more sophisticated models show significant predictive improvement over EUT.

However, even these models are still unable to explain widely observed violations of monotonicity, as well as violations of transitivity and invariance. A well-known example is the **Ellsberg paradox**. The examples given earlier in Tables 5.2 and 5.3, relating to the Allais paradox, involve situations where objective probabilities are known, in other words risky situations. However, frequently people face situations where objective prob-abilities cannot be calculated; these are referred to as situations involving uncertainty or **ambiguity**. There is a well-known paradox here also, first investigated by Ellsberg (1961). Suppose that there are two urns, 1 and 2. Urn 2 contains 100 balls, 50 red and 50 blue. Urn 1 also contains 100 balls, again a mix of red and blue, but the subject does not know the proportion of each. Thus choosing from Urn 1 involves a situation of ambiguity, whereas choosing from Urn 2 involves risk. Subjects are asked to make two successive choices. Both choices consist of two gambles, each of which involves a possible payment of $100, depending on the color of the ball drawn at random from the relevant urn. These choices are illustrated in Table 5.4.

**Table 5.4**   The Ellsberg paradox

| Choice 1 | A1 – ball is drawn from Urn 1 | $100 if red, $0 if blue |
|---|---|---|
| | A2 – ball is drawn from Urn 2 | $100 if red, $0 if blue |
| Choice 2 | B1 – ball is drawn from Urn 1 | $100 if blue, $0 if red |
| | B2 – ball is drawn from Urn 2 | $100 if blue, $0 if red |

Ellsberg's experiments showed that A2 is generally preferred to A1, while B2 is pre-ferred to B1. These choices are not only inconsistent with EUT, but also with SEU. The choice of A2 implies a subjective probability that less than 50% of the balls in Urn 1 are red, while the choice of B2 implies the opposite, that more than 50% of the balls in Urn 1 are red.

The general conclusion to be drawn from the experiments is that people do not like situations where they are uncertain about the probability distributions of a gamble, that is, situations of ambiguity. This phenomenon of **ambiguity aversion** has been commonly found, not just in experiments, but also in the field, as demonstrated in the introduction to the chapter in relation to financial trading. Furthermore, there is neuroeconomic evi-dence that provides a basis for the phenomenon. A study by Hsu and colleagues (2005) involved asking subjects to make choices under conditions of both risk and uncertainty. Under conditions of uncertainty there is more activation of the ventromedial prefrontal cortex (VMPFC) and the amygdala (associated with a primitive fear response), while there is less activation of the nucleus accumbens (NAcc), which relates to expectation of reward. Thus it appears that people value uncertain outcomes less than when the out-comes are risky, as their brains are searching for missing information.

This finding of common occurrence in both experimental and field studies applies to all the violations mentioned here, and includes the various anomalies described by Camerer (2000), illustrated in Table 5.1. The nature of these violations is described in the next section, which is concerned with the exposition of PT; this is classified by Starmer (2000) as a non-conventional theory.

## 5.3   Prospect theory

The first question at this stage is: what constitutes the difference between a conven-tional and a non-conventional theory? All the theories described so far, including EUT, have essentially been models of preference maximization, assuming that agents behave *as if* optimizing some underlying preference function. As we have noted in the last two chapters, the form of the function makes no claim regarding underlying psychological mechanisms or processes. On the other hand, as we have also seen, behavioral models try to model the psychological processes that lead to choice, and Starmer (2000) refers to these as **procedural theories**. Prominent features of these models include the existence of **bounded rationality** and the consequent use of decision **heuristics**. Bounded rationality implies that the agent has both imperfect information in a complex and dynamic decision environment, and limited computational ability; the agent's objectives may also be imperfectly defined. Thus the concept of optimization becomes more complex, with constraints of time, computational resources, and often conflicting objectives. In such situations the use of heuristics becomes necessary; these are computational shortcuts that simplify decision-making procedures. Since the late 1970s a variety of these non-conventional theories have been developed, but without any doubt PT has been by far the most influential of these (see Klaes, 2015c). Thus this section concentrates on a detailed discussion of this particular theory. In the concluding section of the chapter some of the other procedural theories are discussed and compared.

PT was originally developed in the KT paper of 1979, and then extended in a later paper by the same authors in 1992, being renamed cumulative PT. We shall see, however, that most of the elements of the theory have important precedents, in particular the work of Markowitz (1952) and Allais (1953). PT models choice as a two-phase process: the first phase involves editing, while the second involves evaluation. The use of an editing phase is the most obvious distinguishing characteristic of PT from any of the theories discussed in the previous section. The second feature that distinguishes PT from these theories is that outcomes are measured as gains or losses relative to some reference point. These features, and the other features of PT are now discussed.

### Editing

This phase consists of a preliminary analysis of the offered prospects, which has the objective of yielding a simpler representation of these prospects, in turn facilitating the evaluation process. Certain heuristic rules and operations may be applied, not necessarily consciously, to organize, reformulate and narrow down the options to be considered in the next phase. These operations include coding, combination, segregation, cancellation, simplification and the detection of dominance.

1   **Coding** – Empirical evidence suggests that people normally perceive outcomes as gains or losses relative to some reference point, rather than as final states of wealth or welfare. This aspect is discussed in more detail in the next section under evaluation.

2   **Combination** – Prospects can sometimes be simplified by combining the probabilities associated with identical outcomes. For example, the prospect (100, 0.30; 100, 0.30) will be reduced to (100, 0.60) and evaluated as such. The operation of combining is also referred to as **coalescing**.

3   **Segregation** – Some prospects contain a riskless component that can be segregated from the risky component. For example, the prospect (100, 0.70; 150, 0.30) can be segregated into a sure gain of 100 and the risky prospect (50, 0.30). Likewise, the prospect $(-200, 0.8; -300, 0.2)$ can be segregated into a sure loss of 200 and the risky prospect $(-100, 0.2)$.

4   **Cancellation** – This aspect was described earlier in relation to the independence axiom. When different prospects share certain identical components these components may be discarded or ignored. For example, consider a two-stage game where there is a probability of .75 of ending the game without winning anything and a probability of .25 of moving onto the second stage. In the second stage there may be a choice between (4,000, 0.80) and (3,000). The player must make the choice at the start of the game, before the outcome of the first stage is known. In this case the evidence in the KT study suggests that there is an **isolation effect**, meaning that people ignore the first stage, whose outcomes are shared by both prospects, and consider the

choice as being between a riskless gain of 3,000 and the risky prospect (4,000, 0.80). The implications of this effect, in terms of inconsistency in decision-making, are considered later, in the section on decision-weighting.

5    **Simplification** – Prospects may be simplified by rounding either outcomes or probabilities. For example, the prospect (99, 0.51) is likely to be coded as an even chance of winning 100. In particular, outcomes that are extremely improbable are likely to be ignored, meaning that the probabilities are rounded down to 0. This part of the editing phase is often performed first, and the sequence of the editing operations is important, because it can affect the final list to be evaluated. As we shall see, the sequence and method of editing can depend on the structure of the problem.

6    **Detection of dominance** – Some prospects may dominate others, meaning that they may have elements in common, but other elements involve outcomes or probabilities that are always preferable. Consider the two prospects (200, 0.3; 99, 0.51) and (200, 0.4; 101, 0.49). Assuming that the second component of each prospect is first of all rounded to (100, 0.5), then the second prospect dominates the first, with the outcome of the first component being the same, but its probability being greater.

As has already been stated with regard to the isolation effect, there are various aspects of the editing process that can cause anomalies such as inconsistencies of preference, which will be discussed later. The KT editing heuristic has therefore been criticized on various grounds. For example, Quiggin (1982) has argued that the editing process is redundant if the preference function is appropriately specified. He has also argued that the final stage of detecting dominance, while it may induce monotonicity, has the side-effect that it admits violations of transitivity. Quiggin refers to this as an 'undesirable result'. Starmer (2005) argues that this comment, and other criticisms of PT, is motivated by 'a pre-commitment to preference theories which satisfy normatively appealing criteria such as transitivity and monotonicity' (p. 282). He further argues that such a pre-commitment is misplaced in the light of direct empirical evidence. This issue will be discussed further later when more examples have been examined.

## *Evaluation*

Once the editing phase is complete, the decision-maker must evaluate each of the edited prospects, and is assumed to choose the prospect with the highest value. According to PT, the overall value of an edited prospect, denoted $V$, is expressed in terms of two scales, $v$ and $\pi$. The first scale, $v$, assigns to each outcome $x$ a number, $v(x)$, which reflects the subjective value of that outcome. The second scale, $\pi$, associates with each probability $p$ a decision weight $\pi(p)$, which reflects the impact of $p$ on the overall value of the prospect.

The first scale entails an explanation of **reference points**, **loss-aversion** and **diminishing marginal sensitivity**, while the second scale entails an explanation of **decision-weighting**, or weighted probability functions. These four aspects of PT are discussed at length in the next four sections, since they are core concepts to which repeated reference is made throughout the remainder of the text. There is one other element that is often ascribed to PT, concerning the framing of decisions, but this aspect is discussed in the next chapter, in the context of mental accounting.

A mathematical exposition of the basics of the KT model can now be given, which is essentially taken directly from the 1979 paper. As far as the first scale is concerned, the EUT utility function $u(x) = x^b$ is replaced by the following value function:

$$v(x) = \begin{cases} (x-r)^\alpha & \text{if } x \geq r \\ -\lambda(r-x)^\beta & \text{if } x < r \end{cases} \qquad (5.9)$$

There are four parameters in this model:

$r$ = reference point
$\alpha$ = coefficient of diminishing marginal sensitivity for gains
$\beta$ = coefficient of diminishing marginal sensitivity for losses
$\lambda$ = coefficient of loss-aversion

The second scale, for decision-weighting, involves an inverted S-shaped curve, similar to that shown in Figure 5.2, with the following form:

$$\pi(p) = \frac{p^{\gamma}}{(p^{\gamma} + (1-p)^{\gamma})^{1/\gamma}} \tag{5.10}$$

There is now a fifth parameter, gamma which determines the curvature of the function. All of these parameters are explained in the following sections of the chapter, with numerical examples.

The original KT model was concerned with simple prospects of the form $(x, p; y, q)$, which have at most two non-zero outcomes. In such a prospect, one receives $x$ with probability $p$, $y$ with probability $q$, and nothing with probability $1 - p - q$, where $p + q \leq 1$. A prospect is **strictly positive** if its outcomes are all positive, i.e., if $x, y > 0$ and $p + q = 1$; it is **strictly negative** if its outcomes are all negative. A prospect is **regular** if it is neither strictly positive nor strictly negative.

The basic equation of the theory describes the manner in which $v$ and $\pi$ are combined to determine the overall value of regular prospects.

If $(x, p; y, q)$ is a regular prospect (i.e., either $p + q < 1$, or $x \geq 0 \geq y$, or $x \leq 0 \leq y$), then

$$V(x, p; y, q) = \pi(p)\, v(x) + \pi(q)\, v(y) \tag{5.11}$$

Where $v(0) = 0$, $\pi(0) = 0$, $\pi(1) = 1$. As in utility theory, $V$ is defined on prospects, while $v$ is defined on outcomes. The two scales coincide for sure prospects, where $V(x, 1.0) = V(x) = v(x)$. Equation (5.11) generalizes EUT by relaxing the expectation principle described earlier.

As a simple example, take the situation of tossing a coin where the outcome of heads results in a gain of \$20 while the outcome of tails results in a loss of \$10. We can now express the utility of this regular prospect below:

$$V(20, .5; -10, .5) = \pi(.5)\, v(20) + \pi(.5)\, v(-10)$$

The evaluation of strictly positive and strictly negative prospects follows a different rule. In the editing phase, as described earlier, such prospects are segregated into two components: (i) the riskless component, i.e., the minimum gain or loss which is certain to be obtained or paid; (ii) the risky component, i.e., the additional gain or loss which is actually at stake. The evaluation of such prospects is described in the next equation.

If $p + q = 1$ and either $x > y > 0$ or $x < y < 0$, then

$$V(x, p; y, q) = v(y) + \pi(p)[v(x) - v(y)] \tag{5.12}$$

That is, the value of a strictly positive or strictly negative prospect equals the value of the riskless component plus the value-difference between the outcomes, multiplied by the weight associated with the more extreme outcome. For example:

$$V(400, .25; 100, .75) = v(100) + \pi(.25)[v(400) - v(100)]$$

The essential feature of equation (5.12) is that a decision weight is applied to the value-difference $v(x) - v(y)$, which represents the risky component of the prospect, but not to $v(y)$, which represents the riskless component.

The following four sections discuss the main elements of the KT model of PT, including the additions of cumulative PT, which relate to the last of the elements. In each case

PT is compared with other theories, and the relevant empirical evidence from various laboratory and field studies is examined.

## 5.4  Reference points

*Nature*

In PT outcomes are defined relative to a reference point, which serves as a zero point of the value scale. Thus the variable $v$ measures the value of deviations from that reference point, i.e. gains and losses. As Kahneman and Tversky say:

> This assumption is compatible with basic principles of perception and judgement. Our perceptual apparatus is attuned to the evaluation of changes or differences rather than to the evaluation of absolute magnitudes. When we respond to attributes such as brightness, loudness, or temperature, the past and present context of experience defines an adaptation level, or reference point, and stimuli are perceived in relation to this reference point. (p. 277)

It should be noted that this element of PT was not an innovation of the KT model. It has a considerably longer history, involving in particular aspects of the work of Markowitz (1952) and Helson (1964), although we will see later that the Markovitz model differs in other important respects from the KT model. The concept of reference points is indeed part of folklore in some respects. For example, readers who are familiar with the children's story 'A Squash and a Squeeze' will recognize the wisdom of the old man in advising the woman who complains that her house is too small. After cramming all her animals into the house, and then clearing them all out again, she finds that her house now seems large.

It is often assumed in analysis that the relevant reference point for evaluating gains and losses is the current status of wealth or welfare, but this need not be the case. In particular, the relevant reference point may be the expected status rather than the current status, an example being given in the discussion of anomalies. We will return to this aspect of the determination of the reference point later.

As with the other three central components of PT, it is now useful to consider the psychological and neuroscientific foundations of the concept, and then to explain its application by means of a number of examples, discussing how the concept helps to explain certain anomalies in the EUT.

*Psychological foundation*

Evolutionary psychologists attempt to go beyond describing mental attributes and try to explain their origins and functions in terms of adaptations. It can be seen that the psychological concept of a reference point is related to the broader biological mechanisms of **homeostasis** and **allostastis**. Both of these have fundamental functions that appear to have evolved as adaptations. **Homeostasis** is a well-known biological principle, whereby various systems in the body have an optimal set point, and deviations from this point trigger negative feedback processes that attempt to restore it. Examples are body temperature, the level of blood sugar and electrolyte balance. The term **allostasis** was introduced by Sterling and Eyer (1988) to refer to a different type of feedback system whereby a variable is maintained within a healthy range, but at the same time is allowed to vary in response to environmental demands. Heart rate, blood pressure and hormone levels are variables in this category. Thus when we exercise both heart rate and blood pressure are allowed to rise in order to optimize performance. Wilson and colleagues suggest that happiness is also a variable in this category; this issue is discussed further in Chapter 11.

A simple physical or biological illustration of the phenomenon of reference points is the experiment where a person places one hand in cold water and the other in hot water for a certain time, before placing both hands in the same container of lukewarm water. The subject experiences the strange sensation of one hand now feeling warm (the one that was in cold water), while the other hand feels cool (the one that was in hot water). It appears that the visible evidence from the eyes that both hands should feel the same is unable to override the separate reference points of previous temperature in the brain. We shall see that these fundamental evolved adaptation mechanisms underlie many of the anomalies in the neoclassical model.

Other senses also involve the use of reference points. Our visual systems are prone to the same sort of error as described above with the water experiment. A classic example of this is the Delboeuf illusion (1865) relating to visual perception. Consider the diagram below:

**Figure 5.3**   The Delboeuf illusion

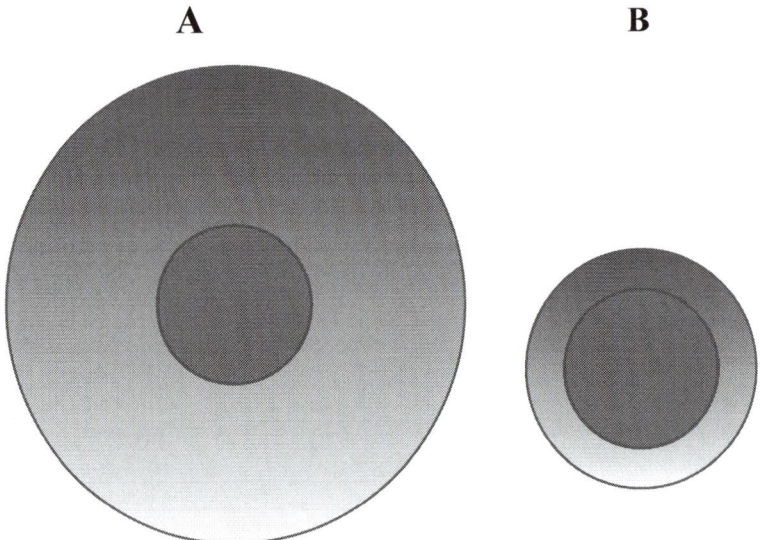

The inner circle on the right appears bigger than the inner circle on the left. This is true regardless of how long we look at the diagram, and even when we are aware of the illusion. The illusion is caused by the fact that we tend to use the outer circle as a reference point, so that it is the comparative sizes of the inner and outer circles in each case that affect our perception, not the absolute sizes.

Another example of a similar visual illusion concerns the perception of color. We do not perceive colors as they actually are, but make automatic adjustments to allow for background light. This generally allows us to make better judgments of the true color of objects, which is very important in terms of biological fitness. However, as Woodford (2012) has noted: 'Perceived brightness depends on the contrast between an object's luminance and the background level of luminance to which they eye has adapted, rather than on the object's absolute level of luminance.' Again this can be seen with a variation of the Delboeuf illusion, as seen in Figure 5.4.

In this case the inner circle on the left appears brighter or lighter than the inner circle on the right because it is contrasted against a darker background, even though both inner circles have the same absolute level of luminance.

**Figure 5.4**   The luminance illusion

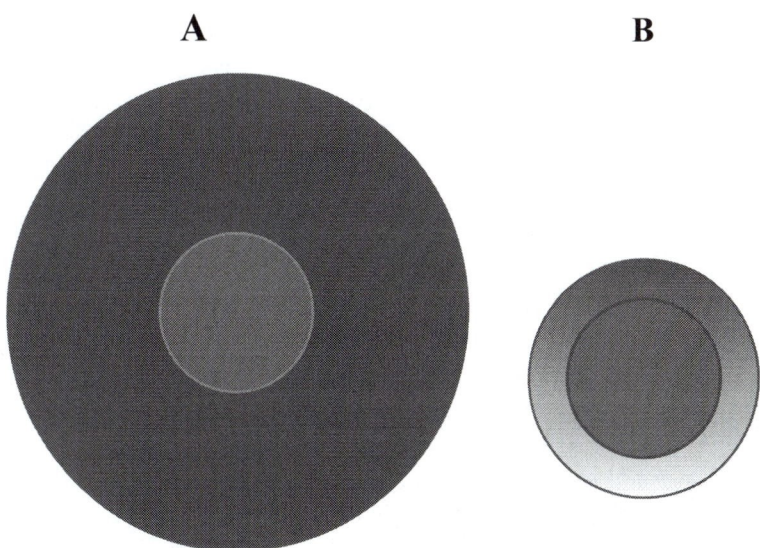

*Neuroscientific foundation*

We have already seen in Chapter 3 that there is strong evidence for the existence of reference dependence in terms of the phenomenon of the dopaminergic reward prediction error (DRPE or RPE), which is based on the difference between anticipated and obtained reward. In experimental neuroscientific studies risk is normally introduced into the decision-making situation by asking subjects to perform a series of gambling tasks, and using fMRI. There are complications in neuroscientific analysis because of the possibility of confounds, which is discussed in more detail later in relation to decision-weighting. Two studies, De Martino and colleagues (2006) and Windmann and colleagues (2006) have examined the differential responses of subjects to punishments and rewards in gambling tasks, and both support the existence of framing effects and reference dependence, with differences in OFC activity in particular. Caplin and Dean (2010) use an axiomatic approach that eliminates the confound problem and also find evidence for reference dependence based on expectations mediated by dopamine release.

There is another analytical problem here however, described in Chapter 2, relating to the correlation-causation situation. As Fox and Poldrack (2009) point out, at the present it is difficult to determine whether the observed results reflect the neural causes or neural effects of reference dependence. Further research with lesion patients may help to clarify this situation, as again explained in Chapter 2, since it can usually be concluded that the neural deficit is the cause of any differences in behavior.

*Empirical evidence*

It is now time to analyze the effects of the reference point phenomenon on decision-making under risk, applying PT to various real-life situations. At this stage the examples are limited to situations where the reference point phenomenon can be isolated from other elements of PT. Further examples, including those given in Table 5.1, involve a combination of elements, and a discussion of these situations is therefore deferred until later in the chapter.

There are various possible sources of reference points, the main ones being previous experience, expectations, and the status of others. Each of these is now considered in turn.

One of the best known anomalies in EUT is a phenomenon sometimes referred to as the '**happiness treadmill**', which was mentioned in Chapter 3. The average income in the United States has increased by more than 40% in real terms since 1972, yet in spite of having far greater income and wealth Americans regularly report that they are no happier than previously. Similar findings have occurred in other countries. Furthermore, the phenomenon does not appear to be caused by the unreliability of self-reporting data; if other indicators of happiness or unhappiness are examined, such as suicide rates and the incidence of depression, we see a similar story. Suicide rates are at least as high in rich countries, like the US, Japan, Sweden and Finland, as they are in poor countries. Similarly, within the same country, suicide rates tend to be at least as high among affluent groups as they are among poor groups.

There is some evidence that reference incomes may also play an important role in the gender gap in incomes, at least in some professions. Rizzo and Zeckhauser (2007) use data from the Young Physicians Survey and find that males set higher reference incomes and respond more strongly to reference incomes compared with females, and show that this fully explains the gender gap in earnings and earnings growth rates.

Even in situations like winning the lottery, where a large and sustained increase in happiness would be expected, at least according to EUT, empirical evidence indicates that winners report average satisfaction levels no higher than that of the general population within as little time as a year (Brickman, Coates and Janoff-Bulman, 1978).

There is a happier side to the story with this phenomenon, and that is that it works in both directions. People who have suffered some kind of major personal tragedy, such as the loss of a loved one or serious injury, also tend to recover quickly in terms of reported happiness level. As indicated in the previous chapter, both of these regressions to normal levels of satisfaction tend to be unexpected by those involved, certainly as far as their rapidity is concerned. It is notable that half of prison suicides occur on the first day of imprisonment. Inmates generally adapt quickly to their new environment, in spite of their fearful expectations.

Expectations have an important role to play as far as the reference point phenomenon is concerned. When people expect a pay rise of 10% for example, and then they are awarded just 5%, they tend to be disappointed. Their reference point in this case is not their current pay level but their expected pay level; thus they code and evaluate the pay award as a loss, not as a gain. A study by Abeler and colleagues (2011) indicates that work effort is significantly affected by expectations of rewards. In a series of experiments they find that, when expectations are high, subjects work longer and earn more money than if expectations are low. This finding is supported by a number of previous studies by Bell (1985), Loomes and Sugden (1986), Gul (1991), or Koszegi and Rabin (2006).

An interesting study on expectations that has important policy implications was recently performed by Brown and colleagues (2014). This used various questions from the UK's National Student Survey to examine student satisfaction with factors such as feedback promptness and instructor enthusiasm. The most important finding was that student evaluations were highly related to their expectations, which were often based on their beliefs regarding practices at other universities. These beliefs tended to vary widely, with those students who believed other universities performed well in these areas expressing lower satisfaction with their own university. The authors therefore suggest that universities evaluate quality and satisfaction separately, using objective measures like actual feedback time to assess quality, and subjective measures in student evaluations to assess satisfaction.

Reference points are also strongly influenced by the status of others. We may be delighted with a pay rise of 5%, until we find out that a colleague has been awarded 10%, when we react with fury. In this case the new information shifts the reference point, turning what was initially coded as a gain into a loss. Again, EUT is unable to explain this phenomenon, which will be discussed in more detail in Chapter 10 in connection with fairness and social utility functions.

Another situation where the reference point may not correspond to the current level of wealth is where a person has not yet adapted to the current asset position. The KT paper gives the example:

> Imagine a person who is involved in a business venture, has already lost 2,000 and is now facing a choice between a sure gain of 1,000 and an even chance to win 2,000 or nothing. If he has not yet adapted to his losses, he is likely to code the problem a choice between (–2,000, .50) and (–1,000) rather than as a choice between (2,000, .50) and (1,000). (Kahneman and Tversky, 1979, p. 286)

As will be explained later in the chapter, the phenomena of loss-aversion and diminishing marginal sensitivity cause the person who has not yet adapted to be more likely to take a risk than the person who has adapted to the recent loss.

Shifts in reference points may also arise when a person formulates his decision problem in terms of final assets, as proposed in EUT, rather than in terms of gains and losses. This causes the reference point to be set to zero wealth, and we will see later that this tends to discourage risk-seeking, except in the case of gambling with low probabilities, for example entering lotteries.

Given these different possible sources of reference points it is not surprising that in some situations there may be more than one. Lu and colleagues (2015) have reported that subjects have different types of risk-aversion for both gains and losses depending on whether financial or social reference points were salient. Various studies by Boles and colleagues also indicate that people can form alternative reference points on a post hoc basis after an experience, and that these are influenced by emotional factors in order to result in the best mood regardless of the outcome (Boles and Messick, 1995; Larrick and Boles, 1995; Johnson, Ilies and Boles, 2012). Thus once again emotions and self-serving bias are relevant in this phenomenon.

An example of multiple reference points, again with important policy implications, involves the Delboeuf illusion described earlier. Several studies have shown that people's perceptions of food serving sizes depend on the size of plate on which the food is served (Van Ittersum and Wansink, 2012, 2013; Wansink, Van Ittersum and Payne, 2014). The authors suggest that a change in social norms may help people to consume less food by using smaller plates, and at the same time reduce wastage. Furthermore, some research has indicated that serving size depends on the serving size of others served beforehand. In this case there appear to be two reference points that may be used as anchors (McFerran et al., 2010): the portion size and the body type of others. If other consumers select a large serving, following consumers choose a larger portion, but this portion is significantly smaller if the other is obese than if she is thin. These issues are discussed in Case 5.3 and, along with broader issues, in Case 10.4.

## 5.5  Loss-aversion

*Nature*

In the words of Kahneman and Tversky (1979):

> A salient characteristic of attitudes to changes in welfare is that losses loom larger than gains. The aggravation that one experiences in losing a sum of money appears to be greater than the pleasure associated with gaining the same amount (p. 279).

For example, most people would not bet money on the toss of a coin, on the basis that a heads outcome gives a specific gain, while a tails outcome gives an equal loss. In mathematical terms, people find symmetric bets of the form $(x, 0.50; -x, 0.50)$ unattractive. The phenomenon can be expressed in more general mathematical terms as follows:

$$v(x) < -v(-x) \quad \text{where } x > 0 \tag{5.13}$$

Again, this element of PT is not an innovation; it is discussed, for example, by Galanter and Pliner (1974).

Expression (5.13) can also be used to derive a measure of loss-aversion, often denoted by the coefficient $\lambda$, where $\lambda$ is the ratio $-v(-x)/v(x)$. For example, in Tversky and Kahneman's 1992 study it was found that the median value of $\lambda$ for their college student subjects was 2.25. However, there is no universally agreed measure of loss-aversion. Whereas in the above situation $\lambda$ is measured over a range of $x$ values, it can also be measured as $-v(-\$1)/v(\$1)$. Another measure is to take the ratio of the slopes of the value function, $v'(-x)/v'(x)$, in the loss and gain regions; the meaning of this will become clearer after reading the next section related to the value function.

As with the previous element of PT, it is useful to consider the psychological and neuroscientific foundations of the phenomenon first, before moving on to examine a more detailed analysis of examples, indicating how these explain anomalies in EUT.

### Psychological foundation

Evolutionary psychologists have speculated on the origins of the phenomenon, in terms of its adaptationary usefulness. Pinker (1997) has proposed that, whereas gains can improve our prospects of survival and reproduction, significant losses can take us completely 'out of the game'. For example, an extra gallon of water can make us feel more comfortable crossing a desert; a loss of a gallon of water may have fatal consequences. While such conjectures regarding the origins of the phenomenon are by necessity in the nature of 'just-so' stories, there is no doubt of the existence of the asymmetry in real life, as will be shown when we examine empirical evidence.

A recent theory relating to the psychology of loss-aversion involves the concept of regulatory focus. Instead of explaining behavior in terms of the distinction between 'hot' and 'cold' systems, this theory examines the fundamental motivational aspects of behavior, and strategies related to these aspects. Regulatory focus theory proposes the coexistence of two motivational systems, the **promotion system** and the **prevention system**. These each serve fundamentally important but different needs. The promotion system is concerned with nurturance needs related to advancement, aspirations, and accomplishment, and is marked by a sensitivity to gains versus non-gains. People with promotion focus are more sensitive to positive than to negative changes from neutrality or the status quo, i.e. some reference point. In contrast, the prevention system relates to duties, responsibilities, and security, and is sensitive to losses versus non-losses. Prevention-focused people are more sensitive to negative than to positive shifts from the status quo (Higgins, 2009). Thus, prevention-focused persons should be more concerned about falling below the previous status quo or reference point, a negative change or loss, than should promotion-focused persons. However, the attitude to risk of such persons will depend on the ability to restore the status quo. If this is more likely to be achieved by playing it safe, then they will be risk-averse. However, if restoring the status quo can only be achieved by a high-risk strategy, then prevention-focused persons will be risk-seeking (Scholer et al., 2010). An example of this second situation is the 'end-the-day effect', discussed in the section on empirical evidence.

*Neuroscientific foundation*

We have already seen in the previous chapter that the main neural evidence for loss-aversion comes from studies that indicate that gains and losses are encoded in different ways in different brain regions. However, there is not just a simple two-system model in operation here. When risk is involved, it appears that the neural activity evoked by potential gains and losses is only partially overlapping with that evoked by actual gains and losses.

A study by Tom and colleagues (2007) introduced risk into the decision-making situation by imaging subjects during a gamble acceptability task series, in which subjects decided whether to accept or reject mixed gambles offering a 50% chance of gain and 50% chance of loss. The size of gain and loss were varied across different trials, with gains ranging from $10 to $40 and losses from $5 to $20. The loss-aversion coefficient $\lambda$ was measured to have a median of 1.93. The study reported that a network of regions, including ventral and dorsal striatum, ventromedial and ventrolateral PFC, ACC, and dopaminergic midbrain regions, showed increasing activity as potential gain increased. The loss-aversion asymmetry is shown by the fact that many of these regions showed not just decreasing activity, but a greater decrease in activity for potential losses compared with the increase in activity for potential gains. A more recent study by Caplin and Dean (2010) indicates another type of asymmetry. It suggests that, even in the NAcc, which is activated by dopamine with both gains and losses, the signal is different in each case. For gains the signal has a shorter time lag and is less intense than for losses.

*Empirical evidence*

Over the last thirty years there have been a large number of studies relating to loss-aversion. As with the discussion of reference points, it is helpful to start with a phenomenon where loss-aversion can be isolated from other elements of PT. An example is the observation of asymmetric price elasticities of demand for consumer goods. Price elasticities indicate price sensitivity, measuring the percentage change in quantity demanded divided by the percentage change in price. Loss-averse consumers dislike price increases more than they like the gains from price cuts, and will reduce purchases more when prices rise than they will increase purchases when prices fall. Therefore loss-aversion implies that price elasticities will be asymmetric, with demand being more elastic in response to price rises than in response to price reductions. Such asymmetric responses have indeed been found in the case of eggs (Putler 1992) and orange juice (Hardie, Johnson and Fader, 1993). In terms of measurement, the study by Hardie, Johnson, and Fader found the loss-aversion coefficient to be around 2.4 for orange juice. A more recent study by Mackiewicz and Falkowski (2015) examined price elasticities for six different products (toothpaste, bread, ball pens, shoes, hot tubs and refrigerators), reporting that the price elasticity of demand was on average 40% higher for price increases than price decreases.

One of the best known manifestations of loss-aversion involves differences between prices potential buyers are willing to pay (WTP) for goods and prices potential sellers are willing to accept (WTA) for the same goods, often referred to as **the endowment effect.** Endowment effects are discussed in section 8, since this is an area where PT has attracted significant criticism.

There are various phenomena in financial markets that indicate loss-aversion by investors. One of the best known anomalies is a phenomenon known as the '**disposition effect**' (Shefrin and Statman, 1985), where investors tend to hold on to stocks that have lost value (relative to their purchase price) too long, while being eager to sell stocks that have risen in price. This involves both loss-aversion and reference points, with the purchase price acting as a reference point in this case. EUT is unable to explain this phenomenon easily, since according to this aspect of the NM people should buy or sell based on expectations of the future price, not the past price. Furthermore, tax laws encourage selling losers rather than winners, in order to reduce capital gains tax liability. Although investors sometimes claim that they hold on to losers because they expect them to 'bounce back', a study by Odean (2001) indicated that unsold losers only yielded a return of 5% in the following year, compared with a return of 11.6% for winners that were sold later. Genesove and Meyer (2001) have reported a similar disposition effect in the housing market; owners appear to be unwilling to sell their properties for less than they paid for them, and therefore tend to hold on to them too long before selling when the market goes into a downturn. However, a more recent study by Barberis and Xiong (2009) questions the ability of PT to explain the disposition effect in stock markets. They test the relationship between stock price movements and traders' realization of gains and losses and find an opposite result to that predicted by PT. The problem here is that there is a difference between frequency of portfolio evaluation (maybe twice a year) and frequency of checking portfolio values (maybe once a month), and the predictions of PT depend on assumptions regarding whether investors realize utility only at a point of evaluation, or every time they check values. The disposition effect is discussed further in the next chapter in the context of mental accounting.

A further anomaly in financial markets concerns the mood of investors in business cycles. A study by Garcia (2013) constructed a measure of investor sentiment from 1905 to 2005, based on the financial news in the *New York Times*, and observed how this was affected by recessions and expansions. They found that, while a movement of one standard deviation in sentiment during an expansion was associated with a 3.5% rise in the DJIA, a movement of one standard deviation during a recession was associated with a 12% fall. Kuhnen (2015) claims that this asymmetry, or pessimism bias, is driven by people reacting more to low outcomes in the negative domain relative to the positive domain.

Loss-aversion has also been observed in the labor market. A study by Card and colleagues (2012) examined the effect of disclosing pay information relating to employees at the University of Southern California on a website. They observed an asymmetric response to the information about peer salaries: workers with salaries below the median for their pay unit and occupation reported lower pay and job satisfaction, while those earning above the median reported no higher satisfaction.

Another anomaly of EUT that can be explained by PT concerns the **'end-of-the-day effect'** observed in racetrack betting. Bettors tend to shift their bets toward long shots, and away from favorites, later in the racing day (McGlothlin, 1956; Ali, 1977). In this case again both loss-aversion and reference points are involved. Because the track stacks the odds against bettors in order to make a profit, by the last race of the day most of them are suffering losses. It appears that most bettors also use zero daily profit as a reference point; they are therefore willing to bet on long shots in the last race, since a small bet can generate a sufficiently large profit to break even for the day. Some studies indicate that this effect is so large that conservatively betting on the favorite to show (a first, second or third place finish) in the last race is profitable, even allowing for the track's biasing of the odds. It is important to note that EUT cannot account for this phenomenon if bettors integrate their wealth, meaning that they regard gains and losses from the last race on one day as being in the same category as gains and losses on the next outing.

A more recent study of the 'end-of-the-day effect' by McKenzie and colleagues (2016) finds somewhat conflicting results and indicates a more nuanced interpretation. This was an experimental study rather than a field study, but it found that bettors like to bet more on outsiders in the last race regardless of whether they had won or lost up to that point, or how much. The authors suggest that this may be due to a preference for 'going out with a bang'. Although the findings are different, the explanation may be similar to that for consumers' preference for rising consumption profiles over time. Once again, loss-aversion is a crucial factor.

An excellent study of loss-aversion in terms of detail and methodology relates to professional golf (Pope and Schweitzer, 2011). There are a number of reasons why this study is significant: (1) it relates to highly experienced players, who should have taken advantage of any learning effects; (2) it involves high stakes in a competitive environment, so there is no lack of incentive as far as optimizing behavior is concerned; and (3) it involves a situation where there is a natural reference point, par, for each hole played, so that a bogey or any score above par would be considered a loss. This study is discussed in more detail in Case 5.2, but the conclusion is that even the best professional golfers exhibit loss-aversion.

Further anomalies involving loss-aversion, combined with other effects, are discussed in more detail in another case study at the end of the chapter, and also in the first two case studies in the next chapter. These involve endowment effects, the equity premium puzzle and the downward-sloping labor supply curve.

In general it can be concluded that there is robust evidence supporting the existence of loss-aversion in both experimental and field studies, with different kinds of subjects and goods. Many of these studies have also measured the loss-aversion coefficient, and the results have been summarized by Abdellaoui, Bleichrodt and Parashiv (2007). The estimates vary between 1.43 and 4.8, but it should be noted that the values are not strictly comparable; not only do they utilize different measures of loss-aversion described earlier, but they make different assumptions regarding the form or shape of the value functions and probability weighting functions described in the next two sections.

There have also been a number of recent studies investigating and reviewing the factors determining loss-aversion and its boundaries (Ariely, Huber and Wertenbroch, 2005; Camerer, 2005; Novemsky and Kahneman, 2005a, 2005b). It is appropriate to discuss these more fully in the context of mental accounting in the next chapter, but one finding can be mentioned at this stage: it appears that loss-aversion may be attenuated in circumstances involving time constraints (Chan and Saqib, 2013). They report that 'people under time pressure no longer consider the hedonic impact of losses to be greater than that of gains, but roughly to be more equal, relative to those under no such constraints.' The rationale is that, because people consider time to be a resource, and the loss of time under time pressure is a loss of resource, this additional loss places them further along the loss function, thus experiencing diminishing marginal sensitivity to further losses and attenuating loss-aversion.

## 5.6  Shape of the utility function

*Nature*

There is an ongoing debate in the literature regarding this issue. We will consider four main possibilities here: (1) the traditional concave function of the NM; (2) the Friedman–Savage (FS) function; (3) the Markowitz (M) function; and (4) the prospect theory (PT) function.

1   *The neoclassical model utility function*

    As already discussed, this has a concave shape, caused by the law of diminishing marginal utility. The implication of this is that there is risk-aversion at all levels of wealth.

2   *The Friedman–Savage utility function*

    Friedman and Savage (1948) observed that the traditional concave function failed to explain various widely observed phenomena, such as gambling. They proposed a

**Figure 5.5**    Friedman–Savage utility function

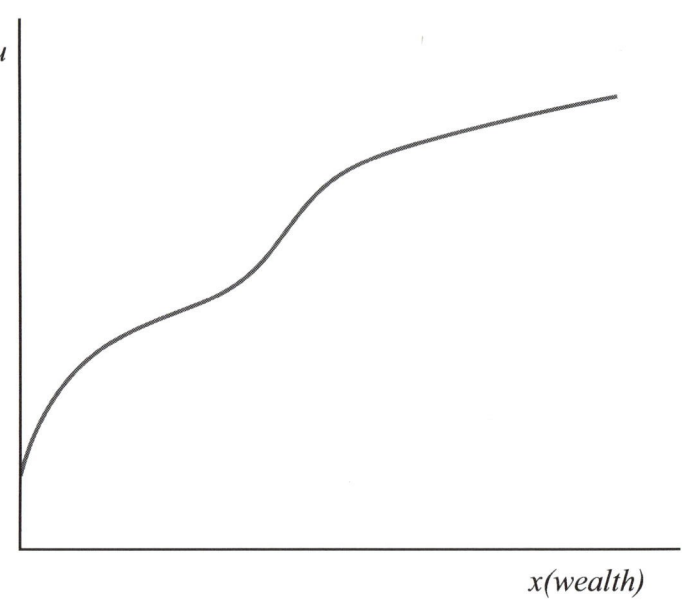

function that had two concave regions, with a convex region between them, in order to explain these anomalies. This is shown in Figure 5.5.

Although the FS utility function does explain some anomalies of the NM function, it still fails to explain various empirical observations. For example, it predicts that in the middle region of wealth people will be willing to make large symmetric bets, for example betting $10,000 on the toss of a coin. In reality people do not like such bets, as was pointed out by Markowitz (1952).

**3    *The Markowitz utility function***

Markowitz proposed various amendments in order to remedy the failings of other functions to explain empirical data. He anticipated the work of Kahneman and Tversky by including both reference points and loss-aversion in his analysis. The shape of his utility function was S-shaped in the regions of both gain and loss. However, as can be seen in Figure 5.6, in the middle region of small gains and losses between points A and B, the function has a reversed S-shape. The implications of this shape of function are that people tend to be risk-seeking for small gains (explaining most gambling), and risk-averse for small losses (explaining why many people take out insurance). However, people would be risk-averse for large gains and risk-seeking for large losses.

It should be noted that this graph also takes into account the other two elements of Markowitz, that are also features of PT: reference points (measuring outcomes in terms of gains and losses); and loss-aversion (the function is steeper in the loss domain than in the gain domain).

**4    *The Prospect Theory utility function***

In PT risk-aversion may be caused by two factors. One factor is the nature of the decision-weighting factor ($\pi$), discussed in the next section. The other factor is the phenomenon of **diminishing marginal sensitivity**, which determines the shape of the function $v(x)$. Kahneman and Tversky proposed a utility function that featured diminishing marginal sensitivity in the domains of both gains and losses. The marginal value of both gains and losses generally decreases with their magnitude (Galanter and Pliner, 1974); this is essentially an aspect of the well-known feature of the NM, the law of diminishing returns.

**Figure 5.6**  Markowitz utility function

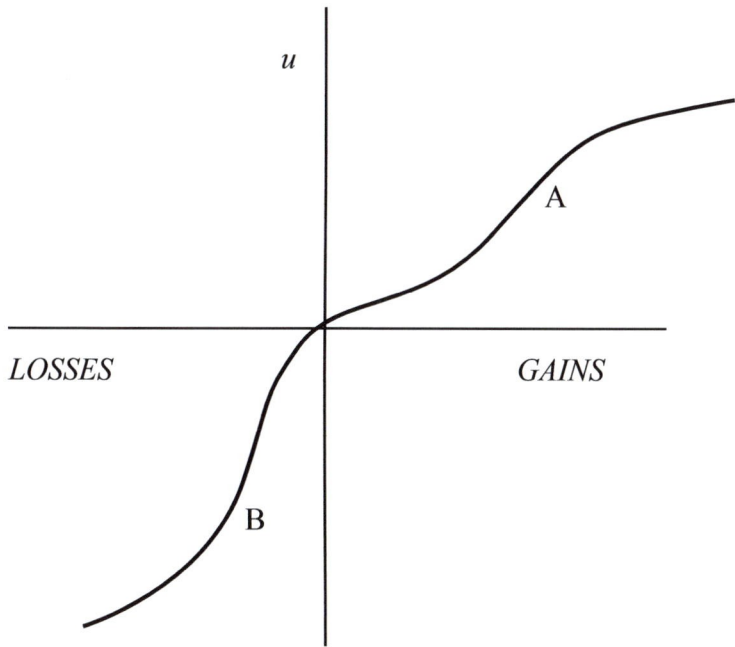

As we have seen earlier, the PT value function was parameterized by Kahneman and Tversky (1992) as a power function:

$$v(x) = \begin{cases} (x-r)^\alpha & \text{if } x \geq r \\ -\lambda(r-x)^\beta & \text{if } x < r \end{cases}$$

(5.9) repeated

where $\alpha$, $\beta > 0$ measure the curvature of the value function for gains and losses respectively, and $\lambda$ is the coefficient of loss-aversion.

The relationship is shown graphically in Figure 5.7.

It can be seen that in PT the value function for changes of wealth is normally concave above the reference point and usually convex below it. In mathematical terms this can be expressed as follows:

$$v''(x) < 0 \text{ for } x > 0 \text{ and } v''(x) > 0 \text{ for } x < 0 \tag{5.14}$$

This type of function implies that diminishing marginal sensitivity generally causes risk-aversion in the domain of gains and risk-seeking in the domain of losses. For example, when faced with the prospects of (200, 0.5) and (100) people generally choose the latter, since the gain of 200 does not usually have twice as much utility as the gain of 100. In mathematical terms, $v(200) < 2v(100)$. However, if we reverse this situation in order to consider people's attitudes to losses we find that people generally prefer the prospect $(-200, 0.5)$ to $(-100)$. They are prepared to gamble in this situation, since the loss of 200 does not usually have twice as much disutility as the loss of 100. In mathematical terms, $-v(200) < -2v(100)$. Kahneman and Tversky named this phenomenon the **reflection effect**, meaning that the preference between negative prospects is the mirror image of the preference between positive prospects.

**Figure 5.7**  PT utility function

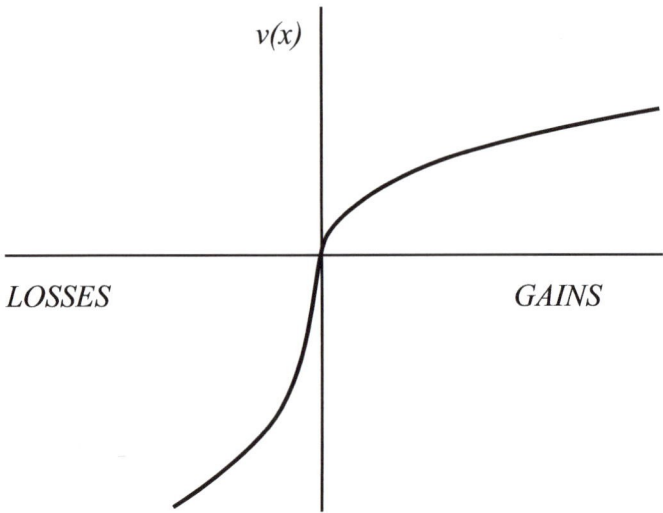

*Psychological foundation*

In the words of Kahneman and Tversky (1979):

> Many sensory and perceptual dimensions share the property that the psychological
> response is a concave function of the magnitude of physical change. For example,
> it is easier to discriminate between a 3° and a change of 6° in room temperature,
> than it is to discriminate between a change of 13° and a change of 16°. We propose
> that this principle applies in particular to the evaluation of monetary changes.
> (p. 278)

As with the other elements of the KT model, evolutionary psychologists like to go beyond
the descriptive statement above and speculate on how such a mental adaptation can have
evolved. It appears that in many situations it is relative changes rather than absolute
changes that are the key to survival and reproduction. For example, when one is hungry,
a kilogram of meat is extremely useful (compared with zero or a very small amount); ten
kilos is not much more useful, unless there are a lot of mouths to feed, since the additional
amount could not be stored in our ancestral environment.

However, there does appear to be one exception to diminishing marginal sensitivity,
in the loss region. As was mentioned in the discussion of loss-aversion, a really large loss
can have fatal consequences. The implication of this is that people may be risk-averse for
very large losses, while being risk-seekers in the case of smaller losses. Examples of such
situations are given in the discussion of anomalies later.

*Neuroscientific foundation*

There are a number of problems in attempting to establish a neuroscientific basis for
diminishing marginal sensitivity in the utility function. First, as we have seen in the previous chapter, there are different kinds of utility, and the difference between decision and
experienced utility is an important one in terms of neural correlates. Anticipatory utility is
also relevant. When subjects receive an immediate reward following a decision it is impossible to disentangle the combination of different utilities involved, since at present the
fMRI technique lacks sufficient temporal resolution to do this. One approach is to design

studies where the relevant reward is delayed and temporally separated from the decision, as in buying a stock or a lottery ticket.

Second, there are problems with confounds, since in practice it is difficult to separate the effects of the shape of the value function from the effects of the shape of the decision-weighting function. As a simple example of this, people may appear to give a relatively low value to receiving a large gain, but this may be due to the assignment of a low decision weight to the receipt of the gain rather than a low utility. This is explained in more detail in the next section.

One consequence of these problems, and others, is that different studies have produced some conflicting results. An example here is the role of the amygdala in responding to stimuli of different valences. It was originally believed that the amygdala was activated only when negative stimuli were given, resulting in a fear or anxiety response. However, later studies have indicated that there is activation in the amygdala in some cases when a positive stimulus involving some kind of reward is administered. At this point therefore there is still much that is unknown regarding neural response systems to rewards and punishments of different magnitudes, and it can be concluded that it is not yet clear how neural activity relates to the S-shaped value function proposed by PT.

## Empirical evidence

We will start by comparing EUT and PT as far as the shape of utility functions is concerned. Diminishing marginal sensitivity is also a feature of EUT as well as PT, but when combined with reference points and loss-aversion it has different implications in PT compared with EUT.

Let us consider the reflection effect. As an empirical demonstration of this effect, the KT paper examined the attitudes of a sample of 95 respondents to positive and negative prospects and found the following results: when choosing between the prospects (4,000, 0.80) and (3,000) 80% preferred the second prospect (a sure gain), but when choosing between the prospects $(-4,000, 0.80)$ and $(-3,000)$ 92% preferred the first prospect, taking a risk of making a greater loss. The reflection effect had also been observed by other researchers before the KT study, for example Markowitz (1952) and Williams (1966a).

EUT regards diminishing marginal utility and the concavity of the utility function as being the cause of risk-aversion. It tends to explain risk-aversion in terms of expected values and variances. However, when the prospects of the losses in the previous example, $(-4,000, 0.8)$ and $(-3,000)$, are compared, the second choice has both higher expected value and lower variance, and therefore should be preferred according to EUT. As seen earlier, the empirical evidence of the KT study contradicts this prediction, with 92% of their sample preferring the first prospect.

EUT also has problems explaining various attitudes towards insurance. It may seem initially that taking out insurance implies risk-aversion, as implied by EUT. However, by assuming a concave utility function throughout the domain of the level of assets, EUT implies risk-aversion is universal. This is contradicted by the fact that many people prefer insurance policies that offer limited coverage with low or zero deductible over comparable policies that offer higher maximal coverage with higher deductibles. Thus taking out insurance may be risk-averse compared with not taking out any insurance at all, but some policies, which may be popular, may be risk-seeking compared with others.

There is one phenomenon related to insurance which may appear to be an anomaly for both PT and EUT. This concerns attitudes to **probabilistic insurance**. This type of policy involves the purchaser paying a fraction of the premium of full insurance, but only gives the probability of the same fraction of paying out if an accident occurs. It appears that such a policy involves more risk than standard insurance. Empirical evidence from the KT study indicates that such insurance would not be popular, which appears to contradict the predictions of the PT model. This apparent anomaly in PT, along with certain tendencies for risk-seeking in the gain domain mentioned earlier, can only be explained after a discussion of decision-weighting in the next section.

So far we have compared the EUT and PT utility functions in terms of empirical evidence. However, it can also be seen that there are important differences between the PT function and the Markowitz (M) function. Markowitz noted the presence of risk-seeking in preferences among positive as well as negative prospects, and, as we have seen, he proposed a utility function that has convex and concave regions in both the gain and loss domains. The Markowitz function has received some empirical support from a study by Jullien and Salanié (2000), which related to racetrack betting. This study found that the utility function for small amounts of money was convex. Another study by Levy and Levy (2002) has also claimed to contradict the PT function and support the Markowitz model.

These studies raise some important issues:

1   How does the PT model explain activities like gambling? This widely observed empirical phenomenon appears to imply risk-seeking in the gain domain.

2   How does the PT model explain why people take out insurance? This is also a common activity, and seems to imply risk-aversion in the loss domain.

It is only possible to discuss the Jullien and Salanié and Levy and Levy studies, and examine the apparent anomalies in the PT model, after a discussion of the remaining element of the model, decision-weighting.

## 5.7  Decision-weighting

*Nature*

As with some of the previous elements of PT, which feature in other theories prior to the original KT paper, decision-weighting is not a unique element of PT. Various conventional theories incorporate decision-weighting, notably rank-dependent EUT. This is also the area where there are some substantive differences between the original 1979 paper (henceforth referred to as original PT, or OPT) and the revised 1992 paper, which introduces the term '**cumulative prospect theory**', or CPT. The latter version is more complex, but more satisfactory in a number of ways. In particular it is more general, applying to situations involving uncertainty as well as those involving risk, and it is also better supported empirically, fitting a wide number of studies by different researchers in different countries. However, in order to better understand the development of the theory, we will discuss the original version first before extending it.

As with the other elements of the KT model, it is appropriate to start with a quotation from the 1979 paper:

> In PT, the value of each outcome is multiplied by a decision weight. Decision weights are inferred from choices between prospects much as subjective probabilities are inferred from preferences in the Ramsey-Savage approach. However, decision weights are not probabilities: they do not obey the probability axioms and they should not be interpreted as measures of degree or belief (p. 280).

There are actually two reasons why decision weights may be different from objective probabilities, and it is important to distinguish between them, even though they may have the same biasing effect, as we will see. These reasons relate to **estimation** and **weighting**.

The first aspect relates to situations where objective probabilities are unknown, while the second relates to situations where these probabilities are known but do not necessarily reflect decision preferences according to EUT.

**1**    *Estimation of probabilities*

People are often lousy at estimating probabilities of events occurring, especially rare ones. They overestimate the probability of dying in plane crashes, or in pregnancy, or suffering from violent crime. An example of overestimating low probabilities, concerning playing the lottery, was given in Chapter 4. The California lottery, one of the biggest in the world, requires matching six numbers between 1 and 51 in order to win the main prize. The odds against doing this are over 18 million to 1. In other words, if one played this lottery twice a week, one could expect to win about every 175,000 years. It was found by Kahneman, Slovic and Tversky (1982) that people overestimated the odds of winning by over 1,000%.

Another example of situations where people are often bad at estimating probabilities is where conditional probabilities are involved, as we have also seen in Chapter 4. A simple example is where, after several consecutive coin tosses turning up heads, people are inclined to think that tails is more likely on the next toss (in this case the objective probability should be known but appears to be rejected). A more complex example involving conditional probabilities is given by Casscells, Schoenberger and Graboys (1978), and relates to a situation where a person takes a medical test for a disease, like HIV, where there is a very low probability (in most circumstances) of having the disease, say one in a thousand. However, there is a chance of a false prediction; the test may only be 95% accurate. Under these circumstances people tend to ignore the rarity of the phenomenon (disease) in the population and wildly overestimate the probability of actually being sick. Even the majority of Harvard Medical School doctors failed to get the right answer. For every thousand patients tested, one will be actually sick while there will be 50 false positives. Thus there is only a 1 in 51 chance of a positive result meaning that the patient is actually sick.

**2**    *Weighting of probabilities*

The 1979 paper by Kahneman and Tversky concentrates on the discussion of those decision problems where objective probabilities, in terms of stated values of $p$, are both known and adopted by respondents. In such situations decision weights can be expressed as a function of stated probabilities: $\pi(p) = f(p)$. These decision weights measure the impact of events on the desirability of prospects, and not the perceived likelihood of these events, which was discussed above in the context of estimation. As an illustrative example, consider the tossing of a fair coin, where there is an objective probability of 0.50 of winning 100 and the same probability of winning nothing. In this case it is usually observed empirically that $\pi(0.50) < 0.50$, meaning that there is risk-aversion.

There are a number of important characteristics of the weighting function that were observed by Kahneman and Tversky. Most obviously, $\pi$ is an increasing function of $p$, with: $\pi(0) = 0$ and $\pi(1) = 1$.; this means that impossible events are ignored and the scale is normalized so that $\pi(p)$ is the ratio of the weight associated with the probability $p$ to the weight associated with a certain event. In addition there are three important characteristics of $\pi$ which violate the normal probability axioms in EUT: **subadditivity**, **subcertainty** and **subproportionality**. These are now discussed in turn.

The characteristic of subaddivity relates to situations where p is small. For example the KT paper found that the prospect (6,000, 0.001) was preferred to (3,000, 0.002) by 73% of the respondents. This contravenes the normal risk-aversion for gains and diminishing marginal sensitivity described in earlier elements of PT, and can only be explained by a weighting function involving subadditivity.

In the above example: $\pi(0.001)v(6,000) > \pi(0.002)v(3,000)$

Since $v(3,000) > 0.5\ v(6,000)$      because of diminishing marginal sensitivity (concavity of $v$)

$\pi(0.001)v(6,000) > \pi(0.002)v(3,000) > \pi(0.002)0.5v(6,000)$

Cancelling $v(6,000)$ from both sides of the first and last terms,

$\pi(0.001) > 0.5\pi(0.002)$

$\pi(0.5 \times 0.002) > 0.5\pi(0.002)$

In general terms the subadditivity principle can be expressed as follows:

$$\pi(rp) > r\pi(p) \quad \text{for } 0 < r < 1 \tag{5.15}$$

The overweighting of probabilities illustrated above was also observed by KT in the domain of losses. They observed that 70% of their respondents preferred the prospect $(-3,000, 0.002)$ to the prospect $(-6,000, 0.001)$, which shows the reflected preferences of the previous example. However, they did not find that this principle applied to larger probabilities, for example where $p = 0.90$. The significance of these findings is discussed in the section relating to anomalies.

The second principle of subcertainty can be illustrated by a couple of examples coming from studies by Allais (1953). Allais noted that people tend to overweight outcomes that are considered certain, relative to outcomes that are merely probable. He found that 82% of his respondents preferred the prospect (2,400) to the prospect (2,500, 0.33; 2,400, 0.66). Yet 83% of his respondents preferred (2,500, 0.33) to (2,400, 0.34).

Thus in the first case: $v(2,400) > \pi(0.66)v(2,400) + \pi(0.33)v(2,500)$

While in the second case: $\pi(0.33)v(2,500) > \pi(0.34)v(2,400)$

Thus $v(2400) > \pi(0.66)v(2400) + \pi(0.34)v(2,400)$

Dividing by $v(2,400)$,

$1 > \pi(0.66) + \pi(0.34)$

In general terms the subcertainty principle can be expressed as:

$$\pi(p) + \pi(1 - p) < 1 \tag{5.16}$$

One main implication of subcertainty is that preferences are generally less sensitive to variations in probability than EUT would suggest. This is illustrated in the graph in Figure 5.8, where: $\pi(p)$ is less steep than the 45-degree line.

The discontinuities of the function at low and high probabilities reflect the phenomenon that there is a limit to how small a decision weight can be attached to an event, if it is given any weight at all. The implication is that events with very low probabilities are ignored, or given a weight of zero, and there is then a discrete quantum jump to a minimum decision weight that is applied to events that are regarded as just sufficiently likely for them to be worth taking into consideration. A similar effect occurs at the upper end of the probability spectrum, where there is a discrete jump between certainty and uncertainty.

A final characteristic of decision-weighting functions is that they involve subproportionality. This means that they violate the independence or substitution axiom of EUT. For example, the KT study found that 80% of respondents preferred the certainty of (3,000) to the uncertain prospect (4,000, 0.8), but when these outcomes had their probabilities reduced by a common factor of a quarter, the situation was reversed. Thus 65% of their respondents preferred the prospect (4,000, 0.2) to the prospect (3,000, 0.25).

**Figure 5.8**  A typical PT weighting function (1979 version)

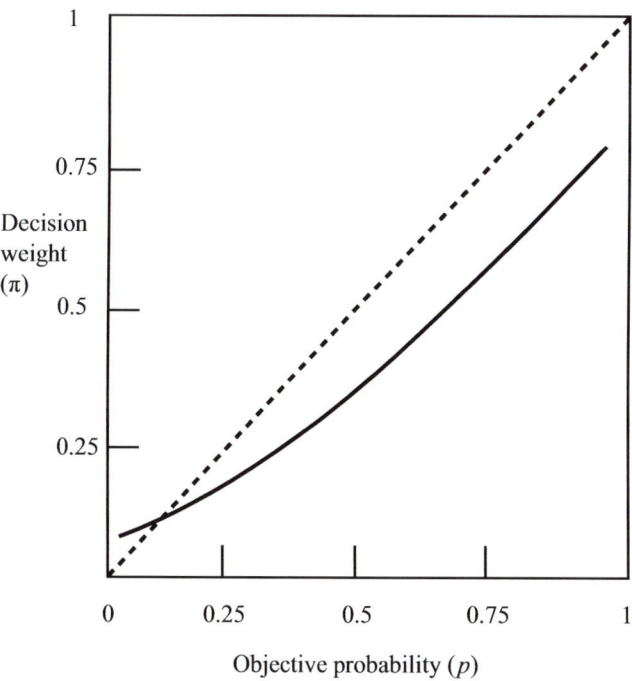

The independence axiom was stated in formal terms near the beginning of the chapter. In more simple terms this principle states that if a prospect A $(x, p)$ is preferred to prospect B $(y, q)$ then it follows that any probability mixture $(A, r)$ must be preferred to the mixture $(B, r)$. In the example above $r = \frac{1}{4}$. In contrast the subproportionality principle of PT states the following:

$$\frac{\pi(pq)}{\pi(p)} \leq \frac{\pi(pqr)}{\pi(pr)} \qquad 0 < p, q, r \leq 1 \tag{5.17}$$

This means that, for a fixed ratio of probabilities, the ratio of the corresponding decision weights is closer to unity when the probabilities are low than when they are high. In more simple terms, people judge probabilities that are the same compared in relative terms (1 to 0.8 and 0.25 to 0.2) to be more similar when probabilities are small (0.25 is judged more similar to 0.2 than 1 is to 0.8).

This completes the description of the original version of decision-weighting in the 1979 paper. However, certain empirical anomalies were later observed, described in the final subsection, and the revised 'cumulative prospect theory' was developed in the 1992 paper. The essential difference in general terms is that the principle of diminishing marginal sensitivity is now applied to weighting functions as well as the utility function. In the words of Tversky and Kahneman (1992):

> Diminishing sensitivity entails that the impact of a given change in probability diminishes with its distance from the boundary. For example, an increase of 0.1 in the probability of winning a given prize has more impact when it changes the probability of winning from .9 to 1.0 or from 0 to 0.1, than when it changes the probability of winning from 0.3 to 0.4 or from 0.6 to 0.7. Diminishing sensitivity, therefore, gives rise to a weighting function that is concave near 0 and convex near 1 (p. 303).

In CPT, sometimes called second-generation PT, the probability weighting function is used in a rank-dependent way. Decision weights are assigned cumulatively, starting with the largest gain and working downwards, and a mirror-image method applies to assigning weights to losses. A numerical example will help explain this. Consider a lottery that gives monetary gains of $0, $5 and $10 with respective probabilities 0.5, 0.3 and 0.2. The weight for the largest gain, $10, is determined by a direct transformation of the relevant probability, giving a weight of $w(0.2)$. The decision weight for the next largest gain, $5, is defined as $w(0.2 + 0.3) - w(0.2)$. It should be noted that the sum of the weights for the $5 and $10 gains is $w(0.5)$, which is the sum of the transformation of the corresponding probabilities. The advantage of this innovation in second-generation PT is that it maintains stochastic dominance, unlike OPT.

The weighting function, for both gains and losses, therefore has an inverted S-shape, shown in Figure 5.7. This is again similar to the weighting function used in many conventional rank-dependent EUT models. Instead of using the symbol $p$ to denote decision weights, the symbol $w(p)$ is used, and the general shape of the function is described by the following mathematical form, the same as (5.10):

$$w(p) = \frac{p^{\gamma}}{(p^{\gamma} + (1-p)^{\gamma})^{1/\gamma}} \tag{5.18}$$

The parameter $\gamma$ determining the curvature of the function may be different for losses compared with gains. As Tversky and Kahneman point out, this form has several useful features: it has only one parameter, $\gamma$, thus maintaining parsimony; it is versatile, in accommodating weighting functions with both convex and concave regions; and it does not require $w(0.5) = 0.5$ as a point of symmetry for the curve. Related to this last feature, the most important advantage of the form is that it fits empirical data well, as we will see shortly.

The practical implications of these modifications to the weighting function are that, instead of having a simple twofold attitude to risk, involving risk-aversion for gains and risk-seeking for losses, there is now a more complex fourfold pattern: risk-aversion for gains and risk-seeking for losses of high probability; risk-seeking for gains and risk-aversion for losses of low probability. As we will see in the last part of this section, this refined model fits better with empirical observations.

There have been other attempts to parameterize the decision-weighting function, involving more complex two-parameter models, for example Lattimore (1992) and Prelec (1998). These produce a similar inverse-S-shaped function to that shown in Figure 5.9, and are difficult to distinguish from the KT version in analyzing empirical data.

### Psychological foundation

There are various puzzles regarding the attitudes to risk described above. First, there is the issue concerning why we are bad at estimating probabilities, particularly those of rare events. Second there is the issue regarding why we are usually risk-averse when gains are at stake, but risk-seeking when losses are involved. Finally, there is the issue of exceptions: why are we sometimes risk-seeking for gains, particularly when probabilities are low? Evolutionary psychologists have ventured a number of theories relating to these issues, and there is some interesting evidence both from other species and from neuroscientific studies.

As far as the first issue is concerned, it appears that we are bad at estimating probabilities for events that have no resemblance to those that have occurred in our

**Figure 5.9**    A typical PT weighting function (1992 version)

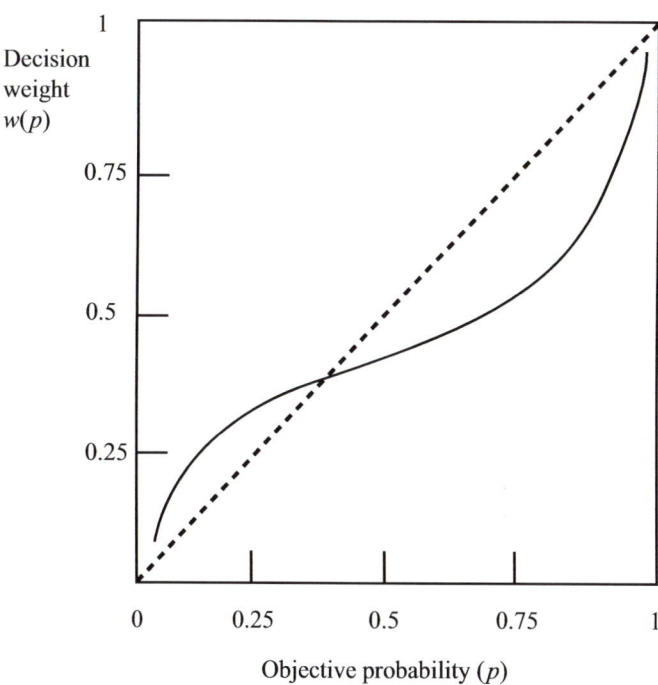

evolutionary past. Betting on the lottery is obviously in this category. Complex problems involving conditional probabilities would also often fall into this category of unfamiliarity. On the other hand, events that were a high risk in our evolutionary past, such as death in pregnancy or through violent assault, tend to be overestimated in importance in our current environment (Slovic, Fischhoff and Lichtenstein 1982; Glassner 1999).

As an interesting corollary, there is evidence that some animals are extremely good at estimating probabilities in situations that directly affect their survival. One might not expect woodpeckers to be exceptionally good mathematicians, but in one respect they seem able to solve a problem that would stump many skilled humans (Lima 1984). In a laboratory experiment, woodpeckers were presented with two kinds of artificial trees, both of which had twenty-four holes. In one group they were all empty, while in the other six of the holes contained food. The problem facing the wood peckers was similar to the one facing oil wildcatters: to determine how many holes to try before moving on. If they left too soon they would be deserting a tree that may still contain food, but if they stayed too long they missed out on opportunities elsewhere. Using sophisticated mathematics it can be calculated that the woodpeckers would maximize their food intake by leaving a tree after encountering six empty holes. In the study it was found that the average number of holes tried by the woodpeckers was 6.3, remarkably close to perfect. Furthermore, when the number of empty holes was varied in the experiment, the woodpeckers changed their behavior accordingly.

What is the implication of this? It is not that woodpeckers are better mathematicians than humans. However, the process of natural selection has honed the instincts of woodpeckers over millions of years. Those ancestral woodpeckers who were better at solving this problem, through some neurological superiority, were more likely to pass on their genes, with the same capacity, to future generations, Over time competition between woodpeckers would ensure that only the most successful would survive and breed, so that today's woodpeckers have adapted extremely well to solving their perennial problem. We shall see that this process of natural selection can lead to the building of extremely effective mechanisms for solving problems, particularly in the domain of behavioral game theory.

However, returning to human behavior, there is at least one other important factor that is relevant in terms of explaining our poor estimation of probabilities. Our senses of perception have become attuned through natural selection to become highly selective, filtering out 'noise' and trivia, and external events have to compete for our attention. We tend to give more weight to events that attract our attention for whatever reason. In modern times the media play an important role here. Because events like plane and train accidents receive much media coverage, they attract our attention more than car accidents, and this affects our estimation of probabilities, causing us to overestimate them.

Let us now consider the second issue mentioned above. What explains the general pattern of risk-aversion for gains? Once again animal studies are instructive. In general animals often appear to be risk-averse, for example in competition for mates. Such competition rarely results in fatal injuries. Often there are displays and shows of strength to begin with; if this fails to discourage one of the contenders, the situation may escalate to some form of sparring. This preliminary 'sizing up' usually results in one or other contender backing down, except when the rivals are very evenly matched. This rarity of intra-species lethal combat was once explained by biologists in terms of group selection, meaning that the phenomenon was good for the species as a whole. However, this group selection explanation has been long discredited, at least in this context (Williams 1966b), with biologists now favoring individual selection, at the level of the 'selfish gene', to use another expression from Dawkins (1976). In simple terms, the aphorism 'those who fight and run away live to fight another day' is appropriate.

This leads us to the third main issue. There are obviously situations where humans are risk-seeking in the region of gains. What can account for this? Again it is necessary to consider animal studies and neurological research, as well as human studies. A study of macaque monkeys by Platt and McCoy (2005) has demonstrated that, like humans, they are fond of a gamble. An experiment indicated that they preferred an unpredictable reward of fruit juice to a reward of a certain amount, where the expected values of both prospects were the same. The experiment also showed that the monkeys still preferred to gamble even when the unpredictable prospect delivered a series of miserly portions. Platt's conclusion was: '… it seemed as if these monkeys got a high out of getting a big reward that obliterated any memory of all the losses that they would experience following that big reward.' It is also notable that the gambling behavior was mirrored by neuronal activity in the brain region associated with the processing of rewards.

In simple terms, there are situations where it does pay most species to take risks, even life-threatening ones. Were it not for this propensity to take such risks the human race would never have ventured forth to populate the whole planet, and would have stayed concentrated in Africa, where *homo sapiens* originated about a hundred thousand years ago. There are still a few tribal societies in existence today where life is very much as it was then. The Yanomamö in South America are such a tribe, surviving by hunting and small-scale farming. Violence is a way of life for this tribe, with a quarter of the men dying from this cause. The killers in turn are often killed by relatives of their victims. The question therefore arises: why do Yanomamö men risk killing each other? An extensive, long-term study by the anthropologist Chagnon (1988) has revealed that those who kill and survive end up having more wives and babies. The study compared 137 Unokais (men who had killed at least one other man) and 243 non-Unokais in the tribe. The Unokais had on average 1.63 wives and 4.91 children, while the non-Unokais averaged only 0.63 wives and 1.59 children.

Therefore taking risks can obviously pay dividends. However, it appears that there is no particular strategy regarding risk that is optimal for all individuals within a population in all situations. We have already seen in the Scholer and colleagues (2010) study discussed in the section on loss-aversion that some people display a motivational system that appears to be prevention-focused, while other people display a motivational system that appears to be promotion-focused. Prevention-focused people are loss-averse, but may display either risk-aversion or risk-seeking, depending on the potential for restoring a particular status quo. Thus attitudes toward risk depend both on an individual's motivational focus and on the particular environmental situation with which they are faced.

## *Neuroscientific foundation*

One conclusion that can be drawn from the above discussion is that our brains require mechanisms built into them over the course of evolution that provide rewards for taking risks. These mechanisms are biochemical in nature, and the most important one involves the neurotransmitter dopamine. Evidence suggests that some people have a variation of the dopamine D4 receptor gene, sometimes referred to as the 'novelty seeking' gene. This variation can lead to a number of variations in behavior patterns (Benjamin et al. 1996). Studies have shown how such variations affect migration (Chen et al. 1999) and sexual behavior (Hamer 1998). A discussion of how far such a gene might spread throughout a population is deferred until the chapter on behavioral game theory, since it involves an explanation of the concept of an evolutionarily stable strategy (ESS). At this stage it just needs to be noted that such a gene bestows certain advantages on its possessor (the tendency to take more opportunities), but also certain disadvantages (the tendency to come to grief when taking such opportunities). This also helps to explain why different individuals have a different motivational focus and different attitudes to risk.

As far as probability weighting is concerned, studies attempting to identify neural correlates of distortions in this characteristic have a fairly recent origin. Paulus and Frank (2006) estimated a non-linear probability weighting function using a gamble-certainty-equivalent paradigm. They reported that activity in the ACC was correlated with the non-linearity parameter, with subjects who had more ACC activity for high versus low prospects tending also to have more linear or objective weighting of probabilities.

Another study by Hsu and colleagues (2009) has also estimated non-linearities in probability weighting, showing a significant correlation between behavioral non-linearity in gambling tasks and non-linearity of striatal response. A study by Berns et al. (2007) examined probability-weighting distortions for aversive outcomes, such as the prospect of receiving an electric shock. These researchers reported that there was fairly wide-scale overweighting of low-probability aversive events recorded in a number of brain regions, including dorsal striatum, PFC, insula, and ACC.

Again these studies raise the issue of cause and effect, as is so often the case with identifying neural correlates of behavior. However, as mentioned earlier, future studies involving subjects with brain lesions may clarify the position, if subjects with lesions in certain areas tend to have linear probability weighting.

## *Empirical evidence*

Some of the anomalies in EUT have already been discussed in the previous sections. However, some further explanation of these phenomena is necessary, and a number of others can also be discussed. In particular we are now in a position to show that PT is in general better at explaining various real-life phenomena than EUT, or any of the conventional models extending EUT. As Camerer (2000) has observed in a review and comparison of PT with other theories, PT, and in particular cumulative PT, can explain not only the same observations that EUT can explain, but also the various anomalies that cannot be explained by EUT.

Let us begin by examining empirical evidence supporting the inverted S-shaped weighting functions for both gains and losses. Tversky and Kahneman (1992) performed a study with graduate students to reveal their preferences in terms of certainty equivalents (CEs) for a number of prospects. Table 5.5 gives a sample of results that were observed, showing the expected values (EVs), median CEs, and attitudes to risk for each prospect.

**Table 5.5**    Empirical results related to weighting function

| Prospect | Description of prospect | EV ($) | Median CE ($) | Attitude to risk |
|---|---|---|---|---|
| (0, 0.05; $100, 0.95) | gain, high probability | 95 | 78 | Averse |
| (0, 0.05; −$100, 0.95) | loss, high probability | −95 | −84 | Seeking |
| (0, 0.50; $100, 0.50) | gain, medium probability | 50 | 36 | Averse |
| (0, 0.50; −$100, 0.50) | loss, medium probability | −50 | −42 | Seeking |
| (0, 0.95; $100, 0.05) | gain, low probability | 5 | 14 | Seeking |
| (0, 0.95; −$100, 0.05) | loss, low probability | −5 | −8 | Averse |

*Source: Compiled with data from Tversky and Kahnemann (1992), Table 3.*

Thus with the first prospect the subjects were prepared to pay an average of $78 dollars to obtain an expected value of $95, showing risk-aversion. In general, if the CE > EV this indicates risk-seeking for both gains and losses, while if the CE < EV this indicates risk-aversion for both losses and gains.

Similar results have been obtained using an evolutionary model featuring a stochastic foraging environment in which conditions are autocorrelated over time (Mallpress et al., 2015). Using a rigorous evolutionary approach based on reproductive value, this study indicates that optimal risk preferences can be strongly influenced by the options currently available, because these provide information about the likely future conditions and hence the need to take risks.

These empirical results can be presented in a table displaying the **four-fold attitude to risk**, shown in Table 5.6.

**Table 5.6**    Four-fold attitude to risk

| | GAINS | LOSSES |
|---|---|---|
| Chances are high (95% probable) | Fear of disappointment, risk averse: "A bird in hand ..." | Hope to avoid loss, risk seeking "The tragedy of human existence" |
| Chances are low (5% probability) | Hope of large gain, risk seeking lotteries | Fear of large loss, risk averse, insurance |

This data can be transformed in order to draw a decision-weighting function. We do not have to take into account diminishing marginal sensitivity as far as the utility function is concerned in this case, since all the amounts of money involved are the same in this example, $100. Thus attitude to risk is affected only by diminishing marginal sensitivity in the decision-weighting function. The plotting of this function requires the calculation of the ratios of the certainty equivalents of each prospect ($c$) to the non-zero outcome ($x$). Thus for the first prospect in Table 5.5 this ratio $c/x = 0.78$. One can interpret this ratio as a subjective or weighted probability, in that a subject may know the objective probability of gaining $100 is 0.95, but because of risk-aversion they really perceive the probability as 0.78

**Figure 5.10**   Empirical decision-weighting function for TK data

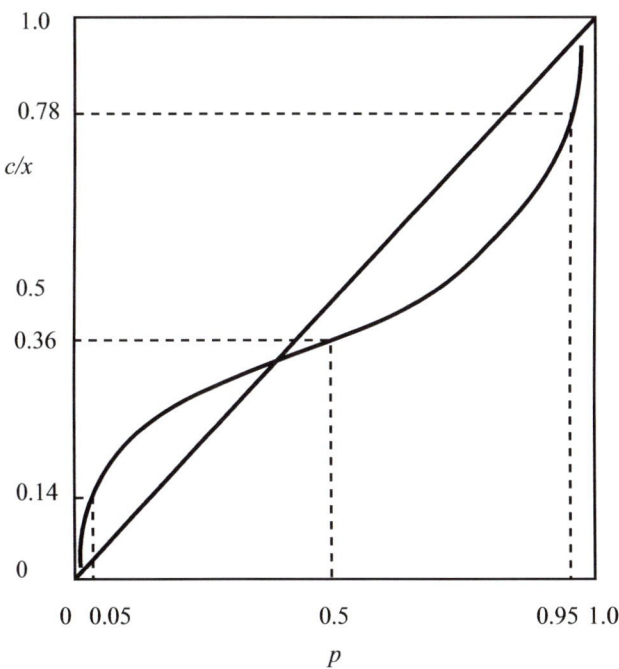

in terms of decision-making. From the small sample of results above a decision-weighting function is drawn, in this case for gains, shown in Figure 5.10. It should be noted that the 45° line, where $c/x = p$, represents risk-neutrality; points above the line occur where $c/x > p$, implying risk-seeking, while points below the line occur where $c/x < p$, implying aversion. In the case of decision-weighting functions for losses, the situation is reversed: points above the line represent risk-aversion and points below the line represent risk-seeking. It should also be noted that the curve is not symmetrical, since $w(.5) = 0.36$.

The graph above relates only to a very small sample of observations, for the sake of simplicity. However, when applied to a much larger sample of the TK observations, the general shape of the function fits well, for both gains and losses. The graph confirms the predictions of PT in terms of risk-seeking for gains of low probability and risk-aversion for gains of high probability, with this pattern being reversed for losses. In the TK sample as a whole, 78% of the subjects were risk-seeking for gains of low probability, while 88% were risk-averse for gains of high probability. 80% were risk-averse for losses of low probability, while 87% were risk-seeking for losses of high probability.

The empirical observations of the 1992 TK study have been replicated in a number of other studies. A particularly notable study was carried out by Kachelmeier and Shehata in 1992, and was one factor leading to a revision of the original version of PT. This study was carried out in China, and due to the prevailing economic conditions there, the investigators were able to offer substantial rewards of up to three times normal monthly income. The main finding was that there was a marked overweighting of low probabilities; this resulted in pronounced risk-seeking for gains. In the highest payoff condition described above, and with a probability of winning of 0.05, certainty equivalents were on average three times larger than expected values.

Many other studies, in a variety of different fields, provide general support for cumulative PT when it is compared with EUT. Insurance is a good example of a field where appropriate comparisons can be made. According to EUT, people buy insurance at a cost greater than the expected monetary loss because they have a utility function that is concave throughout, making them risk-averse in the domain of losses. Thus they dislike large losses disproportionately compared to the small losses of paying insurance premiums. The problem with this explanation is that in many situations people do not buy insurance voluntarily. For example, car insurance is compulsory by law in many countries or states (and even then many people drive uninsured). This failure to buy insurance is easier to reconcile with PT, where the utility function is convex for losses. Furthermore, cumulative PT can also explain why people *do* sometimes buy insurance in terms of the overweighting of low probabilities, or risk-aversion for low probabilities of loss, rather than in terms of the large disutility of loss, as with EUT.

One aspect of insurance provides crucial evidence regarding the validity of the two theories, and this concerns probabilistic insurance, described earlier. According to EUT, if there is a small probability, $r$, that the policy will not pay out, then a person should be prepared to pay approximately $(1 - r)$ times as much as the full premium for probabilistic insurance. For example, if there is a 1% chance that the claim will not be paid in the event of an accident, then a person should be prepared to pay about 99% of the full premium. However, empirical evidence indicates that people have a strong dislike of probabilistic insurance. A study by Wakker, Thaler and Tversky (1997) showed that people were only willing to pay 80% of the full premium in the situation above. On the other hand, cumulative PT can explain this once again in terms of the overweighting of low probabilities; since probabilistic insurance does not reduce the possibility of loss to zero, such a prospect is unappealing. Thus, in the words of Camerer (2000, p. 300):

> Prospect theory can therefore explain why people buy full insurance *and* why they do not buy probabilistic insurance. Expected utility cannot do both.

We find a similar problem for EUT when it comes to explaining the popularity of gambling and the equity premium on stocks compared with bonds. EUT can explain the former by assuming a convex utility function for money, causing risk-seeking, but, given this assumption, stocks should return *less* than bonds, which is patently untrue over the long term. The equity premium is discussed in detail in the first case study in the next chapter. Gambling is explained by PT once again in terms of the overweighting of low probabilities, rather than a convex utility or value function. This can apply to all forms of gambling, from horseracing to playing the lottery.

Various aspects of playing the lottery have already been discussed. There is one further phenomenon here that adds support to the PT model. People like big prizes disproportionately. Although EUT can explain this with the additional assumption of a convex utility function, the overweighting of low probabilities in PT can also be relevant. Larger states or countries tend to find that their lotteries are more appealing and more widely played. One might expect that the larger prizes offered would be offset by the lower probability of winning, but this appears not to be the case.

As far as gambling on horseracing is concerned, there is further interesting evidence available. There is a significant bias toward betting on long shots rather than on favorites. This bias can be measured in terms of the proportion of total money bet on long shots and comparing this with the proportion of times such horses actually win. Studies by Thaler and Ziemba (1988) and Hausch and Ziemba (1995) indicate that long-shot horses with 2% of money bet on them only win about 1% of the time. The overweighing of low probabilities appears to be a relevant factor here. However, if one takes account of the study by Jullien and Salanié (2000) mentioned earlier, the convexity of the utility function for some amounts of gain may also be relevant.

There is another side to the story above, and that is the aversion towards betting on heavy favorites. In this case the Jullien and Salanié (2000) study found that there was a highly non-linear weighting function for losses, causing probabilities of losses to be strongly overweighted. For example, it was found that $\pi(.1) = 0.45$ and $\pi(.3) = 0.65$.

Thus it seems that, while people like to gamble, they are disproportionately afraid of the small possibility of losing when they bet on a heavy favorite.

There is one final aspect to this racetrack betting situation which has broader implications, and this is the 'gambler's fallacy', sometimes referred to as the '**the law of averages**', which was discussed in the previous chapter. Long shots are frequently horses that have lost several races in a row. Gamblers often believe that they are therefore 'due' for a win in these circumstances. The phenomenon is the same as the situation where a coin comes up heads on several consecutive tosses and people believe that there is then a greater chance that the coin will come up tails on the next toss.

There is some recent evidence regarding gender bias as far as decision-weighting is concerned. Fehr-Duda and colleagues (2011) report that women who are in a good mood tend to be more optimistic than men in terms of overestimating low probabilities. It appears from this study that mood has no such influence on probability estimation by men. However, we have seen in the previous chapter that probability estimation can be influenced by the phenomenon of visceral fit, which is obviously related to mood. Again it appears that more research needs to be done in this area, to examine not only how different visceral factors affect probability estimation, but how these different factors may have different effects based on gender.

While this subsection reviews some of the evidence supporting PT in terms of probability weighting, Section 5.8 will provide a more extensive review of empirical evidence in general terms, comparing PT with EUT and other conventional theories.

## 5.8  Criticisms of prospect theory

PT has now been around for over three decades. During that time, not surprisingly considering its non-conventional nature and radical implications, it has attracted numerous criticisms. It is important also to distinguish between OPT and CPT, since different criticisms may apply in each case. Some of the criticisms have been theoretical, and some empirical. In the first case it has been claimed that the theory contains contradictions, is incomplete, or lacks clarification, whereas in the second case the claims are that empirical data violates the assumptions of the theory and that the theory makes incorrect predictions. It is not possible to examine all the criticisms of PT in both its forms here, so our approach is to focus on the ones that have received the most attention in the literature.

In terms of theory we will discuss four main criticisms here: the lack of normative status; internal contradictions; incompleteness; and the determination of reference points. Empirical criticisms relate to: violations of the combination principle; violations of stochastic dominance; the failure to explain the Allais paradoxes; violations of gain-loss separability; the nature of the utility function; endowment effects; the discovered preference hypothesis and misconceptions; and the nature of framing effects. Many of these empirical criticisms have come from various studies by Birnbaum; Birnbaum (2008) summarizes 11 paradoxes where 'prospect theories lead to self-contradiction or systematic false predictions'. It is not appropriate to examine all of these in detail here, but we shall discuss the most fundamental ones.

Once these criticisms have been discussed, it is then possible to consider alternative decision models and come to certain conclusions regarding the current state of decision theory.

### *Lack of normative status*

The most fundamental, although not necessarily the most serious, criticism relates to the normative aspects of the theory. Kahneman and Tversky propose PT as a descriptive rather than a normative theory. The authors treat the EUT model as the normative model to be used as a benchmark, but in rejecting its usefulness as a descriptive model, they do not propose any norm or norms to replace it. While the editing phase of the model adds explanatory power to the model in the descriptive sense, by introducing elements of bounded rationality and decision heuristics it not only makes the model less parsimonious, but it also makes it **indeterminate**. Thus the model loses the simplicity and tractability of EUT and some conventional models which optimize a single variable.

Let us now consider the nature of this indeterminacy. In general terms this is caused by the fact that, like other procedural models, there are features of the model that are underdetermined by the theory, such as the order in which certain operations are performed in the editing phase, the location of reference points, and the shape of the probability weighting function. The issue of the determination of reference points is discussed later in the section. As far as the weighting function is concerned, the cumulative function in equation (5.9) is unlikely to be accurate in detail. In the words of the 1992 study:

> We suspect that decision weights may be sensitive to the formulation of the prospects, as well as to the number, the spacing and the level of outcomes. In particular, there is some evidence to suggest that the curvature of the weighting function is more pronounced when the outcomes are widely spaced. (p. 317)

The evidence referred to here comes from Camerer (1992).

However, the main problem related to normative status concerns violations of both monotonicity and transitivity. Examples of these are given later in the section. Many economists would question whether it is even possible to have theories of 'preference' that violate transitivity. Certainly it becomes more difficult to talk about people maximizing any preference function, although not impossible as we will see. We shall also see that most recent theories of decision-making adopt the same descriptive rather than normative approach, in order to account for the violations of monotonicity and transitivity which have been widely observed.

### Internal contradictions

These criticisms come in particular from Birnbaum (2008), who also reports many studies that are claimed to violate PT empirically which will be discussed later. Birnbaum draws attention to the editing rules, which he states are 'imprecise, contradictory, and conflict with the equations of PT. This means that OPT often has the misfortune (or luxury) of predicting opposite results, depending on what principles are invoked or the order in which they are applied.' The reason why Birnbaum uses the term 'luxury' in the above context is that the contradictions mean that PT can explain most empirical results *ex post* simply by applying the editing rules selectively. Unfortunately the downside of this characteristic is that the theory is claimed to be difficult to use for prediction purposes on an *ex ante* basis. This has unfortunate consequences also as far as the explanation of the Allais paradoxes is concerned, as we shall see. To illustrate the problem, consider the example in Table 5.7.

Each gamble is represented by an urn containing 100 marbles that are identical except for their color. The urn for gamble A contains one red and one blue marble, each of which pays $100, and it has 98 white marbles that pay nothing. Urn B contains one red marble paying $100, two green marbles that pay $45, and 97 white marbles that pay nothing. A marble will be drawn at random from whichever urn the participant chooses, the color of the marble determining the prize.

In the initial choice gambles (choice 1), a person must choose between A and B; there are three **branches**, or outcomes, in each case. A branch corresponds to a probability-consequence event, but in gamble A it can be seen that the first two branches are identical in this respect. Because of this feature (actually it is sufficient for them to have the same consequence or pay-off), the combination principle results in gamble A

**Table 5.7**  Combination and cancellation

| Choice | Gamble | Probability-consequence | Gamble | Probability-consequence |
|--------|--------|-------------------------|--------|-------------------------|
| 1 | A | 0.01 probability to win $100 | B | 0.01 probability to win $100 |
| | | 0.01 probability to win $100 | | 0.02 probability to win $45 |
| | | 0.98 probability to win $0 | | 0.97 probability to win $0 |
| | | | | |
| 2 | A′ | 0.02 probability to win $100 | B | 0.01 probability to win $100 |
| | | 0.98 probability to win $0 | | 0.02 probability to win $45 |
| | | | | 0.97 probability to win $0 |
| | | | | |
| 3 | A″ | 0.01 probability to win $100 | B′ | 0.02 probability to win $45 |
| | | 0.99 probability to win $0 | | 0.98 probability to win $0 |

being represented as A′, which would then be compared with B. Thus the combination principle results in the choice being represented as choice 2. However, it can also be seen that the first branch of A and B is identical, therefore according to the cancellation principle the choice between A and B can be reduced to a choice between A″ and B′, as shown in choice 3. People may not have the same attitudes towards choices 2 and 3, resulting in preference reversals and inconsistent results.

## Incompleteness

OPT is often criticized as being incomplete because it only applies to gambles with no more than two non-zero consequences. CPT is more general than OPT for several reasons: (1) it applies to gambles with more than two non-zero consequences; (2) it removes the need for the editing rules of combination and dominance detection, which are automatically guaranteed by the representation of CPT; and (3) it allows different weighting functions for positive and negative outcomes. Another possible aspect of incompleteness of both forms of PT concerns reference points, discussed next.

## The determination of reference points

Some economists view it as a weakness of PT that reference points are not determined endogenously. The determination of reference points is necessary in order to estimate the incidence and effects of loss-aversion; a good example of this problem relates to the endowment effect, discussed in Case 5.1. If subjects are given something for free in an experiment they are likely to value this object differently than if they had 'earned' it in some way (Cherry et al., 2002). In practice however it is difficult to construct an experimental design where subjects can experience real losses without destroying the incentive to take part. The Cherry and colleagues study overcame this problem by allowing subjects to 'earn' wealth by taking part in a quiz and answering questions correctly. This study is discussed in more detail in Chapter 10 in the context of fairness games.

Kahneman and Tversky, and other supporters of PT, generally use either the existing situation as a reference point, or some anticipated or expected situation. However, more precision regarding the determination of reference points would be an aid to constructing better models of behavior. Certainly more research into how reference points are determined in different situations would be valuable, and this necessitates a detailed theory relating to how people form and adjust expectations. For example, it would be useful to know if different types of saver or investor have the same reference points. Furthermore, an understanding of the process of the dynamic adjustment of reference points over time would aid the analysis of various psychological phenomena; an example is the 'writing off' of sunk costs, discussed in more detail in the next chapter.

### Loss-aversion

This is a key component of PT and implies that most decision-makers find symmetric bets such as lotteries of the form $(0.5, +X; 0.5, -X)$ unattractive. However, a study by Adam and Kroll (2012) indicates that a majority of risk-averse subjects prefer similar symmetric lotteries to a sure thing. Having established that a sample of 50 subjects were all risk averse by comparing their certainty equivalents to a lottery of the form $(0.5, 50; 0.5, 0)$, the study then examined willingness to accept a lottery of $(0.5, Y+X; 0.5, Y-X)$ in preference to a sure thing of $Y$. PT predicts that such subjects would prefer the sure thing because of loss-aversion, but 96% of the subjects played at least one out of 25 lotteries, with an average number played of 15.9. Adam and Kroll suggest that these results provide evidence in favor of a theory of attraction to chance, caused by emotional factors (Albers, 2000).

### Violations of the combination principle

CPT (and many other decision theories like RDU) satisfy coalescing and transitivity, and therefore cannot explain 'event-splitting' effects. Starmer and Sugden (1993) found that preferences depend on how branches are split or coalesced (combined). Birnbaum (1999, 2004, 2007) and Humphrey (1998, 2000, 2001a, 2001b) have reported widespread and robust findings of **event-splitting effects**. In order to gain an understanding of this phenomenon and how it contradicts both OPT and CPT we need to give an example; the one in Table 5.8 below comes from Birnbaum (2004), and presents subjects with two choices, the first between A and B, and the second between A′ and B′. As in Table 5.8, in each

**Table 5.8**    Violations of the combination principle

| A | 85 red marbles to win $100 | B | 85 black marbles to win $100 |
|---|---|---|---|
|   | 10 white marbles to win $50 |   | 10 yellow marbles to win $100 |
|   | 5 blue marbles to win $50 |   | 5 purple marbles to win $7 |
| A′ | 85 black marbles to win $100 | B′ | 95 red marbles to win $100 |
|   | 15 yellow marbles to win $50 |   | 5 white marbles to win $7 |

*Source: Reprinted from* Journal of Mathematical Psychology, *48(2), Birnbaum, M.H., Causes of Allais common consequence paradoxes: An experimental dissection, pp. 87–106, 2004, with permission from Elsevier.*

choice a marble is drawn randomly from an urn, with the color of the marble determining the prize. The subjects must choose which urn to draw from.

It can be seen that A′ is the same as A, with the last two outcomes combined. Likewise, B′ is the same as B, with the first two outcomes combined. Thus, if a person obeys the combination principle, then they should make the same choice between A and B as between A′ and B′. However, Birnbaum (2004) reported that 63% of subjects chose B over A, and 80% chose A′ over B′, a highly significant result.

### Violations of stochastic dominance

CPT and similar theories must satisfy stochastic dominance, as explained earlier. It seems intuitive that people would not choose an option that was obviously stochastically dominated by another option. In order to understand the issue better we will repeat the example given earlier in the chapter from Tversky and Kahneman (1986):

Consider the following pair of lotteries, described by the percentage of marbles of different colors in each box and the amount of money you win or lose depending on the color of a randomly drawn marble. Which lottery do you prefer?

**Option A**

| 90% white | 6% red | 1% green | 1% blue | 2% yellow |
|---|---|---|---|---|
| $0 | win $45 | win $30 | lose $15 | lose $15 |

**Option B**

| 90% white | 6% red | 1% green | 1% blue | 2% yellow |
|---|---|---|---|---|
| $0 | win $45 | win $45 | lose $10 | lose $15 |

*Source: Tversky A., Kahneman D. (1989). Rational Choice and the Framing of Decisions, p.102.*
*In: Karpak B., Zionts S. (eds) Multiple Criteria Decision Making and Risk Analysis Using Microcomputers.*
*NATO ASI Series (Series F: Computer and Systems Sciences) vol. 56. Springer, Berlin, Heidelberg.*

It is transparent in this example that Option B dominates Option A, as we saw earlier. However, there are situations where stochastic dominance is not so obvious. Consider the following example, from the same study by Tversky and Kahneman, which is a slightly modified version of the above problem.

**Option C**

| 90% white | 6% red | 1% green | 3% yellow |
|---|---|---|---|
| $0 | win $45 | win $30 | lose $15 |

**Option D**

| 90% white | 7% red | 1% blue | 2% yellow |
|---|---|---|---|
| $0 | win $45 | lose $10 | lose $15 |

*Source: Tversky A., Kahneman D. (1989). Rational Choice and the Framing of Decisions, p.102. In:*
*Karpak B., Zionts S. (eds) Multiple Criteria Decision Making and Risk Analysis Using Microcomputers.*
*NATO ASI Series (Series F: Computer and Systems Sciences) vol. 56. Springer, Berlin, Heidelberg.*

In this version Option C is basically the same as Option A, but combines blue and yellow marbles into the same category because they both result in a loss of $15. Similarly, Option D is basically the same as Option B, but combines red and green marbles, since they both result in a win of $45. However, the framing of the options makes it more difficult to detect the dominance of D over C. Kahneman and Tversky found that 58% of subjects preferred the dominated option C. Thus, although the authors of CPT were aware of such a violation, CPT itself is not able to explain it.

Birnbaum and Navarrete (1998) also tested for violations of stochastic dominance by asking subjects to compare the following gambles:

A    90 red marbles to win $96          B    85 black marbles to win $96
      5 white marbles to win $14                5 yellow marbles to win $90
      5 blue marbles to win $12                10 purple marbles to win $12

*Source: Compiled with data from Birnbaum and Navarrete (1998), Table 1.*

It should be noted that the representation of the gambles is in a different form from the PT representation, since the focus of Birnbaum's theory is on trees with branches, rather than on prospects. This is explained in the next section in relation to configural weights models. It is easier to see which of the gambles A and B is dominant by showing a 'root gamble', G, which involves 90 red marbles winning $96 and 10 white marbles winning $12. We can now use the principles of combination, cancellation and transitivity to determine dominance. A is dominant over G, and G is dominant over B, therefore A is dominant over B. However, Birnbaum and Navarrete (1998) found that 73% of their student subjects violated dominance in this example and chose B. This result was confirmed in various other similar choices in this study, and was also repeated in Birnbaum, Patton and Lott (1999), with again 73% of another undergraduate student sample violating dominance in various similar problems. Birnbaum (2006) claims that by 2006 he has completed 41 studies with 11,405 participants testing stochastic dominance in various formats, and reports that violation is a very robust finding.

### Failure to explain Allais paradoxes

Different theories explain the Allais paradoxes in different ways. We have already seen that PT was originally constructed in order to explain these paradoxes in terms of editing principles. In order to test the implications of PT, Birnbaum (2007) devised some tests which dissected the Allais paradoxes, by presenting them in gambles of different forms, some using the combination principle, some using the cancellation principle, as illustrated earlier in Table 5.6. Based on empirical data from 200 participants, Birnbaum concludes: 'neither OPT nor CPT with or without their editing principles of cancellation and combination can account for the dissection of the Allais paradoxes' (Birnbaum, 2008, p. 483).

### The nature of the utility function

Another criticism, relating to the utility function, has been raised by Levy and Levy (2002), who claimed to have found evidence contradicting an aspect of PT in a series of experiments which compared the PT and Markowitz utility functions. The Levy and Levy (LL) study argued that the original KT data did not provide a reliable indicator of the shape of utility functions because it always asked subjects to compare prospects that were both either positive or negative. In reality, the LL study claimed, most prospects are mixed, involving situations where there is a possibility of either gain or loss, for example in investing on the stock market. Their study included a number of experiments, asking respondents to choose between such mixed prospects. The main objective was to test whether the data supported the PT model, with the S-shaped utility function, or the M model, with the reversed S-shaped function throughout most of the range. The study used a total of 260 subjects, consisting of business students and faculty from a number of institutions, along with a number of professional practitioners. One of the tasks in the experiments will serve as an example of the methodology. The subjects were asked to consider that they had invested $10,000 in stock and were evaluating the possible returns, choosing between the following two mixed prospects:

**Prospect F:** $(-3,000, 0.5; 4,500, 0.5)$      **Prospect G:** $(-6,000, 0.25; 3,000, 0.75)$

Both prospects are not only mixed, involving the possibility of either gain or loss, but their expected values are the same, 750, and the same for the both the gain and loss components, $-1,500$ and 2,250. According to the PT model, people are risk-averse in the domain of gains; therefore they should prefer the gain of 3,000 with a probability of 0.75 in prospect G to a gain of 4,500 with the probability of 0.5 in prospect F. Similarly, the PT model proposes that people are risk-seeking in the domain of losses; thus they should prefer a loss of 6,000 with a probability of .25 in prospect G to a loss of 3,000 with a probability of 0.5 in prospect F. Therefore prospect G is dominant over prospect F according to the PT model, while the situation is reversed according the M model. The LL study found that 71% of their subjects preferred F while only 27% preferred G. They interpreted this finding as showing strong evidence against the PT model, and, combined with the results of other tasks in their experiments, they concluded that the M model was better supported.

However, The LL study has been criticized in a paper by Wakker (2003). Wakker claims that the data of the LL study can still be used to support the PT model, since the LL study ignored the element of decision-weighting. The LL study justified this on the grounds that the probabilities involved in their experiments were always at least 0.25 in magnitude, and that probabilities in this range should involve a linear weighting function. Wakker disputes this, claiming that non-linearities in this range can have a significant distorting effect, enough to make the results compatible with PT. When we consider the finding of Jullien and Salanié reported above, with losses involving $\pi(.3) = 0.65$, Wakker's conclusion seems to have some justification.

## Violations of gain-loss separability

The gambles described in Tables 5.6 and 5.7 have been positive gambles. Mixed gambles, termed regular prospects in PT, were described earlier, and are evaluated according to expression (5.9), meaning that the gains and losses are valued separately and then added together. This assumes the feature of gain-loss separability. In simple (non-mathematical) terms this means that if you prefer the good part of B to the good part of A, and if you prefer the bad part of B to the bad part of A, then you should prefer B to A. Various empirical studies by Wu and Markle (2008), and Birnbaum and Bahra (2007) have contradicted this feature. Wu and Markle (2008) report a reversal between preferences for mixed gamble and the associated gain and loss gambles such that mixed gamble A is preferred to mixed gamble B, but the gain and loss portions of B are preferred to the gain and loss portions of A. The implication of this is that the argument given in PT for the kinked utility function described in equation (5.12) and illustrated in Figure 5.7 is false. This does not necessarily mean that the utility function is not kinked, but the existence of a kink must rest on a different premise from that given in both OPT and CPT.

## The discovered preference hypothesis and misconceptions

There are some studies that combine a number of objections. The **discovered preference hypothesis (DPH)** developed by Plott (1996) proposes that people's preferences are not necessarily revealed in their decisions. They have to be discovered through a process of information gathering, deliberation, and trial-and-error learning. Subjects must therefore have adequate opportunities and incentives for discovery, and it is claimed that studies lacking these factors are unreliable. Plott argues that most studies that support the endowment effect are in this category, lacking the necessary elements of experimental design that ensure reliability. Binmore (1999) makes a similar claim.

Plott and Zeiler (2005, 2007) pursue this issue further, by performing experiments to test whether subject misconceptions, rather than PT preferences, can account for the gap between willingness to pay (WTP) and willingness to accept (WTA) that PT refers to as the endowment effect. It should be noted that the methodology in this study was different from that in List (2004) and many other studies, because it did not focus on willingness to trade as such, but on the concepts of WTA and WTP, which entail various problems in terms of analysis. Plott and Zeiler (PZ) draw attention in particular to the concept of '**subject misconceptions**', and point out that this is not operationally defined or quantified. It is in effect a compound effect of several effects that PZ identify: misunderstanding an optimal response; learning effects; lack of subjects' attention because of inadequate incentives to give an optimal response; and giving a strategic response. Since these problems apply to much research in experimental economics it is worth giving some explanation regarding each of them and discussing the PZ approach to solving these problems. This approach incorporates the following four elements.

**1**    *Use of an incentive compatible elicitation device*

When subjects are asked to state a WTP or WTP they are essentially in a kind of auction scenario, and this is not the same buying/selling scenario as the normal marketplace. This lack of familiarity may cause subjects to misunderstand how to give an optimal response. Therefore an important principle in the PZ study was to use an **incentive compatible elicitation device**. A common technique used in experimental economics in such situations to elicit valid responses is the **Becker-DeGroot-Marschak (BDM)** mechanism. This mechanism pits each buyer and seller against a random bid, which determines the price paid by the buyer and that received by the seller. All sellers stating bids lower than the random bid sell the good, and all buyers stating bids higher than the random bid buy the good. Sellers bidding higher than the random bid and buyers bidding lower do not transact. The purpose of this mechanism is to elicit bids that reflect the true value to each party. The optimal response is to state a bid equal to the subject's true value.

**2**    *Training*

Since it is not obvious to subjects that stating one's true value is On optimal response, especially given that the random bid is determined by a lottery, PZ took time in their study to fully explain the mechanism using numerical examples. An illustration here will clarify the situation. Say a seller's true value is $6, but they overbid, stating $7, maybe under the misapprehension that this may cause the buyer to bid higher, as in many real-life situations. This is an example of a **strategic response**, where one party to a transaction takes into account the behavior and reactions of the other party. If the random bid is $6.50 they will not transact, and there is an opportunity cost of $0.50, because they are forgoing a transaction that would give them a consumer surplus of $0.50. Now take the situation where a buyer's true value is $6. They may underbid, stating $5, maybe under the misapprehension that this may cause the seller to come down in price, again as in real-life situations. If the random bid is $5.50, they will not transact, and will again forgo $0.50. The training was therefore designed to ensure that subjects understood the nature of the BDM mechanism, and therefore stated bids that represented their true values.

**3**    *Practice rounds*

This procedure allows subjects to 'learn though using the mechanism while still educating themselves about its properties'. Subjects can also ask questions and the experimenter can check that subjects are understanding the nature of the task.

**4**    *Anonymity*

Anonymity in decisions and payouts is important because otherwise subjects may again be inclined to make strategic responses, either to impress other subjects or to impress the experimenter.

PZ (2005) found that, while they could replicate the WTA-WTP gap in the study of Kahneman, Knetsch and Thaler (1990) using an experimental procedure lacking in controls, when they implemented the full set of controls described above the gap was not observed. PZ concluded that this ability to 'turn the gap on and off' constituted a rejection of the PT interpretation of the gap as being an endowment effect, in favor of the theory of subjects' misconceptions as being the cause.

The PZ study is certainly a valuable and informative one in many ways, but its conclusion has one main weakness. This is that the methodology is 'all-or-nothing', in the sense that either there is very little experimental control, or various controls are combined together. The result is that a number of effects are confounded together in the 'subjects' misconceptions' category. Plott and Zeiler admit this, giving five possible interpretations of these misconceptions (some of which they reject) in their conclusion. In particular, in the summary of their 2007 paper, they explicitly state that their objections to endowment effect theory do not challenge PT in general. However, like Birnbaum, they claim that a kink in the utility function is not necessary to explain empirical findings, in this case WTA-WTP asymmetries.

Further research is needed, using various degrees of control in the experimental design, to establish whether the switching off of the WTA-WTP gap is mainly due to misunderstanding the optimal response, learning effects, giving some kind of strategic response, or misinterpreting the intentions of the experiment or experimenter. It may be that learning effects, through practice rounds, could be the main factor; this would support the findings of List (2004) reported earlier.

It has been argued that the best type of experimental design to ensure that the requirements of the DPH are met is a **single-task individual-choice** design (Cubitt, Starmer and Sugden, 2001). Such a design can ensure that subjects get an opportunity to practice a single task repeatedly, with the requisite learning effect, and it can also ensure simplicity and transparency, which are difficult to achieve in market-based studies, where tasks are more complex and involve interactions with others. However, when Cubitt, Starmer and Sugden reviewed the results of nine different experiments involving such a design, they found that the results still violated the independence axiom for consistent choices in Allais-type situations, discussed earlier. Another study by Loomes, Starmer and Sugden (2003) also questioned the interpretation of the disappearance of the WTA-WTP gap under market experience. These researchers note that:

> even after repeated trading, individuals' valuations of given lotteries remain subject to a high degree of stochastic variation, arguably reflecting many subjects' continuing uncertainty about what these lotteries are really worth to them. (p. 166)

Having mentioned these results and conclusions, we can now consider an associated problem with the PZ conclusion. If subjects did not have a clear understanding of the experiment they may have been inclined to state certain values which did not reflect their true values, perhaps still giving a strategic response. Although Plott and Zeiler think this unlikely, it would mean that their results do not provide evidence rejecting the occurrence of the endowment effect in the real world outside the laboratory. Recent field studies confirm the existence of the endowment effect under most real-world conditions, although they also report that the economic environment does play a role in affecting people's perceived reference states and consequently on their valuations (Köszegi and Rabin, 2006; Knetsch and Wong, 2009).

## *The nature of framing effects*

Inconsistent results have been reported as far as the ability of PT to explain framing effects. Different types of framing effect have been demonstrated by Levin and colleagues (1998): standard risky choice, attribute framing and goal framing. This study claimed that PT probably best explains the first type of effect, but not the other two. It also doubted that PT could interpret the empirical evidence of risky choices in different contexts. A similar conclusion was reached by Wang and Johnston (1995), who indicated that framing effects are context-dependent, rather than being a generalized phenomenon. Other evidence suggests that a framing effect depends on task, content and context variables inherent in the choice problem (Wang, 1996; Fagley and Miller, 1997).

A further body of research criticizes the original approach of Tversky and Kahneman (1981) and their illustration of framing effects in a situation sometimes referred to as the '**Asian disease**' problem. People are informed about a disease that threatens 600 citizens and asked to choose between two undesirable options (Tversky and Kahneman 1981). In the 'positive frame' people are given a choice between (A) saving 200 lives with certainty, or (B) a one-third chance of saving all 600 with a two-thirds chance of saving nobody. Most people prefer A to B here. In the 'negative frame' people are asked to choose between (C) 400 people dying with certainty, or (D) a two-thirds chance of 600 dying and a one-third chance of nobody dying. In this case most people prefer D to C, in spite of the fact that A and C are identical results or 'prospects' and B and D are identical results. As well as illustrating framing effects and preference reversal, this example also illustrates loss-aversion (saving lives is seen as a gain, while dying is seen as a loss).

Several studies have argued that this approach actually confounded two different effects: a framing effect and a reflection effect (Arkes, 1991; Kühberger, 1995; Levin et al., 1998; Chang, Yen and Duh, 2002). This distinction now needs to be explained in some detail in order to understand the implications.

A framing effect depends on whether the problem is framed in a positive or negative *frame*, which depends on the negation 'not'. A reflection effect depends on the *domain* of the problem, meaning whether it relates to a gain or loss. To illustrate this difference, statement A – '200 people will be saved' – represents both a positive frame and a positive domain, whereas statement C – '400 people will die' – involves both a negative frame and a negative domain. It is therefore argued that, because frame and domain correlate perfectly in the TK treatment of the Asian disease problem, it is impossible to disentangle the framing and reflection effects. On the other hand, it can be claimed that the statement '400 people will not be saved', although identical in meaning with statement A, involves a negative frame but a positive domain. Similarly, the statement '200 people will not die' is identical in meaning with statement C, but involves a positive frame with a negative domain. Thus by restating A and C, it is possible to test PT against other theories as far as explaining framing effects is concerned. This aspect is discussed in the next section.

## 5.9  Recent theories and conclusions

It should not be inferred from the discussion above that these have been the only criticisms of PT; we have concentrated on these issues since they have attracted the most discussion in the literature. In response to the various theoretical and empirical issues and problems raised, a number of new theories or models of decision-making under risk and uncertainty have been proposed over the last two decades, some even predating CPT, which have claimed to surmount these problems and explain empirical findings in a more satisfactory way. It is impossible to survey all these models here, but six main ones will be considered: (1) third-generation PT; (2) probabilistic mental models (PMM); (3) fuzzy-trace theory (FTT); (4) the priority heuristic; (5) imprecision theory; and (6) configural weights models.

### Third-generation prospect theory (PT3)

It makes sense to discuss this first, since it builds on the elements of both the first (1979) and second (1992) versions of PT. Schmidt, Starmer and Sugden (2008) proposed $PT^3$ as a model that extends the predictions of PT in an area in which the theory had previously been silent, the situation where reference points are uncertain. Therefore $PT^3$ can be applied to situations where decision-makers are endowed with lotteries and have the opportunity to sell or exchange them, for example where they buy insurance or sell stocks, unlike the original versions of PT. Furthermore, $PT^3$ was intended to explain two commonly observed anomalies in EUT: (1) discrepancies between WTA and WTP valuations of lotteries; and (2) preference reversals in gambles involving what are referred to as **P-bets** and **$-bets**. These concepts were originally developed by MacCrimmon and Smith (1986).

Some detailed explanation here will aid an understanding of both methodology and the relationship between uncertainty, preference reversals and transitivity. A P-bet offers a relatively large probability of a modest sum of money and a residual probability of zero.

A $-bet offers a smaller probability of a considerably bigger prize and a larger chance of zero. Respondents are asked to place certainty equivalents on each bet and also to make a straight choice between the two bets. A common preference reversal observed here is that people place a higher money value on the $-bet, but choose the P-bet. As an example, consider the following two prospects:

**$-bet:** A = (0.1, $140)    certainty equivalent of $14
**P-bet:** B = (0.8, $15)    certainty equivalent of $12

A has the higher certainty equivalent, but people often still prefer B, the P-bet. If we now refer to prospect C as a sure bet of $13 (or any sum between $12 and $14), this would result in the following ordering of preferences:

$$P \geq \$, \$ \geq C, C \geq P$$

which violates transitivity.

In order to generalize PT to apply to situations with uncertain reference points, Schmidt, Starmer, and Sugden (2008) propose two components: (1) a definition of 'gain' or 'loss' relative to stochastic reference points, known as reference acts; and (2) a rank-dependent method of assigning decision weights to any act $f$, relative to any reference act $h$.

In its most general form PT[3] incorporates the approach of Sugden (2003) in terms of using reference-dependent subjective expected utility (RDSEU), and proposes a value function of the form:

$$V(f, h) = \Sigma_i \, v(f[s_i], h[s_i]) \, W(s_i; f, h)$$

Where $W(s_i; f, h)$ is the decision weight assigned to state $s_i$ when $f$ is being evaluated from $h$. PT[3] also uses parameterizations relating to utility functions and probability weighting functions whose validity has already been established by previous versions of PT. Schmidt, Starmer and Sugden claim three main advantages of this modeling approach:

1   Generality – it is more general than previous versions of PT, applying to three key aspects of preferences: attitudes to consequences, attitudes to probability, and attitudes to gain and loss.

2   Parsimony – the model is as simple as possible given its application above; only one parameter is involved for each of the three aspects.

3   Congruence with reality – when the model is applied to existing evidence it explains both the anomalies mentioned earlier, in that it predicts both WTA and WTP discrepancies for lottery valuations and the preference reversal with P and $ bets.

Regarding the last advantage, the explanation of preference reversal is significant, in that it is based on 'the interaction of empirically plausible degrees of loss-aversion, diminishing sensitivity and probability weighting' rather than being caused by the violation of procedural invariance, which had been the interpretation of many psychologists. Applying these three different factors to the example above, this means in simple terms that people value the $-bet more than the P-bet because of overweighting of low probabilities, they value the sure bet more than the P-bet because of loss-aversion, and they prefer the P-bet to the $-bet because of diminishing marginal sensitivity.

Schmidt, Starmer and Sugden do not propose that PT[3] accounts for all preference reversals of the P and $ bet type; they acknowledge that violations of procedural invariance are important, in that different methods of eliciting information can influence decisions, but they claim that, given its psychological plausibility and the way their model fits the evidence, PT[3] does play a significant role in the explanation of preference reversal.

*Probabilistic mental models*

According to the theory of probabilistic mental models (PMM) (Gigerenzer et al., 1991), people first attempt to construct a local mental model (LMM) of the task given to them, and then utilize it to solve the problem using long-term memory and elementary logical operations. If, as in any complex problem, this process is not possible, then a PMM is constructed using probabilistic information generated from long-term memory. Thus PMM theory suggests that a decision-maker solves a problem by applying inductive inference, meaning that they put the specific decision task into a larger context. The theory explains framing effects in terms of the inferences people make when presented with incomplete information.

We can compare PMM with PT by examining how each views the Asian disease problem. PT explains the Asian disease problem by using different reference points for different comparisons. Statements A and B are worded in terms of people being saved, both involving a *perceived* positive domain (the actual domain is negative since people are still dying); thus in the domain of gains people are risk averse and prefer option A to B. On the other hand, statements C and D are expressed in terms of people dying, involving a negative perceived domain, or losses. In this domain people are risk-seeking, and therefore prefer option D to C.

By contrast, according to PMM, when people edit the statement '200 people will be saved' they may infer that maybe over time more than 200 will be saved. On the other hand, the statement '400 people will die' may be edited so that it is inferred that maybe more than 400 people will eventually die. Thus when statements A and C are expressed differently, with negative frame and positive domain and vice versa, it is possible to test PMM theory against PT. For example, when asked to compare A': 400 people will not be saved' with B: 1/3 chance that 600 will be saved, and 2/3 chance that 0 will be saved, PT predicts that A' will be favored, while PMM theory predicts that B will be preferred, interpreting A' to mean that maybe more than 400 people will not be saved.

This is the approach taken by Chang and colleagues (2002), who test PT against two competing models: probabilistic mental models and **fuzzy-trace theory** (Reyna and Brainerd, 1991), discussed next.

*Fuzzy-trace theory*

Fuzzy-trace theory (FTT) proposes that people prefer to reason using simplified representations of information, that is, the gist of the information, rather than using exact details. For example, both numerical outcomes and probabilities are represented dichotomously; this means that the Asian disease options can be simplified as follows:

Statement A:   Some people will be saved.
Statement B:   Some people will be saved or nobody will be saved.
Statement C:   Some people will die.
Statement D:   Nobody will die or some people will die.

In choosing between A and B, the first part of the statement is common to both options, thus the choice centers on the difference 'nobody will be saved', and A is preferred to B. Similarly, in choosing between C and D the difference is 'nobody will die', and D is preferred to C. Therefore, given the original four options FTT makes the same predictions as PT. However, option A' now becomes: 'some people will not be saved', which cannot be compared directly with B. Likewise, option C' becomes 'some people will not die', which cannot be compared directly with D. Under these circumstances, according to FTT, people are forced to think in more detail about the problem, calculating expected values, and choosing according to their attitudes to risk.

The study by Chang and colleagues (2002) attempts to test the different theories against each other by performing two experiments. In both cases the experiments are expressed in terms of an investment decision problem, but in the first case the options are presented in the same way as the original Asian disease problem, with A being compared to B and C being compared to D. The results confirm all three theories and it is impossible to test for differences between them. However, in the second experiment A′ is compared to B and C′ is compared to D. In this case all three theories make different predictions. Chang and colleagues find that FTT explains the results best, since there is no significant difference between responses according to whether the frame is positive or negative. Thus they conclude that there is no framing effect in the situation where domain and frame are different, confirming the study of Stone (1994). They find further evidence in favor of FTT in the comments of subjects relating to the scenario. In the first experiment only 18% of the subjects (undergraduate business students) mentioned the calculation of expected values in their comments. By contrast, in the second experiment they find that 35% of the subjects refer to the calculation of expected values.

However, there is one main shortcoming of the Chang and colleagues study, which is admitted by the authors. This is that the subjects are not asked to indicate their perceived problem domain or problem frame. For example, the study assumes that option A′ (400 people will not be saved) involves a perceived problem domain of gain. This assumption is certainly questionable, since it can be argued that the reference point used here may be that all people will be saved, and that therefore A′ involves a perceived loss. If this is indeed the case then the predictions of PT are confirmed. More research needs to be done in this area to ascertain how people perceive problem domains.

There are important policy implications of framing effects, in particular in the type of accounting situation described by Chang and colleagues. Over the last two decades there have been numerous accounting scandals in both the USA and Europe involving the reporting of financial information to both shareholders and auditors. If framing effects are better understood, this may enable government legislators and standard setters, like the International Accounting Standards Board, to better determine both the kind of information and presentation of information so as to prevent fraud and deception.

## The priority heuristic

In its philosophy this model is similar to the two above, being a later development of them, and can be regarded as part of the 'fast and frugal heuristics' research program (Gigerenzer and Goldstein, 1996; Gigerenzer et al., 1999, Gigerenzer, 2004). The priority heuristic originated with Brandstätter, Gigerenzer and Hertwig (2006), who proposed it as a simple sequential cognitive process in contrast to more complicated models involving non-linear transformations of utilities and probabilities on top of EUT. The priority heuristic is a three-step process, consisting of a priority rule, a stopping rule, and a decision rule, as follows:

**Priority rule**  Go through reasons in the order: minimum gain, probability of minimum gain, maximum gain, probability of maximum gain.

**Stopping rule**  Stop examination if the minimum gains differ by 1/10 (or more) of the maximum gain; otherwise, stop examination if probabilities differ by 1/10 (or more) of the probability scale.

**Decision rule**  Choose the gamble with the more attractive gain (probability). The term attractive refers to the gamble with the higher (minimum or maximum) gain and the lower probability of the minimum gain.

Brandstätter, Gigerenzer and Hertwig (2006) report that their empirical findings show that the priority heuristic can explain the Allais paradox and the same four-fold pattern of risk attitudes as CPT. Furthermore, they claim that it can explain certain observed intransitivities which cause preference reversals that cannot be explained by CPT. In view of its simplicity, the principle of Occam's razor would tend also to favor its application.

It has been noted by its authors that the priority heuristic is designed to apply to difficult decisions where trade-offs are inevitable. Brandstätter, Gigerenzer, and Hertwig

(2008) extend their approach by advocating what they refer to as an Adaptive Toolbox Model of risky choice. This employs the priority heuristic as a second stage of a decision-making process, where the first stage involves seeking a no-conflict solution. This in turn means searching for dominance, and if that fails, applying a similarity heuristic. This first stage is similar to the approach of Rubinstein (1988, 2003), which is explained in Chapter 8 in the context of intertemporal choice. Only if the first stage is unable to detect a no-conflict solution does the second stage involving the priority heuristic apply.

There have been various criticisms of the priority heuristic and the fast and frugal heuristics program. At the empirical level, Birnbaum (2008) claims that the priority heuristic fails to explain various observed results. There has also been criticism at the theoretical level. The model is proposed as a process model rather than an 'as-if' model, but it has been claimed that there are a number of components of fast and frugal heuristics that involve questionable assumptions, making the program in general psychologically implausible (Dougherty, Franco-Watkins and Thomas, 2008).

### The Take-the-First heuristic

This is another example of a 'fast-and-frugal' heuristic, which applies in situations where decision options are open-ended as opposed to being a defined set presented to the decision-maker, and where time constraints are important. Both of these conditions are relevant in many common decision scenarios, such as choosing a tie to wear in the morning or which traffic lane to drive in. The first task for the decision-maker is obviously to generate a list of possible options. The Take-the-First (TTF) heuristic suggests we should take the first decision that our minds generate in this situation (Johnson and Raab, 2003; Raab and Johnson, 2007). The rationale for this heuristic is that our minds tend to generate better options first, with later ones being less appropriate or beneficial, and time constraints may prevent a long scrutiny of all possible alternatives. For example, doctors may only have a matter of minutes to save a patient's life in the emergency room. Hepler and Felz (2012) suggest that the TTF heuristic may be appropriate in many sports situations, and tested the theory in a basketball context. They reported that: (1) subjects used the heuristic on a majority of the trials (70%); (2) earlier generated options were better than later ones; (3) first options were meaningfully generated; (4) final options were meaningfully selected; and (5) more confident subjects used the heuristic more frequently and generated fewer options than less confident subjects.

### Salience theory

This can also be regarded as related to the 'fast and frugal' heuristics approach, being a theory of choice among lotteries in which the decision-maker's attention is drawn to precisely defined salient payoffs (Bordalo, Gennaioli and Shleifer, 2012). It suggests that decision-makers represent lotteries as having decision weights which are distorted in favor of salient payoffs, where salience is a function of contrasts between payoffs. An important implication for consumer behavior is that people compare attributes where contrasts are greatest. The study claims that this model fits many empirical phenomena related to risk-seeking and makes accurate predictions related to preference reversals.

### Imprecision theory

The basic premise of this theory is that many choices that people make involve a degree of uncertainty or imprecision. This idea has a long history, but it has only been since the mid-1990s that models of imprecision, often referred to as **stochastic decision models** since they involve a random error, began to be formulated. These models essentially took some form of deterministic model, like EUT, as their base, and then added a stochastic component. The main purpose was to explain certain violations involving preference reversal that could not be explained by purely deterministic models. There is a common finding in empirical studies that subjects make preference reversals even when faced with the same pairwise choice problem twice within the same experiment. Studies by Starmer and Sugden (1989), Camerer (1989), Hey and Orme (1994) and Ballinger and Wilcox (1997) indicate that between one-quarter and one-third of subjects switch preferences on repeated questions.

These violations again relate to the editing phase of the choice process, involving framing effects. An early model developed by Loomes and Sugden (1982, 1987) was called **regret theory** and was discussed earlier. This approach was explicitly designed to take into account both violations of monotonicity and transitivity. This theory has the further advantage that it posits a preference function that can be maximized, giving the model normative status. However, experiments by Starmer and Sugden (1998) suggest that regret theory does not explain all the observed violations. Loomes and Sugden (1995, 1998) also propose a **random preference** model, which posits that people act on preferences based on a core theory, but the parameters to be applied in any context vary randomly, for example the degree of risk-aversion. However, this and other stochastic models failed to account for more than a subset of the systematic deviations, i.e. preference reversals, commonly observed.

More recently Butler and Loomes (2007) have developed and tested a model that appears to account for a greater number of observed preference reversals. It involves a model originally developed by MacCrimmon and Smith (1986) based on P-bets and $-bets. As we have seen in the discussion of PT[3], a P-bet offers a relatively large probability of a modest sum of money and a residual probability of zero. A $-bet offers a smaller probability of a considerably bigger prize and a larger chance of zero. Respondents are asked to place certainty equivalents on each bet and also to make a straight choice between the two bets. The preference reversal observed here is that people place a higher money value on the $-bet, but choose the P-bet, and this result violates transitivity, as we have already seen.

Butler and Loomes (2007) varied the standard procedure to allow for imprecision by allowing participants to respond in any of four ways, rather than just two. Thus instead of just offering the simple alternative: (1) prefer A; (2) prefer B, they offered four choices: (1) definitely prefer A; (2) think I prefer A but am not sure; (3) think I prefer B but am not sure; (4) definitely prefer B. The study concluded:

> in the absence of very precise "true" preferences, respondents faced with equivalence tasks may be liable to pick one value from an imprecision interval, with their perception of the range of this interval, and their selection of a particular value from within it, both liable to be influenced by various "cues" or "anchors". (p. 293)

An important anchor turned out to be the starting point of the iterative procedure for determining certainty equivalents. This procedure, and the problems involved, is discussed in more detail in Chapter 7 in the section on methodology.

Another important conclusion by Butler and Loomes was that 'all methods of eliciting those preferences, with or without incentives, are vulnerable to procedural effects of one kind or another.' They reject the idea of a 'gold standard' in terms of procedure.

## Configural weights models

These represent a family of models rather than a single model. Three main versions have been developed in recent years: rank-affected multiplicative weights (RAM); transfer of attention exchange (TAX); and gains decomposition utility (GDU). It goes outside the scope of this text to describe these in detail here, so we will concentrate on describing the main common features, and how they compare and contrast with PT.

There are three common factors: (1) both types of model are descriptive rather than normative; (2) both use reference-dependent utility or value functions; and (3) both are psychological models, so that they use 'psychophysical' utility and decision-weighting functions based on psychological theory.

The most fundamental difference is that in configural weights models people treat gambles as trees with branches rather than as prospects or probability distributions. Branches with lower consequences receive greater weight, as a consequence of risk-aversion; thus these models do not rely on non-linear utility functions, although they do not rule them out. Weights depend in part on the rank of a branch with the set of total outcomes. Configural weights models generally violate the principle of combination or coalescing, and the principle of cancellation, used in PT.

Different models use different methods for assigning weights. In the RAM model, the weight of each branch of a gamble is the product of a function of the branch's probability multiplied by a constant that depends on the rank and augmented sign of the branch's consequence (Birnbaum, 1997). The augmented sign is positive for branches with lower consequences and negative for branches with higher consequences. A middle-ranked branch in a three-branch gamble has an augmented sign of zero. The decision situation is best illustrated by a simple binary gamble, like tossing a coin, shown in a tree diagram in Figure 5.11. The augmented sign for the lower consequence, tail, would be positive, thus increasing its weight, while the augmented sign for the higher consequence, head, would be negative, decreasing its weight.

The TAX model also represents the utility of a gamble as a weighted average of the utilities of the consequences, with the weights depending on probability and rank of the branches. The main difference is that in TAX the branch weights result from transfers of attention from branch to branch. This is how Birnbaum (2008) describes TAX:

> Intuitively, a decision maker deliberates by attending to the possible consequences of an action. Those branches that are more probable deserve more attention, but branches leading to lower valued consequences also deserve greater attention if a person is risk averse. In the TAX model, these shifts in attention are represented by weights transferred from branch to branch. (p. 470)

Again we can use Figure 5.11 for illustration.

**Figure 5.11** TAX model

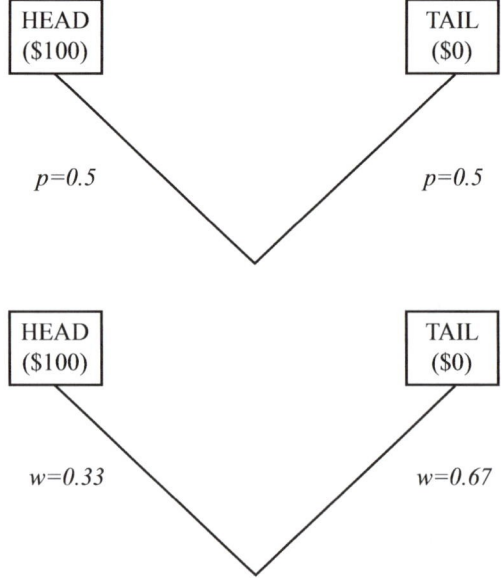

Let us assume for simplicity that the utility function is linear and identical with money value. In the first diagram it can be seen that the expected value of the gamble is $50. Both branches have equal probabilities, so this has no affect on attention in this example; however, the lower valued consequence, tail, receives more attention, and it is assumed in the second diagram that a weight of 1/6 or 0.17 is transferred from the probability of a head to the probability of a tail, thus giving this consequence a decision weight of 0.67 compared to a weight of 0.33 for a head. A person would then value the gamble at $33. This example illustrates also how the TAX model accounts for risk-aversion, without resorting to a non-linear utility function.

The GDU model takes the approach of decomposing multibranch gambles into a series of two-branch gambles. Thus a three-branch gamble is resolved in two stages: first, the chance to win the lowest consequence, and otherwise to win a binary gamble to win one of the two higher prizes. The binary gambles are represented by the RDU model described in Section 5.2.

The main advantage of configural weights models claimed by Birnbaum (2008) is that they explain many of the 11 paradoxes left unexplained by PT in either form. He furthermore claims that TAX in particular is able not only to explain all 11 paradoxes, but to predict them using parameters estimated from previous data, thus avoiding one of the methodological issues discussed in Chapter 2.

## Conclusion

Perhaps at this stage the main conclusion that readers may have arrived at is that there are too many theories of decision-making under risk. This would echo the criticism of Fudenberg (2006) mentioned in Chapter 2, that there are too many theories in behavioral economics in general. On the face of it, we would agree with this conclusion; one unfortunate consequence is that it is easy for students to become confused, since there appear to be so many contradictions and conflicts. However, we believe that there are two important factors that need to be considered in this context that will help to guide the student of behavioral economics, and point the way to the future: (1) common factors; and (2) differentiation between phenomena and explanations for phenomena.

**1**   *Common factors*

It has already been seen in the discussion of configural weights models that these models share a number of common factors with PT. This aspect of common ground can be generalized to most recent models of decision-making. However, it is easy to overlook this, since academics have an inevitable tendency to stress differences rather than similarities when they want to get papers published in journals. Maybe we should label this a 'publishing bias', which produces a 'polarization effect', so that the stances of different researchers appear to be more different than they really are. The most important factors which recent theories tend to share relate to having: a descriptive rather than normative approach; reference dependence; loss-aversion; and a psychological basis underlying the model. It is probably fair to say that any new models or extensions of existing ones will share these features. Reference dependence and loss-aversion appear to be fundamental psychological features, and we have seen that these features are also well supported by neuroeconomic studies. As we have also seen in Chapter 2, many researchers believe that progress can only be made by moving beyond 'as-if' models and utilizing process models that incorporate such psychological and neural features explicitly. However, at present there is a lack of clarity relating to the nature of some of these features, and this brings us on to the second factor.

**2**   *Differentiation between phenomena and explanations for phenomena*

We have already seen in the discussion of endowment effects that it is important to distinguish phenomena from explanations of these phenomena. There may often be several theories or explanations as to why a particular effect occurs. Thus it helps to avoid confusion if separate terms are used for phenomena and explanations. This differentiation is important with other fundamental concepts as well, such as risk-aversion and loss-aversion (Schmidt and Zank, 2005). We have also seen that there are different ways of accounting for risk-aversion. PT and many other models do this by using non-linear utility functions. Birnbaum and Stegner (1979) on the other hand propose that people place more weight on lower valued consequences because of asymmetric costs of over- and underestimating value. This was illustrated in Figure 5.9. A similar distinction applies to the concept of loss-aversion. PT and other theories often define loss-aversion in different ways, as we have seen, but they again attribute loss-aversion to the nature of the utility function, with a kink or asymmetry at the reference point. In contrast, configural weights models account for loss-aversion by a transfer of weights.

Of course the different models obey or violate different principles, and as a result make different predictions. As has now been said several times, the ultimate test rests on empirical evidence relating to these predictions, provided that such evidence is correctly obtained, analyzed and interpreted. At this point such evidence is still indecisive, which is why there are so many models still being considered. Many studies have indicated the need for further research in order to determine with greater certainty which models have more real-world application and which do not. Some studies have been quite specific regarding what type of research is needed here. For example, Birnbaum (2008) states:

> What has not yet been done is the assessment of the behavior of individuals over a large number of replications with a larger number of properties tested within the same person. (p. 497)

The advantage of such studies is that it would become possible not only to determine appropriate models in general, but also to see whether different models apply to different people. In the meantime Birnbaum suggests, and we would agree, that it is best to assume that everyone can be represented by the same model, while different people may have different parameters in that model. We can also conclude at this stage that the appropriate model for descriptive purposes will not in general be EUT, but some form of process model. Although it is not yet clear which model or models will turn out to be superior, it is at least clear that process theories like PT and configural weights theories both explain and predict better than EUT.

As a final concluding point it should be noted that there are other anomalies in EUT, and most other theories and models, which are not easily explained by any additional assumptions that are consistent with the NM. Some of these have been mentioned in Chapter 3. For example, one factor is that people appear to value control, even when this conveys no rational advantage. A study by Langer (1975) indicated that people who were allowed to choose their entries in a lottery valued their tickets more highly than those who were simply assigned entries at random. When researchers offered to buy the tickets back from the subjects they found a huge difference: those subjects who were assigned tickets were willing to sell them for an average of just under two dollars, while those who selected their own entries demanded more than eight dollars. Another anomaly that is discussed in Langer's study involves the same factor of illusory control over events. When people played a game of chance against an opponent, the appearance of the opponent affected the amount that players were willing to bet. The game simply involved drawing a playing card, with the higher card winning. Half the bettors played against a well-dressed and confidently acting opponent, while the other half played against opponents who acted in a bumbling manner and wore ill-fitting clothes. Of course the chance of winning is a half in either situation, yet bettors were willing to bet 47% more when faced with opponents who appeared inferior.

This factor of control, however illusory, is likely to be one factor why people regard car travel as less risky than train or air travel. PT can accommodate this apparently irrational tendency in terms of the overweighting of certain probabilities, although it should be noted that in this case again the probabilities are not necessarily low. A different weighting function may be involved in these situations, in the same way that the Jullien and Salanié study found different weighting functions for losses compared with gains.

In more general terms, the strong desire to be in control appears to be an important reason why the majority of people still believe in the phenomenon of free will (Wegner 2001). Again, evolutionary psychology has proposed an explanation for this emphasis on control. In our past our ancestors developed a very useful cause-imputing mental adaptation which enabled them to impute and analyze causes of events. It was often better from a survival point of view to impute an incorrect cause of an event than to consider the event as being causeless. For example, if one's goods disappeared overnight, it might have been better for one's future prospects to blame the wrong person for stealing the goods than to believe that the goods just vanished without a cause. A strong desire for accountability has always been a prominent feature of most criminal justice systems in all kinds of different societies. This aspect of social fairness and punishment is discussed in detail in Chapter 10.

It seems fitting to end this conclusion by commenting on the main criticism of PT discussed earlier, its lack of normative status. In the past there has been too much reliance on axioms like monotonicity and transitivity in spite of mounting empirical evidence of their violation. Models like PT have been rejected because they permit such violations. For example, Quiggin (1982) commented that the implication in PT that certain choices may violate transitivity was 'an undesirable result'.

Economics as a science needs to reject assumptions that are proved invalid, and in turn reject theories based on these assumptions which are incapable of accurate prediction. It should not be rejecting theories that disavow such assumptions and by doing so predict well. As Starmer (2000) states:

> there should be no prior supposition that the best models will be ones based on the principles of rational choice, no matter how appealing those may seem from a normative point of view. (p. 363)

Therefore it is inappropriate to use normative criteria, as many economists have done, to evaluate a descriptive model. PT and other recent theories may be less neat and parsimonious than EUT and conventional extensions of EUT, but they are undoubtedly better predictors, and explain various paradoxes. In time normative versions of recent theories may be developed, once economists obtain a better understanding of phenomena like the learning process and reactions to incentives, but lack of normative status is not necessarily a weakness of any theory of decision-making.

## 5.10  Summary

- Expected utility theory (EUT) rests on three main axioms: transitivity, continuity and independence. In addition assumptions are usually made regarding expectation, asset integration and risk-aversion.
- In EUT risk-aversion is caused by the utility function being concave.

- Conventional extensions to EUT relax the independence axiom in several ways, but still maintain monotonicity and transitivity.
- Some conventional models incorporate probability weighting, thus including subjective evaluations of both outcomes and probabilities.
- A prospect consists of a number of possible outcomes along with their associated probabilities.
- Prospect theory (PT) states that decision-making under risk involves two phases: editing and evaluation.
- The editing process involves coding, combination, segregation, cancellation, simplification and detection of dominance.
- The evaluation of prospects in PT involves four main principles: reference points, loss-aversion, diminishing marginal sensitivity and decision-weighting.
- Reference points are points denoted as zero on the value scale, with outcomes having values measured as deviations from this reference point, that is, in terms of gains and losses.
- Reference points are often the current level of assets or welfare, but may also involve expectations of the future. Sometimes people may not have yet adjusted to the current situation, so their reference point may relate to a past situation.
- The biological basis of reference points is related to the processes of homeostasis and allostasis.
- Reference points can explain the anomaly of EUT referred to as the 'happiness treadmill'.
- Loss-aversion means that the disutility from losses is greater than the utility from gains of the same size.
- Loss-aversion can explain anomalies like the 'disposition effect' and the 'end-of-the-day' effect.
- There is neuroscientific evidence for the psychological phenomena of reference dependence and loss-aversion.
- Diminishing marginal sensitivity means that people become increasingly insensitive to larger gains and losses. Thus the value function is S-shaped, being concave in the region of gains and convex in the region of losses. This may cause risk-aversion for gains and risk-seeking for losses, depending on decision-weighing.
- Decision-weighting means that outcomes are weighted not according to objective probabilities, as in EUT, but according to decision weights.
- Decision weights may differ from objective probabilities for two reasons: people are often bad at estimating probabilities; and even if such probabilities are known or stated, people may weight them subjectively.
- People frequently overweight low probabilities.
- Decision-weighting can explain many anomalies in EUT, such as gambling and insurance, in particular probabilistic insurance.
- PT has been criticized on various grounds, theoretical and empirical: the lack of normative status; internal contradictions; incompleteness; and the determination of reference points. Empirical criticisms relate to: violations of the combination principle; violations of stochastic dominance; the failure to explain the Allais paradoxes; violations of gain-loss separability; the nature of the utility function; endowment effects; the discovered preference hypothesis and misconceptions; and the nature of framing effects.
- There are various recent models of decision-making which claim to explain and predict better than PT; the priority heuristic, imprecision theory, and configural weights models are prominent among these.

## 5.11  Review questions

1   John McEnroe has been quoted as saying 'the older I get, the better I used to be'. Explain this is terms of PT.

2   How does Pinker's three-act tragedy relate to the NM and to PT?

3   How do EUT and PT differ in their views of risk-aversion and risk-seeking?

4   Use two numerical examples to explain the difference between risk-aversion and risk-seeking.

5   Explain the endowment effect in terms of the experiment with pens and mugs. What principles of PT are relevant here?

6   Explain the 'end-of-the-day effect' in gambling in terms of PT.

7   Give an example of an experiment where neuroeconomics has been helpful in explaining people's behavior.

8   Why is the decision-weighting function important in PT?

9   Give three reasons from behavioral economics why people tend to prefer travelling by car than by plane.

10  Explain the difference between a descriptive and a normative theory. How do EUT and PT compare in these respects?

11  Use a numerical example to explain the principles of cancellation and dominance.

12  Explain the steps in the priority heuristic process.

13  Explain the nature and purpose of imprecision theory.

14  Describe the fundamental difference between PT and configural weights theories.

15  Show, using a numerical example, how the TAX model accounts for risk-aversion.

## 5.12  Review problems

1   **EUT**

A student is considering studying for a test tomorrow, but is tempted to go out and party with friends. He believes that the test could be either easy or hard, with equal probability, and estimates that he will achieve the marks shown below:

|        | Easy | Hard |
|--------|------|------|
| Study  | 90   | 75   |
| Party  | 75   | 55   |

The student believes his utility function is given by $u = \sqrt{x}$, where $x$ is the number of marks achieved. He also estimates that studying involves a cost of 2 units of utility. Determine the course of action that maximizes the student's utility.

2   **Prospect Theory**

The student now changes his beliefs regarding his utility function, since he realizes that he is affected by loss-aversion relative to a reference mark of 75. His value function is now given by:

$$v(x) = \begin{cases} (x-r)^{0.5} & \text{if } x \geq r \\ -2(r-x)^{0.5} & \text{if } x < r \end{cases}$$

If the cost of studying is 7 units on the v-scale, determine the student's best course of action.

3  **Prospect Theory**

Before making the decision above the student views some previous tests and updates the estimated probabilities of the test being easy or hard accordingly. His revised estimates are: P(easy test) = 0.3; P(hard test) = 0.7. Do these revised probability estimates affect his choice of action?

## 5.13  Applications

Three case studies are included in this chapter, all of them relating to anomalies in EUT that have been observed in the field. The cases illustrate in particular the importance of reference points, and how they are determined in different circumstances, and the phenomenon of loss-aversion, along with its consequences.

---

### Case 5.1    The endowment effect

According to the NM, ownership or entitlement should not affect the value of goods. This assumption relates to the Coase theorem, which states that the allocation of resources will be independent of property rights. There are two main exceptions to the Coase theorem: (1) income effects may affect tastes; and (2) transactions costs may discourage trade. In addition to these exceptions, there are certain other situations where economists have proposed that value may be affected by ownership: (3) where ownership has conveyed experiential effects, causing people to value items they have owned for some time; and (4) where buyers and sellers need time to adjust to and learn market conditions, which may have recently changed.

Apart from the above exceptions, the NM predicts that buyers and sellers should not on average demand different prices for the same good, that is, the willingness to pay (WTP) of buyers should not differ significantly from the willingness to accept (WTA) of sellers. Stated in different terms, the NM assumes that indifference curves are unaffected by ownership. However, many anomalies have been observed over the years. For example, a number of hypothetical surveys have shown that in the case of hunting and fishing rights the WTA of sellers has been between 2.6 and 16.5 times as large as the WTP of buyers. In a real exchange experiment, it was found that the ratio for deer hunting rights was 6.9 (Heberlein and Bishop, 1986). Another such experiment found that the ratio for lottery tickets was 4.0 (Knetsch and Sinden, 1984).

A particularly comprehensive and detailed study was performed by Kahneman, Knetsch and Thaler in 1990. One important objective of this study was to isolate any endowment effect from any of the other circumstances mentioned above that might cause discrepancies between WTP and WTA. For example, the researchers carried out a number of experiments with tokens first, to accustom the subjects to the situations. As expected, these induced-value experiments showed no difference between the WTP and WTP for tokens. However, when the experiments were repeated with consumer goods, using mugs and pens, significant differences appeared. Four trials were performed with the subjects (Cornell University students), in order to eliminate any learning effect over time, but it was found that there was very little difference between the trials. There were 44 subjects involved, divided into two equal groups, one with the property right to the good which they could sell, and the other without the ▶

property right initially, but in a position to bid for it. It was also stressed to the subjects that it was in their interest to state their true willingness to pay and accept in the questionnaires, because after the four trials one trial would be taken at random, the market-clearing price (MCP) would be calculated from the responses, and the relevant transactions would then take place. Thus, if the subjects with the property right indicated a WTA at or below the MCP they would then sell at this price, while subjects without the property right who indicated a WTP at or above the MCP would then buy at this price.

The following results were recorded:

**Mugs** – The median WTP soon settled to $2.25 after the first trial, while the median WTA was a constant $5.25 throughout all the trials. An average of 2.25 trades took place with each trial, compared with an expected 11 (50% of the 22 pairs of subjects would be expected to have the potential buyer value the good more than the seller).

**Pens** – The median WTP was a constant $1.25, while the median WTA varied between $1.75 and $2.50. An average of 4.5 trades took place per trial, compared with the expected 11.

The authors of the study came to the following conclusions:

**1** There was evidence contradicting the NM – People's preferences do depend on entitlements.

**2** Indifference curves depend on the direction of trade – An indifference curve showing acceptable trades in one direction may cross another indifference curve showing acceptable exchanges in the opposite direction.

**3** Endowment effects reduce the gains from trade – The volume of trade will be lower than predicted by the NM. This is not because of inefficiencies like transaction costs, but because there are less mutually advantageous trades available.

**4** Endowment effects will be different for different goods – They are unlikely to exist at all for money tokens, or for goods that are purchased explicitly for the purpose of resale, or for goods where perfect substitutes are available at a lower price. The effects are likely to be strongest 'when owners are faced with an opportunity to sell an item purchased for use that is not easily replaceable'. Examples given are tickets to a sold-out event, hunting licenses in limited supply, works of art, and a pleasant view.

**5** Endowment effects can also apply to firms and other organizations – For example, firms may be reluctant to divest themselves of divisions, plants or products, and they may be saddled with higher wage levels than newer competitors.

There has been considerable laboratory evidence from numerous studies over many years that supports the existence of endowment effects in the traditional sense. These effects relate to the situation where an owner of a good, or seller, places a higher value on it than a non-owner, or buyer. According to PT this phenomenon arises through a combination of reference points and loss-aversion. The owner or seller's reference point involving possessing the item, while the buyer's reference point does not involve possession; the seller's loss in a transaction is greater than the buyer's gain in the transaction.

However, Plott and Zeiler (2005, 2007) point out that the term is now used to refer to two different phenomena, only one of which refers to endowment in the strict sense. Moreover,

▼

we have already seen in Chapter 3 that the term 'endowment effect' is problematical because it is now used to refer to a theory or explanation for a phenomenon, rather than the phenomenon itself (Plott and Zeiler, 2007). Therefore there are two main kinds of criticism of the 'endowment effect': (1) the effect does not really exist, when it is tested for under proper controlled conditions; and (2) the effect may exist, but it is caused by factors other than those proposed by PT. We will examine each criticism in turn.

Many studies refer to differences between willingness to pay (WTP) and willingness to accept (WTA) as an endowment effect. This does not necessarily involve endowment, since sellers may not have been endowed with the good originally. Plott and Zeiler (2005, 2007) note that sellers may have come into possession of a good for many reasons, such as earning income to buy it, rather than it being gifted to them like 'manna from Heaven'. Thus there is not just a single phenomenon occurring. Evidence suggests that WTA by sellers may depend significantly on how they came into possession of the good.

As suggested by the original study by Kahneman, Knetsch and Thaler (1990), the endowment effect appears to vary according to the type of good, and in particular does not seem to occur for exchange goods. For example, a study by Svirsky (2014) finds that, while there appears to be an endowment effect for chocolate coins, there is no such effect when these coins are described as tokens, or for money.

Further complications are raised by other possibilities. For example, the influence of the experimenter is an important factor. Subjects may interpret the choice of the good endowed by the experimenter as an indicator of relative quality. Furthermore, social preferences may be relevant if the endowed person regards the good as a gift from the experimenter, and therefore does not want to reject it for that reason.

Another relevant factor concerns learning effects. If the seller has had time to thoroughly inspect the good to fully learn its value, this increases WTA. Some economists have expressed the belief that the endowment effect is merely the result of a mistake made by inexperienced consumers and through time these consumers will learn 'better' behavior that conforms to the NM (Knez, Smith and Williams, 1985; Coursey, Hovis and Schulze, 1987; Brookshire and Coursey, 1987; Shogren et al., 1994). Some of these researchers have also reported empirical findings that do not support the endowment effect hypothesis. More recently List (2004) has conducted a large-scale study involving more than 375 subjects who actively participated in a well-functioning marketplace. The purpose of the study was to test the predictions of PT in terms of the endowment effect against the predictions of the NM. Further details of the study are described in Case 5.1, but here it is sufficient to note that all subjects actively traded sportscards and memorabilia. In the experiment they were endowed with either a candy bar or a mug of similar market value, and asked whether they would like to trade. List found that both inexperienced and experienced consumers did not trade as much as predicted by the NM, revealing an endowment effect as people tended to value the good they were endowed with more than the other product. However, for 'intense' consumers who traded in their usual market at least 12 times monthly, and for dealers, there was no reluctance to trade and therefore no evidence of an endowment effect. List's conclusion was that experience in the market did indeed tend to eliminate the endowment effect, and that furthermore there was a transference of this experience, meaning that experience in the subjects' normal market of sportscards and memorabilia transferred its effects to trading other goods. In a more recent study involving a field experiment that exogenously induces market experience, List

▶

(2011) finds confirming evidence that market experience alone can eliminate the endowment effect.

Let us now consider the second criticism of the endowment effect, which is that it is caused by factors other than loss-aversion related to reference points. Birnbaum (2008) explains the endowment effect in terms of a configural weights model. It has been proposed by Birnbaum and Stegner (1979) that exchange asymmetries between WTA and WTP could be explained in terms of asymmetric costs to buyer and seller. A buyer makes a worse or more costly error by overestimating value than by underestimating value, whereas for a seller the more costly error is to underestimate value rather than overestimate it. The result is that, in a configural weights model, buyers assign greater weight to lower estimates of value and sellers assign greater weight to higher estimates of value. Birnbaum claims that various empirical studies involving judgments of buying and selling prices of either 'sure things' of uncertain value, like used cars and stocks, or standard risky gambles, support this explanation of the endowment effect and are not consistent with the loss-aversion explanation (Birnbaum and Stegner, 1979; Birnbaum and Zimmermann, 1998).

The conclusion, at least based on existing research, is that not only is the endowment effect an ambiguous term, but also that both its causes and the circumstances of its effects remain controversial issues in behavioral economics.

**Questions**

1   Explain why the term 'endowment effect' is ambiguous.

2   Explain how PT can explain endowment effects.

3   Explain how configural weights theories explain endowment effects.

4   Explain, with aid of a graph, how the endowment effect may cause indifference curves to cross, contrary to the NM.

5   Wimbledon tickets are allocated by a lottery process. Given that there is a secondary market for such tickets, what implications does the endowment effect have in this situation?

6   We have seen that studies by List (2004) and Plott and Zeiler (2005) argue that the endowment effect is not present under various circumstances. What circumstances may eliminate the endowment effect?

## Case 5.2   Loss-Aversion In Golf

We have seen that loss-aversion is a fundamental bias that is anomalous with the NM. However, many economists believe that this and other types of bias tend to be eliminated in market situations when the stakes are high, competition is great, and traders are experienced. The study by Pope and Schweitzer (2011) is of seminal importance in this respect because it is a field study as opposed to an experiment, and by studying behavior of professional golfers in PGA tournaments, it satisfies the conditions of high stakes, competition, and experience. Furthermore, the study involves a situation where the reference point is highly salient, a par score for each hole, and thus it allows for a precise test of the

▶

existence of loss-aversion. Because the outcomes of a tournament, and the payoffs golfers receive, depend on their overall scores over 72 holes (four rounds), EUT predicts that golfers should have the same incentive to hole any putt, regardless of whether the putt is to make a par score, or to make a birdie (one stroke below par) or an eagle (two strokes below par). On the other hand, PT predicts that golfers have more incentive to make a par putt than a below-par putt because of loss-aversion. Thus there is an opportunity here to test the two theories directly against each other in a market setting. In reality there are problems of confounds, which also need to be addressed. Therefore this study is valuable for two reasons: (1) it is a good test of the existence of behavioral biases; (2) it is a good example of how a field study can be designed and implemented to test theories.

The study examined putts, analyzing a sample of 2.5 million putts in total, using laser measurements of distance. Although the study considered all putts, the majority of the putts were either for par or for a birdie. If a player misses a par putt, then they may register this as a loss, whereas this would not occur for a birdie putt; making the latter putt would be registered as a gain. There is an alternative explanation: par putts are more likely to be second putts on the green than birdie putts, so players may focus more on holing these putts to avoid 'three-putting'. However, this is still a loss-aversion explanation, but using number of putts on the green as a reference point rather than par for the hole.

The means of testing the theories was to estimate a regression function with probability of holing a putt as a function of effort and a number of relevant putt characteristics, like distance from the hole. The central hypothesis was that, with a PT value function incorporating loss-aversion, golfers would invest more effort in holing par, bogey and double-bogey putts than birdie or eagle putts. This method allows the comparison of the proportion of par putts made with the proportion of birdie putts. The main finding is that the birdie putts are made 2% less often than comparable par putts, thus supporting the loss-aversion theory. The term 'comparable' is important, because of the existence of a number of possible confounding factors. Most obviously, birdie putts are generally of longer distance, so distance has to be controlled for, and this was possible through accurate measurements of distance from the hole. Thus it was possible to compare putts on the same hole in the same tournament that were within one inch (2.5cm) of each other. In addition, the authors considered and controlled for a number of other confounds or contrasting explanations to loss-aversion:

1  *Players attempting par putts may have learned something about the green conditions after having already attempted and failed a birdie putt.* Learning may also occur by watching a partner putt. These learning effects were controlled for by using dummy variables in the regression analysis relating to number of putts already taken on the green by both the player and the partner.

2  *Players attempting birdie putts may be starting from a more difficult position on the green, because of a longer approach shot.* This effect was controlled for by dividing all the greens into different sections and using dummy variables for the different sections.

3  *Player-specific factors may be relevant.* Some players may be long drivers but poor putters. In this case they may be more likely to be in a position to attempt a birdie putt, but also less likely to hole it. These fixed effects were accounted for in the analysis.

4  *Hole-specific factors may be relevant.* Some holes may have easy fairways but difficult greens and vice versa. Thus with an easy fairway it might be more likely to have a birdie putt, but this putt may be more difficult. Again these fixed effects were accounted for.

**5** *Tournament-specific fixed factors may be relevant.* This means that a player in a better position in the tournament may be more likely to be going for a birdie or eagle putt, and may also have a greater incentive to hole it. This effect was controlled for by using a dummy variable to take into account a player's overall score in the tournament.

**6** *Players may be overconfident on birdie putts.* A good drive or approach shot may result in the possibility of a birdie putt, and also induce a state of overconfidence. As we have seen, overconfidence can reduce performance. However, in observing golfing performance, the study finds that there is positive rather than negative autocorrelation between hole scores, meaning that a low score on one hole tends to be associated with a low score on the following hole. The authors infer from this result that there is also likely to be autocorrelation between quality of stroke on each hole, so that a good drive or approach shot is likely to be followed by a good putt, whereas overconfidence would produce the opposite result.

**7** *Players may be more nervous on birdie putts.* This is likely to be related to position in the tournament, and as seen in (5) above, this was controlled for. Furthermore, nervousness should be more relevant in later rounds when there is more pressure to perform well, but in fact it was observed that the performance differential between par and birdie putts was reduced in later rounds.

Thus all these alternative explanations for the performance differential between par and birdie putts can be eliminated. As well as the general finding supporting the existence of loss-aversion, the study reports two more interesting findings. The second finding is that the difference between par putts holed and birdie putts holed is most marked in the first of the four tournament rounds, and that the effect is less than half as large in the fourth and final rounds. This is also in keeping with the theory of loss-aversion, combined with shifting reference points. The existence of par as a reference point is likely to be most salient in the first round. By the final round the scores of the other players are likely to become a more important reference point, in particular the score of the leader; thus after the first round scores are generally measured in terms of strokes behind the leader.

A final finding of importance concerns risk-aversion. According to PT people tend to be risk averse for gains of relatively high probability and risk-seeking for losses of relatively high probability (professionals make both birdie and par putts with a frequency over 80%). The implication is that golfers should be more cautious in attempting birdie putts than in attempting par putts. A cautious putt errs on the side of being short, since a putt that is too long frequently involves a more difficult follow-up putt with a less predictable line and slope. Pope and Schweitzer find that birdie putts do indeed tend to fall short more often than par putts, thus supporting another aspect of PT.

Perhaps it is appropriate to leave the final word regarding loss-aversion to the most famous golfer of the last two decades, Tiger Woods:

> Any time you make big par putts, I think it's more important to make those than birdie putts. You don't ever want to drop a shot. The psychological difference between dropping a shot and making a birdie, I just think it's bigger to make a par putt. (Pope and Schweitzer, 2011, pp. 144–145)

**Questions**

1   Compare the predictions of the EUT with prospect theory as far as putting is concerned.
2   Explain the nature of reference points in a PGA tournament with four rounds.
3   Explain the nature of confounds and contrasting explanations in this study.
4   Explain how the study tests for risk-aversion.

---

**Case 5.3**   Serving size and eating habits

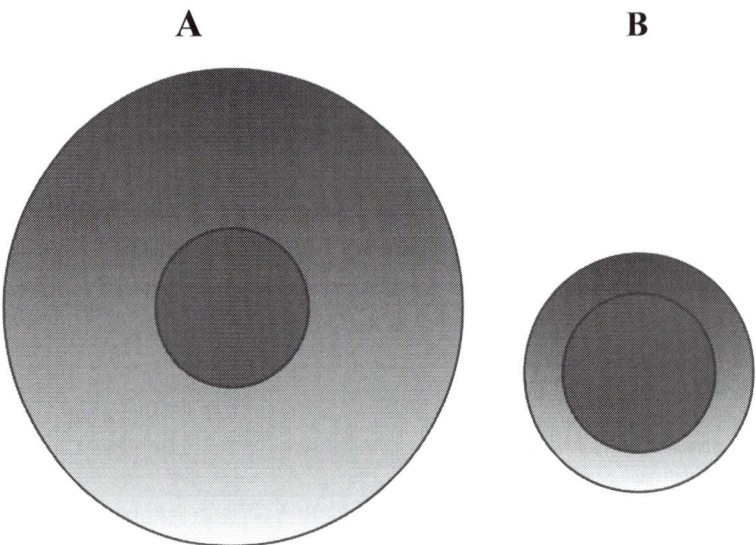

A                                                 B

The diagrams above illustrate the Delboeuf illusion, first described in 1865.

**Questions**

1   Which of the inner circles is bigger?
2   What concepts in behavioral economics are relevant in this illusion?
3   How do you think the illusion is relevant if we are trying as individuals to reduce our food consumption?
4   How does the serving size of others around us affect our own serving size?
5   How do you think an understanding of this illusion might help restaurant owners?

# CHAPTER · 6

# Mental Accounting

Sometimes we get lucky. After gambling for a while in the casino we find we have more money than we came in with. We may even keep these winnings in a different pocket to distinguish it from 'our own' money. We also find that we are more inclined to gamble with this money than with our original money. Behavioral economists refer to this phenomenon as the 'house money effect'. We are less risk-averse with gains than we are at the status quo.

It might be thought that this phenomenon is of limited importance. Yet some economists believe that this behavioral phenomenon related to risk-aversion has played an important part in the housing bubble leading up to the financial crisis of 2007–2008. House prices more than doubled in the USA from 2000 to 2006, creating large gains in wealth for many people. These gains were, at least initially, unexpected and viewed as unearned. Both factors led to a big increase in consumer spending – and further investment in housing, given that consumers were less risk-averse in terms of spending these gains. This spending on housing also became seen as a low-risk investment once house prices became expected to continue increasing at fast rates, often over 10% a year. Increased spending on housing drove prices still higher, fueling a vicious circle. The circle was initially seen as virtuous for those making gains, but an unsustainable bubble was created, leaving a large number of home-buyers vulnerable to a downward turn in the market. When this occurred, many people found themselves trapped in a negative equity situation – they owed more money on their mortgages than their houses were worth.

## 6.1  Nature and components of mental accounting

The term mental accounting was introduced by Thaler's landmark article 'Mental accounting and consumer choice' (1985); just as the last chapter drew heavily on the two papers by Kahneman and Tversky on prospect theory (PT), this chapter draws heavily on two papers by Thaler, the original 1985 paper and the update, 'Mental accounting matters', in 1999. Thaler draws parallels between the accounting process as used by firms and the mental accounting process used by individuals, defining mental accounting as follows:

> Mental accounting is the set of cognitive operations used by individuals and households to code, categorize and evaluate financial activities. (Thaler, 1999, p. 183)

Thus mental accounting encompasses a broad range of human behavior, which as we shall see is not just restricted to financial activities. Like PT, mental accounting theory (MAT) was developed to overcome descriptive anomalies in the standard model, and it incorporates the basic elements of PT in its formulation. It helps us to develop a better understanding of the psychological processes that underlie choices and decisions.

Thaler's papers refer to three components of the mental accounting process:

- The perception of outcomes, and the making and evaluation of decisions.
- The assignment of activities to specific accounts.
- The determination of the time periods to which different mental accounts relate.

These three components are now discussed, summarizing the material in Thaler's papers, and reorganizing the content so that some of the original material covered in the first area, such as opening and closing accounts, is now discussed under the third area. In addition, two other aspects are covered in this chapter: (1) an updating of empirical evidence relating to mental accounting, including both behavioral and neuroeconomic studies, and (2) policy implications relating to the behavior of markets and institutions. There is a separate section on policy implications, whose purpose is to examine the effects of mental accounting by individuals on the behavior of markets and institutions. In practice, however, it is impossible to completely disentangle this aspect from the material relating to empirical evidence; for example, we cannot understand how consumers react to different types of product offering without considering different marketing strategies.

## 6.2  Framing and editing

*Implications of prospect theory*

Mental accounting is concerned with how people perceive and evaluate situations when there are two or more possible financial outcomes, in particular with how people combine these outcomes. For example, purchase decisions, even for a single item, always involve both a cost and a benefit. Such decisions become more complex when there are special offers like discounts, prize draws or two-for-one offers. Multiple purchases, when the items are complementary, like buying a holiday with airfare, hotel, car rental, meals and so on, are also more complex. Sequential outcomes also need to be evaluated. For example, do people prefer to win two separate lotteries paying $50 and $25 respectively, or a single lottery paying $75? EUT, based on the invariance principle, would indicate that people would be indifferent between the two outcomes. However, Thaler found that in a survey 64% of subjects predicted that the two-time winner would be happier.

PT contains some important implications as far as this process of evaluating joint outcomes is concerned. Thaler summarized these in his 1985 paper:

1   Segregate gains (because the gain function is concave due to diminishing marginal sensitivity).
2   Integrate losses (because the loss function is convex, again due to diminishing marginal sensitivity).
3   Integrate smaller losses with larger gains (to offset loss-aversion).
4   Segregate small gains from larger losses (the utility of a small gain can exceed the utility of slightly reducing a large loss, again due to diminishing marginal sensitivity).

Thus the first principle can explain the finding regarding lottery preferences. A similar factor may explain the finding that people prefer multiple discounts to a single one amounting to the same thing; for example people prefer a 20% off plus a further 25% off to an equivalent 40% off (Chen and Rao, 2007; Chen et al., 2012). However, as we will see in Section 6.5, there may be other factors involved in this preference.

These principles have some important implications for marketing strategy, in terms of what Thaler refers to as 'hedonic framing'. For example, instead of marking down a price from $20 to $18, and framing this reduction as 'new low price' or 'now only $18', it may be better to use a **reference price** of $20, and emphasize the $2 discount. This is based on the fourth principle above, sometimes referred to as the 'silver lining' principle. There is a further reason for framing the discount in this way, as will be seen in the next section in relation to transaction utility. Thaler (2016) also applies the fourth principle to the situation where car dealers are trying to sell off old models, where he suggests that offering rebates is more effective than discounting price, on the basis of segregating small gains from large losses.

Of course, we have seen in the previous chapter that some of the principles of PT have been questioned, for example gain-loss separability. Empirical evidence, in particular related to product bundling, may shed some light here, and this will be considered in the remainder of the section.

### Hedonic editing

Whereas framing is concerned with the external description of events that is given to a subject, editing is concerned with the internal process whereby the individual codes or 'parses' the information. The lottery example above can be used as an illustration. According to PT, people tend to evaluate the outcomes separately, coming to the conclusion:

$$v(\$50) + v(\$25) > v(\$50 + \$25) \quad \text{or in more general terms:}$$
$$v(x) + v(y) > v(x + y)$$

This is obviously a positive, rather than a mixed gamble. The principles of hedonic editing can also be applied to another well-known anomaly in EUT, the 'jacket-calculator saving' situation mentioned at the beginning of the first chapter. It appears anomalous that people are prepared to drive for 20 minutes to save $5 on an item when the normal cost is $15, but not when it is $125. If people use the 'minimal' account frame of EUT related to the cancellation principle, then the issue is simply one whether it is worth traveling for 20 minutes to save $5, and the normal cost of the item is irrelevant. Similarly, if the 'comprehensive' account frame is used, where all other factors such as current wealth and expected future earnings are taken into consideration, the cost of the item whose price is reduced is irrelevant. This is another application of the invariance principle.

The editing process of MAT, however, can account for the difference in choice. Whereas EUT considers $v(\$5)$ as the value of the saving regardless of the item whose cost is reduced, MAT regards the savings on each item as a difference between two values. Thus the saving on the $15 item is coded as $v(-\$10) - v(-\$15)$, whereas the saving on the $125 item is coded as $v(-\$120) - v(-\$125)$. Because of the diminishing marginal sensitivity of the loss function the first saving has a greater utility than the second. We shall see in the next section, as with the framing of discounts, that there is another possible explanation for this phenomenon in terms of transaction utility.

A similar process appears to be at work when we examine how the concept of credit is edited by consumers. Cryder and Xiao (2014) find that consumers code a 'credit' as a gain, and compared with the term 'loan', consumers with a credit mindset tend to respond quicker to gain-oriented words, view credit as a larger windfall gain, and have increased happiness and an additional interest in spending. Thus using the term 'credit' changes psychophysical representations of spending. Whereas typical spending is coded as a loss, Cryder and Xiao (2014) hypothesize that spending credit is psychologically represented as the reduction of a gain, a hedonically less painful prospect than incurring an equivalently sized loss, as predicted by PT.

Another important area of application of the concept of hedonic editing is in the insurance industry. People generally dislike the idea of deductibles, because of loss-aversion. The use of rebates or no-claims bonuses is preferred by the consumer, since rebates appear as a gain, or silver lining, while the extra premium paid may not be valued that highly because of diminishing marginal sensitivity. A study by Johnson and colleagues (1993) asked subjects to compare two offers of auto insurance cover, one with a deductible frame and one with a rebate frame. The results are shown below:

1    Deductible frame – premium of $1,000 for one year

    This policy has a deductible of $600 which will be subtracted from the total claims against the policy. In other words, if you make any claims against the policy, the company will give you the total amount of the claims minus the deductible.

If your claims in one year total less than $600, the company will pay nothing. If your claims exceed $600, the company will pay all of the amount above $600.

2    Rebate frame – premium of $1600 for one year

With this policy, a rebate of $600 minus any claims paid will be given to you at the end of the year. In other words, if you have no claims against the policy, the company will give you $600 back at the end of the year. If you do file one or more claims, you will get back $600 minus the amount the company paid out for your claims. Should the total claims exceed $600, the company will give you no rebate but will pay the claims.

The reader can verify that the two policies offer the same financial terms, in the sense that the subject will end up with the same state of wealth regardless of whether they make claims and how much they claim. In fact the first policy should be preferable if the discounting of future values is taken into account, since the second option essentially involves giving the company an interest-free loan of $600 for a year. However, the study found that only 44% of subjects would accept the first option, while 68% of subjects would accept the second option.

Hedonic editing is also relevant in the consideration of the phenomenon of endowment effects, in the sense of exchange asymmetries, described in the previous chapter. The key issue here is the location of the appropriate reference point; any gains above this will be valued less highly than losses below the reference point. Again the insurance industry provides some instructive examples. In this case we do not need to rely solely on survey or experimental evidence, but can refer to empirical observations from naturally occurring situations. Johnson and colleagues (1992) compare the situations in New Jersey and Pennsylvania, where changes in insurance laws allow us to examine real choices. Both states introduced the option of a reduced right to sue in case of pain and suffering, in return for lower insurance rates. However, the laws in the two states differed in terms of the default option. In New Jersey the default option was the reduced right, so motorists have to pay extra for the full right. In Pennsylvania the default option was the full right, so motorists have to opt out in order to get a discount. The result was that in New Jersey only about 20% of motorists chose to acquire the full right, whereas in Pennsylvania about 75% of motorists retained the full right to sue (Insurance Information Institute, 1992). While other factors that affect this decision may vary between the two states, the huge difference in results appears to provide important evidence in favor of this aspect of MAT.

Generally speaking, empirical evidence supports the Hedonic Editing Hypothesis (Thaler and Johnson 1990), that people edit multiple outcomes in a manner that is optimal, in other words that they behave according to the four principles outlined earlier in the section. The only exception concerns the second principle: people appear to prefer to segregate rather than integrate losses. Thaler and Johnson established this by asking questions regarding people's temporal preferences regarding losses, on the basis that a preference for two outcomes on the same day implied integration while a preference for the outcomes being a week or two apart implied segregation. They inferred from this that a loss a short time prior to another one would *increase* the sensitivity of the person to another loss rather than decrease it. A longer time period to recover from a loss would reduce the sensitivity to the second loss. It should be noted that this exception does not imply that people are behaving in a non-optimal manner in terms of the maximization of hedonic utility, but rather that the loss-aversion factor in PT needs to be refined to take into account the observed behavior.

There are important implications of hedonic editing for marketing practices, particularly relating to sales promotions and product bundling; some of these are discussed next and a more general discussion follows in section 6.5.

*Evaluation of outcomes and decision-making*

It was stated earlier that even the simplest purchase decision, involving a single item with no special offers, involves multiple outcomes: the benefit or value from consumption and the cost paid. The standard model frames the net value of the purchase in terms of benefit minus cost. In reality the phenomenon of loss-aversion makes this coding of the purchase hedonically inefficient. Both Kahneman and Tversky (1984) and Thaler (1985) therefore reject the idea that costs are necessarily viewed as losses.

Thaler proposes instead that there are two types of utility that consumers gain from a transaction, as we have seen in Chapter 3:

1   Acquisition utility – this represents the value of the good obtained relative to its price, equivalent to the concept of consumer surplus.
2   Transaction utility – this corresponds to the perceived value of the 'deal', in other words the difference between the reference price and the price paid.

We have already seen in previous chapters that consumers frequently act under conditions of cognitive load, so cognitive ease is an important consideration in making choices. A study by Liu (2014) suggests that this may lead to '**utility blindness**', so that consumers may focus more, or entirely, on transaction utility for many of their transactions, since this is easier to compute than acquisition utility. Only when consumers have the mental resources and time available, combined with a certain level of involvement, may they enter into more complex computations of acquisition utility. The effects of price promotion are further discussed in the section on policy implications.

The evaluation process also becomes more complex when product components are bundled together in a **product bundle**. Sometimes this happens naturally, for example when computers are bought with screens and cars with stereo systems. Other times sellers deliberately bundle products together, which may be complementary, but may also be substitutes if the intention is to offer the consumer variety. Thaler (1999) claims that in this situation using a **consolidated price** for the bundle is preferable to using a **partitioned price** in terms of consumer evaluation. He states two advantages of this form of framing: first, it integrates losses in terms of the costs to the consumer; and second, it prevents raising the salience of the expense of individual items. He uses examples of luxury packages to illustrate this, like a Club Med vacation or a *prix fixe* dinner. This issue is discussed further in the final section of the chapter on policy implications.

Evidence supporting the mental accounting approach to the editing of consumer preferences comes not only from behavioral studies in the field but also from various neural imaging studies (Bechara et al., 1999; Kuhnen and Knutson, 2005; Knutson et al., 2007). These show that distinct neural circuits related to anticipatory affect provide critical input into subsequent purchase decisions, indicating that there is a tradeoff between the potential pleasure of acquisition and the pain of paying. Knutson and colleagues (2007) used event-related functional magnetic resonance imaging (fMRI) to investigate how consumers weigh preferences and prices in a three-phase dynamic process: consumers see the product first, then the price, and then have to make a choice whether to buy or not. Their results indicate that the first phase involves the nucleus accumbens (NAcc), indicating that this brain region is involved in the subjects' reaction to products. Subjects' subsequent reaction to price information was reflected in activation of the mesial prefrontal cortex (MPFC) and the insula. More specifically it was observed that excessive prices deactivated the MPFC while activating the insula. The authors note:

> price alone could not account for the correlation between MPFC activation and
> the price differential ... These findings are consistent with the idea that people
> do not react as much to absolute price as to the price relative to what they think

is acceptable for a given product (Thaler, 1985) (making it difficult to determine whether prices are high or low without knowing their associated product). (p. 152)

Thus, rather than there being a general sense of arousal during a purchase decision process, different parts of the brain are activated or deactivated at different times in response to different stimuli. The authors conclude that:

The findings are consistent with the hypothesis that the brain frames preference as a potential benefit and price as a potential cost. (p. 153)

As noted in the first chapter, this study also shows that brain activation can be used to predict purchase decisions above and beyond self-report variables. The authors furthermore conclude that 'fMRI prediction methods may eventually prove most useful in situations where people's behaviour and self-reported preferences diverge' (p. 155).

## 6.3   Budgeting and fungibility

Just as firms set budgets or targets for spending in various categories, and allocate expenses to different categories, so do individuals. However, for individuals the budgets do not just relate to spending, they also relate to other monetary categories such as income and wealth. Studies also indicate that people appear to maintain different accounts for time (Leclerc, Schmidt and Dube, 1995; Rha and Rajagopal, 2001; Saini and Monga, 2008). The characteristic of **fungibility** relates to the substitutability of different budget categories; if budgets are fungible, overspending in one category can be compensated by underspending in another category and vice versa. According to the neoclassical model (NM), if the marginal utility of a good or service is greater than its marginal cost, then it should be worth buying, and therefore complete fungibility should exist, with no need for budgeting. We now need to consider the relevant empirical evidence, and the implications regarding the behavioral approach compared with the NM.

### *Consumption budgeting*

Thaler (1999) suggests that the allocation of spending to different categories serves two purposes. The first is to facilitate comparisons or trade-offs between different uses of funds; for example, should I spend the money I saved this last three months on a holiday or a new computer? The second purpose is to act as a self-control device; for example, if I have already spent my weekly budget on eating out at restaurants, then I'll have to wait until next week before I eat out again.

Evidence suggests that different individuals and households conduct this budgeting of spending in quite different ways. Sometimes the allocation can be very strict and formalized, for example involving the putting of certain sums of money into different labeled envelopes on a regular basis. In other cases the allocation can be looser, less formalized and less frequent. In general poorer individuals or families tend to have budgets defined over shorter periods, like weeks or months, whereas wealthier individuals and families may have annual budgeting periods. For example, Heath and Soll (1996) find that most of their MBA student subjects had weekly food and entertainment budgets.

Various studies indicate a lack of fungibility for different spending categories. For example, Hastings and Shapiro (2013) find that, when gasoline prices rise, consumers have a tendency to switch to lower octane gasoline, to a greater extent than would be predicted by income effects alone. This suggests that consumers have a 'gas money' category in their spending budget. They also appear to have categories for gift card spending. Helion and Gilovich (2014) find that consumers tend to buy hedonic rather than utilitarian items when they use gift cards rather than paying by cash or credit card, and they tend to buy items that are typical of a particular retailer when they use a retailer-specific gift card (Reinholtz, Bartels and Parker, 2015).

The fungibility of spending categories has also been investigated by observing the reactions of consumers to unexpected price changes and in-store coupons. Both of these would be expected to have a wealth effect according to the standard model, but observed behavior indicates that the effects are greater than those predicted by the NM, operating through the perceived liquidity of consumers. Janakiraman, Meyer and Morales (2002) find that unanticipated price increases reduce consumers' tendencies to buy discretionary goods, while unanticipated price reductions increase it. Furthermore, they find that the mechanism is different in each case. The unexpected price increases cause increased small-deal sensitivity, whereby consumers dislike buying goods at the regular price, but tend to buy goods on offer at small discounts. However, unexpected price reductions appear to cause a simpler illusory wealth effect, with increased purchases but no change in small-deal sensitivity.

Unexpected coupons also appear to have the effect of increasing the number of unplanned purchases. Heilman, Nakamoto and Rao (2002) find that surprise coupons increase consumers' basket size by about 12%, both in terms of items purchased and dollars spent. Moreover, the incremental purchases tend to be either 'treats', products that are cognitively related to that which was promoted, or products shelved in close proximity to that which was promoted. Some similarities to these results were obtained by Milkman and Beshears (2009). They found that online grocery shoppers spent on average $1.59 more when redeeming a $10-off coupon, and that this extra spending tended to be on goods that the shopper did not normally buy, that is, these were likely to be 'treats'.

A paradox regarding consumption budgeting, at least according to the NM, is that people are often delighted to receive gifts that they would never buy for themselves. Following the NM, the standard advice for gift-giving is that gifts of cash are best, since a gift in kind can only be as good as cash at best, and then only if it is something that the recipient would have bought anyway. Yet people are delighted to receive gifts like iPods, holidays, clothing items and expensive bottles of wine. Of course, there are various explanations regarding why people enjoy receiving gifts:

1  *The marginal cost of the gift to the recipient is zero* (ignoring any complications like feelings of reciprocal obligations, discussed in Chapter 8). Therefore, as long as the marginal utility is positive, it will improve the welfare of the recipient. However, many people appear to experience feelings of joy on receiving gifts that indicate that the marginal utility may exceed the marginal cost even if the recipient were to pay it.

2  *There is a marginal utility associated with gratitude.* The receiver of the gift may be gratified that the giver has such a good opinion of them that they choose to buy them a gift. This is again assuming that the receiver does not believe the giver was acting in a strategic way, for example expecting a favor in return.

3  *The recipient may be 'liquidity constrained'.* Therefore the recipient is unable to afford the good or service, even by borrowing funds. However, there are many situations where this is obviously not the case.

The appropriate psychology of gift-giving and receiving takes into account lack of budget fungibility and self-control factors. People tend to have specific budgets for the items mentioned above: expensive consumer durables, holidays, clothing and wine. If these budgets are exceeded in any time period consumers do not trust themselves to keep to their budgets in later time periods. For example, a person may have a weekly budget of $100 for eating out at restaurants. This may involve one good meal per week. It would be dangerous for the consumer to exceed this, as this would set a new reference point at a higher level of consumption. If this reference point were to become established it would cause not only the budget to be exceeded, but would also make it hard to revert to the original consumption level because of loss-aversion. However, a free meal or voucher would not allow a new reference point to become established, as this would be regarded as a special occasion. There are a number of applications of this psychology. Examples are sales contests and prize draws, where prizes tend to have high value relative to most people's budgets.

Some research into the mental accounting process suggests that, rather than being a rigid and categorical process, it tends to be a pliant, malleable and self-serving process (Soman and Gourville, 2001; Cheema and Soman, 2002; Cheema and Soman, 2006). In particular many small and routine expenses are either not coded, or are allocated to a miscellaneous category equivalent to 'petty cash'. This means that they are not subject to normal accounting controls; an example of this was seen above, where people prefer to pay with small rather than large denomination bills. Cheema and Soman (2006) find that people are more likely to incur expenses when they are ambiguous to the extent that they can be allocated to more than one expenditure category at the discretion of the consumer. However, there are conflicting effects here. Cheema and Soman (2008) also report that partitioning an aggregate quantity of a resource, such as food or money, into smaller units reduces the quantity or rate of consumption of that resource. The reasoning here is that more purchasing decisions are required in this situation, increasing transactions costs, and this increases the attention factor and salience of the purchasing decision. This is particularly important in self-control situations, such as the tendency to overeat. For example, Cheema and Soman (2008) found evidence of reduced consumption of chocolates and gambling when transactions were partitioned. However, they also stress the importance of clearly defined partitions as far as self-control is concerned. In the two examples mentioned the partitions were clear. If there is ambiguity present, then there is more scope for consumers to be self-serving in terms of allocating the resource into a particular category.

There is also evidence that consumer budgets are influenced by the time frame involved. Ülkümen, Thomas, and Morwitz (2008) examined and compared the budgeting processes for consumers over monthly and yearly periods. They found that yearly budgets are higher than the equivalent monthly budgets, and are closer to recorded expenses. They proposed two reasons for this: first, the narrow monthly frame caused consumers to omit various expense categories which they included in the longer yearly frame; and second, the uncertainty and low confidence related to the longer period caused an upward adjustment.

## *Income budgeting*

People often find it difficult to classify transactions in terms of income or wealth. For example, should one treat a windfall gain as a source of income or as an addition to wealth? In other situations there may be a clear distinction; a tax refund or an increase in salary obviously fall into the income category. However, there appear to be some common 'rules' that apply to both situations. Evidence suggests that people classify both sources and uses of funds on a serious-frivolous scale (O'Curry, 1997; O'Curry and Strahilevitz, 2001). Windfall gains may be regarded as frivolous whereas a pay rise would be serious. Going to the cinema may be frivolous, but paying the rent is serious. Furthermore, O'Curry finds that people match the seriousness of the source of gain with the use to which it is put, again indicating a lack of fungibility. This finding is also supported by Kooreman (2000), who reported that spending on children's clothing is much more sensitive to changes in the designated child allowance than to other income sources.

Another finding regarding the fungibility of income categories relates to the payment of dividends by firms. In principle firms could return profits to shareholders either by paying dividends or by repurchasing shares. If dividends are taxed at a higher rate than capital gains, as in the USA, tax-paying shareholders should prefer the repurchase of their shares to receiving dividends. The standard model would thus predict that firms would never pay dividends under these tax conditions. Shefrin and Statman (1984) have proposed a mental accounting explanation for the payment of dividends. This explanation involves self-control aspects, and a principal-agent model of self-control developed by Thaler and Shefrin (1981) and discussed in detail in Chapter 8. Dividend payments make it easier to follow the rule: it is okay to spend the payments but don't touch the principal. When shares are repurchased it is more difficult for shareholders to determine how much of the resulting cash inflows they can afford to spend without dipping into capital.

Shefrin and Thaler (1992) also explain another observed anomaly in the standard model, where many people simultaneously borrow and yet take too few income tax exemptions in order to receive a large tax refund from the Internal Revenue Service (IRS). Again this is a self-control device to prevent overspending, and in particular to allow saving. The tax refund would be classified as a 'serious' source of funds on O'Curry's scale, making it easier to use the funds for saving. There is substantial evidence for this. When the Economic Growth and Tax Relief Reconciliation Act was passed in 2001, returning a record (at the time) $38 billion to taxpayers, a survey indicated that only 22% of households planned to spend the rebate, with the vast majority planning to save it (Shapiro and Slemrod, 2003). This issue relating to how people view tax rebates is discussed further in connection with wealth budgeting and also in terms of government policy.

### Wealth budgeting

The two dominant hypotheses in the NM regarding spending and saving are the **life cycle** and **permanent income hypotheses** (Modigliani and Brumberg, 1954; Friedman, 1957). According to both of these hypotheses people try to smooth their consumption patterns over their lifetimes to maintain a consistent standard of living. The implication of this is that in mid-life, when people generally have their highest earnings, they should save most, while younger and older people with lower incomes should dissave. Furthermore, wealth is treated as being perfectly fungible, so that any change in wealth should produce an identical effect on consumption, no matter what is the source of the wealth change. A pay rise, a lottery win, a capital gain on the stock market and an expected inheritance would all cause the same effect, assuming they were all of the same discounted net value (see Chapter 7 for more detail on discounting).

There is considerable evidence, however, that people do not behave according to the above predictions, and have much shorter time perspectives. Their consumption tends to be overly sensitive to their current income, so that young and old people spend too much, and middle-aged people spend too little. Soman and Cheema (2002) claim that their research reinforces other findings that 'consumers are unable to correctly value their future incomes, and that they lack the cognitive capability to solve the intertemporal optimization problem required by the life-cycle hypothesis'. Of course the conventional argument in the NM is that people do not necessarily need to consciously solve this problem; they may still behave *as if* they have solved the problem, maybe under the constraints of market forces. However, Soman and Cheema go on to argue that consumers, particularly inexperienced ones, use information such as their credit limit as a signal of their future earnings potential. Credit limits are not the kind of market constraint that is likely to lead consumers to optimizing behavior. One reason for this concerns self-control problems discussed in the next two chapters.

Moreover, the evidence suggests that wealth is not fungible and that people classify wealth into different categories in two main ways. The most obvious classification is according to liquidity. Cash in hand is most liquid, followed by money in checking and money market accounts. Savings and time deposits are less liquid, and then come stocks and bonds. Next in the hierarchy is home equity. This has become more liquid in recent years, with the prevalence of home equity loans, but most people still aim to pay off their mortgage by the time they retire. This aspect of home equity is discussed in more detail in Case 6.3. At the far end of the scale comes the 'future income' account, which relates to future expected earnings and long-term savings like retirement accounts, or whole life policies. The marginal propensity to consume (MPC) from these different categories varies enormously: for current assets the MPC is nearly unity, while for future income it is close to zero. This indicates a clear lack of fungibility which is totally in contrast with the life cycle and permanent income hypotheses of the standard model.

A second method of classifying wealth concerns the distinction between 'realized' and 'paper' wealth gains and losses. 'Paper' gains and losses are mainly caused by changes in the values of stocks or real estate, but may also be caused by revaluations of inventory. In general the MPC tends to be much lower with 'paper' gains, especially if these are reversible, as with a stock market gain (Cheema and Soman, 2002).

There is now an abundance of studies that indicate various anomalies in the NM related to the fungibility of wealth. These anomalies relate to the use of credit cards, attitudes towards stock returns, segregation of asset types as investments, and the impact of social interactions. These issues are now discussed.

**1**    *Use of credit cards*

There are a number of studies showing that ways in which people use credit cards violate the assumptions of the NM in terms of perfect fungibility of assets and utility maximization. Prelec and Simester (2001) report that with real transactions of high value willingness-to-pay (WTP) is substantially higher when credit card use is required compared with the situation when cash is required. More specifically they observe that in a sealed bid auction for tickets to a Boston Celtics basketball game WTP was up to 100% higher when credit cards were required for the transaction rather than cash. This phenomenon is related to payment decoupling, discussed in the next section.

There is also evidence that the simultaneous use of credit cards and savings accounts violates the NM. Bi and Montalto (2005) observe that the average debt of US households with credit cards was over $8,000 in 2004, yet most of these households with credit cards also hold financial assets, with nearly 40% of them holding positive liquid assets of more than one month's income. Why do people borrow funds at 10% while they are accumulating funds in liquid accounts yielding less than 2%? It appears that this use of revolving credit means that some people view liquid assets as a special or emergency fund, but do not view a line of credit in the same way. A similar study in the UK by Gathergood and Weber (2014) sheds further light on this 'co-holding puzzle'. They find that about 12% of their sample hold on average £3,800 of revolving consumer credit incurring relatively high interest charges, which they could immediately pay off using liquid assets. However, they also report that these co-holders are financially literate, with above average income and education. It therefore appears that this lack of fungibility is explained by self-control factors, involving the desire to prevent impulsive spending. Thaler and Shefrin (1981) claim that people may have a rule that they save at least a given proportion of their salary, maybe for their children's education, and never withdraw from this fund. Such a rule prevents the usual type of internal arbitrage that characterizes the NM. Yet, as Shefrin and Statman (1984) state: 'The underlying rationale is straightforward. By prohibiting withdrawals from the "college fund", the possibility of not replenishing that fund because of a weak will is avoided.'

However, it appears that credit cards may not be the last resort as far as liquidity is concerned. Recent evidence suggests that some people may not use credit cards as a source of funds even when they have substantial liquidity available from them, and instead prefer to take out payday loans (Agarwal, Skiba and Tobacman, 2009). Just as in the case with preferring the use of credit cards to savings, this is irrational, in fact even more so: typical payday loans involve an annualized interest rate of several hundred percent. This preference may be based on the desire to use credit card liquidity as an emergency reserve, or it may be caused by the fact that credit card liquidity for these households declined substantially in the 12-month period leading up to the payday loan, or it may simply be caused by ignorance of annualized payday loan rates.

2    *Attitudes towards stock returns*

It has been reported that a combination of loss-aversion and narrow framing explains the behavior of stock returns and volatility (Barberis and Huang, 2001). This study also finds that this behavior is better explained by 'individual stock accounting' rather than by 'portfolio accounting'. This means that investors are loss averse over individual stock fluctuations rather than over the fluctuations of their portfolios as a whole. This is explained below.

3    *Segregation of asset types*

According to the NM, investors evaluate each investment choice according to its impact on their aggregate wealth or portfolio. However, it appears that investors tend to consider each decision as unique, isolating the current choice from other choices. This phenomenon is referred to as **narrow framing** (Kahneman and Lovallo, 1993; Kahneman, 2003). Thus they tend to allocate funds among different portfolio assets as if the individual assets are independent parts of the investment portfolio.

Rockenbach (2004) performed a controlled laboratory study to test whether investors split their funds between safe and risky assets as if each of the two asset types represented separate portfolio layers or mental accounts. The subjects in the experiments, who consisted of both students and investment professionals, repeatedly allocated funds among stocks, call options and risk-free bonds. The main finding was that the pricing of the option suggested that subjects saw stocks and options as substitutes and in a separate class from risk-free bonds. In keeping with these findings, Choi, Laibson, and Madrian (2009a) have reported that investors, when choosing their asset allocation for 401(k) accounts, sometimes ignore the asset allocation of other accounts where the employer makes matching contributions. It has also been reported that the timing of transactions is relevant as far as narrow framing is concerned. A study by Kumar and Lim (2008) found that stock trades that were more clustered together in time exhibited less of a narrow framing effect, resulting in more diversified portfolios, than trades that were more separated in time.

The studies discussed above indicate that people tend to evaluate portfolio items individually rather than in total when the issue concerns risk and volatility. However, there is some conflicting evidence here. When the issue concerns the evaluation of lottery portfolios people often prefer an aggregated evaluation rather than a segregated one. A good example is the one originally formulated by Redelmeier and Tversky (1992). This involves a simple lottery with outcomes ($2,000, 0.5; −$500, 0.5). If this lottery is played twice the outcomes can be represented as ($4,000, 0.25; $1,500, 0.5; −$1,000, 0.25). The framing effect here is that people are more likely to play this repeated lottery if the outcomes are aggregated than if they are segregated. However, the effects of aggregation appear to be context-specific. Langer and

Weber (2001) report that people also prefer 'venture' lotteries when the outcomes are aggregated; such lotteries involve a high probability of loss, but a chance of a big gain. On the other hand, 'loan' lotteries, where there are low-moderate probabilities of large losses, tend to be evaluated better when the outcomes are segregated. There are as yet no conclusive studies regarding situations where the 'lotteries' in the portfolio are heterogeneous rather than being identical. This issue regarding the representation and evaluation of outcomes has important implications for the policies of investment funds and hedge funds, since they want to know how their client investors will view different methods of representing the outcomes of the same portfolio.

4   *Emotional accounting*

Levav and McGraw (2009) have introduced a term '**emotional accounting**' to explain people's behavior in the kind of situation where people acquire increased wealth under unpleasant circumstances, for example when people receive money from a contentious life insurance settlement, or from a suit for a wrongful death of a child. They propose that such a gain has a negative affective tag attached to it, and this has important consequences as far as spending is concerned. The authors suggest that people tend to adopt two strategies here: hedonic avoidance and laundering. The first strategy means that people avoid spending on products that provide enjoyment, because of feelings of guilt that this would arouse. The second strategy, complementary to this, is that people tend to spend instead on 'virtuous' or utilitarian goods, such as investing in education, or making donations to charity. This is particularly relevant when people feel some responsibility for the unpleasant circumstances, and is related to the 'moral cleansing' notion of Tetlock (2002). Further evidence of laundering, or spending on utilitarian products as an attempt to resolve conflicted feelings, is provided by Ramanathan and Williams (2007).

People also often acquire assets as a result of a social interaction of some type. Some researchers have investigated the reactions of subjects who were asked to value either the purchase or sale of items possessing some social significance, under various different social circumstances. It appears that reactions in these situations are again often emotionally charged, and that some trade-offs are regarded as taboo (Fiske and Tetlock, 1997; Tetlock et al., 2000). For example, people do not like to value friendships in terms of improved living conditions. The effects of these social interactions are discussed in detail in Chapter 10, but at present it is sufficient to note that they appear to induce people to posit a social or emotional value to objects that is quite independent of the item's monetary value. For example, a person may be highly reluctant to sell a ring that was bequeathed to them by a parent. This phenomenon reinforces endowment effects and reduces the fungibility of assets.

5   *The 'denomination effect'*

Another interesting application of fungibility concerns the '**denomination effect**' (Raghubir and Srivastava, 2009). This effect is that the likelihood of spending is lower when an equivalent sum of money is represented by a single large denomination (e.g. one $20 bill) relative to many smaller denominations (e.g. 20 $1 bills). People tend not to like 'breaking' large denomination bills when purchasing items, as they view this as a significant decrease in their wealth, whereas using small denomination bills to pay does not have the same psychological effect. Furthermore, it was reported that people preferred to receive large denomination bills as change from a purchase, as a self-control device. It also appears that people prefer to spend used or worn notes rather than crisp new ones when they make payment (Di Muro and Noseworthy, 2013). In this case the lack of fungibility arises not from self-control factors but from disgust and a fear of contagion, discussed in Chapter 4.

## Time budgeting

This is one area where research findings appear to be conflicting. Rha and Rajagopal (2001) investigate whether people do perform mental accounting regarding time; they find that people do appear to maintain separate accounts for time based on the context. For example, people view time spent driving or waiting differently depending on the context; there is a significant difference between perceptions of work time versus non-work time. Furthermore, they find that 'people attempt to match the time spent on different activities based on source of gain of time'. Thus people try to utilize time received from a particular category within the category itself. This finding is analogous to that of Kooreman (1997) described earlier, indicating that people try to match expenditure category with income category in the case of children's welfare benefits. There is a further analogy with consumption accounting, in that people appear to have a miscellaneous category that can be used as a 'buffer source'. Thus sleep time can be used to finish activities that are relatively under more time pressure.

However, several studies have indicated that people treat time differently from money in a number of situations. For example, choices tend to be risk seeking for losses of money but relatively risk-averse for losses of waiting time (Leclerc, Schmitt and Dube, 1995). Similarly, Okada and Hoch (2004) have found that people display greater WTP for riskier options when they pay in time rather than money. We shall also see in Chapter 7 that people tend to discount time differently from money, with important consequences for the phenomenon of procrastination.

Another study (Duxbury et al., 2005) appears to show contrary findings for time compared with money in the classic jacket-calculator situation described earlier. The authors report similar results to those discussed earlier in terms of the trade-off between time spent (20 minutes) and money saved ($5), but subjects react differently when the direction of the effect is reversed, when the trade-off is between money spent and time saved. The authors report an absence of mental accounting effects in this case. Their conclusion is that 'mental accounting effects may be context-specific and suffer from a lack of generality'.

This conclusion appears to be in keeping with the findings of Saini and Monga (2008), who conclude from their experiments that people tend to use heuristics more often in decisions involving temporal expenditures rather than money expenditures. They propose that the reason for this is that temporal expenditures are harder to account for. An example is a parent trying to decide how many universities to visit for her child; it is much easier to estimate the costs involved than the time. As a result of this case of bounded rationality, the parent may use a heuristic such as a rule that one should always evaluate three options, or doing the same thing as a friend.

Soster, Monga and Bearden (2010) also find that consumers think differently about money and time. In a study of movie patrons, 400 patrons spent either time (filling out a 7-minute survey) or money ($3) during the summer. In return, they received a movie ticket they could use either later in the summer (same accounting period) or in the fall season (different accounting period). 'The season mattered when people had spent time – they were more likely to return to watch a movie when they had a summer ticket rather than a fall ticket', the authors write. 'The season did not matter when people had spent money – movie attendance for the two seasons was similar.' In the minds of consumers, the authors explain: 'Today's expired time cannot be recouped by tomorrow's time and today's spare time cannot be added to tomorrow's time.'

On the other hand, if someone spends too much money one day she can maintain a desired state of wealth by spending less the next. 'As such, people are likely to keep an account of monetary costs, not only during the accounting period in which they are incurred, but also in subsequent periods.' This discussion of time budgeting leads us on to the next aspect of mental accounting, where the relationship between different time periods is discussed in more detail.

## 6.4  Choice bracketing and dynamics

The evaluation and decision-making situations so far considered have essentially related to either single transactions or product bundles. We can consider this approach as essentially a cross-sectional one in terms of examining different components of a transaction at the same period of time. However, it has already been seen that, especially in self-control situations, evaluations can be made over different time frames. Therefore it is now necessary to take a time-series approach to evaluation and decision-making. 'Choice bracketing' refers to how people segregate or aggregate choices over time periods.

### Opening and closing accounts

In any accounting system decisions have to be made when to leave accounts open and when to close them. A number of examples from different decision situations will be discussed here: buying and selling stock; reporting earnings; sunk costs; and payment decoupling.

**1**  *Buying and selling stock*

   If a stock in one's portfolio has fallen in value, but is retained, that is, the account is left open, then there is a 'paper' loss. Not surprisingly such losses are less painful than 'realized losses' that occur when the account is closed and the stock sold. Decisions in this area are particularly interesting when an investor needs to raise cash, maybe to buy new stock, and has to choose between selling a stock that has fallen in value and a stock that has risen in value. The NM predicts that a rational investor should sell the stock that has fallen, since losses are tax-deductible while gains are subject to capital gains tax. However, Odean (1998) finds that investors were more likely to sell stocks that had increased in value rather than stocks that had decreased; this phenomenon is referred to as the '**disposition effect**'. In addition, he finds that the stocks sold subsequently outperformed the stocks bought, underlining further the irrationality (in the conventional sense) of the strategy. It thus appears that unrealized losses in particular are not coded as losses in the same way as realized losses, and do not cause the same degree of loss-aversion. This effect has been investigated in some detail over the last 15 years.

   Oehler and colleagues (2003) report similar findings in their experiments as far as the general preference to sell winners rather than losers. They find that the disposition effect is only reduced under the strong pressure of mechanisms like a dealer market, when the last price is assumed as a reference point, rather than the purchase price. In this kind of situation market forces can overcome the mental accounting bias. The authors comment colorfully that when investors use purchase price as a reference point 'they die hard in all market settings'. However, the authors also note that markets do not collapse in their experiments, due to disposition investors' reluctance to trade. Their explanation is that there is a coexistence of two or more groups of investors, including both disposition investors and momentum traders. Another study of the disposition effect, by Frydman and Rangel (2014), provides evidence that qualifies the above conclusion somewhat. They find that the disposition effect can be debiased to some extent by reducing the salience of purchase price information. In a stock trading experiment they report a 25% reduction in the effect when purchase price information is absent compared with when it is displayed prominently on screen. Kubinska, Markiewicz and Tyszka (2012) also find that the disposition effect is more marked among contrarian rather than momentum traders, meaning those traders who buy and sell in a pattern that is in contrast to prevailing market sentiment.

Other research indicates that belief and probability biases play an important role in explaining the disposition effect. These involve the 'gambler's fallacy' and self-evaluation factors. Kadous and colleagues (2014) also propose that it is necessary to distinguish between what they call 'self-regard', which is global in nature, and self-confidence, which is domain-specific, since the term 'self-esteem' can relate to both of these and cause a confound. The reason for this is that they found the effects of self-regard and self-confidence to work in opposite directions. The disposition effect was associated with low self-regard, since such investors would face cognitive dissonance if they sold losers, and a threat to self-image. However, the disposition effect was associated with high self-confidence, since such investors had sufficient confidence to hold on to losers and tend to hold them for longer.

A study by Chang, Solomon and Westerfield (2016) sheds further light on the role of cognitive dissonance in the disposition effect. Investors may be more willing to sell stocks that have risen in value since purchase than stocks that have fallen because to do the latter may be seen as an admission that they may have made an error of judgment. The evidence suggesting this comes from the fact that when investors delegate the decisions to money fund managers the disposition effect disappears and is replaced by an opposite effect. Furthermore, increasing the salience of the delegation was found to increase the extent of the reverse-disposition effect. Thus cognitive dissonance theory can explain contrary aspects of investor behavior, where investors in individual stocks show a disposition effect but managers investing in mutual funds exhibit the reverse effect.

Brigden and Häubl (2012) report another interesting finding regarding stock prices, which also has implications for the disposition effect, in that the effect of a falling stock price appears to be greater when a stock slowly loses value compared with when it falls quickly. They attribute this to salience, so that a rapid fall is immediately apparent and is more likely to cause a sale, whereas a slower fall may escape notice for a while and, when it does become apparent, sale may appear a relatively unattractive option because it is being compared to superior, previously foregone opportunities.

2    *Reporting earnings*

Firms as well as individuals make use of discretion when reporting earnings in official announcements. Such discretion is created in a number of ways, but in particular involves the timing of the recording of revenues and expenses. If a firm wants to boost its reported earnings it can 'pre-book' revenues that it has not yet received, and delay recording costs or spread them over several time periods. A study by Burgstahler and Dichev (1997) indicates that firms are reluctant to announce losses or earnings decreases. Small reported gains and increases are much more common than small reported losses and decreases, conforming to the predictions of PT regarding loss-aversion.

This is not the only aspect of PT corroborated by the above study. Large gains appear to be trimmed down in order to allow more scope for improvement in the following accounting period, confirming the predictions of having diminishing marginal sensitivity to gains and the use of reference points. Furthermore, whereas small losses may be massaged into small gains, moderate losses tend to be somewhat inflated, again as predicted by the diminishing marginal sensitivity characteristic.

**3** *Sunk costs*

Consumers frequently have to decide when to open and close mental accounts when the purchase decision and consumption are separated in time. This can happen for several reasons: some goods have to be booked in advance, like theater or airline tickets; some goods and services are durables, like cars and domestic appliances, yielding benefits over a substantial period of time; and some goods are stored, like frozen food, and are consumed at a later date. In all these cases payment occurs before consumption. In other cases consumption occurs before payment, and these cases are discussed in the next subsection.

If payment is made before consumption, and there is no rebate if the consumer changes his mind later, then the consumer is faced with a sunk cost. Economists define such costs as being those that do not vary according to a particular decision; they do not have to occur before the decision is made. According to the NM sunk costs should not affect the decision to consume. For example, the decision to drive through a blizzard to watch a game should not be affected by whether a ticket has already been purchased or not. Similarly, the decision to buy a theater ticket should not be affected by whether one has just lost a ticket and needs to buy another one. However, there is considerable evidence that sunk costs do affect decisions (Kahneman and Tversky, 1984; Arkes and Blumer, 1985; Gourville and Soman, 1998; Prelec and Loewenstein, 1998).

Kahneman and Tversky (1984) find that consumers are less willing to replace a lost theater ticket than if they had lost an equivalent amount of money. This is in keeping with the fungibility research described earlier; replacing a lost ticket involves further spending in the same category, while losing money does not. Arkes and Blumer (1985) find that season ticket holders to a theater group who paid full price were initially more regular attenders than those who had received a discount, but that there was no difference in attendance in the second half of the season. Gourville and Soman (1998) find that members of a health club who pay dues twice a year attend more frequently in those months when the dues are paid.

Thus it appears that sunk costs do affect consumer behavior, but are eventually written off. What is the mental accounting explanation for this? Again, as with product bundling, it appears that salience is the relevant factor. If a cost has just been paid it is salient in the mind, and if the payer does not consume the relevant good or service the cost is then edited as a loss. Loss-aversion thus leads to consumption. A similar phenomenon appears to be relevant when people have their temporal horizons limited. A study by Strough and colleagues (2013) reports that students whose attention had been drawn to their mortality, or who were instructed to imagine that their time as a student was coming to an end, were less likely to pay attention to sunk costs.

Another situation where sunk costs are relevant is the decision to replace a durable. Heath and Fennema (1996) show that consumers tend to depreciate durables on a linear basis over time, but mental depreciation depends not just on time but on frequency and the quality of past usage (Okada, 2001). Okada finds that people are more likely to prefer a trade-in for their existing good than to buy a new good with an equivalent discount. Okada's experimental study gave consumers a choice between (1) trading in an existing camera for $80, and (2) buying the new one for a $80 discount from the regular price of $200. The standard model predicts that people would prefer the second option, since they get to keep their old camera. However, in the experiment 56% of the subjects preferred the first option, and only 44% the second. It might be claimed that this result is caused by a general 'trade-in effect', where people prefer trade-ins to discounts, but this explanation is eliminated by the study showing that there is no bias towards the first option when the old camera was won by lottery. Therefore it appears that a mental accounting explanation is required. This allows consumers to depreciate items purchased based on their endowment value and receive a transaction value on trade-in that more than offsets the transaction value of the discount in the second option. This explanation is supported by more recent evidence that in trade-in situations consumers place more importance on getting a good value for the used product than on getting a good price for the new product, notably in the automobile market (Zhu, Chen and Dasgupta, 2008). There are policy implications here that will be discussed later.

**4    *Payment decoupling***

The situations described above relate to those where payment occurs before consumption. In other situations consumption occurs before payment. This occurs when goods are bought on credit, and it also happens when people receive money for performing a job or task before performing it.

Decoupling is particularly obvious with the use of credit cards. It has already been noted that WTP can be significantly increased by the use of credit cards rather than cash (Prelec and Simester, 2001). Stores also would not be willing to pay 3% or more of their revenues to card companies unless credit cards were effective in increasing spending. The most obvious effect of credit card use is that it enables liquidity-constrained individuals to buy goods they would otherwise be unable to purchase. Also the NM predicts that payment later rather than in the present should be preferred on a discounting basis, provided that the card is paid in full and no interest is charged. However, in practice the average household with credit cards has an outstanding debt that is not paid off monthly, as we have already noted. Furthermore, Prelec and Loewenstein (1998) make the point that, other things being equal, consumers prefer to pay before rather than after. Therefore there must be some mental accounting factors related to decoupling that are relevant in the preference for credit cards. Two different effects can be identified:

1    The use of credit cards reduces the salience of the costs of the purchase. Thus Soman (1997) finds that students leaving the campus bookstore were much more accurate in remembering the amount of their purchases if they paid in cash than if they paid by credit card.

2    Credit card bills aggregate a number of items together, so that each individual item loses salience. As Thaler (1999) notes, the impact of an individual purchase of $50 is less than the impact of an additional $50 item in a bill for $843. This reduction in salience is related to the principle in PT and mental accounting regarding the integration of losses due to diminishing marginal sensitivity.

In neural terms, this reduction in salience is likely to be related to the deactivation of the insula. As seen earlier in the discussion of the study by Knutson et al. (2007), insula activation seems to be related to the anticipation of pain, or the displeasure of paying an excessive price. Further neuroeconomic research in this area of paying by credit card rather than cash, although presenting methodological difficulties, would be revealing. It may ultimately suggest certain policy implications in terms of solving this self-control problem. There are other policy implications of using credit cards that will be considered in section 6.5.

When people are paid before doing a job as opposed to afterwards as is usual, which again amounts to consumption occurring before payment, then there are also important effects on attitudes, preferences and choices. Siemens (2007) finds that as more time elapses between receiving money and performing the associated task, then people tend to report less job satisfaction, are less willing to do the job again and are more likely to regard the payment as unfair. Essentially the same psychological phenomenon is occurring here as that described earlier in relation to sunk costs: people tend to forget the earlier payment/consumption as it becomes less salient over time. Therefore when required to perform a task later this task appears more onerous.

Additionally we have seen that payment and consumption can also be separated, or 'decoupled', even when they are basically simultaneous in time but the product consists of a bundle so that consumers are unable to allocate costs directly to particular components. Thaler (1999) comments that in general consumers don't like the experience of 'having the meter running', since this draws unwelcome salience to the cost of specific components of a product bundle. This '**flat rate bias**' is particularly prominent in telecommunications. Most telephone customers prefer a flat rate service than paying by call when the bill would be the same under both circumstances (Train, 1991), and even when paying by call would cost them less (Prelec and Loewenstein, 1998). America Online (AOL) found that when they introduced a flat rate internet service in 1996 they were so swamped by demand that customers had trouble logging on to the service, earning the company bad publicity. However, in spite of consumer preferences for flat rates, firms often use more complex pricing strategies to maximize profits which take advantage of consumers' overconfidence, as will be seen in the next section related to policy implications.

Payment decoupling also has effects on usage of durables and services. Soman and Gourville (2001) find that in an experimental situation skiers with a four-day lift pass are more likely to miss the last day skiing than if they buy the pass on a daily basis. Furthermore, in a field study they find that customers with multi-performance theater tickets are more likely to miss performances than those buying tickets separately. Decoupling is particularly important in the health club industry, where self-control problems are evident. If people pay an annual fee this first of all creates a mental commitment on the part of the consumer. From that point for the rest of the year the marginal cost per visit is zero, thus making it easier to make the decision to exercise than in the pay-per-visit scenario.

## Prior outcome effects

We have already seen that in certain gambling situations, like betting on racehorses, prior outcomes can affect attitudes to risk. For example, people are more likely to bet on long shots in the last race of the day (the 'end-of-the-day effect'). The mental accounting explanation is that people tend to close their betting accounts at the end of the day and are loss-averse. Since the majority of punters are in a loss position by the time of the last race, they are often prepared to take a risk on a long shot in order to break even by the end of the day. This increased willingness to take risk after prior losses in general terms is sometimes also referred to as the 'break even effect'.

Thaler and Johnson (1990) find similar results in their experiments with MBA students playing with real, but small, stakes. Gamblers in casinos are often observed to keep money that they have won during the day in a separate pocket (or mental account) from their 'own' money; Thaler and Johnson refer to this phenomenon as the '**house money effect**', and gamblers tend to be risk-seeking with such funds. On the other hand, they tend to be risk-averse if they are in a losing position and probabilities and possible gains are moderate; only if there is a chance to break even, usually with a low probability of a relatively high gain, do they seek risk. This behavior tends to apply to experienced gamblers such as poker players, not only casual gamblers (Smith, Levere and Kurtzman, 2009).

Experiments tend usually to be limited to small stakes relative to overall wealth, but Gertner (1993) has found supporting evidence regarding the daily closing of accounts by observing the behavior of contestants in a television game show called 'Card Sharks'. Winners of the show on a particular day had to predict whether a card picked at random from a deck would be higher or lower than a card that was showing. The odds of winning vary from certainty to about even. After making the prediction the contestant can then make a bet on the outcome of between 50% and 100% of the amount they have won that day (on average about $3,000). Gertner finds that today's winnings strongly influence the size of the bet; in contrast cash won on previous days has virtually no effect. Thus cash won today is treated in a separate account from cash won the day before, a finding even more remarkable considering the difference in time between the shows in real time may be only a few hours, and previous winnings have not yet been collected.

This well-observed path dependence where risk attitudes depend on prior gains and losses is also evidenced by neuroeconomic studies. A study by Hytönen (2014) uses fMRI scanning to establish that these behaviors involve the use of affective brain processes rather than deliberative ones, once again indicating the importance of the dual systems theory of decision-making.

### Myopic loss-aversion

When gambles or lotteries are combined, they are evaluated differently from when their outcomes are presented singly. In general people tend to be more willing to take risks if they combine many bets together than if they consider them one at a time. Myopic loss-aversion (MLA) is another example of the more general phenomenon of narrow framing discussed earlier, where prospects are evaluated singly rather than as part of an overall portfolio. Sometimes the term '**narrow bracketing**' is used to describe this type of intertemporal narrow framing, the phenomenon where evaluation periods for decision-making are short. It appears to be a common phenomenon in various fields of activity, and the first two case studies at the end of the chapter are both concerned with different aspects of narrow bracketing.

In order to explain the mechanics of MLA it is useful to examine how the process of repetition affects the evaluation of gambles. A good example to illustrate the effect of repetition of gambles is the one described by Thaler (1999) and originally analyzed by Samuelson (1963). The outcomes of an individual bet are represented as ($200, 0.5.; −$100, 0.5). If an individual has a loss-aversion factor of 2.5 they would reject this bet, since it would give them a loss-aversion adjusted expected value of −$25. However, if the bet is played twice the outcomes become ($400, 0.25; $100, 0.5; −$200, 0.25). In this situation the loss-aversion adjusted expected value is +$25, and the combined bet would be acceptable. Therefore in order to explain why many people reject attractive small bets it is necessary to consider both loss-aversion and a segregated mental accounting approach.

Benartzi and Thaler (1995) have adopted such an approach in analyzing what has become known as the **equity premium puzzle (EPP)** (Mehra and Prescott 1985). The equity premium is the difference between the rate of return on equities (stocks) and a safe investment such as treasury bills. The puzzle is that this difference has historically been very large, averaging about 6% per year over the last 80 years. Later studies have developed and broadened the MLA approach to the puzzle (Barberis, Huang, and Santos, 2001). The EPP is discussed in the final section and in Case 6.1.

### The diversification heuristic

A further anomaly in consumer behavior, again related to narrow framing, is observed when simultaneous choices between goods are compared with sequential choices. The diversification heuristic was first observed by Simonson (1990). He gave students the opportunity to choose between six snacks under two different conditions: (1) sequential choice: subjects picked one of the snacks at each of three class meetings held a week apart; (2) simultaneous choice: on the first class meeting subjects selected three snacks to be consumed over the next three weeks. Simonson observed that there was much more variety seeking in the simultaneous choice condition than in the sequential choice condition: in the former 64% of the subjects chose three different snacks, whereas in the latter only 9% of the subjects made this choice. Simonson suggests that this anomaly can be explained by variety-seeking serving as a choice heuristic. This may be a useful evolutionary psychological mechanism in many situations, when consumption is in the immediate future. However, the heuristic may be misapplied in other situations, where consumption is over a longer period. The error represents a failure of predicted utility to accurately forecast future experienced utility.

The effect has been referred to as '**diversification bias**' by Read and Loewenstein (1995) who observed a similar phenomenon among trick-or-treaters on Halloween night. An experiment involved children calling at two adjacent houses. At one house the children were allowed to choose between two treats (sequential choice), whereas at the other they were told to choose whichever two they liked (simultaneous choice). The results showed strong diversification bias in the simultaneous choice condition: every child selected one of each treat. However, in the sequential choice condition only 48% of the children selected different treats. The contrast is particularly notable since in each condition the treats are put into the same bag, or portfolio, and consumed later.

Diversification bias is not restricted to children and students. A similar kind of diversification bias has been observed in investors by several studies (e.g. Samuelson and Zeckhauser, 1988; Benartzi and Thaler, 1998; Benartzi and Thaler, 2001; Hedesström, Svedsäter and Gärlin, 2004). There appears to be a general tendency to divide retirement funds fairly evenly over the range of assets on offer. This is sometimes referred to as the **1/*n* heuristic,** on the basis that if there are *n* assets on offer the amount 1/*n* will be invested in each. This rule is apparently of ancient origin, according to a quotation in the Talmud from about the fourth century, advising that a person should allocate their assets 'a third into land, a third into merchandise and keep a third at hand' (Benartzi and Thaler, 2001, p. 79). However, the unfortunate result is that the composition of people's portfolios can be easily skewed by manipulating the range of assets on offer. For example, with just two funds, one for stocks and one for bonds, there would tend to be a 50/50 split; but if another fund for stocks is added to the range of possible assets, the proportion of the portfolio invested in stocks would tend to jump to two-thirds. A study by Hedesström, Svedsäter and Gärlin (2004) investigated the behavior of a large sample of citizens in the Swedish premium pension scheme; the authors find evidence of the same diversification bias and use of the 1/*n* heuristic. A more recent experimental study by Morrin and colleagues (2012) suggests that people may actually use two different heuristics when it comes to investing retirement funds. One heuristic involves dividing investments into all available categories, labelled 1/*n*#; another heuristic involves spreading total funds equally among all chosen funds, labelled 1/*n*$. The authors find that choosing from larger fund assortments appears to tax cognitive resources, resulting in a reduced tendency to invest in all available funds (1/*n*#) but an increased tendency to spread the invested dollars evenly among the chosen alternatives (1/*n*$). Another recent study by Bateman and colleagues (2016) also examines investment decisions for retirement plans and finds that asset allocation information for pre-mixed investment options (normally presented as a pie chart or a table) had the largest impact on choices. Experimental subjects preferred investment options with more, and more evenly weighted, asset class allocations, a significant variation from the standard 1/*n* heuristic.

This behavior has important implications for public policy in terms of the design of both retirement saving plans and privatized Social Security systems. We can now start to examine some of these implications.

## 6.5   Policy implications

So far in this chapter we have concentrated largely on examining the non-NM behavior of individuals, particularly consumers. This behavior has important implications for the behavior of institutions such as firms and governments, and for markets. It is generally assumed here that these institutions respond rationally to the non-NM behavior of individuals, with certain exceptions. The obvious question at this point is: why make this asymmetric assumption? As noted by DellaVigna (2009) a key difference is experience. Firms tend to be specialized, have access to large amounts of data, and have the ability to analyze it more effectively. They are also subject to competition, so that firms that do not respond appropriately tend to be driven out of the market. Even when firms do have biases that cause nonstandard behavior, in particular the principal-agent problem, they still have incentives to respond to the nonstandard behavior of consumers. The same applies to employers, financial institutions, and politicians when they respond to the non-NM behavior of workers, savers and investors, and voters. We also see an important pattern as far as welfare is concerned: when agents have non-NM preferences, such as loss-aversion or self-control problems, but have rational expectations, firms are likely to respond with welfare maximizing offers; however, when agents also have non-rational expectations, firms rationally respond to these by magnifying the bias, leaving agents worse off.

In this section we examine responses in five main categories: (1) individual agents; (2) marketers; (3) labor markets; (4) financial markets; and (5) government policy. The first category needs some explanation. Agents are often aware or at least partially aware of their own biases, and can take steps to overcome them or compensate for them, particularly where there are self-control issues. This type of situation and the strategies involved are discussed again in Chapter 8 in connection with intertemporal decisions.

### Individual agents

One major implication is that people should allocate expenses to unambiguous categories to avoid overspending. The study by Cheema and Soman (2006) indicates that people are more likely to spend if there is ambiguity in the categories used. An extreme example of such a self-control device is where cash is placed in labeled envelopes for specific uses. There are also implications here for gift-giving; we have seen that people may be delighted to receive a gift that they would never buy for themselves, being outside their budget for that category of expenditure.

Another type of self-control device for consumption relates to the restriction of cash withdrawals from banks or ATMs to small amounts. This may be an effective commitment if there is no opportunity to withdraw more cash in the near future. In a similar manner consumers may limit their purchases to small amounts, as suggested by the study by Cheema and Soman (2008). Smokers may buy packs of ten cigarettes for example, which again may be an effective commitment if there is no opportunity, or if it is inconvenient, to buy further cigarettes later. This last example is interesting because it violates two economic principles. First, it is normally cheaper to buy most goods in larger quantities. Second, it contradicts a principle of PT described earlier, that losses should be aggregated because of diminishing marginal sensitivity. The fact that people do violate both of these principles in reality is a testimony to the importance of self-control problems and the lengths that people will go to in order to overcome them. Wertenbroch (1999) neatly sums up this tendency in the title of his feature: in order to limit their consumption, 'consumers pay more for less of what they like too much' (see Wertenbroch, 1998). According to Prelec and Simester (2001), we should always leave home without our credit cards; their use causes us to overspend and undersave. Another problem with credit cards is that they tend to encourage the use of inappropriate anchors. Some evidence suggests that naïve consumers use their credit limits and minimum payments as anchors for the amount they can afford to spend and the amount they should pay monthly respectively. Such behavior would cause a rapid escalation of debt.

Another area of behavior where commitment may be beneficial for consumers is when pre-payment for a good or service is possible. Hochman, Ayal and Ariely (2014) provide experimental evidence that pre-payment can increase commitment to pre-paid options, and also increase motivation and engagement in any relevant tasks.

There are also policy implications regarding time budgeting. Again people may budget time into different categories for self-control reasons. The author, for example, may have a time budget related to writing five pages a day. Other tasks, such as doing housework, repairing the table or paying a bill may be foregone in achieving this target. Furthermore, it should be stressed that it is not only onerous tasks that may be foregone; playing sudoku may also have to go by the wayside. However, some of the activities foregone may actually have a greater productivity in financial terms than the writing of the five pages. The fifth page may have an estimated marginal revenue of £20, but the time taken to write this page may mean being late with paying a bill at a cost of £50. This time budgeting may not appear to be rational according to the NM. The issue here, discussed earlier in Chapter 3, concerns self-signaling. If the author slips behind the five-page target, this may be viewed as a lack of self-control, with a resulting loss of self-respect; if the target is repeatedly missed this loss of self-respect may possibly lead to the abandonment of the writing project altogether. Thus seemingly irrational allocations of time budgets may in the long term serve an important purpose.

## *Marketers*

There are a number of policy implications here, and we will focus on some of the most important ones.

**1**   *Sales promotions*

As stated earlier, the concept of hedonic editing has important implications in this area of strategy. Much research has been carried out regarding the effectiveness of different types of sales promotions, comparing consumer response to price versus non-price promotions, but until recently there has been an inadequate theoretical explanation for the differential response. Jha-Dang and Banerjee (2005) utilize a mental accounting theoretical framework to explain observed differences in effectiveness. They test in the laboratory consumer response to three different types of promotions of the same monetary value:

**1** *Extra product promotion* – An additional amount of the product is provided at the same price.

**2** *Price off promotion* – A temporary price reduction below the regular price is given.

**3** *Premium promotion* – A separate complementary product is provided free.

The first method does not segregate gains, since the gain is in the same form as the product bought, whereas the other two methods do segregate gains, with the gain from the promotion being either monetary or in the form of a complementary product. The authors had hypothesized that the second and third types of promotion would prove more effective and found that their experimental evidence supported this hypothesis.

Price promotions involve several psychological processes on the part of the consumer, with implications for marketing that are often counter-intuitive. For example, it may be better to offer no discount than a low discount in some circumstances (Cai, Bagchi and Gauri, 2016). A zero discount may become a reference point, being regarded as a normal price, but a low discount of say 5% may be compared with a higher discount being a reference point. Thus a low discount may yield a low transaction utility and result in lower sales than a zero discount. Consumers may either buy elsewhere or wait, expecting a larger discount in the future.

A number of studies have indicated that multiple discounts may be more effective than a single one amounting to the same thing. This effect was described earlier in the context of the implications of PT and the segregation of gains. However, there may be other reasons for consumers preferring a multiple discount, for example 20% off, plus another 25% off, rather than an equivalent 40% off (Schley, 2013). One reason is the 'face value' effect, meaning that consumers wrongly perceive the first offer as amounting to a total of 45% off. Another reason is that consumers may perceive a multiple discount, regardless of the percentages involved, as being a rare offer. A fundamental psychological insight is that consumers value rarity or scarcity, and are prepared to pay more for products that they perceive as being scarce. Thus limited offers, where either the amount of the product on sale or the time period of the offer are limited, tend to increase sales.

A potential problem with discounting concerns a rebound effect when the discount is removed. In particular this may occur if the discount results in a reduction in the internal reference price of consumers. Bambauer-Sachse and Dupuy (2012) report that various factors appear to affect this adjustment of the internal reference price, notably level of involvement, savings presentation, and price-confidence of the consumer. More price-confident consumers experience a smaller adjustment of the internal reference price than less price-confident consumers.

Bearing in mind what has already been said in previous chapters regarding the importance of emotional factors in the buying decision, it should be no surprise that such factors are also relevant in determining how consumers react to price promotions. As we have already seen, as transaction utility becomes relevant, this increases cognitive ease. This in turn results in an increase in the importance of visceral or emotional factors as cognitive load is reduced. Aydinli and Bertini (2012) report that this influences behavior when consumers are faced with a choice between two snacks, one with greater cognitive appeal and one with greater affective or emotional appeal. The authors find that, as predicted, a 50% discount on both snacks causes a switch in preference from the former to the latter compared with when both snacks are at full price.

2    *Free offers*

There appears to be an ever-increasing tendency for firms to offer goods, and in particular services, for free, for example Facebook, Google and Wikipedia (Hossain and Saini, 2013). These authors suggest that such a strategy is more effective at increasing sales or usage of hedonic rather than utilitarian products. In many cases free offers are combined with other required goods, and are often termed 'freebies'. There appears to be conflicting evidence regarding the effectiveness of this kind of strategy. Obviously, the aim of the seller here is to increase sales of the bundle as a whole, and thus increase profits, even allowing for the costs of throwing in the freebie. However, a study by Kamins, Folkes and Fedorikhin (2009) has found that this kind of offer decreased the price that consumers were willing to pay for each product in the bundle when sold individually. This study suggests that consumers react to such bundles by not only regarding the freebies as being of low quality, but by regarding the other products as being of lower quality also. Thus this kind of promotion could have a long-term damaging effect on overall sales. However, a more recent study by

Palmeira and Srivastava (2013) finds that consumers may have a higher WTP for the product after the promotion is retracted when it was offered for free than when it was offered at a low, discounted price. The reason once again is related to reference points. Consumers may regard the discounted price as a reference point, inferring a low-quality product. However, they are less likely to do so for free offers, instead using the price of the focal purchase as an anchor to make inferences about the quality of the freebie.

**3**   *Bundling*

The free offers described above involve a particular type of bundling, but in more general terms bundling occurs whenever two or more products are sold as a single package. There are basically two alternative pricing strategies here, these being consolidated pricing and partitioned pricing. Once again, there is conflicting empirical evidence regarding the evaluation of consolidated prices versus partitioned prices (Drumwright, 1992; Wang, 1996; Johnson, Herrmann and Bauer, 1999). Thaler recommends consolidated prices, based on the mental accounting principle of aggregating losses. An example of a preference for partitioned prices, thereby segregating losses, comes from a study by Choi and Li (2014), who show that consumers may be prepared to pay $92 plus $5 shipping, but not a total of $97. The authors qualify their conclusion by saying that it may only apply to hedonic goods but not utilitarian goods, on the basis that people are more inclined to ignore unfavorable information with hedonic goods, and thus not pay attention to surcharges that may cause negative feelings.

Actually the conflicting evidence should not be surprising in the light of the notion of Kahneman and Tversky (1984) that prices are 'legitimate exchange for value received' and should be treated as proxies for the goods and services acquired. Thus prices do not merely represent a cost or loss, they can also be viewed as proxy for a benefit. With this in mind, price partitioning may segregate losses, reducing consumer evaluations, but at the same time it may segregate gains, improving evaluations. Therefore price partitioning may have a net effect on evaluations that is either good or bad, depending on the circumstances.

There have been various studies that have examined the circumstances which may influence overall consumer evaluations of product bundles. Brough and Chernev (2012) show that the mental classification of goods into different categories, in particular expensive versus inexpensive, can play an important role, and lead to the anomaly that people may be prepared to pay more for an expensive item alone than for the expensive item bundled together with an inexpensive one. This anomaly suggests that the inexpensive product is actually detracting from the value of the expensive one. There are different possible explanations for this. It may be that the bundling of the products suggests that the expensive good is of lower quality, or it may be that the high price of the expensive product on its own is suggesting a higher quality.

Chakravarti and colleagues (2002) have investigated the effects of partitioning for complementary products. They agree with Thaler regarding the general point that partitioning raises the salience of the price of the components, but add that it also differentially raises the salience of different aspects of the product depending on the component that is partitioned. They conduct an experiment with refrigerators, which are bundled with an icemaker and a warranty. The icemaker is a consumption-related accessory, while the warranty is a performance-related accessory. They found that partitioning both the icemaker and the warranty significantly improved consumer evaluations, but the effect was greater with the consumption-related accessory. However, the investigators warn that in other circumstances partitioning a performance-related accessory could have unfavorable consequences, drawing attention to a factor that may cause negative associations for the consumer.

Another example of a situation where salience is important is bundle promotions, where consumers receive a discount when they buy a certain number of units. It might be thought that this kind of promotion would have the main effect of boosting sales of the promoted product. However, a study by Foubert and Gijsbrechts (2007) found that the main effect was actually to cause brand switching. The authors reasoned that the purchase quantity requirement was often too high to cause consumers to buy much more of the same product, but the salience of the product caused by the promotion induced brand switching.

4   *Disaggregated pricing*

We have seen that consumers tend to set budgets in different categories, but also tend to have a 'petty cash' category to cover miscellaneous small expenses. Firms can take advantage of this aspect of mental accounting by disaggregating prices, particularly for services or consumer durables. A common marketing ploy for selling relatively expensive durables and services is to express the price in terms of an amount per day (Gourville, 1998), sometimes referred to as a 'pennies-a-day' strategy. Thus a $500 per year health club membership might be expressed as 'less than $10 per week' or 'only $1.37 per day'. At first sight this may again seem to violate the principle from PT that small losses should be aggregated because of diminishing marginal sensitivity. However, in this situation there are two other principles working in the opposite direction that may be more dominant. First, reference points are important. Whereas large expenses are often compared with other large expense categories, small expenses may be compared with other items in other budget categories. This means that mental accounting principles related to fungibility are also relevant. Thus consumers may balk at the $500 sum because it exceeds their budget for health maintenance, but the $10 per week sum may be allocated as a petty cash item and be acceptable.

5   *Pricing structure*

It was stated earlier that consumers often prefer to pay flat rates for products, like cellular phone service. However, firms often take advantage of a non-NM feature of consumer beliefs described in Chapter 3, overconfidence. People tend to underestimate their usage of 'recreational' goods like phone and internet service, and also are overconfident regarding the precision of their demand forecasts. Firms can take advantage of this by offering tariffs with included quantities at zero marginal cost (e.g. free minutes), followed by steep marginal charges. Similarly, in rental markets firms can charge moderate flat rates combined with large late fees (Grubb, 2009). Other aspects of payment decoupling are discussed in Chapter 8, in relation to intertemporal decisions and self-control factors.

6   *Cash versus credit cards*

It has already been seen that there are a number of reasons why people may prefer to pay by credit card than by cash, largely due to the effects of salience and the greater feeling of loss when paying by cash. However, there is a flip side to this, in terms of the post-transaction situation. Shah and colleagues (2015) report that post-transaction connection is greater when payment is made by cash, resulting in greater emotional attachment to the product, a greater commitment to the seller, and a greater brand loyalty in terms of a higher likelihood of repeat purchase. The psychological mechanism here may involve cognitive dissonance, in that, like the disposition effect, people may be more reluctant to admit that a cash purchase was a mistake than a credit card purchase. Thus a company relying heavily on credit card purchases may make more sales initially but may also have more fickle customers.

7    *Trade-in pricing*

In the discussion of sunk costs it was seen that there is evidence that people place more value or importance on the good being traded in than the good being purchased. There is also evidence, particularly in the automobile industry, that dealers take advantage of this. In the words of Iorio (2005): 'Car dealers have the bad habit of giving you more for your trade-in than they actually are. They do this by artificially inflating the price of the car you're purchasing and then artificially inflating the trade-in allowance.' As a response to this response, some car buying guides and public policy makers advise car buyers to keep the two transactions separate, and to agree on the price of the new car before negotiating a trade-in price.

## Labor markets

An important aspect of behavior in labor markets that involves mental accounting is money illusion, as seen in Case 1.2. In labor markets this translates into loss-aversion with respect to nominal wage losses, but not real wage losses. For example, Kahneman, Knetsch and Thaler (1986) found that 62% of respondents judge unfair a wage cut of 7% when there is no inflation, but only 22% of respondents judge unfair a 5% increase when there is 12% inflation, even though both situations represent a 7% cut in real wages. Employers tend to respond to this bias by resisting nominal wage cuts, except in times of severe recession when prices may be falling. They may prefer instead to lay off workers. The optimal solution, for both employers and workers, actually varies from country to country according to labor laws and customs. In Europe it is more common to reduce wages by reducing the length of the working week, rather than firing workers which tends to result in industrial action and high compensation payments. This essentially amounts to an egalitarian work-sharing solution. We shall see in Chapter 10 that aspects of social interaction and fairness are important in this issue.

Another aspect of the labor market where mental accounting is relevant concerns the nature of the labor supply curve. The theory of labor supply in the standard model predicts that the supply curve will be a standard upward-sloping one, where workers will work longer hours at higher wages. This theory is based on the concept of intertemporal substitution, meaning that when wages are high workers will substitute work for leisure, as the opportunity cost of leisure is higher at the higher wage. If people have diminishing marginal utility of leisure time, then they will be inclined to give up more leisure as the wage increases. According to many behavioral theories, however, workers may have reference-dependence for total earnings, leading them to be '**target workers**', who aim to achieve a particular level of total earnings each time period, for example per week. In this case a higher wage rate would lead to a lower level of hours worked, and a downward-sloping supply curve. The shape of this supply curve has important public policy implications in terms of predicting the effects of changes in tax and transfer programs.

In practice, however, the theory has been difficult to test empirically, since a number of conditions need to be satisfied. An ideal testing situation would involve the following factors:

1    *The increase in wages should be temporary*. Otherwise the effect of the increase will be compounded with other effects related to future expected wealth.

2    *Wages are relatively constant within a day*. This allows workers to use the level of wages earlier in the day to act as a guide in prompting them how many hours to work later in the day.

3    *Wages vary from day to day, and are uncorrelated*. This allows an investigation into how workers adjust their hours to the wage rate on a daily basis, without being able to use the previous day's wage rate as a guide to how long to work the next day.

The first study to take account of these factors and test the behavioral model against the standard model was conducted by Camerer and colleagues (1997), and involved cab drivers in New York City; the details of this study are presented in Case 6.2. The main conclusion of the study was that reference dependence was important, and there was strong evidence that these workers were target workers, supporting a behavioral model against a standard model.

However, this study has been criticized on a number of grounds, notably by Farber (2005, 2008). For example, there is what econometricians refer to as an identification problem; it has been claimed that shifts in the supply curve would lead to observations showing an inverse relationship between hourly wage rates and hours worked, but these would actually be points on the demand curve not the supply curve. Another problem is that in the Camerer and colleagues study the wage rate was calculated by dividing total earnings by the number of hours worked. Any upward error in hours worked would cause a downward error in the calculation of the wage rate, thus exerting a negative bias on the estimated relationship. More recent studies by Fehr and Goette (2007) and Farber (2008) have overcome these econometric problems, but the results are not conclusive in some areas. The Fehr and Goette study involved another field experiment, this time with bike messengers, who, like cab drivers, are able to choose how long to work within a shift. In response to a temporary increase in wage of 25%, they report two main findings: (1) they work 30% more shifts; and (2) within each shift, they do 6% fewer deliveries. The problem here is that it can be claimed that both of these results are compatible with both the NM and the behavioral target worker hypothesis. The NM can explain the finding of fewer deliveries in terms of increasing fatigue among workers working longer hours. The behavioral approach explains the findings in terms of reference dependence combined with loss-aversion.

Farber (2008) uses the same population of workers, cab drivers, as the Camerer study, but finds only weak evidence of reference dependence. In particular he finds that the reference point may vary substantially from day to day for any particular driver, and also that most shifts end before the reference income level is reached. More recently, the conflicts between the Camerer and colleagues and Farber studies have been reconciled to a considerable degree in a study by Crawford and Meng (2011). This uses the same data relating to cab drivers as before, but modifies Farber's econometric strategy, basically adopting the reference-dependent approach of Köszegi and Rabin (2006). This approach involves targets or reference points for both income and hours worked, unlike the original Camerer and Farber approaches. Loss-aversion is still incorporated in the model, so that workers who work longer hours than their target suffer from loss-aversion. Furthermore, targets are endogenously determined, based on rational expectations for both income and hours worked, which it is assumed have been learned from experience. On the basis of this revised model but using the original data from Camerer and colleagues, Crawford and Meng conclude that reference dependence 'is an important part of the labor-supply story'.

### Financial markets

As with other areas, there are many examples of situations where mental accounting principles are relevant in understanding the behavior of financial markets. We have already seen, for example, that the diversification heuristic is important in guiding the behavior of investors. Before we consider another application it is important to note that in financial markets more than in any other area there is a belief that the market will eliminate behavioral deviations from the standard model. Three main reasons are generally given for this:

1   Aggregation – individual deviations will tend to cancel each other out in the market as a whole.

**2**    Experience and expertise – the most important agents in financial markets tend to be skilled experts, who do not suffer from the same biases as normal people.

**3**    Competition – agents who are biased will be driven out of the markets, since they will make bad decisions and be unable to compete.

Some of these objections to behavioral models have been discussed earlier, and some aspects of them and related evidence are discussed in more detail in the following application. In general it seems fair to conclude that the evidence is mixed. Some studies indicate that in markets dominated by experts biases tend to be disappear or at least be less pronounced; however, one study (Haigh and List, 2005) showed the opposite, that experts showed even more bias than non-experts.

A particularly important application of mental accounting relates to MLA and the EPP. As we have already seen, the equity premium is the difference in the rate of return on equities (stocks) and a safe investment such as treasury bills. The puzzle is that this difference has historically been very large. The equity premium in the USA has averaged about 6% per year over the last 80 years, although this has been measured in different ways with different results. Part of this difference can be attributed to risk, but Mehra and Prescott (1985) show that the level of risk-aversion necessary to explain such a large difference in returns is implausible. They estimate that a coefficient of relative risk-aversion of about 30 would be necessary to explain the historical equity premium.

Benartzi and Thaler (1995) explained the EPP in terms of loss-aversion rather than risk-aversion. They note the risk attitude of loss-averse investors depends on the frequency with which they close their accounts and reset their reference points. When investors evaluate their portfolios very frequently, with an extreme case being every day, then there is nearly a 50% chance of stocks going down rather than up, with the result that loss-aversion makes stocks an unattractive investment. If on the other hand investors evaluate their portfolios rarely, like every ten years, there is only a low probability of stocks falling over such a long period, so loss-aversion is not an important factor. Benartzi and Thaler hypothesize that investors have preferences described by PT, and then ask how often people would have to evaluate the changes in their portfolios to make them indifferent between the (US) historical distributions of returns on stocks and bonds. Their simulations suggest that a period of about 13 months would achieve this, implying that if most people evaluate their portfolios once a year the EPP is solved.

This attitude towards evaluation is termed myopic loss-aversion, since such a strategy is not in the long-run interests of investors. Many studies have shown that if a longer evaluation period is enforced, then investors take more risks (Gneezy and Potters, 1997; Thaler et al., 1997; Benartzi and Thaler, 1999; Gneezy, Kapteyn and Potters, 2003). The study by Thaler and colleagues manipulated the frequency with which subjects make investment decisions between stocks and bonds, with three different possibilities: eight times a year, once a year, and once every five years. In the two longer-term situations subjects invested about 67% of their funds in stocks, while with the more frequent evaluation subjects only invested about 41% of the funds in stocks. Benartzi and Thaler (1999) asked university staff members how they would invest retirement funds, choosing between stocks and bonds. The authors this time manipulated the method of representing returns, either displaying the distribution of one-year rates of return or showing the distribution of 30-year rates of return. Subjects who viewed the one-year rates invested the majority of their funds in bonds, while those shown the 30-year rates invested 90% of their funds in stocks.

Some studies of MLA indicate that professionals are as prone to the phenomenon as more naïve or inexperienced investors. Gneezy, Kapteyn and Potters (2003) find that 'market prices of risky assets are significantly higher if feedback frequency and decision flexibility are reduced'. They conclude that 'market interactions do not eliminate such behavior or its consequences for prices'. Haigh and List (2005) find that, although there are differences between the behavior of professionals (from the Chicago Board of Trade) and students, the behavior of the traders actually displayed a greater tendency to MLA than that of the students. There is therefore something of a conflict between these studies and the study of Oehler and colleagues (2003) discussed earlier. The latter study indicated that the strength of market forces may suppress behavioral anomalies such as the disposition effect, but this does not appear to be applicable to MLA. The Haigh and List study is also interesting in that it contrasts with the List (2004) study discussed in the previous chapter, where there was evidence that market experience reduces the endowment effect.

There are also some recent studies that question the applicability of MLA in general. Two other main explanations for the EPP have been proposed: ambiguity-aversion (Anderson, Hansen, and Sargent, 2003); and disappointment-aversion (Ang, Bekaert and Liu, 2005; Fielding and Stracca, 2007). Langer and Weber (2005) argue that the relation between myopia and the attractiveness of a lottery sequence is less general than suggested in previous research. They extend the concept MLA to myopic PT, providing experimental evidence that for specific risk profiles myopia will not decrease but increase the attractiveness of a sequence. Another study by Aloysius (2005) claims that the results obtained in the study by Benartzi and Thaler (1999) can be explained in terms of ambiguity-aversion caused by bounded rationality rather than MLA. The ambiguity in this case relates to uncertainty regarding the specification of the investor's model of stock returns. By contrast, Maenhout (2004) finds that the degree of concern relating to this ambiguity would have to be implausibly high to fully account for the equity premium. A more recent study by Kliger and Levit (2009) finds support for the MLA explanation, by examining evidence from the Tel Aviv stock exchange. This study examined the situation when trading in some securities was shifted from daily to weekly trading, increasing the length of the evaluation period; the MLA hypothesis predicts that risk-aversion would fall causing expected returns to fall, and indeed this is what the study observed. Another recent study by Glätzle-Rützler, Sutter and Zeileis (2015) finds no evidence for MLA among a sample of 755 adolescents, although in other respects these subjects behaved as expected in terms of investment decisions.

Conflicting theories and conflicting evidence point out the need for further research into the EPP. Benartzi and Thaler have in fact revised their theory regarding the relationship between the EPP and MLA since their 1995 paper. One main weakness of the original model was that it was not an intertemporal model involving consumption choice, which is the essence of the puzzle in broader terms. People make investment decisions over the long term ultimately in order to maximize their overall consumption.

### Government policy

There are also other significant implications of mental accounting processes for public policy. Some of these relate to activities where the government is directly involved in terms of provision, such as state pensions and medical care, and others relate to areas of activity where the government wants to influence the market, for example with environmental policies or social policies. In many cases the government wants to 'nudge' people into making decisions that are better for them, in terms of being judged better by the decision-makers themselves (Thaler and Sunstein, 2008). Thaler and Sunstein make the important and often-overlooked point that all decisions take place within a frame, for example deciding whether to be paid once a month or twice a month; furthermore, there is no such thing as a 'neutral' frame, and attempts to provide one may be misguided. Many of the policies involve aspects relating to intertemporal decisions and social interaction, which are discussed in later chapters, so we will concentrate on the mental accounting aspects at this stage, starting with public provision.

**1**    *Public services*

In many countries services such as health care and pensions have mixed provision, with both the public and the private sector having a role. The state is often regarded as providing a safety net, so that the less privileged sectors of the population receive at least some minimum standard of provision. In the USA the Medicare system of health care for the elderly, along with Medicaid for low income groups, is an example. This system was radically overhauled in 2003, with the changes coming into effect in 2006, aiming to provide a better, more comprehensive service with more choice, at an estimated cost of half a trillion dollars. However, Part D of the system, relating to drug provision, has come in for much criticism, especially related to its choice architecture. It is claimed that this is confusing and cumbersome, offering too many choices with too little guidance. As seen in Chapter 4 in connection with menu effects, too much choice can be a problem, causing people to make worse rather than better decisions. Confusion can cause people to defer making a decision, sticking with the status quo. Furthermore, in an attempt to achieve neutrality, default options were chosen at random. This is misguided, again because of the existence of 'status quo' bias, also discussed in Chapter 4. People tend to anchor on an existing situation, and accept it, even if it is significantly suboptimal. Thus people may end up continuing on a particular drug program, even when a better/cheaper drug is available.

Another important issue in public policy relates to contributions to pension funds or retirement savings plans and provision for the elderly. Saving for retirement is a well-documented self-control problem. Although the reasons for this are discussed in Chapter 8, one important implication follows from what has already been said regarding the liquidity of assets. People are more likely to leave their savings alone if such savings are in unambiguous illiquid accounts, like retirement accounts. Furthermore, governments can encourage savings in this form by providing the relevant tax incentives, like individual savings accounts (ISAs) in the UK. As with health care, this is an area where public and private sector provision complement each other. If more people are covered adequately by private provision, this reduces the burden on an increasingly strained public sector. This increasing strain arises because of the aging of the population in all developed countries, and has not been helped by the financial crisis in 2007–2008 and subsequent public spending.

**2**    *Government influence*

Government policy can influence market behavior in a number of ways. First of all, it can mandate or encourage changes in the framing of choices. Retirement savings is a good example. Although there are several factors that are relevant here, for example moral hazard, it has been found in many countries that there are three main problems in the private sector:

**1** An insufficient number of people are enrolled.
**2** The majority of people do not make sufficient contributions to allow for a comfortable retirement, because of the self-control and discounting problems discussed in Chapters 7 and 8.
**3** People allocate their contributions badly among different investments.

All these problems involve framing. There is strong evidence that enrollment can be increased simply by changing the default option to enrolling rather than not enrolling. Until recently the 'default option' in many pension schemes has been to opt out. A report by the Pensions Commission in the UK in 2011 recommended establishing a new national savings scheme where the default option is to contribute; studies have indicated that this might double the enrolment rate.

However, this does not address the second problem: how can we save more in the first place? One method of achieving this is to integrate savings plans with spending accounts. For example, credit card plans exist whereby not only must the whole balance be paid in full each month, but an additional payment is included to be placed in a savings account. This method takes advantage of the principle of integrating losses due to diminishing marginal sensitivity.

There is also some evidence that suggests that if higher contributions are presented as a default option in employment contracts, people are more likely to accept them. On the other hand, they tend to be unwilling to actively opt to pay higher contributions when lower contributions are presented as the default option. Again status quo bias is the problem here. Thus the choice of default is vital in the framing of choices. Default options are often regarded as 'normal' or endorsed by the default setter, thus causing the bias.

As far as the third problem is concerned, evidence also suggests that portfolio allocations can be substantially altered by framing choices differently. Benartzi and Thaler (2001) found that allocation to stocks rather than bonds varied from 34% to 75% in different retirement savings plans, the national average being 57%, according to how many of each type of asset was offered in the plan. When there were four bond funds and only one stock fund to choose from in the plan the allocation to stocks was 34%, whereas when there was only one bond fund and five stock funds, allocation to stocks was 75%. In this case it is the diversification heuristic that is skewing the allocations. People generally tend to underinvest in stocks, because of MLA, as explained earlier, so a nudge in terms of the framing of investment options might help people to make better decisions in terms of fund allocation.

Status quo bias can be a problem in other aspects of policy where the government wants to change behavior. For example, the current policy in most countries regarding organ donation is that people have to carry a donor card if they wish to donate, in other words they have to opt in. In view of the shortage of organs like kidneys, and the number of deaths related to this, some doctors (and others) have proposed that this default should be changed so that people have to opt out. Evidence suggests that this change would result in a substantial increase in organ donation.

Another area where framing is of great importance is tax and transfer policies. In this case it is the government itself that is responsible for framing the nature of its policies. Studies by Epley, Mak, and Idson (2006) and Epley and Gneezy (2007) indicate that people are more likely to spend income that is unexpected and perceived as unearned. Their experiments showed that income received as a rebate is less likely to be spent than income that is expressed as a bonus. Having considered and rejected various explanations for this, the investigators proposed that rebates were perceived as a return to the status quo (encouraged by government rhetoric in the USA in 2001), whereas bonuses were perceived as gains relative to the status quo. Reversals of losses were seen as being more valuable than gains. The psychology involved is similar to the 'house money' effect described earlier in the chapter. Furthermore, the experiments performed in the study by Epley, Mak and Idson (2006) indicated that people receiving the smaller rebates ($300) recalled spending a higher proportion of it than those receiving the larger rebates ($500 and $600). There are various possible interpretations here, but a mental accounting explanation is that smaller amounts are less likely to be earmarked for a particular budget category of spending/saving, and are more likely to be placed in a miscellaneous 'petty cash' category, thus stimulating immediate spending. Thus it might be possible for the government to stimulate more spending in the economy by spreading out rebate payments and making smaller payments, while keeping the total rebate bill the same.

Epley and Gneezy (2007) also propose that the contrast in people's attitudes to reversals of losses compared with gains, whereby returns to the status quo may be seen as more valuable than gains, is relevant for other aspects of government policy. For example, environmental policy, counter-terrorism policy and anti-obesity policy may all be more effective if they are framed as returns to a previous more desirable state than as gains compared with the current undesirable state. Given the importance of these policies to the welfare of the nation, further research in this area is seen as a high priority.

Attention and salience are also relevant as far as government influence is concerned. With so many messages being aimed at us every day by a variety of sources, it takes a special message to have a persuasive effect, overcoming what Thaler and Sunstein call the 'yeah, whatever' heuristic. Salience can also be relevant in environmental policy, where the government is trying to encourage consumers to use less of a resource. For example, to reduce use of oil a government may require all new cars sold to advertise their fuel economy figures. Of course consumers are free to choose to ignore this information, or edit it out, but if it is prominent enough this may be difficult. 'Smart' meters for electricity, gas and water allow consumers to monitor usage on an hourly basis. This might not normally be salient, but if the relevant utility introduces 'intermittent' billing processes based on these meters this may make the usage more salient. Gilbert and Graff Zivin (2014) use data from such smart meters to estimate that consumers reduce usage by 0.6–1% following receipt of an electricity bill.

Social factors, such as the desire for conformity may also be relevant here, and these factors apply in particular to what are often seen as social problems like smoking, binge drinking, and teenage pregnancy. In all cases it can be difficult for government policy to overcome the relevant status quo bias and 'yeah, whatever' heuristic. These factors will be discussed further in Chapter 10, but one aspect is worth mentioning here. When habits are costly, like smoking, there are also implications in terms of the mental accounting processes of aggregation versus disaggregation. Governments may want to achieve the opposite of firms, in terms of discouraging the consumption of goods or services regarded as undesirable. Therefore instead of expressing costs in terms of an amount per day or week, the government may want such costs to be evaluated by consumers over a period of a year or longer. Government anti-smoking campaigns may thus stress yearly costs. As a result, instead of viewing the cost of smoking as £5 per day, which may fall into the petty cash category, the consumer may come to view the cost as nearly £2,000 per year, a more daunting expense.

## 6.6  Summary

- Mental accounting is the set of cognitive operations used by individuals and households to code, categorize and evaluate financial activities.
- There are three main aspects of mental accounting: (1) the perception of outcomes and the making and evaluation of decisions; (2) the assignment of activities to specific accounts; and (3) the determination of the time periods to which different mental accounts relate.
- Prospect theory (PT) has various implications for mental accounting, in particular four principles: (1) segregate gains; (2) integrate losses; (3) integrate small losses with larger gains; and (4) segregate small gains from large losses.
- Transactions confer two different types of utility: acquisition utility and transaction utility.
- Products are frequently sold as bundles of components, in which case the price may be consolidated or partitioned.

- Determining whether the price should be consolidated or partitioned is important in marketing strategy since it affects consumer responses. Each method may prove preferable in different circumstances, depending on how it increases the salience of particular product characteristics.
- Various neural imaging studies provide supporting evidence for the mental accounting process in terms of editing and evaluating outcomes.
- There is a large body of evidence that mental accounts for consumption, income, wealth and time are not fungible, as is assumed in the neoclassical model (NM).
- Fungibility means that different types of account within some aggregate variable, like consumption or wealth, are perfectly substitutable.
- In consumption budgeting some people may have fixed budgets for particular categories of spending, while others may have more flexible budgets and categories. More flexibility tends to cause people to spend more than they would with less flexibility.
- People often classify types of income on a serious-frivolous scale, and match increases in income in one category with increases in spending in the same category.
- In wealth budgeting, the NM assumes that people smooth consumption over their lifetimes, and treat different types of wealth as being fungible. Anomalies relate to the use of credit cards, attitudes towards stock returns, segregation of asset types as investments, and the impact of social interactions.
- Like any accounting system, mental accounting requires making decisions regarding when to open and close accounts.
- Typical situations when such decisions have to made are: buying and selling stock; reporting earnings; depreciating sunk costs; and payment decoupling.
- Payment decoupling means that spending and consumption cannot be directly matched, even when they are simultaneous. The consequence is that we cannot easily allocate a consumption item to a particular cost.
- An example of payment decoupling is when people pay a flat rate for something, like internet use, which does not depend on the hours of use. People tend to like this option rather than 'having the meter running'; this is known as 'flat rate bias'.
- Prior outcomes affect attitudes to risk in subsequent situations. The 'house money effect' appears to be common, where gains encourage risk-seeking, but only in regard to recent gains.
- Myopic loss-aversion (MLA) also appears to be a common phenomenon, where people evaluate their portfolios too frequently, leading them to be too risk-averse in the long run and forgoing returns.
- Diversification bias is observed in a number of situations, especially notable where investors use the $1/n$ heuristic in selecting from a range of assets to include in their portfolios.
- There are several normative or policy implications of mental accounting processes; these relate to agents themselves, marketers, labor markets, financial markets and governments.

## 6.7  Review questions

1  Explain why people may drive for 20 minutes to save $5 on a $15 calculator but not for a $125 dollar jacket. What principle of PT is relevant here?

2  Explain the mental accounting rule 'segregate small gains from large losses', and give an example relating to marketing.

3  Why are people more reluctant to replace a $20 theater ticket if they have lost it than if they have lost $20 cash? What principle of the standard model does this violate?

4    Why would people prefer to pay by credit card and pay 12% interest when they have a savings account with sufficient funds paying them only 3%?

5    Explain what is meant by 'emotional accounting', giving an example.

6    Explain what is meant by disaggregated pricing; why would marketers use such a tactic?

7    Explain why governments might want to use the opposite type of policy to disaggregated pricing, and instead aggregate prices or costs to the consumer.

8    Explain the factors that are relevant in trade-in pricing.

9    Explain why default options are important, giving two examples.

10   Explain what is meant by a 'target worker', and why such workers behave in contrasting ways to the predictions of the standard model of labor supply.


## 6.8   Applications

Three case studies are now discussed. The first two relate to different aspects of MLA, while the last one relates to fungibility and consumption budgeting.

### Case 6.1 The equity premium puzzle

The EPP is that, over the long term, stocks have consistently outperformed bonds by a large margin. It is certainly one of the most hotly debated topics in financial economics. The debate was largely sparked off by a paper by Mehra and Prescott (1985). They reported that, on the basis of US data for about 100 years from 1889 to 1978, the average annual real return to stock was 7%, while the average annual return to Treasury bills was 1%, indicating a risk premium between risky and safe assets of about 6%. The authors claim that such a large premium is a puzzle because, according to conventional economic models, it implies an astronomical coefficient of risk-aversion, in excess of 30. In order to aid an interpretation of this value, Mankiw and Zeldes (1991) provide an example: a person with such a degree of risk-aversion would be indifferent between a gamble with a 50% chance of a consumption of $100,000 and a 50% chance of a consumption of $50,000, and a certain consumption of $51,209. This does not seem reasonable in the light of other empirical data. Furthermore, the puzzle does not seem confined to the USA. A study by Canova and De Nicoló (2003) finds that 'the basic features of the equity premium and risk-free puzzles remain regardless of the sample period and the country considered'. The risk-free puzzle can be viewed as the converse of the EPP, as it poses the apparent anomaly of why the risk-free rate is so low.

At present investigators are divided into three main camps: those who do not believe that there is a premium at all, those who have proposed some kind of explanation, and those who have reviewed the different explanations, and believe that the puzzle remains. The purpose here is not to discuss all these different approaches in any detail, but rather to focus on one particular explanation by Benartzi and Thaler (1995), which involves the behavioral aspects of PT and mental accounting. Before explaining this approach however, it is worthwhile gaining an overall perspective by giving a brief overview of the three main camps mentioned above.

Those investigators who do not believe in the existence of the premium point to various problems and ambiguities related to measurement. Perhaps the most fundamental

▶

issue here is the distinction between the historical premium and the expected or *ex ante* premium. Ibbotson and Chen (2003) estimate that the *ex ante* premium over the period 1926–2000 in the USA was about 1.25% lower than the historical premium. A second issue relates to the choice of risk-free asset. Most studies use either Treasury bills or long-term Treasury bonds, usually with a maturity of 20 years. Jones and Wilson (2005) estimate that over the period 1871–2003 the historical equity premium was 4.79% on bonds and 3.85% for bills. However, in certain periods the difference has been much larger. In the period 1990–2003 the equity premium was only 2.05% for bonds, but 6.32% for bills. Jones and Wilson also discuss a third measurement issue: the use of geometric means versus arithmetic means. They use the former measure, on the basis that they are more appropriate in a long-term time series study. The difference is notable; Jones and Wilson estimate that arithmetic means, as used in the Mehra–Prescott study, tend to be 1.6–1.8% higher than geometric means. A final measurement issue concerns whether returns should be described in nominal or real terms. Benartzi and Thaler (1995) argue that nominal measures are often more appropriate, for two reasons: first, returns are usually reported in nominal terms; second, simulations suggest that investors cannot be thinking in real terms, otherwise they would not be willing to hold Treasury bills over any evaluation period, since they always yield negative prospective utility. Although these measurement issues muddy the waters as far as obtaining a precise measure of the size of the equity premium, most researchers still believe that the historical premium is significantly large.

Over the last 20 years there have been many attempts to explain the puzzle. Some of the better known models are:

1  Generalized expected utility (Weil,1989; Epstein and Zin, 1989)

2  Habit formation (Constantinides, 1990; Ferson and Constantinides, 1991; Hung and Wang, 2005; Meyer and Meyer, 2005)

3  Imperfect markets or market frictions (He and Modest, 1995; Luttmer, 1996; Zhou, 1999)

4  Ambiguity or uncertainty (Olsen and Troughton, 2000; Aloysius, 2005)

5  Delayed consumption updating (Gabaix and Laibson, 2001)

6  Fluctuating economic uncertainty or consumption volatility (Bansal and Yaron, 2004)

Finally, there are a considerable number of commentators who have surveyed the above models and results, and conclude that the EPP is still a puzzle, for example Kocherlakota (1996), Chapman (2002) and Oyefeso (2006).

The Benartzi and Thaler (BT) approach combines two important elements:

1  A utility function described by PT, involving reference points, diminishing marginal sensitivity, a weighted probability function, and loss-aversion. The authors note that this function has something in common with the habit formation explanation, in that both models involve reference points.

2  A mental accounting process whereby portfolios are evaluated at regular intervals, and accounts are 'closed'.

The authors then proceeded to ask two questions:

1  What evaluation period would investors have to use in order to be indifferent between a portfolio consisting entirely of stocks and a portfolio consisting entirely of five-year Treasury bonds?

**2**  Given the evaluation period determined above, what combination of stocks and bonds would people hold in order to maximize prospective utility?

The authors based their answers to the above questions on simulations using historical data for the USA from 1926 to 1990 involving monthly returns on stocks, bonds and bills. They find that the evaluation period in the first question was about 13 months, in terms of nominal returns, and about ten months for real returns. They then find that the optimal position for investors involves 30–55% of the portfolio invested in stock. The prospective utility function is virtually flat over this range. These results broadly match empirical findings; institutional investors have about 53% of their portfolios in stocks, while individuals allocate their funds between stocks and bonds on about a 50–50 basis.

Having derived results to these two questions, the authors proceed to ask two further questions:

**1**  Which aspects of PT drive the results?

**2**  How sensitive are the results to alternative specifications?

They find that loss-aversion is the main determinant of the outcomes, whereas the specific functional forms of the value function and weighting functions are not critical. When the parameters in the model are changed in specification this also does not appear to significantly affect the length of the evaluation period. For example, if actual probabilities are used instead of a weighting function, the period is reduced by one or two months.

The BT study also examines the relationship between the equity premium and the length of evaluation period. They find that the premium falls from 6.5% for a one-year period to about 3% for a five-year period, 2% for a ten-year period and 1.4% for a twenty-year period. The authors then comment that investors with a twenty-year horizon are able to reap the reward of an economic rent of 5.1% if they are able to resist the temptation to count their money often: 'in a sense, 5.1% is the price for excessive vigilance.'

These reduced premiums estimated by the BT study are matched by calculations by Jones and Wilson (2005). The risks of loss in terms of investing in stocks rather than bonds are reflected in the probability of a negative premium for the period of evaluation. This probability is particularly relevant in the BT model which is driven strongly by loss-aversion. Jones and Wilson estimate that the probability of a negative premium falls from 41% for a one-year period to 33% for a five-year period, 25% for a ten-year period and 17% for a twenty-year period.

The final element in the BT paper contains a solution to the puzzle of organizational MLA. While individuals may be strongly tempted to count their money frequently, why should this apply to institutional investors like pension funds who should have every reason to take a long-term evaluation period? The answer given is that the reason for organizational MLA lies in an agency problem. The fund managers in such institutions have to report results on an annual basis, and are held accountable for these short-term results. Bearing in mind the competitive nature of these funds, there may be a 'tragedy of the commons' here, in that managers may be tempted to trade off better short-term results for better long-term results, knowing that their rivals are in the same situation. Such game theory considerations are discussed in Chapter 9.

---

**Questions**

1  Explain the statement: 'in a sense, 5.1% is the price for excessive vigilance.'
2  What is the significance of the probability of a negative premium?
3  Is the equity premium likely to remain at the historical level in the future?
4  How have studies since the BT study of 1995 shed light on the phenomenon of the EPP and the MLA explanation?

---

## Case 6.2 Why you can't find a cab on a rainy day

These conditions are satisfied well by one particular group of workers: cab drivers. On some days they are busy, and their hourly wage rate is higher, while other days are quieter, causing a lower rate. Drivers are in a position to determine the number of hours they work on a daily basis, depending on their average hourly wage for that day. A study by Camerer and colleagues (1997) examined data relating to New York City cab drivers between 1988 and 1994, using three different samples totaling 1,826 observations. These observations related both to different drivers and to the same drivers on different days. The investigators relied on data from trip sheets that drivers fill out daily, checked against the records of the meters inside the cabs. Hours worked were calculated by measuring the time taken from when the first customer was picked up to when the last customer was dropped off. Daily wage rates were calculated by dividing total daily revenue (not including tips) by hours worked.

The objective of the study was to test two competing hypotheses:

1  NM – upward-sloping supply curve, with positive wage elasticity.
2  behavioral model – downward-sloping supply curve, with negative wage elasticity.

The latter model involves the supposition that workers are target workers, meaning that they aim for a daily income target, and stop working when they reach that target. This implies a more specific hypothesis regarding wage elasticity. Wage elasticity measures the percentage change in hours worked in response to a 1% change in the wage rate. If workers aim for a daily income target then the wage elasticity should be −1. The implications of this behavior in terms of economic theory are discussed further below.

The investigators used ordinary least squares regression to estimate the relationship between hours worked against the wage rate, using logarithms of both variables in order to estimate the wage elasticity. Thus their model is in the form:

$$\ln H = a + b \ln W$$

where $H$ represents the number of hours worked per day, $W$ represents the hourly wage rate and $b$ represents the wage elasticity.

They obtained separate results for each sample and certain subsamples. The simple correlations between log hours and log wages are all negative for the three main samples: −0.503, −0.391 and −0.269. Although these correlations are not very high, for the two largest samples, totaling 1,506 observations, the regression coefficients are not only negative but statistically significant at the 5% level. Furthermore, the two estimates of wage elasticity are −0.926 and −0.975, both very close to −1.

The study also investigated how elasticities varied with both experience and payment structure. Drivers were divided into two groups, according to whether they had more or less than three years of experience. The hypothesis relating to experience was that the more experienced drivers would learn that they could earn more by driving more on high-wage days and driving less on low-wage days. This would cause them to have a more positive elasticity. This hypothesis was indeed confirmed: there is a marked difference between the elasticities for experienced and inexperienced drivers. Indeed in two of the samples the elasticity is positive.

It was also hypothesized that the way drivers pay for their cabs would affect elasticity. Drivers fall into three main categories here: those who rent daily for a 12-hour shift; those who rent weekly or monthly; and those who own their own cabs. The first group has a relatively low negative elasticity (−0.197), while the elasticities for the other two groups are −0.978 and −0.867 respectively, suggesting that they are target workers.

The issue of optimality is also raised in the study. It is estimated that if drivers worked the same number of hours in total, but redistributed on the basis of working a constant number of hours per day, they could increase their earnings by an average of 5%. Furthermore, assuming that their utility function for leisure is concave, this fixed-hours rule would also improve total leisure utility. It was also estimated that, if drivers reallocated their total driving hours as if the wage elasticity were +1, they could increase earnings by 10% on average.

The study concludes by considering different explanations for the results. Four possible explanations are rejected:

1   *Drivers are 'liquidity-constrained'.* This means that they do not have enough cash to pay daily expenses and cannot borrow. If this is the case they could not afford to stop driving on low-wage days. However, cab owners are not liquidity constrained (the medallion licences they own are now valued at about $250,000), and yet their wage elasticities are still negative.

2   *The calculation of the working hours and wage rate does not take into account actual hours worked.* It may be that on quiet days drivers finish late, but take a lot of unrecorded breaks. This would cause total hours worked to be lower and the wage rate to be higher. However, in one of the samples the breaks were recorded and excluded; this made no difference to the results.

3   *Drivers finish early because being busy and carrying a lot of passengers is tiring.* However, a survey of the cab fleet managers revealed that most of them thought that fruitlessly searching for fares on a low-wage day was more tiring than carrying passengers.

4   *The data is biased, since it only takes into account days worked, or 'participation', not the days when drivers chose not to work at all.* It may be that there is a tendency to work unexpectedly on some days, this being correlated with working long hours. However, drivers usually operate on a fixed-shift schedule, with penalties for not showing up, making unexpected participation of little importance.

Having rejected the four explanations above, the authors conclude that daily income targeting is the best explanation for the results obtained. As with the previous case study

▶

relating to the equity risk premium, the essential behavioral factor here is MLA. Drivers have a reference point in terms of a daily income target, and are averse to any shortfalls or losses compared to this target. Any gains have progressively less marginal utility because of the concavity of the utility function. The question then is: why do they have an evaluation period of such a short time as one day? This seems an extreme example of 'narrow bracketing'. The authors of the study propose two explanations for this:

1  *Daily income targets serve as a useful heuristic*. It is easier to use this rule than to try to estimate the marginal utility of work time and compare it with the marginal utility of leisure time for each day.

2  *Daily income targets serve as a useful self-control device.* If longer evaluation periods are used, it becomes easy for drivers to slack off and finish early, with the intention of making up for lost time and income later in the week or month. The situation is similar to that of an author with a daily target of pages written, discussed earlier in the chapter. Furthermore, as the study notes: 'a drive home through Manhattan with $200–$300 in cash from a good day is an obstacle course of temptations for many drivers, creating a self-control problem that is avoided by daily targeting.'

As a final point the authors of the study comment on the difference between experienced and inexperienced drivers. Experienced drivers are less likely to be target earners, and closer to being optimizers. The study suggests that there may be two reasons for this:

1  Drivers learn to optimize through experience.

2  Non-optimizing target-earners are weeded out by a selection process.

### Questions

1  Why can't you catch a cab on a rainy day?

2  Explain the differences between the predictions of the standard model and its behavioral alternative.

3  Explain why target earners have a wage elasticity of $-1$.

4  Explain the meaning of the statement: 'furthermore, assuming that their utility function for leisure is concave, this fixed-hours rule would also improve total leisure utility.'

5  Explain why daily targeting is 'myopic'.

6  Explain why daily targeting is related to self-control factors.

7  Explain how the studies by Farber and Fehr and Goette support or do not support the conclusions of the Camerer and colleagues study.

### Case 6.3  The housing market and debt

House prices in the USA more than doubled between 2000 and 2006, according to the well-known Case-Shiller index of 20 major cities. Between 2006 and 2011 they declined by 22%, as the housing bubble burst. By mid-2016 they had recovered considerably, but were still about 5% lower than the 2006 high, and 20% lower after adjusting for inflation. US real estate is the largest asset class in the world, currently valued at around $26 trillion, with outstanding mortgage debt at around $11 trillion (Economist, 2016a). The fact that much of this debt is owned abroad means that the risk of default remains a threat to the global financial system.

Since 2010, when the Dodd-Frank Act was passed with a variety of changes in financial regulation, the US government has been largely content to let the housing market be. After all, the fancy derivatives that 'caused' the financial crisis in 2007 have largely disappeared, banks have much larger buffers of equity now, and new regulations are in place to protect borrowers and determine the design of new mortgages. Conventional measures of house affordability, in terms of price–income ratio and price–rent ratio, are at around their long-term averages over the last 30 years (Economist, 2016a). Yet there are still many reasons for behavioral economists to be concerned. These reasons relate to: (1) attitudes to risk and moral hazard; (2) attitudes to debt; (3) incentives for financial institutions; and (4) incentives to politicians.

**1**  *Attitudes to risk and moral hazard*

It is often argued that investors and lenders have learned their lesson from the financial crisis. In particular, it was widely assumed before the crisis that house prices would continue to rise, and this was reinforced by the representativeness heuristic. The recent fall in prices has resulted in more realistic expectations. However, there are recent signs that some lending practices are slipping in terms of risk taking. For example, there has been an increase in loan-to-value (LTV) ratios, with reportedly a fifth of these now being 95%. Income-to-loan ratios may also be falling (Economist, 2016a). The moral hazard situation has actually increased since the financial crisis, since there is now a greater involvement of federal government. State institutions (Federal National Mortgage Association, Federal Home Loan Mortgage Corporation, General National Mortgage Association, Federal Housing Association, Veterans Association) between them either own or guarantee $6.4 trillion of loans, and between 65% and 80% of new loans have a federal guarantee (Economist, 2016). The result is that the additional loan risk is not a result of behavior by the banks, who may be tightening their criteria, but is caused by other institutions who have entered the market since the financial crisis.

**2**  *Attitudes to debt*

There are various problems in behavioral terms here. A fundamental one concerns reference points. Household debt fell slightly following the crisis, but has now virtually returned to pre-crisis levels, close to $12.6 trillion at the end of 2016, nearly 80% of GDP. Student debt and car loan debt are on the rise in particular. Consumers are now used to high levels of debt, so it does not cause so much concern as in previous years. We will also see in the next two chapters that consumer impatience and inconsistent time preferences also play an important role here: consumers want to enjoy goods and services now, and will worry about paying for them later.

**3**  *Incentives for financial institutions*

These have been drastically altered since the crisis, because of the increased activity of federal institutions and increased regulations. Fewer mortgages are being originated and these are going increasingly to the more affluent consumers. Thus federal institutions are increasingly taking on the risk of lending to poorer, higher-risk households, and this risk is being funded by the taxpayer, at an estimated $150 billion a year (Economist, 2016a). These institutions are not required to maintain the same capital buffers as are now required of the banks.

**4**  *Incentives to politicians*

The situation might be less worrying if it could be reasonably claimed that politicians, meaning law-makers, were on top of it. However, there appears to be a huge complacency in this area. There are two main reasons for this. First, it is claimed that the relevant actions have already been taken in terms of increased regulation. Capital buffers are now twice what they were before the crisis, the derivatives market is more highly regulated, as is the mortgage market. In fact many in the Republican camp believe that these steps have already been excessive, and need to be rolled back somewhat. The second reason relates to the opening and closing of mental accounts: the political cycle is 4–5 years, but cycles of financial crisis are much longer, at least 10–15 years. Thus current politicians do not need to worry about the next crisis; when it occurs they will probably no longer be in office – it will be somebody else's problem.

## Questions

1   Describe the framing effects that are mentioned in the case regarding house affordability, and explain how these may make it appear that the housing market is not currently in crisis.

2   What are the dangers of federal involvement in the housing market?

3   Explain why consumer debt may not be fungible, and the implications of this.

4   Explain the role of the representativeness heuristic in the housing and debt markets.

# PART·III

# Intertemporal Choice

# CHAPTER · 7

## The Discounted Utility Model

## 7.1  Introduction

Intertemporal choices relate to decisions involving trade-offs between costs and benefits occurring in different time periods. Governments, firms and individuals are all faced with such decisions on a frequent and ongoing basis, for example: investing in roads, schools and hospitals; building a new factory or launching a new product; buying a new car, spending on a vacation or joining a health club. Economists have been interested in such decisions since at least the days of Adam Smith, but the current model that is generally used by most economists, as well as by governments and firms, is the discounted utility model (DUM), originally proposed by Samuelson in 1937. The widespread use of the model seems strange to many practitioners in behavioral economics, in view of the fact that Samuelson himself had significant reservations regarding both the normative and the descriptive aspects of the model, and that many anomalies have been observed over the last few decades.

Because the topic of intertemporal choice is so broad in scope, the structure in the previous chapters is somewhat modified. Up to this point we have started with the fundamental aspects of the neoclassical model, observed the anomalies and then extended the model, introducing behavioral modifications. In this chapter, however, we will concentrate entirely on describing the DUM (as the relevant aspect of the NM), and examining its implications and anomalies. Only in the next chapter will we move on to discuss alternative behavioral models. At that point we will see that various factors discussed in previous chapters are relevant in terms of formulating such models.

In this chapter therefore we begin by considering the historical origins of the DUM, before describing the essential features of the model. The discussion of origins is important, since many of the more recent behavioral developments are in many ways a reversion to much earlier work involving psychological and sociological factors. We shall also see in the next chapter that recent theories of intertemporal choice also incorporate elements of theory from evolutionary biology and neuroeconomics. After the features of the DUM are described, its many anomalies are discussed. The nature and causes of these anomalies involves a discussion of the complex concept of time preference, which is deferred until the next chapter. Finally, various policy implications of the DUM are considered.

## 7.2  Origins of the discounted utility model

Although Adam Smith was the first economist to discuss the importance of intertemporal choice as far as the wealth of nations was concerned, it was Rae who essentially provided a psychological foundation for a theory of intertemporal choice.

### *John Rae and the desire for accumulation*

In the early nineteenth century Rae (1905 [1834]) identified 'the effective desire for accumulation' as being the key psychological factor determining a society's decisions to save and invest, which in turn determined a country's rate of economic productivity and growth. Rae also identified four psychological factors that either promoted or inhibited this desire, and which varied across different societies. The two promoting factors were:

1  *The bequest motive* – to accumulate resources for one's descendants.
2  *The propensity to exercise self-restraint* – this involves the intellectual capacity to foresee probable future outcomes of decisions, and the willpower to put long-term interests ahead of short-term ones.

The two inhibiting factors described by Rae were:

1  *The uncertainty of human life* – there is no point in saving for the future if it is unlikely that we will have much of one. Rae summed this up by saying:

> When engaged in safe occupations, and living in healthy countries, men are much more apt to be frugal, than in unhealthy, or hazardous occupations, and in climates pernicious to human life.

2  *The urge for instant gratification exacerbated by the prospect of immediate consumption* – Rae again expresses this in vivid terms:

> The actual presence of the immediate object of desire in the mind by exciting the attention, seems to rouse all the faculties, as it were, to fix their view on it, and leads them to a very lively conception of the enjoyments which it offers to their instant possession.

### Two different approaches

Later theorists developed two different views of time preference stemming from Rae's work. One view took the approach that the default situation was that people weighted the present and future equally, but the discomfort of delaying gratification caused people to weigh future outcomes less heavily than present ones (Senior, 1836). The second view took the opposite approach, proposing that people generally only considered immediate utility, but the anticipation of future utility might on occasion more than offset any loss of current utility, causing them to delay gratification (William Jevons, 1888; Herbert Jevons, 1905). Both approaches emphasize the importance of current feelings, but explain variations in time preference between people in different ways. According to the first approach people vary in terms of the discomfort they experience in delaying gratification. According to the second approach variations in time preference arise because of people have different abilities to anticipate the future.

### Böhm-Bawerk and trade-offs

The next major development in the theory of intertemporal choice came from Böhm-Bawerk (1889). He, and later Pigou (1920), introduced the notion that people generally underestimate future wants, leading to a time preference pattern biased towards the present. It should be noted at this stage that this notion does not involve a discounting of future outcomes; instead it is the utility of these outcomes that is underestimated. This is a key distinction that will be discussed in more detail later in the chapter.

Böhm-Bawerk introduced another important innovation in the theory of intertemporal choice: such choices were seen as trade-offs in terms of allocating resources to oneself in different periods of time, similar to trade-offs in allocating resources between consuming different current goods.

### Irving Fisher and indifference curve analysis

The final development before the introduction of the discounted utility model came from Irving Fisher (1930). He formalized much of the work outlined above, extending the Böhm-Bawerk framework of analysis in terms of using indifference curves to illustrate the relevant trade-offs. Current consumption was plotted on the horizontal axis and future consumption (usually for the following year) was plotted on the vertical axis. The concept of the marginal rate of substitution between current and future consumption was also applied; this depended both on time preference and diminishing marginal utility.

It should also be emphasized that Fisher discussed at length the psychological factors affecting time preference. Thus he not only took account of future wealth and risk, he also referred to the four factors described by Rae, and to foresight, which is the other side of the coin of Böhm-Bawerk's notion of the underestimation of future wants. Fisher also stressed the importance of fashion:

> This at the present time acts, on the one hand, to stimulate men to save and become millionaires, and, on the other hand, to stimulate millionaires to live in an ostentatious manner. (p. 87)

The reason for underlining the fact that these early pre-DUM developments in the theory of intertemporal choice all took different psychological factors into account is that the DUM itself swept away the explicit consideration of these psychological factors, condensing them into a single construct: the discount rate. The implications of this 'revolution' need to be discussed at some length in the remainder of this chapter.

## Samuelson and the discounted utility model

Samuelson introduced the DUM in 1937 in a short article modestly titled: 'A Note on Measurement of Utility'. Apart from commenting that the comparison of intertemporal trade-offs required a cardinal as opposed to ordinal measure of utility, it extended Fisher's indifference curve analysis, essentially limited to the comparison of two periods, to multi-period situations. However, as noted above, it combined all the psychological factors involved in time preference into the single parameter of the discount rate. The nature of the model can be best described in mathematical terms. It specifies an intertemporal utility function $U_t(c_t,...,c_T)$ which describes the utility at time $t$ of the consumption profile $(c_t, c_{t+1}, c_{t+2},...)$ starting in period $t$ and continuing to period $T$. The model incorporates the general axioms of the NM described in previous chapters regarding the completeness, transitivity and independence principles. The DUM then goes on to assume that a person's intertemporal utility function can be described by the following specific functional form:

$$U_t(c_t,...,c_T) = \sum_{k=0}^{T-t} D(k)u(c_{t+k}) \qquad \text{where } D(k) = (1/1+\rho)k$$

This is essentially a similar expression to equation (1.1), where the second component is expanded. The term $u(c_{t+k})$ can be interpreted as the person's instantaneous utility function, meaning their perceived well-being in period $t + k$. The term $D(k)$ refers to the person's discount function, meaning the relative weight that the person attaches in time period $t$ to their well-being in period $t + k$. Finally, the term $\rho$ refers to the person's discount rate, meaning the rate at which they discount expected future utilities. This term therefore combines all the various psychological factors involved in time preference that were discussed earlier.

It will aid an understanding of the workings of the model, as well as the implications and anomalies discussed later, if a simplified example is examined at this stage. Let us take the following consumption profile, measured in thousands of dollars per year over a period of the next three years: (20, 20, 20). We will also assume for simplicity that these consecutive equal amounts of consumption yield equal amounts of utility. It should be noted that this assumption violates some of the behavioral factors considered in earlier chapters, such as the effects of reference points, habit formation and the desire for increasing consumption profiles (the 'happiness treadmill'). These complicating factors will be discussed later in terms of their implications for the DUM.

Since the measurement of utility is in arbitrary units of 'utils', we can consider the utility profile as consisting of the terms (20, 20, 20). It is assumed that the model is discrete and that the utilities are all received at points in time at the end of each period, rather than being continuous flows throughout each period. This may appear unrealistic but the DUM can be modified to transform it into a continuous-time model; the utility function becomes an integral of a negative exponential function. For simplicity we will use the discrete form of the model. If the consumer discounts future utility at the rate of 10% per year the current utility of the consumption and utility profiles can now be calculated as follows:

$$Ut(20, 20, 20) = \frac{20}{1 + 0.1} + \frac{20}{(1 + 0.1)^2} + \frac{20}{(1 + 0.1)^3} = 49.74 \qquad (7.1)$$

This calculation illustrates an important feature of the DUM: it closely resembles the compound interest formula used in calculating net present values. This analogue with the common technique for evaluating financial investments has been largely responsible for the rapid assimilation of the model by economists, particularly after Koopmans (1960) showed that the model could be derived from a set of axioms or basic principles that are superficially plausible. The model also gained normative status, as it was shown that an exponential discounting function was consistent with rationality, in the sense that it resulted in dynamically consistent choices. Other economists, including Lancaster (1963), Fishburn (1970) and Meyer (1976), have since provided alternative axiom systems for the DUM, further increasing its perceived legitimacy and popularity.

## 7.3   Features of the discounted utility model

There are a number of features of the DUM that now need to be examined, since these relate to the implicit psychological assumptions underlying the model. These features have been analyzed and their validity critically reviewed by Frederick, Loewenstein and O'Donoghue (2002), and the following discussion draws extensively from that review.

*Integration of new alternatives with existing plans*

It is a common assumption in most decision or choice situations relating to the standard model that people evaluate new alternatives by integrating them with existing plans. This means that if a person is offered a prospect A (say, investing $10,000 now to gain $15,000 in three years), the effects of this prospect on the person's whole consumption profile must be considered. Thus if the person currently has the consumption profile $(c_1,...,c_T)$, then they must estimate their new consumption profile if they were to accept prospect A, for example $(c'_1,...,c'_T)$. Prospect A would then be accepted if $Ut(c'_1,...,c'_T) > U_t(c_1,...,c_T)$.

Although this approach may seem logical from a normative point of view, meaning that people should want to integrate new alternatives in order to maximize welfare, we have already seen in previous chapters that this places unrealistic demands on people's mental capacities. People may not have well-formed consumption profiles relating to all future periods, and they may be unable or unwilling to reformulate such plans every time that new prospects are encountered. The next section relating to anomalies in the DUM will examine empirical evidence regarding people's behavior in this regard.

## Utility independence

It is assumed in the DUM that it is simply the sum of all the discounted future utilities, for example the value of 49.74 in equation (7.1), which is relevant in terms of making intertemporal choices. This ignores the possibility that the distribution of utilities over time may be relevant. As we shall see, people may prefer a flat or rising utility profile to a falling one, or a pattern of dispersion of utilities rather than a concentrated pattern. This assumption is also related to the next one.

## Consumption independence

It is assumed in the DUM that a person's welfare in any time period is independent of consumption in any other period. This means that preferences over consumption profiles are not affected by the nature of consumption in periods in which consumption is identical in the two profiles. It is therefore analogous to the independence axiom in expected utility theory (EUT). As Frederick, Loewenstein and O'Donoghue (2002) state:

> Consumption independence says that one's preference between an Italian and
> Thai restaurant tonight should not depend on whether one had Italian last night
> nor whether one expects to have it tomorrow. (p. 357)

It should be noted that neither Samuelson nor Koopmans proposed that this assumption had either normative or descriptive validity. Indeed we will review a number of empirical anomalies in the remainder of this chapter and the next.

## Stationary instantaneous utility

The DUM generally assumes that the instantaneous utility function is constant over time, meaning that the same activity yields the same utility in the future, viewed from the future, as now. For example, if activity A is expected to yield 20 utils in 3 years' time, the current utility of A, which can be written as $u_0(A)$, will be discounted to about 15 utils (at a 10% discount rate). However, it is assumed that the utility of A in three years' time, $u_3(A)$, will still be 20 utils. This implies that people's preferences do not change over time, an obviously unrealistic assumption.

Evidence suggests that people tend to exaggerate the degree to which their future preferences will resemble their current ones, a phenomenon referred to as **projection bias** (Loewenstein, O'Donoghue and Rabin, 2003). Thus they may expect to like the music of Oasis in 20 years because they like it now, but then find in 20 years' time that they can't stand it.

## Stationary discounting

It is assumed in the DUM that people use the same discount rate over their lifespan. In contrast, there is considerable evidence that discounting rates vary according to age. Mischel and Metzner (1962) have found that willingness to delay gratification increases with age, implying that older people have a lower discount rate. However, the relationship between discounting and age appears to be a complex one. In an experimental study of respondents between the ages of 19 and 89 it was found that older people discount more than younger ones, and that middle-aged people discount less than either group (Read and Read, 2004). Similar results were found by Harrison, Lau and Williams (2002).

A more detailed study by Halfmann, Hedgcock and Denburg (2013) introduces two further parameters into the relationship between discounting and age: cognitive ability/impairment and gain/loss. Their conclusions suggest an even more complex situation, since they find that both cognitive impairment and losses versus gains are relevant to discount rates. For gains they find that middle-aged subjects discount at the same rate as older impaired subjects, while older unimpaired subjects discount at a lower rate than either of them. The picture is somewhat different for losses: in this case middle-aged subjects discount at the same rate as older unimpaired subjects, while older impaired subjects discount at a higher rate than either of them. Thus it appears that older impaired subjects discount both future gains and future losses more highly than unimpaired subjects. It should be noted, however, that this is not irrational, given the shorter expected lifespan and lower quality of life of such subjects.

### Constant discounting

The DUM assumes that at any period of time the same discount rate is applied to all future periods. In mathematical terms this means that, given the discount function:

$$D(k) = [1/(1+\rho)]\,k$$

at time period $t$ the same per-period discount rate $\rho$ is applied to all periods in the future. This condition ensures time-consistent preferences; since the standard model views time-consistent preferences as being rational, and inconsistent preferences are usually seen as irrational, this feature of the DUM is often perceived to be legitimate. However, there is plentiful empirical evidence that discount rates are not constant over time, but rather tend to decline. Inconsistent time preferences have been widely observed. This evidence, and alternative models of accommodating it, is reviewed in the next chapter.

It should also be noted at this stage that constant discounting is not a sufficient condition for consistent time preferences to exist. Stationary discounting is also necessary. If discounting is not stationary, then in the following time period $t + 1$ one may observe the different, but still constant, discount function:

$$D_{t+1}(k) = [1/(1+\rho')]\,k$$

where $\rho' \neq \rho$. For example, the evidence in the Read and Read study mentioned above suggests that, as people enter middle age, $\rho' < \rho$. In this situation discounting is constant in both periods t and t + 1, but the discount rate changes with the passage of time. The consequence of this is that once again time preferences will be inconsistent.

### Independence of discounting from consumption

Another assumption of the DUM is that all forms of consumption are discounted at the same rate. Without this assumption it is impossible to reduce the discount rate to a single parameter or to talk about a uniform time preference. As Frederick, Loewenstein and O'Donoghue (2002) put it:

> We would need to label time preference according to the object being delayed – "banana time preference", "vacation time preference", and so on. (p. 358)

There is indeed evidence that different products are discounted at different rates (Train, 1985), and even that different attributes of products are discounted differently. For example, Soman (2004) has found that perceived effort and perceived price are discounted differently. Do-it-yourself products involve effort in terms of consumption and appear more attractive when the purchase is planned for some time in the future. When purchase is immediate such products appear less attractive, implying that perceived effort is discounted more heavily than price. Once again the consequence is preferences that are inconsistent over time.

## Diminishing marginal utility and positive time preference

Although these two features are not essential elements of the DUM, in practice most analyses involving intertemporal choice assume that both conditions exist. In actuality both elements predate the DUM, since Fisher (1930) emphasized the importance of each of them in his indifference analysis approach. Indifference curves generally require the assumption of diminishing marginal utility or concave utility functions. The implication of this condition is that it might cause people to delay consumption until later time periods. For example, when we eat a delicious and generously portioned meal we may prefer to leave some of it for the next day, or, if at a restaurant, take the remaining portion home in a doggy bag.

It should be noted that this effect of diminishing marginal utility operates in the opposite direction to the normal direction of time preference. Normally time preference is positive, meaning that people apply a positive discount rate to future utilities. For this reason many economists have not been happy with Fisher's approach, on the grounds that it confounds the effect of diminishing marginal utility with 'pure' time preference. However, we shall see in a later section that it is very difficult to define the term 'pure' time preference, since there are in reality a number of confounding factors, not just the phenomenon of diminishing marginal utility.

## Evolutionary biology, neuroscience and the discounted utility model

Although the economic model of the DUM was developed without any reference to evolutionary biology, it is worthwhile considering evolutionary aspects at this stage, first modeled by Rogers (1994). Evolutionary theory suggests a sound reason why all animals should discount future outcomes. To consider this we need to recall that biological or inclusive fitness operates at the level of the gene rather than the individual. Mothers prefer consuming now, to increase their own offspring, to saving and passing an equal amount of consumption to their daughters later, to increase the daughters' offspring. This is because only half of one's genes is passed on to one's offspring, so a mother is more closely related to her daughters than to her granddaughters (twice as closely in fact). This is the biological basis for impatience or discounting the future. However, if the return for saving is high enough, passing on consumption to the future would pay, since the increase in the number of grandchildren would more than compensate for the fact that they were less closely related. Rogers (1994) estimated the rate of time preference based on this simple evolutionary model to be about 2% per year. This estimate and the methodology involved have been questioned by other studies, but a discussion of this aspect is best left until the next chapter.

A further evolutionary factor underlying time preference and discounting is that individuals who have children earlier are then able to have more offspring in total, an evolutionary advantage, so that such individuals would come to dominate the population over time (Robson, 2002). However, as with the previous factor, the theory is complicated by the fact that the relationship between consumption and number of offspring is an indirect one. For example, it may be better for an individual to delay having offspring by consuming more now to build greater body size first.

Evolutionary theory also has something to say about discount rates in the DUM, which are assumed to be both stationary and constant. Chu, Chien and Lee (2010) propose that non-stationary discounting is supported by evolutionary theory, involving a U-shaped discounting function over time, with both younger and older people having higher discount rates than middle-aged people. This conforms to the findings of Read and Read (2004) and Harrison, Lau and Williams (2002) described earlier.

Basic evolutionary models suggest that people should have time-consistent preferences. The argument is as follows: if maximizing lifetime fitness involves a particular intertemporal trade-off between outcomes over two dates in the future, as time moves on and these dates become closer, nature should choose current preferences so that this trade-off is unaffected (Robson, 2002). Thus, if initially we prefer to have offspring three years in the future rather than two, then in one year's time our preference will remain the same as far as deferring having offspring is concerned, that is, we will prefer having offspring in two years' time rather than one. However, once again, if we consider additional factors relating to the basic model, the implications are that it may be more appropriate to use a non-constant discounting function, such as the hyperbolic discounting model, rather than the exponential one of the DUM. These additional factors are examined in the next chapter.

Evolutionary biology and neuroscience can also shed some light on the feasibility of the DUM in terms of the assumption of stationary discounting. Adolescents do not yet have a full developed prefrontal cortex (PFC), and this may explain why they appear to be more impatient than older adults, having a higher discount rate. Similarly, age-related cognitive impairment is also associated with damage in the PFC, explaining a higher discount rate for older impaired subjects. Furthermore, as people age, their expected future lifespan shortens and uncertainty relating to the future increases. This should cause the discount rate for all adults to increase once they reach a certain age, although we have already seen that empirical studies do not always show this.

## 7.4  Methodology

Before discussing anomalies in the DUM, it is necessary to consider the methodology used by investigators in empirical studies that measure discount rates. Many aspects of the methodology described also apply to other areas of research, but this discussion is particularly important in the current context, given the enormous variation in results reported: studies have computed discount rates varying from minus 6% (delayed rewards are preferred) to infinitely positive. An understanding of the different methods employed by researchers will in turn aid an understanding of the sources of these variations, as well as the anomalies and alternative models to the DUM described later. Some general aspects of methodology have already been discussed in Chapter 2, particularly relating to the nature of different types of empirical study; the more specific aspects that need to be explained at this stage concern the elicitation of relevant information regarding time preference, and the calculation of the discount rate.

### Elicitation of information

Four experimental procedures tend to be used: choice tasks, matching tasks, rating tasks and pricing tasks.

1  *Choice tasks*

   This is the most common experimental method for eliciting discount rates. Subjects are typically asked to choose between a smaller, more immediate reward and a larger, more distant reward. The obvious disadvantage of this technique is that it only provides a lower or upper limit to the discount rate. For example, if people prefer a sum of $110 in one year to $100 now this merely tells us that their discount rate is *at least* 10%. In order to yield more precise results investigators have to offer a series of many different choices, so that if people prefer $110 in one year, they are then asked if they prefer $120, and so on. Thus usually a bracket can be calculated for each subject. Apart from the complications and length involved, another problem with the technique is that is subject to an anchoring effect, discussed in Chapter 3. Subjects tend to be influenced unduly by the first option offered. One way in which this problem can be countered is by using **titration procedures**. These present subjects with responses that are successively at opposite ends of a spectrum. For example, a first question might ask subjects to choose between $100 now and $101 in one year, while the next question asks them to choose between $100 now and $1,000 in one year; then the next question might compare $100 now with $102 in a year, followed by $100 now and $500 in a year, as the procedure gradually narrows down to a central range.

**2** *Matching tasks*

With this method subjects give open-ended responses which equate two intertemporal options. For example, they may be asked how much money they would require in one year to be equivalent to receiving $100 now. Such a technique has two advantages over the procedure of choice tasks. First, an exact discount rate can be computed from a single response, without the need for asking a series of questions. Second, there is no anchoring problem, since the responses are open-ended.

However, there are various problems that arise with the matching task procedure, which can lead to misleading results. One prominent problem is that subjects tend to use crude rules for making judgments. For example, it is quite common for people to use a 'times *n*' rule for generating future reward equivalents, meaning that they multiply the present amount by the number of years to obtain an equivalent delayed reward. Thus subjects may state that $100 now is equivalent to $500 in five years' time. Such a rule does not necessarily mean that subjects are responding in ways that do not correspond to real-life behavior, but this suspicion is reinforced by a second problem, that results are highly inconsistent according to the method of matching used. When subjects are asked for example to state the future reward that is equivalent to a specified current reward they tend to use a much higher discount rate than when they are asked to state the current reward that is equivalent to a specified future reward (Frederick, Loewenstein and O'Donoghue, 2002, p. 387).

The same kind of inconsistency has been found when questions have been framed in terms of matching amount of reward and time of delay. For example, a study by Roelofsma (1994) asked one group of subjects to state the amount of money they would require to compensate for delaying the delivery of a purchased bicycle by nine months, obtaining a median response of 250 florins. However, when another group of subjects was asked how long they would be willing to delay delivery of the bicycle in return for the compensation of 250 florins, the mean response was only three weeks, implying a discount rate twelve times as high.

These highly inconsistent results obtained with matching procedures shed doubt on the reliability of the procedure in general, while simultaneously demanding some kind of psychological explanation. As with other cases of inconsistency and preference reversal one of the consequences is that normative models of behavior become problematical to develop. This aspect is discussed in more detail in the next chapter in the section related to policy implications.

**3** *Rating tasks*

With this procedure subjects are asked to rate outcomes in different time periods in terms of either like or dislike. Thus an ordinal scale is used as opposed to a cardinal and ratio-based scale. The advantage is that this imposes less of a computational strain on subjects, but the disadvantage is that results are less well differentiated. For example, if a person rates $150 in one year as being preferable to $100 now, it is not clear if the difference in preference is large or small.

4    *Pricing tasks*

This procedure involves eliciting a willingness to pay (WTP) by respondents in order to receive or avoid a particular outcome in the future, expressed in either monetary or non-monetary terms (like an extra year of life or a specified amount of pain). Like rating tasks, this procedure allows the manipulation of time between subjects, since each individual may evaluate either the immediate or delayed outcome in isolation.

## Methodological issues

It can be seen from Case 7.1 that even experimental studies have produced a wide variation in reported discount rates. This is because, although controls have been used, different controls have been used in different studies. To give a flavor of this we will take one of the most controlled studies, performed by Harrison, Lau and Williams (2002), and examine the principles underlying its experimental design and the issues raised. They asked a representative sample of 268 people from the Danish population the basic question: do you prefer $100 today or $100 + x tomorrow? The format of their experiment modified this question is six ways:

1    *Use of choice tasks*

Twenty different amounts were offered as the B option to compare with a standard A option in order to estimate narrow boundaries for an individual's discount rate.

2    *Random payments used as incentives*

Subjects were simultaneously asked several questions with varying amounts of $x$, with one question being selected at random for actual payment after the end of the experiment. The objective was to avoid income effects that might affect the answers to later questions. This is a standard mechanism among researchers for ensuring participation, motivation and reliable responses. The main problem with this method is that it does not allow for learning effects to take place (Starmer, 2000).

3    *Use of 'front-end delay'*

Both early and later options were in the future. Thus, instead of asking for example whether subjects preferred $100 *now* or $100 + x in six months, the investigators asked whether subjects preferred $100 *in 1 month* or $100 + x in seven months. This avoids the problem, mentioned in Chapter 2, that there could be a confound between the effects of 'pure' time preference and transactions costs in the future. Receiving money in the future always involves some transactions cost, as it has to be collected in some way and there is a possibility of the experimenter defaulting. If both options involve future payment this effect is controlled for. This is an important control device, which has not been used in many studies. Comment on the results is given later.

4    *Use of different time horizons*

Four time horizons were used: 6 months, 12 months, 24 months and 36 months. Some subjects were randomly assigned to answer questions relating to a single time period while others were asked questions relating to all periods. Using both methods allows the evaluation of the effect of the subjects' consideration of multiple time periods.

5    *Information relating to the subjects' market rate of interests is elicited*

The objective here was to examine the possibility that subjects' discount rates were censored by market rates. This means that the interest rates reported by subjects do not reflect 'pure' time preference, but are determined by the market rates they face. For example, if someone can borrow at 6% they might prefer $105 in one year to $100 now, since borrowing the $100 would be more expensive.

**6**    *Provision of the annual interest rates associated with delayed payment*

This facilitates comparisons between the options in the experiment and external or market options.

The format of this experimental design does not permit the testing of all the effects discussed in section 7.5 on anomalies, for example the 'sign effect' and the 'magnitude effect', but it does succeed in controlling for some important problems relating to misconceptions and confounds. However, there is one issue that merits some further discussion here. The authors report that:

> Our results indicate that nominal discount rates are constant over the one-year to three-year horizons used in these experiments. (p. 1606)

Some commentators have concluded from this that the use of front-end delay, by eliminating the confound related to transactions cost, provides supporting evidence in favor of the constant discounting characteristic of the DUM and against hyperbolic discounting. The issue of hyperbolic discounting is discussed in the next chapter, but the merits of this claim need some clarification. Closer inspection of the study's results indicates that the 6-month discount rate was actually 34.9%, the 12-month rate was 29.0%, and the 24-month and 36-month rates were 27.4% and 27.9%. Thus the claim that a constant discounting rate applies throughout the *whole* period is misleading. What would be revealing here is the use of a shorter front-end delay, of a day or a week, and an estimation of discount rates for periods shorter than 6 months. This kind of empirical evidence would facilitate the evaluation of the constant discounting claim.

However, there is one other major methodological problem that has not been discussed so far. Usually rewards, and costs, in both experiments and field studies are expressed in monetary terms. Thus any discount rates based on monetary data are based on the implicit assumption that utility is a linear function of money. Both standard and behavioral economic theory generally propose a logarithmic function, based on either risk-aversion or diminishing marginal sensitivity. In order to compensate for this effect more recent research has proposed alternative mechanisms for estimating time preferences, for example the convex time budget of Andreoni and Sprenger (2012) and the double multiple price list (DMPL) of Andersen and colleagues (2008). It goes beyond the scope of this text to discuss these methods, but the reader should be aware of the nature of the problem. To shed some light on this, it has been reported (Estle et al., 2007) that consumable goods (which yield utility directly) are discounted more steeply than monetary rewards. The authors of the study propose that this may be because money is fungible, and can be used to buy anything. However, this finding suggests that the attempt to find an empirically revealed universal discount rate is ill-founded.

### Calculation of the discount rate

It is also a worthwhile exercise at this point to review the mathematics behind the calculation of discount rates, since different methods can be used here. The simplest method involves the standard compounding formula used in net present value and internal rate of return calculations in evaluating investment decisions. This formula can be represented below:

$$F = P(1 + r)^n \tag{7.2}$$

where $F$ = future value, $P$ = present value, $r$ = discount rate, and $n$ = number of time periods. For example, if subjects match the value of \$500 in 10 years to \$100 now, the method above would calculate the discount rate as follows:

$$500 = 100(1 + r)^{10}$$

This yields a discount rate of about 17% a year.

However, most empirical studies do not use the above method of calculation because it involves **discrete compounding**, usually with yearly periods, as in the above example. Instead it is usually preferred to use **continuous compounding**. This involves using an exponential function:

$$F = Pe^{nr} \tag{7.3}$$

This formula can be manipulated to solve for the value of $r$ as follows:

$$r = \frac{\ln (F/P)}{n} \tag{7.4}$$

If the same values in the discrete example above are substituted into the exponential function, the implied discount rate is 16%. When continuous compounding is used the implied discount rates are always lower than with discrete compounding, and the difference between the two methods becomes greater as discount rates increase. For example, if the future equivalent in the above situation was \$1,000 instead of \$100, (as would happen if a subject was using the 'times $n$' rule), then discrete compounding would yield a discount rate of 26% while continuous compounding yields 23%.

Discount rates can also be calculated on either an average or a marginal basis. For example, subjects might be indifferent between receiving \$100 now, receiving \$120 in one year, and receiving \$160 in five years. Using continuous compounding this implies a discount rate of 18.2% over the next year (between year 0 and year 1), and an average discount rate of 7.8% per year over the next five years (between year 0 and year 5). However, it may be useful in some situations to consider the marginal discount rate per period. In the situation above the marginal discount rate between year 1 and year 5 is 7.2% per year.

## 7.5  Anomalies in the discounted utility model

Many anomalies in the DUM have already been noted, in terms of the features of the model described earlier, and the manner in which such features do not appear to be confirmed by empirical evidence. Many other anomalies arise due to factors discussed in the previous two chapters, relating to prospect theory and mental accounting. These further anomalies relate to: the 'sign effect'; the 'magnitude effect'; the 'delay-speedup' asymmetry; preference for improving sequences; the 'date/delay effect'; and violations of independence and preference for spread. These factors are now discussed in turn.

### The 'sign effect'

This effect means that gains are discounted more than losses, as proposed by prospect theory. For example, a study by Thaler (1981) asked subjects how much they would be willing to pay for a traffic ticket if payment could be delayed for periods of three months, a year, or three years. The responses indicated that people used much lower discount rates than in situations where monetary gains were involved. This study was an experimental and hypothetical one, but in this situation it should be practical to conduct a field study, since local government authorities maintain records of fines and dates of payments. In many cases the implied discount rate used by such authorities is very large, with fines often doubling in a matter of a few weeks. The main problem with analyzing such a study would be the existence of confounding factors discussed in the previous section. In this case people may forget to pay, or delay payment in the hope of evading the fine altogether (if authorities fail to follow up on all tickets issued).

At the extreme end of the loss-discounting spectrum, there are several studies that indicate that many people prefer to incur a loss immediately rather than delay it (Mischel, Grusec and Masters, 1969; Yates and Watts, 1975; Loewenstein, 1987; Benzion, Rapoport and Yagil, 1989; MacKeigan et al., 1993; Redelmeier and Heller, 1993; Hardisty, Appelt and Weber, 2012). This implies a negative discount rate for losses, and an interpretation of this phenomenon is given shortly in connection with the magnitude effect.

Various theories accounting for the 'sign effect' have been proposed. Bilgin and LeBoeuf (2010) introduce the term **'temporal loss-aversion'** as an explanation. In a series of experiments these investigators found that intervals preceding losses seem shorter than intervals preceding gains, and that this effect is driven by perceptions of the quality of the interval end point rather than by the quality of the interval itself. For example, for a person moving jobs to a new city in a couple of months' time, if that person is not looking forward to the move, the interval may appear to be shorter than it would for the person who is looking forward to the move. If the interval is perceived to be shorter, then a smaller discount rate would be used. This temporal loss-aversion may occur because the subjective size of the effect is greater, or because losses may attract more attention than gains. There are other psychological factors related to this kind of loss-aversion. Anticipatory utility, or in the case of losses, disutility, is important. As we have seen in Chapter 3, people do not like the idea of a loss 'hanging over' them, and may prefer to endure the pain of the loss immediately and 'get it over and done with'. Thus people are motivated to maximize savoring events that they look forward to and minimize the dread associated with unpleasant events in the future.

Bilgin and LeBoeuf (2010, p. 528) venture an evolutionary explanation for this phenomenon: 'when danger is imminent, it is likely more adaptive to err in the direction of exaggerating the proximity of the danger because perceiving dangers as temporally near may galvanize necessary coping resources.' This is particularly true for unexpected dangers, Bilgin and LeBoeuf claim, and one of their experiments found that unexpected losses loomed nearer than expected ones.

## The 'magnitude effect'

Studies that vary outcome size often find that large outcomes are discounted at a lower rate than small ones (Thaler, 1981; Ainslie and Haendel, 1983; Loewenstein, 1987; Benzion, Rapoport and Yagil, 1989; Holcomb and Nelson, 1992; Green, Fry, and Myerson, 1994; Kirby, Petry and Bickel, 1999; Hardisty, Appelt and Weber, 2012). For example, in Thaler's study subjects were indifferent between $15 immediately and $60 in a year, $250 immediately and $350 in a year, and $3,000 immediately and $4,000 in a year. These matching preferences indicated discount rates of 139%, 34% and 29% respectively.

This phenomenon requires a psychological explanation, especially since the effect works in the opposite direction to the effect of diminishing marginal utility. The discount rates calculated for Thaler's study above are based on the monetary values, not the actual utilities. If utilities were used to calculate discount rates instead of monetary values, then, assuming the law of diminishing marginal utility applies, the differences in discount rates between small and large amounts would be even greater.

Hardisty Appelt and Weber (2012) find that there is also an interaction between the 'sign effect' and the 'magnitude effect'. They find that, although large gains are discounted at a lower rate than small gains, large losses are discounted at a higher rate than small losses. For example they find that a $10 loss is discounted by −6% over six months, while a $1,000 loss is discounted by −13% over the same period. They propose that both sign and magnitude effects can be explained by '**resolution theory**'. This emphasizes the importance of present bias, meaning that consumers have a psychological desire to resolve both gains and losses immediately. For gains people want the gain immediately to avoid the deprivation of waiting, and they also want to have any loss immediately to close their mental account on the loss and avoid the feeling of the loss looming over them in the future.

### The 'delay-speedup' asymmetry

Studies have also investigated the effect of changing the delivery time of outcomes. These changes can be framed as either delays or accelerations from some reference point in time. For example, Loewenstein (1988) has found that subjects who didn't expect to receive a VCR for another year would pay an average of $54 to receive it immediately (a perceived gain). However, those subjects who thought they would receive the VCR immediately demanded an average of $126 to delay its receipt by a year (a perceived loss). Other studies have confirmed these findings in situations where the outcomes involved payments, that is, negative outcomes, rather than positive ones like the delivery of a product. In these situations subjects demand more to accelerate payment (a perceived loss) than to delay it (a perceived gain).

We can note that these results are predicted by prospect theory. Two elements of the theory are involved: reference points and loss-aversion.

### Preference for improving sequences

The DUM predicts that, total undiscounted utility being equal, people will prefer a declining sequence of outcomes to an increasing sequence, since later outcomes are discounted more heavily. Thus, given the two consumption profiles (50, 60, 70) and (70, 60, 50) over three consecutive time periods, the DUM predicts that people will prefer the latter to the former. In contrast, many studies have shown that people prefer improving profiles. For example, Loewenstein and Sicherman (1991) have found that, for an otherwise identical job, most subjects prefer an increasing wage profile to a declining or flat one. Hsee, Abelson and Salovey (1991) have found that an increasing salary sequence was rated as highly as a decreasing sequence that conferred a much larger monetary amount. In addition to these studies involving gains, some investigators have examined sequences of losses. Varey and Kahneman (1992) have found that subjects strongly preferred a sequence of decreasing discomfort to a sequence of increasing discomfort, even when the overall sum of discomfort over the interval was otherwise identical. Chapman (2000) investigated the responses of people to hypothetical sequences of headache pain, with the sequences being matched in terms of total pain; durations varied from one hour to as long as 20 years. For all durations, between 82% and 92% of the subjects preferred sequences of pain that were declining rather than increasing. Thus in general, for both gains and losses, people prefer an improving sequence to a sequence where outcomes are deteriorating.

These findings are in line with various effects reported in Chapter 3, for example expectations effects and anticipatory utility, and reference points. In particular it is worth recalling the colonoscopy studies of Redelmeier and Kahneman (1996), where remembered utility, which in turn may determine decision utility, may differ from real-time utility. Remembered utility, or disutility, may depend more on utility at the end of the sequence rather than at the start, as predicted by the peak-end rule.

## The 'date/delay effect'

While all the effects described above involve objective changes and manipulations of outcomes and time periods, recent research has also indicated that people may make different intertemporal choices when logically identical situations are presented or framed in different ways. Studies by Read and colleagues (2005) and LeBoeuf (2006) find that people use lower discount rates in situations when time periods are described using end dates than when the same time periods are described as extents. For example, the LeBoeuf study asked subjects the following two questions (on February 15):

1   How much money would you want to receive *in eight months* to be equivalent to receiving $100 now?

2   How much money would you want to receive *on October 15* to be equivalent to receiving $100 now?

Although the two questions are equivalent in logical terms, it was found that people generally demanded a larger amount in answering the first question, implying a higher discount rate when a future gain is framed in terms of extent. Similar results are reported when outcomes are expressed as losses rather than gains, and in a number of experiments when the time intervals until outcomes occur vary between two months and two years.

LeBoeuf (2006, p. 61) proposes a psychological explanation for this phenomenon, utilizing aspects of both prospect theory and mental accounting:

> When consumers consider an interval demarcated by a date, the date may be construed as relatively abstract point in time, and consumers may not even compute the interval's length. In contrast, when that same interval is described as an extent, by definition, the amount of time is highlighted … Thus consumers may attend more to interval length when facing an extent.

If the interval length is perceived as being longer it follows that a higher discount rate will be used. There are various policy implications of this finding, and these are discussed in the next chapter.

## Violations of independence and preference for spread

As mentioned in the previous section, the assumption of consumption independence implies that preferences between two consumption profiles should not be affected by the nature of consumption in periods in which consumption is identical in the two profiles. Again, there is evidence that suggests that consumers may respond differently in situations that are logically equivalent. For example, Loewenstein and Prelec (1993) have found that when people are given a 'simple' choice: (A) dinner at a fancy French restaurant next weekend or (B) dinner at the same restaurant on a weekend two weeks later, most people prefer the first option, the sooner dinner. This is predicted by the DUM, as people discount the utility of the later event more heavily. However, the investigators observed different results when subjects are offered an 'elaborated' choice: (C) dinner at a fancy French restaurant next weekend and dinner at home on a weekend two weeks later, or (D) dinner at home next weekend and dinner at the French restaurant on a weekend in two weeks. In this decision situation most people prefer the second option. Since the most likely event for subjects is to have dinner at home, the 'elaborated' options

(C) and (D) amount to the same as the 'simple' options (A) and (B). Thus there appears to be a framing effect, causing preference reversal.

The psychological explanation here appears to be that the 'elaborated' options draw attention to the sequence of outcomes over time, and, as seen above, people prefer an improving sequence.

Loewenstein and Prelec (1993) also observe a preference for spreading outcomes, again a violation of independence. An experiment involved subjects hypothetically receiving two coupons for fancy restaurant dinners, and asking them when they would use them. Two different conditions were used, one involving a two-year time limit and the other involving no time limits. Results indicated that subjects scheduled the two dinners later with the two-year limit (8 weeks and 31 weeks) than when there were no limits (3 weeks and 13 weeks). It appears that framing the offer with a two-year limit causes the subjects to spread their outcomes over a longer period if the two-year horizon is longer than the implicit time horizon used by subjects who face no time limits. This is another example of an anchoring effect.

There is also evidence that people have a preference for spreading incomes as well as consumption, a phenomenon referred to as 'income smoothing'. A natural experiment occurs in California, where about a half of the United School Districts give teachers the choice of receiving their annual salaries in 10 or 12 monthly payments. The DUM would predict that teachers should choose 10 payments and earn interest on their savings. However, in reality about 50% of the teachers choose 12 instalments, even though over a long period of time the interest foregone is considerable (Mayer and Russell, 2005). The psychological explanation, supported by a survey of the teachers, is that the 12 monthly payment option, by spreading the receipt of incomes, facilitates self-control over spending.

### Implications of anomalies

With other aspects of the NM violations of the model, for example preference reversals, are often perceived by subjects as being mistakes once they are pointed out. However, this is frequently not the case with the anomalies described above. A few examples will illustrate this important point:

**1**    *The 'sign effect'*

When within-subjects studies are compared with between-subjects studies, the size of the sign effect is greater with the first type of study. Thus when subjects are exposed to both gains and losses the disparity in discount rates is greater than when subjects are only exposed to either gains or losses but not both. If the 'sign effect' were regarded as a 'mistake' by subjects, one would expect the disparity to be smaller or non-existent in within-subjects studies where subjects could directly compare their responses to losses and gains.

**2**    *The 'magnitude effect'*

The evidence here is similar to that relating to the 'sign effect'. Frederick and Read (2002) have found that when subjects evaluate both small and large amounts the disparity in discount rates is greater than when they evaluate only small or large amounts. Once again this runs contrary to what one would expect if the anomaly was regarded as a 'mistake', since the comparison of the small and large amounts would provide an anchoring effect.

**3**    *Preference for improving sequences*

In the study by Loewenstein and Sicherman (1991) it was explained to subjects that a decreasing wage profile ($27,000, $26,000...$23,000) would enable them to consume more in every period than the corresponding increasing wage profile ($23,000, $24,000...$27,000) with the same nominal total. However, this did not affect the behavior of the subjects, who continued to prefer the increasing profile.

The significance of this behavior is that, at least in many situations, people do not regard the anomalies described as being mistakes, or errors of judgment. Actually, this should not be surprising, since at the outset the DUM was not presented as either a valid descriptive or normative model. Unfortunately, as it has gained rapid and widespread acceptance by economists and other practitioners, the DUM has covertly gained a reputation in terms of descriptive and normative validity.

Therefore, after reviewing the DUM and its shortcomings, the task is now to examine other models of intertemporal choice which have better descriptive and normative validity. This is the subject of the next chapter.

## 7.6  Summary

* Early scholarship relating to intertemporal choice emphasized the importance of psychological factors in determining preferences.
* The discounted utility model (DUM) compressed the influences of all factors affecting time preference into a single parameter, the discount rate.
* The originator of the DUM, Samuelson, never intended the model to be either normative or descriptive in terms of validity.
* The DUM has eight primary features: integration of new alternatives with existing plans; utility independence; consumption independence; stationary instantaneous utility; stationary discounting; constant discounting; independence of discounting from consumption; and diminishing marginal utility and positive time preference.
* Empirical research may involve either field studies or experimental studies. The latter may involve either real or hypothetical rewards/losses. Either type of study may be between-subjects or within-subjects.
* Experimental studies may involve choice tasks, matching tasks, pricing tasks and rating tasks. The first two techniques are most common.
* Discount rates can be calculated on either a discrete or continuous compounding basis. The latter method, involving an exponential function, is more common.
* There are a large number of anomalies in the DUM: the 'sign effect'; the 'magnitude effect'; the 'delay-speedup' asymmetry; preference for improving sequences; the 'date/delay effect'; and violations of independence and preference for spread.
* The anomalies in the DUM should not be regarded as mistakes or errors in judgment. Instead they imply that the model lacks both descriptive and normative validity.

## 7.7  Review questions

1  Explain what is meant by consumption independence, giving an example.
2  Explain the difference between stationary discounting and constant discounting.
3  Describe the method of using choice tasks to elicit information, discussing any problems and how they may be overcome.
4  Describe the method of using matching tasks, discussing any problems that tend to arise in practice.
5  Explain what is meant by 'front-end delay', and the advantage of using this experimental method.

6    Explain what is meant by a negative discount rate; under what circumstances might people have a negative discount rate?

7    Explain what is meant by 'delay-speedup asymmetry', and how it is related to prospect theory.

8    Explain what is meant by a violation of independence in intertemporal choice, giving an example. What might cause this violation?

## 7.8  Applications

At this stage of our analysis of intertemporal choice we are not really in a position to examine and evaluate individual situations, since we have not yet discussed alternative behavioral models that aim to overcome the shortcomings of the DUM. Therefore the analysis of particular specific situations will be delayed until the next chapter. There is therefore only one application included here; this is a general overview of empirical studies measuring discount rates conducted over a 25-year period.

### Case 7.1 The measurement of discount rates

In a landmark article in 2002 entitled 'Time discounting: A critical review', the authors Frederick, Loewenstein and O'Donoghue summarized in a table the implicit discount rates from all the studies that they could find between 1978 and 2002 where such discount rates were reported or could easily be calculated. The table lists 42 studies, and describes the type of study, the good involved, whether real or hypothetical rewards/losses were involved, the elicitation method, the time range, the annual discount rate, and the discount factor. The discount factor ($\delta$) is calculated by using the expression $\delta = 1/(1 + r)$. As we shall see in the next chapter, it can be more convenient mathematically to use the discount factor instead of the discount rate in expressing various phenomena. The table is reproduced below:

**Table 7.1**  Empirical estimates of discount rates

| Study | Type | Good(s) | Real/ hypo rewards | Elicitation method | Time range | Annual discount rate | $\delta$ |
|---|---|---|---|---|---|---|---|
| Maital and Maital (1978) | experimental | money and coupons | hypo | choice | 1 year | 70% | 0.59 |
| Hausman (1979) | field | money | real | choice | undefined | 5% to 89% | 0.95 to 0.53 |
| Gateley (1980) | field | money | real | choice | undefined | 45% to 300% | 0.69 to 0.25 |
| Thaler (1981) | experimental | money | hypo | matching | 3 months to 10 years | 7% to 345% | 0.93 to 0.22 |

▶

| Study | Type | Good(s) | Real/ hypo rewards | Elicitation method | Time range | Annual discount rate | δ |
|---|---|---|---|---|---|---|---|
| Ainslie and Haendel (1983) | experimental | money | real | matching | undefined | 96000% to ∞ | 0.00 |
| Houston (1983) | experimental | money | hypo | other | 1 year to 20 years | 23% | 0.81 |
| Loewenstein (1987) | experimental | money and pain | hypo | pricing | immediate to 10 years | −6% to 212% | 1.06 to 0.32 |
| Moore and Viscusi (1988) | field | life years | real | choice | undefined | 10% to 12% | 0.91 to 0.89 |
| Benzion et al. (1989) | experimental | money | hypo | matching | 6 months to 4 years | 9% to 60% | 0.92 to 0.63 |
| Viscusi and Moore (1989) | field | life years | real | choice | undefined | 11% | 0.90 |
| Moore and Viscusi (1990a) | field | life years | real | choice | undefined | 2% | 0.98 |
| Moore and Viscusi (1990b) | field | life years | real | choice | undefined | 1% to 14% | 0.99 to 0.88 |
| Shelley (1993) | experimental | money | hypo | matching | 6 months to 4 years | 8% to 27% | 0.93 to 0.79 |
| Redelmeier and Heller (1993) | experimental | | hypo | rating | 1 day to 10 years | 0% | 1.00 |
| Cairns (1994) | experimental | money | hypo | choice | 5 years to 20 years | 14% to 25% | 0.88 to 0.80 |
| Shelley (1994) | experimental | money | hypo | rating | 6 months to 2 years | 4% to 22% | 0.96 to 0.82 |
| Chapman and Elstein (1995) | experimental | money and health | hypo | matching | 6 months to 12 years | 11% to 263% | 0.90 to 0.28 |
| Dolan and Gudex (1995) | experimental | health | hypo | other | 1 month to 10 years | 0% | 1.00 |
| Dreyfus and Viscusi (1995) | field | life years | real | choice | undefined | 11% to 17% | 0.90 to 0.85 |
| Kirby and Marakovic (1995) | experimental | money | real | matching | 3 days to 29 days | 3678% to ∞ | 0.03 to 0.00 |

| Study | Type | Good(s) | Real/ hypo rewards | Elicitation method | Time range | Annual discount rate | δ |
|---|---|---|---|---|---|---|---|
| Chapman (1996) | experimental | money and health | hypo | matching | 1 year to 12 years | negative to 300% | 1.01 to 0.25 |
| Kirby and Marakovic (1996) | experimental | money | real | choice | 6 hours to 70 days | 500% to 1500% | 0.17 to 0.06 |
| Pender (1996) | experimental | rice | real | choice | 7 months to 2 years | 26% to 69% | 0.79 to 0.59 |
| Wahlund and Gunnarson (1996) | experimental | money | hypo | matching | 1 month to 1 year | 18% to 158% | 0.85 to 0.39 |
| Cairns and Van der Pol (1997) | experimental | money | hypo | matching | 2 years to 19 years | 13% to 31% | 0.88 to 0.76 |
| Green, Myerson, and McFadden (1997) | experimental | money | hypo | choice | 3 months to 20 years | 6% to 111% | 0.94 to 0.47 |
| Johanneson and Johansson (1997) | experimental | life years | hypo | pricing | 6 years to 57 years | 0% to 3% | 1.00 to 0.97 |
| Kirby (1997) | experimental | money | | pricing | 1 day to 1 month | 159% to 5747% | 0.39 to 0.02 |
| Madden et al. (1997) | experimental | money and heroin | hypo | choice | 1 week to 25 years | 8% to $\infty$ | 0.93 to 0.00 |
| Chapman and Winquist (1998) | experimental | money | hypo | matching | 3 months | 426% to 2189% | 0.19 to 0.04 |
| Holden, Shiferaw, and Wik (1998) | experimental | money and corn | real | matching | 1 year | 28% to 147% | 0.78 to 0.40 |
| Cairns and Van der Pol (1999) | experimental | health | hypo | matching | 4 years to 16 years | 6% | 0.94 |
| Chapman, Nelson, and Hier (1999) | experimental | money and health | hypo | choice | 1 month to 6 months | 13% to 19000% | 0.88 to 0.01 |
| Coller and Williams (1999) | experimental | money | real | choice | 1 month to 3 months | 15% to 25% | 0.87 to 0.80 |
| Kirby, Petry, and Bickel (1999) | experimental | money | real | choice | 7 days to 186 days | 50% to 55700% | 0.67 to 0.00 |

| Study | Type | Good(s) | Real/ hypo rewards | Elicitation method | Time range | Annual discount rate | δ |
|-------|------|---------|--------------------|--------------------|------------|----------------------|---|
| Van der Pol and Cairns (1999) | experimental | health | hypo | choice | 5 years to 13 years | 7% | 0.93 |
| Chesson and Viscusi (2000) | experimental | money | hypo | matching | 1 year to 25 years | 11% | 0.90 |
| Ganiats et al. (2000) | experimental | health | hypo | choice | 6 months to 20 years | negative to 116% | 1.01 to 0.46 |
| Hesketh (2000) | experimental | money | hypo | choice | 6 months to 4 years | 4% to 36% | 0.96 to 0.74 |
| Van der Pol and Cairns (2001) | experimental | health | hypo | choice | 2 years to 15 years | 6% to 9% | 0.94 to 0.92 |
| Warner and Pleeter (2001) | field | money | real | choice | immediate to 22 years | 0% to 71% | 1.00 to 0.58 |
| Harrison, Lau, and Williams (2002) | experimental | money | real | choice | 1 month to 37 months | 28% | 0.78 |

*Source: Frederick, S., Loewenstein, G. and O'Donoghue, T. Time discounting and time preference: A critical review.* Journal of Economic Literature, *XL, June 2002, pp. 351–401, Table 1, with permission from the American Economic Association.*

## Questions

1   What factors might account for the huge variability in the estimates of discount rates?

2   Does there appear to be any relationship between the size of discount rates and whether rewards are real or hypothetical?

3   What is the implication of a negative discount rate, and what might cause this?

4   Is there any evidence of methodological progress, in terms of a convergence of estimates as time goes on? What is the significance of any lack of progress?

# Alternative Intertemporal Choice Models

Why would we place the alarm clock on the other side of the room from the bed? Well, we don't need to do that any more. Now we can buy Clocky, the alarm clock that jumps off the bedside table and runs away when we try to snooze it, sounding its alarm. A comment on YouTube said that it would be even better if the clock could be designed to run and hide under the bed, to make it even harder to get at.

So the question now becomes: why would we buy something that makes life harder for us, and that causes us to curse in the morning when we can't turn it off? Clocky is all about commitment. When we go to bed at night we want to make sure we wake up on time in the morning. But when we wake up we suffer from a preference reversal, and we want to stay in bed. Our morning self is a different person from our evening self, and this pattern is repeated day after day. The result is that our evening selves learn about the weaknesses of our morning selves and try to overcome these by making a commitment that our morning self is unable to avoid. This pattern of preference reversal over time is a very common one in various facets of our lives; we are always yielding to temptation and procrastinating, and at the same time trying to take measures to prevent our future selves from doing so.

## 8.1  Time preference

The most obvious characteristic of the table at the end of the previous chapter is the very wide disparity between different measures of the discount rate, even within the same study as well as between studies. Thus it is not simply differences in methodology in terms of experimental design that account for these variations. The primary reason for the variability is the existence of confounding factors in the measurement of time preference. This raises the fundamental issue of what constitutes time preference. It is necessary to understand this concept and the factors involved if we are to address and explain the anomalies related to the discounted utility model (DUM). We shall see in the second section of the chapter that these anomalies are frequently related to self-control problems. The third, fourth and fifth sections of the chapter then discuss various alternative models to the DUM, while the sixth section examines the relevant empirical evidence from behavioral, evolutionary and neuroeconomic studies. The seventh section concludes with the discussion of various policy implications related to the models and the evidence.

First, we need to examine the various confounding factors involved in the measurement of time preference.

### Consumption reallocation

Most studies use monetary rewards as payoffs rather than consumption. When discount rates are calculated it is normally assumed that rewards and losses are consumed immediately at the same point in time that they are received, and that they do not affect the pattern of consumption at other time periods. For example, if a reward of $100 is to be received in one year, it is assumed that this amount will be consumed immediately rather than causing a stream of higher consumption over a prolonged time period after one year. Furthermore, it is assumed that this reward is not anticipated, in terms of increasing consumption in time periods before it is received. It is obvious from empirical observation that both aspects are unrealistic. Ideally the calculation of discount rates should take into account the effects of rewards and losses on the whole lifetime pattern of consumption.

## Intertemporal arbitrage

When rewards are tradable, like money, intertemporal choices may not reflect time preference directly, but may be caused by intertemporal arbitrage. For example, if a person prefers $100 now to $150 in five years' time, this may be because they can invest $100 now at the market rate of interest and make it worth more than $150 in five years. When financial markets are efficient it can be argued that discount rates will converge on the market rate of interest, rather than being a direct reflection of time preference. Of course market interest rates are affected by time preference, but they are also influenced by many other factors, such as default risk, uncertainty, liquidity and so on.

However, there is a heavy weight of empirical evidence that financial markets cannot explain intertemporal choices, since discount rates generally are much higher than market interest rates. For example, people with substantial savings earning 4% a year interest should not prefer $100 today over $120 in one year if financial markets are efficient, yet many do. Such choices and preferences imply either that people are ignorant about the operations of the markets or that they are unable to use the markets properly for some reason. It appears therefore that discount rates do take into account time preference, and other factors, in ways that the market interest rate does not.

## Concave utility

As can be seen from the table in the case study at the end of the previous chapter, the majority of empirical studies involve monetary rewards, and base the calculation of discount rates on the monetary amounts. As was mentioned briefly in the previous chapter it is misleading to calculate discount rates on this basis, since it is implicitly assumed that utility increases linearly with monetary amounts. This assumption is in direct contradiction to both the neoclassical model (NM) and the principles of prospect theory. An example will illustrate the effects of relaxing this assumption and instead incorporating a concave utility function, as proposed by prospect theory. Say that the average response of a group of subjects is that they are indifferent between $100 now and $150 in five years. The imputed discount rate (assuming no consumption reallocation) is 8.1% a year on the basis of the monetary amounts. However it may be that the $150 has only 30% more utility than $100 (this is also ignoring the effect of inflation, which is considered later). Using utility as the basis for discounting, the imputed discount rate is only 5.2%. This shows that utility discount rates are lower than monetary discount rates when utility functions are concave.

In terms of empirical findings, Chapman (1996) attempted to allow for the concavity of the utility function by estimating a utility function from the monetary amounts, and found that the discount rates calculated from the utility function were indeed substantially lower than the monetary discount rates. However, it is difficult empirically to conduct a reliable study to estimate utility discount rates, bearing in mind the problem of consumption reallocation discussed earlier. For example, although it may be possible to estimate that $150 has only 30% more utility than $100, what is relevant are the streams of utility that flow from the reward of $150. A consumer may respond by spending an extra $30 a year over the next five years, and a person's utility function may not be concave over such small amounts.

## Uncertainty

Future rewards and costs are almost invariably associated with uncertainty in practice. Thus in field studies it is particularly difficult to avoid this confound, regardless of whether rewards and costs are expressed in monetary terms or in other ways. For example, even if we can be sure that a particular electrical appliance will save us a certain amount of electricity in the future (which is unlikely in itself), we cannot be sure what will be the future price of electricity.

In experimental studies it might appear that investigators could avoid this confound by assuring subjects that delayed rewards will be delivered with certainty. This is indeed the common practice in such studies, but whether respondents can accept this situation from a subjective point of view is questionable. It may be that there is an unconscious psychological mechanism that automatically relates delay to uncertainty. One reason for such a mechanism is that, even if rewards are certain in monetary or other terms, our valuation of these may change over time, since utilities change as tastes change in ways that are not entirely predictable. For example, in the future we come to value money less and health more than we do today. Therefore there will always be an element of uncertainty relating to future tastes and utilities.

Furthermore, some experimental studies have compounded this problem by introducing ambiguity into the situation. For example, a study by Benzion, Rapoport and Yagil (1989) asked respondents to imagine that they had earned money, but when they arrived to receive payment they were told that the 'financially solid' public institution that had promised to pay them was 'temporarily short of funds'. They were then asked to specify future amounts of money that would make them indifferent to receiving the amount of money that they had been promised immediately, with varying amounts of delay. The methodological problem here is that there is an inconsistency in terminology: financially solid institutions should not become temporarily short of funds. The latter expression introduces an element of uncertainty into the subject's consideration.

One finding that seems beyond doubt here is that discount rates are significantly affected by uncertainty. This is established by studies that introduce objective uncertainty. For example, in a study by Keren and Roelofsma (1995), one group of subjects was asked to choose between 100 florins immediately and 110 florins in one month, while another group was asked to choose between a 50% chance of 100 florins immediately and a 50% chance of 110 florins in one month. With the first group 82% preferred the smaller immediate option, but, when rewards were uncertain, only 39% of the second group preferred the smaller immediate reward. Thus a much higher discount rate is implied when rewards are certain compared with the uncertain situation.

### Inflation

Most studies ignore the effect of inflation in the calculation of discount rates, assuming that the utility of $100 now is the same as the utility of $100 in ten years at the times they are received. In practice people are likely to discount future monetary rewards according to their experiences with and expectations of inflation. Furthermore, there is another element of uncertainty here, as the effect of future inflation on purchasing power becomes more uncertain as the duration of delay increases.

### Expectations of changes in utility

It was stated above that our tastes often change in unpredictable ways. However, some of these changes are partially predictable. Again, we have seen earlier that people often prefer rising consumption profiles, and this preference is anticipated. The factors underlying this phenomenon are examined in Case 8.3, along with the implications. At this point we can observe that it has two effects on preferences and discounting, which operate in opposite directions. The more obvious effect is that, if we expect to have higher consumption levels in the future, the marginal utility of $100 of consumption now is greater than the marginal utility of $100 of consumption in five years, because of the effect of the law of diminishing marginal utility. This effect exerts an upward bias on discount rates.

However, there is another effect at work here. People may wish to defer consumption to later periods in order to have a rising consumption over time, but they may lack the self-control to save sufficient income earned now to provide for this future consumption. In such a situation people may welcome some sort of commitment device that allows them to have more money in the future without the opportunity to spend it earlier, in the same sort of way that they may commit to paying into a pension fund. We have already seen something of this effect in the case of the teachers who preferred to be paid 12 times a year rather than 10. In this situation people may prefer to receive the money in the future rather than immediately. This effect exerts a downward bias on discount rates.

## Anticipatory utility

This is another phenomenon that has been discussed earlier, in Chapter 3. For example, people may wish to defer consumption of a restaurant dinner, since the anticipation of the future utility may increase total utility. The modeling of this factor is discussed in a later section, but at this stage we can observe that the effect is to exert a downward bias on discount rates and can also cause reverse time-inconsistency of preferences.

## Visceral influences

Again this factor was discussed in Chapter 3, and is modeled in a later section. The prospect of an immediate reward (the 'actual presence of the immediate object of desire' in Rae's terms) may stimulate visceral factors that temporarily increase the attraction of the reward. However, like uncertainty, it is difficult to unravel these influences from time preference. It is argued by Frederick, Loewenstein and O'Donoghue (2002) that if the visceral factors increase the attractiveness of the immediate reward without affecting its enjoyment (decision utility rather than experienced utility), then 'they are probably best viewed as a legitimate determinant of time preference'. On the other hand, if visceral factors do affect experienced utility, then 'they might best be regarded as a confounding factor'.

## What is time preference?

The presence of the various confounding factors described above raises the fundamental issue concerning the definition of time preference. In particular, the issue involves whether time preference is a unitary construct. This has aroused much debate in the psychology literature. There is a general consensus that psychological constructs or traits must satisfy the following three criteria:

1 *Constancy*

Constructs tend only to be useful when they remain constant within the same person over time. For example, many studies have shown that people's scores on intelligence tests change little over time.

2 *Generality*

Constructs or traits should be able to predict a wide range of behaviors, rather than just a single, narrow aspect of behavior. Intelligence is again a good example of such a trait. Impulsiveness is another example. Impulsive people make rash decisions without much (or any) thought, like purchase decisions, which they frequently regret afterwards.

### 3    *Correlation between different measures*

Valid constructs can be measured in different ways that correlate highly with one another. In the case of intelligence it is difficult to devise tests that measure a cognitive skill where test results are not correlated. Tests of personality characteristics such as impulsiveness are similar. People who rate as impulsive on one question are likely to rate as impulsive on other questions.

The construct of time preference does not satisfy these criteria well, unlike the so-called 'Big Five' personality traits of openness, conscientiousness, extraversion, agreeableness and neuroticism. In terms of constancy, there is some evidence that the ability of children to delay gratification is significantly correlated with other variables much later in life, such as academic achievement and self-esteem (Mischel, Shoda and Peake, 1988; Shoda, Mischel and Peake, 1990; Ayduk et al., 2000). However, this only constitutes evidence of construct validity to the extent that these other variables are expressions of time preference, which some people would question.

On the other hand, there is a considerable body of evidence that discount rates for different rewards and costs are at best only weakly correlated. Fuchs (1982) found no correlation between experimental studies involving hypothetical monetary rewards and real-world behaviors involving time preference, such as seat belt use, smoking, credit card debt, and the frequency of exercise and dental check-ups. Chapman and Elstein (1995) and Chapman, Nelson and Hier (1999) have found only weak correlations between discount rates for money and for health. Furthermore, Chapman and Elstein (1995) found no correlation between discount rates for losses and rates for gains. The main evidence of correlations involves addictive behavior: smokers tend to invest less in human capital, having flatter, as opposed to rising, income profiles (Munasinghe and Sicherman, 2006); heroin addicts tend to have higher discount rates for monetary rewards (Kirby, Petry and Bickel, 1999).

It should be noted here that low correlations between different aspects of behavior involving time preference do not necessarily provide definitive evidence that time preference is not a unitary construct. For example, people may show a low discount rate for monetary rewards, implying that they value future revenues highly, but show a high discount rate for health-related factors, because they do not exercise. There are many possible explanations why people might engage in such seemingly inconsistent behavior: (1) they may have a strong aversion to exercise; (2) they are too busy earning income for their future to exercise; (3) they may value monetary rewards more than their health, maybe because they can bequeath them to their children; and (4) they do not believe that exercise is necessary for good health.

Furthermore, one should add that high correlations would not provide definitive evidence for a unitary construct either. As is the case with other social phenomena, time preference and time-related behaviors may themselves be correlated with other factors, such as intelligence and social class. These factors would have to be identified and controlled in order for a study to provide proper evidence.

What can be concluded regarding time preference from such diverse and incomplete findings? Frederick, Loewenstein and O'Donoghue (2002) suggest that a useful approach may be to revert to a pre-DUM model and 'unpack' time preference into its more fundamental psychological components: **impulsivity**, **compulsivity** and **inhibition**. The advantage of doing this is that each of these characteristics can be measured reliably, and each explains and predicts different aspects of behavior. These terms and their influences are now discussed.

Impulsivity refers to the extent to which people act in a spontaneous, unplanned manner. Impulsive people may act without making conscious decisions, and their behavior tends to reveal a high discount rate for many types of activity, such as credit card use.

Compulsive people tend to make plans and stick to them. Thus they may exercise regularly, get medical check-ups regularly, always use a seatbelt and pay bills on time. Generally such repetitive behaviors imply low discount rates for the relevant activities. Inhibition involves the ability to inhibit 'knee-jerk' responses or impulsive behavior that may follow visceral stimuli. People who are inhibited may be criticized for not following their instincts, for example in terms of sexual behavior, but they may also be praised for their willpower, when it comes to refraining from eating junk food. The ability to resist visceral influences implies a low discount rate for the relevant behaviors, with more importance being attached to the future effects of such behaviors. The relevance, and indeed the very meaning of the term 'willpower', is discussed in the next section.

A final observation regarding time preference is that, as with aspects of behavior discussed in other chapters, research in neuroscience is making progress in terms of locating specific areas in the brain which influence or determine the three psychological factors described above (Damasio, 1994; LeDoux, 1996). The fact that different brain areas appear to be involved in affecting these factors would seem to be sufficient justification for unpacking the concept of time preference. Further progress in the neuroscientific field may shed more light on the interrelationships between these psychological characteristics, and their relationships with other aspects of behavior. This issue is discussed further in the sixth section, related to empirical evidence.

Now that the concept of time preference has been discussed in some detail, and its component factors examined, we can turn our attention to the consideration of the most important anomaly related to the DUM, time-inconsistent preferences, which are a manifestation of self-control problems.

## 8.2  Time-inconsistent preferences

*Nature*

We have seen that intertemporal decision-making often relates to situations where people are faced with choosing whether to undertake an activity that involves a cost sooner and a benefit later. Investment goods have this characteristic, for example investing in one's education. Other types of decision involve a benefit sooner and a cost later, as is the case with leisure goods, for example watching TV or eating junk food. Frequently the cost involves an opportunity cost, for example saving for one's retirement means forgoing consumption in the nearer future in order to consume more in the further future. In many of these situations the opportunity cost relates to an activity regarded as unpleasant in the near future, like dieting, undertaking an exercise regime, or giving up smoking. Thus the decision-maker may frame the choice as being between gaining a benefit (the pleasure of eating junk food, relaxing on the couch or inhaling tobacco) sooner versus gaining a different benefit (improved health) later. Since the long-term benefits in these situations are normally considered to exceed the short-term ones, the basic trade-off can be regarded as 'smaller-sooner' (SS) versus 'larger-later' (LL). The essence of this kind of self-control problem, which we can refer to as '**temptation**', is that when the SS benefit is still some way in the future people make the decision to forgo it in favor of the LL benefit; however, as time moves on and the proximity of the SS benefit becomes more immediate, the SS benefit also becomes more appealing, and people 'yield to temptation' and reverse their previous decision. This reversal is known as a time-inconsistent preference (TIP).

When payoffs are negative, involving costs, the SS versus LL trade-off relates to a different kind of self-control problem: **procrastination**. In this context we can think of procrastination as meaning unanticipated delay. An example is starting a project that involves a deadline; if it is started earlier the cost is relatively small, but if it is delayed then the cost is larger in terms of the greater effort and stress involved. In this case, when the SS cost is some way in the future people prefer SS to LL; however, as time moves on and the SS becomes immediate, people tend to switch to preferring LL and put off starting the project. Of course this situation still involves temptation; we may be tempted to do other more pleasurable activities than start the project.

In practice both field studies and experimental studies have shown that such inconsistent time preferences are common. Casual observation and personal experience also indicate the common nature of such situations. For example, we may decide now that at the restaurant this evening we will resist the temptation to have a tasty dessert, because that would not be good for our future health. Yet later, when the dessert trolley comes round (better restaurants know the power of visceral influences, and therefore display the tempting goods under our noses), we yield to temptation and indulge ourselves.

Experimental studies have shown the phenomenon of TIPs in a more precise and quantitative manner. For example, Ainslie and Haslam (1992) reported that:

> a majority of subjects say they would prefer to have a prize of a $100 certified check available immediately over a $200 certified check that could not be cashed before 2 years; the same people do not prefer a $100 certified check that could be cashed in 6 years to a $200 certified check that could be cashed in 8 years. (p. 69)

It is important to see how this would affect a subject's behavior. When presented with the second choice they will prefer to wait for the larger amount in eight years, but sometime later, within the next six years, their preference will switch to the smaller amount being received sooner. This implies that the discount rate used by the subjects is greater over the short time horizon than over the long time horizon. Similar results have been found with choices involving a wide range of goods apart from both real and hypothetical cash rewards, for example health, food and access to video games.

Studies using matching tasks as opposed to choice tasks have confirmed these findings, as discussed by Thaler (1981) and Benzion, Rapoport and Yagil (1989). Subjects were asked to state the money amounts where they would be indifferent between $x at time $t$ and $y immediately, with both $x$ and $t$ being variables. This permits the direct computation of discount rates for different time periods, and it has been repeatedly found that the discount rate is a decreasing function of $t$. Of course, as we saw in the previous chapter, this kind of methodology lends itself to the confound influence of transactions costs, since there is no front-end delay with the payment of $y.

### Reverse time inconsistency (RTI)

This term was introduced by Loewenstein (1987) to describe situations where people initially preferred the SS reward, but then later changed their preference to the LL reward, thus switching preferences in the opposite direction to that more normally observed. He proposed that for 'vivid and fleeting' consumption, like Halloween candles or expensive wines, the explanation lay in the effect of anticipatory utility, with people choosing to delay consumption in order to prolong savoring the moment.

There will be a discussion of explanations of both reverse time inconsistency and 'normal' time inconsistency later in the chapter, but it should be noted here that further studies have observed RTI in different situations from that in the Loewenstein study. Sayman and Önçüler (2009) observed RTI in five different experiments, involving both a two-level loyalty reward program and hypothetical monetary rewards. In the two-level reward program customers of a café could receive one free croissant when they had bought ten croissants, (SS) or two free croissants when they had bought 15 (LL). Of the 47 subjects participating, 19 (40%) showed RTI switching from the SS to LL after they had bought ten croissants. Only nine (19%) of the subjects showed standard time inconsistency, with the remaining subjects showing time-consistent preferences, either sticking with SS or sticking with LL.

In the other experiments in this study, the monetary rewards varied from $7 to $25. In all the experiments the delays were in the range between a few days up to four weeks. Other studies observing RTI have used larger rewards, equivalent to about $1,400, and delays up to two years (Holcomb and Nelson, 1992; Albrecht and Weber, 1997; Scholten and Read, 2010). Sayman and Önçüler (2009) find that RTI is relatively more likely to be observed when the delay to and between the two rewards is short.

### Issues and protocols

When the DUM was examined in the previous chapter it was seen that the model assumed both constant discounting (at any period the same discount rate was used to discount outcomes in all future periods) and stationary discounting (the same discount rate was used in all future periods as in the current period). Under these assumptions people would have preferences that were time-consistent.

However, there is an additional complication that needs to be addressed before considering different approaches to explaining TIPs. The delayed gratification (DG) situations considered above, and in most empirical studies, involve SS and LL costs and benefits that are fixed at the outset in terms of both amount and time of delivery. There are some real-life situations where this does not apply. In fact one of the landmark experiments by Mischel and Ebbesen (1970) that is often quoted as an example of time inconsistency did not involve this protocol. In this experiment the subjects, young children, were offered a choice between a smaller reward that was constant and continuously available from the outset and a larger reward that was fixed in amount but uncertain regarding its delivery time. The experimenter simply informed the subjects that he would be leaving the room 'for a while' and that sometimes he was absent for 'a long time'. A real-life example of this kind of decision situation is where one is waiting for a bus and deciding how long to wait before calling a taxi (Rachlin, 2000). In this case both forms of transport represent a cost, with the taxi being the larger cost, so initially one waits for a bus. However, after a certain length of wait, one may estimate that it may take longer than initially expected to catch the bus and that it is better to hail a taxi, since these are continuously available. Superficially this appears to be a switch from preferring a smaller cost sooner to a larger cost later, and thus another example of TIPs and a violation of the assumptions of constant and stationary discounting. In fact this is not necessarily the case given the change in protocol.

In the above type of situation a critical factor affecting the decision is the subjective probability distribution relating to the temporal delay of the larger cost or benefit. This prior distribution also entails a conditional distribution for expected remaining delay, which may be continuously updated in rational Bayesian terms. Different situations may involve different prior probability distributions, and these may have quite different decision implications. Since this dimension of intertemporal decision-making is both realistic and significant, it is worth describing it in some detail before discussing various approaches to explaining TIPs. The following description draws heavily from McGuire and Kable (2013), but omits some of the mathematical elements.

People may have essentially three possible prior probability distributions for events involving uncertain time duration or delay, like waiting for an experimenter to return, depending on past experience of similar situations. One possible distribution is Gaussian or normal, for example where people are estimating the life of an electrical component like a battery. In this case the conditional distribution for expected remaining life features a declining value as time passes. If such a distribution applied to children waiting for an experimenter to return, so that a longer wait implied an expected shorter time for him to return, then there should be no switch in preferences from LL to SS since the LL is expected sooner as time passes and its discounted utility increases.

A second type of prior probability distribution is an exponential, where the conditional distribution for expected remaining delay features a constant value over time. An example might be continually rolling a die and waiting for it to show a six. In this case the past waiting time has no influence on expected remaining time (for rational individuals), so that if children expected an experimenter to return after 5 minutes this expectation would not change as time passes and children wait longer. As with the previous situation there should be no switch in preferences from LL to SS, as the discounted utility of LL remains the same over time.

However, there is third possible type of prior probability distribution, associated with a power function in mathematical terms. This is also referred to as a heavy-tailed distribution, since it allows for a more frequent occurrence of extreme events than the previous two distributions. An example might be waiting for the return of an email, or waiting for a bus if there is no recognized schedule. In this case the conditional distribution for expected remaining delay features an increasing value as time passes. If children are explicitly told in an experiment that it may be a long time before the experimenter returns, they might entertain such a probability distribution, and expect the remaining delay to increase as they wait longer. In such a situation a switch from preferring LL to SS is predicted, since the discounted utility of LL is declining over time. A similar situation could apply to waiting for a bus, where delay is associated with cost. In this case the switch would be from an expected smaller cost sooner to a larger cost (of hailing a taxi), as the expected 'sooner' waiting time increases as time passes and no bus comes, thus increasing the expected cost of delay.

It is important to note here that with this last type of situation involving a heavy-tailed prior probability distribution the switch in preferences is not time-inconsistent, but is actually predicted by the DUM. The reason for this is that the anomaly of TIPs is only present when there is no new information appearing over time. With the prior heavy-tailed probability distribution, the conditional distribution for expected remaining time is continuously updated in Bayesian terms, so no news, like the experimenter not returning or no bus arriving, is still news, and this new information causes a rational switch in preferences.

## Approaches

Now that the nature of TIPs has been described in detail, we can see that there is really a two-fold challenge for behavioral economists here:

1   Determining the psychological processes underlying and explaining the anomaly of TIPs.
2   Developing alternative models that explain and predict observations better.

Over the last two or three decades there have been many attempts to address these issues, and these are discussed in the next three sections. We shall see that some approaches have focused more on the first issue than the second, and some more on the second issue than the first. We can classify the approaches into three general categories: hyperbolic discounting; modifying the instantaneous utility function; and more radical models. The first of these has received the most attention by researchers.

## 8.3  Hyperbolic discounting

*Nature of hyperbolic discounting*

The first economist to discuss alternatives to the constant discounting approach of the DUM was Strotz (1955), who did not see any normative value in the approach. Strotz also realized the implication of relaxing the assumption of constant discount rates in terms of the existence of TIPs. Although he did not propose any specific mathematical form of discount function as an alternative, he did draw attention to the case of declining discount rates. This really forms the basis of hyperbolic discounting: people tend to be more impatient in the short run, using a higher discount rate, and become more patient over longer periods of time. This phenomenon is referred to as **present bias**. However, it should be noted from the outset that the existence of present bias does not provide conclusive evidence of a hyperbolic discounting situation. There is an important confound here, because a modified instant utility function can also explain present bias, as explained later in the chapter. This confound is particularly obvious in the model of Lee and colleagues (2013), so it is worthwhile discussing this before describing hyperbolic discounting in more detail, particularly since it illustrates clearly the two challenges mentioned in the previous section. Lee and colleagues propose that consumers feel an emotion of psychological discomfort when they are considering deferring consumption, due to a feeling of loss of control. This causes them to want to regain control, which it turn causes them to use a higher discount rate for the immediate future. We will return to this model for further discussion later.

The first formal models involving hyperbolic discounting were constructed by Chung and Herrnstein (1967) and Phelps and Pollak (1968). This work has later been developed, in particular by Ainslie (1975; 1986; 1991; 1992) and by Laibson (1997; 1998).

In order to clarify the terminology and facilitate the understanding of the mathematics of the various models, let us begin by distinguishing between the terms **discount rate**, **discount factor**, **per-period discount factor**, and **discount function**. In the conventional discounting model of the DUM, the discount rate $\rho$ is constant and corresponds to the interest rate at which future utilities are discounted. The discount factor is the proportion by which each period's utility is multiplied in order to calculate the present value of the utility. In the constant discounting model the discount factor is given by $1/(1 + \rho)^t$. The per-period discount factor $\delta$ represents the proportion by which each discount factor is multiplied to compute the discount factor for the following period. In the DUM this is again constant, being given by $1/(1 + \rho)$. The discount function describes the relationship between the discount factor and time, showing the total effect of discounting over a range of time periods. The discount function in the DUM can therefore be described as $D(t) = \delta^t$, and this is referred to as an exponential discount function. Thus if a person has a utility function $u(x_0, x_1, x_2 \ldots x_0)$, the utilities in the periods 0, 1, 2,…$t$ are discounted by 1, $\delta$, $\delta^2$,… $\delta^t$. It should be noted that the time variable is treated as being discrete in this case, only assuming whole numbers.

These concepts are best illustrated by an example and a graph. In the DUM we will assume that the value of $\rho = 0.1$. It follows that $\delta = 0.9091$. After ten time periods the discount factor will have the value of $0.9091^{10} = 0.3856$. Thus a utility of 100 units expected in ten years will have a discounted present utility of 38.56 units. A graph of this discount function is shown in Figure 8.1.

The original hyperbolic discount function introduced by Chung and Herrnstein (1961) was based on experimental studies with animals, and took the form $D(t) = 1/t$. Herrnstein (1981) also developed another special case of hyperbolic function, where $D(t) = (1 + \alpha t)^{-1}$.

Phelps and Pollak (1968) used a modified version of this function, referred to as a **quasi-hyperbolic function**. This is described below:

$$D(t) = 1 \quad \text{if } t = 0$$
$$\beta\delta^t \quad \text{if } t > 0$$

In general $\beta < 1$, implying that the discount factor between the current period and the next is lower than the discount factor in later periods. Thus it can be said that $\beta$ measures the degree of present bias. In the limiting case where $\beta = 1$ the quasi-hyperbolic function reduces to the exponential function of the DUM. It should also be noted that this model, often referred to as the $(\beta,\delta)$ model, can also accommodate RTI, by allowing $\beta > 1$. According to the $(\beta,\delta)$ model, in contrast to the DUM, the utilities in the periods 0, 1, 2,...$t$ are discounted by 1, $\beta\delta$, $\beta\delta^2$,... $\beta\delta^t$.

Phelps and Pollak (1968) originally introduced this functional form in order to study intergenerational altruism, and the function was first applied to individual decision-making by Elster (1979). The pure, generalized hyperbolic function was originally introduced by Harvey (1986) and has been further developed by Prelec (1989, 2004) and Loewenstein and Prelec (1992). It has also been discussed in various contributions by Ainslie and Laibson mentioned earlier. This is a continuous function, taking the form $D(t) = (1 + \alpha t)^{-\beta/\alpha}$. The $\alpha$-coefficient determines how much the function departs from constant discounting. The limiting case, as $\alpha$ goes to zero, is the exponential discount function $D(t) = e^{-\beta t}$, in its continuous form. In Figure 8.1 it is assumed that $\alpha = 100{,}000$ and $\beta = 3{,}500$, again to give a function that intersects the others half way through the ten-year period.

## Implications of hyperbolic discounting

The primary implication of hyperbolic discounting is that time preferences will be inconsistent. We have already seen that there is a large body of empirical evidence that supports the theory of dynamic inconsistency in preferences. It is instructive to illustrate this effect of hyperbolic discounting with a simple example at this stage, and for this purpose we

**Figure 8.1**   Shapes of discount functions

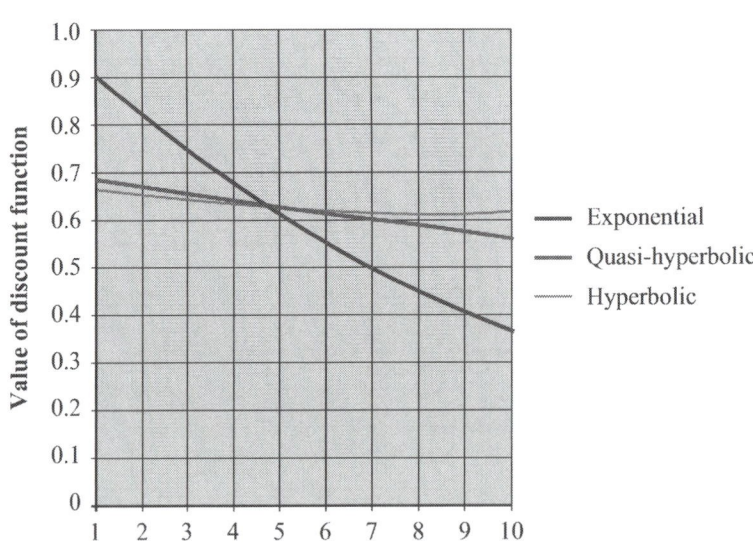

can use the values in the study of Ainslie and Haslam (1992), mentioned earlier. Let us assume that subjects have $\beta = 0.6$ and $\delta = 0.9$, and they are faced with the choice between receiving \$100 in six years' time (the SS reward) or \$200 in eight years' time (the LL reward). In this simple example both payoffs and time periods of delivery are fixed from the outset, unlike some of the examples described earlier in the chapter.

We can now write:

$V_0$ (\$100 in 6 years) = 0.6(0.9)$^6$ (100) = \$31.9
$V_0$ (\$200 in 8 years) = 0.6(0.9)$^8$ (200) = \$51.7

Thus at the present time the \$200 in eight years is more appealing. However, in six years' time the situation has changed so that:

$V_6$ (\$100 now) = \$100
$V_6$ (\$200 in two years) = 0.6(0.9)$^2$ (200) = \$97.2

At this point the value of the immediate receipt of \$100 exceeds the value of the \$200 in two years, and the subjects' preference has reversed. This example illustrates a 'temptation' situation. A comparison of exponential and hyperbolic discounting is shown in Figures 8.2 and 8.3. This is useful in illustrating the differences between naïve and sophisticated consumers, which is explained shortly.

We can also see how the $(\beta, \delta)$ model describes a procrastination situation, by considering the mirror image of the problem above and changing both payoffs into negative ones, so that the first payoff is $-\$100$ in six years and the second one is $-\$200$ in eight years. At the current time the smaller discounted cost of $-\$31.9$ of the SS is preferable to the larger discounted cost of $-\$51.7$ of the LL. However, in six years' time, subjects will prefer to switch to LL, with its lower discounted cost of $-\$97.2$ compared with the immediate cost of $-\$100$ of the SS.

The reason for the effectiveness of the $(\beta, \delta)$ model lies in its assumption of a higher discount rate between the current period and the next (for normal time inconsistency),

**Figure 8.2**   Exponential discounting and consistent time preferences

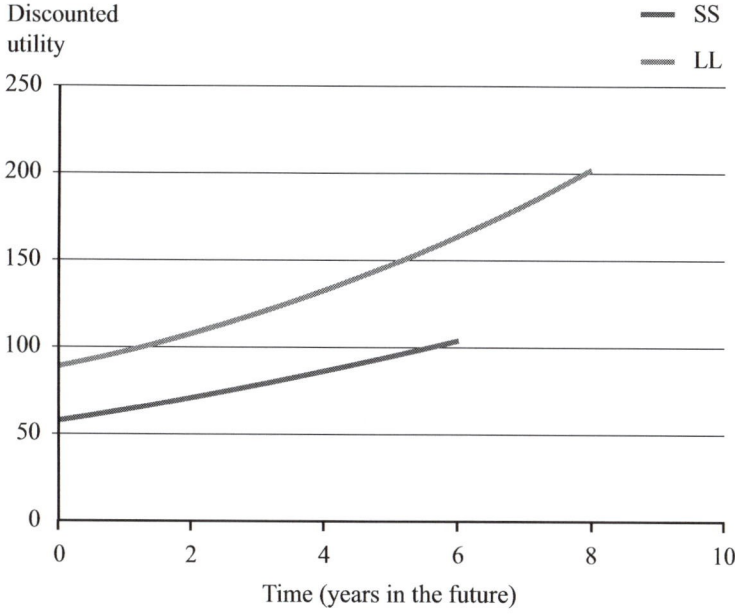

**Figure 8.3**    Hyperbolic discounting and inconsistent time preferences

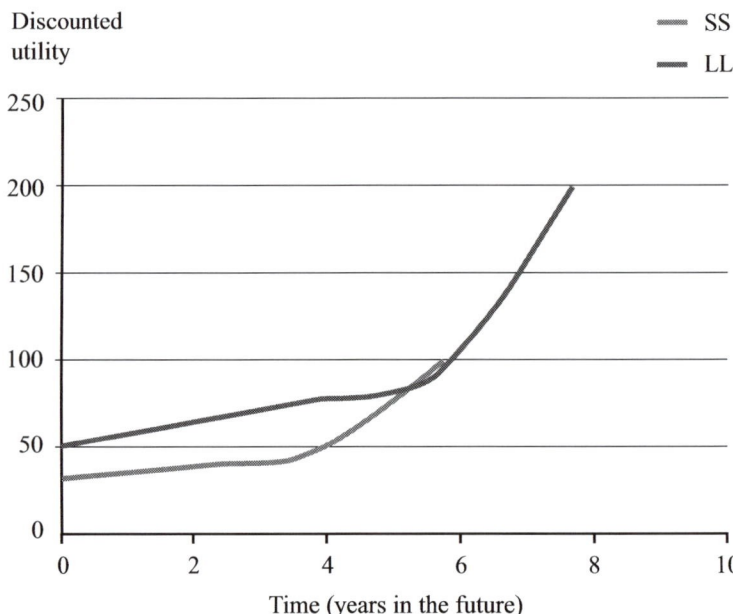

but a constant discount rate thereafter. The per-period discount rate between now and the next period is $(1 - \beta\delta)/\beta\delta$, whereas the per-period discount rate between any two future periods is $(1 - \delta)/\delta$, a smaller value.

The manner in which such present bias and inconsistency affects behavior depends on the degree of self-awareness of subjects, in terms of how aware they are that their preferences will change over time. There are two extreme situations: people may be completely '**naïve**', believing that their future preferences will be identical to their current ones. This would imply that people do not learn at all from past experience of changing preferences. It was assumed in the above numerical example that subjects were of this type. Naïve agents think that they will use a constant discount rate in the future, but will actually discount hyperbolically. If we refer to the person's belief regarding the value of their $\beta$ as $b$, then $\beta < b = 1$. Thus these consumers believe their preferences in the future are shown in Figure 8.2, seeming that LL will always be preferable to SS, and they will therefore not anticipate any forthcoming conflict.

The opposite extreme is where people are completely '**sophisticated**', and can predict accurately how their preferences will change over time. In this case $\beta = b < 1$. In this case consumers realize that their preferences in the future are shown in Figure 8.3, and anticipate a conflict when the preference reversal occurs. Thus sophisticated individuals have a key advantage over naïve ones, in that they can pre-commit to certain courses of action that prevent them from yielding to a preference reversal later. We saw an example of such a **commitment** in the introduction to the chapter, concerning alarm clocks. In reality it appears that most people lie somewhere in the middle of the naïve–sophisticated spectrum, meaning that $\beta < b < 1$, although there is limited empirical evidence regarding this aspect.

A good illustration of the differences between the behavior of exponential discounters, naïve and sophisticated hyperbolic discounters, which incorporates commitment, is given by Ho, Lim and Camerer (2006). They give a hypothetical numerical example relating to the situation of buying and consuming potato chips. They use a three-period model as follows:

1   *Purchase decision*: this involves a choice between a small (one serving) bag or a large (two servings) bag which involves a quantity discount.

2    *Consumption decision*: this involves a choice between consuming one serving or two, and an instantaneous utility related to consumption. If the smaller bag is purchased in the first period, only one serving can be consumed, but purchase of the larger bag offers the choice between consuming a single serving and leaving the other to a later period, or consuming both servings in the same period. Thus buying a smaller bag acts as a commitment in this case, as far as eating less and improving health is concerned.

3    *Health outcome*: this is adverse because chips are bad for you, but is much worse if two servings are consumed rather than one.

Under these conditions, and using reasonable parameters for discounting and outcomes, the authors conclude that each group of discounters may behave differently:

1    *Exponential discounters*: these may buy a large bag to benefit from the quantity discount, but only consume a single serving in the second period to avoid the worst health outcome.

2    *Naïve hyperbolic discounters*: these may buy a large bag, believing that they will behave like the exponential discounters and only consume one serving in the next period. However, in the second period they discount hyperbolically, applying a high discount factor to the adverse health effects in the third period, and they end up consuming both servings.

3    *Sophisticated hyperbolic discounters*: these may choose the small bag as a self-control or commitment device, knowing that in the next period they would be unable to resist the temptation of consuming both servings if they bought the large bag.

A numerical example will illustrate this situation. We assume for simplicity that $\delta = 1$ (so that exponential discounters do not discount future outcomes at all) and that $\beta = 0.5$. Let $c$ = number of servings consumed in any time period, and $p$ = the price per serving. We assume $p = 1.5$ for a small bag, and $p = 1$ for a large bag, to reflect the bulk discount. We model the utility flows as follows:

1    At the purchase decision ($t_0$) there is negative utility given by $U_0 = -cp$, which is the cost of purchasing the chips.

2    At consumption decision ($t_1$) there is instantaneous utility given by $U_1 = 1 + 5c$

3    Health outcome occurs with a one-period lag after consumption and is negative, given by $U_2 = 3 - 6c$.

It is now possible to calculate utilities for the three different types of consumer, rational, naïve and sophisticated, in the relevant time periods, for each consumption decision, in order to see how each type of consumer will behave. Table 8.1 shows the situation for rational consumers.

**Table 8.1**    Rational consumers (exponential discounters)

| $t$ | S | L(1) | L(2) |
|---|---|---|---|
| 0 | −1.5 | −2 | −2 |
| 1 | 6 | 6 | 11 |
| 2 | −3 | −3 + 6 = 3 | −9 |
| 3 | | −3 | |
| PV$_0$ | 1.5 | 4 | 0 |
| PV$_1$ | N/A | 6 | 2 |

There are three possible decisions:

1    S refers to purchasing a small bag, limiting consumption to one serving in the following time period.

2    L(1) refers to the purchase decision to buy a large bag and then consume a single serving in the next time period. It is assumed that the remaining serving is consumed in time period 2, so in this time period there is a health outcome of −3 related to consumption in the previous period and a positive consumption utility of 6, yielding a net utility of 3. In time period 3 there is the negative health outcome of −3 related to consumption in period 2.

3    L(2) refers to the decision to buy a large bag, and then consume both servings in the next time period.

It can be seen from the table that the rational consumer who discounts exponentially will maximize $PV_0$ at the purchase decision by choosing L(1), buying a large bag and planning to consume one serving in the next period, with the remaining serving being consumed in $t_2$. When $t_1$ is reached, the consumer will still maximize utility by sticking to his plan and consuming a single serving in each of the next two time periods.

Let us now consider the situation for naïve consumers. This is shown in Table 8.2.

**Table 8.2**    Naïve consumers

| $t$ | S | L(1) | L(2) |
| --- | --- | --- | --- |
| 0 | −1.5 | −2 | −2 |
| 1 | 3 (6) | 3 (6) | 5.5 (11) |
| 2 | −1.5 | 1.5 | −4.5 |
| 3 | | −1.5 | |
| $PV_0$ | 0 | 1 | −1 |
| $PV_1$ | N/A | 6 | **6.5** |

Expected utilities at $t_0$ are shown first; some of these utilities are revised at $t_1$, because of present bias, and are shown in brackets. As with rational consumers, naïve consumers maximize expected utility at $t_0$ by choosing L(1), purchasing the large bag, planning to consume a single serving in each of the following two time periods ($PV_0 = 1$). However, once they reach $t_1$ these consumers will maximize expected utility by switching to L(2), which is perceived to have $PV_1 = 6.5$ compared with $PV_1 = 6$ for the L(1) plan.

Sophisticated consumers have complete knowledge of the change in utilities in the future, and therefore realize that they will change preferences at $t_1$. Since at $t_0$ L(2) is the worst of all the options, with $PV_0 = -1$, sophisticated consumers will therefore commit to S to prevent the switch to L(2) in the future.

If the utilities of actual behavior are measured from the viewpoint of the first period then the exponential discounters end up with the most utility in this example ($PV_0 = 4$), because they benefit from the discount. Sophisticated consumers end up with $PV = 0$. The naïve hyperbolic discounters end up worst off ($PV_0 = -1$), because of the adverse health effects that they discount heavily compared to the benefits of consumption when they get to the second period. However, we should not conclude that sophisticated hyperbolic discounters will always end up better off than naïve ones. If they anticipate that they will eventually succumb to temptation, they are more likely to succumb earlier (in an 'unraveling' effect) than naïve discounters.

This model therefore explains consumption patterns for both investment goods and leisure goods. Investment goods have an immediate cost but a delayed benefit, whereas leisure goods (like eating junk food or watching TV) have an immediate benefit but a delayed cost. Let us call the immediate payoff $x_1$ at time $t = 1$ and the delayed payoff $x_2$ at time $t = 2$. Therefore the investment good has $x_1 < 0$ and $x_2 > 0$, while the leisure good has $x_1 > 0$ and $x_2 < 0$. We can now consider and compare three different concepts from an *ex ante* viewpoint when $t = 0$: (1) how much $(\beta, \delta)$ consumers *want* to consume, (2) how much such consumers *actually* consume, and (3) how much naïve consumers *expect* to consume.

1   Consumers want to consume at $t = 0$ if $\beta\delta x_1 + \beta\delta^2 x_2 > 0$, or $x_1 + \delta x_2 > 0$.
2   Consumers actually consume at $t = 1$ if $x_1 + \beta\delta x_2 > 0$.

   Investment goods have $x_2 > 0$, and since this is multiplied by $\beta$, which is smaller than 1, the result is that these agents underconsume investment goods. Similar reasoning indicates that they overconsume leisure goods ($x_2 < 0$).
3   Naïve consumers expect to consume if $x_1 + b\delta x_2 > 0$.
4   Since $b < \beta$, these consumers overestimate their consumption of investment goods and underestimate their consumption of leisure goods.

## Advantages of hyperbolic discounting

There are two main advantages of the $(\beta, \delta)$ model, described below.

1   *Analytical tractability*
   The model maintains most of the analytical tractability of the exponential model. It is again a discrete function, and after period 1 the per-period discount factor is $\delta$, the same as the exponential function. In Figure 8.1 it is assumed that $\beta = 0.7$ and $\delta = 0.98$, since this produces a function that crosses the exponential function half way through the ten-year period for ease of comparison.
2   *Congruence with reality*
   The model fits empirical findings well, mimicking the qualitative property of the hyperbolic discount function. This can be seen in Figure 8.1 where hyperbolic, quasi-hyperbolic and exponential functions are compared. DellaVigna (2009) summarizes several studies that support the $(\beta, \delta)$ model, explaining anomalies in the DUM. These studies relate to: excessive preference for membership contracts in health clubs (DellaVigna and Malmendier, 2006); positive effects of deadlines on homework grades and preference for deadlines (Ariely and Wertenbroch, 2002); preference for pre-teaser rather than post-teaser interest rates in credit card take-up (Ausubel, 1999); liquid credit card debt combined with simultaneous illiquid wealth accumulation (Laibson et al., 2017); demand for illiquid savings as commitment devices (Ashraf, Karlan and Yin, 2006); demand and default for payday loans (Skiba and Tobacman, 2008); and default settings in retirement savings plans (Madrian and Shea, 2001; Cronqvist and Thaler, 2004). The findings of these studies are discussed in more detail in the section related to empirical evidence.

## Criticisms of the hyperbolic discounting approach

It is fair to say that hyperbolic discounting has entered into the mainstream of behavioral economics, largely due to its well-documented empirical superiority over the exponential model and its analytical convenience. However, it has not been without its critics. It should be noted that these critics are largely not defenders of the traditional DUM, but are proponents of newer and more radical models.

Let us examine criticisms from defenders of the DUM first. These fall mainly into three categories, all of which have been mentioned earlier:

1   *Failure to use front-end delay*. This results in a confound with transactions costs explained in the previous chapter.

2   *Use of hypothetical rewards*. This may lead to unreliable results due to a lack of incentives compared with the use of monetary rewards.

3   *Failure to provide information relating to the annual interest rates implied in the different options*. Most studies simply give the options in terms of choice or matching tasks without such information. Coller and Williams (1999) found that discount rates were significantly lower when annual interest rate information is provided.

The first two criticisms have largely been countered over the last decade by numerous field studies involving hyperbolic discounting, many of which were summarized earlier in the section. These studies have often involved situations with delayed SS rewards or costs and these rewards and costs have been real rather than hypothetical.

As far as the third criticism is concerned, it has been sometimes suggested that there are legal requirements in many countries that require the provision of such information, and that this makes the provision of interest rate information a realistic condition. This may be true in different types of lending/borrowing situation, but the majority of intertemporal choice decisions are not of this type. When we are debating whether to eat a dessert, or join a health club, or tidy the garage, these are not situations where interest rate information is realistically going to enter the decision process.

Furthermore, as was discussed at the end of the previous chapter, studies that have incorporated the desired control elements, such as that by Harrison, Lau and Williams (2002), have not eliminated the non-constant discount rate phenomenon. While rates did not vary much between one and three years, rates were higher for the six-month time frame. Many hyperbolic discounting studies show higher rates for periods less than a year.

We will now move on to consider criticisms from proponents of newer discounting models. One more recent theory that has been proposed as being superior to hyperbolic discounting is **subadditive discounting**. The concept of subadditivity has been discussed in Chapter 5, and when applied to discounting it implies that people are less patient (i.e. have higher discount rates) per unit of time over shorter intervals regardless of when they occur. Thus the theory suggests that people would have a higher discount rate for a daily period than for a monthly period, even if the daily period were at a relatively distant point in the future. Read and Roelofsma (2003) conclude that subadditive discounting is superior to hyperbolic discounting in terms of explaining empirical results for both choice and matching tasks.

However, the main criticism that has been aimed at hyperbolic discounting, which applies also to subadditive discounting, is that it lacks a psychological foundation. It is basically a descriptive theory rather than an explanatory one. Although one can say that the $(\beta,\delta)$ model *describes* 'temptation' and procrastination self-control problems, this begs the question *why* people should use such a discounting method, particularly since it does not appear to result in optimizing welfare, and therefore is maladaptive in evolutionary terms. For example, a study of procrastination by students has shown that those with TIPs performed worse than those with consistent preferences, and this was true even with sophisticated students who had full awareness of their time inconsistency (Wong, 2008).

Even though the phenomenon has been widely observed among animals as well as humans, and has been studied by researchers in many disciplines, its strongest proponents have failed until recently to provide a good psychological foundation for it. Most researchers have entirely ignored this aspect, and of course this is quite legitimate from the standpoint of the traditional approach of the NM, which is only concerned with behavior, not psychological processes. However, given that there are alternative theories to explain the same behavior, which have different implications, it is worthwhile to examine psychological foundations, and a number of theories have been forthcoming over the last ten years. One model that has been proposed is the perceived time model (Kim and Zauberman, 2009). In this model hyperbolic discounting occurs because people show *diminishing sensitivity* to longer time horizons and because of *time contraction* (one year is perceived to be less than four times three months).

Another recent theory, described earlier, concerns the psychological discomfort related to losing control when consumption is deferred (Lee et al., 2013), with the resulting need to regain control causing present bias. A third recent theory concerns the concept of psychological connectedness (Bartels and Rips, 2010), described later in connection with multiple-self models.

In the last two decades some researchers have also attempted to find underlying biological causes for hyperbolic discounting. The challenge here is to find the possible evolutionary origins of such a psychological mechanism, in terms of how it might have increased inclusive fitness compared with the more intuitively appealing exponential discounting approach (Robson, 2002; Samuelson and Robson, 2007, 2009). These explanations are discussed in the section on empirical evidence, in terms of evolutionary biology.

## 8.4   Modifying the instantaneous utility function

In the previous chapter we described various anomalies observed in the DUM, and in the first section of this chapter many of these are viewed as confounds as far as measuring time preference and discount rates are concerned. It can be argued that it is more appropriate to treat these confounding factors as additional aspects of the instantaneous utility function. Models that attempt to achieve this are now discussed.

### Habit formation models

There is a long tradition of habit formation models in economics, going back to Duesenberry (1949). His hypothesis that the level of consumption depended on a past peak of consumption was based on the idea that current utility depends not only on current consumption but on past consumption:

$$U_t = f(C_t, C_{t-1}, C_{t-2}, ...)\tag{8.1}$$

In most models all the values of past consumption are combined together into a composite variable, $Z_t$, that may be exponentially weighted to give more importance to more recent periods, and that is increasing with past consumption. The utility function then becomes:

$$U_t = f(C_t, Z_t)\tag{8.2}$$

Thus the more a person has consumed in the past the more utility current consumption will yield, causing the person to consume more now. It should be noted that this ignores the possibility of shifting reference points, discussed shortly, which would have the opposite effect. This model can be applied in macroeconomic terms to all consumers and all goods, or on a microeconomic basis to particular goods. For example, Becker and Murphy (1988) have used a habit formation model to examine the effects of past and future prices on the current consumption of addictive goods. These models have also often been used to explain the equity premium puzzle discussed in Case 6.1. We will examine their relevance again in Case 8.2, which concerns the relationships between savings, consumption and growth.

As mentioned above, shifting reference points have important implications for habit formation. Another important factor related to habit formation is diminishing marginal sensitivity. Since both of these factors are elements of prospect theory, a more complete discussion of habit formation necessitates an examination of prospect theory models. We will also see in a later section that there are some important policy implications related to habit formation, especially as far as food intake and diet are concerned.

### Prospect theory models

Perhaps the single most salient characteristic of prospect theory is its use of reference points, as explained in Chapter 5. When a person's reference point for current consumption is past consumption, a reference-point model is identical with a habit formation model. However, this is only a special case of the more general reference-point model. Reference points can also be dependent on expectations of the future, or on social comparisons, as we have seen. The importance of social comparisons is considered in Case 8.3, in connection with the preference for rising consumption profiles.

Other important features of prospect theory that affect the instantaneous utility function are loss-aversion and diminishing marginal sensitivity. Loewenstein and Prelec (1992) have used a utility function incorporating such features in order to explain the anomalies of the 'magnitude effect', the 'sign effect', and the 'delay-speedup' asymmetry discussed in the previous chapter. The factor that is particularly important in their analysis is the concept of the **elasticity of the utility function**. The elasticity concept 'captures the insight that people are responsive to both differences and ratios of reward amounts' (Frederick, Loewenstein and O'Donoghue, 2002). Thus a person may be indifferent between receiving $10 now and $20 in a year, but prefer $200 in a year to $100 now. It may appear that a lower discount rate is being used for the larger amounts; however, in reality the person may have a constant time preference in the two options but may be more responsive to the difference between $100 and $200 than to the difference between $10 and $20.

Similarly, the Loewenstein–Prelec model can explain both the 'sign effect' and the 'delay-speedup' asymmetry in terms of loss-aversion, with people discounting gains more than losses. In the case of the 'delay-speedup' situation it needs to be recognized that any shift in consumption either forwards or backwards in time is made less desirable by loss-aversion, since although one gains consumption in one period, one also loses consumption in another period (when it was originally expected). Thus the gains from accelerating consumption are not as great as the losses from delaying it. Reference-point models incorporating loss-aversion have also been applied to draw conclusions regarding the permanent income hypothesis (Friedman, 1957). According to the conventional log-linear version of the permanent income hypothesis model, changes in future income, while affecting the level of consumption, will not affect the rate of consumption growth; consumption in all future periods will be increased or decreased by the same proportion in every period. However, as shown by Bowman, Minehart and Rabin (1999), a decrease in future incomes may not reduce current consumption very much because of loss-aversion, thus causing future consumption to fall by a greater amount as people are forced to adjust. Consumption growth may therefore respond more to future income decreases than to future income increases, and two studies by Shea (1995a and 1995b) lend some support to this hypothesis.

The characteristic of diminishing marginal sensitivity also has implications for habit formation models, especially when combined with shifting reference points. This concept has different effects over different time frames, and for different types of consumption, so we will start by considering a fundamental example, food. Of all self-control problems the tendency to overeat and the corresponding health problems related to obesity are among the most serious. We have already seen the nature of some of these problems in Chapter 4, particularly related to the studies by Wansink (2005, 2006, 2009). The central theme in these studies is that there are many anchoring effects that determine how much we eat, like size of plate, number and sex of eating companions, and whether we are watching TV at the same time. The role of diminishing marginal sensitivity essentially relates to satiation. In the short term, which in the case of food can be over the normal course of a meal, or even over a few days, we tend to become satiated as we eat more food in general or more food of a particular type (Epstein et al., 2009). The same study found that people react in the same way to sexual stimuli of a particular type as far as diminishing marginal sensitivity is concerned, and of course it is well known that reactions to recreational drugs are similar. However, over the longer term, the diminished sensitivity can lead to a shifting of the reference point to a higher level of consumption. Hence drug-takers need to increase their dosage over time to get the same 'fix' or high. The physiology underlying this phenomenon, in terms of chemical receptors and the function of neurotransmitters is fairly well known in this situation, but varies somewhat from case to case. With food intake much research still needs to be done in terms of how diminishing marginal sensitivity and shifting reference points operate, and also how they vary from person to person. Some policy implications of these aspects are discussed in a later section.

## Anticipatory utility models

We have seen in Chapter 4 that people derive utility from anticipation of future consumption as well as from current and past consumption. This effect can be expressed in a manner parallel to the habit formation model and equation (8.1):

$$U_t = f(C_t, C_{t+1}, C_{t+2},...) \tag{8.3}$$

This phenomenon works in the opposite direction to the normal direction of time preference, for both gains and losses. Thus we may prefer to delay consumption of certain products where anticipatory rewards are important, and accelerate bad outcomes rather than have them hanging over us (Loewenstein, 1987; Hardisty et al., 2012). We have seen earlier that such preferences associated with anticipatory utility can explain reverse time inconsistency. There are certain exceptions to this phenomenon: waiting for a good outcome can be frustrating, while one may prefer to delay the possibility of a bad outcome to avoid spoiling the weekend (for example, when students take a test). It should be noted that if there is uncertainty regarding the outcomes this adds another dimension to the situation, as the emotions of hope and anxiety enter the picture. Such visceral influences are discussed shortly. If a normal discounting approach is taken, without modifying the utility function, the result is that different discount rates will be calculated with different goods, as is often observed in empirical studies. In this case the reality is that the utilities have not been modified to allow for anticipation and that if this is done the discount rates may actually be constant.

## Visceral influence models

The nature of visceral influences has been discussed earlier, both in this chapter and in Chapters 3 and 4. A number of studies have shown that visceral factors can affect discount rates in different ways. Some studies have examined mood in general, finding that when either positive or negative mood is induced in experimental subjects this tends to increase patience (Drichoutis and Nayga, 2013). This relates to discount rates in general. In other cases we have seen that the temporal proximity of an outcome may increase its desirability. This may cause a higher rate of discount to be computed for near-future outcomes when factors like anger, hunger, lust and sleeplessness are involved, thus seeming to support the hyperbolic discounting approach. We have also seen that psychological discomfort caused by deferment of a reward may in turn cause a desire to regain control and thus present bias (Lee et al., 2013). Another model involving a trade-off between two different visceral factors has been proposed by Thomas and Park (2012). The trade-off is between the positive visceral reaction to receiving an immediate reward and the feeling of anticipated regret of forgoing a larger delayed reward. The authors claim that this may reduce present bias in 'tightwads' who are more disposed psychologically to feel regret, but not in 'spendthrifts' who are less disposed to feel regret.

In all the above studies there is a proposed relationship between visceral factors and the discount rate. However, it may be more appropriate to modify the instantaneous utility function to allow for a momentary increase in utility in certain circumstances (Loewenstein, 1996, 2000). It should be noted that temporal proximity of the outcome is only one of these circumstances. Other cues may also be important, for example spatial proximity, or the presence of associated sights, sounds or smells.

The influence of visceral factors is more complicated than just the effect on the instantaneous utility function. It has been found, for example, that when people are under their influence they tend to overestimate how long their effect will last, while when people are not under their influence they tend to underestimate the magnitude of their effect in the future. People also tend to perceive immediate emotions as being more intense than previous emotions, a phenomenon referred to as '**immediacy bias**' (Van Boven, White and Huber, 2009). This bias may be caused by salience or by greater availability of information regarding the present emotion. When people are reminded that information about emotions naturally decays from memory, this tends to reduce immediacy bias.

Another effect of visceral factors leads to a paradox, in that people may not want to want certain things, even expressing their preference for not doing something while they are actually doing it, like taking drugs. This phenomenon relates to the difference between wanting and liking, so it may be more meaningful to state that people may not want to *like* certain things. Obviously self-control factors are relevant here, and the concepts of temptation and willpower. These will be further discussed in later sections, in the context of multiple-self models and policy implications.

## 8.5  More radical models

In Chapter 5 we saw that it was possible to distinguish between conventional modifications to expected utility theory and non-conventional alternatives. However, even these non-conventional alternatives, like prospect theory, are really best viewed as extensions of the standard model rather than outright rejections of it. Similar considerations apply to the DUM, but it is more difficult here to draw the line between the conventional and the non-conventional. So far the alternative models to the DUM that we have examined have involved modifying either the discount function or the instantaneous utility function. Even here though some of the modifications involve non-conventional factors related to prospect theory. The models examined in this section involve more radical differences from the DUM, although in some cases they are still often considered conventional models, like the dual-self model of Fudenberg and Levine (2006). The reason for this lack of clarity, or blurring of distinctions, is that intertemporal models are more complex than static models of preference, consisting of more components. This has led to a hybridization of models, in that some components of a model may be 'conventional' while other components may be 'non-conventional'. Furthermore, the issue is also becoming more complicated as time passes and more 'radical' models become integrated into mainstream theories. These aspects are best explained in more detail as we examine the individual models.

## Projection bias

This is an example of a phenomenon that has been discussed earlier. People's tastes change over time, and there is a general tendency to underestimate the magnitude of these changes. The presence of visceral influences, discussed above, is only one of the factors that can cause this; habit formation and the shifting of reference points are two other important factors that can cause the same phenomenon. This bias is contrary to the assumption of rational expectations in the standard model, which implies that people can forecast changes in their tastes accurately. It has been modeled by Loewenstein, O'Donoghue and Rabin (2003), who review extensive evidence for the phenomenon. In the case of habit formation the utility function in equation (8.2) may be appropriate as the instantaneous utility function at time $t$: $U_t = f(C_t, Z_t)$. This can be expressed more simply as $U_t(C_t, Z_t)$, where $Z_t$ again represents a composite variable reflecting past consumption. At time $t + 1$ an individual's true instantaneous utility function may be $U_{t+1}(C_{t+1}, Z_{t+1})$, and their expectation of this function at time $t$ may be $\tilde{U}_{t+1}(\hat{C}_{t+1}, Z_{t+1} | Z_t)$. This represents expected utility in time $t + 1$ of expected consumption in time $t + 1$ and past consumption up to that period, given the current level of past consumption at time $t$. According to the projection bias model:

$$U_t(C_t, Z_t) < \tilde{U}_{t+1}(\hat{C}_{t+1}, Z_{t+1} | Z_t) < U_{t+1}(C_{t+1}, Z_{t+1})$$

This can be modeled more precisely using a weighted function to indicate how accurately people forecast future utilities:

$$\tilde{U}_{t+1}(\hat{C}_{t+1}, Z_{t+1} | Z_t) = \alpha[U_t(C_t, Z_t)] + (1 - \alpha)[U_{t+1}(C_{t+1}, Z_{t+1})] \qquad (8.4)$$

where $0 \leq \alpha \leq 1$

The higher the value of $\alpha$, the greater the degree of projection bias, meaning that there is a greater tendency to underestimate future utilities.

This phenomenon, which resembles myopia, has important policy implications, for individuals, firms and governments. For example, people may consume more of a good now, underestimating the effect that this will have on future utility, and therefore underestimating future consumption, or the desire for future consumption, of the good. In this situation people may discount future consumption too highly as far as the maximization of welfare in terms of experienced utility is concerned. The policy implications are discussed in the next section.

## Mental accounting models

The features of mental accounting were discussed extensively in Chapter 6, and it was seen that these involved the aspects of framing and editing, fungibility, and choice bracketing. We now need to examine the effects of these behavioral aspects on intertemporal choice and discounting.

One of the main implications of lack of budget fungibility is that different discount rates are applied to different goods. We have seen that small purchases may be classified as 'petty cash', with the result that people may be more inclined to spend on these, using a higher discount rate. Goods involving a larger expenditure, such as durables, may be evaluated more carefully, using a lower discount rate.

There are also a number of implications of choice bracketing which contradict the predictions of the DUM. We have seen that people often prefer to prepay for various expenses to avoid the 'pain of paying' later for something they have already consumed (Prelec and Loewenstein, 1998), whereas the DUM predicts a preference for paying later. Furthermore, they may prefer to receive payment for work after rather than before performing it, again in contradiction to the DUM. We have also discussed the preference for payment decoupling, which may lead to fixed-fee pricing with zero marginal costs, as for example with many health club membership schemes. This is another contradiction of the DUM, which predicts a dislike for upfront fees. This situation is examined in more detail in Case 8.1.

Another anomaly of the DUM observed earlier, that relates to choice bracketing, is the preference for spread of consumption. Loewenstein and Prelec (1993) found that people tend to prefer to spread the 'treats' of dining at a fancy French restaurant, although in this case there was also a preference for an improving sequence of outcomes, as predicted by prospect theory. The preference for spread is a separate phenomenon, and appears to be related to anticipatory utility.

### Strength depletion models

The central notion behind these models is that people's capacity for self-regulation is a limited resource (Baumeister and Heatherton, 1996), and in the face of continuous temptation becomes exhausted leading to preference reversals (Baumeister et al., 1998; Muraven, Tice and Baumeister, 1998). The authors provide evidence from various experimental studies to support this model, showing for example that emotional upset tends to reduce physical stamina, and that suppressing forbidden thoughts can lead to giving up more quickly in attempting to solve insoluble anagram puzzles. The capacity for self-regulation is viewed as a physiological factor and, just as with physical exertion, requires effort to be sustained, resulting in fatigue.

The main problem with these models at present is that they lack a precise neuro-physiological foundation, instead relying on a somewhat nebulous concept of 'willpower'. The only neural correlate identified in the models is the level of blood glucose in the brain, which is a heavy user of this essential fuel. However, this cannot explain why particular experiences, like listening to certain music, can either drain or bolster 'willpower', without any effect on blood glucose.

### Multiple-self models

The term multiple-self has an element of ambiguity that needs to be clarified from the outset. First the concept can be applied to the situation where the 'self' is a dynamic and ever-changing entity over time. This is most clear when we compare our current self, in terms of attitudes, values and beliefs, with our self in some period well in the past; sometimes we have difficulty understanding our past selves and may indeed be embarrassed by them. However, the term multiple-self can also be applied to situations at a particular point in time, when there appear to be conflicts between our short-term 'self' and our long-term 'self'. Models of this situation are often referred to as dual-self models, for example that of Fudenberg and Levine (2006) discussed later.

All these models are inspired by the observation that self-control problems are commonplace, and often involve forms of commitment described in the discussion of hyperbolic discounting. Indeed the term 'self-control' can be considered meaningless *unless* there is more than one 'self'. It begs the questions:

1    Who is doing the controlling, if not the self?
2    Why is there a need for self-control, if there is just a single self seeking to maximize some kind of preference function?

Furthermore, there is significant neuroscientific evidence that we have two separate systems that are involved in intertemporal decision-making. This is discussed in the next section.

There are a variety of multiple-self models. Some models involve a near-sighted or myopic self and a far-sighted self who are in conflict and alternately take control of behavior (Winston, 1980; Schelling, 1984; Ainslie and Haslam, 1992). These models are criticized by Frederick, Loewenstein and O'Donoghue (2002) on the grounds that they fail to explain why either type of self gains control, and they do not capture the fundamental asymmetry between the far-sighted and near-sighted selves. Far-sighted selves can make commitments to control the behavior of near-sighted selves, but not vice versa. An example is where the far-sighted self leaves the alarm clock across the room from the bed, so that the near-sighted self cannot just slam it off quickly in the morning and go back to sleep.

As noted by Frederick, Loewenstein and O'Donoghue (2002), 'few of these multiple-self models have been expressed formally, and even fewer have been used to derive testable implications that go much beyond the intuitions that inspired them in the first place'. However, as they also point out, this is not so much a failure of the models themselves as an indication of the complexity of the underlying phenomena. Certainly the models do help to explain the existence of various self-control strategies, and can also, with the aid of game theory, provide a much-needed psychological foundation for hyperbolic discounting.

A recent psychological foundation for hyperbolic discounting is provided by another multiple-self model involving the theory of psychological connectedness (Bartels and Rips, 2010). In general we are more psychologically connected to our proximate selves in the future, because key personality characteristics and preferences are less likely to change. We are likely to be less psychologically connected to our more distant selves. This theory, supported by experimental evidence, can therefore account for present bias. The theory of psychological connectedness can also account for different propensities to behave in an unethical way (Hershfield, Cohen and Thompson, 2012). If a person has a strong sense of connectedness with their future self, and is considering acting in a potentially unethical way, they can access the feelings that their future self will feel, for example guilt and shame, and this may prevent them from engaging in such behavior. However, people who lack a sense of continuity with their future selves will fail to recognize the future emotional consequences and be less inhibited in terms of ethical misconduct.

## *Dual-self models*

A variation of the above model has been proposed by Thaler and Shefrin (1981), along the lines of principal-agent theory. The far-sighted self is the principal or 'planner', while there is a sequence of near-sighted selves who constitute the agent or 'doer'. Thus the model captures the asymmetry aspect. The far-sighted planner is concerned with future utilities whereas the near-sighted doer is only concerned with the instantaneous utility function at a particular point in time. The planner is at least partially aware of the conflicts that will occur in the future, for example when the dessert trolley comes around, and can adopt commitment strategies to control the behavior of doer, by perhaps only going to restaurants that do not serve tempting desserts. This type of principal-agent model involves aspects of game theory discussed in the next chapter.

A further type of dual-self model is also based on game theory, in this case relating to social interaction and the choice between cooperation and defection (Elster, 1985b). This is fundamentally a prisoner's dilemma situation on a repeated basis. Self-control requires the continued cooperation of a series of instantaneous selves. As we will again see in the next chapter, there is a tendency for an unraveling sequence of defection, whereby sequential selves repeatedly give in to temptation. There is also a self-signaling effect here, which has been discussed in Chapter 3, Section 3.5, whereby giving in to temptation signals the next self that they lack the self-control to commit themselves to avoiding temptation in the future, thus destroying confidence and 'willpower'.

The most well-developed model of this type is arguably the dual-self model of Fudenberg and Levine (2006). This actually rejects hyperbolic discounting and for this reason may be termed a conventional model. However, it also incorporates elements of prospect theory and mental accounting which are unconventional. The Fudenberg–Levine (FL) model posits a patient long-run self and a sequence of myopic short-run selves. These selves are involved in playing a game in a sequence of stages. The long-run and short-run selves share the same preferences over the outcomes in each stage, but they regard the future differently. The short-run self is impatient and has 'baseline preferences' only for the current stage, while the long-run self also has preferences for future stages. Each stage consists of two phases. In the first phase the long-run self can choose a self-control action that influences the utility of the short-run self. This means that, at some cost in utility for both selves, the long-run self can choose preferences other than the baseline preferences. In the second phase, once its preferences have been determined, the short-run self takes the final decision. This whole process is illustrated in Case 8.1 related to joining a gym and exercising.

Fudenberg and Levine emphasize the advantages of their model over hyperbolic discounting, in that it produces a single equilibrium for behavior, rather than the multiple equilibria that are associated with hyperbolic discounting and the multiple-self model. While being analytically simpler and making more precise predictions, they claim that it can explain empirical facts just as well.

There are a number of predictions or implications of this model. For example, the authors find that self-control costs lead to longer delays. They also develop a banking-savings model where it is predicted that people will use self-control in limiting the amount of pocket cash that they have available to spend later in a nightclub scenario. This behavior invokes the notion of a commitment, which is further developed in the next chapter in the context of game theory. It is notable that this aspect of the model incorporates mental accounting concepts, in that bank cash is regarded differently from pocket cash in terms of the marginal propensity to consume. The concept of a reference point is also used, in that the amount of pocket cash is used as the reference point for spending, not one's total wealth. It is important that the constraint on spending here is not liquidity, since in principle one could write a check or use a credit card in the night club. However, these are 'non-anonymous' accounts, meaning that spending from them will result in an identifiable transaction later, which may cause self-recrimination – or recrimination from one's partner. Cash on the other hand is an anonymous account, as we discussed in Chapter 6 on mental accounting. Fudenberg and Levine also explain Rabin's 'risk paradox' in a similar way: people are averse to taking small risks which involve pocket cash, but do not have similar risk-aversion for large gambles that involve bank cash.

One final implication of the model is important. It proposes that the costs of self-control are non-linear, meaning that an increase in self-control involves an increasing marginal cost. The underlying principle here is that self-control is an exhaustible resource, and that therefore the law of diminishing returns applies, as discussed earlier in the context of strength depletion models. The consequence is that increasing cognitive load or emotional stress reduces self-control. The empirical evidence regarding the various aspects of the FL model is discussed in the next section.

Dual-self models have also been proposed by psychologists, neuroscientists and evolutionary biologists, and there is an element of consilience here, in that findings in different disciplines using different approaches have tended to come to similar conclusions. Brocas and Carrillo (2008a) approach the subject from the neurological basis of brain modularity, where there is ample evidence (examined in the next section) that the brain not only consists of different systems, but also that these systems are in conflict in various ways. They propose three main sources of conflict: asymmetric information, temporal horizon, and incentive salience. So far we have concentrated mainly on the second of these sources, although the first is relevant in the 'planner-doer' model. Brocas and Carrillo propose that decreasing impatience and hyperbolic discounting emerge as a result of these two conflicts. However, there is another 'dual-self' aspect related to incentive salience that has been referred to in Chapter 4 related to wanting and liking. Robinson and Berridge (2003) and Berridge (2003) show that there is one system that mediates the feeling of pleasure and pain (the 'liking' system) and a different system that mediates the motivation or incentive to seek pleasure and avoid pain (the 'wanting' system). The evidence relating to this is discussed later in relation to neurological studies.

Evolutionary biologists have proposed dual-self models to explain the origins and development of morality (for a summary, see Frimer, Schaefer and Oakes, 2014). In this case there as an agent, who is the executor of actions, and is purely selfish, and a moral actor, who watches over the selfish agent and regulates his actions in order to ensure that the individual cooperates with others in the relevant group in order to be accepted and receive the benefits of belonging to the group. This is necessary for survival and reproduction if cooperative groups outcompete discordant groups and lone individuals in accessing finite resources. This aspect of behavior is discussed in more detail in Chapter 10 in the context of social preferences.

### The procedural approach

In the discussion of hyperbolic discounting it was noted that its most important failing was the lack of a psychological foundation. Rubinstein (2003) both disputes the empirical evidence for hyperbolic discounting, and provides an alternative framework for decision-making which he claims does have a legitimate psychological foundation. Like various other models we have seen, Rubinstein's approach is based on a heuristic process. This proposes that the decision-maker uses a procedure that applies similarity relations, involving a money dimension and a time dimension, in a series of three steps.

The objects of choice in intertemporal situations can be described as being in the form $(x, t)$, where $x$ is received with a delay of t units of time. Thus a decision-maker may have to compare two choices: A = $(x, t)$ and B = $(y, s)$. According to Rubinstein (2000) many decision-makers go through the following three steps:

1  *Search for dominance*

   If $x > y$ and $t < s$ then A dominates B, since it is preferable in both dimensions (a larger reward is received sooner).

2  *Search for similarities in the two dimensions*

   If the decision-maker finds similarity in one dimension only, he determines his preference using the other dimension only. For example, if x is similar to y, but $t > s$, then B is preferred to A, since the rewards seem similar, but B involves less delay.

3  *Use of a different criterion*

   If the first two stages do not give a result, some different criterion must be used (Rubinstein is not specific regarding the nature of this).

Rubinstein conducts three experiments to test how the procedural approach explains behavior compared with hyperbolic discounting. It is worth describing the first experiment here, since it will aid an understanding of the different models and how they compare. This experiment was performed in 2002 with a total of 456 students on a between-subjects basis involving choice tasks and money. Different students were asked to answer either question 1 or 2 below:

Q1  Choose between the following two options:
    a) Receiving $467.00 on June 17, 2004
    b) Receiving $607.07 on June 17, 2005

Q2  Choose between the following two options:
    a) Receiving $467.00 on June 16, 2005
    b) Receiving $467.39 on June 17, 2005

55% of the subjects chose delay in question 1, while only 46% chose delay in question 2. According to the procedural approach the 39 cents difference in question 2 is too small to be meaningful, causing subjects to tend to prefer the shorter delay, even by only one day. In question 1, however, neither amount nor time period are similar, so subjects have to resort to the third step of the approach. Rubinstein comments that the results contradict any hyperbolic discounting approach. The one-day discount rate implied by the preference for earlier delivery in question 2 is lower than the one-year discount rate implied by the preference for delay in question 1.

While this example does not provide conclusive evidence in favor of the procedural approach, when combined with the results of the other two experiments, it does pose significant questions regarding the hyperbolic discounting model. It can also be observed that Rubinstein's results contradict the subadditive model of discounting, which predicts a greater one-day discount rate.

## 8.6  Empirical evidence

There are three main sources of empirical evidence regarding intertemporal decision-making models: (1) behavioral studies; (2) evolutionary biology; and (3) neuroeconomic studies. A number of these studies have already been discussed briefly in previous sections, in order to explain the nature of specific models, but we are now in a position to take an overall view to see how the evidence sheds light on the various models as a whole.

Before examining these further sources we should bear in mind certain important principles in terms of how this empirical evidence can be interpreted. First, it is necessary to realize that some theories described so far are not mutually exclusive, but may instead be complementary. This applies to hyperbolic discounting in particular, which can be combined for example with multiple-self models. On the other hand, while 'planner-doer' models may be compatible with visceral factor models, these are both mutually exclusive with hyperbolic discounting. A second and related principle involves reductionism: different theories apply at different levels. Hyperbolic discounting is a purely economic 'explanation'; underlying it may be a psychological explanation related to psychological connectedness. Similarly we shall see that dual-self models may be reliant on psychological evidence related to 'hot' and 'cold' decision-making processes, which in turn may be reliant on neurological studies relating to brain systems. A third point involves confounds: some studies provide evidence that does not distinguish between different theories, meaning that the evidence can be explained by different theories, even though they are in principle contradictory. Studies that provide evidence that can distinguish between theories are particularly important.

## Behavioral studies

Perhaps the most important general finding of many recent empirical studies is that there are significant correlations between discount rates and various aspects of lifestyle and behavior. Some of these, for example Chabris and colleagues (2008), find relatively low correlations but still report that discount rates are a better predictor of smoking, drinking and obesity than attitudes to risk and uncertainty. Sutter and colleagues (2013) examine adolescents aged between 10 and 18, and find that their discount rates calculated from experiments are already a good predictor of lifestyle choices such as smoking, drinking, obesity, saving and conduct at school. Various cross-sectional studies in different countries have shown a relationship between discount rates and obesity (Zhang and Rashad, 2007; Weller et al., 2008; Ikeda, Kang and Ohtake, 2010; Van der Pol, 2010), with obese individuals being less patient. Some studies also report a link between different lifestyle behaviors associated with discounting, notably obesity and savings rates, both at a country level (Komlos, Smith and Bogin, 2004) and an individual level (Smith, Bogin and Bishai, 2005). Other time-series studies find a relationship between discounting at an early age and behavior at a later age. For example, Seeyave and colleagues (2009) use a sample of US children and find that time preference at age 4 is correlated with being overweight at age 11.

Another general finding concerns the relationship between language and time preference. Chen (2013) examines differences between languages which grammatically associate the future and the present, like German, and those which clearly distinguish between them, like English, in terms of how they relate to the time preference of speakers. He examines nine multilingual countries where both types of language are spoken and finds that those populations speaking languages with a weak future-time reference, like German, have lower discount rates in terms of saving more, smoking less, being less obese, and practicing safer sex. While this is certainly an interesting finding, it is problematical in terms of conclusions, since it leaves open the cause-and-effect issue. Differences in language may cause differences in behavior, or differences in behavior may cause differences in language, or both may be caused by underlying differences in psychological and cultural disposition.

We have already mentioned a number of studies that provide evidence for hyperbolic discounting (HD). Some of this research has also estimated parameter values for the $(\beta,\delta)$ model. DellaVigna and Malmendier (2006) study health club membership, and find that a model involving $\beta = 0.70$ and $\delta = 0.9995$ fits their data. The Laibson and colleagues (2009) study estimated $\beta = 0.70$ and $\delta = 0.96$. Paserman (2008) uses job search data to estimate $\beta = 0.40$ and $\delta = 0.99$ for low-wage workers and $\beta = 0.89$ and $\delta = 0.99$ for high-wage workers, assuming sophistication. Skiba and Tobacman (2008) allow for partial naïveté, estimating $\beta = 0.53, b = 0.90$, and $\delta = 0.45$. It is notable that borrowers of payday loans have a very high discount rate, otherwise the enormous interest rates on such loans would not be acceptable. Another study that may provide evidence for HD versus exponential discounting was performed by Lerner and colleagues (2013), but in this case there is a confound, since the study investigates the relationship between the negative mood of sadness and discounting, with the main finding being that sadness increases present bias, but does not reduce patience in general.

It should also be noted that other studies do not support the existence of present bias and HD, but this may be because of another confound related to receiving monetary rewards. The confound arises because it is the timing of consumption that is relevant for discounting purposes rather than the timing of the reward. A recent study by Augenblick and colleagues (2015) avoided this problem by examining the discounting of both effort tasks and monetary rewards, and find that subjects exhibit considerably more present bias in the effort task situation.

A problem with many HD studies is that they were typically designed to test the theory of non-constant hyperbolic discounting versus constant exponential discounting; they were not designed to test HD against other behavioral theories, like visceral influence models that modify the instantaneous utility function, and therefore cannot discriminate between the two theories. Thus when we observe a preference reversal, like switching from a LL reward to a SS reward, we need to ask if this is because of a change in the discount factor being used or because of a change in perceived utility of the reward. Furthermore, there are other possible explanations: perceived probabilities or attitudes to risk may have changed, or the experimental protocol may be different in terms of the perceived timing of costs and benefits. We have already seen that subjects may have different prior probability distributions regarding delay. This means that evidence of preference reversal is not necessarily proof of non-constant discounting (Gerber and Rohde, 2010).

Examples of research that discriminates between different theories are the studies by Mischel (1974) and Mischel and colleagues (1992). Children were placed in a room by themselves and taught they that they could summon the experimenter by ringing a bell. They would then be shown a superior and inferior prize and told that they would receive the superior prize if they could wait successfully for the experimenter to return. One main finding was that the children found it harder to wait for a delayed reward if they were made to wait in the presence of either one of the immediate or delayed reward objects. This finding is particularly important since it provides evidence for the visceral factor theory as against the non-constant discounting theory. According to the latter children should be more willing to wait in the presence of the superior delayed reward. This result does not indicate that the hyperbolic discounting theory is false in general, merely that it may not be the best explanation of behavior in certain situations.

A number of behavioral studies also provide evidence of increasing costs of self-control, meaning that our facility for self-control is a limited resource, and becomes increasingly costly to utilize as cognitive load increases. An example of this phenomenon is described in the paper by Fudenberg and Levine (2006), which reports an experiment by Shiv and Fedorikhin (1999), where subjects were asked to memorize either a two- or a seven-digit number, and then walk to a table with a choice of two desserts, chocolate cake and fruit salad. In one treatment the actual desserts were on the table, whereas in a second treatment the desserts were represented by photographs. It was hypothesized that:

1    Subjects would face a self-control problem regarding the cake, in the sense that it would have a higher emotional or visceral appeal, but be less desirable from a 'cognitive' viewpoint.

2    Subjects' reactions were more likely to be determined by emotional reactions when cognitive resources were constrained by the need to remember the longer number.

3    The 'cognitive overload effect' would be greater when subjects were faced with actual desserts rather than with their pictures.

All three hypotheses were supported by the experimental results. When faced with real desserts, subjects who were asked to remember the longer number chose the cake 63% of the time, while subjects given the two-digit number only chose the cake 41% of the time, a statistically significant difference. However, when faced with pictures of the desserts, the choices were 45% and 42% respectively, an insignificant difference. These results can also be explained by the dual-self model, in that the long-run self, faced with increasing cognitive costs, is less well able to exert self-control. The FL paper also notes that the increasing marginal cost of self-control implied by the Shiv and Fedorikhin study contravenes one of the axioms proposed by Gul and Pesendorfer (2001) in relation to self-control, specifically the axiom relating to set-betweenness. This axiom was discussed in the context of EUT in Chapter 5, where we saw that evidence did not support it in that context either.

More recent studies by psychologists have generally supported the theory of increasing costs of self-control, for example Gailliot and colleagues (2007), Vohs and colleagues (2008), Burger, Charness and Lynham (2010), Fedorikhin and Patrick (2010), Usta and Häubl (2010), and Bucciol and Piovesan (2011). Bucciol, Landini and Piovesan (2013) find that exposure to temptation reduces the productivity of young children, aged 6 to 13, but not older children. This is in keeping with the findings of the Mischel studies described earlier.

However, the empirical evidence regarding the costs of self-control and its effects is sometimes surprising and conflicting. Myrseth, Fishbach and Trope (2009) and Zhang and Shrum (2009) find that self-control improves when temptation is present. Grubliauskiene and Dewitte (2014) and Duh, Grubliauskiene and Dewitte (2016) also suggest that pre-exposure to temptation can increase self-control, in both adults and children, by preparing them mentally to resist. Thus we are presented with a view of self-control that is analogous to physical ability. In the short term it declines with use as physical resources are exhausted, but over the long term it can increase as the body adapts to the stress.

Van Dillen, Papies and Hofmann (2013) propose that the effect of cognitive load and self-control is mediated by an attention factor. They concede that cognitive load may reduce self-control once the tempting good has already received attention from the consumer, but propose that, if attention is diverted from the good before it becomes tempting, self-control may not be affected. Thus a conference delegate immersed in a scientific discussion with a colleague may notice a chocolate cake at the buffet, but not be tempted like a typical holiday tourist.

Burger, Charness and Lynham (2010) study procrastination by students, and report two main findings. First, unlike previous studies, they find that the imposition of interim deadlines for a fairly long-term project (five weeks) does not improve performance in terms of completing a given task. Second, they find that in the short term over a two-day period, exposure to temptation reduces productivity in the first day, but actually increases the probability of completing a task over the whole two-day period. The authors suggest that this may be due either to the self-signaling effect of exerting willpower, or to the suffering on the first day creating a commitment to persevere and 'see things through' on the second day.

Fedorikhin and Patrick (2010) find that although positive mood generally facilitates resistance to temptation as far as healthy food choices are concerned, any emotional arousal accompanying this mood can reduce this resistance by increasing the cognitive load. For example, the study indicates that watching an exciting video clip while in a positive mood is more likely to be associated with choosing M&Ms as an unhealthy snack rather than grapes as a healthier option. Thus it is not just the kind of mood, but also the intensity of feeling, that affects choice.

Another finding that is perhaps counter-intuitive comes from a recent study by Usta and Häubl (2010). One might expect the delegation of decision-making to others, such as physicians or financial advisers, to reduce the cognitive load and stress factor. However, the study finds that such delegation, while reducing actual decision-making effort, depletes self-regulatory resources and impairs subsequent ability for self-control. Even recalling past episodes of such delegation has the same effect. The authors propose that the reason for this is that delegation of decision-making poses a threat to self-esteem, in terms of viewing oneself as a free agent. In support of this reasoning, the study finds that the depletion of self-regulatory resources does not occur when subjects are given the opportunity to affirm their sense of free agency.

The Gailliot and colleagues (2007) study takes a reductionist approach, explaining the phenomenon of increasing costs of self-control in physiological terms: self-control relies on glucose (as do brain processes in general), and this is a limited energy source.

The study showed that acts of self-control, like coping with thoughts of death or stifling prejudice during an interracial interaction, reduced glucose levels, and this impaired self-control on subsequent tasks. Furthermore, consuming a glucose drink eliminated these impairments.

This kind of reductionist approach, coupled with neuroeconomic studies, is an important aid in discriminating between different theories related to intertemporal decision-making, and in particular achieving an understanding of TIPs. As can be seen from the studies surveyed above, much further research is necessary in this area in order to clarify a number of current issues.

## Evolutionary biology

Similar experiments to the ones described above have also been performed with non-human animals, such as rats and pigeons, in particular to test whether they also have TIPs and present bias (Ainslie, 1975). In general this appears to be the case, with individual differences between animals just as with humans, but once again there is a problem with confounds, since non-human animals may hold different prior probability distributions. Thus any observed preference reversals may still exhibit constant exponential discounting and not be irrational.

In terms of evolutionary biology, it might seem that basic neo-Darwinian principles would favor the evolution of a brain that is a cohesive entity. This would not necessarily rule out the possibility of brain modularity with different systems for different functions, but one might suppose that these systems would not be in conflict, as in multiple-self and dual-self models. However, there is now extensive evidence that such conflicts occur in various areas such as memory, information processing and motivation. The approach of Brocas and Carrillo (2008a and b), and the model of the brain they propose to account for the three conflicting areas of asymmetric information, temporal horizon and incentive salience, in many ways parallels the tradition in economics of modeling the firm as a nexus of agents with conflicting objectives. Yet this raises the fundamental issue: why would the process of natural selection favor the evolution of a brain with such inbuilt conflicting systems?

Different scientists from different disciplines have approached this problem from different angles, exhibiting a remarkable degree of consilience. The ethologist and evolutionary biologist Dawkins (1976) argues that selection occurs primarily at the level of the gene, and this is bound to result in conflicts at the level of the individual. Related to this is the fact that most of the genetic material within our bodies is actually 'foreign', for example the bacteria in the gut, without which we could not survive. The evolutionary psychologists Tooby and Cosmides (1992) argue that many of our internal conflicts are a consequence of our evolutionary past, and are no longer adaptations, in the same way as our taste for sugary, fatty foods is no longer adaptive for humans living in developed societies. The economist and dietitian Arthur de Vany (2011) argues along similar lines, in particular proposing that the brain's demand for glucose is often in conflict with the tendency of the pancreas to release more insulin which reduces the glucose level in the blood, storing it in muscle and fat tissues rather than letting it go to the brain. He attributes the conflict to the modern over-availability of simple carbohydrate, high glucose foods that send our insulin soaring and then crashing. De Vany credits his ideas in turn to a work by Peters and colleagues (2004), which presents a neuroeconomic model of competition for energy resources. Wang and Mariman (2008) focus on the physiological consequences of this competition, proposing that the modern tendency towards insulin resistance, leading to type-2 diabetes, obesity and associated health problems, is a result of the brain's strategy to protect its supply of glucose. However, the result of this internal competition need not necessarily be bad. Livnat and Pippenger (2006) show that competition between different sub-systems may actually lead to improved biological outcomes, just as in a free market economy competition tends to improve welfare.

Moving on to more specific aspects of evolutionary biology, it might at first appear that natural selection would favor constant exponential discounting over hyperbolic discounting and decreasing impatience. After all, how could TIPs serve as an adaptation in terms of improving our prospects of survival and reproduction? This is an issue where much research is still needed to clarify the situation. Robson and Samuelson (2009) propose that the existence of **aggregate uncertainty** can result in non-constant discounting and present bias with decreasing impatience; they claim this may be a more basic phenomenon that preference reversals. Aggregate uncertainty refers to systematic uncertainty where all individuals are faced with the same uncertainty, like the possibility of an earthquake or a flood. Unsystematic or idiosyncratic uncertainty is individual-specific, like the possibility of being attacked or robbed. Robson and Samuelson argue that evolution has caused us to have the belief that idiosyncratic uncertainty is controllable, since we can often take steps to avoid these kinds of danger. Therefore we tend to have a greater fear of uncontrollable aggregate uncertainty. However, they conclude that although this can account for present bias, it should not lead to preference reversals.

It has also been proposed that in our ancestral past there was a lack of savings technology. An animal recently hunted and killed had to be eaten very quickly before the meat deteriorated. This is an obvious cause of present bias. A more sophisticated theory suggests that an ultimate cause of hyperbolic discounting is the survival advantage of being able to quickly access mentally ratios related to the probability of relative amounts of food in foraging patches or the relative size of rival groups. Thinking in terms of ratios means that the difference between one and two days (weeks, months or years) in the future is the same as the difference between two and four days, not two and three days. This provides the mathematical basis for hyperbolic discounting versus exponential discounting.

## Neuroeconomic studies

Studies in the 1990s by Damasio (1994), LeDoux (1996) and Bechara and colleagues (1999) tended to support the psychological theories of dual systems of decision-making as far as temporal horizon is concerned. Damasio showed that patients with damage in the ventromedial prefrontal cortex had an impaired ability to engage in long-term planning while appearing emotionally flat, meaning that events that would normally make people happy or sad did not seem to register with them emotionally. LeDoux and Bechara both provided evidence that the amygdala played a crucial role in the expression of impulsive and emotional behavior. Bechara (2005) has also gone on to distinguish between an impulsive system (mainly the ventral striatum and amygdala) that processes information about immediate rewards, and a reflective system (mainly the ventromedial and dorsolateral prefrontal cortex and anterior cingulate) which processes information about future rewards. This in many ways parallels the 'planner–doer' model of Thaler and Shefrin (1981) in terms of principal and agent, and is also similar in this way to the model proposed by Brocas and Carrillo (2008a).

McClure and colleagues (2004) take the analysis one step further. Using the fMRI technique, they found that decisions relating to immediately available rewards involve the preferential activation of parts of the limbic system associated with the midbrain dopamine system, including the paralimbic cortex. In contrast, with intertemporal choices generally, regions of the lateral prefrontal cortex and posterior parietal cortex are engaged uniformly. The study also found that:

> The relative engagement of the two systems is directly associated with the subjects' choices, with greater relative fronto-parietal activity when subjects choose longer term options (p. 503).

The authors hypothesize that:

> short-run impatience is therefore driven by the limbic system, which responds preferentially to immediate rewards and is less sensitive to the value of future rewards, whereas long-run patience is mediated by the lateral pre-frontal cortex and associated structures, which are able to evaluate trade-offs between abstract rewards, including rewards in the more distant future. (p. 504)

McClure and colleagues (2004) conclude that the interaction between short-sighted and far-sighted systems provides neuroscientific support for hyperbolic discounting.

The evidence in this study is also supported by comparisons with advanced primates, who have substantially smaller prefrontal cortexes than humans, and with subjects with prefrontal brain damage. In both cases individuals are heavily influenced by the availability of immediate rewards, and are unable to delay gratification or plan ahead.

However, the conclusions of McClure and colleagues (2004) have been challenged by Glimcher and colleagues (2007) and Glimcher (2009). They argue that there is no compelling evidence for concluding that the brain is divided into emotional and rational areas, and that in monkeys research has shown that activity in the posterior parietal cortex predicts preferences for both immediate and delayed rewards, with no suggestion of the existence of dual systems. It should be noted that Glimcher does not doubt the notion that emotions affect decision-making; he suggests, like Bechara, that the amygdala may be involved in this respect.

More recent research by Heatherton and Wagner (2011) and Lopez and colleagues (2014) provides conflicting evidence, supporting the dual system hypothesis. Using fMRI data they conclude that temptation rewards are processed by an impulsive system, in particular the nucleus accumbens, and that activation of this system may in turn activate the opposing self-control system based on the prefrontal cortex (PFC). In view of these conflicting studies it is clear that more research is needed at the neurological level to clarify the situation regarding the role of different brain areas in the context of temptation and self-control.

Some research in neuroeconomics relates to other aspects of intertemporal decision-making which have important policy implications, for example general inhibitory mechanisms related to temptation. Berkman, Burklund and Lieberman (2009) propose that there is a general inhibitory network in the brain, and show that inhibitory signals are not completely task specific, but can spill over to unrelated domains and result in unintentional inhibition of unrelated responses, termed an 'inhibitory spillover effect'. Tuk and colleagues (2015) provide evidence supporting this hypothesis by observing subjects performing simultaneous tasks requiring self-control, concluding that the strength depletion model does not apply to simultaneous task situations.

Another area of neuroeconomic research relates to dietary habits. Rangel (2013) examines problems people have with dieting and finds that there are certain vicious circles of cause and effect that make dieting especially difficult from a physiological viewpoint. First, there is the problem of homeostasis, in that after dieting for a while people tend to 'plateau', as their metabolic rate slows down to adjust to the lower calorie intake. This slowdown is mitigated by neural factors and the endocrine system. Another problem is that a bad diet, in terms of eating a lot of junk food, can cause cognitive impairment, which then reinforces the bad diet. The junk food can also cause problems related to insulin control, more specifically a 'roller-coaster' ride of high blood glucose after eating followed by low blood glucose after the insulin is released, which in turn causes neural signals to eat more sugar. These problems related to obesity are discussed further in the section on policy implications.

## 8.7  Policy implications

There are a number of normative aspects as far as policy implications are concerned that arise from the models of intertemporal choice discussed here. These relate to individuals, firms and governments.

### Individuals

We have seen that the main implication of the various models presented in this chapter is that people have self-control problems, meaning dynamic conflicts over time causing preference reversals. These problems relate in particular to temptation, where we switch from preferring a larger benefit later to a smaller benefit sooner, and procrastination, where we switch from preferring a smaller cost sooner to a larger cost later. In both cases we come to regret our decisions later in retrospect, because we are not optimizing our behavior. An example from the DellaVigna and Malmendier (2006) study described earlier is the finding that 80% of monthly members of the health clubs ended up paying more per visit on average than they would have paid if they had chosen a different option of paying for ten-visit blocks, because they overestimated their gym usage. Furthermore, the study found evidence that these members did not learn from their mistakes, by changing their membership plan later once they realized their low usage; instead they continued with their monthly plans. They were also slow to cancel their monthly memberships, with an average delay of over two months between last gym visit and cancellation, losing even more money. This situation is discussed in more detail in Case 8.1.

Failure to optimize behavior also arises in situations where people tend to underestimate usage. Miravete (2003) examined people's choice of telephone calling plan when South Central Bell changed their tariff structure. The new structure involved either paying a flat monthly rate, or paying a fixed rate plus call charges. Again the study finds that many people chose the wrong option, but in this case people tended to be quicker to learn from their mistakes. Whereas 40% of people initially chose the wrong option, paying too much, two months later this proportion was reduced to 33%. Not all studies of situations where naïve consumers underestimate usage present such an optimistic picture. Heidhues and Köszegi (2010) find that naïve consumers overborrow on both credit cards and subprime mortgages, where the baseline repayment terms are cheap. However, there are large penalties for delaying repayment, and the study finds that these consumers end up paying the penalties, thus suffering large welfare losses.

It is important to realize that the issues above related to present bias and optimization do not arise with the constant exponential discounting of the DUM. With the constant discounting model, as stated earlier, there is no conflict between short term and long term: one path of action will at all times seem preferable. The only exception to this is the situation where people have heavy-tailed prior probability distributions for delay, as we have seen; in this case long-term rewards are expected further and further into the future as time goes on, and it therefore makes sense to switch to the SS reward. In the example where one yields to the temptation of having the dessert one had previously not intended to have, according to the DUM one will at all times either want the dessert or not want it; there is no scope for the exertion of willpower. If the discounted benefits of eating the dessert exceed the discounted costs one will indulge, and if they do not then one will not indulge. The important implication here, discussed extensively by Ainslie (2001) in his book *Breakdown of Will*, is that in the DUM the concepts of temptation and willpower are redundant. Of course, present bias is not the only factor related to non-optimization in some cases; overconfidence and self-serving bias are also relevant.

The role of **self-awareness** is always important in good decision-making, and it is particularly important in the context of self-control situations. Psychological conflict arises because the subject will normally remember that their preference in the past was different, and, if the subject is sufficiently self-aware, they will also realize that in the future they will come to regret their action if they indulge, because from that future standpoint, discounted costs exceeded discounted benefits.

The main implication of self-awareness is that people will make commitments to prevent them from taking later actions that fall into the category of 'vices'. We have already seen some examples of this, relating to buying an alarm clock that is difficult to turn off, and buying a small bag of chips rather than a large one. Plentiful evidence of such commitments provides a 'smoking gun' as far as hyperbolic discounting, TIPs, and self-awareness are concerned. Ancient references to such commitment devices include the story of Ulysses ordering his shipmates to tie him to the mast so that he could listen to the song of the sirens without being lured onto the rocks and shipwrecked. Burnham and Phelan (2001) provide some off-the-wall modern examples: smearing one's brownie with mayonnaise when given lunch on a plane, and posting one's internet cable to oneself. Both actions are designed to prevent later indulgence when preferences have changed, but obviously they are only possible if a certain degree of self-awareness is present. Other common forms of commitment involve the use of whole life insurance policies and illiquid savings accounts, paying health club memberships for a year where there is no refund or cancellation option, leaving one's credit card at home when going shopping, or using a debit card instead of a credit card (King and King, 2011).

A good example of commitment from sophisticated subjects concerns an experiment conducted by Ariely and Wertenbroch (2002). This involved executive education students at MIT, who had to write three papers in a semester for a particular class. One group was given evenly spaced deadlines throughout the semester for the three papers, while the other group was allowed to select their own deadlines. The penalty for an overdue paper was the same in each case. Although it was possible for the second group to have made all their papers due at the end of the semester, in the experiment many did in fact commit to spacing out their deadlines. It was also notable that those who did have evenly spaced deadlines, whether externally or internally imposed, performed better than those who did not. Thus it appears that the more sophisticated subjects, who foresaw self-control problems, made the commitment involving evenly spaced deadlines, and as a result improved their welfare.

As already stated, people generally lie somewhere in the middle of the spectrum of self-awareness, and O'Donoghue and Rabin (2001) introduced a model of partial self-awareness that accounts for various aspects of observed behavior, although it was specifically designed to account for the phenomenon of procrastination. In this model people are aware that they will have self-control problems in the future, but they underestimate the magnitude of the problems. The authors observe that, when people choose from a menu of options involving costs and benefits at different times in the future, they may now eschew an option involving immediate action and relatively small benefits in favor of an option involving action and greater benefits in the long term. However, later on, they may forsake the latter option in favor of another option that involves action and even greater benefits still further in the future. Thus preferences may constantly shift, with actions continuously being delayed. For example, we may decide not to tidy the garage this week, because we plan to redecorate it next month. Next month we may decide that redecoration of the garage is not as important as fencing the garden. While this model cannot explain all types of procrastination, for example where a given task is continuously delayed, it does have important policy implications. The same authors have investigated other causes of procrastination (O'Donoghue and Rabin, 2008), and find that procrastination is more likely in multistage projects when the costs of completing the different stages are more unequal, and in particular when the later stages are more costly. Furthermore, if the cost structure is endogenous, people are prone to choose cost structures with lower costs early on, but this is likely to cause them to start but not finish projects. Commitment to finish rather than just start projects is an important policy implication in this case.

Another interesting example of commitment has been researched by Frank and Hutchens (1993), and involves the preference for rising wage profiles. This preference has been discussed earlier, and is also the subject of Case 8.3. It is argued that the main pressure for rising wage and consumption profiles is a social one, and that if the workers involved can commit to restricting their wages in the short term in return for the promise of higher wages later in their careers, they can improve their welfare. Although the authors admit that their evidence is insubstantial quantitatively, it is highly suggestive. To our knowledge there has been no extensive study of the phenomenon discussed by Frank and Hutchens, and it is probable that the primary reason for this is the lack of available data for a wide range of professions.

All of the examples of commitment described to this point involve deliberate actions. There have also been a number of studies, particularly in the psychology literature, where commitment does not involve such action, but instead involves the automatic involvement of the emotions. Although economists such as Becker and Akerlof had broached this subject earlier, Hirshleifer (1987) and Frank (1988) were the first economists to develop a formal theory of the emotions as commitment, based on game theory. Since that time there has been considerable input from various fields, including political scientists, psychologists and neuroscientists. Until the work of Hirshleifer and Frank there had been much puzzlement regarding the usefulness of emotions such as anger, envy and hatred, all of which are commonly viewed as 'negative' emotions, in contrast to the 'positive' emotions such as love, joy and pride. Negative emotions often caused people to take actions that were self-destructive, and therefore they seemed to serve no Darwinian purpose, meaning that it was difficult to see why they had evolved. The main contribution of Hirshleifer and Frank was to propose a theory that such emotions served as a credible commitment, deterring others from taking advantage of us. Thus, although such emotions might cause short-term harm (and long-term harm in individuals where they are excessive), in most individuals they serve to promote our long-term welfare.

A number of misunderstandings tend to occur regarding the Hirshleifer–Frank model. First of all, there is a difference between the capacity to feel an emotion and the actual feeling of the emotion. As Elster (1998) has observed, an irascible person may rarely feel anger, because others may take care not to provoke the person's anger. To correct another misunderstanding, the theory does not mean that the capacity for anger is always 'good' for us, anymore than the capacity for pain is always good for us; it simply means that on average it has served people well in the past, or in biological terms it has improved our inclusive fitness. The theory also does not mean that we should always display anger when it is provoked; sometimes it is better to keep calm, particularly in view of social conventions.

Finally, it should be noted that emotions would not be necessary as commitment devices if the DUM and constant discounting were applicable. According to the DUM, if someone offends us, a 'rational' calculation of self-interest will tell us how to react, in terms of whether to punish the offender, how and when; there is no conflict between short-term and long-term interests.

Hyperbolic discounting models may describe such situations well in many cases, but as far as lending insight into their nature and normative aspects, multiple-self models have a significant advantage. This is because they can highlight the essential asymmetry involved between the current or myopic self and the meta-self that is at least partially aware of future changes in preferences. As already stated, the meta-self can make strategic commitments to constrain the later behavior of the myopic self, but the reverse cannot happen. For example the person who finds it difficult to rise in the morning may place the alarm clock on the other side of the room to ensure that the myopic self does not simply slam it off immediately it rings the next morning, but the myopic self cannot reply in any strategic manner to such a commitment.

Commitments can be either external or internal. External commitments, once made, become less controllable by the individual, and therefore are most effective because they do not depend so much on the person's willpower. Putting money into an illiquid life insurance policy is an example. Some people even using blogging as an external commitment, since public announcements of intention involve a loss of face if the person then reneges on their commitment. The disadvantage of external commitments is that they lack flexibility if a person's circumstances change. Internal commitments involve making personal or private rules, for example saving 10% of one's salary every month, but these are more vulnerable to temptation.

For individuals therefore, the key to maximizing experienced utility over the long run may be the use of appropriate strategic commitment devices that constrain the future desires of the myopic self. It is also important, as we have seen, that the meta-self is aware of the changing preferences that inevitably occur. Of course, it will never be possible for any meta-self to have rational expectations to the extent that all future preferences will be accurately predicted; however, the more able people are to learn from past experience regarding such changes, the more likely it is that they will be successful in anticipating future changes and conflicts, and taking appropriate action.

A further implication of the fact that agents have only incomplete information about future preferences is that abstinence may be a better policy than moderate consumption, as illustrated in Case 5.1. In situations involving the possibility of addiction, such as gambling, smoking or drinking, an abstinence rule, though a second-best rule, can act as a commitment device against inefficient learning that would lead to future excesses (Carrillo, 2004).

However, there is a final twist to this situation that we have also touched on earlier, and this relates to self-signaling. When the self-control problem is repeated, as is often the case, a yielding to temptation (or 'defection') in the first round can lead to a loss of self-confidence, thus making defection more likely in the next round and so on. Thus a far-seeing self may envisage the likely succession of failures if too harsh a rule is made initially, and decide instead to adopt a less strict policy as far as commitment is concerned. This aspect relates to a more general issue of planning for the future, where again there are counterintuitive conclusions. Townsend and Liu (2012) report that in a number of experiments planning does not benefit everyone. In particular, it does not benefit those who are in poor goal-standing related to past goals and achievements. Planning may instead set themselves up for failure, since it will cause emotional stress which in turn will detract from their performance.

It is therefore difficult to draw definite conclusions regarding how individuals should make commitments in self-control situations. The main general conclusion is that those agents who know themselves, and can predict their future selves, best are also best able to maximize their own welfare in terms of experienced utility.

One other aspect of self-control problems that has important policy implications concerns the effects of diminishing marginal sensitivity and shifting reference points. For controlling food intake there are a number of relevant factors in particular:

1   There is a multisensory system in operation, involving visual, olfactory and gustatory senses. The interdependence of seeing, smelling and tasting foods is not well-known at present, but it may be possible that if just one of these senses suffers from diminishing sensitivity in eating a meal, this may override the other senses. On the other hand, diminishing sensitivity may only occur when all three senses are affected.

2    The phenomenon of diminishing marginal sensitivity is highly specific to different foods (Epstein et al., 2009). People who eat meals with more varied foods, or whose intake in general is more varied, tend to eat more in total. This is especially true of sugary and fatty foods, where a large number of convenient snacks are available. When we eat a monotonous diet we eat less as diminishing sensitivity sets in much earlier.

3    People vary as to how much they can consume before diminishing sensitivity occurs. There is evidence that obese people are not affected until larger intakes are consumed (Epstein et al., 1997; Temple et al., 2007). This may be because obese people have shifted their reference points to higher levels, or it may be an independent genetic factor in operation.

4    Diminishing sensitivity is delayed when people perform other activities while eating, like watching TV or reading a book (Epstein et al., 1997, 2005; Temple et al., 2007). This may be because these environmental distractors affect memory. People whose memories are impaired, such as amnesiacs, can eat one meal immediately after another.

There is a need for further research relating to these factors affecting diminishing marginal sensitivity, but some of the policy implications for people suffering from self-control problems with food intake are obvious.

Most of the policy implications described above relate to increasing self-control. Some more recent research has instead focused on the other side of the problem, reducing temptation. In some cases abstinence can achieve this, but other strategies are also possible. Papies and colleagues (2015) propose a strategy of 'mindful attention', which aims at regulating attention to view one's current thoughts and feelings as 'passing events in the mind'. Thus temptations lose their salience. A similar strategy is suggested by Milyavskaya and colleagues (2015), who adopt a neuroscientific approach based on the dual systems described in the previous section. They point out that temptation rewards are processed by an impulsive system, in particular the nucleus accumbens, and that activation of this system may in turn activate the opposing self-control system based on the PFC. Therefore they recommend increasing the 'want-to' motivation factor as a means of reducing activity in the impulsive system, which in turn means that there is no need for the self-control system to 'work harder'. Another recent study, by Mead and Patrick (2016), again recommends reducing temptation, in this case by a strategy of 'unspecific postponement' of a reward, which amounts to saying to oneself: 'I'll have it some other time.' This strategy also relies on self-signaling, so that successful postponement sends a message that one is strong enough to overcome temptation.

There is one other strategy that can be effective in reducing temptation, sometimes referred to as 'intermittent goal-striving' (Coelho do Vale, Pieters and Zeelenberg, 2016). This involves planned deviation from goal-oriented behavior in the short run in the pursuit of long-term goals. An example is a dieting program over three months, which allows for one day a week of 'bingeing'. Such deviations allow for the replenishment of self-regulatory resources, as well as positive mood feelings and an ability to develop coping strategies. The authors report that experimental evidence suggests that this type of strategy may help rather than hinder the achievement of long-term goals, as long as the deviations are planned.

## Firms

Many policy implications for firms are the flip side of those for individuals, since firms may be able to exploit the weaknesses of naïve consumers in particular, increasing their profits at the expense of consumer welfare. However, the picture is not quite so simple as this, since firms' policies aimed at the exploitation of naïve consumers may actually in turn be exploited by sophisticated consumers and benefit such consumers, as we shall see.

In general there has not been as much research relating to policy implications for firms as there has been for individual agents or governments. However, DellaVigna and Malmendier (2004) have shown that dynamic inconsistencies and other anomalies regarding timing of rewards and payment have important implications for contract design in the case of both **investment goods** and **leisure goods**. Investment goods are defined as those where there are immediate costs, in terms of money and effort, and delayed benefits, for example health club memberships. Leisure goods involve immediate benefits and delayed costs, such as credit card financing. DellaVigna and Malmendier (2004) construct sophisticated models of consumer and firm behavior, the mathematics of which are omitted here, and investigate various possibilities according to the degree of naiveté of consumers and different market conditions. They find that empirical evidence from various industries confirms the predictions of the models. The authors summarize their findings in terms of three main implications:

1  *Firms should price investment goods below marginal cost.*

   Naïve consumers tend to overestimate usage of such goods, and therefore overestimate the value of the discount on marginal cost. For example, in the health club industry it is common to have a zero marginal cost for users, who mainly pay annual or monthly fees (DellaVigna and Malmendier, 2006). Price discrimination cannot explain such a practice, since more frequent users with less elastic demand would be charged a higher per-usage price, and this type of strategy by firms is not commonly observed. As far as sophisticated consumers are concerned, they can use the high initial cost as a form of commitment. This situation is examined in more detail in Case 8.1.

2  *Firms should price leisure goods above marginal cost.*

   In this case naïve consumers underestimate future usage, for example credit card financing. They are therefore attracted by offers that have favorable initial terms. Sophisticated consumers can take advantage of this by paying off their outstanding balances each month, and therefore borrowing for up to six weeks free of charge, since many card companies do not charge annual fees. Mobile phone companies have similar charging schemes, with free minutes per month, but high charges for excess time. Naïve consumers may be attracted by the free minutes, but tend to underestimate their phone usage and may therefore end up paying high monthly bills. Mail order firms use similar attractive offers with free books or CDs, but high charges for additional items. DellaVigna and Malmendier (2004) note a slightly different strategy in the gambling industry. In this case hotels, notably in Las Vegas, charge attractive low rates for accommodation and dining, since naïve gamblers underestimate their gambling activity and losses. Thus for the hotels the gambling activity subsidizes their core business. Again, sophisticated consumers can take advantage of this strategy by staying and dining in the hotels, but take in shows or play golf rather than gamble.

3  *Firms should charge back-loaded fees and introduce switching costs for all goods.*

   It is common for credit card companies to have introductory or 'teaser' offers, like zero interest rate charges on balance transfers for limited periods like six months. After the initial period the interest rates usually rise very significantly, typically to about 10% above prime or base rates. As we have already seen in the study by Heidhues and Kőszegi (2010), such a strategy is profitable since naïve consumers underestimate the amount of their borrowing after the teaser period is over (Ausubel, 1999). **Switching costs** relate to the costs, both in money and effort, of either switching to a new provider or cancelling the agreement. For example health clubs typically offer automatic renewal, and only allow members to cancel their memberships in person or by letter, rather than by email or by phone. The result is that users tend to remain members longer than otherwise. DellaVigna and Malmendier (2004) found that there was an average period of over two months between a member's last usage and the cancellation of their membership.

DellaVigna and Malmendier also draw conclusions regarding the welfare effects of these policy implications. They observe that, for sophisticated consumers, market interactions need not reduce their welfare. In fact they may gain if they are in effect being subsidized by naïve consumers, as is the case with credit card financing. In addition, market mechanisms encourage firms to create commitment devices that allow sophisticated consumers to increase their long-run welfare, for example by investing in life insurance policies. However, for naïve consumers who have non-rational expectations, two adverse welfare effects are noted. First, there is an overall reduction in efficiency in terms of net surplus to consumers and producers. Second, in monopoly there is a redistribution of surplus from consumers to producers, who are able to take advantage of the lack of consumer awareness to increase their profits. In perfect competition the second effect is eliminated, but this situation rarely arises in reality. These adverse effects on the welfare of naïve consumers also have implications for government policy which are discussed shortly.

Another area where there are policy implications is the effects of promotions. Although many aspects of promotions have been discussed in earlier chapters, one factor that has not yet been mentioned concerns their effect on the patience of consumers. Shaddy and Lee (2012) find that promotions make consumers both more willing to spend money to avoid waiting and less willing to wait to obtain additional money. Of course, this is not necessarily a good thing for firms, since we have seen that promotions may have a damaging effect on brand loyalty, increasing consumer fickleness.

There are also policy implications in principal-agent situations. Yilmaz (2013) conducted a study comparing exponential discounters with sophisticated hyperbolic discounters and found that, when facing a sophisticated agent, it is optimal for the principal to reward the good performance more and punish the bad performance more in the early period, relative to the optimal wage scheme for a time-consistent agent.

## Government

The models of intertemporal choice presented in this chapter have significant implications for a number of areas of government policy. The following aspects are now discussed: (1) incomplete self-knowledge; (2) addiction; (3) savings; (4) investment; (5) social security; (6) social projects; (7) environmental policy; (8) recreational drugs; and (9) food consumption and obesity.

In many areas some kind of 'nudge' policy is possible; in the words of Thaler and Sunstein (2009), this means trying to 'influence choices in a way that will make choosers better off, *as judged by themselves*'. The italics are the authors' own, to draw emphasis to the last part of the definition, and yet this aspect is still often misunderstood by critics. The nudge concept is discussed further at the end of the section.

**1**    *Incomplete self-knowledge*

DellaVigna and Malmendier (2004) have shown that naïve consumers are not able to maximize their welfare, even if there is perfect competition. There is a role for a paternalistic government to intervene in such situations, if it can obtain more information regarding the future preferences of these consumers than the consumers themselves. Heidhues and Köszegi (2010) recommend the prohibition of large penalties for deferring small amounts of repayment, and recent regulations in the US credit card and mortgage markets have indeed moved in this direction. While this may be possible in some circumstances, the information requirements for policy intervention are large, and even then intervention may not be a complete remedy. It may well be that, as DellaVigna and Malmendier recommend, the best policy is to educate naïve consumers as far as possible regarding their lack of self-awareness. Duflo, Kremer and Robinson (2011) examined the behavior of Kenyan farmers investing in fertilizer, finding that they exhibited present bias and tend to procrastinate by delaying purchases. They estimate that an appropriate government policy for maximizing average welfare is to offer small, time-limited discounts, rather than either allowing a free market or paying large subsidies.

2    *Addiction*

Addiction is of course one specific area where incomplete self-knowledge is relevant. However, there are certain tax implications in this case that have been ignored by the main body of public finance literature. Of particular interest here is a study by Gruber and Köszegi (2001), which arrives at two main conclusions. First, there is evidence that smokers are forward-looking in their smoking decisions, in that announced but not yet effective tax increases lead to both increased sales and reduced consumption. This apparently contradictory behavior implies that smokers are rational to the extent of buying more while the price is lower, while at the same time reducing consumption in anticipation of the price rise. Second, given the empirical evidence regarding TIPs, there is a justification for basing taxes not only on the external costs imposed by smokers but also on the internalities that they impose on themselves. Internal costs for smoking are far greater than external ones, with the study estimating that a pack of cigarettes costs $30.45 in terms of lost life expectancy. The authors estimate that optimal internality taxes are probably at least $1 per pack in the USA.

3    *Savings*

Naïve individuals tend to overestimate their ability to save for the future and do not take advantage of available commitment devices to help them save more. Laibson (1997) has argued that as new and liquid financial instruments have proliferated since the 1980s, due to the deregulation of banking systems in various countries, this problem has been aggravated. While deregulation may have increased competition and efficiency, one undesirable result has been that many automatic commitment devices in the form of illiquid savings instruments have disappeared. The policy implications are further complicated by changes in mandatory retirement laws in many countries. Diamond and Köszegi (2003) use a multiple-self model to argue that recent changes may cause people to save more in order to retire earlier. Governments, however, often want people to retire later in order to reduce the financial burden on public finances. Trying to encourage people both to save more and to retire later is a major problem facing many governments. A Danish study by Chetty and colleagues (2014) suggests that a policy of raising retirement contributions through passive decisions, such as automatic increases in employer contributions, is more successful in increasing total savings than subsidies that involve active decisions to invest in retirement accounts, which mainly result in a switch of funds from one account to another. There is also some evidence that those who are most financially illiterate tend to have higher discount rates (Meier and Sprenger, 2013); thus they may discount the benefits of having financial information and choose to remain illiterate in this respect. The problem of inadequate saving has been particularly prevalent in the UK since 2010, where household saving has fallen from nearly 6% of disposable income to −1%. In response to this, and the concerns expressed by the Bank of England, the Financial Conduct Authority and debt charities, both the major political parties have pledged in their election manifestos to give debtors more legal protection from bailiffs, charges and interest, and give them more 'breathing space' in which to settle their debts. Although this may relieve hardship in the short run, the problem with this type of policy is that once again it creates moral hazard, incentivizing households to take on yet more debt. It would appear that improving financial literacy is a better long-run policy in this case. Further implications of the savings problem for government policy are discussed in Case 8.2.

**4**    *Investment*

We have seen that TIPs can lead to procrastination. Entrepreneurs who are sophisticated in terms of being aware of this tendency may make the commitment of foregoing free information in order to avoid procrastination and invest now. Brocas and Carrillo (2004) argue that this phenomenon may lead to excessive investment in the economy and entry mistakes. They further argue that government intervention, forcing investors to acquire information before making investment decisions, may reduce interest rates and lead to an overall improvement in welfare in the economy as a whole.

**5**    *Social security*

People receiving social security benefits, in cash or in other forms, tend to receive these benefits on either a weekly or a monthly basis. Cash benefits are usually paid weekly. However, the food stamp program in the USA operates on a monthly basis. Providing benefits in the form of food stamps is in itself an automatic commitment mechanism, since it prevents recipients from using the benefits to buy goods regarded as undesirable by the government. However, given a self-control problem and a lack of other forms of commitment, monthly provision may lead to excessive consumption in the first part of the month. Shapiro (2005) provides evidence that caloric intake declines by 10% to 15% over the food stamp month, providing further evidence for TIPs and against the permanent income hypothesis. It may therefore be that this program would improve welfare if it operated on a weekly basis, although these improvements would have to be balanced against the increased transaction costs for both recipients and government.

**6**    *Social projects*

Such projects relate to major infrastructure investments, like building roads, schools, hospitals, power stations and railways. Governments must determine an appropriate official discount rate to apply to costs and benefits in order to make optimal investment decisions. Evans and Sezer (2004) observe that countries have used very different approaches in this area. For example, Germany bases its 3% real rate on financial market data, while France has applied an 8% real rate based on the marginal product of capital. In 2003 the UK switched from a 6% real rate, based mainly on the cost of capital, to a 3.5% real rate based entirely on social time preference, which Evans and Sezer argue is the appropriate rate to use. For public investment decisions it might initially seem that TIPs and self-control problems may not apply, but governments may also be inclined to place short-run electoral benefits before longer-run budgetary considerations. In this case they might use high official discount rates. Evans and Sezer examined official discount rates and estimated social time preference rates (STPRs) in six major countries: Australia, France, Germany, Japan, the UK and the USA. The only major country where the official discount rate is less than the estimated STPR is Germany, where the 3% official discount rate is less than the estimated STPR of 4.1%. France appears to have a large discrepancy, applying the rate of 8% whereas the estimated STPR is only 3.5%. Such a policy could lead to severe public underinvestment, to the cost of future generations.

**7**    *Environmental policy*

This is another area where bad decisions can harm future generations. Once again procrastination is a major problem. There are on the one hand good reasons for waiting until reliable evidence is available before making major global decisions that could impose large and immediate costs. However, some authors have argued that TIPs have been one of the main problems of enforcing and enlarging the scope of the Kyoto protocol (Winkler, 2006). Additional problems are involved here, relating to the 'tragedy of the commons' situation, discussed in Chapter 9, and the degree of uncertainty. It is argued by Newell and Pizer (2003) that this uncertainty also relates to appropriate future interest rates used for discounting purposes, and that such rates should be much lower than the present rate, being only a half of this rate in a hundred years. These authors estimate that such a procedure would nearly double the net present value of the benefits of environmental protection policies.

**8    *Recreational drugs***

Historically US laws have been very strict regarding sales of such drugs, imposing severe penalties, but not so strict regarding possession. This policy may have a perverse effect on behavior, as noted by Fudenberg and Levine (2006). Severe penalties have the effect of increasing the fixed cost of making a transaction, causing consumers to buy larger quantities in each transaction. Such stockpiling is likely to lead to greater consumption, as we saw in the hypothetical example involving potato chips. Fudenberg and Levine, along with other economists, have therefore recommended legalization of such 'temptation' goods, combined with a high excise tax, similar to the policies used in many countries in relation to cigarettes. Such a policy provides a greater incentive to reduce consumption of harmful products.

**9    *Food consumption and obesity***

Obesity is an increasing global problem, and is discussed in more detail in Case 10.4. Over a third of US adults are estimated to be obese, defined as having a body mass index (BMI) over 30. The costs of obesity are difficult to estimate, for two main reasons. First, it is related to many different medical conditions and adverse health effects, notably heart disease and type-2 diabetes, but also conditions such as hypertension, liver disease and joint problems. The second reason is that obesity incurs both direct costs on health and medical services, often funded by governments, and indirect costs, such as increased absenteeism from work, disabilities and lower productivity, incurred by individuals and employers. In the USA the direct costs of obesity-related illness in terms of medical care have been estimated at $190 billion, or over 20% of all medical spending (Cawley and Meyerhoefer, 2012). Furthermore, it has been estimated that as much as 90% of obesity is preventable through appropriate lifestyle and nutrition policies. This issue thus presents a huge challenge to governments. Most experts stress that the problem is highly complex, and that solving it requires a multifactorial approach, involving environmental, social, geographical, and educational components, as well as medical and economic.

It can be claimed that obesity is often the result of TIPs, and people yielding to the temptation of a smaller sooner reward. Therefore, in general, correctional policies involve either making this reward smaller or making the later reward larger. Education of the public, in the broadest sense, is necessary to convey the message. However, when we move on to policy specifics, many problems arise. Two general problems are that in many countries and cultures obesity has become a social norm, with no stigma attached (Lin and McFerran, 2012), and that people react negatively to government communications perceived as attempts to persuade or coerce (Liu and Fitzsimons, 2013).

One line of policy to combat the problem is a traditional one in economic terms: taxes on offending goods. These are now being implemented in some countries, particularly on high-sugar soft drinks. However, the evidence for their effectiveness has not been forthcoming, even with taxes as high as 17.5% (Wansink, Hanks and Just, 2012; Shah et al., 2013). This may seem surprising given the availability of low-calorie substitutes. The Shah and colleagues study did indicate that stigma may be more effective at deterring consumption.

Another line of policy concerns food labeling. There are some important framing effects here. Nutrient information, including calorie content, is often ignored as being too much to read and interpret in a supermarket shopping situation (although online shoppers may welcome this). The principle of cognitive ease is again relevant here. In this context, star ratings, or color codes, provided they are not ambiguous, may be useful (Rohr et al., 2015). Perhaps even more useful are exercise equivalents in terms of calories burned (Goswami and Urminsky, 2015).

Food labeling is a clear example of a nudge policy. At this point a more detailed account of the nature of nudges is necessary, especially since there is some misunderstanding and controversy regarding their use. Nudges refer to strategies that manipulate the **choice architecture** of the decision-maker in order to promote choices that individuals would judge as being best for themselves under conditions of perfect information, unlimited cognitive abilities, and perfect self-control. The concept of choice architecture is central to nudging, and refers to the framing of the decision environment. This may include visual design, sound or musical factors, the positioning of potential purchase items, listing of choices on a menu and types of anchor. According to the invariance principle of the NM these should have no effect on decisions, but, as we have already seen in many chapters, there is a large body of empirical evidence that contradicts this axiom.

When the concept of a nudge was originally promoted in the eponymous book by Thaler and Sunstein (2009) the authors pointed out that there was one common false assumption and two common misconceptions regarding the concept. The false assumption is that almost all people, almost all of the time, make choices that are in their best interest or at the very least are better, by their own lights, than the choices that would be made by third parties. Again, there is abundant evidence that this is invalid, for example: around 20% of people in developed countries are now classified as obese; in the USA there are about 500,000 premature deaths each year caused by alcohol and cigarette consumption; drinkers and smokers are willing to pay third parties, like Alcoholics Anonymous, to help them choose better consumption sets.

Libertarians sometimes argue that people should still be free to make their own choices even if these turn out to be bad ones. The counter to this argument involves the two misconceptions referred to above. The first misconception is that there is a viable alternative to nudging. In reality there is always some kind of choice architecture, even if this is not deliberately manipulated, and although we may regard this as 'neutral', this is often a status quo, or worse, undesirable. For example, consider the following choices facing a cafeteria owner in terms of arranging the food:

1   Arrange the food so as to make people better off.
2   Arrange the food randomly.
3   Arrange the food to make people as obese as possible.

The first option may appear paternalistic, but the other two seem undesirable in terms of customer welfare.

The second misconception is that nudging involves some kind of coercion, like limiting people's choice of options or imposing costs on them. Some government policies definitely do this, like banning smoking in public places or putting taxes on sugary drinks; however, the cafeteria owner does not impose costs on consumers by arranging the food to encourage the consumption of fruit and discourage the consumption of dessert. In other situations, like where a government changes the default option for a pension or healthcare plan, the additional costs are negligible in terms of the cognitive effort of opting out of the default option and selecting another alternative.

Thaler and Sunstein describe their approach as 'libertarian paternalism', where people are not forced into making decisions of a certain type, but are 'nudged' by the framing of the decision situation into making decisions that later on in retrospect they believe were in their best interests. They suggest that this is especially important in the areas of health care and saving for retirement. In particular, they are critical of recent legislative changes in US health care on a number of grounds, such as the randomization of default settings for choices and the offering of too many choices, which they suggest is confusing to many people. Furthermore, the authors suggest that the 'nudge' approach can be applied to a wide variety of social policies, such as environmental policy, involving fuel economy and electricity usage, smoking, littering, teenage pregnancy and filing tax returns.

Many economists have criticized the 'nudge' approach. As we have seen, some express the opinion that people should be free to make their own mistakes. Actually, this misses the point: nudge policies *do* leave people free to make their own mistakes, but they are less likely to make mistakes – if the government gets it right. This is where the true problem of nudge policies lies, in the law of unintended consequences. There is some evidence that this may occur in the health insurance market in the USA, if consumers are nudged to overcome inertia and make better individual choices. It has been estimated that the problem of adverse selection may be exacerbated, with less healthy people facing much higher premiums, and as a result there may be an aggregate welfare loss (Handel, 2013).

## 8.8  Summary

- There are many confounding factors involved in the measurement of time preference.
- Time preference does not appear to be a unitary psychological construct, since it does not satisfy the three main criteria of constancy, generality and correlation between different measures.
- It may be more useful to decompose time preference into three main elements: impulsivity, compulsivity, and inhibition.
- Hyperbolic discounting involves applying higher discount rates to time periods nearer in the future, and lower ones to periods further away.
- Hyperbolic discounting has become widely applied in behavioral economics because it describes empirical data much better than the exponential discounting of the DUM. In particular it explains TIPs, which are an anomaly in the DUM.
- The existence of TIPs is the cause of many self-control problems. This is particularly true when visceral factors are present.
- The main strategy used by individuals confronted with self-control problems is to make commitments. This is only possible for self-aware or sophisticated agents. External commitments involve less willpower than internal ones.
- The concepts of temptation and willpower are redundant in the DUM, since a particular path of action will always dominate preferences.
- Emotions are an important form of commitment. These are internal, but to a large extent uncontrollable. The expression of emotion is the controllable element.
- The main criticism of the hyperbolic discounting approach is that it is purely descriptive, and does not consider underlying psychological factors.
- Alternative behavioral models involve modifying the instantaneous utility function. Such models also can explain TIPs.
- More radical models involve the concepts of projection bias, mental accounting models, multiple-self models, dual-self models, and the procedural approach.
- Models should not be seen as being mutually exclusive; many can be complementary to each other, and may operate at different levels of explanation in a reductionist manner.

- There are a number of policy implications of these behavioral models, for individuals, firms, and governments. These relate particularly to self-control problems and commitment.
- Nudge policies may be useful for firms, and especially governments, to use in order to encourage consumers to behave in ways that are consistent with their long-term interests, and are later recognized by consumers as such.

## 8.9  Review questions

1   Describe the various confounding factors involved in the concept of time preference.
2   Explain the meaning of temptation and procrastination in terms of how they relate to inconsistent time preferences.
3   Explain how the $(\beta,\delta)$ model of quasi-hyperbolic discounting can explain preference reversals, using a numerical example.
4   Discuss the advantages and disadvantages of hyperbolic discounting.
5   Compare and contrast hyperbolic discounting and visceral factor models as approaches to explaining preference reversals.
6   Explain the contribution of prospect theory models to understanding intertemporal preferences.
7   Explain the nature of multiple-self models and how they address preference reversals.
8   Explain the meaning of the term commitment in connection with self-control problems, and discuss its role in addressing these problems.
9   Discuss the role of neuroeconomic evidence in understanding and developing models of intertemporal decision-making.
10  Explain what is meant by the term 'nudge' as far as government policy is concerned, giving examples.

## 8.10  Applications

The applications considered here all involve TIPs, self-control problems and the making of effective commitments. The first two cases involve the common problems of exercising and saving. The third case, related to the preference for rising consumption profiles, also involves social preferences. The last two cases involve the impacts of behavioral factors in the financial markets.

---

### Case 8.1  Price plans for gym memberships

We have already mentioned various policy implications following from studies by DellaVigna and Malmendier (2004, 2006). One particular situation these authors examined was the optimal pricing structure for firms facing consumers with hyperbolic preferences for gym memberships. They developed a three-stage model as follows:

**Period 1**
The firm offers the consumer a membership plan with a membership fee $F$ and a per-use fee $p$. The consumer either accepts or rejects the contract.

▶

---

### Period 2

If the consumer accepts the contract, he or she pays $F$ and then makes the decision whether to exercise ($E$) or not ($N$). If the consumer chooses $E$, he or she incurs a cost $c$ which relates to the personal effort of exercising, and also pays the firm the usage fee $p$. If the consumer chooses $N$, then there is no cost $c$ or usage fee $p$.

### Period 3

If the consumer chooses $E$ then there is the delayed health benefit $b$; this is obviously not received if the consumer chooses $N$.

The firm incurs a setup cost of $K$ whenever a consumer accepts the contract, and a unit cost $a$ if the consumer chooses $E$. The consumer is also assumed to be a hyperbolic discounter with parameters $\beta$, $b$ and $\delta$, as explained in the section on hyperbolic discounting. For simplicity, the firm is assumed to be time-consistent with a discount factor $\delta$.

For the naïve hyperbolic discounter choosing to exercise, the decision process can be described as follows:

### Period 1

The utility from choosing $E$ is $\beta\delta$ ($\delta b - p - c$), and the payoff from $N$ is 0. Therefore the consumer chooses $E$ if $c \leq \delta b - p$.

### Period 2

Choosing $E$ only gives a utility of $\beta\delta b - p - c$, so the consumer actually chooses $E$ only if $c \leq \beta\delta b - p$, a smaller amount than in period 1.

Thus we can see that the naïve hyperbolic discounter, by misinterpreting his or her own future discounting process, overestimates the net utility of $E$ when buying the membership. Such consumers choose to exercise less often than they planned to when buying the membership.

The sophisticated consumers on the other hand are under no illusions regarding their propensity to exercise and correctly predict their choice of $E$.

Assuming profit maximization, DellaVigna and Malmendier predict that, for time-consistent consumers (with $\beta = 1$), the firm simply sets $p^*$ (the optimal per-use fee) equal to the marginal cost $a$. However, for hyperbolic discounters with $\beta < 1$, the optimal pricing contract involves setting the per-use fee below marginal cost ($p^* < a$), and the membership fee $F^*$ above the optimal level for time-consistent consumers. There are two reasons for this result:

1   Sophisticated consumers like the lower per-use fee because it serves as a commitment device for increasing the probability of exercising. They know that they will be tempted to skip going to the gym unless the per-use fee is low.

2   The higher membership fee allows the firm to exploit the overconfidence of naïve consumers. They will be willing to pay the higher membership fee because they overestimate their frequency of usage and the resulting benefits.

DellaVigna and Malmendier also present empirical evidence in support of their model. They showed that firms in the health club industry typically charged high membership fees and low, often zero, per-use fees. More specifically, they found that the average membership fee was about $300 per year. Most gyms also have the option of paying no membership fee but paying a higher per-use fee (about $15 per visit) instead. The study found that the average gym member goes to the gym so rarely that their actual per-use cost works out at about $19 per visit. These consumers would be better off not buying the membership and just paying on a per-use basis. Therefore this forecasting mistake allows us to conclude that many gym members behave like they are naïve hyperbolic discounters.

## Questions

1  Compare and contrast the purchasing decision in the health club situation with the purchasing situation modeled earlier in the chapter relating to buying potato chips.

2  If naïve consumers learn to become more sophisticated, how is this likely to affect their buying behavior and firms' strategy in the health club industry?

3  Explain the implications if a health club were to abandon a fixed fee structure and just charge a relatively low per-use fee of $10.

## Case 8.2  The savings problem

Over the last 20 years household savings rates in many of the rich OECD countries have fallen sharply. The so-called Anglo-Saxon countries – America, Canada, Britain, Australia and New Zealand – have the lowest rates of household saving. Americans on average, save less than 1% of their after-tax income today compared with 7% at the beginning of the 1990s. In Australia and New Zealand personal saving rates are negative, as people borrow in order to consume more than they earn.

Other countries with rapidly aging populations, especially Japan and Italy, have also seen their personal saving rates plummet, though from a higher level. The Japanese today save 5% of their household income, compared with 15% in the early 1990s. Only a few of the rich countries, notably France and Germany, have avoided this pattern of reduced saving. Germans saved around 11% of their after-tax income in 2004, up slightly from the mid-1980s.

In the USA the overall trend in saving masks sub-trends in the components of saving. Evidence suggests that while saving of high-income earners has proved stable, middle-income saving has collapsed, and low-income earners are increasingly dissaving (Bunting, 2009).

This general trend in the rich countries raises a number of issues:

1  What is the appropriate way to measure a country's savings?

2  Are rich countries saving enough?

3  What kinds of government policy are effective in encouraging saving?

All of these issues involve certain aspects of behavioral economics, although some of the aspects are not directly related to intertemporal choice. We will focus on those aspects that are related to intertemporal choice, observing differences between the standard model and its behavioral alternatives.

### The appropriate way to measure savings

The most fundamental point here is that, as far as countries are concerned, it is the total amount of savings by households, firms and governments that is important.

Thus saving by firms in the form of retained profit, and budget surpluses by governments can in principle make up for any deficit by households. However, there appears to be at least some interrelationship between these different categories. A theory called **'Ricardian equivalence'** holds that increases in public saving are cancelled out by falls in private saving as individuals anticipate future tax cuts. An OECD study (de Mello, Kongsrud and Price, 2004) of 16 rich countries between 1970 and 2002 has found that, on average, about half of any improvement in public finances is offset by lower private saving in the short term, and about two-thirds in the long term. However, in the USA, one of the most extreme cases of low national saving, the offset was smallest. This raises policy issues discussed later.

As far as the household saving rate is concerned, this is calculated by subtracting consumption spending from after-tax income. One measurement problem is that the definitions of both income and spending that statisticians use in the national accounts often bear little resemblance to what people think of as saving and spending. Realized capital gains, for instance, are not included in income, even though the taxes paid on capital gains are deducted from income. There is an aspect of mental accounting that is relevant here. As seen in Chapter 6, people tend to classify income and wealth into different accounts and their marginal propensities to spend and save from these different accounts are also very different. For example, people tend to have a high MPC with current income, but a much lower one for various categories of wealth, like capital gains. We shall see that this lack of fungibility has important implications for government policy.

## Adequacy of saving

There are both macro- and microeconomic aspects of this issue, and both have become the subject of highly controversial debate amongst economists and policy-makers in recent years. The macroeconomic aspects relate to the function of saving in the economy as a whole, and in particular its role in funding investment and stimulating growth. We are not so much concerned with this issue here, although many economists would say that, with a current net national savings rate of only 2%, the US economy would definitely benefit from a boost in saving as far as economic growth is concerned. As a result of fiscal stimulus and multiple bailouts, the budget deficit for 2010 is estimated at 9% of GDP, a historical high. Investment tends to be low, and the sustainability of overseas borrowing is questionable.

The main issue from a behavioral point of view concerns the microeconomic aspects of saving: are individuals saving enough? In the last decade at least four studies have suggested that people in the USA are not saving enough, while at least another four studies have suggested that they are saving enough. The reason for the disagreement is that different studies are based on different assumptions regarding expected earnings, attitudes to saving, retirement age, desirable levels of consumption during retirement, government policy and other crucial factors that affect savings adequacy.

In order to address the issue of savings adequacy we must consider the three main motives for individual saving:

1  Precautionary – people want to insure against a sudden drop in income.

2  Consumption smoothing – people often wish to consume more than their income when they are both young and old, and therefore save most in their middle age.

3  Bequest motive – people want to leave assets to their children.

Therefore the issue whether people are setting aside enough from their current income depends on assumptions regarding what those people will want to consume or bequeath in future, what wealth they have already accumulated, and what returns on those assets will be.

In the 1990s many economists argued that in the USA individual saving was insufficient, notably Bernheim (1993). However, more recent studies have argued the opposite case, for example Engen, Gale and Uccello (1999) and Scholz, Seshadri and Khitatrakun (2006). The last of these studies concluded that 80% of US households had accumulated adequate saving.

However, the main weakness of these more optimistic studies lies in the assumptions made. First, they include individuals' equity in their house as part of their financial assets. Again the fungibility issue is relevant here. While there is some evidence in both the USA and the UK that increases in property values have fueled increased consumption, people still do not treat such wealth in the same way as other forms of wealth. Not only are such unrealized paper gains subject to reversal, but there is also an endowment effect here; many old people are reluctant to sell their house to finance their retirement consumption. If only half an individual's house equity is included, the most optimistic study suggests that just under 60% of US households have adequate savings.

A second important assumption in the studies mentioned is that future state pension benefits will be paid as promised. Given the budgetary pressures posed by the baby-boomers in many countries, a reduction in benefits is quite probable, particularly in the USA. For poorer Americans, any cut in promised pension benefits would significantly reduce the adequacy of their current saving. Projected payments from social security exceed the value of all other financial assets for the bottom one-third of the income distribution.

In the UK, where the government's level of pension provision is set to replace a much smaller proportion of earnings than in the USA, the situation is similar. A recent report by Britain's Pension Commission argued that, given downward trends in the occupational pensions provided by employers and the erosion of state pensions, 60% of workers over 35 are not saving enough.

A third assumption concerns the rate of return on savings. In recent years, the biggest difference between high-saving and low-saving OECD countries has been the return on assets. A recent report from the McKinsey Global Institute (MGI, 2005) observes that between 1975 and 2003 asset appreciation was responsible for almost 30% of the increase in the value of household financial assets in the USA, whereas in Japan high saving rates made up for negative returns on assets. Based on current rates of return and saving patterns in big industrial economies, the McKinsey study is not optimistic regarding the adequacy of global wealth accumulation. There is currently much uncertainty regarding future rates of asset appreciation.

## Implications for government policy

How can governments increase the amount households save? Tighter monetary policies would certainly help. In the USA in particular policy has been loose by most standards for many years, encouraging borrowing at the expense of saving. Most governments also use tax incentives to some extent. The simplest incentive would be to switch from an income-tax structure, where tax is deducted twice (once from company profit and again when people receive investment income), to a consumption-based structure. However, governments tend to limit such a switch because it is regressive in nature, shifting the tax burden from rich to poor.

Some government policies have the effect of reducing saving rather than encouraging it. For example, in the USA eligibility for welfare assistance such as food stamps is phased out if a couple has assets over $3,000. In the UK, the means-tested pension credit, designed to help pensioners, has the perverse result of making saving for workers on low incomes an unattractive proposition: for every pound of savings income they can incur marginal tax rates of at least 40%. However, the new pension system that came into operation in 2011 should address some issues, by incorporating a default of participation in the scheme, with a 4% level of income contribution.

One major alternative tax incentive has been to shelter retirement accounts, in effect subsidizing them. In the USA the subsidy on retirement-saving accounts is 27% of the value, amounting to 1% of GDP in terms of foregone tax revenue. There is a debate regarding the effectiveness of this policy, with some economists arguing that it merely displaces saving from one form to another, without increasing overall saving. However, a study by Venti and Wise (1989) concluded that 'the vast majority of IRA (US individual retirement account) saving represents new saving, not accompanied by a reduction in other saving'. These results were confirmed using a different methodology by Feenberg and Skinner (1989).

In summary, there are three main aspects of behavioral economics that have important policy implications in terms of the adequacy of saving:

**1** *Fungibility*

Different forms of saving and wealth are not treated as being fungible or substitutable. This is demonstrated by the evidence from the Venti and Wise study and the Feenberg and Skinner study. Governments can make use of this lack of fungibility to encourage more saving.

**2** *Self-control and commitment*

IRAs, like other retirement accounts, are illiquid, since they involve a 10% tax surcharge if money is withdrawn before the investor reaches 59½ years old. Venti and Wise (1989) commented that some may regard this illiquidity as an advantage since it helps ensure behavior that otherwise would not obtain. As stated earlier, the general trend in global financial markets towards greater liquidity may have discouraged saving by removing such commitment devices. Therefore governments can encourage more saving by creating additional commitment devices in the form of illiquid savings accounts with tax incentives, such as individual savings accounts (ISAs) in the UK.

**3** *Framing*

The desire to save, particularly for retirement, can be much influenced by the way in which the options in retirement plans are framed, as noted in Chapter 5. Poorer people, for example, are more likely to be enrolled in private retirement plans if that is the employer's default option than if workers have to elect to enroll. A study by Madrian and Shea (2001) indicated that shifting to automatic enrolment raised participation among poorer workers from just over 10% to 80%. UK pension policy has now moved in this direction. This kind of 'nudge' policy is very much endorsed by Thaler and Sunstein (2008).

### Questions

**1** Why have different studies come to different conclusions regarding the adequacy of saving?

2  Explain why the putting of money in a retirement account might not reduce other forms of saving.

3  Explain why fungibility is an issue as far as increasing saving is concerned.

4  In what circumstances is illiquidity of assets a desirable characteristic?

## Case 8.3 The desire for rising consumption profiles

Frank and Hutchens (1993) have investigated the factors that may cause wage profiles to rise in ways that are not explained by increases in productivity. In particular they examined the cases of airline pilots and intercity bus drivers, both of whom have relatively constant productivity over most of their careers, but who have average annual earnings at the end of their careers 600% higher and 50% higher respectively than at the start of their careers. The authors rejected four existing explanations of the rising wage profiles, relating to investment in firm-specific capital, binding contracts, risk-aversion and adverse selection, before proposing a theory relating to commitment. The workers involved had to commit to accepting lower earnings than was justified by their productivity in the early years of their careers. It was further argued that such commitment is more likely in circumstances where much of the social activity of the workers involved is with fellow workers, and they showed that this is indeed the case with the two groups of workers they studied. Although the evidence in the study was by no means conclusive, being limited to only two groups of workers, it is highly suggestive.

### Questions

1  What are the behavioral factors underlying a preference for rising wage and consumption profiles?

2  Explain why pilots and bus drivers have relatively constant productivity over their career.

3  Explain why investment in firm-specific capital cannot satisfactorily account for rising wage profiles as far as airline pilots and intercity bus drivers are concerned.

4  Explain the role of commitment in causing rising wage profiles, and why social activity with fellow workers is important as far as the likelihood of commitment is concerned.

## Case 8.4 Payday loans

The payday loan market has attracted much publicity in recent years, since the financial crisis of 2007–8, with payday lenders receiving much criticism and facing tighter regulation in many countries. In the UK, lenders like Wonga have used large-scale advertising campaigns in various media, and its ad with puppets of pensioners has become notoriously controversial. The criticism has centered on the exploitation of vulnerable borrowers, who are excluded from

▶

more traditional methods of borrowing like bank loans, overdrafts and credit cards, because of a bad credit history. This exploitation has been alleged to involve a lack of transparency over repayment terms and charges, deliberate attempts to confuse or mislead customers, and the use of intimidatory tactics to secure repayment, like sending threatening letters from fictitious lawyers. Some payday borrowers claim to have suffered emotional stress and to have been forced into a debt trap, borrowing more and more to repay existing debt.

What is a payday loan? Essentially these are small, short-term, unsecured loans, in the UK usually between £50 and £2,500, which are designed to be repaid when the borrower receives their next paycheck, normally within four weeks. The borrower signs and submits a post-dated check for the loan amount plus interest and any charges, which the lender can cash at the end of the specified period.

In the UK the typical borrower is young, without children or dependants, and is below average income, but not subprime. The demographics of the market are somewhat different from the USA, where borrowers are often older, with dependants, and in the subprime category, because they either cannot substantiate their income, or have a bad credit history. It also appears that the market in the UK is typically viewed as a short-term source of finance, whereas in the USA it is often used on a more repeated long-term basis.

On the basis of survey evidence in the UK (Burton, 2010), it appears that payday borrowers perceived three main advantages of payday loans compared with borrowing from a bank:

1  Speed – loans were quick to arrange, particularly with online lenders.

2  Convenience – there was less administration involved in terms of forms to fill and checks for the lender to make. Some lenders appeared willing to lend 'with no questions asked'.

3  Clarity – banks terms on overdrafts and credit cards were often seen as confusing, whereas payday lenders often presented their repayment terms on the basis of amounts of £100, which made it easier for customers to see how much money they would have to repay.

Since many borrowers had suffered bad experiences with banks following the financial crisis, they perceived payday lenders as being an attractive alternative, with speed and convenience being more important than cost (Burton, 2010). After using the payday loans market borrowers had mixed reactions. Some still viewed it as an attractive alternative source of finance to be used in occasional emergencies, but others, particularly low-income borrowers, found that it led to a vicious circle of debt, as they used the market repeatedly, being tempted to borrow more and more over time, in some cases borrowing from many lenders simultaneously.

It was in response to a number of complaints that the Office of Fair Trading (OFT) began an inquiry into the market in 2012. The OFT then referred the market to the Competition Commission in 2013, on the basis that a few large payday loan operators were dominating the market and charging excessively for their services. More recently, in 2014, the overall regulator of the financial markets in the UK, the Financial Conduct Authority (FCA), has intervened with tighter regulation of the payday lenders. In particular, the FCA has imposed three different caps on charges:

1  A cap on the maximum interest rate that can be charged, at 0.8% per day.

2  A cap on the maximum fee that can be charged, at £15.

**3** A cap on the maximum total amount that any borrower has to repay, no matter how overdue their payment is, at twice the original amount borrowed.

An illustration of these caps can be given, where £100 is borrowed for 30 days: if payment is made on time, the total payment is £124; if payment is made 30 days late, the total payment is £166.60; if payment is made 90 days late, the total payment is capped at £200. In addition to the above caps, various other regulations were introduced by the FCA, such as limiting the number of times a loan can be rolled over to twice, and limiting the number of times payment can be claimed from a borrower's account to twice. The government has also intervened in the market, by allocating £38 million to the Credit Union Expansion Scheme in 2013, viewing credit unions as a viable alternative to banks and payday lenders, especially for low-income borrowers.

Reaction to the effects of regulation has been mixed. The Consumer Finance Association (CFA), which represents a number of payday lenders, claims that it has had an undesirable effect on borrowers by restricting their sources of funds. The number of payday lenders has fallen from 240 in 2013 to between 30 and 40 in 2015 (Peachey, 2015). The CFA reports that there has been a 68% fall in short-term lending in that period, with 80% of loan applications now being rejected (CFA, 2015). They furthermore claim that 4% of these rejected applicants have turned to illegal loan sharks, who tend to charge extortionate interest rates and use intimidatory tactics. They may also resort to using overdrafts and paying bills late, both expensive options.

Debt charities contest this view. Citizens Advice report a 53% decrease in payday loan issues referred to them between April and June 2015, and claim that this shows that the regulation has had a beneficial effect on borrowers. Other charities claim that there is no evidence that frustrated borrowers are increasingly turning to loan sharks.

In general, it appears that payday loan restrictions do reduce the number of loans given. Similar evidence is reported in the USA, where a study by McKernan, Ratcliffe and Kuehn (2013) used nationally representative data from the 2009 National Financial Capability State-by-State Survey to examine the relationship between the state-level restrictions and consumer use. The authors find that prohibition of payday loans reduces the use of such loans by 32%. The main issue surrounds whether this reduction benefits consumers or not.

The two contrasting attitudes above can be illustrated by the following quotations:

> "High-cost credit is not the answer to financial difficulties" (Gillian Guy, chief executive of Citizens Advice).

> "The demand for short-term credit does not go away with a reduction in supply; consumers still require access to small sum short-term loans to manage their finances effectively" (CFA Report, 2015).

## Questions

**1** What behavioral biases may cause people to be more inclined to take out payday loans?

**2** Explain the case for regulating the payday loan market.

**3** What problems may arise in regulating the market?

**4** Is there any scope for a nudge policy by the government in this situation?

**5** Advise a sophisticated consumer who is considering taking out a payday loan.

## Case 8.5 Financial crashes

Financial crashes are not a new phenomenon. Probably the first one that has been reasonably well documented is known as 'tulip' mania in Holland in the seventeenth century. In March 1637 some single tulip bulbs sold for as much as ten times the annual income of a skilled craftsman. When prices fell, many investors were ruined and the Dutch economy suffered a significant blow. Crashes continued in various forms in various countries throughout the eighteenth and nineteenth centuries, and in the twentieth century there were several global crashes, notably the Wall Street Crash in 1929. Although this was most noted in the 'black' days of late October, most of the fall in stock prices occurred over a longer period from 1930 to 1933, with the stock index falling 80% from its peak in September 1929. The biggest one day fall in the Dow Jones index (in percentage terms) occurred on October 19, 1987, when it fell by 22.6%. However, contrary to many expectations, the market recovered quickly, reaching its previous peak in barely 15 months. The most recent global crash, which began in August 2007, saw the Dow Jones losing about 50% of its value over an 18-month period. The market took about five years in this case to reach its previous peak. The 1929 crash was followed by the Great Depression, and it took 25 years before the Dow Jones returned to its 1929 peak. Even this period will be exceeded by Japan's stock market. The Nikkei 225 index reached an all-time peak of 38,957 at the end of 1989, but fell 82% from this over the 20-year period to March 2009. In September 2015 the index was still over 50% less than the 1989 peak.

Financial crashes are not limited to stock markets. The financial system can come under severe strain whenever there is a bubble in an important asset which then bursts. The asset can be tulip bulbs, but these days is more likely to relate to real estate or financial instruments whose value is based on real estate, like derivatives. However, the general cause of any crash is the same: excessive speculation in an asset causes a bubble in its price, and then at some point investors lose confidence in the asset, and in their rush to sell it cause the bubble to burst and the price to tumble. As prices fall, this causes a further loss of confidence, and further selling ensues, causing the price to fall further in a vicious circle. In modern markets, where information is rapidly disseminated on a global basis, prices can fall very quickly if investor panic sets in.

Mainstream economic theory has a hard time explaining bubbles and crashes. The reason for this is that it proposes that the pricing of financial assets is determined by the efficient market hypothesis (EMH). The EMH, in its most popular weak form, stipulates that all public information is instantly incorporated into current asset prices. In the case of stock markets the relevant information relates to anything that is perceived to affect the future profits of firms. Therefore stock prices should follow a random walk, as they only respond to new information. It is thus extremely unlikely that the frequently observed volatility would occur since it does not appear rational that long-run profit expectations should change by as much as 20% within a few days. Furthermore, assuming profits remain a fairly constant proportion of GDP, the EMH predicts that national stock market indices should only be able to grow in the long run at the same rate as nominal GDP, typically 4% to 7% a year for developed countries. During bubbles stock markets often go up much faster than this for sustained periods of several years.

The 2008 crash was more complex than other previous ones because it involved derivatives to a large extent, in particular collateralized debt obligations (CDOs). These instruments

▶

were a result of a new bank lending model, particularly in the mortgage market. This market traditionally involved just two parties, the borrower and the lender. From the late 1990s the market developed into a much more complex model, sometimes called the 'originate-and-distribute' model. This typically involved at least six parties, whose roles are briefly described below:

**1** Borrowers – in many cases these were in the subprime category, meaning that they would not qualify for a mortgage in the traditional model, either because of low and unstable incomes, or because of a bad credit history.

**2** Mortgage brokers – borrowers would approach brokers rather than banks directly, to make it easier to shop around. Brokers would evaluate offerings from different banks, qualify borrowers, and advise them on the best deal. In return they received commission from the borrowers (and sometimes from lenders).

**3** Commercial banks – these were high-street banks or similar institutions, who lent the money to borrowers, and then received a stream of income consisting of repayments of principal and interest. However, in many cases they then sold the mortgages on in packages to other institutions, mainly investment banks. The streams of income would then be passed on to the investment banks who purchased the mortgage packages.

**4** Investment banks – these institutions then securitized the mortgages. This means that they used them as collateral and issued securities whose value was based on this collateral. These securities resembled bonds, and buyers received interest on them, this interest being paid out of the income received from the mortgages. However, some of these mortgage-backed securities (MBS) were transformed into more complex instruments, by combining the collateral of mortgages, of all types, with other instruments, including low-risk US Treasury bonds. The securities based on this hybrid collateral were called CDOs, and tended to be divided into different layers, or tranches, of different risk in terms of priority of payment. The top tranche had a prior claim on any income from the collateral, and were normally given a AAA rating by a ratings agency, typically paying around 4% interest. The second tranche then had the next claim on any remaining income, normally having a BBB rating (still investment grade), and typically paying around 7%. The lowest tranche then had the final claim on any remaining income, usually was not rated, and often was retained by the investment bank.

**5** Rating agencies – these institutions are responsible for evaluating the risks of investment instruments, in terms of risk of default on interest or principal. There are two main firms in this market, Moody's and Standard and Poor's (S&P), who control 80% of the global market. There are many different gradations of risk, with the top rating being AAA, representing very low risk of default. Investors have tended to use these ratings as being very reliable indicators of risk, thus perceiving the top tranche of CDOs to be similar in risk to US government bonds.

**6** Institutional investors – these are financial institutions who invest people's money on their behalf, the most important being pension funds and insurance companies. These institutions were the main buyers of CDOs on a global basis, perceiving them to be a highly attractive investment – the same risk as US government bonds (for the top tranche), but paying a much higher rate of interest (around 4% interest compared with around 1%).

So what went wrong? Many factors are relevant here, but mainstream economics has identified two that are particularly important:

▶

1 Lack of transparency – the risk involved in CDOs was difficult to assess because of the complexity of the instrument. Rating agencies justified their low risk assessment on two grounds:

   a) If borrowers defaulted, the assets would revert to the investment bank, and with property prices continually rising, these assets would increase in value. Thus default risk was not really a problem.

   b) The collateral was diversified, so even if some assets in it declined in value, others were likely to rise.

   It turned out that these grounds were spurious, since borrowers defaulted in large numbers, causing property prices to fall. The fall amounted to around 30% over two years. Collateral therefore fell in value, earning no income, and the value of the CDOs in turn fell dramatically. Many became virtually impossible to sell, and the investment banks and institutional investors holding them were hit badly. But why did so many borrowers default?

2 The agency problem – in the traditional banking model the banks as lenders had much to lose if they made bad loans and were therefore motivated to qualify lenders properly. Thus there was no subprime market. In the new banking model there were various kinds of moral hazard, meaning that parties did not suffer the consequences of taking risks if these turned bad. Two main examples follow:

   a) Brokers are agents of the borrowers and of the banks, but do not pay the consequences if there is a default. Their reward is from commission, so they are motivated to urge loans to borrowers who are not qualified, and who then prove unable to repay the loan.

   b) The originators of the loans, typically commercial banks, have no intention of holding on to them, since they want to resell them. Therefore they again do not suffer the consequences of default, and are more ready to make loans than they would be in the traditional model.

The explanation of the crash above is simplified considerably, and it ignores the role of instruments like credit default swaps, and government-sponsored enterprises like Fannie Mae and Freddie Mac in the mortgage market (both of which had to be bailed out by the US government). It also ignores the role of a global savings glut, originating in Asia, which tended to push interest rates down in many other countries.

Although the 2008 crash was more complicated in term of its causes than previous crashes, there have been a number of behavioral factors in terms of investor psychology that have played an important role in addition to the factors described above.

## Questions

Explain the role of the following behavioral factors in the 2008 financial crash:
1  Overconfidence
2  The representativeness heuristic
3  Confirmation bias
4  The beauty contest game
5  Conformity bias

# PART·IV

# Strategic Interaction

# CHAPTER · 9

## Behavioral Game Theory

The movie *Dr. Strangelove* features a device called the Doomsday Machine, which is designed to automatically destroy life on Earth if there is a nuclear attack against the former Soviet Union. Furthermore, the device is impossible to untrigger. This seemingly foolhardy characteristic is essential for producing the desired deterrent effect on the enemy. It ensures that the decision-making process is irrevocable, eliminating the possibility of any human interference, thus rendering the device an entirely credible commitment as a retaliatory defense weapon.

The movie is a black comedy regarding the nuclear arms race between the USA and the Soviet Union. This arms race had many flashpoints in the 1960s, notably the Cuban Missile Crisis in 1962, and has often been used to illustrate key aspects of game theory, both between nations and within nations. US and Soviet leaders wanted to deter the other country from attacking them, and appear strong to their citizens, without overburdening their countries by excessive spending on defense. Behavioral factors featured prominently during the Cold War stand-off. They were important for example during the Cuban Missile Crisis, as initially President Kennedy overreacted angrily to Soviet Premier Khrushchev's abrasive tone in his speeches. It took time for the appreciation to gain hold in the Oval Office that this was normal in Khrushchev's speeches relating to US–Soviet relations, and was essentially due to the speeches being aimed at pleasing a Soviet audience.

## 9.1  Nature of behavioral game theory

In the previous chapter we considered some aspects of game theory in general, since some of these concepts were necessary in order to understand how intertemporal preferences affect behavior. In particular we have seen that game theory is relevant whenever there is interdependence in decision-making. In some cases the game was played between a firm and consumers, as in Case 8.1 involving price plans for gym memberships; in other cases the game was played between different 'selves', specifically an impatient short-run self and a patient long-run self. We have also come across several important game theoretic concepts already, such as strategies, sequence, commitment and payoffs.

As we shall discuss below, there is a general debate in the literature on whether standard game theory, which ultimately rests on the core assumptions of the NM regarding economic rationality, should be regarded as 'behavioral' to begin with. Equally, much of current advances in game theory turn on a general aim of modeling behavioral elements of strategic interaction. Overall, these insights from game theory are relevant to behavioral economics and it is important to understand their foundations. In this chapter we therefore consider more general applications of game theory in behavioral economics. In order to discuss these applications it is necessary to introduce the basic elements of game-theoretic analysis in more detail.

The essence of interdependent decision-making situations is that when decision-maker A takes a decision (for example, regarding price, entry into a market, whether to take a job), it is rational for A to consider the reactions of other decision-makers to what it does, usually assuming that they act rationally, and how these reactions will affect their own utility or profit. It must also take into account that the other parties, in selecting their reactive strategies, will consider how A will react to their reactions. This can continue in a virtually infinite progression. In one way, the setting is straightforward and familiar. We encounter it in games of strategy, such as tic-tac-toe, checkers (draughts), or chess. If the setting is simple enough, we might be able to identify a winning strategy or one that secures at least a draw, as in tic-tac-toe. But as the example of chess illustrates, games that allow for a significant range of possible moves over long interdependent sequences can pose considerable challenges to human decision-making. As it stands, no winning strategy for chess has been identified. For the student of economic behavior, even simple games of strategic interaction are therefore an insightful testbed for the reach and limits of rational decision-making. And this is true even before one considers that particular moves in an economic context might have uncertain outcomes attached to them as a result of not only strategic or endogenous uncertainty, that results from the complexity of the interactions between economic agents, but also exogenous uncertainty, where it may be unknown, for example, to what extent a given player can be assumed to act rationally.

Strategic interaction is relevant to all areas of economics; some examples are: the setting of interest rates by the central bank in macroeconomic policy; oligopolistic pricing in microeconomics; wage negotiations and strikes in labor economics; bidding in financial economics; and trade negotiations in international economics. Game theoretic situations also occur in politics, sociology, warfare, 'games' and sports, and biology, which makes the area a unifying theme in much analysis. The main pioneering works in economics were Von Neumann and Morgenstern (1944) and Nash (1951), but their contributions were taken up rapidly during the second half of the twentieth century by many authors in economics and game theory today has become one of the key conceptual tools of economic analysis.

## Elements of a game

The concept of a game, as we are now using it, applies to a large variety of situations that we do not normally refer to as games. A good example is the standard prisoner's dilemma (PD) game, shown in Table 9.1. The narrative motivating the classic PD situation goes as follows: two prisoners are held in separate cells, accused of committing a crime. They cannot communicate with each other, so each does not know how the other is acting. The prosecutor, knowing that a conviction can only be secured on the basis of a confession, offers lenient treatment to the first defendant stepping forward with a confession. If neither confesses, the prosecutor can only get them convicted on other minor offenses, each receiving a one-year sentence. If one confesses while the other does not, the one confessing will be freed while the other one receives a harsh ten-year sentence. If both players confess they will each receive a five-year sentence.

**Table 9.1**  Prisoner's dilemma

|  |  | Suspect B | |
|---|---|---|---|
|  |  | Confess | Not Confess |
| Suspect A | Confess | 5, 5 | 0, 10 |
|  | Not Confess | 10, 0 | 1, 1 |

When discussing the PD in class, students sometimes point out, the type of 'confession' underlying the game really amounts to 'snitching', and corresponds to defecting from a status quo where, prior to being arrested, both individuals might have expressed a commitment to each other not to 'snitch'. Defecting increases one player's payoff at the expense of the other player. As we will discuss in Chapter 10, empirically, economic behavior is often motivated by norms such as fairness, which can be incorporated into the NM through 'other-regarding preferences'. More generally, as we discuss below, institutional factors such as norms may be an important external determinant in the resolution of game-theoretic situations.

We will use the notation introduced in Table 9.1 throughout our discussion of game theory. The values in the table represent payoffs. In the PD case, they stand for jail sentences; the payoffs for Suspect A are the left-hand values, while the payoffs for Suspect B are the right-hand values. The objective for each suspect in this case is obviously to minimize the payoff in terms of jail time. The structure of this kind of game in terms of the relationships between the payoffs is relevant to many economic situations, and we will return to it frequently in both this chapter and the next.

Thus we can say that chess, poker and rock-paper-scissors are games in the conventional sense, as are tennis and football (either American football or soccer). However, games in the technical sense used in this chapter also include activities like going for a job interview, a firm bargaining with a labor union, someone applying for life insurance, a firm deciding to enter a new market, a politician announcing a new education/transport/health policy, or a country declaring war. What do these diverse activities have in common?

The following are the key elements of any game:

1   *Players* – These are the relevant decision-making identities, whose utilities are interdependent. They may be individuals, firms, teams, social organizations, political parties or governments.

2   *Strategies* – These can be defined in different ways. In some cases the term strategy refers to a complete plan of action for playing a game. In other cases a strategy simply involves the choice of a single action, like 'confessing' in a PD game. It is important to understand that in many games there may be many actions involved. A complete plan means that every possible contingency must be allowed for. In this chapter, in keeping with common convention, we will use the term 'rule' for a complete plan of action, and reserve the term 'strategy' for a specific action or move. Strategies often involve either '**cooperating**' or '**defecting**'. In the game theory context, 'defection' refers to a strategy where one player chooses an action that increases their own payoff at the expense of the other player(s). Cooperation involves making a risky move where the opponent(s) may take advantage of you and reduce your payoff, in the hope that if they return the favor both or all of you may be made better off as a result.

3   *Payoffs* – These represent changes in welfare or utility at the end of the game, and are determined by the choice of strategy by *each* player. It is normally assumed that players are rational and have the objective of maximizing these utilities or expected utilities. Notice that the word *each* is important; what distinguishes game theory from decision theory is that in the latter outcomes only depend on the decisions of a single decision-maker. In game theory, we look at the outcome that results from the strategic interdependency of the players' decision-making.

The **normal-form representation** of a game specifies the above three elements, as shown in Table 9.1. Players are assumed to move simultaneously by default, so these kinds of situation can be represented by tables or matrices. The normal-form representation helps to clarify the key elements in the game.

When the players do not move simultaneously, and the sequence of moves is important, it is necessary to use an **extensive-form representation**, which usually involves a **game tree**. The concept of a game tree is illustrated in Figure 9.1; this is an example of an **ultimatum game**. In this type of game there are two players, and as with many games where the sequence of moves matters, there is a proposer (P) and a responder (R). In its standard form, a certain sum of money, frequently $10, represents a value of the gain to the proposed deal if R accepts P's offer. If R declines, this gain from exchange, or surplus, would be lost. In the ultimatum game, P offers a share of the surplus $x$ to R, leaving themselves $10 - x$. In the game shown in Figure 9.1 it is assumed that if P determines an even split out of 10 the game ends, and that the only possible uneven split is (8, 2).

**Figure 9.1**   Extensive form of ultimatum game

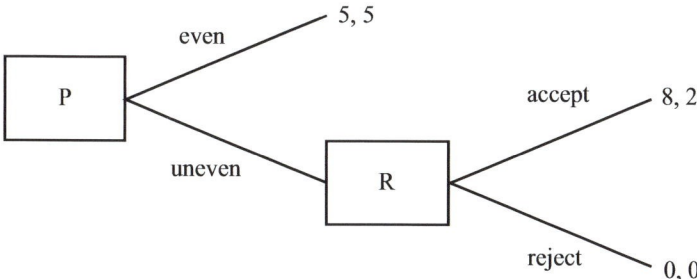

The extensive-form representation involves four elements:

1   A configuration of **nodes** and branches running without any closed loops from a single starting node to its end nodes.
2   An indication of which node belongs to each player.
3   Probabilities that 'Nature' (an external force) uses to choose branches at random nodes.
4   Payoffs for each player at each end node.

Nodes therefore represent decision points for a particular player. External influences can also be incorporated by introducing 'Nature' as a player. For example, Nature may decide that it rains or not, at a certain level of probability. Once a game is available in its normal- or extensive-form representation it is possible to analyze it for plausible outcomes. These will be equilibria of play, in the sense that they will depict those choices of strategy by each player that are compatible with each other. The equilibria for both this game and the PD are discussed in the next section.

## Types of game

There are many different types of game theory situation, and different methods of analysis are appropriate in different cases. It is therefore useful to classify games according to certain important characteristics.

1   *Cooperative and non-cooperative games*
    In cooperative games the players can communicate with each other and collude. They can also enter into third-party enforceable binding contracts. Much of this type of activity is expressly prohibited by law in developed countries. Many of the games that are of interest in economic situations are of the non-cooperative kind. This type of game involves forming self-enforcing reliance relationships, which determine an equilibrium situation. The nature of such equilibria is discussed in the next section. We shall also see that many games involve a mixture of cooperation and competition, and this is true of the basic 'one-off' PD game.

2   *Two-player and multiplayer games*
    PD situations are obviously two-player games. However, this kind of game is capable of being extended to consider more than two parties, as we have seen in the previous chapter, in the context of public goods games. Having more players tends to increase the likelihood of defection, particularly in the 'one-off' situation, referred to as a '**one-shot**' game. One version of such a situation is sometimes referred to as '**the tragedy of the commons**'. This applies in cases where property rights are untradeable,

insecure or unassigned, for example where pollution is involved. The reasoning is that with more players it is important to defect before others do; only if defectors are easily detected and punished will this be prevented. The depletion of fish stocks in the North Sea due to overfishing, and the resulting conflicts, are an example of the tragedy of the commons. In other situations, instead of the resource being overused, it is undersupplied, as with public goods like street lighting and hospitals. With multi-player games there is also the opportunity for some of the players to form coalitions against others, to try and impose strategies that would otherwise be unsustainable.

**3**   *Zero-sum and non-zero-sum games*

With zero-sum games, sometimes called constant-sum games, the gain of one player(s) is automatically the loss of another player(s); thus the sum of the gains (and losses) of the players is constant. This can apply for example in derivatives markets, where certain transactions occur between two speculators. However, most situations involve non-zero-sum games; furthermore, even when monetary gains and losses offset each other, the utilities of such gains and losses may not do so, because of loss-aversion.

**4**   *Complete and incomplete information*

In the version of the PD presented in the previous chapter it was assumed that all the players knew for certain what all the payoffs were for each pair of strategies. In practice this is often not the case, and this can also affect strategy. In some cases a player may be uncertain regarding their own payoffs; in other cases they may know their own payoffs but be uncertain regarding the payoffs of the other player(s). For example, an insurance company may not know all the relevant details regarding the person applying for insurance, a situation leading to adverse selection. Likewise, bidders at an auction may not know the valuations that other parties place on the auctioned item. Games with incomplete information are unsurprisingly more difficult to analyze.

**5**   *Static and dynamic games*

**Static games** involve **simultaneous moves**; the PD game is a simultaneous game, meaning that the players make their moves simultaneously, without knowing the move of the other player. In terms of analysis the moves do not have to be simultaneous in chronological terms, as long as each player is ignorant of the moves of the other player(s). Many life situations involve **dynamic games**; these involve **sequential moves**, where one player moves first and the other player moves afterward, knowing the move of the first player. The ultimatum bargaining game is an example of a dynamic game. The order of play can make a big difference to the outcome in such situations.

**6**   *Discrete and continuous strategies*

Discrete strategies involve situations where each action can be chosen from a limited number of alternatives. In the PD game there are only two choices for each player, to confess or not confess; thus this is a discrete strategy situation. In contrast, a firm in oligopoly may have a virtually limitless number of prices that it can charge; this is an example of a continuous strategy situation. As a result the analytical approach is somewhat different, in terms of the mathematical techniques involved.

**7**   *'One-shot' and repeated games*

The distinction between these two types of situation has already been discussed in the previous chapter. Many short-run decision scenarios in business, such as pricing and advertising, are best analyzed as repeated games, in that there is a continuous interaction between competitors, who can change their decision variables at regular intervals. Some of these games may involve a finite number of rounds, where an end of the game can be foreseen, while others may seem infinite or open-ended. Long-run decisions, such as investment decisions, may resemble the 'one-shot' situation; although the situation may be repeated in the future, the time interval between decisions may be several years, and the next decision scenario may involve quite different payoffs.

## Behavioral game theory and standard game theory

Standard game theory (SGT) generally involves four main assumptions, which have left it exposed to criticism: (1) people have correct mental representations of the relevant game; (2) people choose fully rationally; (3) equilibria are reached instantly, since there are no time lags due to learning effects or other factors; and (4) people are motivated purely by self-interest. In many ways, these assumptions are consistent with the NM as we have introduced it in Chapter 1. It is through the language of game theory that the NM has found its way into many branches of modern economics.

We will see that, in spite of these behaviorally quite restrictive assumptions, SGT does not necessarily perform badly in many situations, when its predictions are compared with empirical findings. Indeed, in many 'one-shot' games, both static and dynamic, and involving complete and incomplete information, its predictions can be quite accurate. This applies in particular to 'market-like contexts involving the interaction of many mutually anonymous agents capable of forming complete, third-party enforceable contracts' (Eckel and Gintis, 2010, p. 110). However, as Goeree and Holt (2001) have noted, changes in payoffs can result in significant anomalies, discussed in later sections. In other games, like bargaining games and iterated games, its predictions may be way off track; for example, in the ultimatum bargaining game in Figure 9.1, B may be outraged by the uneven offer and reject it because it violates social norms of fairness. We will examine this kind of situation in more detail in the next chapter. However, we often find that, by relaxing the SGT assumptions, and adding certain new parameters within the basic game-theoretic framework, we can improve fit and prediction significantly. This is in keeping with the general approach of behavioral economics regarding the modification and extension of the neoclassical model (NM).

Camerer (2009) has stated that there are four main elements of behavioral game theory, corresponding to relaxations of the four assumptions of SGT mentioned above:

**1**  *Representation*

This refers to how a game is perceived or mentally represented. Often players perceive a game incorrectly or have an incomplete representation of a game, and SGT tends to ignore this aspect.

**2**  *Initial conditions*

These involve the players' beliefs about the game situation. SGT assumes that these are correct, and that actions match beliefs. Behavioral game theory takes bounded rationality into account, either by proposing limits on strategic thinking (as in cognitive hierarchy theory) or by assuming players make stochastic mistakes because of 'noise', meaning unwanted information that interferes with intended signals.

**3**  *Learning*

This is relevant in repeated games, where players can learn from their own and others' payoffs, other players' strategies, and can also learn about what other players are likely to do. This factor is ignored in SGT.

**4**  *Social preferences*

Players have preferences regarding not only their own payoffs, but also those of others, and the distribution of these payoffs, and these are ignored in SGT.

Thus throughout the rest of the chapter we will be considering models that go beyond the core assumptions of SGT. However, we will be focusing on the first three elements described above. The impact of the fourth factor, social preferences, will be examined in the next chapter.

In the models that we will discuss in this chapter we will find two strands of analysis in how behavioral aspects have found application in game theory, distinguished by the source of behavioral insight:

1  *A sound basis of experimental evidence*

   This entails an examination and evaluation of many empirical studies, to see what anomalies arise with the relevant SGT model, and modifying it accordingly.

2  *A sound basis in the discipline of psychology*

   The models are not only constrained by empirical evidence, they are also based on theory from psychology.

Before we continue, a final methodological point needs to be made regarding the difference between standard and behavioral game theory. In Chapter 1, we noted that in many respects, the conceptual 'stand-off' between standard economics and behavioral economics has given way to wide-spread appreciation of behavioral elements in practically all areas of economic research today, so that it is more meaningful to use the NM as a benchmark from which to assess both the range of behavioral models that we now find in the economic literature, and those models in modern economics that are more closely wedded to the NM. In game theory, this picture is more pronounced. While it is true that many analyses based on SGT do in fact seek to address various behavioral elements of strategic interaction, they typically retain several strong rationality and equilibrium assumptions. This is even the case with authors who explicitly seek to go beyond some of the core assumptions of SGT. Gintis (2009) has expressed the underlying behavioral skepticism by noting that while the empirical anomalies of that rational choice model are relevant and need to be addressed, this is best done by generalizing the model rather than dismissing it:

> a dismissal of traditional decision theory may be emotionally satisfying, but it is immature, short-sighted, and scientifically destructive. There is no alternative to the traditional decision-theoretic model on the horizon ...: the theory is mostly correct, and where it fails, the principles accounting for failure are complementary to, rather than destructive of, the standard theory. (p. 246)

Compare this with the original intent of behavioral economists, who set out to '*replace inaccurate modeling principles with more psychologically reasonable ones*' (Camerer, 1997, p. 185; emphasis added). Game theory, whether under the behavioral label or not, is typically more closely related to the NM than other areas of behavioral economics. This should not come as a surprise. The very starting point of game theory, to look at individuals interacting strategically, implies a significant commitment to rational decision-making. Our discussion of game theory here and in the following chapter will therefore follow a more eclectic approach than other chapters. Our aim is mainly to illustrate, through a range of selected examples, how behavioral dimensions are present and are taken up in game theoretic models.

## 9.2  Solution concepts

In analyzing a given game, we want to find out which strategies the players will reasonably choose. As we shall see, there is a particular equilibrium concept in SGT, called a Nash equilibrium, that picks out combinations of strategies across players that are mutually consistent in the sense that in equilibrium each player plays a best response to the chosen strategies of all other players. We will motivate this solution concept gradually. Assume, in line with SGT, that the players are rational utility maximizers, and expect this also of each other. We can now consider different ways of trying to identify how the game will be played, depending on the payoff profile faced by players. We can: (1) try to identify **dominant strategies**; (2) try to eliminate **dominated strategies**; (3) look for **Nash equilibria**; and (4) in the case of sequential-move games, look for **subgame perfect Nash equilibria**.

To keep the exposition simple, we will limit our discussion here to discrete strategies, and initially only consider pure strategies. In the next section we will then look at a generalization of the concept to include mixed strategies, and will discuss other types of equilibrium also.

### Strategic dominance

If we look at a discrete set of strategies open to each player, and limit ourselves to strategies that are 'pure' in the sense that players need to commit to playing exactly one of the moves available to them, a natural question to ask is whether we can identify a strategy that represents a winning move for any of the players, in the sense that it yields the highest payoff *irrespective of what other players do*. For the case of two players A and B, and A being able to choose between two strategies $S_1$ and $S_2$, we can define this as follows:

1   *Dominant strategies*

A strategy $S_1$ is said to strictly dominate another strategy $S_2$ for player A if, given any collection of strategies that could be played by B, playing $S_1$ results in a strictly higher payoff for A than does playing $S_2$. In other words, player A has a **strictly dominant strategy** available if it yields the highest payoff compared to the other available strategies, for every possible strategy of B. Rational players will always adopt a dominant strategy if one is available. Equally, they will assume their opponent will adopt a dominant strategy, which will allow them to pick their best response to this strategy even if they themselves do not have a dominant strategy available. Therefore, in any static game involving discrete strategies, we should always start by looking for a dominant strategy.

We can discuss this process in the PD situation described earlier. Table 9.2 is a repeat of this situation. Consider the choice of A between confessing and not confessing, given B's choice of either 'confess' or 'not confess'. If B confesses, A is better off confessing, since A will then only get five years rather than a ten-year sentence. If B does not confess, A is still better off confessing, since A will get off free rather than serving a year. It is thus clear that irrespective of B's choice, it is always strictly better for A to confess. In other words, confessing is a dominant strategy for A. Conversely, 'not confess' is a **dominated strategy**, since it is a strategy dominated by 'confess'. Because the game is symmetrical, the same holds for B. Thus we can say that if A and B are fully rational they will both confess.

We now can see why the PD setting is called a dilemma in SGT, since by the assumptions of SGT, players will pick strategies that lead to an outcome that leaves them worse off than if they had both stood firm and not confessed. It can therefore be said that in the PD situation the dominant strategy outcome is **Pareto-dominated**. This means that *there is some other outcome where at least one of the players is better off*

**Table 9.2**   Dominant strategies in the prisoner's dilemma game

| | | Suspect B | |
| --- | --- | --- | --- |
| | | Confess | Not Confess |
| Suspect A | Confess | 5, 5 | 0, 10 |
| | Not Confess | 10, 0 | 1, 1 |

*while no other player is worse off.* Clearly, the combined payoff for A and B would be higher, in the sense of lower sentences for both, if they both did not confess; but this is not relevant to the choice of strategy by each player, which takes solely individual payoffs into account. Even if B were to play 'not confess', A would be better off confessing, and in that case even go free.

**2    *Iterated dominance***

What would happen if one player did not have a dominant strategy? This is illustrated in Table 9.3, which is similar to Table 9.2 but with one payoff changed. There is now an asymmetry in the matrix of payoffs, because a confession by A if B does not confess results in a two-year sentence, maybe because A has had a prior conviction. Although B's dominant strategy is unchanged, A no longer has a dominant strategy. If B confesses, A is better off also confessing, as before, but if B does not confess, A is better off also not confessing. There no longer is a strategy available to A that yields the highest payoff irrespective of B's choice.

**Table 9.3**   Iterated dominant strategy equilibrium

|  |  | Suspect B | |
|---|---|---|---|
|  |  | Confess | Not Confess |
| Suspect A | Confess | 5, 5 | 2, 10 |
|  | Not Confess | 10, 0 | 1, 1 |

Does this mean that we can no longer infer how A will reasonably play this game? Not quite. Note that B still has a dominant strategy. This means that A can rule out that B will play 'not confess', since this strategy is dominated for B by 'confess'. But once A removes B's 'not confess' from the strategy space, 'confess' becomes a dominant strategy for A. Through iterative elimination of dominated strategies, we can therefore determine how A will want to play. Thus the equilibrium is the same as before. The general rule for identifying best-response strategies through iterated dominance is to successively identify dominated strategies and remove them from further consideration. With games involving a greater number of possible strategies or players this becomes more difficult to determine and places increasing burden on the underlying rationality assumption.

*Nash equilibrium*

The situation becomes more complicated when neither player has a dominant strategy. This means that we are no longer considering a PD, since the structure of the payoffs has changed, as shown in Table 9.4. Now the table is symmetrical again, but both suspects now get a two-year sentence if they confess when the other suspect does not confess.

**Table 9.4**   Game with no dominant strategy

|  |  | Suspect B | |
|---|---|---|---|
|  |  | Confess | Not Confess |
| Suspect A | Confess | 5, 5 | 2, 10 |
|  | Not Confess | 10, 2 | 1, 1 |

It is no longer possible to identify a dominant strategy for either player in this game. But a consideration of best-response behavior still allows us to identify strategy pairs between the two players that together represent a rational choice of strategy. To see this, imagine we could identify a strategy pair that, for each player, depicts the best response to what is the best response of the other player. This, in a nutshell, is the concept of a **Nash equilibrium**. There are two such equilibria in Table 9.4:

1    If B confesses, A is better off confessing; and given this best response, B's best reply is to confess.

2    If B does not confess, A is also better off not confessing; and given this best response, B's best reply is not to confess.

The same equilibria could also be expressed from the point of view of determining B's strategy:

1    If A confesses, B is better off confessing; and given this best response, A's best reply is to confess.

2    If A does not confess, B is also better off not confessing; and given this best response, A's best reply is not to confess.

Both A and B will clearly prefer the second equilibrium, but there is no further analysis that we can perform to further differentiate between the two equilibria in a way that would allow us to infer whether the players would choose one over the other. This presents a problem for strategy selection if the game is repeated, as will be seen later.

The concept of Nash equilibrium is an extremely important one in game theory, since many games lack dominant strategies and cannot be solved through iterated dominance either. In the next section we will examine cases where not even Nash equilibria in pure strategies exist, so that we need to take recourse to mixed strategy equilibria.

1    *Nash equilibrium and evolutionarily stable strategies*

The attractions of Nash equilibria for SGT are obvious. As long as every player expects that a particular Nash equilibrium will be played, it is rational for them to play it too. Nash equilibria therefore exhibit self-reinforcing properties. There is another aspect of Nash equilibria that deserves mention in this context, in that a special class of Nash equilibria are of relevance in evolutionary game theory (Maynard Smith and Price, 1973; Selten, 1980). These special Nash equilibria are characterized in terms of equilibrium strategies known as evolutionarily stable strategies (ESS). Broadly speaking, in a sufficiently large population of organisms that each play a given genetically fixed strategy when randomly interacting with one another in a way that determines reproductive success, that strategy is evolutionarily stable if it persists against invading strategies once it is prevalent in the population. Take the strategy of 'confess' in Table 9.4. Clearly, this strategy will only have a chance to persist against 'not confess' if the payoff of using 'confess' against 'confess' is equal to or greater than the payoff from using 'not confess' against 'confess', which is the case in this example. Were this condition not met, then 'not confess' would come with a higher 'reproductive' value and an initially small population of 'not confessing' invaders might eventually eclipse the incumbents. As it turns out, the Nash equilibrium is an ESS equilibrium in the present case. More generally, it can be shown that every ESS equilibrium is a Nash equilibrium (but not the converse).

2    *Subgame perfect Nash equilibrium*

There is another refinement of the concept of Nash equilibrium that is relevant to our further discussion below and in the next chapter when we look at dynamic games. These kinds of games are more transparent if depicted in extensive-form. We will use the ultimatum game in Figure 9.1 for illustration, which is repeated in Figure 9.2.

**Figure 9.2**  Extensive form of ultimatum game

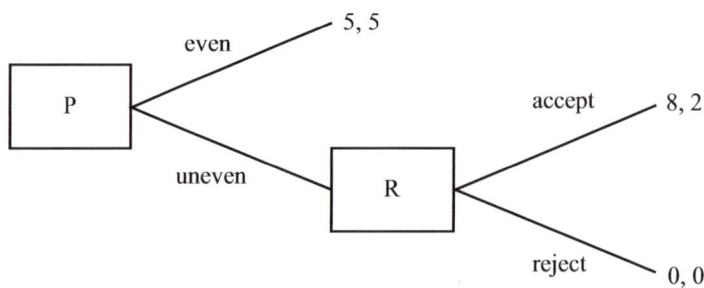

A **subgame** is the continuation game from one of the nodes of the game as depicted in extensive form (assuming for simplicity that at every node there is only one state of nature) to the end nodes which follow from that node. Thus there is a subgame in Figure 9.2 at the decision node for R. **Subgame perfection** means that players play their equilibrium strategies if the subgame is reached. **Subgame perfect Nash equilibrium (SPNE)** is an equilibrium for the complete game where players play their equilibrium strategies in each subgame. In order to determine the SPNE for a game we have to use the method of **backwards induction**. This means thinking forward and working backward, and we will see that this often unnatural method is the key to successful strategy in many situations. In the ultimatum game in Figure 9.2 it means that, in order to determine P's optimal, or equilibrium, strategy, we must first consider R's situation. R must make a decision if P goes for an uneven split. According to SGT (ignoring social preferences), a rational R will accept the uneven split, since a payoff of 2 is better than 0 from rejecting the offer. Working backwards, we can now say that P will therefore decide to go for an uneven split, since a payoff of 8 is better than the 5 from an uneven split. Thus the SPNE for the game is (uneven, accept/uneven).

It should be noted that SPNE is more restrictive than Nash equilibrium, since it assumes that Nash equilibrium must apply in all sub-games, as well as in the overall game. In the ultimatum game above there are two Nash equilibria, but only the one determined above is subgame perfect. The other Nash equilibrium is (even, reject/uneven). In the second case, if P anticipates that R will reject an uneven offer, P will decide to go for an even split, so this is a best response. If P goes for an even split, R does not get a chance to respond (it is assumed in this game). However, although (even, reject/uneven) is a Nash equilibrium, it is not subgame perfect, since R should not reject an uneven split according to SGT.

### Empirical studies of simple games

Even in simple static games with complete information there are often anomalies in terms of discrepancies between predictions based on SGT and actual observed behavior. One example, discussed by Goeree and Holt (2001) is the 'traveler's dilemma' (TD) game. In this game two players independently and simultaneously choose integer numbers between (and including) 180 and 300. Both players are paid the lower of the two numbers, and, in addition, a positive amount $R$ is transferred from the player with the higher number to the player with the lower number. For example, if one player chooses 200 and the other chooses 240, they receive payoffs of $200 + R$ and $200 - R$ respectively. Since R is positive, the best response is to undercut the other player by 1 (if their decision were known), and both players will iterate to a dominant strategy equilibrium of choosing the lower bound of the range, in this case 180. It should be noted that the size of $R$ does not affect the equilibrium in this game. Goeree and Holt (2001) found that SGT predicted behavior well when the cost of having the higher number was large ($R = 180$), with 80% of all subjects in their experiment choosing the SGT equilibrium strategy. However, when the cost of having the higher number was low ($R = 5$), the SGT prediction was way off target, with about 80% of the subjects this time choosing the highest number in the range of 300. This result will be commented on in the conclusion of the section.

Other anomalies in simple games have been noted, including the one-shot PD. There is a tendency to cooperate here, in both experiments and in real life, which is not predicted by SGT, where we have seen that the dominant strategy equilibrium is for both players to defect. Since there are multiple theories relating to the causes of this anomaly, a discussion of it is best left until after the examination of repeated games, as many PD games in real life are of this variety.

So far we have discussed anomalies related to Nash equilibrium. Another weakness related to this concept is that in many game situations there are multiple equilibria, and SGT is silent regarding which of these is more likely. One example of this kind of game is a 'minimum-effort coordination game', again investigated by Goeree and Holt (2001). In this game two players simultaneously choose 'effort' levels, in the range from 110 to 170, with a cost; the payoff for each player is a joint product, consisting of the minimum of the two efforts, minus the product of the player's own effort and a constant cost factor, $c$, where $c < 1$. In this game any common effort in the range is a Nash equilibrium, because a unilateral 1-unit increase in effort above a common starting point will not change the minimum but will reduce one's payoff by the cost of the effort, $c$. Similarly, a 1-unit decrease in effort will reduce the payoff by $1 - c$, meaning that it will reduce the minimum product by more than the savings in effort cost. SGT cannot therefore produce predictions regarding what level of effort players are likely to make in a one-shot game of this type. It does, however, predict that the cost of effort should not affect the equilibria in general terms, so long as $c < 1$. On the contrary, Goeree and Holt found that when the cost of effort was low ($c = 0.1$), behavior was concentrated at the highest effort level of 170, while when the cost of effort was high ($c = 0.9$) efforts were concentrated at the lowest possible level.

There are other examples of coordination games with multiple equilibria where there are 'focal points', but these involve a more complex analytical approach and are discussed in the section on iterated games.

*Behavioral conclusions*

Although there are both anomalies and areas where SGT is silent, for the most part the contradictions and observed behavior are 'generally consistent with simple intuition based on the interaction of payoff asymmetries and noisy introspection about others' decisions' (Goeree and Holt, 2001, p. 1402). Most people would not be surprised that a greater cost of error or effort would reduce the value of players' decisions in the traveler's dilemma or coordination games. We will also see that this conclusion of Goeree and Holt tends to apply to other empirical anomalies related to other types of game discussed in later sections.

## 9.3  Mixed strategies

*Pure and mixed strategies*

All the strategies so far discussed have involved what are called 'pure' strategies. A pure strategy always responds in the same way to a given situation, or, in more technical terms, it involves the selection of exactly one action at each decision node. However, there are many games where there is no Nash equilibrium in pure strategies. This applies to 'trivial' games like matching pennies and rock-paper-scissors, and to real-life games like poker, tennis, and football (both American and soccer). For example, in rock-paper-scissors, if A plays rock, B's best response is to play paper (paper wraps rock); however, A's best reply to B's best response is to play scissors (scissors cuts paper), not rock, and thus there is no Nash equilibrium here, or if any other action is taken by either player, in terms of pure strategies. On the other hand, we will see shortly that there is an equilibrium in terms of mixed strategies.

We can introduce the idea of a mixed strategy by considering the generic game referred to as '**Battle of the sexes**' (**BoS**). The nature of this game is that a pair of players, one of each sex, want to spend an evening out together, but they have different interests. A wants to watch a boxing match, but B wants to go to the ballet. In this situation a simplified payoff table can be illustrated by Table 9.5. As before, row payoffs are given first and column payoffs second.

If both players go to the ballet, B has a fine time, but A does not enjoy himself, except for having the company of his partner. The situation is reversed if they both watch boxing. On the other hand, if each does their own thing, it is assumed that they are miserable without each other's company. In this situation the reader should be able to verify that there are two Nash equilibria in terms of pure strategies: either they both go to the ballet, or they both watch boxing.

**Table 9.5** Battle of the sexes

|   |   | B | |
|---|---|---|---|
|   |   | **Ballet** | **Boxing** |
| **A** | **Ballet** | 1, 2 | 2, 10 |
|   | **Boxing** | 0, 0 | 2, 1 |

There is also another equilibrium in terms of mixed strategies. This should be easy to see in common sense terms, at least if the situation is a repeated game: half the time they go to the ballet, and half the time they watch boxing. This type of equilibrium is referred to as a **mixed strategy equilibrium** (**MSE**), since there is no tendency or incentive for the players to depart from it. In this case there is no mathematical computation necessary to determine the MSE, since the payoff table is symmetrical. If the payoffs are asymmetrical the MSE is more complex to determine, as we will see in the next section.

*Unpredictability*

In spite of the title 'Battle of the sexes', this game is essentially a game involving cooperation, as is the PD. In both cases the players are trying to coordinate their actions. However, in competitive games the key to success is often unpredictability. If an opponent can detect a pattern in your behavior, then they will beat you. This applies to the games mentioned earlier where there is no equilibrium in pure strategies. For example, if your opponent knows that you are going to play rock each time, they will always play paper and beat you. Equally, if they detect that you play an alternating pattern of rock, then scissors, then paper, they will also be able to beat you by selecting the appropriate responses of paper, rock and scissors. Any detectable pattern can thus be beaten.

Let us consider the well-known situation in tennis where one player is serving and the other is receiving. This is a good example to use for several reasons: (1) both players have two main possible actions: server can serve to forehand or backhand, and receiver can move to forehand or backhand; (2) these actions are repeated many times between the same two players in a match, enabling any pattern to be detected; and (3) an extensive field study (Walker and Wooders, 2001) has been conducted to compare theoretical predictions with empirical observations. We can consider this a simultaneous game, since, at least at the top level of the game, the receiver must anticipate the direction of the serve and decide what direction to move in before the server hits the ball if they are to have a reasonable chance of making a return.

A simplified form of this situation is illustrated in Table 9.6, where the server's payoff is 0 if the serve is returned and 1 if it is not. This is a zero-sum game, so the receiver's payoff is 1 if a return is made and 0 if not. It is assumed at this point that if the receiver anticipates wrongly he will fail to make a return, but if he anticipates correctly he will return successfully.

**Table 9.6** Game with no Nash equilibrium in pure strategies

|  |  | Receiver's move | |
|---|---|---|---|
|  |  | Forehand | Backhand |
| Server's aim | Forehand | 0, 1 | 1, 0 |
|  | Backhand | 1, 0 | 0, 1 |

In terms of Nash equilibrium, if the server aims to the forehand, the receiver's best response is to move to the forehand; obviously the server's best response to this best response is to serve to the backhand. The situation is reversed if the server aims to the backhand, so there is no Nash equilibrium in pure strategies. This means that there are two significant differences between this situation and the BoS game discussed earlier. We have already noted that in this case the players are in competition with each other, rather than trying to cooperate with each other. The game in this case is also a zero-sum game: if one player gains, the other automatically loses the same amount (ignoring loss-aversion). This situation arises in more general terms whenever one player wants a coincidence of actions, while the other player does not. This happens in many real-life situations, not just in recognized games: employers want to monitor employees who shirk, while shirkers want to avoid being monitored; the tax authorities want to audit those who evade taxes, while evaders want to avoid being audited; attacking armies want to gain an element of surprise, while defenders want to avoid being surprised. The question therefore arises: how does each player determine an optimal strategy, maximizing payoffs, in this kind of situation?

*Randomization*

As stated earlier, the key to success is unpredictability. This is achieved by a process of randomization. In the example in Table 9.6 the optimal strategy for each player, that is, the MSE, is to randomize their actions so that half of the time they serve or move in one direction and half of the time they go the other way. Randomization in this case means that the players must each act in such a way that it is as if they are tossing a coin to determine their action at each play. Only by randomizing their actions can they avoid their opponent detecting a pattern in their play, allowing the opponent to anticipate their actions and beat them.

However, it is important to realize that the tossing a coin analogy is only appropriate when payoff matrices are symmetrical, like in the simple tennis example and the BoS game (randomization is not necessary there, since the players are trying to cooperate rather than compete, and a simple alternating scheme would suffice). When payoffs are asymmetrical the MSE involves a more complex type of randomization, and it has to be calculated. Randomization may seem like 'madness' in terms of being the basis of a strategy, but there must be method in it if it is going to be a sensible, or optimizing, strategy. There must be a pattern in one's lack of pattern. This seeming paradox can be illustrated by a more realistic development of the tennis example in Table 9.6. We will now consider the situation where payoffs are no longer either 'succeed/fail' or (1,0), but allow for degrees of success. In other words we are now going to consider a game involving continuous rather than discrete payoffs. Table 9.7 indicates the probabilities of the server beating the receiver and the complementary probabilities of the receiver returning. This table is adapted from the excellent and highly readable book by Dixit and Nalebuff (1991), *Thinking Strategically*.

**Table 9.7**   Mixed strategy equilibrium

|   |   | Receiver's move | |
|---|---|---|---|
|   |   | Forehand | Backhand |
| Server's aim | Forehand | 10%, 90% | 70%, 30% |
|   | Backhand | 80%, 20% | 40%, 60% |

This situation is still a zero-sum game (the probabilities or payoffs in each cell always add up to 100%), but it is not symmetrical since the receiver's forehand is stronger than their backhand. This can be seen from the fact that if the receiver correctly anticipates a serve to their forehand they will make a successful return 90% of the time, while if they correctly anticipate a serve to their backhand their success rate is only 60%. In order to understand how the MSE is derived from the optimal strategies for each player, let us consider first of all the pattern of 50/50 randomization so far discussed, which we will see is suboptimal for both players. The server wants to maximize the percentage of winning serves (minimize the percentage of successful returns) and the receiver wants to do the opposite.

If the server serves to the forehand half the time and to the backhand half the time, the server's success rate when the receiver moves to their forehand will be $0.5(10\%) + 0.5(80\%) = 45\%$, while their success rate when the receiver moves to their backhand will be $0.5(70\%) + 0.5(40\%) = 55\%$. Thus the average success rate for the server is 50% (and it is also 50% for the receiver). However, this figure assumes that the receiver is moving to forehand and backhand on a 50/50 basis. We can now see that this is not optimal for the receiver, since by moving to their forehand all the time they can improve their success rate from 50% to 55%, and thus reduce the server's success rate to 45%. How then can we derive an optimization strategy for each player?

The key intuition here is to see that when a player is optimizing their strategy there is no incentive for the opponent to change their strategy. As long as the opponent can gain by changing their strategy, one is not optimizing one's own strategy, as seen in the example above when both players start with a 50/50 randomization pattern. Thus player A (the server) maximizes their payoffs when B (the receiver) is indifferent between their actions (moving to forehand or backhand). The solution can be obtained by using some simple algebra. Let A serve to the forehand in the proportion $p$, and to the backhand in the proportion $(1 - p)$. Similarly, let B move to the forehand in the proportion $q$, and to the backhand in the proportion $(1 - q)$. In order to compute the optimal strategy for A therefore we must equate B's payoffs from moving in either direction:

Average payoff from moving to forehand $= p(90) + (1 - p)(20) = 70p + 20$
Average payoff from moving to backhand $= p(30) + (1 - p)(60) = -30p + 60$

$70p + 20 = -30p + 60$
$100p = 40$
$p = 0.4$ or $40\%$

Thus the server's optimal strategy is to serve to forehand 40% of the time and to backhand 60% of the time. Only with these proportions is the receiver unable to exploit the situation to their own advantage, and to the server's disadvantage.

The optimal strategy for the receiver can be calculated in a similar way. In this case the server's payoffs from serving in either direction must be made equal:

Average payoff from serving to forehand = $q(10) + (1 - q)(70) = -60q + 70$
Average payoff from serving to backhand = $q(80) + (1 - q)(40) = 40q + 40$

$-60q + 70 = 40q + 40$
$-100q = -30$
$q = 0.3$ or $30\%$

Thus the receiver's optimal strategy is to move to forehand 30% of the time and to backhand 70% of the time. Only with these proportions is the server unable to exploit the situation to their own advantage, and to the receiver's disadvantage.

We can also compute the overall success rate ($s$) for the server if they use their optimal strategy and the receiver reacts accordingly:

$$s = 0.4\{0.1(0.3) + 0.7(0.7)\} + 0.6\{0.8(0.3) + 0.4(0.7)\} = 0.52 \text{ or } 52\%$$

The corresponding success rate for the receiver is therefore 48%.

A number of things can be observed regarding the MSE of optimal strategies here. The first general point is that the MSE is always identical to both a **maximin** and a **minimax** strategy for each player. This means that the server is trying to maximize their own minimum payoff, which will result if the opponent is optimizing their own strategy. We have seen for example that if the server randomizes on a 50/50 basis the receiver can exploit this to reduce the server's overall success rate to 45%. Therefore the 50/50 pattern is not a maximin strategy; the minimum payoff is maximized at 52%. A similar line of reasoning applies to the receiver. Likewise, a minimax strategy (sometimes called 'minimax regret') means that each player is trying to minimize the maximum payoff for their opponent; this follows from the zero-sum nature of the game.

Another observation is that, like many predictions of game theory, the solution is not an intuitive one. While it is not as counterintuitive as some predictions we will come across, it may seem strange that the receiver should move to their stronger forehand so little, only 30% of the time. This is because the server is serving more to the more vulnerable backhand, and it therefore pays the receiver to move to that side more often.

## Empirical studies of mixed strategy equilibrium

It is all very well to say that a server should serve to the forehand 40% of the time on a random basis, but how can the server actually achieve this? A number of empirical studies have been performed going back to the 1950s examining this randomization process, and how successful it is in achieving MSE. Almost all of these studies have involved experiments, and these have become more sophisticated and more revealing over time, as various design flaws have been eliminated.

Many psychologists and neuroscientists believe that the brain incorporates some kind of randomizing mechanism (for a survey, see Glimcher, 2003), but the precise operation of this has not yet been studied in detail at the physiological level. What has emerged from empirical studies, however, is that this mechanism is far from perfect. Although results from different studies vary in their conclusions, the general pattern is that departures from MSE, while often small, are usually statistically significant. These departures can be observed both in games requiring randomization and in direct randomization tasks where subjects are asked to generate a sequence of random responses. There are three main aberrations from a correct pattern of randomization:

1   *People produce too many runs of numbers in a sequence*

    A run is a succession of similar responses. In order to explain this factor it is help-ful to give an example. Take the sequence THHTHTTH. This sequence has eight responses, and six runs. The maximum number of runs of eight is obtained if the responses alternate each time.

2   *People alternate their responses too much*

    This observation is similar to the first, and probably has the same psychological foun-dation, as we will see later. This phenomenon is also commonly observed in real life; for example, people avoid betting on lottery numbers that have recently won, until it is 'their turn' to win again.

3   *People generate samples that are too balanced*

    There is a tendency for people to assume that large sample properties are also observed in small samples. We can use the previous example of the heads-and-tails sequence to illustrate this phenomenon. Obviously, in a large sample one would expect the total numbers of heads and tails to be approximately equal; however, in a small sample there is statistically a relatively high probability of the sample being biased. The probability of obtaining an exactly 50/50 distribution of heads and tails in a sequence of eight coin tosses is only 0.27.

In spite of these general findings there are some interesting results regarding learning. As mentioned earlier, there have been some field studies examining the performance of professional players in certain games in terms of their abilities to randomize success-fully. We have seen that successful randomization can be judged by observing whether expected payoffs are equal with each action. For example, if a tennis player is randomiz-ing properly, his success rate will be the same serving to the forehand as serving to the backhand. Several studies have now been performed in this area, one in tennis (Walker and Wooders, 2001) and two in European football (Palacios-Huerta, 2003; Chiappori, Levitt and Groseclose, 2003). Walker and Wooders studied ten big tennis matches in the period 1974–1997, concentrating on long matches in order to provide a larger sample of points. They observed in particular the proportions of winning points when servers served to the right or left. The football studies examined both the direction of penalty kicks and the direction of goalkeeper moves. The main finding in all studies is that win rates from different actions are approximately the same, supporting the hypothesis that professional players at least can successfully randomize to achieve MSE. Walker and Wooders note that the pro tennis players still have a tendency to over-alternate, although much less than the results observed in experimental studies.

As a final comment regarding these empirical studies it is relevant to consider the conclusion of Walker and Wooders:

> The theory (of MSE) applies well (but not perfectly) at the 'expert' end of the spectrum, in spite of its failure at the 'novice' end. There is a very large gulf between the two extremes, and little, if anything, is presently known about how to place a given strategic situation along this spectrum. (p. 1535)

There is another empirical anomaly that has been observed with games involving MSE, and this relates to situations where payoffs are asymmetrical, and as a result players cease to randomize on a 50–50 basis. Goeree and Holt (2001) investigated this anomaly using a 'matching pennies' game, which essentially has the same payoff structure as the tennis game: one player is trying to match strategies (like the returner) and the other is trying to mismatch strategies (like the server). Goeree and Holt found that the standard MSE prediction of a 50–50 division of choices was highly accurate when the payoffs were symmetrical, but was way off when payoffs were asymmetrical. It should be noted that changing one player's payoffs should not affect their strategy according to SGT, since their strategy should be based on the *other* player being made indifferent between the two alternatives. However, when one player's payoff for matching strategies of 'left-left' was quadrupled (with other payoffs unchanged), this increased the proportion of players choosing the 'left' strategy from around the predicted 50% to 96%. Furthermore, their opponents seemed to anticipate this, with 84% of them iterating to the appropriate mismatching response of 'left-right'. A similar opposite pattern was observed when the 'matching' players had their payoffs for 'left-left' reduced to about half of the original level: they chose the 'right' strategy, and again this move was largely anticipated by their opponents.

## Behavioral conclusions

At this point the main question we have to ask concerns the causes of the aberrations from MSE observed in empirical studies: what is the psychological foundation for such aberrations? Rapoport and Budescu (1997) propose that there is a combination of two factors at work: limited working memory and the representativeness heuristic. Gintis (2009) proposes a different approach to the issue, focusing on social norms and correlated equilibrium. We will examine each explanation in turn, since they focus on quite different aspects.

**1**   *Limited working memory and the representativeness heuristic*

This essentially relates to the concept of bounded rationality. In their model subjects remember only the previous $m$ elements in their sequence and use the **feature-matching heuristic,** which is an aspect of the representativeness heuristic, a phenomenon discussed in more detail in Chapter 3. This means that they choose the $m + 1$st element to balance the number of heads and tails choices in the last $m + 1$ flips, ignoring small sample variation. If the memory length is not very long, subjects will tend to over-alternate when asked to generate a random sequence. In binary experiments with coin tosses this model suggests that memory length is about seven characters. As an illustration of this model, in the sequence of heads and tails given earlier, the first seven results involve 4T and 3H; therefore feature-matching requires that the 8th result be H.

An interesting observation concerning the over-alternation tendency is that this tendency is *not* present in young children. Contrary to many other psychological errors, where people improve as their minds develop, this is one case where the opposite occurs. It seems that only the prolonged experience and exposure to harsh market forces of seasoned professionals can overcome this tendency, at least to some extent.

One interpretation of MSE that is commonly favored in terms of explaining the observed aberrations is that players do not need to actually randomize with perfection, as long as other players cannot guess what they will do. This implies that bounded rationality is symmetrical. In this case MSE can be described as being an **'equilibrium in beliefs'**. This means that players' beliefs about the probable frequency with which their opponent will choose different strategies are correct on average, and make them indifferent about which strategy to play. For example, in our tennis scenario described earlier, if a receiver estimates that there is a 40% chance the server will serve to his forehand, he will be indifferent about which way to move. Empirical studies where players have been given the opportunity to randomize explicitly, but have declined to do so, have indicated that a population of such players can still achieve aggregate results close to those predicted by MSE (Bloomfield, 1994; Ochs, 1995; Shachat, 2002). These findings lend some support to the 'equilibrium in beliefs' hypothesis.

A final question arises at this point. Is there any rival theory that can produce better predictions than MSE? Some results indicate that a model involving **quantal response equilibrium (QRE)** may achieve this. According to QRE players do not choose the best response with certainty (as is the case with the other equilibria so far discussed), but '**better respond**' instead. This means that they choose better responses (with higher payoffs) with higher probabilities. There is some psychological foundation underlying such a model, given the existence of bounded rationality, 'noise', uncertainty, and problems of encoding and decoding information. The jury is still out on the virtues of QRE versus MSE but QRE is increasingly regarded as an important concept to distinguish SGT from more behaviorally inclined strands of game theory (Bonau, 2017).

**2**  *Social norms and correlated equilibrium*

Gintis (2009) claims that the correlated equilibrium is a much more natural equilibrium than the Nash equilibrium, and can increase welfare compared with MSE. The notion of a correlated equilibrium originated with Aumann (1987). Essentially the correlated equilibrium relies on a 'choreographer' to determine a rule of play, acting as Nature and making the first move in the game. The players then play a Nash equilibrium, each assuming that the other player(s) obey the rule. A couple of examples will illustrate. The simplest one involves determining which side of the road to drive on. It is easy to see that there are two Nash equilibria, with both drivers either driving on the left or both driving on the right. The weakness of the Nash equilibrium concept is that it provides no indication of what each driver should do; obviously they could signal, a factor considered in a later section, but it would be much easier if there was a common norm that both drivers universally obeyed. This is of course the situation that exists in almost all countries. A slightly more complex example relates to the BoS game described earlier. There were two Nash equilibria there, and a further equilibrium in mixed strategies. To determine the equilibrium in mixed strategies we have to let $P_A$ = the probability of A going to the ballet and $P_B$ = the probability of B going to the ballet and then set the payoffs of the other player's strategy equal for each player, just as in the tennis example. We find that in equilibrium $P_A = 1/3$ and $P_B = 2/3$. If we apply these probabilities to the payoffs we can calculate the expected payoffs as follows:

Expected payoff to A = 2/9(1) + 5/9(0) + 1/9(2) = 2/3
Expected payoff to B = 1/9(2) + 5/9(0) + 2/9(1) = 2/3

However, it can easily be seen that both players can improve on this by following a pure strategy determined by a norm. For example, the norm may be that both players go to boxing on Monday to Friday, and then to the ballet at the weekend. In this case A's average payoff will be 5/7(2) + 2/7(1) = 12/7 and B's average payoff will be 5/7(1) + 2/7(2) = 9/7. In this case any 'matching' norm that both players follow is better than MSE, because the payoffs are low in MSE since both players 'mismatch' most of the time.

We will see that correlated equilibrium is also relevant in repeated games where iteration and backward induction are important. The nature and importance of social norms will be discussed in more detail in the next chapter.

It can be seen once again that observed empirical anomalies often correspond to intuitions; in this case, with more complex game situations, the existence of bounded rationality and the use of heuristics are important factors.

## 9.4  Bargaining

Bargaining refers to the process by which parties agree to the terms of a transaction. It has been a focus of attention for economists certainly since the time of Edgeworth (1881), with his well-known 'Edgeworth box', which showed the range of outcomes which represented optimality for both parties. In the 1950s economists, notably Nash (who was really a mathematician) began to use game theory in their approach to the problem of determining optimal outcomes. Nash in many ways foreshadowed the work of more recent researchers, using a two-level approach. At one level he investigated the ways in which parties determined how to come to an agreement (unstructured bargaining), and at another level he examined the nature of the solution that the parties would arrive at, given a certain set of rules for the bargaining procedure (structured bargaining).

From the 1960s economists began to apply the methods of experimental economics to these twin problems, comparing empirical results with theoretical predictions. This then allowed theories to be modified in line with such results, suggesting certain psychological processes and phenomena that have become incorporated into the body of behavioral game theory.

It should also be stated at this point that bargaining games are considered in more detail in the next chapter, since they involve the concepts of social norms and fairness.

### Unstructured bargaining

This kind of bargaining allows the players to use any kind of communication, not restricting the type of message or the order of offers made. Nash (1950) had proposed a unique Pareto-optimal solution that maximized the product of the utility gains for each player above the so-called 'disagreement point'. However, many early experimental studies in the 1970s produced results that did not agree with the Nash solution. The reason for this finding was that these studies did not consider how monetary payoffs mapped into utilities as far as attitudes to risk were concerned (they usually assumed risk-neutrality).

Roth and Malouf (1979) used a '**binary lottery**' technique to induce risk-neutrality. This method requires some explanation. Players are asked to bargain over the distribution of a number of lottery tickets. For example, if they bargain for sixty tickets out of a hundred, they have a 0.6 probability of winning a fixed cash prize. This technique assumes that players are indifferent between compound lotteries and their single-stage equivalents, for example if they are indifferent between having a 0.5 chance of having 60 tickets and having 30 tickets with certainty. However, the experiments of Kahneman and Tversky have shown that this assumption is highly dubious, as we have seen in the discussion of prospect theory in Chapter 5. Therefore the use of lottery tickets as payoffs may not in itself yield different results from using monetary payoffs.

The study by Roth and Malouf indicated that, when tickets gave the same monetary prize ($1) to each player, the players bargained nearly universally to a 50/50 split with a negligible amount of disagreement. However, when the prize of a ticket to the second player was three times the value of the prize to the first player ($3.75 to $1.25), there tended to be two **focal points** for the bargaining solution. The main focal point was the split of 75/25 in favor of the first player, which equalized the expected payoffs (the first player had three times as many tickets, but for a prize of a third of the amount of the second player). However, there was a second focal point, again involving a 50/50 split. One result of having two focal points rather than one was that the average rate of disagreement was higher, at 14% of the transactions. Roth and Murnighan (1982) duplicated this result.

Another focal point effect was found in a study by Roth and Schoumaker (1983), relating to the past history of the players. The experiment began with some players playing against a computer that was programmed to give a generous share to these players, without the players' knowledge. When these players began to play against other human players, with all players' histories being known, there was a '**reputation effect**', such that players who had been successful in the past were able to negotiate more favorable outcomes later.

Other studies have shown that focal points can be determined purely by chance, meaning by factors that are totally irrelevant to the bargaining transaction. Mehta, Starmer and Sugden (1992) found that allocating playing cards on a chance basis to players affected their demands in bargaining situations. When both players had equal numbers of aces they easily bargained to a single focal point of a 50/50 split. However, unequal allocations of ace cards resulted in dual focal points, one with a 50/50 split and another according to the 'irrelevant' distribution of aces, so that a player with 3 aces out of 4 often demanded 3/4 of the pot, and players with only 1 ace often demanded only 1/4 of the pot.

We shall see that the underlying factor behind these different focal points is the phenomenon of '**self-serving' bias**, discussed in Chapter 3. People tend to prefer interpretations of information that are favorable to themselves – a good example being that the vast majority of people believe they are better-than-average drivers. In the Roth and Malouf study (1979), it was the second players, with the higher prize, who were proposing 50/50 splits, rather than splits which gave the players the same expected payoff. Self-serving bias is a major factor preventing the negotiation of agreements in many real-life bargaining situations in business and international relations. The question is: can the problem be solved and how?

There is certainly evidence that the problem can be solved in experimental situations. The first case study at the end of chapter reviews a series of studies by Loewenstein and colleagues (1993) and Babcock and colleagues (1995, 1997) relating to legal situations where a plaintiff is suing a defendant for damages relating to an accident, with the legal costs to each party mounting as the case takes longer to settle. The authors find various ways in which the probability of settlement can be increased, for example by assigning the roles of plaintiff and defendant *after* the players have read the relevant information about the facts of a case.

It may be objected at this point that these results relate to experiments, not to field studies, and it is difficult, if not impossible, to apply the different protocols used to real-life situations. Obviously plaintiffs and defendants in real legal cases do not get assigned roles after accidents and similar events have already occurred. However, there are certain policy implications arising from the Babcock and colleagues (1996) study, where subjects were asked to list weaknesses in their case. The resulting large increase in settlement rate suggests that mediation can be very useful in many situations, where mediators can point out all aspects of the case, including weaknesses overlooked by the different parties. They may also be able to suggest compromise solutions in complex situations, when there are many variables involved, that the principals in the transaction may not be able to envisage on their own. Certainly organizations like the World Trade Organization and United Nations can play a role here in conflicts in international relations. Given recent perceived 'failures' by both these institutions, it must be noted that the success of such organizations depends on the will of parties outside the main conflict to find a solution.

### Structured bargaining

The general nature of the structure used in experiments has been for the players to alternate offers over a finite or infinite period. It is usually not advisable for a player to make two consecutive offers, since this tends to be viewed as a sign of weakness. Since these games are sequential, they are referred to as dynamic games. There is also a cost of delay if an offer is rejected, since continued negotiations in reality tend to involve some kind of opportunity cost, such as lost profit and wages in an industrial dispute. A factor of major importance in the outcome of these situations is the discount rate/discount factor of each player. Players with lower discount rates (higher discount factors) have an advantage in such games, if discount rates are common knowledge, since they can afford to be more patient. Since the 1980s many experiments have been conducted using a number of variations in procedures: the most important variables have been the number of rounds of offers, the size of discount rate, and the relationship between the rates of the players.

A simple example of a two-stage bargaining game is one where each player gets to make a single proposal for how to split a pie, with the amount of money to be divided falling from $5 in the first stage to $2 in the second. The first player proposes a split of $5 that is either accepted (and implemented) or rejected, in which case the second player proposes a split of $2 that is either accepted or rejected by the first player. If this second offer is rejected then both players end up with payoffs of zero.

In standard or classical game theory the method of solving dynamic games of this kind is to use **backwards induction**, or the '**foldback**' method. This method starts by examining the end of the game first and working back towards the beginning. In the second stage of the game described above a rational second player would demand $1.99, since the first player should accept the remaining $0.01 rather than get nothing. Therefore in the first stage the first player should offer $2, anticipating that the second player will accept this. In general with this kind of game the first player should offer the amount that the pie is reduced to in the second round. We will comment on this approach in the next section, since backwards induction is involved in both dynamic games and repeated games, and in practice it tends to predict badly in many situations (Binmore and Shaked, 2010a).

## Bargaining with incomplete information

In many real-life situations the players have asymmetrical information, typically knowing more about their own payoffs than about those of the other player. For example, in auctions buyers know their own valuation of the item, but not often that of the seller, and vice versa. The simplest situation here is a first-price sealed-bid auction with two bidders, where both players make simultaneous bids, with the prize going to the highest bid at the same price as the bid. For example, each bidder's value for the prize may be equally likely to be $0, $2 or $5, with bids constrained to be in integer amounts, with ties being decided by a coin toss. The equilibrium in SGT is described as Bayesian Nash, which specifies an equilibrium bid for each value of the bidder. It can be shown (though the calculations are somewhat tedious) that the equilibrium bids in this example are $0, $1 and $2 for values of $0, $2 and $5 respectively (Goeree and Holt, 2001, p. 1413).

The above game is a static game. Many bargaining games with incomplete information are dynamic, and can involve several stages. This makes the bargaining situation more complicated, since not only are players trying to maximize their utilities, but they are also aware that the offers and bids that they make and accept or reject convey information regarding their valuations that are often detrimental to their interests. This aspect of the game involves the concept of **signaling**, discussed in more detail in Section 9.6.

## Empirical studies of bargaining games with complete information

We will begin by discussing games with complete information, since these are simpler to analyze. Early experiments by Binmore, Shaked and Sutton (1985) used a protocol that involved two two-round games, with a common discount factor ($\delta$) of 0.25, and in the repetition of the game player 1 in the first game became player 2 in the second game. The results again indicated that there were two focal points: one involving a 'fair' 50/50 split, and another involving the SPNE of 75/25. This split is a SPNE since the pot of £1 was reduced to £0.25 in the second round of both games if player 1's initial offer was refused; thus it makes no sense (ignoring social preferences and reciprocity) for player 2 to refuse any offer above £0.25. Another notable finding was that in the second game initial offers shifted to the single focal point of the SPNE, suggesting a learning effect. It was suggested that player 1 in the second game, having experienced the situation of being player 2 in the first game, now realized that it made no sense to make an initial offer of more than £0.25. Further studies involving a similar kind of 'role-reversal' protocol have indicated a similar learning effect, but not as rapid as in situation above.

A later study by Neelin, Sonnenschein and Spiegel (1988) used an experimental protocol that involved two-round, three-round and five-round alternating offer games, with common discount factors of 25%, 50% and 34% respectively, and with the SPNE being $1.25 in each case. Although the study found that initial offers in the two-round game were heavily concentrated around the SPNE, initial offers in the three-round and five-round games were not. In all three types of game the initial offers tended to be concentrated around the size of the pie in the second round. This suggests that the subjects, as business and economics students, had learned about backwards induction or had worked it out for themselves for one step, but were unable to apply the technique beyond this to determine the SPNE for three-round and five-round games.

Experiments by Ochs and Roth (1989) provided some evidence, though still weak, that transactions do approximately attain SPNE. The most important finding concerns counter-offers. Not only were these commonly refused in the second and third rounds, but they were frequently 'disadvantageous'. In other words a majority of players were making counter-offers that would leave them less well-off than if they had accepted the original offer. For example, it makes no sense to reject an offer of $3 out of a $10 pot if this rejection then reduces the size of the pot to $2.50 in the next round. Similarly, it makes no sense to reject the offer of $3 if the pot is then reduced to $3.50 and one makes the counter-offer of $1, since one would only gain $2.50 even if the counter-offer is accepted. There are two possible explanations for this phenomenon of disadvantageous counter-offers:

1    Players had social preferences that inclined them to reject unequal offers.

2    Players had limited computation abilities, failing to realize that rejecting an offer in one round would limit their gains to less than this in later rounds.

As stated earlier, the first explanation is discussed in the next chapter. There have been several studies investigating the second factor, and in particular the strength of the learning effect. Although the original study by Binmore, Shaked and Sutton (1985) suggested a strong learning effect over just two games, later studies (Ochs and Roth, 1989; Bolton, 1991; Harrison and McCabe, 1992; Carpenter, 2003) indicated much slower or insignificant learning rates. Camerer and colleagues (1994) and Johnson and colleagues (2002) have designed experiments to achieve two aims: (1) isolate social preferences by having players play against a computer, and (2) investigate the thinking processes of subjects by tracking their demands for information in the different rounds of the game. They have reported three main findings:

1    Players tend not to make equilibrium offers even when social preferences are not involved.

2    Players tend not to look ahead one or two periods to consider what will happen if an offer is rejected.

3    Players can learn to look ahead, using backward induction, if they are explicitly taught to do so, since this process appears not to occur naturally.

The experimental protocols discussed up to this point have all involved fixed-discounting games. Other studies have examined situations where there are fixed costs of delay. This situation may apply in legal cases or industrial disputes where costs are generally independent of the size of the pie. The most interesting finding here that has been consistently reported (Binmore, Shaked and Sutton, 1989; Rapoport, Weg and Felsenthal, 1990; Forsythe, Kennan and Sopher, 1991) is that divisions of the relevant pies tend to be very uneven, more in keeping with SPNE, unlike the frequent even splits in fixed-discounting games. The challenge for researchers is that social preferences should apply equally to each situation, so why the difference? More research needs to be conducted regarding learning in each situation; differences in learning may account for the observed disparity.

## Empirical studies of bargaining games with incomplete information

In bargaining situations with incomplete information we have once again two main aspects to consider: (1) how to organize these situations in terms of bargaining structure, and (2) how to determine solutions in terms of the kind of equilibrium that will prevail.

In terms of the first aspect, Valley and colleagues (2002) have found that communication improves the efficiency of trade. A trade is efficient if a transaction occurs when a buyer's valuation exceeds a seller's valuation. In typical sealed-bid mechanisms where both parties submit a threshold price that they will trade at, trade will not be 100% efficient, since both parties will tend to 'shave' their bids according to the predictions of game theory. This means that buyers will bid less than their true valuation, while sellers will bid more than their true valuations. The crucial finding in the Valley and colleagues study was not so much the fact that communication improves trade efficiency, but the manner in which it does so. It appears that bargainers tend to coordinate on a single price that they will both bid. This coordination takes the form of 'feeling each other out', searching for clues regarding the other player's valuation, while still maintaining a fair amount of bluffing as to their own valuation – we are not talking about mutual truth telling here for the most part. It also seems from this pioneering study that face-to-face communication is more successful at improving trade efficiency than written communication.

With regard to the second aspect, some studies have found that solutions in terms of bidding tend to conform surprisingly well to SGT predictions. The reason that this is surprising is that the predictions are hardly intuitive, as we shall see shortly. Most studies have focused on the **sealed-bid mechanism**, or **bilateral call market**, as it is often referred to in financial markets. In this kind of market both buyers and sellers make sealed bids, and a transaction occurs at the half-way price if the buyer's bid exceeds that of the seller. If the buyer's bid ($v$) is below that of the seller ($c$) no transaction takes place. We will take an example used by Daniel, Seale and Rapoport (1998). If the buyers' and sellers' valuations ($V$ and $C$) are uniformly distributed over the space (0,200) for the buyer and (0,20) for the seller, the game-theoretic predictions are as follows:

Sellers' bids will be a linear function of their valuations, according to the equation:

$$c = 50 + 2/3C$$

Buyers' bids will follow a **piecewise linear** pattern. This means that, when drawn graphically, the function consists of three linear segments joined together. In mathematical terms, the buyer's predicted bidding pattern is shown below:

When $V \leq 50$, $v = V$
When $50 \leq V \leq 70$, $v = (50 + 2V)/3$
When $V > 70$, $v = 63.3$

These predictions suggest that sellers should ask a price much higher than their actual valuation or costs, while buyers should mostly make a flat bid of 63.3, as long as their valuation is at least 70; these predictions are both strong and counter-intuitive, making for a revealing empirical test. Although the empirical findings from the study by Daniel, Seale and Rapoport (1998) do not indicate a sharp piecewise linearity in buyers' valuations, they do confirm the predictions in two main ways:

1    Buyers bid a smaller fraction of their valuations when their valuations are high.
2    Sellers mark up their costs very considerably.

The authors replicated these results, in terms of generally confirming game-theoretical predictions, when the parameters of the experiments were somewhat changed, for example with a larger range of sellers' valuations. They also found a significant learning effect, in that buyers started by bidding too high and then after ten rounds learned to reduce their offers substantially.

### Behavioral conclusions

In the study by Goeree and Holt (2001) the subjects performed very much as predicted by SGT in the 'shrinking pie' game described earlier (p. 371), where the pie started at $5 and then shrunk to $2 in the second round. The average offer observed in the study was $2.17, compared to the SGT prediction of $2. However, when the pie was shrunk from $5 to only $0.50 in the second round, the first player subjects diverged considerably from the SGT prediction of offering only $0.50 in the first round: the average offer was $1.62, with 28 out of the 30 offers being above $0.50. This type of situation will be discussed in more detail in the next chapter, since the main reason for the divergence appears to involve social preferences and the concept of fairness.

As far as games with incomplete information are concerned, let us return to the simple example of the auction game described earlier, where each bidder's value for the prize may be equally likely to be $0, $2 or $5. We saw that the equilibrium bids in SGT in this example are $0, $1 and $2 respectively. Goeree and Holt (2001) find that the Bayesian Nash equilibrium predicts well in this situation, with 80% of the bids matching the equilibrium. However, just as we have seen in other examples, they find that changing the payoffs, while not affecting the equilibrium, does affect behavior and causes divergences from predictions. In this case, changing the values to $0, $3, and $6 reduced the proportion of Nash bids to 50%. Goeree and Holt hypothesize that these deviations from Nash behavior seem to be sensitive to the costs of deviation. This is an important general conclusion, since it applies to other games described previously, and also to games described later in the chapter involving coordination, like the 'stag hunt' game (see page 384). Goeree and Holt also point to the possibility of risk-aversion, which is again a factor in coordination games.

## 9.5  Iterated games

### Iteration and dominance

We have seen in the second section of the chapter that it is often easy to solve games with a dominant equilibrium, particularly if there are only two strategies available for each player in a two-player game. In more complex situations we can iterate to a dominant equilibrium by eliminating dominated strategies. We shall see that some situations can involve many steps of iteration, even an infinite number. Given this increased complexity, there is therefore a slight departure from the structure of previous sections, in that empirical studies are discussed throughout the section. The main objective here is to examine how players conduct iterations in different game situations, in particular how many steps they take, using empirical investigation; we can then draw certain conclusions regarding the underlying psychological mechanisms involved, particularly relating to beliefs about other players.

It is useful to start with a simple two-step game, using an example from Beard and Beil (1994). They used a sequential game with two players, and by varying the payoffs in a number of ways, they were able to investigate how much player 1 was willing to bet on player 2 obeying dominance. The basic version of the game is shown in Table 9.8.

**Table 9.8**   Iterated dominance game

|  | | Player 2 | |
| --- | --- | --- | --- |
|  | | Left | Right |
| Player 1 | Left | 9.75, 3 | |
|  | Right | 3, 4.75 | 10, 5 |

Player 1 moves first, and if she moves left that ends the game; she earns $9.75 for herself and $3 for player 2. On the other hand, if player 1 moves right, player 2 then gets to move next. If she acts in pure self-interest, she will move right also, earning $5 rather than $4.75 from moving left. This response will also earn $10 for player 1, which is slightly higher than the $9.75 she would receive if she moved left at the start. Thus the iterated dominant equilibrium is (right, right). However, there is a risk to player 1 in playing right, since if player 2 does not obey dominance she will only get $3.

In this baseline experiment 66% of player 1s played left, showing a general mistrust of player 2. In the event this mistrust proved justified, since when player 1 played right, player 2 only responded by playing right 83% of the time. This percentage means that the expected payoff for player 1 from playing right turned out to be only $(3 \times 0.17) + (10 \times 0.83) = \$8.81$, worse than the payoff from playing left.

The investigators then varied the payoffs as follows:

1  Less risk – lower payoff for player 1 moving left.
2  More assurance – lower payoff for player 2 if (right, left).
3  More resentment – higher payoff for player 2 if player 1 moves left.
4  Less risk, more reciprocity – higher payoff for player 1 if (right, left), and higher payoffs for player 2 if player moves right.

When there was less risk, more assurance or more reciprocity for player 1, this increased willingness to play right; when playing right created more resentment, they were less likely to play right. However, it was notable that in all the scenarios above player 2s always responded by playing right if player 1 had played right; in other words, player 2s obeyed dominance. This experiment leads to a general conclusion that has since been confirmed by many other studies: players tend to believe that other players are less likely to obey dominance, that is, be rational, than they actually are. This is particularly true when the cost of irrationality is small (Goeree and Holt, 2001). On the basis of the experiment above there could be a number of explanations for this; for example, player 1s may have incorrect beliefs regarding the social preferences of player 2s. However, this explanation tends to be ruled out by empirical findings from 'beauty contest' games, described next.

*Beauty contest games*

The name for this revealing type of game originated with Keynes's *General Theory of Employment, Interest, and Money* in 1936. He likened investment on the stock market to a beauty contest where competitors have to pick out the prettiest faces, the prize being awarded to the competitor whose choice most nearly corresponds to the average preference of the competitors as a whole. As Keynes explained the situation:

> each competitor has to pick, not those faces which he himself finds prettiest, but those which he thinks likeliest to catch the fancy of the other competitors, all of whom are looking at the problem from the same point of view. It is not a case of choosing those which, to the best of one's judgment are really the prettiest, nor even those which average opinion genuinely thinks the prettiest. We have reached the third degree where we devote our intelligences to anticipating what average opinion expects the average opinion to be. (p. 156)

This situation can be easily modeled into a simple game for experimental purposes. The standard form of this game is to ask a group of players to select a number from 1 to 100. The winner is the player whose number is closest to a certain fraction ($p$), say 2/3, of the average of all the players. The purpose of the experiment is to examine how many rounds of iteration players perform. If players choose randomly or uniformly the average will be 50, so 2/3 of this number gives 33. This choice reveals one step of reasoning. The second step is to reason that if other players use one-step reasoning and choose 33, then their best choice is 22. A third step would be to assume that other players use two steps and therefore choose 15. It can be seen that there are an infinite number of possible iterations in this game, and the resulting iterated dominant Nash equilibrium is 0. Nagel (1995) found that the average choice was about 35, with frequency 'spikes' at 33 and 22. More comprehensive experiments were carried out by Ho, Camerer and Weigelt (1998), confirming the general finding that players performed only one or two steps of iteration. Camerer (1997) found similar results with different types of subjects: psychology undergraduates, economics PhDs, portfolio managers and CEOs. In field studies involving contests for readers of financial magazines offering substantial prizes, the results also tend to be similar, with spikes at 33 and 22, but with a somewhat lower average number. About 8% of contestants chose the equilibrium of 0.

There are two possible conclusions from these experiments: either people are generally unable to iterate beyond a couple of steps, or they do not believe that other people are capable of doing so. In order to come to more definite conclusions we have to examine results from other games.

*Iterations leading to decreased payoffs*

A good example where further iteration reduces payoffs is a so-called '**centipede**' game. This is a sequential game involving two players and a repeated number of moves. At each move a player can take 80% of a growing pie (leaving the other player with 20%) and end the game, or they can 'pass' and let the other player move, with the pie doubling with each move. This kind of game is also known as a **trust** game, since the players can benefit by trusting the other players, at least to some extent. Experiments were carried out with this game by McKelvey and Palfrey (1992), using an initial pie of $0.50 and four moves. A game tree for this game is shown in Figure 9.3.

If the players pass on all four moves they end up with $6.40 and $1.60, a substantial improvement over the initial situation of $0.40 and $0.10. However, if we solve the game by backwards induction, the dominant strategy at the last move is to take; the same is true at the second-to-last move, and so on right back to the first node. Thus the iterated

**Figure 9.3** Centipede game

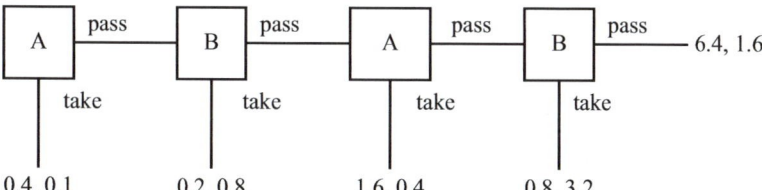

dominant solution is to take at the first move. Passing at the first node would violate four steps of iterated dominance. We can see that this is a kind of game that 'unravels', resulting in a PD-type of result, meaning one that is Pareto-dominated by passing on all moves. It also resembles PD in that self-interest causes a mistrust of cooperation by the other player.

So much for the theoretical equilibrium according to SGT. In practice McKelvey and Palfrey found that the game tended not to unravel until towards the end. In four-move games only 6% to 8% of players took on the first move, with this percentage increasing at each node reaching 75% to 82% on the last move. In six-move games, where the end pie is $2^6$ or 64 times the initial amount, only 1% or less of players took on the first move. Only with high stakes, and after learning through five trials, did the fraction of players taking at the first move increase significantly, to 22%.

Similar results have been found in other experimental games that have a similar structure to the centipede game, for example multiple-strategy PD games. Experiments have also been conducted involving continuous strategies (like the beauty contest game), rather than discrete strategies, for example pricing in imperfect competition. In general players tend to demonstrate two to four steps of iterated dominance in their initial choices.

A similar kind of unraveling effect was noted in the previous chapter, in relation to the dual-self model. When sophisticated consumers are aware that eventually they will most likely succumb to temptation of some kind, they may decide to give in now and indulge themselves. This is one situation where sophisticated consumers may end up worse off than naïve consumers, who may resist temptation for a while, being unable to predict that they will eventually give in.

## *Iterations leading to increased payoffs*

In some games further iteration improves payoffs. A good example is the so-called '**dirty faces**' game, which has been posed as a riddle for many decades. In its original form (Littlewood, 1953) there are three ladies, A, B and C, in a railway carriage, all of whom have dirty faces and all of whom are laughing. A then realizes from the reactions of her companions that she must be laughable. Her reasoning is that, if B saw that A's face was clean, she would infer that C was laughing at her, and therefore stop laughing. Since she is still laughing, this must mean that A's face is dirty. In this situation A is assuming that B is sufficiently rational to draw inferences from the behavior of C.

This kind of situation can be modeled experimentally by constructing a game where players know the 'types' of other players, but not their own type. Such an experiment was performed by Weber (2001). Players are of two types, X and O, with probabilities of 0.8 and 0.2. There are two possible strategies, Up or Down. An Up move gives no payoff to either type. A Down move gives a payoff of $1 to type X and -$5 to type O. Players take it in turn to move, and the game ends when one player plays Down. If players know nothing of their type the expected payoff of playing down is negative, so they should choose up (assuming risk-neutrality). Being in state X is like having a dirty face, and playing Down is equivalent to knowing you have a dirty face. The players are commonly told that at least one of them is type X. If a player observes that the other player is O they can infer immediately that they are type X and play Down on the first move. If a player observes that the other player is X, they cannot infer their own type on the first move of the game. They will both therefore play up on the first move. This will then inform each player that the other has observed that they are type X. Therefore both players should play Down on the second move.

Weber observed that in the XO protocol 87% of the subjects displayed rationality, using one step of iterated reasoning. However, in the XX situation, only 53% of subjects played Down on the second move, using two steps of iterated reasoning. Camerer (2003) notes that the subjects in this experiment were Caltech students, who are selected for their skills at doing logic puzzles, so that this result of only about half of people performing two steps of iteration may be an upper bound in abstract games like this.

## Behavioral conclusions

The results of the games like the 'dirty faces' game tend to indicate that the reason why people do not generally perform multiple iterations is not just that they doubt the ability of others to perform in this way; they often have 'limited computability'. However, to obtain really decisive evidence on this issue, experiments have to be performed which examine not just people's choices of strategy, but the decision rules that they use to arrive at such choices. Such experiments have been conducted by Stahl and Wilson (1995) and Costa-Gomes, Crawford and Broseta (2001).

These experiments are similar in nature to those performed by Camerer (1994) and Johnson (2002) described in the discussion of mixed strategy equilibrium, in that they require subjects to look at certain information in specific locations on a computer screen, thus revealing the information used and steps performed in arriving at decisions. Non-equilibrium (in the SGT sense) models of this type are often referred to as '**level-***k*' models. A pioneering study involving such a model was performed by Stahl and Wilson (1995); they classified subjects into five main types:

1   Level-0 (choosing each strategy equally often).
2   Level-1 (assuming others are level-0 and best responding to them).
3   Level-2 (assuming others are level-1 and best responding to them).
4   Naïve Nash (assuming others will play Nash equilibrium).
5   Worldly Nash (assume some play Nash, but that others are level-1 or level-2).

The study estimated from using 12 different games that about 18% of players were in the first category, 20% in the second, only 2% in the third, 17% in the fourth and 43% in the fifth.

The study by Costa-Gomes, Crawford and Broseta (2001) reported that 45% of subjects were naïve, meaning choosing strategies with the highest average payoff, while many were classified as optimistic, meaning using a maximax strategy (maximizing their maximum payoff). They also noted that 10% of subjects violated one step of iterated dominance, with this fraction rising to 35% and 85% for two and three steps.

Camerer, Ho and Chong (2004) have proposed a **cognitive hierarchy (CH) theory**, which is based on both the theory and empirical evidence in many of the studies described in this section. Their model proposes a Poisson frequency distribution to describe the proportions of players using different numbers of steps in thinking ($K$). The objective here was to provide a model that has both a sound psychological basis and a sound empirical basis in order to predict equilibrium conditions in iterated games. The model can also be used to predict initial situations for learning models. The model is parsimonious and easy to use, because the Poisson distribution involves only a single parameter: its mean and variance are identical ($\tau$). Those players using 0 steps correspond to level-0 in the Stahl and Wilson classification; those using $K$ steps anticipate the decisions of lower-step thinkers, and best-respond to the mixture of those decisions using normalized frequencies. Empirical studies suggest that a value of $\tau$ around 1.5 is appropriate in many games. The authors have tested the model using first-period data from a large number of experimental games, and it has always predicted at least as well as the SGT Nash equilibrium. When the CH model is compared with QRE, which also tends to predict better than Nash equilibrium, it has two main advantages: (1) it is more sophisticated in psychological terms; and (2) it has more empirical appeal, since it can account for probability 'spikes' in choosing strategies that are often observed in experiments.

A couple of recent empirical field studies have supported the CH model. One of these examined behavior in the Swedish lottery game, LUPI (Östling et al., 2011). In this game players choose integers from 1 to 99,999, and the lowest unique positive integer wins (hence the name LUPI). Given that about 50,000 people play this lottery each day, the Nash equilibrium prediction is approximately equal choice of numbers from 1 to 5,000, a sharp drop-off in choice between 5,000 and 5,500, and very few choices above 5,500. This prediction was fairly accurate for the first seven days of play, but actual behavior involved too many choices of low numbers, too few between 2,500 and 5,000, and too many numbers above 5,500. A CH model estimated the pattern of choices somewhat better, with a value of $\tau = 2.98$, somewhat higher than was found in the experimental data. Another field study by Brown and colleagues (2012) investigated why moviegoers seem to ignore the fact that movies that are not reviewed before they are released tend to be low in quality. Using a CH model, the study estimates that a value of $\tau = 1.26$ fitted the data best, close to earlier lab estimates from experimental data. As Camerer (2009) observes, this naïve strategy by moviegoers leads to greater box-office profits from withholding poor movies from review.

There have also been a couple of recent studies that have indicated that CH models incorporating level-$k$ thinking are not always superior to other models. A study by Choi (2012) examined social learning in networks, where some players in the core of the network had more extensive information links with other players, while players in the periphery had fewer links. Choi found that in various experimental treatments where the CH model was applied the dominant cognitive type was closely related to the Bayesian-rational type. This supports the accuracy of SGT predictions for environments with this kind of choice architecture, and seems at variance with the findings of the studies reported above. However, Choi resists making direct comparisons with those studies indicating the importance of bounded rationality for two reasons:

1    The experiments in the Choi study involve dynamic games, whereas previous studies supporting CH models involved static models. Choi hypothesizes that cognitive reasoning at higher levels is easier in dynamic games than in static games.

2    Choices involving higher levels of reasoning, like Bayesian rationality, are often the same as choices made using lower levels of reasoning. In order to test what levels of reasoning are being applied careful experiments need to be performed that distinguish between these different levels.

Another study by Crawford, Gneezy and Rottenstreich, henceforth CGR, (2008) has also indicated that CH models do not tell the whole story in terms of reasoning in complex decision situations. This study examined coordination games where focal points were possible. These games are essentially of a BoS type, where the players are trying to match outcomes. The example quoted in the earlier section on MSE involved the activities of watching ballet or watching boxing. In this case focal points were not relevant since, it was assumed, neither choice was salient. However, in some coordination games certain choices may be salient because of their label. A famous example is Schelling's (1960) experiment where he asked subjects to choose independently and without communication where in New York City they would try to meet each other. Obviously the subjects wanted to match choices to maximize their payoff. This game is somewhat different from BoS because it was assumed that the players had no preference regarding location or strategy, as long as the choices matched. Despite innumerable possible choices of meeting place, the majority of subjects chose Grand Central Station, the most salient traffic hub of the time. Interestingly, choice would probably be more difficult now; both Times Square and Ground Zero would be competitors. The main finding of the CGR study was that the power of focal points to coordinate choices is limited, because the effect of label salience is easily overcome by payoff salience; the result is that even very small payoff asymmetry can cause coordination failures. The study used the labels '$X$' and '$Y$' in one treatment, with the reasoning being that '$X$' should be salient. This proved to be true, so that in the situation where payoffs for matching choices, either $XX$ or $YY$, were symmetrical ($5 for each player in either case), it was found that 64% of the subjects coordinated on the $XX$ focal point. This was well above the MSE prediction of 50%. However, when the payoffs were slightly changed to an asymmetrical situation, so that coordination at $X$ rewarded player 1 with $5 but player 2 with $5.10 while coordination at $Y$ rewarded player 1 with $5.10 but player 2 with $5, the coordination rate fell to only 38%, well below the MSE prediction of 50.5%. This result suggests a failure of iterative reasoning consistent with level-$k$ models.

However, the CGR study also used a different choice treatment, involving a *pie* chart divided into three equal sectors (like the Mercedes-Benz logo), and with the bottom sector shaded. Thus players could choose 'right', 'left' or 'bottom', with the objective again being to coordinate choices. In this treatment it was found that coordination can persist even with asymmetric payoffs, so that even without labels the bottom sector was salient enough to overcome payoff salience. The empirical results here were sometimes not consistent with CH or level-$k$ predictions, but suggest instead a notion of collective rationality called '**Schelling salience**' or '**team reasoning**'. With this kind of reasoning 'players begin by asking themselves, independently, if there is a decision rule that would be better for both than individualistic rules, if both players followed the better rule' (Crawford, Gneezy, and Rottenstreich, 2008, p. 1448). In this case the better rule was to choose bottom rather than try to maximize individual payoff. These results are also consistent with the findings of Mehta, Starmer, and Sugden (1994a and b) and Bardsley and colleagues (2010).

In some cases bounded rationality may not be a factor at all in explaining why people do not play a Nash equilibrium solution. Instead a notion similar to the 'team reasoning' described above may be responsible for determining strategy, indicating again the importance of social norms and correlated equilibrium. Let us take the repeated PD game as an example, in which the payoff structure is as follows:

- temptation (defect, other player cooperates) = 4
- reward (cooperate, other player cooperates) = 3
- punishment (defect, other player defects) = 1
- sucker (cooperate, other player defects) = 0

The approach in SGT is to use backwards induction. Assuming a finite number of rounds known by both players, say 100, each player would defect in round 100. On that basis each player would then defect in round 99, and so on all the way to the first round. Thus the equilibrium strategy is to defect on all rounds, resulting in a total payoff of 100. There are many rules that a 'choreographer' could make that would improve the payoffs to both players. A simple one is to play tit-for-tat, starting off in round 1 by cooperating. If both players adopt this 'nice' strategy then both will end up cooperating for all 100 rounds, and receive a total payoff of 300. It can be easily seen that this correlated equilibrium is indeed much more natural than the Nash equilibrium of continual defection, as Gintis (2009) claims. This conclusion is also well-supported by empirical evidence from experimental studies with repeated PD games, where both experienced and inexperienced players tend to cooperate much more than predicted by SGT. Furthermore, this example is an illustration supporting the claim by Binmore and Shaked (2010a) that the rule of backward induction is frequently not applied empirically, even when other-regarding preferences are taken into account.

In summary, it appears that there is no single model that can fully explain all decision behavior in iterated games. In some of these games players may be fully rational with SGT predictions proving accurate. However, in many iterated games players appear to be highly heterogeneous, operating with different levels of thinking. Although patterns of iteration vary somewhat from game to game, people usually do not do more than two or three steps of iterated dominance, where the elimination of one's own dominated strategies is counted as the first step. However, there is evidence from some experimental games, particularly more complex ones where people are far from equilibrium at first, that learning takes place and that they perform further iterations as successive rounds of the game take place (Rubinstein, 1989). These learning aspects are discussed in the final section of the chapter. In other games it also appears that team reasoning is an important factor. However, as the CGR study concludes, 'it remains puzzling that team reasoning plays an important role in subjects' responses to *Pie* games, but not to *X-Y* games' (p. 1456). CGR speculate that the use of team reasoning depends on Pareto-dominance relations among coordination outcomes and their degree of payoff conflict, but there is obviously a need for more systematic research in this area in order to determine the relative importance of Bayesian rationality, level-k models and team reasoning and the contexts in which each is prevalent.

## 9.6   Signaling

*Nature and functions of signaling*

Many types of game feature asymmetric information, where one player wants to convey information to the other player(s). Such information does not necessarily have to be true. Actions taken by players that are designed to influence the beliefs and behavior of other players in a way favorable to themselves are often referred to as **commitments** or **strategic moves**. In order to be effective these signals or strategic moves must have **credibility**. This characteristic requires two factors:

1   *Affordability by the signaler's type*

    Someone wanting to obtain a good job may want to signal that they are this 'type' of person by investing in an expensive education or training program. A union striking for higher wages must be able to afford to go on strike, taking into consideration the foregone wages.

2   *Non-affordability by other types*

    A firm producing an inferior, unreliable product cannot afford to give a decent warranty for it. Thus good warranties are credible signals that products are of high quality. Profitable firms may use advertising as a signal of this type. Firms lacking a sound financial foundation may be unable to spend on advertising, so consumers may view advertising as a signal that a firm is well-established.

Signaling is widely used, not just in situations commonly related to economics and business, but also in politics, international relations, sport, warfare and biology. In general it may be used to achieve either competitive or cooperative objectives.

There are also situations where signaling occurs without there being any intention to influence the behavior of other parties. For example, when we see an athlete winning a race, and he is wearing a particular brand name of shoes, then this sends a signal that this brand is of good quality. Of course, if the athlete is sponsored by the shoe manufacturer, in this case the signal is deliberate. The issue that arises with unintentional signaling is how people value these signals compared to private information, such as occurs when they try the shoes on in a shop to see how comfortable they are. This aspect is discussed in the next section, in relation to learning.

### Signaling and competition

One of the most interesting aspects of signaling in a competitive context is that it may appear to be inefficient or self-defeating, since it limits the actions of the signaler. Some examples from the various fields mentioned above may help to illustrate the seemingly paradoxical nature of much signaling.

We have just observed that much advertising seems wasteful of a firm's resources, particularly if it is not directly aimed at increasing awareness or perceptions of the quality of the product advertised. A similar type of business activity, which may superficially seem to be against a firm's interests, is the use of a '**most favored customer clause**' (MFCC). Essentially what this involves is a guarantee to customers that the firm will not charge a lower price to other customers for some period in the future; if it does, it will pay a rebate to existing customers for the amount of the price reduction, or sometimes double this amount. This is particularly important in consumer durable markets. The reason why this strategy is ingenious (and disingenuous) is that it serves a dual purpose:

1   Ostensibly, it creates good customer relations – Many customers are concerned when they are considering buying a new consumer durable that the firm will reduce the price of the product later on. This applies particularly when there are rapid changes in technology and products are phased out over relatively short periods, like computers and other electronics products.

2   The MFCC creates a price commitment – It would be expensive for the firm to reduce price at a later stage, since it would have to pay rebates to all its previous customers. Thus other firms are convinced that the firm will maintain its price, and this causes prices to be higher than they would be without such commitment, contrary to consumer expectations.

In politics it is common for people to make statements like they will never raise taxes, or they will limit immigration. Of course it can always be maintained that talk is cheap, but politicians may have much to lose by reneging on such commitments, and making embarrassing U-turns, especially if the relevant policies form a major part of their electoral platform (their 'type'). Their reputations may be irredeemably tarnished by such actions.

In the field of international relations, countries or groups of countries, often try to influence other countries that are non-compliant in certain regards (like researching and building nuclear weapons) by imposing trade sanctions. These sanctions may hurt the countries imposing them, for example by reducing the availability of oil and increasing its price. On the other hand, if they hurt the non-compliant country more, they may be successful in forcing it to act in the intended manner. However, it is notable that in practice many sanctions have failed to achieve the intended response. When imposed against poor countries, like Iraq and Iran, they mainly affect the poor and can be transformed by dictatorial leaders into a different signal, meaning that the Western countries imposing them want to damage their welfare. It might be said that Western leaders in this situation are not using enough iterations of strategic thought.

Moving on to the field of sport, we can use an example from tennis that was described earlier in the discussion of mixed strategies. It was seen that a server who knows that his opponent's backhand is relatively weak will tend to serve in that direction more frequently (but not exclusively, since his moves then become predictable). If his opponent then improves his backhand with practice, in a later match this may be signaled by moving more to the backhand. The server's response is to serve more to the opponent's forehand, which is stronger. The non-intuitive conclusion can be generalized to other sporting (and non-sporting) situations: by improving our weak points we force our opponents to deal more with our strengths.

Some of the most dramatic examples of signaling come from the field of warfare. The example frequently given here is that of Cortes burning his boats when he invaded Mexico to conquer the Aztec empire (although the historical accuracy of this event is dubious). This drastic form of commitment had two effects. First, it caused his soldiers to fight harder than otherwise, since they knew that they had no alternative. The second effect involves a further iteration in strategic thought: the natives lost morale, since they knew that their enemy was now implacable and would not stop until they had either conquered their land or were completely wiped out.

Signaling also seems to play an important role in evolutionary biology. Biologists were stumped to find an evolutionary explanation for the peacock's tail, until Zahavi (1975) proposed the '**handicap principle**'. The puzzle was that the lavish tail of the peacock was very expensive to maintain in terms of scarce resources; surely natural selection would eliminate such an extravagance? Zahavi proposed that the peacock's tail, by indeed being a handicap, served as a signal to potential mates that the owner must be very healthy, and therefore desirable, in order to be able to afford to maintain such an extravagance. This aspect of sexual selection has also attracted the attention of social scientists. Some have suggested that certain self-destructive habits of young people in particular, like smoking, binge drinking, doing drugs or reckless driving, may also be interpreted as a similar signal; only 'hard', and therefore desirable, individuals can maintain such habits.

It should be noted at this stage that not all signals involve commitments of the type illustrated here. We shall see in the next section that signals can also be used to ensure coordination and cooperation.

## Signaling and cooperation

Many games involve more than one equilibrium, as we have seen in previous sections. Even PD situations, when repeated under certain conditions, may give rise to different equilibrium strategies. In terms of everyday situations, one of the simplest is determining which side of the road to drive on. This is obviously a coordination game, with players trying to match strategies (unless they like playing 'chicken', but that is a different game). The original situation here must have arisen thousands of years ago, with people driving wagons along trails. Obviously there are two possible equilibria, left or right for both players, with roughly equal payoffs in each case. There are a number of stories that claim to explain the origin of driving on one side or the other. In the USA, for example, the fact that wagon-drivers held whips mainly in their right hand may have caused a preference for driving on the right to avoid hitting passers-by. In the UK the prevalent practice of mounting one's horse from the left side may have accounted for the opposite equilibrium being selected.

What these examples demonstrate is that different equilibria may offer different payoffs, with one being preferred over the other in terms of favoring both players. However, there is no principle (like dominance or iterated dominance) that guarantees the attainment of the favorable equilibrium. This situation is modeled by the stylized '**stag hunt**' game, which is described in Table 9.9.

**Table 9.9**  Stag hunt game

|  |  | Hunter B | |
|---|---|---|---|
|  |  | **Stag** | **Rabbit** |
| **Hunter A** | **Stag** | 2, 2 | 0, 1 |
|  | **Rabbit** | 1, 0 | 1, 1 |

The essence of this game is that hunting a stag successfully requires the coordination of two hunters. Success brings a big payoff, but hunting stag is risky, since if the other hunter does not cooperate, the payoff is zero. Hunting rabbit is safer, since this can be done on one's own, and one is guaranteed a payoff of one. There are two Nash equilibria in this game: both hunters hunt stag, or both hunters hunt rabbit. Hunting stag is clearly preferred by both, since it is Pareto-dominant. However, this may not be a focal point because the hunters may be risk-averse, preferring to pursue the '**maximin**', or **risk-dominant strategy** of hunting rabbit. A 'maximin' strategy selects the strategy that maximizes the minimum payoff. A risk-dominant strategy is defined as one that minimizes joint risk, measured by the product of the cost of deviations by other players to any one player who does not deviate (Harsanyi and Selten, 1988). In the example above, if a hunter plays stag and the other hunter deviates and plays rabbit, the cost to the hunter not deviating is 2. The same applies if the roles are reversed, so the joint risk of the stag-stag strategy is 4. If both hunters hunt rabbit, there is no cost to deviation and therefore zero joint risk.

When empirical tests have been performed in stag-hunt situations, it appears that people tend to be risk-averse. In experiments by Cooper and colleagues (1990) 97% of players played the inefficient equilibrium, with no players going for the efficient one. It should be noted that in this experiment the efficient equilibrium only gave a payoff of 25% more than the inefficient equilibrium, not 100% more, as in the example in Table 9.9. Increasing the difference in payoffs may change the results significantly, but we are not aware of any experiments with efficient equilibria awarding payoffs in the order of twice the inefficient payoffs.

The only way that the preferred equilibrium can be reached (ignoring outside options) is by signaling. The Cooper and colleagues study found that signaling by just one player, in effect allowing him to indicate that he intended to play stag, resulted in an increase in the number of players playing the payoff-dominant equilibrium from 0% to 55%. When both players were allowed to signal this fraction increased to 91%.

A note of caution is necessary here regarding the benefits of signaling for the purposes of coordination in cooperative games. Two-way communication does not always improve payoffs compared with one-way communication in games with more than one equilibrium. In BoS games the key difference in the structure of the game compared with 'stag hunt' is that preferences are asymmetrical. Players again want to match strategies, for example by both going to the ballet or both watching boxing, but each player has a different preference. Cooper and colleagues (1990; 1994) found that, without signaling, players mismatched strategies 59% of the time. One-way signaling allowed one player to indicate that they would play their preference, and this reduced mismatching to just 4%. However, when both players signaled, there was a conflict as both indicated their different preferences, resulting in mismatching rising back up to a 42% rate.

### Empirical findings from signaling games

Many signaling games are complex in structure compared to the games so far discussed. This is because, in competitive situations, at least one player has a type, and some players want to reveal their type while others want to hide it. Other players must try to guess this type from the actions of these players, using iterated thinking. A relatively simple illustration is where an employee is hired by an employer. The employee knows her type in terms of whether she is a high productivity ($H$) worker or a low productivity ($L$) worker, but the employer cannot observe this directly. At the start the employer is only able to use **prior probabilities** of each type occurring, based on past experience. For example, there may be a 50/50 chance of the employee being either $H$ or $L$. During their employment workers may put in varying degrees of effort ($E$). The employer has to judge the type of worker from the amount of effort that they put in, using effort, which they can observe, as a signal of productivity. An employer can use this information regarding effort to revise the prior probabilities; this process of **Bayesian updating** was explained in Chapter 4. Employers sack workers whom they perceive to be $L$, but to do this they have to monitor workers, which is costly. $L$ workers may put in more costly effort in order to persuade the employer that they are really of the $H$ type. In turn, $H$ workers may work harder than otherwise in order to distinguish themselves from the $L$ workers, increasing their effort to a level that is unsustainable or too costly for the $L$ workers.

In general, equilibria in these situations are often referred to as **pooling equilibria** or **separating equilibria**. A pooling equilibrium occurs when the different types make the same move, for example if both types of worker put in the same effort, and then it becomes impossible for the other player to detect type. A separating equilibrium occurs if different types make different moves, in this case putting in different amounts of effort. It may be too costly for $L$ workers to exert a lot of effort, but not for $H$ workers, who may find it worthwhile to put in the extra effort to distinguish or separate themselves from the $L$ type. An example of experiments related to monopoly and new firm entry is given in Case 9.3, relating to a situation modeled by Cooper, Garvin and Kagel (1997a and b). These experiments manipulated the payoff variables for both the new entrant and the monopolists in order to examine how this would affect the type of equilibrium observed.

### Behavioral conclusions

In one-shot games signaling does not always produce Nash equilibria. As seen in other game situations, a change in payoff structure can cause deviations. Goeree and Holt (2001) found that in a situation where there were multiple equilibria involving pooling, with both types of sender sending the same signal, the observed behavior of subjects in their experiment contradicted this, and there was a separation of sender types for about 80% of the senders.

We can also see from experiments involving dynamic games with several stages that separating equilibria are more likely when dominance violation prevents one type from successfully imitating the move of another type. In this case, high-cost monopolists found it unprofitable to produce as much output as low-cost monopolists. However, it does take some time for the low-cost monopolists to learn to produce more output than they would otherwise do, because of the iterations involved. Similar experiments, for example those by Camerer and Weigelt (1988) on trust and reputation, and by Chaudhuri (1998) on production quotas and ratchet effects, also indicate the importance of learning processes, as players take time to adjust their beliefs and behavior. Furthermore, they do not always do so in the optimal direction, or by the same extent as is predicted by theory.

We therefore now need to examine these learning processes.

## 9.7  Learning

### Learning and game theory

We have seen that learning, meaning changing behavior through experience, occurs in many different types of game, although it is ignored by SGT. However, up to this point we have been examining behavior in these different classes of game in order to draw conclusions about empirical behavior. This involves studying game behavior for its own sake, as an end in itself. For example, we have examined stag hunt and BoS games in order to see how people coordinate their behavior and cooperate. The objective at this final stage is different. We want to use games in general, rather than a particular class of games, as a means to an end: the fitting and testing of different models of learning. In this situation we are not so much concerned with the observation that, for example, people tend to form a separating equilibrium in the monopoly/entry game under certain conditions. Instead we are interested in how this observation sheds light on different models of learning.

## Learning theories and models

Many different theories of learning have been proposed over the years. These include evolutionary dynamics, reinforcement learning, belief learning, anticipatory (sophisticated) learning, imitation, direction learning, rule learning and experience-weighted attraction (EWA) learning. Although all of these will be described to some extent, and the relationships between them explained, we will focus attention on four main classes of learning theory: reinforcement, belief learning, EWA and rule learning.

Most learning models involve the concept of '**attraction**'. Strategies are evaluated according to certain criteria discussed shortly, to calculate attraction values that are updated in response to experience. Learning models differ in terms of the basis of these criteria or elements of attraction. It is helpful at this stage to introduce some notation regarding these elements. It is assumed here for simplicity that other players all use the same strategy as each other, for example the $k$th strategy; otherwise $s_{-i}$ is a vector.

$s_i^j$ = the $j$th strategy (out of $m_i$ strategies) of player $i$
$s_{-i}^k$ = the $k$th strategy (out of $n_i$ strategies) of other players
$s_i(t)$ = the actual strategy chosen by player $i$ in period $t$
$s_{-i}(t)$ = the actual strategy chosen by other players in period $t$
$\pi_i(s_i^j, s_{-i}^k)$ = the payoff to player $i$ from playing $s_i^j$ when others played $s_{-i}^k$
$b_i(s_{-i}(t))$ = player $i$'s best response to the other players' strategies in period $t$

We can now move on to describing these elements of attraction, using the stag hunt game from Table 9.9 for illustration. There are seven pieces of information that may be relevant in different learning models; it is assumed in this example that player $i$ is A, and that he decides to hunt stag while the other player B hunts rabbit:

| | | | |
|---|---|---|---|
| **1** | $i$'s choice | $s_i(t)$ | hunt stag (S) |
| **2** | $-i$'s choice | $s_{-i}(t)$ | hunt rabbit |
| **3** | $i$'s received payoff | $\pi_i(s_i(t), s_{-i}(t))$ | 0 |
| **4** | $i$'s foregone payoff | $\pi_i(s_i^j, s_{-i}(t))$ | 1 |
| **5** | $i$'s best response | $b_i(s_{-i}(t))$ | hunt rabbit |
| **6** | $-i$'s received payoff | $\pi_{-i}(s_i(t), s_{-i}(t))$ | 1 |
| **7** | $-i$'s foregone payoff | $\pi_{-i}(s_i(t), s_{-i}^k)$ | 1 |

Camerer (2003) illustrates how these elements form the basis of attraction for different strategies according to different learning models in a very useful table, reproduced in Table 9.10.

This table clearly and concisely indicates the relevant elements in each learning theory, and allows easy comparisons between the different models. For example, we can now say that the attraction of the strategy of hunting stag before period $t + 1$, according to **reinforcement theory**, can be represented as:

$$A_S(t) = f\{s_i(t), \pi_i(s_i(t), s_{-i}(t))\} \tag{9.14}$$

**Table 9.10**   Information requirements for different learning theories

| Information | Reinforcement | Beliefs | EWA | Sophistication | Direction learning | Imitate average | Imitate best |
|---|---|---|---|---|---|---|---|
| *i*'s choice | X | | X | | X | | |
| −*i*'s choice | | X | X | X | | X | X |
| *i*'s received payoff | X | X | X | | | | |
| *i*'s foregone payoff | | X | X | X | | | |
| *i*'s best response | | | | | X | | |
| −*i*'s received payoff | | | | X | | | X |
| −*i*'s foregone payoff | | | | X | | | |

Source: *Republished with permission of Princeton University Press, from* Behavioral Game Theory, *Camerer, C.F., 2003, Table 6.3, permission conveyed through Copyright Clearance Center, Inc.*

while according to **belief learning theory**:

$$A_s(t) = f\{s_{-i}(t), \pi_i(s_i(t), s_{-i}(t)), \pi_i(s_i^j, s_{-i}(t))\} \tag{9.15}$$

The differences between these different theories of learning are described shortly.

Unfortunately, this is where the easy part ends. In order to estimate a particular learning model the attractions have to be mapped into probabilities of choosing different strategies using some statistical rule, usually involving a fairly complex mathematical function like 'logit'. An explanation of this process goes beyond the scope of this book, but further details are given in Camerer's (2003) excellent book, *Behavioral Game Theory: Experiments in Strategic Interaction.*

All the models are intuitively plausible in general terms, so the next issue concerns the testing of models against each other in empirical terms. This can be done in several ways:

**1**   *Direct testing*

Subjects can be asked what types of information they use in making strategy decisions.

**2**   *Indirect testing*

Experiments can be set up, using computer formats, to observe what information people use.

**3**   *Statistical testing*

This involves using statistical techniques like logit regression and maximum likelihood estimation to find models that both fit the data best and make the most accurate predictions. These two desirable criteria do not necessarily go together, as we will see in the discussion of EWA.

Each of these kinds of test will be considered in comparing the different models, which can now be explained in more detail.

## Reinforcement learning

This theory became popular as an essential component of the behaviorism movement in psychology in the 1920s, being associated with the figures of Watson, Pavlov and Skinner.

This extreme view of human nature dominated the field until the 1960s. Since then it has largely become discredited because the theory fails all the tests described above.

As can be seen from Table 9.10, reinforcement learning theories propose that subjects use very little information in making strategy choices, just their own previous choices and the resulting payoffs. While such behavior may occur in many non-human animals, various empirical studies have indicated that people use further information than this, relating to other elements in the table.

As far as statistical tests are concerned, reinforcement models may predict the direction of learning correctly, but are usually too slow to match the pace of human learning. This is because in many situations, both in experiments and in real life, there is little reinforcement. Reinforcement can only occur if a subject chooses a good strategy (like a dog responding to the sound of a dinner bell); when a bad strategy is chosen the subject is left searching for a better one with little guidance. Even if a good strategy is selected, this may still be suboptimal, but the subject has no indication of this.

### Belief learning

Well-known examples of belief learning in economics go back to the various oligopoly models that can be found in the literature in the wake of the nineteenth-century Cournot model, and which all feature a best response to behavior observed in the previous period. In the 1950s models featuring '**fictitious play**' were proposed (Brown, 1951; Robinson, 1951). In fictitious play, players keep track of the relative frequencies with which other players play different strategies over time. These relative frequencies then lead to beliefs about what other players will do in the next period. Players then calculate expected payoffs for each strategy based on these beliefs, and choose strategies with higher expected payoffs more frequently. The basic fictitious play model weights all past observations equally, but more recent variations of the model give different weights to past observations, reducing weights for observations further back in time. The Cournot model is at the extreme end of this spectrum, where only the most recent observation is taken into consideration. A more recent variation of belief learning has been proposed by Jordan (1991), and involves **Bayesian learning**. In this scenario players are uncertain regarding the payoffs of other players, but have prior probabilities that are updated over time regarding which payoff matrix the other players are using.

As far as empirical testing is concerned, direct measures of the information used by subjects indicate that fictitious play does not explain learning well. Nyarko and Schotter (2002) showed that stated beliefs often deviated from those proposed by fictitious play, even though fictitious play predicts behavior by other players more accurately than the beliefs stated by the experimental subjects. The predictions of the Jordan model have also been tested, with mixed results. The model appears to predict well in a simple situation, but is unlikely to perform well in more complex games. It is difficult to draw definite conclusions in comparing the merits of reinforcement learning compared with belief learning. Different studies have favored different models, and results depend on: (1) the type of game used; (2) the precise specification of the learning model used; and (3) the econometric methods used to test goodness of fit and prediction.

### Experience-weighted attraction learning

This model was introduced by Camerer and Ho (1999a and b) in response to the perceived weaknesses of both the reinforcement and belief learning models. The most obvious problems were that reinforcement learning models assumed players ignored information about foregone payoffs, while belief learning models assumed players ignored information about what they had chosen in the past. Since empirical testing indicated that players seem to use both types of information, the EWA model was created as a hybrid to take into account all the relevant information.

The EWA model is therefore mathematically complex in its construction, containing four parameters. These parameters relate to:

1   The weight placed on foregone payoffs.
2   The decay of previous attractions (due to forgetting or being given less importance as the environment changes).
3   The rate at which attractions grow, this affects the spread of choice probabilities for different strategies.
4   The strength of initial attractions, which depends on prior beliefs. This is updated in Bayesian fashion.

It goes beyond the scope of this book to describe the details of the EWA model, and the interested reader is directed to the original papers, and to Camerer (2003).

When it comes to empirical testing, statistical analysis involving 31 data sets has shown that EWA is generally superior in terms of goodness of fit compared with either reinforcement learning or the weighted fictitious play version of belief learning (Camerer, Ho and Chong, 2002). The model has been criticized as being unnecessarily complex, and including so many parameters that it was bound to fit data better than other models; however, these criticisms ignore the three main strengths of the model:

1   The EWA parameters are not really additional to those in other models. Other models simply implicitly assume certain values for these parameters.
2   The EWA model illustrates the relationship between the reinforcement and belief learning models. By letting certain parameters take on extreme values EWA can become identical with these models.
3   The EWA model not only has a better fit, but it also predicts better (in 80–95% of the studies where comparisons have been made). It is often assumed that these two criteria for a good theory go together, but this is not necessarily true. It is an important point in statistical analysis that the incorporation of additional parameters in a model can improve goodness of fit. However, the ultimate test of the model is **out-of-sample prediction**. It has been shown in a number of studies that models with better fit do not necessarily produce better out-of-sample prediction. The rule used by Camerer, Ho, and Chong (2002), which is fairly common, is to use only 70% of the data for estimating goodness of fit (assuming this allows sufficient degrees of freedom). Then the resulting model based on the 70% sample is tested for goodness of prediction against the remaining 30% of the data.

## Rule learning

The learning models proposed so far all involve a single 'rule' and sticking to it. Stahl (1996; 1999a and b, 2000, 2004) has proposed a model, again a hybrid, that allows people to switch from one rule to another, depending on how these rules perform. A rule is essentially a way of weighting various pieces of evidence, relating to the seven elements of information described in Table 9.10. These rules in turn determine strategies, and the probability that a strategy is played depends on the weight attached to a particular rule; these weights are updated according to how each rule performs over time.

Like EWA, this is a complex, multiparameter, model that is difficult to estimate econometrically. However, it does have a sound psychological basis, and is very flexible. Stahl has shown that, in terms of predicting relative frequencies of choices in a population, rule learning predicts better than other models, including EWA (again using out-of-sample methods).

*Behavioral conclusions*

SGT does not take learning into consideration at all. This means that the equilibrium predicted by SGT does not involve any change in strategies over time as a game is played repeatedly.

A prominent anomaly here relates to repeated PD games. We have seen that the dominant strategy in the one-shot game is to defect. However, it has been repeatedly observed in experiments that in repeated games it is common for players to cooperate. This phenomenon is discussed in more detail in the next chapter, since it involves the concepts of fairness and social preferences.

The SGT prediction provides a benchmark for comparison for learning models, albeit one that should not be difficult to improve on. Indeed, Stahl (2001) has shown that all the models discussed in this section predict considerably better than the standard equilibrium model. As might be expected, the learning models that fit and predict better tend to be more complex, incorporating more information and more parameters. Empirical results are difficult to compare, since different models perform differently in different games. Recent studies of learning have produced highly contradictory results. For example, a meta-analysis by Weizsäcker (2010), combining the results of 13 experiments carried out in other studies, finds that people ignore the choices and payoffs of other players too often. On the other hand, Goeree and Yariv (2015) find that most subjects imitate the average choices of the other players and do not consider their own possible payoffs enough. In general, reinforcement models tend to do better than belief models in simple MSE games, but belief-learning models perform better in coordination games, market games and iteration games. Good learning models should be flexible enough to perform well in terms of fit and prediction on a universal basis. In view of this problem, Camerer (2003) suggests three main challenges for learning theory in the future:

1   Models should allow for **sophistication**. This means they should take into account that players understand how other players learn; in turn this involves taking into account the last two elements of information in Table 9.10, the actual and foregone payoffs of other players.

2   Models should allow for incomplete information regarding foregone payoffs. This again requires greater complexity.

3   Models should allow a greater range of possible strategies, combined with some algorithm for reducing these to a feasible number for comparison purposes. The determination of an appropriate algorithm poses a major challenge, since it relies on research from neuroscience. An example of such an algorithm is the 'somatic marker' hypothesis proposed by Damasio (1994).

## 9.8  Summary

*   Standard game theory (SGT) involves four main assumptions: (1) people have correct mental representations of the relevant games they are playing; (2) people choose fully rationally; (3) equilibria are reached instantly, since there are no time lags due to learning effects or other factors; and (4) people are motivated purely by self-interest. Behavioral game theory relaxes all four of these assumptions.
*   Simultaneous games can be represented in normal form, as matrices, while sequential games are best represented in extensive form, in a game tree.
*   There are various forms of equilibrium that may be found in games: dominant equilibrium, iterated dominant equilibrium, Nash equilibrium, subgame perfect Nash equilibrium and mixed strategy equilibrium.

- There is also an important link between the concept of Nash equilibrium and that of evolutionarily stable strategy (ESS), as a prominent refinement of the former.
- Nash equilibrium is the most general type of equilibrium.
- Mixed strategy equilibrium (MSE) means that players randomize between different strategies in response to a given strategy of an opponent; the objective is to avoid predictability.
- Empirical studies indicate that people make certain general errors in randomization: they generate too many runs in a sequence, alternate too frequently and generate samples that are too balanced. The representativeness heuristic may be largely responsible for this.
- Quantal response equilibrium (QRE) means that players do not choose the best response with certainty, as is the case with other equilibria, but 'better respond' instead, meaning that they choose better strategies with higher probabilities.
- Changes in payoff structure that do not affect the SGT equilibrium can often have cause a large deviation in behavior from equilibrium, in many different types of game.
- Focal points are outcomes in bargaining where the players tend to settle. If a game has multiple focal points the probability of disagreement is much greater.
- Focal points may have a limited effect in determining strategy when there are payoff asymmetries.
- In bargaining games involving iteration, it is observed that people display social preferences and limited ability to look ahead. Both factors cause departures from SGT equilibrium.
- In games involving iteration players do not often perform more than two steps of iteration; they also tend to believe that other players perform less iterations than they do, suggesting self-serving bias.
- The cognitive hierarchy (CH) theory may provide the best model of initial equilibrium in games involving iterations, in terms of both psychological and empirical foundation.
- Team reasoning is also important in understanding how focal points may be determined.
- Signaling may be used both in competitive and cooperative situations.
- Signals must be both affordable by the signaler, and non-affordable by other types in order to be credible.
- Signals in competitive situations may be counterintuitive in nature, restricting the player's possible future moves.
- In cooperative situations, like the stag hunt game, the Pareto-dominant equilibrium (both players hunting stag) may be deemed inferior to the risk-dominant equilibrium (both players hunting rabbit).
- Empirical studies indicate that signaling serves a vital role in helping to achieve the Pareto-dominant equilibrium.
- A pooling equilibrium means that different types of player pool together and settle on the same strategy, as 'inferior' types try to hide their type; a separating equilibrium means that the different types will settle at different focal points, allowing the other player to distinguish between types and adjust strategy accordingly.
- There are a variety of different learning theories and models: reinforcement learning; belief learning; experience-weighted attraction (EWA) learning; and rule learning are the main types.
- More complex models, like EWA and rule learning, tend to both fit empirical data better and predict better out-of-sample. However, at present there are problems comparing different models, in particular because they tend to perform differently in different types of game situation.

## 9.9  Review questions

1   Explain what is meant by a dominant strategy equilibrium.
2   Compare the concept of dominant strategy equilibrium with Nash equilibrium.
3   Explain the structure of the prisoner's dilemma (PD) game, and show how its equilibrium is determined in SGT.
4   Explain what is meant by a mixed strategy equilibrium, and its implications for optimal strategy.
5   Explain the main findings of the study by Goeree and Holt (2001).
6   Explain the meaning of focal points, and the strategy implications.
7   Explain why equilibria in bargaining games are often different from those predicted by SGT.
8   Explain the role of signaling in games.
9   Explain what is meant by a pooling equilibrium and the circumstances under which it may occur.
10  Explain what is meant by EWA learning.

## 9.10  Review problems

1   **Mixed strategy equilibrium**
    Table 9.11 below shows success rates for the receiver in returning a serve in a tennis match.

**Table 9.11**  Receiver's success rates

|  |  | Receiver's move | |
|---|---|---|---|
|  |  | Forehand | Backhand |
| Server's aim | Forehand | 20%, 80% | 75%, 25% |
|  | Backhand | 80%, 20% | 30%, 70% |

a)  Is this a zero-sum game?
b)  Explain why a 50/50 randomization strategy is non-optimal for each player.
c)  Determine the optimal strategy for each player.
d)  Determine the overall success rates for server and receiver, assuming each is using an optimal strategy.

2   **Types of game and equilibrium**
    The table below shows payoffs in a two-player game, where there are two possible strategies: X and Y.

**Table 9.12**  Payoffs in a two-player game

|  |  | Player B | |
|---|---|---|---|
|  |  | X | Y |
| Player A | X | 4, 4 | 0, 1 |
|  | Y | 1, 0 | 1, 1 |

a) Explain the nature of this game, and derive the equilibrium or equilibria.

b) Is this a cooperative or a competitive game?

c) Is there a focal point in the game?

d) Is there any incentive for the players to signal?

## 9.11    Applications

### Case 9.1  Penalty kicking in professional soccer

Where should top soccer players aim their penalty kicks? One might think at first glance that this is a matter of knowing the kicker's strengths and the goalkeeper's weaknesses. Most right-footed kickers are better at aiming to the left of the goal, or the goalkeeper's right. On the other hand more goalkeepers are more proficient at diving to their right. However, as soon as the kicker predictably kicks in one direction the keeper can anticipate this and is more likely to make a save. Also, if the keeper becomes predictable in diving to one direction then the kicker can take advantage of this and aim elsewhere. The key to success then for both players is to be unpredictable and randomize their directions of shooting and diving.

Welcome to mixed strategy equilibrium (MSE), as game theorists refer to it. As is often the case in game theory, the conclusions are often counterintuitive. In MSE each player will maximize their success when they are indifferent regarding the direction to aim or move, since if they have any preference the other player can take advantage of them, which means that they are not optimizing their chances of success.

But does this prediction of game theorists actually predict behavior in terms of penalty kicking in the real world? After all, the calculations required to estimate the correct type of randomization to use involve long, complicated formulas. Maybe somewhat surprisingly, the theory predicts remarkably well, according to a study by Chiappori, Levitt and Groseclose (2003). Apparently most penalty kickers in the top French and Italian leagues are extremely good at mixing things up. This does not mean that these players are also extremely good mathematicians; they merely act 'as if' they were good mathematicians. Learning and natural selection are responsible for the result.

Let us consider the study in more detail. Five factors aided the development of an appropriate model:

1  **Well-defined game structure**

   The game involves two players, and is a zero-sum game. Each player must determine their move before they can observe the other player's move. This assumption can be tested empirically. A penalty kick can travel at up to 125mph, and reaches the goal in 0.2 seconds. Thus keepers must move before the kick is made. However, kickers must also determine direction before they observe the keeper move. This means that the game resembles a 'matching pennies' game.

2  **Well-defined strategy space**

   Both kickers and keepers can move right, left, or stay center.

3  **Well-defined outcomes**

   Preferences are easy to determine: kickers want to score and keepers want to prevent a score. Furthermore, these results involve huge financial incentives at the top level.

▶

▼

### 4   Available data

There is plentiful video recorded data of top league games in France and Italy. These provided a sample of 459 penalty kicks.

### 5   Available history

Players can and do examine histories of opposing teams. In particular keepers are trained to save penalties and know the past history of penalty kickers. There is an asymmetry here though that was observed empirically. While keepers treat kickers as individuals with different strategies based on their past history, kickers treat keepers as being homogeneous.

Yet there is one final twist to the story of game theory and penalty taking. One empirical observation was not predicted by the theory. There is one kicking-direction strategy that produces notably more success than any other: kicking straight down the middle. This is what two of the best players of the last decade, Cristiano Ronaldo and Zinédine Zidane, did in the 2006 World Cup, both with success. Why is there this discrepancy with the theory? The anomaly is explained by a factor that the model in the study does not take into account: private costs and benefits to the kicker. If a kicker has a penalty saved when the ball is aimed to the left or right, the save can be put down to the keeper's skill. However, if the penalty is saved when the kicker aims down the middle he appears an incompetent fool. Thus in the conflict of interests between the individual player and the team, it may be better for the kicker to maximize his own private benefit rather than the benefit of the team, and aim to the left or right.

### Questions

1   What type of game does this resemble, in terms of the games described in the chapter?

2   Construct a table showing the normal form of the penalty game, assuming (1) players only take into account the team's benefits; (2) the penalty kicker is right-footed and is equally able in kicking to the left or right; and (3) the goalkeeper is equally proficient in diving to left or right. Determine the equilibrium of the game.

3   Construct a table showing the normal form of the penalty game, assuming (1) players only take into account the team's benefits; (2) the penalty kicker is right-footed and is 20% stronger in kicking to their left side; and (3) the goalkeeper is 20% stronger in diving to their right side. Determine the equilibrium of the game.

4   Construct a table showing the normal form of the penalty game, taking into account both the team's benefits and individual payoffs, under the same assumptions as the previous question. Determine the equilibrium of the game.

5   Explain the implications of the differences between private and team benefits as far as goalkeepers are concerned.

6   Explain the implications of the differences between private and team benefits as far as team managers are concerned.

## Case 9.2  Bargaining and self-serving bias

In much of the literature on bargaining, failure to reach agreement has often been put down to the problem of incomplete or asymmetric information. The resulting uncertainty was alleged to cause bargaining impasse, since bargainers used costly delay as a signaling device regarding their own reservation values (Kennan and Wilson, 1990; Cramton, 1992). This theory is difficult to test in terms of field studies, and experimental studies have proved difficult because of problems in controlling aspects of the experimental environment.

Loewenstein and colleagues (1993) and Babcock and colleagues (1995, 1996) have proposed a different theory regarding failure to reach agreement. This theory relates to the existence of self-serving bias, where subjects conflate what is fair with their own self-interest. They have conducted various experiments relating to legal situations where a plaintiff is suing a defendant for damages. They developed a tort case based on a trial in Texas, in which an injured motorcyclist sued the driver of the car that collided with him for $100,000.

In the first experiment, subjects were randomly assigned the roles of plaintiff and defendant. They then had the experiment explained to them, along with the rules of negotiation and the costs of failing to reach agreement. Both subjects were then given 27 pages of materials from the original legal case, including witness testimony, police reports, maps and the testimony of the parties. Subjects were informed that the identical materials had been given to a judge in Texas, who reached a judgment between $0 and $100,000 in terms of compensation.

Before negotiation, the subjects were asked to guess the damages awarded, with the incentive of a monetary bonus if their guess was within $5,000 of the actual amount. They were also asked to state what they considered a fair amount of compensation for an out-of-court settlement. None of this information was available to the other party. Subjects were then allowed to negotiate for 30 minutes, with the legal costs to each party mounting as the case took longer to settle, at the rate of $5,000 for every five minutes' delay. If no agreement was reached after 30 minutes, the judge's decision determined the plaintiff's compensation.

Apart from being paid a fixed fee for participation, the 160 student subjects received additional rewards according to the bargaining outcome, with $1 corresponding to each $10,000 of outcome.

Under normal negotiation conditions, where pairs of players are assigned roles as either plaintiff or defendant from the outset before reading the details of the case, there was a large average difference in estimates of damages, with plaintiffs estimating the judge's award to be about $14,500 higher than defendants. However, this study did not itself demonstrate self-serving bias, since other factors might possibly have caused the discrepancy. Therefore a second study, by Babcock and colleagues (1995), varied the protocol. In this experiment there were two groups of subjects. The first group acted as a control group; roles were again randomly assigned and the subjects had the same instructions as in the first experiment. The estimates of the judge's award were even further apart than in the first experiment, averaging about $18,500. Furthermore, 28% of the pairs of bargainers failed to reach agreement. In the second group, the roles of the subjects were only assigned *after* they had read all the case materials. This had a dramatic effect on outcomes: estimates

▶

of the judge's award now varied by an average of less than $7,000, and only 6% of the subjects failed to reach agreement.

This second study therefore demonstrated that self-serving bias occurs in the encoding of information; other studies have confirmed this process, as bias causes people to ignore information that it not favorable to their interests.

Babcock and colleagues (1996) found another way of removing self-serving bias in the above situation. After the players were assigned roles and had read the case information, they were told about the possibility of bias and asked to list weaknesses in their position. Again the results were quite dramatic: there was no significant difference in the estimates of damages by both sides; 96% of the pairs settled, and settled more quickly than in either of the previously described protocols.

### Questions

1   What other factors might improve settlement rates in the type of legal dispute described above? Suggest other experimental protocols that might be used to investigate these factors.

2   Self-serving bias has sometimes been called the opposite: 'self-defeating' bias. Why?

3   What might be the role of self-serving bias in evolutionary terms, bearing in mind that it can be self-defeating?

## Case 9.3 Market entry in monopoly

Cooper, Garvin and Kagel (1997b) performed an interesting and revealing study of market entry in a monopolistic situation. In their experiment, monopolists were classified into two types, high-cost (H) and low-cost (L). A potential entrant was considering entry, but did not know the monopolist's type. The game was a simple sequential game, with the monopolists moving first by determining output, and then the potential entrant moved by deciding whether or not to enter. The game was repeated over a number of periods and cycles, in order to gain some insight into the learning process.

Monopolists moved by determining an output in the range 1–7 units. H firms maximized profit at the output of 2 units and made losses if output exceeded 5 units, regardless of whether the other firm entered. L firms maximized profit at 4 units, and continued to make profit up to the maximum output. Profits were obviously much higher for both H and L firms if the other firm did not enter. For entrants there were two different playing protocols. In the first one (LP), payoffs from entering were generally lower, and the expected value of entry (based on the prior probability of the monopolist being H of 0.5) was less than the payoff from staying out. In the second protocol (HP), payoffs were generally higher for the entrant, and the expected value of entry based on prior probabilities was greater than the payoff from staying out.

In both protocols the monopolist moves first, determining output. A high output in the initial move acts as a signal that the monopoly is of the L type, and therefore the other firm should stay out in order to maximize its own payoff. This signal is obviously more costly for *H* firms than for *L* firms, but there is some incentive for *H* firms to hide their type and aim for a pooling equilibrium, where *E* cannot see what type of firm the monopolist is. If *E* cannot distinguish between the two types of monopolist, he is forced to use prior probabilities, and in the LP protocol this will deter *E* from entry (based on expected values), giving greater payoffs to both *H* and *L* firms.

According to SGT, there are several equilibria in the LP protocol. There are two pure-strategies separating equilibria, where *H* produces an output of 2, while *L* produces either 6 or 7, deterring entry. There are also several pooling equilibria, with both *H* and *L* types producing the same output, any level from 1 to 5. In this case, since *E* cannot observe type, he is deterred from entry, as explained above.

In the HP protocol the SGT equilibrium is different, since it now becomes profitable for *L* firms to produce 6 or 7 units, an unprofitable output for *H* firms, resulting in a separating equilibrium. The higher output is necessary to convince *E* that they are indeed low-cost firms and that entry is therefore not worthwhile. In this situation there are also several partial pooling equilibria where the *H* and *L* types do not make exactly the same choices, but the sets of choices they sometimes make overlap.

In a second version of the experiment (Cooper, Garvin and Kagel 1997a), increased the payoffs of *H* firms at outputs of 6 and 7, so that they were still positive at the highest levels of output instead of making losses as previously. This made it more difficult for *L* firms to give a credible signal and separate, and therefore more difficult for *E* firms to decide whether or not to enter. The objective here was to see how the rate of convergence and the learning rate would be affected; they were predicted to be slower than in the first experiment.

A number of important empirical findings emerged from both of these experiments:

**1**  Players played as 'myopic maximizers' at the start, maximizing payoffs without regard to how their opponent would perceive this action. This applied in both protocols.

**2**  In the first LP protocol, *H* players soon learned to increase output to conceal their type, leading to a pooling equilibrium at the output of 4 units. By the end of all the sessions nearly 70% of the *H* players settled on this output, and nearly all the *L* players. Only 6% of potential entrants entered.

**3**  In the second HP protocol, *H* players again learned to increase their output from 2 to 4 units to try to pool with the *L* players. However, the *L* players then gradually learned to increase their own output to 6 units, to separate themselves from the *H* players, who could not make a profit at such a high output. By the end of the game there was essentially a separated equilibrium, with 80% of *L* players producing 6 units, and nearly half the *H* players producing 2 units. However, there was another spike of *H* players, with 32% of them still trying to conceal their type by producing 4 units. This turned out to be a failed strategy, since all the *E* players entered at all outputs up to and including 5 units.

**4**  In the second experiment convergence was not only slower, as predicted, but there was no real pattern of convergence at all. *H* players tended to average an output of 3 throughout the periods, while *L* players usually produced 4 units, with a gradual upward trend. The result was a partial pooling equilibrium, with overlapping outcomes. Instead of all *E* players entering at the output of 4, as in the first experiment, only 72% entered at this output, as it became more difficult for *E* players to observe type.

▼

**5** When steps of iterated dominance are explained to the subjects, the rate of equilibration is faster.

## Questions

**1** How do the empirical findings from the experiments compare with the predictions of SGT? What new light do they add to our knowledge of game behavior?

**2** Explain what is meant by a credible signal, using the experiments as an illustration.

**3** Explain the relationship between iteration and learning in the context of these experiments.

# CHAPTER · 10

## Social Preferences

When the British rock band Radiohead made its album *In Rainbows* available online from their website in 2007 for whatever price fans were prepared to pay, this seemed like a business blunder. True, sometimes sellers give products away for free to first-time buyers in order to get them hooked, but Radiohead were already a famous band.

One advantage of this tactic was the great favorable publicity that resulted. The album 'sold' more than 1.2 million copies in the first week alone, compared with the 300,000 copies sold in the first week of their previous album in 2003. Another even more important advantage is that the band is able to retain 100% of the revenues, whereas when artists use a recording company they only get to keep a relatively small fraction of the revenues generated.

However, this still raises the issue: why would people pay for music when they can easily get it for free? On average buyers paid £4 ($6) per album in the days following its release. Some online music labels, like Magnatune, have followed a similar strategy, allowing customers to pay what they want for albums, as long as the payment is within a certain price range ($5–$18). On average customers have been paying $8.20, far more than the minimum of $5, and even more than the recommended price of $8. This behavior is completely anomalous to standard economic behavior involving purely selfish preferences.

A study by Regner and Barria (2009) analyzed the behavior using a game-theoretic model of social preferences based on sequential reciprocity. The first move is made by the band, or the online label, offering the music on an open contract basis. This generates goodwill, or positive reciprocity, among customers. Thus they respond to this move by offering to pay substantial sums for the music, which also allows them to avoid feelings of guilt that they would incur if they paid only a small amount for something they enjoy. Regner and Barria conclude that a sequential reciprocity equilibrium corresponds to the observed pattern of behavior, and this was confirmed by a follow-up study by Regner (2015).

This case demonstrates the power of sequential reciprocity in social interactions, and also the significance of psychological game theory, which incorporates emotional reactions like anger, fear, pride, shame, gratitude and guilt into game situations.

---

# 10.1  The neoclassical model

*Nature*

As with other aspects of economic behavior discussed in previous chapters, our starting point is the neoclassical model (NM) and its shortcomings. In the case of social preferences and fairness the key assumption in the NM is that economic agents are motivated purely by self-interest. Indeed, the NM is often referred to as a self-interest model. This assumption is closely related to the rationality assumption discussed in Chapter 3. Advocates of this model tend to agree with an often-quoted statement by Stigler (1981, p. 176):

> Let me predict the outcome of the systematic and comprehensive testing of behavior in situations where self-interest and ethical values with wide verbal allegiance are in conflict. Much of the time, most of the time in fact, the self-interest theory … will win.

Behavioral economists in general tend to take issue with this stance, appealing to a large amount of evidence for various kinds of social preference, such as reciprocity. Before we begin to consider the meaning of these terms and any related evidence, however, it is necessary to clarify one fundamental and often overlooked point in the burgeoning literature relating to this alleged conflict. 'Pure' self-interest models are in many ways a straw man; they represent a simplified situation that is easy to model and apply, in a similar way to the model of pure competition. It is this simplicity that makes the model attractive, not its realism, since only pathological individuals have no consideration for the effects of their behavior on others. Furthermore, such individuals, while motivated by pure self-interest, are extremely unlikely to achieve their objectives, because they alienate others. All normal individuals, even those we would describe as 'selfish', take into account the effects of their behavior on others to some extent, and also take into account the welfare of others. As we shall see, this 'taking into account' may not be deliberate, but be a result of emotions such as guilt, anger, envy, pity, outrage or even disgust. Thus a model based on people acting in their self-interest, which many would claim is part of the NM, is also consistent with people have other-regarding preferences. It is important to understand that there is no fundamental incompatibility here. Likewise, it is also important to understand that *all* behavioral models are essentially extensions of the self-interest model, not negations of it, in the same way that some intertemporal choice models extend and modify the instantaneous utility function. The analogy is a close one, since the pure self-interest model assumes that people maximize utility functions that only take into account self-regarding preferences and are not affected by the utility of others, whereas behavioral models modify this utility function to take into account other-regarding preferences as well. We shall return to this point a number of times in this chapter, since it is the cause of a number of confusions. In order to prevent some of these confusions we will distinguish between 'self-interest' and 'self-regarding preferences'. 'Self-interest' in the broad sense can take other-regarding preferences into account; 'pure self-interest' does not.

## Anomalies

There is an impressive list of anomalies relating to the 'pure self-interest' aspect of the NM, which arise both from field studies and from experiments. The following examples give some flavor to the kinds of behavior that will be examined in the course of the chapter:

- Tipping waiters
- Giving to charity
- Voting
- Completing tax returns honestly
- Voluntary unpaid work
- Working harder when there are no monetary incentives than when there are monetary incentives
- Firms laying off workers in a recession rather than cutting wages
- Monopolies not raising prices when there are shortages
- Contributing to the provision of public goods
- Punishing 'free-riders', even when there is a cost in doing so
- Cooperating in prisoner's dilemma games
- Investing in others, and trusting them to repay
- Making generous offers in ultimatum bargaining games
- Rejecting ungenerous offers in ultimatum bargaining games

These anomalies relate to aspects of behavior that can be described as either **altruistic** or **spiteful**. While altruism can be defined in many ways, as we will see, a basic definition is that it relates to behavior that confers a benefit to others, while involving a cost to the originator of the behavior, with no corresponding material benefit. Tipping waiters at restaurants where one is unlikely to return is an example. Spiteful behavior can be viewed as the flip side of altruistic behavior. This is behavior that imposes a cost on others, while also involving a cost to the originator of the behavior, with no corresponding material benefit. An example is punishing those who throw litter out of their car by yelling at them (the cost may be small in terms of effort, but there is a risk of a hostile altercation). It should be noted that spiteful behavior is not necessarily bad for society; in the above example it may help to enforce valued social norms. It is notable that both altruistic behavior and spiteful behavior confer benefits to the originator that are non-material, or psychological. Case 1.3 gave an illustration of this, and also indicated that the 'warm glow' people feel in gift-giving is supported by neuroeconomic evidence. We will see in examining social preferences that neuroeconomic studies are also particularly revealing in understanding social behavior. This kind of altruism, sometimes called 'warm-glow' altruism, is also referred to as **impure altruism**, to distinguish it from **pure altruism**, where a person experiences a psychic benefit from an increase in someone else's well-being even if they are not responsible for causing this increase. Thus if your car breaks down and I gain satisfaction from giving you a lift, but not if someone else gives you a lift, then this is an example of impure altruism; if I gain satisfaction regardless of who gives you a lift, this is pure altruism. The distinction between these two types of altruism is important, since the evolutionary factors leading to their existence are different in nature. As we will see in more detail later, pure altruism is based on empathy and the mirror neuron system, while impure altruism is related to signaling intentions and reciprocity.

It can also be seen that several of the anomalies above relate to games, some of which were discussed in the previous chapter. As we saw, games in this context refer to situations where there is an interdependency in decision-making. The essence of these interdependent decision-making situations is that when A makes a decision (for example regarding price, entry into a market, whether to take a job), it will consider the reactions of other persons or firms to its different strategies, and how these reactions will affect their own utility or profit. It must also take into account that the other parties, or players, in selecting their reactive strategies, will consider how A will react to their reactions, which again should be taken into account by A and so on. As we have seen in games like the 'beauty contest', this can continue in a virtually infinite progression. In this situation there is often a considerable amount of uncertainty regarding the results of any decision.

Many elements of real-life strategic situations can be simulated in game experiments, which have the considerable advantage of isolating a particular behavioral factor and simplifying analysis. In this chapter we will discuss games related to social preferences, in particular involving trust, bargaining and punishment. In each case the predictions of standard game theory are examined, and compared with empirical evidence, and we will consider how the standard model can be improved by modification and extension. Now that the basic tools of game-theoretic analysis have been described in the previous chapter, it will be easier to understand both the basic model and appropriate extensions.

In order to appreciate the basis of behavioral game theory, it is important to understand the nature of inferences from empirical studies. If empirical data do not 'fit' the predictions of a particular theory involving the use of game-theoretical analysis this does not mean that game theory as a method of analysis is wrong. There are a number of possible conclusions: (1) the utility functions of the players were mis-specified; (2) bounded rationality prevented the players from using the game-theoretical analysis properly; (3) learning factors caused a time lag in terms of reaching an equilibrium situation; or (4) the players misunderstood the nature of the game, or played a different game from that intended by the experimenters.

As we discussed in the previous chapter, game theory is an important element of modern economics that is heavily indebted to the neoclassical model. In its standard form (sometimes confusingly called 'analytical' game theory), we have seen that it makes a number of important assumptions related to the conclusions above: (1) people have correct mental representations of the relevant game; (2) people choose fully rationally; (3) equilibria are reached instantly, since there are no time lags due to learning effects or other factors; and (4) people are motivated purely by self-interest. Behavioral game theory relaxes all four of these assumptions. The first three assumptions were discussed in the previous chapter, along with the implications of relaxing them; in this chapter we will focus on the last assumption, although the first three are still relevant because there is some interdependency between the assumptions.

## 10.2  The nature of social preferences

*Social preferences and fairness*

Fehr and Fischbacher (2005) define social preferences as 'other-regarding preferences in the sense that individuals who exhibit them behave as if they value the payoff of relevant reference agents positively or negatively.' Several things are noteworthy regarding this definition. First, we shall see that it is not just the payoffs of other people that are important, but also their beliefs and intentions that are relevant. Second, these payoffs, beliefs and intentions can be valued positively or negatively, depending on the reference agent. Our perceptions of other people's beliefs and intentions determine whether we are well-disposed or ill-disposed towards them. If we feel well-disposed to the other agent we value their payoffs positively, but if we are ill-disposed towards the agent we value their payoffs negatively. Third, the relevant reference agents may be a person's colleagues, relatives, trading partners or neighbors, depending on the situation (Fehr and Fishbacher, 2005).

The concept of fairness is central to understanding social preferences, since it determines people's beliefs regarding how both the costs and benefits of people's behavior should be distributed. These beliefs in turn affect how people value the payoffs, beliefs and intentions of others. It is not proposed here to discuss what is fair and what is not. Indeed that would be contrary to the approach of this book, which takes the view that 'fairness is in the eye of the beholder'. A society's view of what is fair can change hugely over the course of centuries and even decades; two hundred years ago slavery and hanging people for stealing a sheep were acceptable in many countries. Some societies today regard the stoning of adulterers to death and 'honor killings' of family members for unapproved love affairs as being acceptable, or even as moral obligations. Even over relatively short periods of time people tend to adjust their values of fairness as circumstances change. The purpose of this section is to examine the factors that determine judgments of fairness in general terms. It is useful to follow the approach of Kahneman, Knetsch and Thaler (KKT) (1986), who identify and describe three of these, based on empirical research. Although their discussion relates to the context of profit-seeking by firms, the factors can be applied to more general situations. The key concept in this approach is **dual entitlement**, meaning that both parties in a transaction are entitled to certain considerations. If we extend the KKT approach, these transactions do not have to be monetary in nature, but can incorporate any kind of cost and benefit. There are three main elements in this concept of dual entitlement:

1   *Reference transactions*
    Market transactions can relate to a price, a wage or a rent. However, we should also consider the broader context of non-market transactions, where some non-monetary cost or benefit is involved, for example where it is customary to bring a bottle of wine to someone's house for dinner. The reference transaction is normally determined by the history of a particular type of transaction, or by prevailing competitive rates.

Thus it may not be regarded as fair for a landlord to increase the rent of an existing tenant, unless rents for similar properties in the area are also increasing, but it may be acceptable to charge a higher rent for a new tenant. The new tenant does not have the same entitlement as an existing one. The basis for this judgment may involve the concept of **moral hazard**, or post-contract opportunism. Once a transactor has made a commitment, like renting a property or taking a job, it may be regarded as unfair if the other transactor takes advantage of this commitment. Sometimes this is referred to as the **'holdup' problem**.

Conflicts may arise in particular when there is more than one reference point. For example, in a wage dispute a union may claim that their wage is unfair because workers of a similar skill in another industry are higher paid, but an employer may claim that their wages have risen faster in recent years than similar workers.

Two observations can be made regarding the reference transaction factor. First, it is in line with prospect theory's emphasis on reference points as far as the perception of gains and losses is concerned. Second, it illustrates that fairness judgments are based on what is normal, or 'norms', rather than what is 'just'. The consequence of this is that not only does the yardstick of what is fair change over time, but also that agents tend to perform, and be expected to perform, fairly in the marketplace. For example, a majority of people tip around 15% in restaurants. An interesting sidelight on this issue is that 'ticket touting', or charging above the standard ticket price in the secondary market, is generally regarded as unfair, and indeed criminal. Theater tickets in London's West End are regularly sold at below a market-clearing price, resulting in continuing shortages for popular shows. In 2006 a tout was fined £9,000 for selling tickets at a 500% markup. Even though people are obviously willing to pay the higher price, and may not have been able to purchase tickets earlier at the standard price, the below-equilibrium standard price is regarded as the reference price and the huge excess causes outrage. We will say more about social norms in the next section, in terms of their nature, origins and functions.

2    *Outcomes to the transactors*

The general principle of dual entitlement means that it is usually regarded as unfair if one transactor makes a gain by imposing a similar loss on the other transactor. Thus if there is a shortage of snow shovels after a big snow fall, an increase in the selling price may be regarded as 'gouging', since such a gain comes at the expense of the buyer. However, it is usually perceived as fair to pass on any increase in cost to the customer, since the seller is not perceived to make a gain in this case. It should be noted that empirical findings suggest that there is an asymmetry here, since reductions in cost are not necessarily expected to be passed on to the customer; the seller's gain is not perceived to be at the buyer's expense.

Once again concepts from prospect theory are relevant in the discussion of reference prices, along with concepts from mental accounting theory. The phenomenon of loss-aversion means that overall welfare is reduced if gains are made at the expense of equal losses in monetary terms, since losers tend to lose more in utility than winners gain. The accounting rules used to make judgments also suggest a lack of fungibility between different types of expense. Out-of-pocket costs, for example paying higher prices, are not judged in the same way as opportunity costs, like not receiving a price reduction. Furthermore, framing effects are important in terms of how the transactors code gains and losses. A loss is perceived as worse than the cancellation of a gain. For example, firms may prefer to offer a discount in a low season rather than reduce prices, since later on it is more acceptable to customers to remove the discount than increase the price. Similarly it is more acceptable for firms not to pay bonuses to employees, however much these were expected, than to cut wages. There is also some evidence that the consideration of outcomes to transactors is relevant in the behavior of oligopolists. Engel and Zhurakhovska (2014) find experimental evidence that oligoposts, as insiders, are less likely to collude when this is likely to cause harm to outsiders in the form of paying a higher price. They attribute this to guilt aversion, ruling out inequity aversion, reciprocity and efficiency as alternative explanations.

**3**   *Circumstances of changing transaction terms*

Kahneman, Knetsch and Thaler (1986) discuss these in a price-setting situation, classifying occasions for change into the three categories of profit reductions, profit increases and increases in market power. However, a more useful general classification, which would fit the empirical findings equally well, may relate to controllable and uncontrollable factors. 'Gouging' actions are therefore generally regarded as unacceptable, and often cause outrage. For example, after the singer Whitney Houston died in 2012, there was a big price hike for some of her albums on the UK iTunes site. This caused considerable customer anger, particularly since a download facility does not involve any scarcity of the product. Another recent example of an alleged 'gouging' situation was widely reported in the British press when the Tesco supermarket chain refused to buy various popular food items, notably Marmite, from the producer, Unilever, in response to a reputed price rise of 10%. Unilever claimed the price increase was due to an increase in costs caused by the decline of the pound after the Brexit vote, but the situation was made more complicated by the fact that Unilever is a Dutch company, and that Marmite is produced in the UK.

Thus, in general, if a firm has an increase in demand that may increase both profit and market power, this may have occurred because of factors outside the control of the firm, and in this case it may be perceived as unfair to increase price. However, an increase in demand caused by the firm producing a better quality product or providing better service may justify a price increase. Similarly increases in cost outside the firm's control causing a fall in profit may justify a price increase, but increases in cost due to inefficiency may not. The same rules apply to changes in wages and rents.

In general exploitation of market power is judged to be unacceptable. What may be relevant to the judgment here is how a transactor gained such market power. Market power based on a superior product or technology may be acceptable, while market power gained by restrictive practices may not. Research findings are limited on this aspect, but it appears that some forms of price discrimination are not regarded as fair, even when substitutes are available.

## Reciprocity

Closely related to the concepts of fairness and dual entitlement is the concept of reciprocity. This term is used in different senses, so it is useful to clarify some issues at this stage. In general, we tend to understand reciprocity in terms of 'tit-for-tat': if people are kind to us, we are kind to them, but if they are unkind we are unkind in return. However, this is a somewhat vague description, and covers a range of different behaviors. Sometimes the term reciprocity refers to the tendency of some people to be conditional cooperators. This means that such people are prepared to cooperate as long as others in the game cooperate, but will 'defect' if others do not cooperate. Defection in two-player games means increasing one's payoff at the expense of others, as discussed in the previous chapter, and in multiplayer games this often amounts to 'free-riding', where a person acts entirely in their self-interest, imposing a cost on others. In one-shot simultaneous games a player often does not know if the other player or players are going to cooperate or not, so expectations are important. These may be based on the history of the other players' strategy.

We will see that the concept of **strong reciprocity** is very important in social preferences, and has fundamental consequences for both private and public policy. Strong reciprocity can be distinguished from 'standard' reciprocity in that, in addition to involving conditional cooperation, it also involves a willingness to punish other players at a cost to the punishing player. An important implication of this is that purely self-interested players will never punish another player, because there no benefits, only costs. We will also see that there are different reasons for punishment. 'Strategic' punishment relates to situations where there is an expected material payoff from punishment. This may occur because punishment has a deterrent effect, causing other players to cooperate more in the future in repeated games, or because if a player does not punish defectors he may in turn be punished. However, for strong reciprocators punishment need not have a material payoff; the benefit may be purely in psychic terms, increasing the player's utility by making them feel better. A strongly reciprocal player therefore responds kindly towards actions that are perceived to be kind and hostilely to actions that are perceived to be hostile. Whether an action is perceived to be kind or hostile depends on the fairness or unfairness of the intention underlying the action (Fehr and Fishbacher, 2005). The existence of strong reciprocators in a multiplayer game has far-reaching implications for behavior and equilibrium, because not only is their behavior different from purely self-interested players, and conditional cooperators, but also their strategies affect the behavior of the purely self-interested players, in particular by making them more inclined to cooperate. Punishment is commonly 'social', where defectors are punished, but it can also be 'antisocial', where cooperators are punished. We will discuss the reasons for the second type of punishment later in the chapter. Models of reciprocity, the evidence relating to them, and the policy implications, will also be examined in later sections.

### *Fairness games and the neoclassical model*

Much insight can be gained into people's perceptions of fairness by examining the results of various games in an experimental setting. Common games that are used to investigate fairness and social preferences are **ultimatum bargaining games**, **dictator games**, **trust games**, **prisoner's dilemma games** and **public goods games**. We have seen a number of examples of these games in the previous chapter. Some games are one-shot games and some are conducted on a repeated basis, and the importance of this distinction will be discussed later, since it is a source of debate and confusion. Games can be varied in several ways to observe differences in behavior, and this aspect is discussed in the next section. The purpose here is to observe differences between the predictions of 'analytical' game theory in the standard model and empirical findings. With these empirical results in mind we can then move on to consider how social preferences can be modeled into a game-theoretic analysis in such a way that the findings can be predicted. The different game situations are now discussed.

1    *Ultimatum bargaining games*

These are two-player games, and, as with most games, involve a proposer (P) and a responder (R). An example was given in the previous chapter. We saw that, in its standard form, a certain sum of money, frequently $10, represents a value of the gain to exchange, or surplus, that would be lost if no trade was made. P offers the sum $x$ to R, leaving themselves $10 - x$. R can either accept the offer or reject it, in which case both players receive nothing.

The basic form of the game is so simple that it does not faithfully represent the more complex bargaining situations in real life, which often involve several stages, but it does offer some important insights as far as fairness is concerned. The SEM, based on 'pure' self-interest, predicts that R will be happy to receive even the smallest amount of money rather than nothing, and that therefore P will propose the smallest amount of money possible (maybe one cent), with R accepting this offer. However, the original study by Güth, Schmittberger and Schwarze (1987) observed that proposers sometimes offered 50% of the surplus and that responders often rejected positive offers. Empirical findings in experiments have consistently confirmed this result, contradicting the predictions of SGT. Some of these studies use the method of eliciting responses described above, while others have asked responders to state a **minimal acceptable offer (MAO)**. The latter method has the advantage that more exact information can be provided, particularly regarding infrequent low offers; a possible disadvantage is that this method may cause an upward bias in responses, meaning that people may demand more (there is a lack of evidence here).

These studies generally indicate that between 60% and 80% of offers are between 0.4 and 0.5 of the surplus, and that there are almost no offers below 0.2. Furthermore, low offers are frequently rejected, with offers below 0.2 being rejected about half of the time. The above findings are also robust as far as increased stakes are concerned. For example, an experiment was conducted with Arizona students where the stakes were $100, and a couple of students rejected offers of $30 (Hoffman, McCabe and Smith, 1996). A similar result has been found with a $400 stake (List and Cherry, 2000), and in countries with low disposable income where the stake was equivalent to three months' expenditure for a typical subject (Cameron, 1999).

One intriguing, and robust, finding from experiments is that 'super-fair' offers, meaning offers of over 50% of the pot, are sometimes rejected (Güth, Schmidt and Sutter, 2003; Bahry and Wilson, 2006; Bellemare, Krger and van Soest, 2008; Henning-Schmidt et al., 2008). This aspect is discussed further in the section on cultural factors.

In summary, the results can be interpreted as showing that responders are angered by proposals that they regard as unfair, and are prepared to punish such unfair behavior at a cost to themselves (being 'spiteful'). At this point we will not explore the issue of what causes such feelings of unfairness, and how much they are innate or determined by culture. This is better left until later in the chapter, after a discussion of variations of this game, other games, and empirical findings.

**2**  *Dictator games*

These are games where the responder's ability to reject an offer is removed, and thus are even simpler. In a one-shot situation they do not even involve strategic thinking (at least in the standard model), since the proposer does not have to consider the reaction of the responder. However, the value of such games is that they establish whether proposers make generous offers because they fear rejection, or whether they are altruistic. Any positive offer by a proposer is altruistic rather than strategic, meaning caused by the fear of rejection. The first comprehensive comparison of ultimatum and dictator games (Forsythe et al., 1994) indicated that dictators offered on average about 20%, much lower than proposers in ultimatum games. Early studies also indicated that average offers are close to the offer that maximizes expected payoffs given the actual pattern of rejections in ultimatum games (Roth et al., 1991), suggesting strategic behavior, but later more sophisticated analyses showed that offers were more generous than payoff-maximizing offers, even allowing for risk-aversion (Hoffman, McCabe and Smith, 1996; Henrich et al., 2001). In the Hoffman, McCabe and Smith study 'dictators' still shared their wealth in about 40% of the observed bargains when the anonymity of the offerer was preserved.

However, these results have also been called into question, on the basis that the wealth of the dictators was not earned. In real-life situations earned wealth may be the more likely situation. Cherry, Frykblom and Shogren (2002) controlled for this factor in an experiment involving three treatments: baseline (unearned wealth), earned wealth and double-blind with earned wealth. Subjects, who were undergraduate students, 'earned' wealth by answering a sample of GMAT questions correctly. In the baseline situations a zero offer was only made in an average of 17% of the bargains. In contrast, in situations where wealth was 'earned', zero offers occurred in about 80% of the bargains. This increased to around 96% in the double-blind situations where the dictators acted in complete anonymity from both the other transactor and the experimenter. The authors therefore concluded that strategic concerns and not fairness were the motivation for other-regarding behavior.

It has also been observed that the status of the dictator relative to the receiver is relevant in determining generosity (Jakiela, 2011). However, the relationships here appear to be complex, with the distinction between earned and unearned status being relevant, as well as cultural factors. In the USA the study reports that unearned status is negatively related to generosity of sharing, but earned status is positively related. However, in Kenya only unearned status is related, in this case positively, with generosity.

In some experiments dictator games are observed by third parties, who have no monetary interest in the game, but who are in a position to punish proposers at a cost to themselves. Fehr and Fischbacher (2004) find that 60% of observers are willing to punish under these conditions, punishing more the lower the proposer's offer. In this case the reason for punishment is different from the reason in ultimatum games, since reciprocity is not involved.

In repeated dictator games in real life, which managers are often faced with, and in particular when decisions may be difficult, for example firing workers and implementing unpopular policies, there is some evidence of ego-depletion effects (Achtziger, Alós-Ferrer and Wagner, 2015). As we have seen with the concept of decision fatigue, these may result in a deteriorating pattern of decisions over time, with such decisions also becoming less prosocial.

**3**    *Trust games*

Trust is the basis of any transaction that does not involve a complete contract that specifies all possible outcomes of the transaction, that is, the vast majority of transactions. This is because most transactions involve costs and benefits in the future where there is always an element of uncertainty. When we buy a good, we assume that it will provide the benefits that we expect; the seller assumes that he will be paid in full. Other types of transaction, like renting a property, taking a job or hiring an employee, lending money involve similar assumptions. Other activities, not normally considered as relating to economic behavior, such as leaving one's front door unlocked, parking on the street, giving to charity and getting married, also are based on an element of trust. In many of these cases we are considering trust in strangers, in other words people with whom we usually do not expect any further interaction, while in other cases we may expect many further interactions, such as in a marriage. This is an important distinction, since we are more inclined to trust those with whom we have already successfully interacted, those with whom we expect to interact repeatedly, or family.

Economists regard trust as a means of reducing transactions costs, since engaging in legal contracts or other forms of commitment is costly (Klaes, 2015e); thus it can be viewed as being 'social capital'. Some economists believe that countries and cultures that are more trusting have higher rates of growth and development; certainly there appears to be a strong correlation here (Knack and Keefer, 1997), but the causation is more complex, because we will see that the existence of trust does not just reduce transactions costs, it also affects behavior in fundamental ways, in particular increasing investment.

In social psychology there is a different perspective on trust. There is less focus on the consequences of trust, in terms of whether it is likely to be repaid or not, and more emphasis on psychological and social factors determining trust, which is a non-consequentialist approach. Dunning and colleagues (2014) emphasize the importance of social norms in establishing an element of trust in initial encounters. This can allow the creation of 'reciprocal reassurance' which can then lead to a virtuous circle of mutual cooperation. The main problem here is determining how these social norms arise in different ways in different cultures, an issue discussed in the next section. In terms of individual psychology, Acar-Burkay, Fennis and Warlop (2014) have suggested that a 'social-cognitive motivation to manage uncertainty' is a key driver of trust, and this is reflected in the **need for closure**. This characteristic varies across individuals, and those with high need for closure tend to have polarized trust relationships according to their social distance from other persons. With people who are close to them they tend to be very trusting, but with others who are socially distance they tend to be very mistrusting. Furthermore, the authors find that people with high need for closure tend not to change these initial trust judgments in the light of later information relating to trustworthiness.

The essence of all interactions involving trust, and games relating to them, is that some kind of investment by the truster ($I$) in the trustee ($T$) is required. This investment is risky because it may not be repaid by the trustee. However, if the return from investment is sufficient, and the investment is repaid sufficiently, the investor will benefit in terms of making a net gain compared with not investing. A typical investment game involves $I$ having an amount $x$ which they can choose to invest or keep. If $I$ invests the amount $y$ (and keeps $x - y$) this earns a return so that it becomes $y(1 + r)$. $T$ must then decide how much of this amount to share with $I$, playing a dictator game at this stage. If $T$ keeps $z$ and returns $y(1 + r) - z$ to $I$, then the total payoffs are $z$ to $T$ and $(x - y) + y(1 + r) - z$, or $x - z + ry$, to $I$. It is therefore possible to measure the amount of trust and the amount of trustworthiness: trust is measured by the size of investment $y$, while trustworthiness is measured by the amount returned, $x - z + ry$.

The neoclassical model predicts that there will be no trust, for the reason that trustees will never return anything. Empirical findings have invariably contradicted this. A study by Berg, Dickhaut and McCabe (1995) used an initial amount $x$ of \$10 and a rate of return $r$ of 2. On average investors invested about 50%; 16% of investors invested the entire amount; and only 6% invested nothing (zero trust). The average amount repaid was about 95% of the amount invested (or a third of the tripled amount), although there was a wide variation. This indicates that the return to trust is around zero, and this result has been confirmed by some later studies. In a study performed in Sweden, Bostedt and Brännlund (2012) find that, even with a high return on investment of 400%, there was less trust shown by trusters than was merited by the behavior of trustees. There appear to be some cross-cultural variations in trust behavior, and these are discussed in the following section.

Trust games are interesting since they allow reciprocity, or at least positive reciprocity, to be measured. This is because the second stage of the game is, as we have seen, a dictator game on the part of the trustee. Therefore, if trustees repay more than they would pay in an ordinary dictator game, any excess must be related to reciprocity. The concept of reciprocity is discussed in detail in Section 10.6, but at this point we can think of positive reciprocity as arising from some feeling of moral obligation on the part of the trustee. In terms of empirical findings, a study by Cox (2004) found that repayments were significantly larger than allocations in a similar dictator game, but that the difference was small, about 10%. Dufwenberg and Gneezy (2000) also found that returns were larger than allocations in a similar dictator game, but in this case the difference was insignificant. Thus it seems that positive reciprocity is not a major factor in trust games.

As with the other games described above, there are variations on trust games, in particular involving many persons or groups. These are discussed in the next section, and also in the section on policy implications related to social and market norms.

**4    *Prisoner's dilemma games***

The PD is perhaps the most well-known game of all, and was discussed in some detail in the previous chapter. The classic PD situation involves two prisoners who are held in separate police cells, accused of committing a crime. They cannot communicate with each other, so each does not know how the other is acting. If neither confesses, the prosecutor can only get them convicted on other minor offences, each prisoner receiving a one-year sentence. If one confesses while the other does not, the one confessing will be freed while the other one receives a ten-year sentence. If both confess they will each receive a five-year sentence. The normal form is shown in Table 10.1, which is a repeat of Table 9.1.

**Table 10.1**   Prisoner's dilemma

|  |  | Suspect B | |
| --- | --- | --- | --- |
|  |  | Confess | Not Confess |
| Suspect A | Confess | 5, 5 | 0, 10 |
|  | Not Confess | 10, 0 | 1, 1 |

The values in the table represent payoffs, in terms of jail sentences; the payoffs for Suspect A are the left-hand values, while the payoffs for Suspect B are the right-hand values. The objective for each suspect in this case is obviously to minimize the payoff in terms of jail time. The problem that they have in this case is that the best combination payoff for the pair of them is for them both not to confess, in other words to 'cooperate' with each other; in this case each suspect will receive a one-year sentence. However, as was shown in the previous chapter, this is not an equilibrium strategy according to the standard game theory of the NM. The equilibrium is for both suspects to confess, or to 'defect', since this is a dominant strategy for players. This equilibrium situation represents a paradox, since they will both end up receiving longer sentences, five years, than if they had cooperated. The equilibrium still applies even if the suspects had agreed to cooperate beforehand; they will still tend to defect once they are separated and do not know how the other is acting.

The reader may wonder at this stage how the type of situation described above relates to social preferences. This is more easily understood if we examine the payoff structure. In any PD situation there is a hierarchy of payoffs, which are frequently labeled as temptation, reward, punishment and sucker's payoff. The relationship between strategies and payoffs is shown in Table 10.2.

**Table 10.2**   Structure of payoffs in prisoner's dilemma

| Strategy pair (self/other) | Name of payoff |
| --- | --- |
| Defect/Cooperate | Temptation    (0) |
| Cooperate/Cooperate | Reward    (1) |
| Defect/Defect | Punishment    (5) |
| Cooperate/Defect | Sucker's Payoff    (10) |

In this light we can see that the PD situation is more related to reciprocity than with fairness. Extensive empirical studies have been conducted for over two decades, and they generally show that in one-shot situations players cooperate about half of the time. Although this plainly contradicts the predictions of standard game theory, it is not clear whether the cooperation is caused by altruism or the expectation of matching cooperation. Therefore the analysis of PD games is a blunt tool for predicting real-world behavior. One interesting finding is that pre-play communication, which according to the standard model should not affect outcomes at all, has a significant effect in terms of increasing cooperation.

As with other games, there are many variations of the standard PD situation. The game as described above involves simultaneous play, or at least each player determines their action without knowing what the other player has decided. If the game is transformed into a sequential play, it resembles a trust game, with the second player acting as a dictator. As we shall see later, many experiments have also been conducted with repeated PD games, sometimes using the same pair of players each time, and sometimes changing the pairs.

Some research has also indicated that the tendency of a player to cooperate or defect in PD games can be estimated from viewing a photo of the player's face. Stirrat and Perrett (2010) find that subjects' behavior during PD games was significantly related to face width: height ratio, with people having wider faces being less likely to cooperate. Furthermore, they find that manipulating this ratio affects subjects' judgments of the cooperativeness of players. Carré, McCormick and Mondloch (2009) find that aggression is also related to lack of cooperation, or trustworthiness and that both of these characteristics are related to face width: height ratio. Rule and colleagues (2013) find that these relationships do not always hold, and suggest further research is necessary to clarify the situation.

## 5 *Public goods games*

Economists define public goods as those goods which have the characteristics of **non-excludability** and **non-rivalry**. This means that they cannot be easily provided to one person without automatically being provided for others, and the consumption of the good by one person does not reduce the amount of the good available to others. Street lighting is a common example. There are also many examples of semi-public goods, like libraries, stadiums, hospitals, roads and fish stocks, which satisfy these characteristics up to a point. In each case one person's consumption or activity causes a negative externality on others. Essentially public goods games are multiple-player PD situations, where the Pareto-optimal solution is for all players to contribute to the maximum (cooperation), but the equilibrium solution according to the pure self-interest of the standard model is to contribute nothing and defect.

Therefore these goods present a problem for public policy, since few people will volunteer to pay for them, or refrain from consumption, hoping to get a '**free ride**' by enjoying the goods that others have paid for. The situations can be easily modeled in experimental games as follows: each of the $N$ players has an endowment of $x_i$ and invests $y_i$ of this resource in a public good that is shared by everyone, and has a total per-unit value of $m$. Player $i$ receives the benefit $x_i - y_i + m\Sigma y_j/N$, where $\Sigma y_i$ represents the sum of the contributions of all the other players. The dominant strategy is to defect by making no contribution, in spite of the fact that all players could collectively benefit most by cooperating and contributing the maximum to the common pool of resources. A number of assumptions are made in this simple model regarding the value of $m$ and the shape of the common utility function.

Empirical evidence again contradicts the standard model, since generally subjects in experiments contribute about half of their resources. There is, however, a wide range of responses, with a majority of players contributing either all their resources or nothing (Ledyard, 1995; Sally, 1995). As with PD games it is difficult to conclude whether people contribute from altruism or because of expectations of cooperation. Furthermore, it is impossible to say whether people defect out of self-interest or whether they have reciprocal social preferences but expect others to free-ride. In order to draw sharper conclusions the structure of the game needs to be tweaked and the consequences examined, as will be seen in the next section. In particular it is interesting to introduce the possibility of punishment at a cost; as we have seen, this allows us to see the role of strong reciprocation. A detailed example of a public goods experiment with such variations is given in Case 10.2. We will see that punishment changes the whole playing of the game in experimental studies: without punishment people tend to 'free-ride' and contribute little, this trend increasing as the game continues; with punishment people contribute far more, with this trend increasing as the game continues.

Another aspect of punishment is often observed in public goods games, referred to as **antisocial punishment**. Unlike the punishment of free-riders, who are punished for contributing too little, antisocial punishment involves the punishment of those who contribute more than average. There are two possible reasons for such an action: (1) low or non-contributors may retaliate in turn against those punishing them, and (2) low contributors may want to deter high contributors from giving large amounts, because this establishes a social norm that makes the low contributors look bad. This second factor is discussed in Case 10.4.

## 10.3  Factors affecting social preferences

The different games described in the previous section have been studied under a wide variety of different conditions that help to shed light on a number of issues related to social preferences. These conditions relate to three main categories of factor: methodological and structural, environmental, and demographic. These factors and their effects are now discussed.

### Methodological and structural factors

These change how experiments are conducted, and include the following factors: repetition and learning, stakes, anonymity, communication, entitlement, competition, available information, number of players, intentions, delay, and the opportunity and cost of punishment. These constitute the most important single variable, particularly since they are to a large extent controllable. This means that, by using clever variations in experiments, individual factors and their effects can be isolated.

**1**  *Repetition and learning*

When ultimatum games are repeated with strangers, there is mixed evidence whether there is a learning effect. Bolton and Zwick (1995) report no learning effect, but other studies have found slight but usually insignificant tendency for both offers and rejections to fall over time (Roth et al., 1991; Knez and Camerer, 1995; Slonim and Roth, 1998; List and Cherry, 2000).

Learning can also occur when players know the offers and MAOs of other players. A study by Harrison and McCabe (1996) indicated that providing such information reduces offers and MAOs to around 15% by the 15th round of play. There may be several reasons for this: responders may cease punishing unfair proposers if they see that others are not doing so; they may 'tire' of punishing, if the desire to punish is a visceral impulse that can be satiated; or they may adjust their perceptions of what is fair. Although it is possible in principle to test if there is a 'tiring' effect by pausing the game for a while and then restarting it, there is at present a lack of research regarding the contributions of any of the above factors.

There is a similar pattern with trust games, PD games and public goods games. When these are repeated with strangers, trust, cooperation and contributions all tend to decline over time (Fehr and Gächter, 2000). The situation is different if punishment is allowed, as seen later. It is also different when games are repeated with the same partners. In this case trust and cooperation become greater over time and contributions become higher (Andreoni and Miller, 1993). Much research has been done with repeated PD games, and various forms of '**tit-for-tat**' (**TFT**) strategy tend to evolve (Axelrod, 1985). Such strategies invoke repaying like-for-like, so defection is punished by defection and cooperation is rewarded with cooperation. The main problem with a simple TFT strategy is that a single defection by one player leads to a debilitating cascade of defections; this is an even more severe problem in real life where 'noise', meaning errors of both judgment and interpretation of responses due to bounded rationality and communications problems, can easily occur.

The success of different strategies in repeated PD situations can be tested by computer simulation, the method pioneered by Axelrod (1985). More recent studies have introduced further complications related to real-life situations, such as playing the game sequentially as opposed to simultaneously, and allowing players to have the option of choosing which other players to play with. Successful strategies tend to be easily understood, 'nice' (tending to cooperate), but prepared to punish (defecting where necessary as a deterrent). Stability over time is not easy to achieve, given the dynamics of different strategies. For example, in a population of players using different strategies against different players, the nastiest strategy, 'always defect' (AD), will do well at first, but then starts to fail, as more AD players play each other and get low payoffs. TFT then gains ground, but because of the weakness of tending to spiral into mutual defection mentioned above, it also starts to lose out to more 'forgiving' strategies, like 'generous' TFT, which occasionally (but unpredictably) forgives defection. 'Generous' in turn allows the rise of even more forgiving strategies, like 'always cooperate' (AC). However, as such strategies spread, this in turn allows the return of the parasitic AD strategy, and a cycle may be initiated (Nowak, May and Sigmund, 1995).

What can be concluded from existing research regarding PD, trust and public goods games in a repetitive context? The general consensus is that in environments where people (1) have frequent interactions with others, (2) recognize these others, (3) remember the outcomes of these interactions, and (4) are in a position to punish these others either by defection or by refusing to play with them (social ostracism in real life), successful strategies tend to be 'nicer' or more cooperative. It should be noted that the threat of being excluded from playing (and not receiving any payoff at all) may be enough to force people to cooperate. We have to be seen to be nice to get people to trust us.

There is one final observation to be made regarding repetition and learning. It has been assumed so far that players are human, and therefore intellectually capable of calculating the effects of strategies in terms of outcomes. It is important to understand that this is not a necessity. As we saw in the previous chapter, there is a branch of game theory in biology, commonly called **evolutionary game theory**, where the players do not have to be intelligent beings in the normal sense. This aspect of game theory was pioneered by Maynard Smith (1976, 1982). For example, bats (Wilkinson, 1984) and fish (Milinski, 1987; Dugatkin, 1991) have been observed to behave according to the predictions of the theory. In the words of Ridley (1996, p. 79):

there is, in fact, no requirement in the theory that the fish understand what it is doing. Reciprocity can evolve in an entirely unconscious automaton, provided it interacts repeatedly with other automata in a situation that resembles a prisoner's dilemma – as the computer simulations prove. Working out the strategy is the job not of the fish itself, but of evolution, which can then program it into the fish.

Thus in evolutionary biology it is the blind mechanistic force of natural selection, not the purposeful behavior of intelligent forward-thinking individuals, which leads to equilibrium. The significance of this phenomenon will be discussed more fully in Section 10.7 related to evidence from evolutionary psychology.

## 2    Stakes

The importance and effect of size of stakes has been discussed before, in both this chapter and earlier ones. One might expect based on this previous discussion that, in ultimatum games, as stakes rise, the *amount* that responders reject should rise, but the *percentage* of the surplus they reject should fall. For example, responders should reject $4 out of $50 more often than $4 out of $10, but should accept 20% out of $50 more often than 20% of $10.

In fact there is mixed evidence that stakes have such an effect, with most studies indicating no significant effect (Roth et al., 1991; Forsythe et al., 1994; Straub and Murnighan, 1995; Hoffman, McCabe and Smith, 1996). Even in the study by Cameron (1999), where stakes were as high as one month's spending, there was little effect. Only a few studies (Slonim and Roth, 1998; List and Cherry, 2000; List and Cherry, 2008) find fewer rejections for larger stakes. Furthermore, the studies also indicate little effect on proposers' offers with higher stakes. The probable reason for this is that subjects may offer closer to 50% rather than much less than 50%, for fear of costly rejection. This fear may well be justified: in the study by List and Cherry (2000) a quarter of the subjects rejected offers of $100 out of $400.

In trust, PD and public goods games the effects of increasing stakes, in terms of the relative size of monetary payoffs, are predictable. When the 'temptation' (defect when other player cooperates) payoff is reduced, and the 'sucker' (cooperate when other player defects) payoff is increased, there is a greater tendency to cooperate. Similarly, when $m$, the marginal rate of social return, is increased in public goods games, contributions increase.

## 3    Anonymity

One recurring problem with experimental studies in general is that the behavior of the subjects can be influenced by lack of anonymity. The knowledge, or suspicion, that their identity may be known either to the investigator or to other subjects may cause subjects to want to appear 'nice' or to please the investigator. Hoffman et al. (1994) found that dictator allocations averaged only about 10% in a double-blind study, significantly less than in other dictator games where the protocol did not involve double-blindness. A similar result was found in Hoffman, McCabe, and Smith (1998), although Bolton, Katok and Zwick (1998) did not find any significant difference between double-blind and other conditions. In ultimatum games it appears that anonymity may reduce rejections slightly but not significantly (Bolton and Zwick, 1995). These findings have been generally supported by a more recent study by Charness and Gneezy (2008), which reports that when players know the family name of their counterparts dictators allocated a significantly larger portion of the pie. However, this information did not have a significant effect on offers in the ultimatum game, where it appears that strategic considerations crowd out tendencies to be generous.

**4**    *Communication*

Several studies show that in dictator games communication by recipients, for example talking about themselves, increases allocations (Frey and Bohnet, 1995; Bohnet and Frey, 1999). In the later study average allocations rose to half, and 40% of dictators gave *more* than half. Even simply being able to identify their recipients had some effect, in terms of reducing the number of dictators leaving nothing. However, in three-person games where there are two recipients for each dictator, but communication only occurs with one of them, dictators are generous only to the recipient with whom they have communicated (allocations being around twice as large). This indicates that communication elicits a target-specific sympathy rather than a general feeling of generosity (Frey and Bohnet, 1997). A study by Xiao and Houser (2005) proposes that people have a strong desire to express negative emotions, and that this is a reward in itself; thus people are less likely to reject offers from unfair proposers if they are able to write a message to them.

**5**    *Entitlement*

The tendency for most offers to be close to 50% of the pot is sometimes attributed to the fact that in most experimental protocols the pot is essentially 'manna from heaven', which is not applicable to most real-life situations. We have already seen that entitlement has important effects on behavior, for example the endowment effect. When dictators or proposers in ultimatum games feel entitled in some way, for example by winning a contest, they make less generous offers (Hoffman et al., 1994; List and Cherry, 2000; Cherry et al., 2002; Jakiela, 2011). In the Hoffman and colleagues study the right to propose an offer was allocated to the person who answered more general knowledge questions. Offers in ultimatum games were reduced by about 10%, while dictators' allocations fell by about half. The Cherry and colleagues study found that the tendency of dictators to make zero offers increased from about 17% to around 80%, with the proportion rising still further in double-blind studies to around 96%. However, it is interesting that recipients did not appear to share the entitlement attitudes of proposers in ultimatum games, since rejection rates increased, even with $100 stakes. There may be a self-serving bias here as far as legitimacy of entitlement is concerned. The Jakiela (2011) study is significant, since it indicates that the relative effects of earned versus unearned status vary between different cultures. Cultural effects are discussed in more detail shortly.

Some experiments have also introduced market scenarios, where the right to be a proposer is auctioned off (Güth and Tietz, 1985, 1986). The finding here is that proposers only offered about a third of the pot, which was in line with the fact that they were paying prices twice as high as those bid by responders in the auction.

**6**    *Competition*

We have already observed that competition has significant effects on judgments of fairness. For example, it is judged to be fair for firms to cut wages if their survival is threatened by competition, but not otherwise (Kahneman, Knetsch and Thaler, 1986). Furthermore, in ultimatum games proposer competition increases offers significantly. Roth and colleagues (1991) conducted a market game where nine players proposed offers (as sellers), and a single recipient (buyer) had the right to refuse the highest offer. Only one offer could be accepted, as is the case where a buyer only wants to buy a single unit. After five or six rounds of play proposals converged on 100%, meaning that all the surplus from trade goes to the buyer. This is in fact the equilibrium according to standard game theory. In a study of responder competition Güth, Marchand and Rullière (1997) found a similar result, but with the effect working in the opposite direction. When a single proposer (seller) was selling a single unit to many competing recipients (buyers), the MAO was found to fall to below

5% of the surplus by the fifth round, while the average offer had fallen to 15%. The gap between offer and MAO indicates that the game had still not found its equilibrium by this fifth stage. Again this confirms the prediction of standard game theory, where the equilibrium is zero, or the smallest unit of money available. These results are discussed further in the following sections.

Some experiments have added outside options to ultimatum games, meaning that players earn non-zero payoffs if offers are rejected (Knez and Camerer, 1995). For example, if a proposer's division of a $10 pie was rejected, the proposer earned $2 and the responder earned $3. A variation of this game awarded half of the surplus ($10 minus the sum of the gains of $2 and $3) to each player. The main result was that the rate of disagreement between proposer and responder rose considerably, to nearly 50% compared with the range of 10–15% in most experiments. It appears that this change in the game's structure affects the players' perceptions of fairness in different ways, with self-serving bias again causing the conflict.

7    *Available information*

Another structural variable that can be manipulated in experiments concerns the information possessed by the players. In ultimatum games, for example, respondents may be in any one of three situations in terms of knowledge about the size of the pie to be divided: (1) perfect information – they know for certain the amount to be divided; (2) incomplete information – they know the possible payoff sizes and their probability distribution; and (3) no information at all. Most studies indicate that responders tend to accept less under conditions of incomplete or zero information (Mitzkewitz and Nagel, 1993; Straub and Murnighan, 1995; Croson, 1996; Rapoport and Sundali 1996). This can be interpreted as giving proposers the benefit of the doubt, since low offers could indicate a small pie. Proposers also tend to take advantage of the situation by offering less. However, a study by Camerer and Loewenstein (1993) found a contrasting result. In this case some respondents had perfect information, while others only knew that the possible pies were $1, $3, $5, $7 and $9, with equal probabilities. In the perfect information situation the average MAO was a typical 30%, but in the incomplete information situation the average MAO was $1.88, which represents about 38% of the average pie of $5. Disagreements were therefore much more common in the imperfect information case.

Information can also be provided regarding the history of players in terms of their previous offers or behavior. This can provide a reference point as far as judgments of fairness are concerned. In both ultimatum games (Knez and Camerer, 1995) and dictator games (Cason and Mui, 1998) there was some positive correlation between the size of offers made by others and own offers, indicating some social influence. In PD games knowledge of the previous behavior of other players has an important effect, particularly if players can choose which other players to play with. As we have seen, a 'bad record' of defection is likely to cause social ostracism in these circumstances, so 'nasty' players will not get a chance to play much and will therefore earn little after a few rounds of play.

8    *Delay*

In fairness games, like the ultimatum game, it has been found that imposing a delay on the responder causes a reduced likelihood of rejection of unequal offers (Grimm and Mengel, 2011). However, if the option of delay is voluntary rather than imposed exogenously, players are unlikely to choose it (Tang, Bearden and Tsetlin, 2009). These findings indicate the importance of emotional or visceral factors when responders are faced with unfair offers.

In the PD game, delay can also be incorporated by making the game sequential instead of simultaneous, and observing the effect on cooperation. A study by

Khadjavi and Lange (2013) examines behavior in PD games, making two relevant comparisons: play in simultaneous games with play in sequential games; and play by female students with play by female prison inmates. They report that there are no significant differences between the two types of player in the simultaneous game; however, in the sequential game there is a significant increase in cooperation by students, but not by inmates. They interpret this finding by proposing that there are no fundamental differences in prosocial preferences versus purely self-interested preferences among the two populations, but that inmates are more likely to believe that other inmates are less prosocial and more self-interested.

**9**    *Multiperson games*

The addition of other players to games that normally involve only two players provides a number of new insights regarding reciprocity and fairness. One general result is that players tend to be mainly concerned with fairness or equality in terms of their own payoffs relative to those of a proposer, rather than compared with the payoffs of third parties. Thus allocations of only 12–15% to other players who are inactive recipients in a three-person game do not seem to concern active responders; overall rejection rates of around 5% have been recorded, showing that they do not care much about how inactive third parties are treated (Güth and Van Damme, 1998). Furthermore, when trust games are played in three-person groups, groups give and repay less, and appear to be disproportionately influenced by the least trusting and trustworthy members (Cox, 2004). In multiperson PD games the likelihood of defection increases, since there is often a race to defect first. This is essentially a 'tragedy of the commons' situation, which can result in global problems like pollution and the depletion of fish stocks. At a more mundane level it can explain why at parties common resources of food and drink are often soon exhausted. If a player trusts some players but not others, he may defect to pre-empt defection by others. These findings, in both experiments and real-world situations, do not present an optimistic outlook for cooperation. However, and fortunately, they are counterbalanced by the following two factors.

**10**    *Intentions*

Humans, and human institutions like legal systems, place great importance on the intentions behind a person's actions as well as on the consequences. Harm caused by accident is not punished as harshly as harm caused deliberately. Furthermore, the intention to cause harm ('conspiracy') is usually punished even if there is no harmful consequence. This view is a universal one in different societies, and therefore appears to be deeply rooted in evolutionary psychology. Simple game theory experiments have established that in ultimatum games MAOs are lower when players are paired with random devices like computers, rather than human proposers (Blount, 1995). Thus it appears that there is a difference in attitude towards inequality compared with attitude towards inequity. It is the latter, meaning a person's perception of being treated unfairly, which seems to cause outrage, more than the perception of inequality. The importance of this distinction will be examined in the next two sections, when inequality-aversion models are compared with reciprocity models that incorporate intentions.

**11**    *Opportunity and cost of punishment*

Punishment is a vital method of enforcing social norms, in particular cooperation. Some writers distinguish between punishment as negative **reciprocity** and punishment as **retaliation** (Fehr and Gächter, 2001). Retaliation is described as relating to situations where players or agents expect future material benefits from their actions. Negative (and positive) reciprocity on the other hand does not entail any expected material benefits. For example, rejecting offers in an ultimatum game represents negative reciprocity on the part of the responder. We have seen that the rewards here are psychological and neurophysiological, as evidenced by neural scanning. A number of studies have shown that a large proportion of subjects, between 40% and 66%, exhibit reciprocity in one-shot situations; the one-shot nature of the situation indicates that this behavior is reciprocal rather than retaliatory (Berg, Dickhaut and McCabe, 1995; Fehr and Falk, 1999; Abbink, Irlenbusch, and Renner, 2000; Gächter and Falk, 2002). Furthermore, studies also show that the desire to punish harmful behavior is stronger than the desire to reward friendly behavior (Offerman, 1999; Charness and Rabin, 2002), indicating that negative reciprocity is stronger than positive reciprocity. This has important consequences for multiperson games.

We have seen that public goods games are particularly prone to defection, or free-riding. Defection may occur out of self-interest, or it may arise because reciprocal types want to punish self-interested types, and this may be the only practical way of doing so. However, as Fehr and Gächter (2000) have shown, if the behavior of players is observable, and if the direct punishment of individual players is possible (at a cost to the punisher), the results of public goods games are radically different. In this study there were four different protocols, all involving four players:

- perfect strangers in each game and no punishment
- perfect strangers with punishment
- same players in repeated game and no punishment
- same players with punishment

In the punishment protocols players could punish any other player by reducing the number of their tokens by $x$, at a cost of $x/3$ to themselves. The existence of a cost is important, not only because it is realistic, but because it enables a distinction to be made between reciprocal and self-interested players. Purely self-interested players will never pay a cost to punish others when there is no material reward.

The results of the four different protocols were vastly different. In the first case, perfect strangers and no punishment, cooperation falls to very low levels in later rounds, with average contribution levels being only 10% of available tokens, and 79% of subjects free-riding and contributing nothing. Even when games were played repeatedly with the same players' cooperation tended to fall, with contributions averaging only about 30% for the last five rounds of the ten-period game. However, when the opportunity for punishment existed, contributions *increased* throughout the rounds, even with perfect strangers. In this case contributions started at 50% and increased to 60%. When games were repeated with the same players, contributions started at 65% and rose to 90% by the end of ten rounds. This is a clear and dramatic demonstration of the power of punishment to enforce cooperation by self-interested individuals. Fehr and Schmidt (1999) have shown theoretically that even a minority of reciprocal subjects is capable of inducing a majority of selfish subjects to cooperate.

There are a number of important policy implications that arise from the above observations that will be discussed at the end of the chapter.

## *Environmental factors*

As we have seen at some length in previous chapters, framing effects are a common phenomenon. It should therefore be no surprise that they play a part in causing differential responses in various games. For example, when ultimatum games are framed in terms of a buyer–seller transaction, where sellers ask a price for a good that buyers can take or leave, offers are reduced by almost 10% while rejection rates remain unchanged (Hoffman et al., 1994). When ultimatum games are framed as dilemmas where resources are shared, with players making sequential claims on a common pool of resources and receiving nothing if the claims add up to more than the pool, then players tend to be more generous, with rejections less frequent (Larrick and Blount, 1997). This may be because the language of 'claiming' creates a sense of common ownership thus inducing a greater tendency to cooperate. It also appears that prompting proposers to consider the likely reactions of responders reduces offers, possibly by increasing the fear of rejection. Hoffman, McCabe and Smith (2000) found that this reduction was in the order of 5–10%.

Framing effects can also be observed in PD and public goods games. For example, when a PD game is framed as a 'social event game', as opposed to an 'investment game', this engenders more cooperation (Pillutla and Chen, 1999). It appears that different terms can trigger different expectations regarding the behavior of other players, leading to reciprocal behavior. This framing effect is particularly noticeable in the case of the Wason test situation, described in Case 10.1.

Environmental factors also play a significant role in affecting 'cheating' behavior. These factors relate to work incentives and culture, display of wealth in the vicinity, and the cleanliness and lighting in the environment. For example, Zhong, Bohns and Gino (2010) have shown that people are more likely to cheat in dim lighting, and also when wearing sunglasses.

### Demographic factors

A considerable body of research has examined the effects of various demographic variables on social preferences. Variables that are frequently studied include gender, age, hormones, academic major, culture and social distance.

**1**  *Gender*

Although there are several significant differences between the genders in terms of fairness and social preferences, there is no simple pattern. Instead there are complex interactions with a number of other factors. Here are some of the main findings:

- In ultimatum games both sexes make similar offers (Eckel and Grossman, 2001).
- In ultimatum games women reject less often.
- In dictator games there appear to be no differences (Frey and Bohnet, 1995; Bolton, Katok, and Zwick, 1998).
- Both sexes demand more from women and offer more to men (Solnick, 2001).
- Women generally punish more (Eckel and Grossman, 1996b).
- Women are cost-conscious punishers; they punish more than men when it is cheap, but less when it is expensive.
- Women are more generous than men in dictator games when recipients have to exert effort to earn rewards as opposed to receiving them as gifts (Heinz, Juranek and Rao, 2012).
- In investment games where subjects can select partners, people tend to prefer to invest in partners of the opposite sex. This cannot be explained by the amount returned, but appears to be caused by tastes and beliefs regarding the trustworthiness of the opposite sex (Slonim and Guillen, 2010).
- While men are not especially generous to attractive women, women offer about 5% more to attractive men than to unattractive men. In fact Schweitzer and Solnick (1999) report that the average female offer to good-looking men was over 50% of the pie, with 5% of females offering almost the whole pie!
  This last interaction is particularly interesting, since it supports field data that looks, and in particular height, are positively correlated with income.
- Men tend to be more competitive and overconfident than women. This may apply in particular to certain professions, like business, or finance (Klaes, Lightfoot and Lilley, 2011; Kamas and Preston, 2012), and appears to be true even in professional sports, like tennis, where one might expect all players to be highly competitive (Wozniak, 2012).

**2   *Age***

Although few studies have been conducted in this area, it appears that children go through three main stages of development as far as social preferences are concerned (Damon, 1980; Murnighan and Saxon, 1998). Before the age of five, they are highly self-interested. Between five and seven they become very concerned with equality, mainly as a method of preventing conflict. After seven they become more interested in equity, for example by relating rewards to inputs or some other measure of entitlement. Some researchers have indicated that this constitutes evidence against the evolutionary psychology approach. For example, Camerer (2003, p. 67) states:

> These facts cast doubt on a strong version of the hypothesis that an instinct for acting tough in repeated interactions evolved because it was adaptive in our ancestral past.

As we shall see, this conclusion can cause misunderstanding, and it is the 'weaker' version of the hypothesis that is important. This is discussed in the section on the role of evolutionary psychology.

**3   *Hormones***

The hormone that is studied most in the context of social preferences is testosterone. Burnham (2007) finds that high testosterone men are more likely to reject low offers in ultimatum games, while Zak and colleagues (2009) find that the administration of exogenous testosterone reduces the proportion offered by proposers. Emanuele and colleagues (2008) find that low serotonin levels are also relevant, being associated with an increased rejection of low offers.

**4   *Academic major***

The evidence appears somewhat mixed in this area. A study by Carter and Irons (1991) found that Economics majors offered 7% less and demanded 7% more in ultimatum games than other majors. This difference applied to both first- and final-year undergraduates, causing the authors to conclude that Economics majors are born self-interested rather than made that way by the subject matter. A side issue is raised here: is this conclusion an example of self-serving bias by economists who want to defend their subject against the alternative conclusion that studying economics makes people more selfish?

Other studies indicate that economics and business students are no different from other majors in terms of offers and MAOs (Eckel and Grossman, 1996a; Kagel, Kim and Moser, 1996), and a couple of studies have even indicated that economics and business students are *more* generous in their offers (Kahneman, Knetsch and Thaler, 1986; Frey and Bohnet, 1995). It is therefore impossible to come to any definite conclusion on this issue at present.

**5   *Culture***

Cultural effects are notoriously difficult to test for, because of problems related to language, experimenter interaction and confounds with other factors. Most cross-cultural studies have involved ultimatum bargaining games. The first detailed study in 1991 by Roth and colleagues examined subjects in four countries: USA, Japan, Israel and Yugoslavia. The main finding was that offers were on average about 10% lower in Japan and Israel, yet rejection rates were also lower. The conclusion was that there appeared to be a different conception in these countries regarding what constitutes a 'fair' offer. It is interesting that a study by Buchan, Croson and Johnson (2004) found an opposite result as far as Japan was concerned, with average offers being higher than in the USA. This may be due to methodological variations, since the latter study used the MAO method whereas the earlier study used the specific-offer method. However, there may be confounding factors here related to the two samples of students.

Some studies have examined the effects of religious factors on social preferences. A study by Ahmed and Salas (2011) finds that priming Christian subjects with religious words in a scrambled sentence promoted prosocial behavior in dictator and PD games.

However, those subjects self-reporting high religiosity did not rate higher in terms of generosity and cooperation. Ensminger and Henrich (2014) find that Islam and Christianity both promote a stronger sense of fairness, but that this sense of fairness may not agree with that of other beliefs.

The most comprehensive studies of cultural differences in social preferences have been conducted by Henrich and colleagues (Henrich et al., 2001; Henrich and Ensminger 2004; Henrich et al. 2005), which examined 20 different cultures, including many primitive cultures in Africa and Asia. An important aspect of this research is that involved an interdisciplinary approach, with contributions from both anthropologists and economists. The research found some very different results regarding average offers in ultimatum games. The Machiguenga in Peru had the lowest average offer rate, with 26% of the pie, whereas two cultures actually had average offer rates above 50%: The Ache in Paraguay and the people of Lamalara in Indonesia.

How can such large differences be explained? It appears that two variables explain the variations to a considerable extent, with a multiple $R^2$ of 68%. These variables are:

i.   *The amount of cooperative activity or economies of scale in production.*
     For example, when members of a society hunt in a group this factor is high, and offers tend to be higher. It is notable that The Machiguenga have a very low level of such cooperation, since the most important social group is the family, and business transactions outside the family are rare.

ii.  *The degree of market integration*
     Markets are integrated when there is a national language and national or large-scale markets for goods and labor. Such integration is also associated with higher offers. There is an important conclusion here: well-developed markets that are more likely to be efficient are less likely to be dominated by pure self-interest.

One final point regarding the Henrich and colleagues findings is worthy of comment, and that concerns the two cultures with average offers above 50%. This appears to involve the '**potlatch syndrome**'. A potlatch is essentially an exhibition or competition of gift-giving which is designed to cause embarrassment or a feeling of obligation in the receiver, and it is, or has been, a feature of some primitive societies in both the South Pacific and the Pacific Northwest. There are also aspects of the same syndrome in many advanced countries. In this case gifts are used as weapons, and what may appear to be positive reciprocity is actually negative reciprocity. The reason why the practice is effective, however, is because it relies on the basic psychological mechanism of the feeling of reciprocity, which appears to be universal in all societies.

This double aspect of reciprocity is also relevant as far as punishment is concerned, and again cultural factors have a large influence. We have already seen that most punishment in public goods games is aimed at low or non-contributors, but sometimes high contributors are punished, this phenomenon being referred to as antisocial punishment. A study by Herrmann, Thöni and Gächter (2008) finds that in Western cities this type of punishment appears to be rare, but in other cities, notably Muscat, Athens and Riyadh, high contributors were punished as much as low contributors. There appear to be a number of correlated factors here: antisocial punishment is associated with a lack of trust and weak social norms of cooperation. Furthermore, there is evidence that lack of trust in strangers is correlated with strong family ties

(Ermisch and Gambetta, 2010), which the authors argue is causal; in large families there is less motivation to deal with strangers, and less experience in such dealings, creating more uncertainty. Since larger, extended family networks are more common in developing countries, it may not be surprising that there is also evidence that lack of trust and weak social norms are negatively correlated with economic growth (Knack and Keefer, 1997). The importance, nature and origins of social norms are discussed in the next subsection.

Stavrova and Ehlebracht (2016) have also carried out an extensive survey relating to trust and cynicism in 41 countries. They report that generally people who are less trusting, or more cynical, tend to be less educated, have lower incomes, have psychological problems and have worse health. They find that less trusting people have lower incomes, even after adjusting for the other factors, and propose that this is because they lose out on opportunities for social cooperation which would improve their economic prospects. However, there is one other interesting finding in this study, and that is that less trusting people actually fare normally in terms of income in societies where others are also less trusting. This finding really confirms what one would predict in repeated PD situations: trust breeds trust and mutual cooperation, while mistrust breeds mistrust and mutual defection.

**6    *Social distance***

Most studies have found that people have more empathy and therefore more positive social preferences towards those others who are closer socially and geographically. However, there have been some recent observations that modify this generality. A study by Charness, Haruvy and Sonsino (2007) examined positive reciprocity in internet interactions pairing people in different countries or different states in the USA, and found in all cases that a substantial minority displayed positive reciprocity, albeit declining with social distance. There has also been a recent natural experiment that relates to this phenomenon, which may have important policy implications. The UK has the third highest level of shoplifting in the world behind the USA and Japan. CCTV is now widely used to detect this crime, and many shops in the UK pay £20 ($32) per week to have a CCTV linked up to the Internet Eyes website, while viewers pay a £13 ($21) annual subscription to access the footage. If a viewer detects a shoplifting incident in real time they can alert the shopkeeper by a simple click of a mouse, and they earn points for flagging up suspicious incidents. The highest scorer each month wins a prize of up to £1,000 ($1,600). Thus this natural situation resembles a public goods game, with the additional factor that people can gain a material reward from punishing free-riders. However, material reward may not be the main incentive. A recent shoplifting incident in southern England was reported by a man living in northern Italy; he claimed he was not motivated by money, saying: 'I feel what I'm doing is ultimately helping someone who lives far away. That can only be a good thing' (Henry and Terraneo, 2010). This is obviously anecdotal evidence, and may not represent average behavior, but it could indicate that there is at least a minority of people with social preferences that extend to others who are far removed from them socially and geographically.

**7    *Social ranking***

Various studies have reported that there is an inverse relationship between social ranking and tendency to cooperate, meaning that those with higher social ranking have less cooperative behavior and intentions (Garcia, Tor and Gonzalez, 2006; Keltner et al., 2008; Poortvliet et al., 2009). Furthermore, a study by Chen and colleagues (2012) finds that there is a correlation between rankings and facial expressions indicating the likelihood of cooperation. In an experiment involving deans of business schools, subjects judged that individuals from higher ranked schools appeared less cooperative, even though they lacked prior knowledge of these rankings.

## Social norms

Fehr and Gächter (2000) define social norms in terms of the following three characteristics: (1) behavioral regularities; (2) based on a socially shared belief regarding how one ought to behave; and (3) enforcement is by informal social sanctions.

The role of social norms in determining social behavior is a highly controversial one. For Binmore and Shaked (2010a) they are fundamental in determining behavior:

> We think it likely that people enter laboratories primed with a variety of social norms, one of which is triggered by the manner in which the experiment is framed. (p. 98)

They go on to claim:

> If the resulting behavior is close to a Nash equilibrium of the game (as in the Ultimatum game), then the social norm is stabilized in the laboratory experiment. If it is not (as in the Prisoners' Dilemma), then the subjects' behavior moves towards a Nash equilibrium. (p. 98)

Binmore and Shaked also support the approach that regards social norms as being culturally determined, and, as we have seen from the Henrich and colleagues and other studies discussed earlier, there is much evidence for this.

However, there are two main problems with this approach. These problems do not relate to its correctness, but to the fact that it begs two questions, currently unanswered (Fehr and Schmidt, 2010):

1   What is the origin of social norms?
2   What is it about the framing of a situation that triggers a particular social norm to operate?

Social norms appear to arise from a process similar to the 'team reasoning' process described in the previous chapter in relation to the selection of appropriate focal points. It was seen that this process has been described by Crawford, Gneezy and Rottenstreich (2008, p. 1448) as follows:

> Players begin by asking themselves, independently, if there is a decision rule that would be better for both than individualistic rules, if both players followed the better rule.

It is now suggested that such a process applies in a broader context, for example situations where there may be rule that is not a Nash equilibrium at all, as far as the original game is concerned, but instead represents a correlated equilibrium of the type described in the previous chapter. This appears to apply particularly to iterated and repeated games, and an example was given in the repeated PD game, where the rule of 'tit-for-tat, starting off with cooperation' results in a much better payoff than the Nash equilibrium, and in fact is Pareto-efficient. We have also seen that in trust games, like the centipede game, empirical studies indicate that players tend to cooperate for several rounds, and again end up with better payoffs than the Nash equilibrium, which is to defect at the first opportunity. Different players in different cultures may play different rules here in terms of how long to cooperate, but there appears to be a general realization that, particularly in games with a large number of stages, the strategy of early cooperation is beneficial. It is notable that the behavior of players does not necessarily move towards a Nash equilibrium with greater experience, either in the laboratory or in the field, although this may happen in some cases, like the repeated PD game.

It is also important to realize that the rules or norms that are developed are not themselves the product of game theory. As Gintis (2009) has argued, they are essentially an 'emergent' phenomenon that arises from the twin forces of gene-culture coevolution and complexity. A simple example will illustrate the point. When it comes to deciding which side of the road to drive on, a repeated game, there are two Nash equilibria, with drivers either always driving on the right or always driving on the left. There is no obvious focal point here, since in either case drivers have equal payoffs. However, in the UK drivers drive on the left and in the USA (and most other countries) they drive on the right; so why have these different norms evolved? There is much conjecture here, but common explanations are as follows:

> UK – Most people found it easier to mount a horse from the left-hand side, thus making it more natural to ride on the left-hand side of the road, and later to drive on that side.
> USA – Many people rode in horse-driven carts or carriages, using a whip. Since most people are right-handed it was safer to ride on the right side of the road, otherwise there was a danger of whipping passersby.

Even if these conjectures are incorrect or incomplete they illustrate the point that social norms are determined by factors other than game theory itself, although they may be reinforced by game theory. The role of social norms in determining social preferences and decisions is discussed further in later sections.

Another important issue concerns the changing of social norms over time. Over centuries there have been huge changes in many countries relating to major social issues such as the role and rights of women in society, the rights of children, marriage, slavery and punishment. Over shorter periods of time we see various norms disappearing and new ones appearing on a smaller scale. For example in the UK, smoking and drink driving are no longer norms as they tended to be a few decades ago, whereas wearing seat belts and bicycle helmets have become norms. All of these aspects of behavior relate to the broader issue of health and safety. The question then arises: what causes these underlying trends, such as a greater concern for health and safety? This goes beyond the scope of this book, but some of the relevant factors will be discussed in the section on policy implications, in particular the increasing concern with the environment and 'green' issues.

## 10.4  Modeling social preferences

*Objectives of modeling*

We have now seen that the standard model, using standard game theory, fails to predict many empirical outcomes, both in real life and in experiments, and in some cases fails badly. It is important to emphasize again that this is not necessarily a failure of game theory as a technique of analysis. There are in general two possible reasons for failing to predict accurately: either people do not engage in strategic thinking in practice (meaning game theory is an inappropriate analytical technique) or the situations are not being modeled realistically, in particular by failing to incorporate social preferences into utility functions. We shall see that there is some truth in both of these factors. For example, we have already seen in the previous chapter that there are some situations where empirical findings indicate a failure to think strategically, like in the 'beauty contest' game.

There is a further point to be made, or rather to be repeated, in this regard. Just as birds do not need to understand the theory of aerodynamics in order to be able to fly, people may behave according to the principles of game theory without necessarily following the logical steps involved. This kind of 'as if' behavior can evolve under the pressures of natural selection, as we have noted earlier in the discussion relating to repetition and learning; recall the apparent mathematical sophistication of woodpeckers. As we have also noted on several occasions, from the first chapter, this 'as if' justification is very commonly used in economics, particularly by supporters of the standard model. However, if standard game theory fails to predict accurately, we may conclude that the 'as if' inference is incorrect, and the model needs to be respecified. This point is further elaborated under the second feature below.

Although the absence of strategic thinking applies to some game situations where the standard model predicts badly, we will see in the remainder of this chapter that it is the existence of more complex strategic thinking that accounts for many anomalies. In these situations improved modeling of situations can lead to accurate predictions of many of the empirical findings, indicating that game theory is still useful as a predictive and explanatory tool.

In the modeling context, the challenge that is posed is that a good model must have two main features, in keeping with other behavioral models in general:

1   *Explanation and prediction* – It must be able to explain the results of a wide variety of different games in terms of *endogenous* parameters. As we have seen earlier in this section, changes in the structure of games can lead to very different empirical results. For example, the introduction of proposer competition and responder competition in ultimatum bargaining games has drastic effects on responses. A good model must be able to account for such differences in a *parsimonious* way, without resorting to ad hoc complications. A further related feature of such a model is that it can make interesting new predictions.

2   *Psychological basis* – This means that models must be based on known psychological mechanisms. It does not necessarily mean that the model actually explicitly incorporates psychological or neurological processes in its mathematical formulation, but it must at least be compatible with such processes, and also be compatible with the results of other studies. This issue will become clearer as we move on to discussing particular models.

In general we will see that all models have certain advantages and disadvantages; the models with more realistic features have a greater psychological richness and predictive power, but their added complexity tends to make them less tractable. Thus a researcher's choice of model will ultimately be determined by the purpose in mind (Falk and Fischbacher, 2005).

## Issues in modeling

Falk and Fischbacher (2005) describe four main questions that models incorporating social preferences need to address:

1   *What is the reference standard as far as equitable transactions are concerned?*
    A common standard here is an equal distribution of payoffs.

2   *How important are intentions?*
    In inequality-aversion (IA) models these are not important at all, but in reciprocity models they are an essential component. This means that it is not just the consequences of a player's actions that are important but their beliefs, and the alternative possibilities of action that are open to them.

3   *What is the purpose of punishment?*
    In IA models the only purpose of one player reducing another player's payoffs is to reduce inequality, but in reciprocity models the motive is retaliation for an unkind

act. Thus with the latter model one should observe both punishments and rewards even when inequality is not reduced.

**4**    *Who is the relevant reference agent?*

This issue arises in multiplayer games. In some models players evaluate fairness towards individuals separately, while in other models the reference agent is the group as a whole.

The empirical findings relating to these questions are discussed in Section 10.7.

## Psychological game theory

We have seen that social preferences are concerned with the distributional consequences of people's actions and people's beliefs regarding underlying motives and intentions. There has been much research over the last 20 years that has shown that people very often care about these aspects, and the branch of behavioral game theory that examines these is now referred to as 'psychological game theory' (PGT). PGT models utilities as being based on beliefs as well as actions (Dufwenberg, 2006), and is used to conceptualize belief-dependent emotions like reciprocity, guilt aversion, regret and shame. The original development of PGT was proposed in a paper by Geanakoplos, Pearce and Stacchetti (1989). A few examples at this stage will help the reader to understand the nature of social preferences, fairness, reciprocity and PGT.

- Ann takes a taxi ride, and tips the driver (Bill) as much as she believes he expects to get. She suffers from guilt if she tips less.

- Carol is offered a piece of candy by a stranger (Dave) sitting next to her on a plane; she likes the candy but refuses to accept it because she believes that by accepting it she will be obligated to the stranger in some way, even if that only means making the effort to strike up some conversation during the flight. She prefers to forgo the candy rather than feel obliged to reciprocate. If she accepts the candy but does not reciprocate she would again feel guilty, because she believes that the stranger would believe that the acceptance of the candy indicates that she is disposed to be friendly and she would be letting him down by not conforming to his expectation. Dave would then also have a lower opinion of her.

- Ellen is worried about her health and consults her family doctor, Frank, who is also a friend. Frank diagnoses a serious illness. Frank realizes Ellen is distressed by her worry, and also realizes that if he prescribes her the most appropriate medicine for her disease, this will also reveal to Ellen the severity of the disease and increase her anxiety. Because Frank cares about Ellen he is reluctant to prescribe her the best medicine; to do so would make him feel guilty for causing her increased distress.

- Gene applies for promotion in his firm. His boss, Henry, writes him an unfavorable report, and his application is rejected. Gene believes that this was partly due to Henry's ignorance regarding the quality and quantity of his work, but was also due to professional jealousy, in that Gene believes that Henry believes Gene is a superior worker and is threatened by him. Gene therefore complains about Henry's conduct to Henry's boss, although this involves more work for him and the risk of retaliation when Henry discovers his disloyalty.

- Irene shares a cake she has bought with Jim and Kayla. Kayla notices that Jim's portion is bigger than hers. She suspects that Irene deliberately gave her a smaller portion, but believes this may be because Irene believes Jim has a greater fondness for cake than she does, so she is not upset. Jim, however, thinks that the unequal portions were accidental, and offers to give Kayla some of his portion, because he would feel guilty for being given the larger portion and accepting it without saying anything.

A number of factors emerge from these quite different situations. First, outcomes or utilities are largely non-monetary, except for the tip, but instead are belief-dependent. Second, people's utilities depend not just on their own beliefs but also on others' beliefs and on other's beliefs about their own beliefs; thus PGT models can be considered as involving a **hierarchy of beliefs**. Third, emotions such as anger, envy, disappointment, blame, pride, shame, gratitude and guilt, or the desire to avoid guilt, are relevant in affecting people's utilities (Geanakoplos, Pearce and Stacchetti, 1989; Battigalli and Dufwenberg, 2007). These emotions crucially depend on our expectations and prior beliefs, which obviously vary from situation to situation. For example, we often care if we cause other people distress, or if they have a lower opinion of us. However, in other situations we may want to cause others distress, or may not care about their opinion of us. All of these factors mean that PGT involves more complexity than standard game theory.

More recently there have been attempts to expand the scope and complexity of PGT further in order to handle many plausible forms of belief-dependent motivation that are illustrated in the examples above. In particular, Battigalli and Dufwenberg (2009) propose four further aspects of development:

1   *Updated beliefs* – PGT originally only allowed initial beliefs to affect a player's utility.
2   *Others' beliefs* – PGT originally only allowed a player's own beliefs to affect his utility, but we can see that sometimes the beliefs of others, for example their respect for him, affects his utility.
3   *Dependence on plans* – PGT, and other traditional game theory, assumes that utilities are affected only by actual outcomes, but unrealized intentions may also influence utility. For example, if we believe another player intended to do us harm, even if their plans were thwarted and the harm was averted, this would still affect our beliefs regarding the other player and our utility.
4   *Non-equilibrium analysis* – PGT, like other game theory, only considers equilibrium situations, but in reality players may not coordinate to reach an equilibrium.

Some of these aspects will be considered further in the next subsection.

### Nature and features of models

In general, current models of social preferences fall into the two main categories referred to above: IA models and reciprocity models. Both of these models maintain the basic assumption in the standard model that players aim to maximize utility, and that players also assume that other players do the same. The models both differ from the standard model in that they enrich or modify the utility function to take into account social preferences. IA models are simpler, because they only incorporate players' first-order beliefs regarding inequality of distribution. They are not PGT models because they do not incorporate a hierarchy of beliefs as discussed earlier, and they take no account of players' emotions beyond a desire for reducing inequality. Reciprocity models are more complex and varied in nature, and can take into account a variety of emotions such as anger, envy, disappointment, blame, pride, shame, gratitude and guilt.

At this stage a couple of simple examples will help to give the reader a flavor of PGT models and some of the implications:

1   *'Surprise gift' game*
    This is a two-player game in which only player 1 moves. Player 1 has two options: he can send player 2 flowers, or he can send chocolates. He knows that player 2 likes either gift, but he enjoys surprising her. Thus if he thinks player 2 is expecting flowers more than chocolates, he will get more utility from sending chocolates, and vice versa

(adapted from Geanakoplos, Pearce and Stacchetti, 1989). In standard game theory there is always an equilibrium in pure strategies if only one player moves; in this game, if we ignore the enjoyment from surprise factor, the pure strategy equilibrium would involve giving the gift which player 1 believes will give player 2 the most utility. However, given the surprise factor, there is a unique mixed strategies equilibrium, where player 1 sends each gift with equal probability.

2    *Disappointment/retaliation game*

This is a sequential game, again adapted from Geanakoplos, Pearce and Stacchetti. It is shown in extensive form in Figure 10.1.

**Figure 10.1**    Disappointment/retaliation game

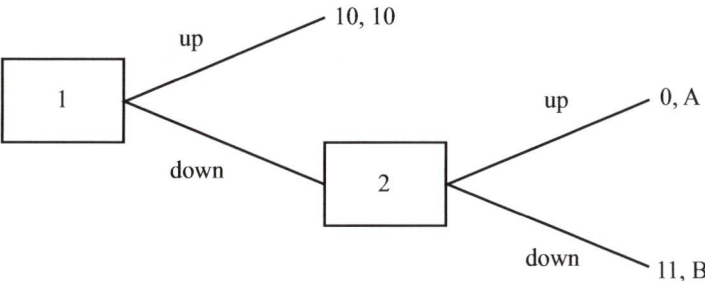

Player 1 only cares about physical outcomes, but player 2's payoffs at two of the terminal nodes depend on his initial expectations. If he is resigned at the start of the game to the idea that 1 will choose down, then A = 1 and B = 5 (these can be regarded as monetary payoffs); therefore 2 chooses down if 1 chooses down, so (down, down) is one credible equilibrium. On the other hand, if 2 is confident that 1 will play up, 2 will be disappointed if 1 plays down, and this alters the values of his payoffs A and B, so that A = 2 and B = 0. In this situation playing up gains utility from harming 1, while playing down loses utility from frustration at 1's betrayal. Therefore, under this belief by 2, the equilibrium is (up, no move). One important implication here is that the backward induction method, used to solve sequential games in SGT, does not work with psychological games. This finding is discussed in later sections.

More specific aspects and concepts related to modeling will be examined in the next two sections, where the psychological foundation and the resulting differences in structure of different models are discussed in more detail. The abilities of the models in terms of explaining empirical results are then discussed in Section 10.7.

## 10.5  Inequality-aversion models

These models assume that people care about their own payoffs, and the relative size of these payoffs compared to the payoffs of others. It should be noted that sometimes such models are referred to as 'inequity-aversion' models. The latter term is less appropriate. The distinction between inequality and inequity was touched on earlier, in the discussions of both intentions and the age factor. The most important point here is that inequality is a neutral term and implies no value judgment, while inequity is a value-laden or normative term involving the subjective notion of fairness. Thus if a human proposer offers less than 50% of the pie in an ultimatum game, this may be rejected by the responder either because of inequality-aversion or because of inequity aversion. As we have seen, this ambiguity can be removed by using a random proposer, like a computer. If rejections occur in this situation, the cause must be inequality-aversion.

Before examining IA models in detail, it is useful to consider the nature of altruism more closely, since altruism is sometimes regarded as the basis of social preferences. This will also aid an understanding of the relevance of the terms 'endogenous', 'parsimonious' and 'ad hoc', used in the previous section in the description of the characteristics of a good model.

As we have already seen, some authors distinguish between **pure altruism**, where a player's utility increases as the utility of other players increases, and **impure altruism**, where a player's utility increases from the act of contributing to others (Margolis, 1982). Thus if I am made happier by lending you my car (and thus making you happier), but not if my neighbor lends you his car, this is impure altruism.

Two fundamental points need to be made at this stage. First, neither of the above types of altruism constitutes pure altruism in the sense that it is sometimes used in psychology (Batson, 1991). **Psychological altruism** refers to the objective of increasing the welfare of others *without* any increase in one's own welfare, either material or psychological. Such a phenomenon is alien to economics, since it cannot be incorporated into any utility maximization model, whether standard or behavioral. In any kind of economic model no factor can affect an individual's behavior unless it can be incorporated in some way into that person's utility function, although Amartya Sen (1977) seems to envisage the reality of psychological altruism. However, current neurological research tends to support the economic model, as illustrated in the last case study in the first chapter.

The second point is that altruism, as defined above, can only explain positive reciprocity; it cannot explain the widespread negative reciprocity observed in empirical findings reported earlier. Any model explaining empirical findings only in terms of altruism would have to incorporate ad hoc complications like changing signs related to the utilities of others. These complications are not explained within the structure of the model itself, meaning that they are exogenous rather than endogenous. This would also make the model lack parsimony, since the model would have to be adjusted to explain different situations.

Therefore any successful model of social preferences must go beyond altruism, since it also has to able to explain spiteful behavior, like the various forms of punishment we have already observed in different types of game.

## The Fehr–Schmidt model

Fehr and Schmidt (1999) proposed a model (FS model), sometimes referred to as a 'guilt/ envy' model, but which the authors actually referred to as a model of inequity aversion. They use the term inequity on the basis that fairness judgments are based on some 'neutral' reference point. They refer to the literature in social psychology regarding social comparisons (Stouffer et al., 1949; Festinger, 1954; Homans, 1961; Adams, 1963), noting that a key insight in this research is that relative material payoffs affect people's well-being and behavior. They also note a number of empirical findings that directly support their hypothesis (Loewenstein, Thompson and Bazerman, 1989; Agell and Lundborg, 1995; Clark and Oswald, 1996; Bewley, 1998). In real-life situations the determination of the relevant reference group and outcome tends to pose modeling problems, but in experimental situations it seems justifiable to assume that the relevant reference group is the other subjects in the study, and that the reference outcome is the average income of these subjects.

In the FS model it is therefore assumed that, in addition to purely selfish subjects, some subjects will also dislike inequitable outcomes. Such inequity could arise from being either worse off or better off than others. An individual's utility function therefore depends not only on their own monetary payoff, but on differences between this payoff and those of others.

This situation can be modeled mathematically as follows:

In a set of $n$ players the social allocation is given by the vector of payoffs

$$x = (x_1, x_2, ..., x_n)$$

The utility function of player $i$ is a function of this vector and is given by

$$U_i(x) = x_i - \alpha_i/(n\text{-}1) \Sigma \max(x_j - x_i, 0) - \beta_i/(n\text{-}1) \Sigma \max(x_i - x_j, 0) \qquad (10.1)$$

Where $\alpha_i$ is a measure of player $i$'s aversion to disadvantageous inequality, and $\beta_i$ is a measure of his aversion to advantageous inequality. Thus the second term in equation (10.1) measures the utility loss from disadvantageous inequality and the third term measures the utility loss from advantageous inequality. Three further assumptions are involved:

1   $\beta_i \leq \alpha_i$, meaning that players suffer less from advantageous than disadvantageous inequality. This certainly seems a reasonable assumption in the light of direct empirical evidence (Loewenstein, Thompson and Bazerman, 1989).

2   $0 \leq \beta_i < 1$, the lower boundary meaning that players do actually suffer from advantageous inequality, rather than feeling a benefit from it. This assumption is certainly questionable (Frank, 1985; Wilkinson, 2004), and Fehr and Schmidt admit the possibility of status-seeking players with negative values of $\beta_i$, but they justify the assumption on the grounds that such players 'have virtually no impact on equilibrium behavior'. The upper boundary $\beta_i = 1$ can be interpreted as meaning that a player is willing to throw away a dollar in order to reduce his relative advantage over player $j$ of the same amount, which seems unlikely.

3   The population of players is heterogeneous, meaning that different players have different values of $\alpha$ and $\beta$. Thus $\alpha$ and $\beta$ have distributions rather than single values for the whole population.

Using the utility function in equation (10.1) Fehr and Schmidt then apply game-theoretic analysis (similar to that used in the previous chapter in relation to continuous strategies) to derive average values of $\alpha$ and $\beta$, sometimes referred to as the 'envy' and 'guilt' coefficients, which are necessary to explain the various empirical results.

The FS model derives a number of conclusions regarding different variations of ultimatum and public goods games. While the neoclassical predicts complete free-riding in public goods games (zero contributions), and no willingness to engage in costly punishment, the FS model predicts that both contributions and punishment will occur if players are sufficiently envious and guilty. The model derives specific conclusions regarding (1) the conditions under which people will free-ride ($\beta_i \leq 1 - m$, where $m$ is the marginal return to the public good), (2) how many free-riders ($k$) it takes to cause everyone to free-ride ($k > m(n - 1)/2$, and (3) how much guilt and envy are necessary for an equilibrium to emerge where there are some positive contributions and punishment (again determined in terms of the endogenous parameters $\alpha_i$, $\beta_i$, $m$, and $c$, the cost of punishment).

The twin strengths of the FS model are:

1   *Simplicity*

The model is simple in form, in terms of the number of parameters involved, and the linearity of the function (although the latter feature can easily be modified).

2   *Robustness*

This characteristic refers to the ability to explain the wide variation in results that are observed from different games. For example, it fits the normal ultimatum game, and the variations with both proposer and responder competition. As far as competition is concerned, the model produces an interesting prediction: in proposer competition, the number of proposers does not affect the equilibrium offer of almost zero, while in responder competition a greater number of responders will reduce the highest equilibrium offer. These contrasting predictions have yet to be confirmed empirically. The nature of empirical evidence and how this relates to different models is discussed in Section 10.7, along with criticisms of the methodology involved.

### The Bolton–Ockenfels model

This model (BO), proposed by Bolton and Ockenfels (2000), is often referred to as an ERC model, because it relates to equity, reciprocity and competition. It is similar to the FS model in many respects, since players care about their own payoffs and their relative share. It is assumed that players prefer a relative payoff that is equal to the average payoff, meaning that they will sacrifice to move their share closer to the average if they are either above or below it.

This situation can be modeled mathematically as follows:

$$U_i(x) = U(x_i, x_i/\Sigma x_j) \tag{10.2}$$

The BO model, like the FS model, uses game-theoretic analysis to derive specific conclusions regarding equilibria in various different games. For example, it predicts that in ultimatum games responders will reject zero offers all the time, and that the rejection rate will fall with increasing percentage offers. It also predicts that ultimatum offers will be larger than dictator offers, and that in three-person games the allocation to inactive recipients will be ignored. These predictions are largely confirmed by empirical findings.

There are three main differences between the BO model and the FS model:

1  The BO model is concerned with relative shares, whereas the FS model is concerned with absolute differences.

2  The BO model only makes a comparison between an individual's payoffs with the average payoff of all the other players. It does not compare each player's payoffs with the maximum and minimum of the other payoffs, like the FS model does.

3  The BO model proposes a symmetrical attitude towards inequality, where guilt and envy are equal in force ($\alpha_i = \beta_i$), whereas the FS model proposes that envy is stronger than guilt.

In all three respects the FS model appears to be superior, in terms of both fitting empirical findings and psychological foundation. A simple demonstration can be given by using a three-person game where the payoff allocation is given by $(x, x - \varepsilon, x + \varepsilon)$. According to the BO model the preferences of the first player should be independent of $\varepsilon$, since the sum of the payoffs will be constant and therefore the relative share of the first player is not affected. However, according to the FS model, as $\varepsilon$ increases, envy of the third player's payoff and guilt regarding the second player's payoff both increase, causing the first player's utility to fall. A study by Charness and Rabin (2000) has confirmed this prediction, and similar empirical findings are reviewed in Section 10.7. However, this conclusion does not mean that the FS model can explain all empirical results in such games, or that it is complete in capturing all the relevant psychological factors, as we shall now see.

## 10.6  Reciprocity models

Reciprocity is based on the idea that people's conception of fairness depends not only on equality or inequality but on people's intentions. As explained in the previous section, altruism only explains positive reciprocity, but any realistic model must also be able to explain and predict the negative reciprocity that is widely observed empirically. In general people can have either 'kind' or 'unkind' intentions towards other people, depending on what we believe are their intentions towards us. Thus intentions depend on beliefs and possibilities. For example, if we have no alternative but to make an unequal offer to someone this is not judged as being as unfair as when we have a choice between making an equal offer and an unequal offer. Empirical evidence relating to this is presented in the next section.

A good starting point for the discussion of reciprocity models is the model proposed by Rabin (1993), since this was the first formal model of this type and the simplest.

### The Rabin model

The central basis of the Rabin model is expressed by the statement:

> If somebody is being nice to you, fairness dictates that you be nice to him. If somebody is being mean to you, fairness allows – and vindictiveness dictates – that you be mean to him. (p. 1281)

The model is a two-player model, in which utilities depend upon beliefs. Player 1's strategy, $a_1$, depends on his belief about the strategy of the other player, $b_2$, and his belief about player 2's belief regarding player 1's strategy, $c_1$. A similar description can be applied to player 2's strategy. On the basis of these beliefs two important constructs can be determined: (1) player 1's 'kindness' to player 2, and (2) player 1's perception of player 2's 'kindness' towards him. The determination and interpretation of these constructs requires a certain amount of intellectual effort, and a fairly detailed exposition of the relevant analysis follows, using a PD situation as an illustration.

1   *Player 1's kindness to player 2*

Given that player 1 has belief $b_2$ regarding player 2's strategy, his own strategy consists of allocating a payoff to player 2 out of a set of possible payoffs. Let the highest and lowest of these payoffs for player 2 be $\pi_2^{max}(b_2)$ and $\pi_2^{min}(b_2)$. We then need to define a fair payoff, $\pi_2^{fair}(b_2)$, which Rabin does by taking an average of the highest and lowest payoffs (although this particular definition does not affect the basic analysis). Player 1's kindness to player 2 can now be expressed as follows:

$$f_1(a_1, b_2) = \frac{\pi_2(b_2, a_1) - \pi_2^{fair}(b_2)}{\pi_2^{max}(b_2) - \pi_2^{min}(b_2)} \tag{10.3}$$

This can be interpreted by saying that player 1's fairness to player 2 is a function of his own strategy $(a_1)$ and his belief regarding player 2's strategy $(b_2)$, and is determined by the fraction of the way above or below the fair point that player 2's actual payoff lies (the numerator), scaled by the range of payoffs player 1 could have dictated (the denominator). Thus if player 2 received a higher payoff than the fair one, the numerator is positive and player 1 is being kind. If on the other hand player 2 receives a lower payoff than the fair one, the numerator is negative and player 1 is being unkind.

2   *Player 1's perception of player 2's kindness*

This perception depends on what player 1 believes player 2 believes player 1 will do $(c_1)$. It can therefore be written as follows:

$$f\!\sim_2(b_2, c_1) = \frac{\pi_1(c_1, b_2) - \pi_1^{fair}(c_1)}{\pi_1^{max}(c_1) - \pi_1^{min}(c_1)} \tag{10.4}$$

Rabin then assumes that player 1's social preferences are given by a three-component utility function:

$$U_1(a_1, b_2, c_1) = \pi_1(a_1, b_2) + \alpha f\sim_2(b_2, c_1) + \alpha f\sim_2(b_2, c_1) f_1(a_1, b_2) \qquad (10.5)$$

The first component of the function, $\pi_1(a_1, b_2)$, represents player 1's direct monetary pay-off. The second component, $\alpha f\sim_2(b_2, c_1)$, represents the utility of player 1's perception of player 2's kindness, where $\alpha$ is a weight showing how fairness converts into money utility (players with no social preferences have $\alpha = 0$). The third component, $\alpha f\sim_2(b_2, c_1) f_1 (a_1, b_2)$, represents the utility of reciprocity; it is a function of the product of the kindness they expect and their own kindness. It should be noted that this term is positive if player 1's generosity is reciprocated by player 2, or if their meanness is reciprocated by player 2. Thus both positive and negative reciprocity yield positive utility, unlike an altruism model.

An equilibrium for the model can then be derived on the basis that players maximize social utilities, assuming rational expectations, $a_1 = b_2 = c_1$. This means that beliefs about the other player's strategy are correct, and that beliefs about the other player's beliefs are also correct. An illustration of the operation of the model can be given in terms of a PD situation, assuming the monetary payoffs are those shown in Table 10.3.

**Table 10.3**  Prisoner's dilemma – monetary payoffs

|  |  | Player 2 | |
|---|---|---|---|
|  |  | Cooperate | Defect |
| Player 1 | Cooperate | 4, 4 | 0, 6 |
|  | Defect | 6, 0 | 1, 1 |

It can be seen that the monetary payoffs correspond to the conditions described in Table 10.2, so that the dominant strategy for each player is to defect, if social utilities are ignored. We now have to calculate social utilities by adjusting the monetary payoffs to incorporate fairness or 'kindness' factors, according to the utility function in equation (10.5). These calculations are shown for each of the four possible pairs of strategies confronting player 1 (player 2's strategies are identical since the monetary payoffs in Table 10.3 are symmetrical).

1   *Cooperate/cooperate*

$$U_1 = 4 + \alpha(4-2)/(4-0) + \alpha(4-2)/(4-0) \times (4-2)/(4-0) = 4 + 0.5\alpha + 0.25\alpha$$
$$= 4 + 0.75\alpha$$

The second term above ($0.5\alpha$) is positive because it is perceived that the other player is being kind, and the third term ($0.25\alpha$) is also positive because there is positive reciprocity.

2   *Cooperate/defect*

$$U_1 = 0 + \alpha(0-2)/(4-0) + \alpha(0-2)/(4-0) \times (6-3.5)/(6-1) = 0 - 0.5\alpha - 0.25\alpha$$
$$= 0 - 0.75\alpha$$

In this case both the second and third terms are negative. Not only is the other player mean, but they are not reciprocating player 1's kindness.

3   *Defect/cooperate*

$$U_1 = 6 + \alpha(6-3.5)/(6-1) + \alpha(6-3.5)/(6-1) \times (0-2)/(4-0) = 6 + 0.5\alpha - 0.25\alpha = 6 + 0.25\alpha$$

The second term is positive since the other player is perceived to be kind, but the third term is negative because player 1's meanness is not reciprocated.

**4**   *Defect/defect*

$$U_1 = 1 + \alpha(1 - 3.5)/(6 - 1) + \alpha(1 - 3.5)/(6 - 1) \times (1 - 3.5)/(6 - 1) = 1 - 0.5\alpha + 0.25\alpha = 1 - 0.25\alpha$$

The second term is negative because the other player is perceived as mean, but the third term is positive since player 1 is reciprocating the other player's meanness.

We can now construct a new payoff table with the social utilities for each pair of strategies. This is shown in Table 10.4.

**Table 10.4**   Prisoner's dilemma – social utilities

|  |  | Player 2 | |
|---|---|---|---|
|  |  | Cooperate | Defect |
| **Player 1** | Cooperate | $4 + 0.75\alpha, 4 + 0.75\alpha$ | $0 - 0.75\alpha, 6 + 0.25\alpha$ |
|  | Defect | $6 + 0.25\alpha, 0 - 0.75\alpha$ | $1 - 0.25\alpha, 1 - 0.25\alpha$ |

In the revised situation the dominant strategy for each player need not necessarily be to defect. The payoff for cooperation given that the other player cooperates is greater than the payoff for defection if $4 + 0.75\alpha > 6 + 0.25\alpha$, that is, if $\alpha > 4$. The implication here is that if people have sufficiently strong social preferences related to fairness there will be a Nash equilibrium situation with two equilibria in pure strategies: cooperate/cooperate and defect/defect. Alternatively the situation could be viewed in terms of a mixed strategy equilibrium.

### The Falk–Fischbacher model

Falk and Fischbacher (2006) constructed another reciprocity model, which proposes a social utility function that incorporates four elements as opposed to the three in Rabin's model. As well as including monetary or 'material' payoffs, kindness and reciprocity, it also takes into account how intentional the kindness of a player is. The FF model has two important variations from the Rabin model: (1) kindness is measured in terms of differences between the payoffs of the different players, rather than in terms of possible payoffs for a single player, and (2) intentions are treated as being dependent on available allocations, both chosen and unchosen. These two variations are now explained in more detail.

**1**   *Measurement of kindness*

In the Rabin model kindness is judged in terms of how much players receive relative to some 'fair' payoff for themselves, which in turn depends on the range of their own possible payoffs. In contrast, the FF model proposes that players judge fairness in terms of the difference between their own expected payoffs and the other player's payoff.

**2**   *Measurement of intentions*

In the FF model there is an intention function, which compares a set of possible payoffs with alternative payoffs. In this case the opportunity cost to the decision-maker is relevant in terms of judging the fairness of their allocation. For example, in an ultimatum game, offering 80%/20% may be regarded as unfair in some situations, but fair in others, depending on what alternatives were open to the decision-maker. If the only alternative was 90%/10%, then the 80%/20% split is likely to be judged fair.

Further details of the FF model are not given here, since it was developed to analyze sequential or extensive-form games, rather than the simultaneous normal-form games illustrated in the tables we have so far used. We saw in the previous chapter that the analysis of extensive form games was more complicated than the analysis of simultaneous games. In standard game theory this involves the use of the foldback method, but as we have seen in the section on PGT, this cannot be applied in psychological games.

### The Dufwenberg–Kirchsteiger model

Dufwenberg and Kirchsteiger (2004) propose a variation of the FF model. Like the FF model and unlike the Rabin model, the DK model relates to sequential reciprocity and also measures fairness in terms of the difference between a player's own expected payoff and the other player's payoff. The DK model is also based on PGT, but extends the analysis to situations where players' beliefs and expectations can change throughout the game, whereas in the original paper by Geanakoplos, Pearce and Stacchetti (1989) initial conditions or beliefs remain constant throughout the game. One consequence of this extension of the analysis is that preference reversals can occur due to a change in the players' beliefs. The DK analysis of a sequential PD game comes to similar conclusions to the Rabin model: if players have high reciprocity sensitivities a twin Nash equilibria solution may result. Both players may cooperate for both material and reciprocity reasons; or they may both defect because of self-fulfilling expectations, with each player believing the other is unkind and being unkind in return.

The DK model also makes some interesting predictions regarding the centipede game, a trust game discussed in the previous chapter. In the DK version of the game, at every node the decision-making player can take (defect) or pass on, in which case their material payoff is reduced by one while the material payoff of the other player is increased by two. A four-stage game is represented in Figure 10.2.

**Figure 10.2** Centipede game with reciprocity

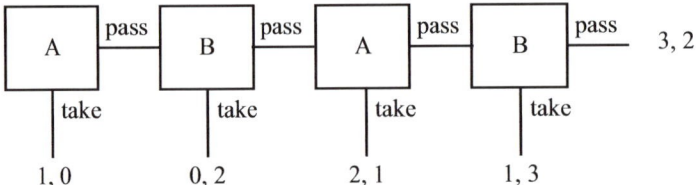

The most interesting prediction here is that it is enough that just one of the players is sufficiently motivated by reciprocity for both players to stay to the last or to the last but one mode. For example, even if A suspects that B will take at the last mode, A may still pass to him at the previous node if B has cooperated up until that point and therefore has established a regular pattern of kindness. The consequence of this is that B may cooperate until the last mode even if he is entirely selfish. Another prediction that follows from this is that the greater the number of stages in the game the more likely the players are to cooperate, since it allows a greater build-up of kindness between them. Dufwenberg (2002) has referred to this process in a psychological game based on motivation by guilt aversion as '**psychological forward induction**'.

We can now see that there are a number of differences between the Rabin and DK models, the most important of which can be summarized below:

1   The DK model applies to sequential games as well as simultaneous games.

2   The DK model applies to games with more than two players.

**3**    The DK model measures kindness in the same units as material payoffs, whereas the Rabin model measures kindness as a ratio.

**4**    The DK model defines the efficiency of strategies as being belief-independent, whereas in the Rabin model the efficiency of a strategy depends on the beliefs of players.

One of the implications of these differences is that Rabin's model assures the existence of an equilibrium in any game where no player is kind. In many games there may also be 'happy' equilibria where both players are kind, but in these cases there must be multiple equilibria, including at least one where no player is kind. We have already seen in the centipede game that the DK model is not so 'gloomy' in its implications, although in other games a 'happy' equilibrium is not guaranteed.

The main advantage that reciprocity models in general have over IA models is that they capture an important psychological factor omitted from the latter type of model. However, as Dufwenberg and Kirchsteiger (2004) themselves admit, their model still omits many of the other psychological factors mentioned earlier in the context of PGT, such as a concern for equality, envy, disappointment and guilt-aversion. These omissions have been addressed by more recent papers by Battigalli and Dufwenberg (2007, 2009). However, the added complexity of the models proposed renders their examination beyond the scope of this book.

## 10.7  Empirical evidence

We have already discussed in Section 10.2 some aspects of empirical evidence in relation to some of the basic games described in the previous chapter, such as PD games, ultimatum games, dictator games and public goods games. However, at that point we were only concerned with comparing empirical findings with the predictions of standard game theory. As in Chapter 8 when examining models of intertemporal choice, we now need to examine empirical evidence in terms of the light it sheds on the different behavioral models. The same general conclusion holds for games involving social preferences as for models of intertemporal choice: it is much easier to show anomalies in the standard model than to compare different behavioral models in terms of how their predictions fit empirical findings. It is important to understand the nature of these difficulties. In standard games, and even in many behavioral games discussed in the previous chapter, players can learn to play some equilibrium because with repetitive play they can come to hold correct beliefs about the opponents' actions (Fudenberg and Levine, 1998). However, 'this may not be enough for psychological games; since payoffs depend on hierarchical beliefs, players would have to able to learn others' beliefs, but unlike actions beliefs are typically not observable ex post' (Battigalli and Dufwenberg, 2009). The consequence of this problem is that players could indeed have the same psychological preferences as proposed by a particular theory, but not behave according to the equilibrium prediction because of mistaken beliefs about beliefs.

Once again findings come from three main sources: behavioral studies, evolutionary biology and neuroscientific studies.

*Behavioral studies*

We can start by comparing the two IA models described earlier. We have already seen that empirical evidence supports the FS model rather than the BO model in terms of comparing a player's payoffs with the maximum and minimum payoffs of other players rather than with their average payoff. Another advantage of the FS model is that it correctly predicts that in public goods games it is the biggest free-riders who are punished, whereas the BO model makes no prediction regarding who is punished.

A final advantage to be mentioned here concerns predictions in variations of the ultimatum game, where rejections result in payoffs of 10% of the original offer. The BO model predicts that, since relative shares are not affected by acceptance or rejection, but payoffs are larger with acceptance, responders will never reject unequal offers, like 80%/20%. In contrast, the standard linear FS model predicts indifference, but modification of the model, to allow concave utilities for money, guilt and envy, can predict rejection. This is much more consistent with empirical results, where the rejection rate by responders of 80%/20% offers may be as high as 50%.

However, there has been heavy criticism of the Fehr–Schmidt methodology from Binmore and Shaked (2010a). These authors report that the FS model has been cited in 2,390 works with uncritical acceptance of the methods, and 'is thought so unproblematic that it is even taught to undergraduates', with a reference to this text. First, it should be noted that virtually all the models described in this text are 'problematic' in some way or other, including prospect theory. This does not mean that they should not be taught to undergraduates, provided the problems are described. Where Binmore and Shaked make a valid point is that in the first edition of this text, although certain limitations of the FS model were described, there was no comment on the methodology. It is not appropriate to discuss the details of Binmore and Shaked's paper (BS) here, and the student is referred to the original work, and to the various responses to it, but the four main grounds of their criticism are summarized below:

1   *Calibration of parameters*

It is claimed that the distributions of $\alpha$ and $\beta$ cannot be estimated from ultimatum game data alone, which leaves the parameters under-identified.

2   *The distribution of parameters is not kept constant*

It is claimed that Fehr and Schmidt sometimes alter their assumptions about the joint distribution of $\alpha$ and $\beta$ without drawing attention to this in order to accommodate or fit new data. In particular BS points out that the distribution used in the FS papers relating to employment contracts (2004, 2005, 2007), which involves 60% of the population behaving according to the SEM (with $\alpha = \beta = 0$) and 40% being inequality-averse (with $\alpha = \beta > 0.5$), is not consistent with the original ultimatum game data. The FS response to this is that the later 40:60 distribution is essentially a simplification of the one originally used.

3   *Predictions are not quantitatively accurate*

The BS paper claims that the FS predictions in various games, including public goods games with and without punishment, auction games and contract games, are no more accurate in general than the predictions from the standard model that do not take into account other-regarding preferences.

4   *Cherry-picking of data and results*

This is really the most serious criticism, and has been touched on above. BS claim that FS throughout their series of papers on inequality-aversion focus on data and predictions that support their model, ignore data or predictions that do not, and fail to make appropriate comparisons with the standard model (or 'money-maximizing' model in BS terms) when such comparisons are not favorable.

Binmore and Shaked go to pains to state that their criticisms are not leveled especially at the FS IA model, but are aimed more generally at the current state of experimental economics. However, Fehr and Schmidt (2010) have defended their methodology against the above claims, and Eckel and Gintis (2010) have also defended the general approach in experimental economics as well as the FS papers specifically. The response to this by

Binmore and Shaked (2010b) has further polarized and broadened the debate. Not only do they claim that FS have not answered any of their criticisms in any substantive way, but they also criticize the work of Gintis (2009), which they claim adopts a similar cherry-picking approach to data and predictions. There is no doubt that this debate will continue for some time.

Having examined and compared the different IA models we can now broaden the discussion and compare IA models in general with reciprocity models. This means we need to address the four issues described in the previous section related to modeling.

**1** *What is the reference standard as far as equitable transactions are concerned?*

There appears to be little controversy here that an equal distribution of payoffs is generally regarded as being fair when these payoffs are regarded as being unearned (Loewenstein, Thompson and Bazerman, 1989; Falk and Fischbacher, 2005). However, as we have already seen, it is rare in reality that payoffs appear as 'manna from Heaven', and when there is an element of 'merit' or entitlement involved we find that preferences can be highly heterogeneous, both within and between cultures.

**2** *How important are intentions?*

This second issue is of fundamental importance in evaluating and comparing IA models with reciprocity models. There is an abundance of empirical evidence that suggests that people do not just care about inequality, they also care about reciprocity and intentions. For example, responders in an ultimatum game may reject 80%/20% offers by a human proposer who stands to gain by making such an offer, but may accept the same split if it is determined by a random process. This clearly shows that the '**consequentialistic**' perspective that proposes that people only consider payoffs, not beliefs and intentions, is inadequate. This finding is supported by a number of studies. For example, Falk and Fischbacher (2005) conducted an experiment based on the ultimatum game, comparing rejections of an (8/2) split when there were different alternatives for the proposer. If the proposer had an alternative of offering an even (5/5) split then 44% rejected the less advantageous (8/2) offer. However, if the alternative was an even less advantageous split of (10/0) then only about 9% of the subjects rejected the offer. Furthermore, if the alternative was a split of (2/8) that was disadvantageous to the proposer, only 27% rejected the (8/2) offer, showing that the majority of subjects did not expect proposers to choose splits that were disadvantageous to themselves.

A more recent study by Falk, Fehr and Fischbacher (2008) confirms some of these findings. This study involved a '**moonlighting game**', where proposers can either give tokens to a responder (which are tripled in value) or can take them away. The responder in turn can then reward or punish the proposer by giving tokens or taking them away at a cost. The game thus combines elements of the ultimatum game, public goods game with punishment and trust games. What is particularly significant is that in one treatment the proposals were generated randomly by a computer, which allows us to see the relevance of intentions. As expected, responders rewarded giving and punished taking, showing strong reciprocity. In the standard treatment there was a slight asymmetry here, in that there was a greater amount of punishment than reward for a given amount of giving or taking by the proposer. Thus on average responders rewarded a gift of six tokens by returning six tokens, but punished a taking of six tokens by taking away eight tokens. So far these results are consistent with an IA model, where people are more averse to negative inequality than positive inequality. However, when the random treatment was used the rewards and punishment were both much smaller, not exceeding two tokens in either direction. Thus, although there is still some evidence of inequality-aversion, the large reduction in rewards and punishment shows that people place a great importance on intentions, not just outcomes.

There is also evidence that the announcement of intentions is important. A study by Hao and Houser (2017) reports that announcement of future actions results in fewer dishonest actions, and that possibly dishonest action taken after it is announced is more likely to be perceived as dishonest than an equivalent action taken without the announcement.

In summary one can say that reciprocity models are more realistic than IA models, although they are analytically more complex since they have to take into account unchosen options as well as those selected. However, the greater mathematical complexity of the analysis may well be worth the trouble, in the light of the greater accuracy of explanation and prediction.

**3** *What is the purpose of punishment?*

Again there is a distinction between IA models and reciprocity models here. According to IA models punishment will only occur if this has the effect of reducing inequalities of material payoffs, while reciprocity models propose that the motive is retaliation for an unkind act, regardless of whether this reduces inequalities. Experiments by Falk, Fehr and Fischbacher (2001) using both ultimatum and public goods games show that inequality-aversion cannot explain much punishment that takes place.

**4** *Who is the relevant reference agent?*

This issue was again investigated by Falk, Fehr and Fischbacher (2001). Their experimental results show clearly that people tend to punish individual defectors rather than the group as a whole, which would include both defectors and cooperators. This represents another refutation of IA models, since these predict that cooperators want to improve their situation relative to the group average, which involves punishing cooperators when this is cheaper than punishing defectors.

Various other significant findings emerge from empirical studies, with a common theme being some kind of asymmetry:

**1** *Asymmetry in reciprocity*

People tend to punish unkindness more than they reward kindness. Croson and Konow (2009) propose two reasons for this: first, an asymmetry in underlying preference that even impartial spectators display, and second, a moral bias in that stakeholders punish more and reward less than spectators.

**2** *Asymmetry in attitudes to punishers and cooperators*

A study by Kiyonari and Barclay (2008) finds that people are more willing to support or reward those who reward cooperators than support those who punished non-cooperators. People did not reward punishers or punish non-punishers. This appears to indicate that people are more inclined to support positive sanctions than negative sanctions.

**3** *Asymmetry in desire to contribute*

We have already seen that in public goods games there is a tendency for contributions to gradually decline, unless there is a possibility for punishment. However, there are various possible reasons for this: (1) people might change their beliefs over time regarding the willingness of others to contribute; (2) people have heterogeneous preferences regarding contributions; and (3) people wish to contribute less than others, so that as the contributions of others decline, their own contribution declines in a 'race to the bottom'. Fischbacher and Gächter (2010) propose that the third explanation is responsible. It has also been reported that, in open-ended projects where duration and outcome are both uncertain, there is not only a tendency for contributions to decline over time, but also a tendency to procrastinate (Bonatti and Hörner, 2011). This suggests a policy of implementing deadlines to eliminate moral hazard.

**4**    *Asymmetry of effects of spiteful preferences*

While we have seen that strong reciprocators have a desire to punish free-riders, and these spiteful preferences promote cooperation, there are also a significant number of free-riders who have a desire to punish cooperators, and this reduces cooperation. These free-riders are not purely selfish, because they are prepared to pay a cost to reduce the payoffs of others, with the purpose of increasing the payoff difference between themselves and cooperators. Falk, Fehr and Fischbacher (2005) find that 13% of the subjects in their study were in this category in a one-shot public goods game. Fehr, Hoff and Kshetramade (2008) conducted an experiment involving a one-shot trust game in India, and find a particularly high proportion of high-caste subjects with spiteful preferences who punish cooperative behavior. When both defection and cooperation are punished, free-riders have less incentive to cooperate, a conclusion also reached by Gächter and Hermann (2010) from experiments in Russia.

**5**    *Asymmetry of conformity bias*

We have already seen that in many environments people like to 'follow the crowd', both because crowds affect the estimation of probabilities and because they affect values, meaning we tend to get to like what others like. However, there is also a tendency, usually a minority one, to want to 'escape from the crowd', often a statement of personal independence. Nakazono (2013) provides an interesting example of this in terms of the forecasts of the Federal Open Market Committee (FOMC) in the USA. He finds that the seven governors on the FOMC make forecasts that follow the previous consensus, possibly indicating both conformity bias and confirmation bias; however, the other members of the FOMC, who serve on a rotating basis, exaggerate their forecasts: they aggressively deviate their forecasts from previous consensus. This suggests that they are aware of the bias of the governors and wish to negate it.

**6**    *Consistent contributors are vital to group cooperation*

Whereas the previous finding has somewhat pessimistic implications for human societies, the finding that a hard core of consistent contributors promotes the development of general cooperation within groups has optimistic implications. This has been recognized by social researchers for some time (Elster, 1985a), but more recent experimental studies have supported these conclusions. Furthermore, they suggest that consistent contributors, who basically have an 'always cooperate' strategy, tend not to suffer any cost from their actions and sometimes gain, at least in repeated multiplayer situations similar to actual societies (Weber and Murnighan, 2008). This has been somewhat of a puzzle in the past, since such contributors can never receive a higher payoff than other players, and can always be exploited by defectors in the short run according to standard game theory. Hence they have been labeled 'suckers'. However, it appears that consistent contributors may receive other payoffs, such as prestige and perhaps sexual access to more partners, which are ignored in SGT, and this may enable them to survive and prosper. Warriors who exhibit self-sacrificial bravery tend to be valued in many societies (Chagnon, 1988, 1990), and an explanation of this phenomenon has been proposed in terms of **costly signaling theory** (Gintis, Smith, and Bowles, 2001; Smith and Bird, 2005). Costly signals act as a credible commitment, in a similar manner to the handicap theory in evolutionary biology (Zahavi, 1975), whereby only meritorious individuals can afford to give a certain signal. It appears that a number of political systems endow prestige on individuals on this basis (Boone, 1998). The effect of such individuals on the group is vital in generating general cooperation, since their behavior encourages conditional cooperators to cooperate more often, by promoting cooperation as the social norm. In this situation punishers of free-riders may be giving a credible signal that only they can afford to pay the cost of punishing. This may in turn cause observers to reward them in ways not considered in SGT. However, in such a system punishment may not even need to be explicit, since people may be shamed into cooperation (Elster, 1985b). The policy implications of social norms are discussed in the next section.

7    *Consensual punishment promotes cooperation most effectively*

In an experiment to compare the effects of a consensual punishment institution versus autonomous individual punishment, Casari and Luini (2009) find that the former promotes a higher level of cooperation. Again social norms appear to be relevant here.

8    *Cooperation in repeated games only tends to evolve if a number of conditions are satisfied*

In experiments involving infinitely repeated games, or simulations of such games where the end of the game is determined randomly, evidence suggests that cooperation is not guaranteed even if an equilibrium involving cooperation exists, and this equilibrium is both **Pareto efficient** and **risk dominant** (Bó and Fréchette, 2011). This is best illustrated by means of an example, and we can use a simple one from the previous chapter to do this, in Table 10.5, which is a repeat of Table 9.4.

**Table 10.5**  Pareto efficiency and risk dominance

|  |  | Suspect B | |
|---|---|---|---|
|  |  | Confess | Not Confess |
| Suspect A | Confess | 5, 5 | 2, 10 |
|  | Not Confess | 10, 2 | 1, 1 |

We have seen that in the above situation there are two Nash equilibria: both suspects confess; and both suspects do not confess (this is obviously not a PD situation, since there are no dominant strategies). The second of these equilibria, involving cooperation, is Pareto efficient, since both players are made better off by not confessing compared with both players confessing. However, the first equilibrium is risk dominant. A risk dominant equilibrium in a 2×2 symmetrical game occurs when the equilibrium strategy is a best response to a mixed strategy where the other player plays each strategy with equal probability (Harsanyi and Selten, 1988). In Table 10.5 the average payoff from confessing is 3.5 years in jail, while the average payoff from not confessing is 5.5 years. Thus the equilibrium of both players confessing, that is, defecting, is risk-dominant in this case, mainly because the 'sucker' payoff from not confessing when the other player confesses is very high. Bó and Fréchette (2011) find that even when equilibria are both Pareto-efficient and risk dominant, these conditions are not sufficient for cooperation to evolve in infinitely repeated games. Only when the payoff from cooperation and the probability of future interactions are high enough do subjects tend to achieve a high level of cooperation.

9    *Overly selfless players are disliked*

This counter-intuitive finding emerged from a study by Parks and Stone (2010). These researchers reported that players in public goods games who contributed more than they withdrew from the common pool were not liked by other players. This may partly explain the phenomenon of antisocial punishment discussed earlier. The other players also did not want to play another game with the selfless players (who were actually computer programs, but were anonymous in the game), even though this should be to their material advantage. Further experiments established that this refusal was not because of the perceived incompetence or unpredictability of the selfless players. Instead two reasons appeared relevant: first, the selfless players were seen as deviating from a social norm (that giving and taking should match), and second, they made the other players look bad. Thus once again, social norms, self-image and reference points are important here. Do-gooders beware.

**10** *The Pay-What-You-Want (PWYW) model may be an effective business model*

The example at the beginning of the chapter of the band Radiohead offering albums at a price determined by buyers may have wider implications as a business model. A study by Gneezy and colleagues (2010) examines the sale of Disneyland souvenir photos and finds that a PWYW method increased revenues compared with selling them at a fixed price. Furthermore, this general finding of the viability of PWYW is confirmed in another field experiment, this time on an ongoing basis. Riener and Traxler (2012) studied the behavior of patrons of a restaurant in Vienna for the first two years after opening, involving about 80,000 visits. Very few patrons offered to pay nothing, less than 1%, and although the average payment fell slightly after the first six months, total revenues increased over the period as a whole.

**11** *There appears to be a relationship between perceived unfairness and health*

A study by Robbins, Ford and Tetrick (2012) found a significant association between perceived unfairness at work and employee stress and psychological dysfunction, and this to some extent was reflected in lower physical health. This may be a complex relationship, since stress and decision fatigue may also cause people to be less prosocial and fair (Achtziger, Alós-Ferrer, Wagner, 2015).

There is finally one general conclusion here, which resembles a general conclusion earlier in the book relating to decision-making under risk and uncertainty: it appears that there may be two types of situation where people have to make decisions involving social preferences. In one kind of situation people tend to automatically apply some kind of social norm, as Binmore and Shaked (2010a) claim, whereas in other situations they play strategically, taking into account beliefs and intentions of other players. Of course, as mentioned earlier, this begs the questions regarding what situations trigger social norms, and which norms are triggered.

## Evolutionary psychology

As we have seen in other areas of economic behavior, evolutionary psychology (EP) plays an important role in understanding social behavior. As far as social behavior is concerned, EP proposes that the human brain developed significantly as people started to live in hunter-gatherer bands or tribes over the last few million years. Cooperation yielded significant advantages in such an ancestral environment, since repeated interactions between people in the same group were frequent, and people learned to recognize others and remember debts. Cooperation was also necessary to provide public goods, including food from big game hunting. Punishment of defectors and free-riders, often in the form of exclusion from the group, or ostracism, was also important in enforcing cooperation. As mentioned above, consistent cooperators may have been rewarded in terms of prestige and access to sexual partners. However, there are a number of misunderstandings concerning the role of EP, and it is important to clarify these.

**1** *Competing versus underlying theories*

The most fundamental misunderstanding is that evolutionary explanations are an alternative to the theories described in the preceding sections. Evolutionary theory is in no way a substitute for these theories; rather it has a complementary role, in terms of explaining how underlying social preferences are formed in the first place. All the theories discussed so far make certain assumptions regarding how conceptions of fairness are determined, and how these conceptions affect our choices in terms of other concepts such as reciprocity and intentions. The fundamental role of EP is to explain how such conceptions developed in our intellectual decision-making processes. EP therefore is best regarded as an underlying theory rather than a competing theory as far as theories of social preferences are concerned. In terms of the hierarchical reductionism explained in Chapter 1, an EP explanation is at a lower level in the hierarchy than the theories described in this section.

**2**  *Questionable status as a scientific theory*

Related to the first criticism is the accusation that EP suffers from an inability to be falsified or to make precise predictions. These are two basic requirements for any scientific theory. However, although EP can be difficult to falsify in some cases, this is because of a lack of available evidence in practice, not because of any principle (unlike for example string theory in physics, or religious 'theories' like the existence of Heaven and Hell). As far as precise predictions are concerned, EP does indeed lead to some very precise, and surprising, predictions, as will be seen in the first case study, on the Wason test.

**3**  *Individual development variations*

One line of criticism of EP is that people are not born with a sense of social responsibility. As we have seen, this takes a number of years to develop, and in the first few years of life infants are almost entirely 'purely' selfish. This is often taken as evidence that the capacities of judging fairness and calculating strategic behavior are inculcated by cultural factors rather than being innate. The falsehood of this argument can be seen by making a direct comparison with sexuality. Most modern psychologists agree that human sexuality does not really develop until puberty (although Freudians dispute this to some extent). However, it is absurd to argue that this is evidence that sexuality is a cultural concept and is not innate. It must be recognized that not all our innate instincts are present at birth; even innate instincts may take some time to fully develop.

**4**  *Cross-cultural variations*

We have also seen that there are considerable variations between cultures as far as certain characteristics like offers and rejections in ultimatum games are concerned. Such variations are also often seen as evidence that EP is not a powerful predictor of social behavior. The essential point here is that EP should not always be seen as a competing explanation for behavior compared with cultural factors (although it may often be). It is not always a case of 'nature versus nurture'; frequently phenomena are best explained in terms of 'nature via nurture', as Matt Ridley (2004) has proposed. Thus, although our brains may be hardwired with certain innate propensities and preferences, these are to some extent malleable by culture. The phenomenon of suicide bombing is an extreme case, where an evolved psychological mechanism geared to improve survival (belief in purpose and supernatural powers) has been hijacked into serving an entirely opposite purpose.

**5**  *One-shot and repeated games*

It is sometimes argued that the tendency to cooperate or reciprocate in one-shot games is evidence against EP. Camerer (2003) makes the point that 'subjects are usually well aware that one-shot games are strategically different than repeated ones'. It should not be inferred that this awareness will necessarily discourage people from cooperating in such one-shot games. This inference overlooks the fact that awareness is not sufficient to deter certain behavior in all cases. To take an extreme example, an alcoholic may be very aware that indulgence after a long period of abstinence may cause a relapse into self-destructive behavior, but this does not deter them, any more than the knowledge that fatty foods cause heart disease discourages people from going to McDonald's. As Camerer also states: 'when our caveman brains play one-shot games in modern laboratories, we cannot suppress repeated-game instincts.'

The point to recognize here is that repeated-game instincts involve guilt and envy, anger and indignation, all emotions that are now hardwired into our psychological make-up. Such emotions cannot be simply disengaged in one-shot situations, even when we are aware of their one-shot nature. However, there is some recent evidence from experiments by Kanazawa and Fontaine (2013) that more intelligent individuals are less likely to cooperate in one-shot PD games, when the one-off nature of the game is explained and anonymity of the players is assured. The authors hypothesize that more intelligent individuals are better able to comprehend any evolutionarily novel situation and adjust their behavior accordingly.

The real challenge for EP, in analyzing social behavior as in other areas, is to produce precise and testable predictions. EP is certainly capable of meeting this challenge, and often produces surprising and interesting results, as seen in Case 10.1.

Arguably the most difficult phenomenon for EP to explain is the evolution of cooperation in a society, and, associated with this, the evolution of morality. It is a fairly common and false belief that EP is unable to do this. A discussion of the evolution of morality goes beyond the scope of this text, but we can discuss some of the research into the evolution of cooperation. The puzzle is to explain how selfish individuals are willing to make the sacrifices necessary for cooperation, since kin altruism can only account for cooperation within the network of an extended family. This remains a controversial issue, with the main controversy centering on the role of group selection. We will not enter this discussion here, since it would involve a lengthy digression.

Some of the research relating to the evolution of cooperation involves simulation in games where hypothetical subjects with heterogeneous social preferences have to compete to survive and reproduce in a dynamic environment over time. As noted by Dekel, Ely and Yilankaya (2007), it is important to consider all types of social preferences and experiment with different protocols to see what types and what preferences come to dominate a population. These results can then be compared with the predictions of EP. Because of the complexity of the interactions of the different parameters and variables in these models, it is often impossible to derive analytical solutions, so simulation is the only feasible method for arriving at predictions.

An example of a prediction based on EP involves a phenomenon called **assortative matching**. This is essentially an application of evolutionary game theory, incorporating signaling, where cooperators are more likely to interact with other cooperators than with non-cooperators. The evolutionary story here is that it is important for cooperators to be able to detect defectors or cheaters, to avoid being suckered. Thus they need to be able to send signals relating to their willingness to cooperate. To be credible these signals tend to be costly. However, it then pays defectors to be able to simulate such signals, and this puts selective pressure on cooperators to become better detectors, so an evolutionary arms race begins. The result of this is that signaling a willingness to cooperate becomes more and more complex, and may well lead to self-deception (Pinker, 1997); it is easier to fake a cooperative signal if we really believe we will cooperate, even if we ultimately defect.

Based on assortative matching, research can then investigate the evolutionary success of preferences for rewarding and punishing. For example, Herold (2012) finds that assortative matching allows rewarders to invade a population of self-interested players. There is also an important interaction between rewarders and punishers, since the entry of rewarders into a population enhances the evolutionary success of punishers, who then come to dominate the population in his model. This result confirms the findings of Kuzmics and Rodriguez-Sickert (2009), who conclude that rewards are costly once you achieve cooperation, while punishments are costly when you don't. Bowles and Gintis (2004, 2013), using a somewhat different punishment protocol in the form of ostracism, also find that punishers survive. The difference here is that ostracism does not involve any cost for the punisher.

Some of the research on the evolution of cooperation involves the study of non-human primates. Certainly there is evidence that both capuchin monkeys and chimpanzees respond negatively to disadvantageous inequity. On the other hand, the evidence regarding whether these species exhibit prosocial attitudes in response to advantageous inequity is ambiguous (Brosnan, 2008), since non-human primates seem mainly concerned with their own payoffs rather than the payoffs of others. However, the evidence that primates exhibit feelings of reciprocity seems beyond doubt. Like humans, other primates appear to be more concerned with the actions of their social partners than with the payoffs of these partners. Thus intentions seem to matter to primates too. Furthermore, their reactions to inequity appear to show several factors related to the emotions that are common to humans. For example, they are prepared to incur a cost to punish 'unfair' treatment, by throwing food back at an investigator, or refusing to cooperate in paired tasks where their partner routinely claims the better reward in an unequal payoff situation (Brosnan and de Waal, 2003). These actions cannot be explained in terms of IA, since they actually result in an increase in inequality. Thus reciprocity in primates is a complex issue, and appears to involve the same kind of emotional commitment devices as with humans. Obviously more research is needed here, perhaps aided by neuroeconomic studies of primate brains in this kind of decision situation. We can now turn our attention to neuroeconomic studies in general.

### Neuroscientific studies

When discussing altruistic and spiteful behavior earlier we were careful to distinguish between material and non-material benefits. Until the beginning of this century the measurement and even the identification of non-material benefits and costs was highly speculative and introspective. Furthermore, many people are reluctant to admit that they actually get a kick out of punishing or reducing the welfare of others; this contravenes social norms in societies with a Judaeo-Christian morality. However, over the last few years, and with the benefit of various types of neural scanning, both identification and measurement of psychic costs and benefits are possible, and this has added significantly to the science of economics in terms of both theory and empirical evidence. We can now consider the implications of certain neuroscientific studies regarding social preferences in general and in particular some of the games described earlier.

First of all, researchers need to know where in the brain to look as far as the recording of rewards from decisions is concerned. O'Doherty (2004) found that not only was the dorsal striatum activated in decisions involving expected monetary rewards, but also that this activation increases as the expected monetary gain grows. Therefore we would expect rewards from punishment or cooperation to be associated with a similar activation. A study by de Quervain and colleagues (2004) examined rewards from punishment in trust games. They used a positron emission tomography (PET) scanning technique and three treatments:

1    Free punishment (F), where player A can punish player B for defecting at the rate of $2 per point at no cost to themselves.

2    Costly punishment (C), where A can still punish B at the rate of $2 per point, but at a cost of $1 per point to themselves.

3    Symbolic punishment (S), where there is just an assignment of punishment points, but no monetary cost to either A or B.

The last treatment was important as a baseline control measure, since neuroimaging scans always measure brain activations in one condition relative to another condition.

The study found that the dorsal striatum was strongly activated in both the F–S contrast and the C–S contrast, indicating that subjects experienced rewards in both situations.

Furthermore, subjects in the C condition who exhibited higher dorsal striatum activation also tended to punish more. The authors concluded that the level of stratum activation was related to the *anticipated* satisfaction from punishment, rather than from the actual punishment. This was because subjects who experienced higher striatum activation in the F condition, even though they were punishing to the same maximal level as subjects with less activation, were willing to spend more on punishment in the C condition.

The de Quervain and colleagues study also found that the ventromedial prefrontal cortex (VMPFC) is activated in the processing of rewards from punishment. It appears from a number of studies that the VMPFC is involved in the integration of separate benefits and costs in the pursuit of behavioral goals (Ramnani and Owen, 2004; Knutson et al., 2007), and the VMPFC is also activated by rewards related to charitable donations (Moll et al., 2006).

Neuroscientific studies involving the VMPFC are also useful in analyzing the phenomenon of conformity bias, discussed in Chapter 4. It was noted then that the frequently observed herding behavior of people can be caused either by a changed perception of probabilities or by an other-conferred utility from following other people. A study by Chung and colleagues (2015) sheds some light on this confound. They study the gambling behavior of subjects in isolation and compare this with their behavior and neural activation after observing the gambling behavior of others. It was found that individual risk attitudes of subjects in isolation were encoded in the ACC and insula, but that these were mediated by the VMPFC when the behavior of others was observed, thus showing that these observations did create an other-conferred utility.

Other studies relating to rewards from cooperation as opposed to punishment have been revealing. Rilling and colleagues (2001; 2004) have examined mutual cooperation with a human partner compared to mutual cooperation with a computer in repeated and one-shot social dilemma games. Results were essentially the same in both studies, but the one-shot situation gives more reliable results, since the repeated game involves a number of confounding influences. The studies show that mutual cooperation with a human partner promotes more striatum activation than cooperation with a computer; the use of the computer partner controls for other influences like the size of reward and effort, so it can be concluded that the observed reward arises entirely from mutual cooperation in the normal sense, meaning with another person.

Antisocial punishment has also been studied in terms of the neuroeconomic factors involved. Pfattheicher, Landhäußer and Keller (2014) examine the role of testosterone and cortisol when players punish cooperators in a public goods game, and find that when cortisol levels are low individuals with elevated testosterone are more likely to engage in this type of punishment than those with normal testosterone levels. However, they do not find the same interaction between cortisol and testosterone for altruistic punishment of free-riders.

As far as fairness is concerned, various brain areas are implicated. Two studies (Tabibnia et al., 2008; Fliessbach et al., 2007) have provided evidence that the fairness of a bargaining offer is associated with activity in the ventral striatum. Studies have also examined the neural processes involved when negative feelings are aroused, for example with unfair offers. Sanfey and colleagues (2003) conducted a study of the ultimatum game using functional magnetic resonance imaging (fMRI) and found that there was greater activation in the insula, the anterior cingulate cortex (ACC), and the dorsolateral prefrontal cortex (DLPFC). A later study by Knoch and colleagues (2006) corroborates these results to some extent. This study used the rTMS technique to disrupt the DLPFC, and found that when the right (but not the left) DLPFC was disrupted this increased people's propensity to accept unfair offers, thus implicating this area of the brain in the judgment of fairness. It appears from this study, and also later studies by Knoch and colleagues (2008) and Spitzer and colleagues (2007), that the DLPFC along with the orbitofrontal cortex (OFC), play a role in moderating self-interested impulses in games where people are tempted to violate social norms and fear punishment. People whose brains show more activation in these areas are more inclined to abide by social norms. The opposite side of this coin is that people with antisocial personality disorder have been shown to display deficient activation in these areas, as well as deficient insula activation (Veit et al., 2002; Birbaumer et al., 2005).

We have seen in Chapter 3 that the insula is implicated in the processing of unpleasant emotions, such as pain, hunger and disgust; it is also activated when we experience negative social feelings, like seeing a price charged that we think is excessive. A study by Harle and Sanfey (2007) sheds further light on people's tendency to reject unfair offers; when negative emotions such as sadness and disgust have already been primed, engaging the insula, this leads to a higher rejection rate of unfair offers. The insula, along with the amygdala, has also been implicated in the decision-making stage of extended coordination games (Hodgson et al., 2012), with the authors suggesting that these brain areas associated with negative affects are activated when subjects consider deviating from a social norm, or losing an established cooperative equilibrium.

Neuroscientific studies also shed some light on inequality-aversion. A study by Tricomi and colleagues (2010) created one 'rich' subject and one 'poor' subject, the first with $80 and the second with $30. The subjects were then asked to evaluate future payments to the other player. Rich subjects valued payments to themselves only slightly more highly than payments to the other subject, while poorer subjects valued payments to themselves much more highly, and valued payments to the other subject negatively. These valuations were closely correlated with activation in the nucleus accumbens (NAcc), an indication of anticipated reward, but there was a different pattern of activity in the VMPFC. Thus it appears once again that separate areas of the brain react differently to social situations: the NAcc is concerned with inequality-aversion, while it appears that the VMPFC has a moderating role in terms of reconciling the conflict between the social preference to equalize payoffs and the purely selfish desire for gain.

In addition, it has been shown that when people's emotions are primed by either fair or unfair behavior in a trust game, this affects their empathy with the player if that player is then subjected to pain (Singer et al., 2006). When the player previously treated them fairly, returning their trust, there was evidence of empathy for their pain in terms of activation of the ACC and anterior insular cortex (AI). When the player had treated them unfairly previously, a difference in reaction between the sexes was observed: while women continued to show some empathy, men no longer showed activation in the ACC or AI, on the contrary showing activation in the NAcc. It seems men may be more likely to take revenge on unfair players than women, while women are more likely to be prosocial. This finding is echoed in some other studies mentioned in the next section. However, a note of caution is in order here: the term prosocial is used in different senses; in economic studies it is usually related to fairness, while in psychology studies it is often related to helping others, or empathy, and the two characteristics are not perfectly correlated. People who value fairness more do not necessarily display more empathy.

A final area of note in this area of social interaction is the processing of own and other rewards. It is known that with both humans and non-human animals group members respond vicariously to benefits obtained by others, and impairments in this capacity contribute to neuropsychiatric disorders in humans, such as autism and sociopathy. The influence of the **mirror neuron system** (**MNS**) is important here. It has been known for some time that the MNS allows monkeys to mimic actions by others, since the same neurons are activated when they observe specific actions by others as when they perform the same actions themselves. More recently it has been found that the MNS is responsible for producing empathy, since it allows people, and some other animals, to experience the emotions of others. Chang, Gariépy and Platt (2013) studied the processing of own and others' rewards in monkeys, finding that own rewards were mainly encoded by neurons in the OFC. Neurons in the anterior cingulate gyrus (ACCg) were found to encode reward allocations to the other monkey, to oneself or to both. Neurons in the anterior cingulate sulcus (ACCs) were found to signal reward allocations to the other monkey or to no one. In this network it was reported that the ACCg was the prime center for computing social rewards.

Zak, Stanton and Ahmadi (2004) and Zak, Stanton and Ahmadi (2007) propose the existence of a human oxytocin mediated empathy (HOME) system, whereby mirror neurons are activated by the release of oxytocin, in turn causing people to be either generous or to punish. Neurobiologists have suspected for some time that this chemical promotes bonding behavior, including maternal care and trust, in a variety of species. A study by Kosfeld and colleagues (2005) supported this hypothesis; it found that the percentage of players who trusted maximally in a social dilemma game increased from 21% to 45% after treatment with oxytocin. The issue then raised was whether oxytocin operated at the level of subjects' beliefs about others' trustworthiness, or whether it operated at the level of the subjects' preferences. The authors concluded that oxytocin does not significantly affect beliefs about the trustworthiness of others, but instead renders subjects less averse to being exploited, thus changing their preferences. A more recent study by Zak and colleagues (2007) sheds further light on the effects of oxytocin. This study found that the administration of oxytocin increased offers significantly in ultimatum games, but not in dictator games. The authors explain this result by proposing that oxytocin increases empathy related to the mental states of others, rather than by increasing altruism *per se*. If the increased offers in the ultimatum games are purely strategic, then this result could be seen to conflict with the Kosfeld and colleagues study, since it would seem that beliefs were being affected rather than preferences.

There appear to be several conflicts in terms of how oxytocin and empathy affect behavior. First, if people witness a distressing scene, such as a car accident, the experience of distress associated with empathy can inhibit generous behavior, so they may be less likely to help victims or people in need of aid in spite of feeling empathy with them (Batson, Fultz and Schoenrade, 1987). Second, mimicry and understanding do not necessarily go together (Khalil, 2011). Thus people may imitate the actions of others who are violent, without performing a rational appraisal of the situation, an unfortunate phenomenon all too often observed in scenes of mob violence. Mob psychology is the flip side of the MNS–oxytocin coin. Obviously, further research needs to be done in this area to clarify the role of both the MNS and oxytocin.

## 10.8  Policy implications

As with other areas of behavior the factors discussed in this chapter have important policy implications, for individuals, firms and governments. In all cases the implications point to different courses of action compared to those suggested by the standard model. Furthermore, we often find that policies designed by firms and governments to achieve certain ends may actually prove to be counter-productive, for a number of different reasons. The examples given in this section will illustrate this counter-productive aspect when social preferences are involved.

### Market norms and social norms

One main factor resulting in counter-productive consequences is the phenomenon of **crowding out of intrinsic incentives**. In general terms this means that the provision of external market-based norms in a transaction may replace pre-existing social norms and change the incentive structure for behavior in an unintended way. Evidence of this phenomenon comes both from field studies and experiments.

Market norms are extrinsic to the individual and are based on the assumption of the SEM that people act purely selfishly and have no social preferences in terms of reciprocity. Fines and monetary rewards are in this category. Social norms on the other hand involve intrinsic values that people have, and are shaped both by a person's individual psychological make-up and by the culture in which the person operates. There is a considerable body of research that emphasizes the importance of social norms in the provision of public goods (Elster, 1989; Ostrom, 1998, 2000; Fehr and Gächter, 2000). An example of the application of the social norms is given in Case 8.3 relating to the desire for rising consumption profiles.

It is helpful at this stage to examine an example where implicit moral incentives are pitted against explicit economic incentives. A study that is often quoted in this respect was conducted by Gneezy and Rustichini (2000). This field study examined a situation at ten Israeli day-care centers, where there was a problem with parents being late picking up their children. The centers had a policy that children were supposed to be picked up by 4 p.m., and delays caused anxiety among the children and teachers had to wait around for parents to arrive. The study lasted for 20 weeks, and for the first four weeks the investigators simply recorded the number of late parents. On average there were eight late pick-ups per week per day-care center. After week 4 a fine was introduced at six of the ten centers, which was the equivalent of $2.50 for a delay of ten minutes or more. This fine was added to the monthly fee of about $380 per child. In the four centers with no fine, which acted as a control group, the number of late pick-ups stayed about the same. However, in the six centers where the fine was enforced the number of late pick-ups *increased* steadily for four weeks, and then stabilized at an average level of about 18 per week, more than twice the original level!

Another study regarding the relative importance of moral and economic incentives was conducted by Titmuss (1971) and related to blood donation. Most people donate blood for altruistic reasons, and are not paid a fee. When a small fee was offered, people tended to give *less* blood than without the fee. It has been hypothesized that the payment of a fee demeaned the act of donating blood, so that people no longer felt good about doing so. However, conflicting results have been reported in the case of organ donation (Deck and Kimbrough, 2013). These researchers find that in the case of deceased organ donation people do respond to market incentives by increasing supply. They also report that a market-oriented policy disproportionally affects the poor. This poses an ethical problem, particularly when the issue is extended to cover live organ donation, as is the case with kidneys. The problem does not just relate to disproportionally affecting the poor. Although larger monetary incentives may increase supply, it should also be noted that being an effective policy is not necessarily desirable; it simply means changing behavior in an expected direction. Levitt and Dubner (2005) note that, in the case of blood donation, large fees may indeed cause more donations, but they may also cause some highly undesirable side effects, like taking the blood of others by force and donating the blood of animals. These effects have already been observed in the market for replacement body organs. The issue of organ donation is discussed further in the section on nudging.

Social norms in terms of environmental policies have also been problematical. A fundamental problem here has been establishing a social norm. Whereas various aspects of safety, such as the wearing of seatbelts in cars and helmets on motor bikes and bicycles, the use of child seats in cars, and the avoidance of drink-driving, have become social norms in many countries over the last few decades, many 'green' initiatives have not been so successful. For example, there is evidence that emergency appeals to reduce electricity usage during peak hours to prevent possible brown-outs are counter-productive (Holladay,

Price and Wanamaker, 2015). This study finds that there is no significant reduction in grid stress during peak hours, but there is increased electricity usage during off-peak hours, with both increased $CO_2$ emissions and greater price volatility. The authors propose this may be due to consumer load-shifting. This study is interesting because it may have broader implications for other types of appeal when there are shortages, such as water, petrol or staple foods. Such appeals may well increase 'panic buying', thus exacerbating the shortage. Rettie, Burchell and Barnham (2014) recommend that such initiatives should be repositioned to that they appear to be 'normal' practice, rather than being targeted towards people who are already environmentally friendly. Thus advertisements stating that nine out of ten people recycle waste products or use energy-saving domestic appliances may help to establish such norms.

A further problem concerns the crowding out of social norms relating to the environment. This has been reported in a study in Switzerland investigating people's willingness to accept a nuclear waste repository in their community (Frey and Oberholzer-Gee, 1997). Initially about half (50.8%) of the respondents indicated a willingness to accept such a facility; however, when the same respondents were asked if they were willing to accept the facility if the Swiss parliament offered substantial compensation to all the residents of the community, the level of willingness dropped sharply to 24.6%.

It now appears that many governments have made serious policy errors by assuming that centralized control over key public resources is vital for efficient use. Standard economic theory predicts that in order to prevent a 'tragedy of the commons' involving overuse and free-riding, common resources such as water supplies, grazing ground, and irrigation systems, need to be controlled by a central authority. However, there is now abundant evidence that such control frequently results in less efficiency and a worsening of environmental problems, by disempowering local groups who previously controlled such resources based on local knowledge and social relationships and placing control in the hands of faceless bureaucrats who were often corrupt (Wunsch and Olowu, 1995; Finlayson and McCay, 1998; Shivakoti and Ostrom, 2002).

Experimental studies have produced similar findings to the field studies above. A meta-analysis of 128 laboratory studies that have explored the effect of extrinsic rewards on intrinsic motivation has found that tangible rewards tend to have a substantially negative effect on intrinsic motivation (Deci, Koestner and Ryan, 1999).

Although the findings above strongly suggest a crowding out of social norms by market norms, there is some evidence that this crowding out does not occur between different social norms. Greenberg (2014) examines the relationship between tipping and holiday generosity at a restaurant using two years of within-customer data. He finds a complementarity between the two types of prosocial norm, rather than a substitution effect, so that tipping rates are higher during the holiday season, particularly among generous tippers.

How can these findings be interpreted? A number of possible explanations have been proposed. One explanation is that the imposition of a fine changes the amount of information available to the players in the game. For example, parents may interpret the fine in terms of the economic and legal options that are feasible for the manager of the center. They may infer from the low value of the fine that the actual cost to the center of a late pick-up is low. Blood donors may interpret any fee paid to them in terms of the value of their donation, and therefore may be discouraged from making a donation if they perceive that this value is small.

However, a more likely explanation is that the introduction of fines and rewards causes a shift in the way that the activities in the game are perceived. Fines and rewards transform the meaning of activities into commercial commodities, to which people attach different monetary values than when such activities are performed out of moral incentives. It also appears that this shift in perception can only occur in situations where subjects had not previously considered monetary rewards and punishments as an option. Once subjects have had their perceptions changed in this direction, they cannot be unchanged. This conclusion is supported by the fact that, when fines were discontinued in the day-care centers after the 16th week, the number of late pick-ups remained at a high level.

We should not conclude from the findings above that monetary incentives in the form of fines and rewards are ineffective. In the day-care center situation the fines were too low to be effective, and were simply seen as representing a low price for being late. To put this into perspective, we should consider the fine of $2.50, or 10 shekels, against the fine for illegal parking of 75 shekels, and the fine for not collecting dog droppings of 360 shekels. Monetary incentives may need to be larger in order to be effective in this particular case.

Another important conclusion relating to all the observed behavior is that **incomplete contracts** may be preferable to complete, or more complete, contracts in many situations. Such incomplete contracts would not specify fines and rewards, but would rely on moral or social incentives for changing behavior in the desired direction. For example, the original contract in the Israeli day-care centers was incomplete, since it did not specify any sanctions for late pick-ups. This issue is discussed further in Case 10.3.

The distinction between market norms and social norms is also relevant in the context of fairness and the concept of a 'just society'. As seen in the recent events related to Trump's election victory in the USA and Brexit in the UK, market forces have caused increased inequality between an 'elite' of skilled professional workers and a mass of manual workers who are either unskilled or whose skills are no longer in demand. The latter group has felt angry and frustrated at being dispossessed, and appear to regard this as a violation of their social norm of fairness. However, in many ways it has become clear that, particularly in the USA, there is a wide disparity in social norms among the general population, with increasing polarization in terms of attitudes to race, immigration, sexual practice and other social issues. Although much research remains to be done in this area, a study by Cappelen and colleagues (2013) reports some interesting findings from an experiment with Norwegian students. The experiment involved a series of risk-taking tasks where students were paired together and asked about their willingness to redistribute gains. Two main findings emerge: (1) although *ex ante* notions of fairness and equality of distribution were popular, there was still a tendency for many subjects to want to redistribute gains *ex post*, that is after the risk-taking choices had been made; and (2) many subjects wished an *ex post* redistribution of gains based on luck, from lucky to unlucky players, but did not wish an *ex post* redistribution based on different choices, that is from risk-takers to non-risk-takers.

Another experiment has examined the perceived fairness of different types of tax system, again indicating another source of counter-productive consequences. Sausgruber and Tyran (2014) conduct an experiment where participants earn incomes from trading and collectively choose one of two possible tax systems to produce a given revenue. They find that a universal tax, imposing the same tax rate on all markets, is regarded as fair, while a discriminatory tax, which imposes a higher tax rate on markets with inelastic demand, is regarded as unfair, even when it is both efficient and results in equal distribution. This result appears to suggest that it is equal treatment rather than equal distribution consequences that is paramount as far as the perception of fairness is concerned.

What are the lessons to be learnt in terms of government policy as far as markets norms and social norms are concerned? First of all it appears that both equality of opportunity and active choice are important criteria for judging fairness; thus if people become richer than others who have the same opportunities, and their wealth is perceived as deriving from choices they made, this inequality is at least to some extent acceptable. Secondly, policies that are perceived as controlling and treat people as untrustworthy are self-defeating, since they reduce people's sense of self-determination and self-esteem, and are self-fulfilling (see Klaes, 2015d). A third lesson is that bureaucrats do not necessarily know better than community residents, who may have much local knowledge gathered over a long period. It now seems that the UK government is learning from these mistakes, since it is trying a large-scale experiment in the opposite direction in terms of its police force. For nearly 50 years the police force has been a centralized authority. Over the last ten years there has been increasing criticism of the current target-based approach, such as catching a certain number of criminals and achieving certain crime detection rates. Many believe this has tied the hands of the police and crowded out intrinsic incentives, so that the police are no longer seen by people as public servants. A bill has been passed that proposes to put police forces in the hands of locally elected commissioners, who would be able to set priorities and budgets, and to hire and fire chief constables. This is intended as a return to real 'community policing'.

## Labor markets

Similar counter-intuitive results to those discussed above have been found in labor markets. Since the seminal work of Akerlof (1982) behavioral economists have frequently modeled these in terms of gift exchange. A **trust contract** refers to a situation where the employer (principal) offers a high wage, trusting the employee (agent) to reciprocate by making a high effort. A **bonus contract** refers to a situation where the principal may reward the agent for making a high effort by making a voluntary bonus payment *ex post*. Both contracts actually involve one player trusting the other, who is in a position to exploit the other player, and both appeal to fairness and reciprocity. However, in spite of this symmetry, there is a distinct asymmetry in terms of the empirical findings. Fehr, Klein and Schmidt (2007) find that trust contracts do very badly and are not profitable, while bonus contracts do very well and are highly profitable. They explain this asymmetry in terms of the different risks involved. The employer faces a higher cost if employees defect by putting in little effort, compared to the employee's cost of putting in a high effort and the employer defecting by not paying a rewarding bonus. Thus contracts work better when the risk of trusting lies with the player for whom the cost of trusting is lower. Fehr, Klein and Schmidt also make two other counter-intuitive conclusions:

1  A higher proportion in the population of agents who value fairness makes trust contracts less acceptable, since fair agents have more to lose from trusting than purely selfish agents.

2  Incomplete contracts may be more efficient than contracts that are more complete, since they allow more flexibility for both employer and employee to act in a trusting and reciprocal way.

Experiments by Fehr and Gächter (2000) have examined different types of labor contract from those described above, relating to the work effort of workers under two conditions: one in which there were explicit incentives in the form of fines if workers were observed shirking, and another where there were no incentives. The relationship between work effort and offered rents was observed, where offered rents are defined as the wage minus the cost of providing a certain desired effort level. In the condition with explicit incentives, the actual work effort did not vary significantly with the rent offered, averaging about 2.5 on a scale of 1 to 10. However, when there were no explicit incentives in the form of fines, work effort increased steadily with the rent offered, reaching a level of 7. Only at low rent levels was work effort lower in the absence of incentives; at moderate and high rent levels work effort was *higher* than when incentives were offered. This result has been confirmed by a later study by Fehr, Klein and Schmidt (2004), as discussed in Case 10.3, where more than 80% of the principals preferred a bonus contract, and both principal and agent received higher payoffs as a result.

In a more recent study, Fehr and Schmidt (2007) investigated the effects of a contract that combined fines with bonuses (stick and carrot), comparing this with a contract that only offered bonuses. It might be thought initially that the combined contract would achieve the best of both worlds, being more general and adding more incentives. However, this was not the finding in their experimental study. Two-thirds of the principals preferred the pure bonus contract, and agents' payoffs were significantly higher with the pure bonus contract.

In this situation, with both extrinsic and intrinsic incentives in operation in the combined contract, it cannot be argued that a simple crowding out of incentives is occurring here. Fehr and Schmidt propose two possible explanations, which are not mutually exclusive:

1   Threats of fines may be perceived by workers as a hostile act, with the result that negative reciprocity causes them to reduce work effort.
2   Threats of fines may send workers a signal that managers are untrustworthy and may pay a smaller bonus than the workers expect, so they react in a self-fulfilling manner, again reducing their work effort.

Sliwka (2007) arrives at similar conclusions. He proposes that when employers try to control employee behavior by using contracts relying on extrinsic incentives, this affects the behavior of employees by sending a pessimistic signal of distrust being the social norm, which may lead employees to conform to this norm and act selfishly. On the other hand, if employers do not rely on this type of contract, this sends a signal that trust is the social norm, and this may encourage conformist employees to act in a trustworthy manner. Thus the moral of these studies, noted in the previous section, appears to be that people respond to signals regarding the social norm: selfish behavior generates selfishness in others, while trust generates trust. Of course this does not apply to all persons, but it may apply to a majority. However, some caution must be urged with this conclusion, since some studies of single firms have indicated that incentive contracts can increase productivity (Gibbons, 1997; Prendergast, 1999; Lazear, 2000). More research is needed to investigate the precise conditions where incentive contracts may work, and when they are likely to be ineffective or even counter-productive.

### Market clearing

According to the neoclassical model markets tend to clear because any shortage or surplus will cause prices to change to eliminate any disequilibrium. Thus if there is a shortage of shovels after a big snowfall, market forces will cause prices to rise as sellers take advantage of the situation to make additional profit. However, empirical evidence suggests that such an action may be judged unfair; in the survey by Kahneman, Knetsch and Thaler (1986) 82% of subjects responded in this way to this specific situation. Buyers may regard such temporary price rises as 'gouging', and boycott the seller in the future. As we have seen, anger and indignation are caused because the offending firm is seen as violating customers' perceived entitlement to a particular reference price. Some states have laws against 'gouging', particularly for essential products like gasoline. In fact, such laws may not be necessary if firms are conscious of likely unfavorable public reactions. An example is given by Olmstead and Rhode (1985), relating to a severe gasoline shortage in California in 1920. SOCal, the dominant supplier, implemented allocation and rationing schemes, with the result that the price was actually lower in California than in the East where there was no shortage. It appears that management at SOCal was concerned about their public image and wanted to appear 'fair'.

A recent shortage of vegetables in Europe in February 2017, caused by bad weather conditions, has resulted in some contrasting policies. In response to the shortage, some supermarket chains in the UK, which imports 50% of its vegetables, rationed shoppers. Thus Tesco limited shoppers to three iceberg lettuces, and Morrisons had a limit of two per visit. Lidl on the other hand increased their price dramatically, to nearly three times the original level. It would appear that Lidl was less concerned with perceptions of fairness, or perhaps management believed that, as a discount store with an established reputation for low prices, their price hike would not be perceived as unfair.

Similar considerations related to market clearing prices may apply when there are surpluses. Overproduction or seasonal factors, for example, may cause a temporary surplus of a product. Of course durable products may be withdrawn from the market and added to inventory, but there is a cost involved with such action. Rather than reducing the price in this situation, which would reduce the reference price, it may be better or more profitable for a firm to offer a discount. Later, when the surplus has disappeared, the discount may be revoked. Revoking a discount involves less hostile consumer reaction than raising price, since it is merely a case of returning to the previous reference price rather than exceeding it; therefore loss-aversion does not occur to the same extent.

## Public goods

The main problem relating to public goods relates to free-riding. According to the standard game-theoretic analysis of the standard model it is difficult to prevent free-riding unless contributions are enforced by public authorities, usually in the form of taxes of some kind. The reason for this, as we have seen, is that it is the 'pure' self-interest of players in such a game situation to defect in terms of not contributing, while it is also in the 'pure' self-interest of other players to defect by not punishing free-riders, since punishment involves some type of cost. Behavioral models that incorporate social utility tend to be more optimistic regarding provision of public goods for two reasons:

1   People may contribute out of altruism, 'pure' or 'impure'. They may also contribute because they expect others to contribute, and therefore they are prepared to contribute themselves out of positive reciprocity.

2   People may be prepared to punish others for not contributing. Such punishment may be in the form of 'whistle blowing' to the authorities in the case of social benefit fraud. Alternatively it may take the form of social ostracism, for example by yelling at people who throw trash on the street. Although there is a cost in punishing others, in the form of time spent or the threat of violent confrontation, this cost may be outweighed by a positive social utility of imposing negative reciprocity.

The empirical studies of Fehr and Gächter (2000), referred to earlier, and a more recent study by Carpenter et al. (2009), provide confirmation that the opportunity for punishment makes a big difference to the outcome of public goods games. Punishment of course does rely on the ability to observe behavior and contributions. The effectiveness of punishment may also depend on the ability to observe who is being punished.

It should be noted that punishment does not have to be in the form of a fine or material loss to be effective. As mentioned earlier in the context of social norms and public policy, ostracism, such as 'naming and shaming', may be at least as effective as material losses in deterring free-riding (perhaps not the most appropriate term for describing consorting with prostitutes!), and ensuring cooperation. A study by Maier-Rigaud, Martinson and Staffiero (2010) supports this conclusion in finding that introducing ostracism increases contribution levels significantly in public goods games, with a net positive effect on the earnings of the group.

## Punishment

In game situations punishment by ostracism or humiliation may be more attractive to individual players than other forms of punishment, because it may reduce or eliminate the cost of punishing. In historical terms, when crime was largely dealt with by the community itself rather than by a centralized authority, social ostracism served as a powerful punishment and deterrent. One main implication here for public policy is that a 'naming and shaming' policy may be effective. Some US cities fight prostitution by posting pictures of convicted 'johns' and prostitutes on websites or on local-access television. As Levitt and Dubner (2005) ask rhetorically in their popular book *Freakonomics*: 'Which is a more horrifying deterrent: a $500 fine for soliciting a prostitute, or the thought of your friends and family ogling you on www.HookersAndJohns.com.' However, punishment by humiliation is a controversial issue. This kind of policy has been widely opposed in schools in the UK. Pupils are no longer told to stand in the corner as a punishment, and a school head recently received much criticism for adopting a policy whereby persistent offenders are required to give a public apology at school assembly.

Another implication for public policy is that a 'whistle blowing' facility may be beneficial. This is, however, also a controversial issue, since it can lead to a 'big brother' state, with neighbors spying on each other. For example, the introduction of ASBOs (Anti-Social Behavior Orders) in the UK was greeted with mixed enthusiasm by the public.

Yet another controversial issue relates to length of sentencing for criminals. The 'three strikes' law in the USA has been heavily criticized for its tendency to incarcerate petty criminals for excessive periods, and indeed the general incarceration policy in the USA has been criticized for being heavy-handed, with high proportions of the population affected, in particular minorities and drug users. However, there is some evidence that 'selective incapacitation' of criminals may be cost-effective under certain circumstances. A study by Vollaard (2013) in the Netherlands examined the effects of a habitual offender law passed in 2001, where criminals with ten offenses on their record could have their sentences increased ten-fold. He finds that, although only a small proportion of the prison population were affected, this policy lowered the rate of burglary and theft from car by about 25% on average, and 40% in the cities where the policy was used most intensively. There were a number of limitations of this study in terms of its conditions, which include the following factors: (1) the average normal sentence (before extension) for the offenses was only a few months, compared with two years or more in the USA for similar offenses; (2) most of the offenders were drug users, with a flat age-crime curve; and (3) there was a strong case of diminishing returns to intensity of application of the law, so that additional extended convictions had a smaller crime-reducing effect. Therefore it is difficult to extend the conclusions of this study to other circumstances in other countries without further research.

## Nudging

Nudging policies have been mentioned several times in different contexts in previous chapters. The key point about such policies, sometimes overlooked by critics, is that the individuals affected by the nudge later come to believe that their decision was in their best interests, in other words that the influence was benign rather than malign. Two further points can be emphasized in the context of social preferences, relating to conformity bias and framing.

We have seen that conformity bias is a very common phenomenon, and governments as well as firms can use it to influence behavior. An example given in Chapter 4 concerns towel usage, whereby a notice in people's hotel rooms stating that the majority of guests reuse towels is effective in increasing reuse. Similar messages may be effective for public health and safety policies, for example relating to using seatbelts, checking smoke alarms and having regular health check-ups. However, we have also seen that people have a desire for autonomy, and this relates to self-serving bias. Thus they may tend to follow the behavior of others to some extent, but they like to perceive that they own their own decisions, since they believe that their decision-making abilities are superior to those of others. The important implication for policy makers is that people do not generally like to be told what to do, and this was an important factor in the Brexit result in the UK in 2016. A study by Suri and colleagues (2014) suggests that in many cases 'asking' is better than 'telling'. More specifically, they recommend that telling people what to do may be necessary initially to cause a change in habits, but this is likely to have only a short-term effect. Asking people to adopt a particular behavior, giving a greater sense of autonomy, may be more effective at changing habits in the long term.

The above study is an example of a framing effect. Other aspects of framing are also very important in nudge policies. We have already seen that, in the context of saving for retirement, choosing appropriate default choices is an important factor. This, along with other menu effects, is relevant in other public policy issues, like helping people to choose appropriate health care plans. Another interesting framing effect is relevant in this context. A study by Aldrovandi, Brown and Wood (2015) finds that using rank-based information is more effective than using comparisons with an average in terms of nudging people to adopt healthier eating habits. For example, telling people that they are in the unhealthiest 10% of eaters is more effective than telling them that they consume 500 calories more than the average person. The authors report from their experiments that providing rank-based information can increase willingness to choose a healthy food by 30% compared with providing information involving comparisons with an average.

## 10.9  Summary

- The neoclassical model is based on the assumption that people are motivated by 'pure' self-interest. The main advantage to this model is its simplicity, but there are many empirical anomalies.
- Behavioral models are also based on self-interest, but modify and extend this concept to include altruistic and spiteful behavior.
- Altruistic behavior relates to behavior that confers a benefit to others, while involving a cost to the originator of the behavior, with no corresponding material benefit. Self-interest is still involved, since there is a psychic benefit.
- Spiteful behavior can be viewed as the flip side of altruistic behavior. This is behavior that imposes a cost on others, while also involving a cost to the originator of the behavior, with no corresponding material benefit. Again the benefit is psychic. Such behavior may sometimes be seen as beneficial to society, since it aids the enforcement of social norms.
- Game theory is an essential tool of analysis in understanding social behavior. This area of theory is involved when there is a strategic interaction between individuals, meaning that each individual has to consider the reactions of others to one's own actions, and is aware that others are considering one's own reactions to their actions.
- Fairness must be regarded as a subjective concept not an objective one; different people and cultures have different attitudes towards fairness, and these attitudes can change greatly over time.

- All attitudes regarding fairness involve the concept of dual entitlement regarding the transactors. Dual entitlement relates to three main factors: reference transactions, outcomes to the transactors and the circumstances of changing transaction terms.
- Different cultures or subcultures within the same country can have different attitudes to fairness, based on different reference transactions.
- Reciprocity is fundamental to the concept of fairness and dual entitlement. In particular, many people are strong reciprocators, meaning that they are prepared to punish defectors at a material cost to themselves.
- Experimental games are useful in establishing attitudes towards fairness; examples are ultimatum bargaining games, dictator games, trust games, prisoner's dilemma games and public goods games. Empirical findings related to these games reveal extensive anomalies in the standard model.
- There are three main categories of variable that affect social preferences: methodological and structural, descriptive, and demographic. The first category is particularly important since it relates to variables that can be manipulated experimentally to reveal the key factors involved.
- Social norms play a vital part in affecting people's attitudes regarding fairness and social preferences, and are determined by gene-culture coevolution in a complex environment.
- Social norms, just like the concept of fairness, can vary within the same country.
- When modeling social preferences, there are two main objectives: explanation and prediction, and a sound psychological basis.
- Psychological game theory (PGT) proposes that utilities are based not just on material payoffs but on beliefs.
- Inequality-aversion (IA) models are based on the assumption that people are envious of others who have more utility than themselves, but also feel guilty if they have more utility than others.
- Reciprocity models are more complex, taking into account how 'kind' people judge others to be, and basing their own kindness on the perceived kindness of other players. This approach has a stronger psychological foundation.
- Behavioral studies indicate that spiteful preferences are asymmetrical in effect. When they result in punishing defectors they promote cooperation, but when they result in punishing cooperators then they cause cooperation to be reduced.
- Consistent contributors, or unconditional cooperators, are vital to the development of a cooperative society. They may survive and prosper in spite of suffering material losses because they send a costly signal of credible commitment, which may result in them receiving rewards in terms of prestige and sexual partnerships.
- Evolutionary psychology (EP) should not be viewed as an alternative approach to economic models; rather it is complementary to them, helping to lend understanding to the underlying psychological foundation of economic models. The real challenge for EP is to provide precise falsifiable predictions.
- Neuroscientific studies support the hypothesis that we, and probably other primates, have areas in the brain that register negative emotions when we feel we have been treated unfairly, and that these negative emotions can result in spiteful preferences.
- There are a number of important policy implications of the behavioral approach that differ from the neoclassical model. In particular, these relate to the contrasts between market norms and social norms. If market norms are introduced in decision situations formerly governed by social norms, for example with fines or incentive contracts, this can result in the crowding out of intrinsic incentives.

## 10.10   Review questions

1    What are social preferences?
2    What factors are relevant in determining the fairness of a transaction?
3    Explain the term 'strong reciprocity', and why it is an important concept.
4    Explain the differences between the Fehr–Schmidt and Bolton–Ockenfels models of inequality-aversion.
5    Explain the difference between IA models and reciprocity models.
6    Explain what is meant by the crowding out of intrinsic incentives, giving two examples.
7    Explain the features of PGT, giving two examples of situations where it is relevant.
8    What do behavioral studies indicate regarding IA models versus reciprocity models in terms of explanation and prediction?
9    What is meant by costly signaling theory? What may it help to explain?
10   In what way are spiteful preferences asymmetrical?
11   Explain why the difference between social norms and market norms is important for public policy. What sort of mistakes do governments tend to make in this regard?
12   What do empirical studies indicate regarding the use of incentive contracts in the labor market?

## 10.11   Applications

The first case study involves a detailed examination of the empirical findings regarding the Wason test and the implications. This is designed to give the reader a better understanding of the role of EP. The second case study involves the policy implications of social preferences.

---

### Case 10.1  The Wason test

One of the main themes in this book is that the human brain is a highly fallible machine, but is fallible in certain predictable ways due to the manner in which it evolved. For example, we have seen that we tend to be bad at calculating and using probabilities, but work much better when probabilities are expressed in terms of frequencies. Similarly, the human brain is often bad at performing **logic**. Logic refers to inferring the truth of one statement from the truth of other statements based only on their form, not their content. A standard example that is normally used relates to the following reasoning: P is true, P implies Q, therefore Q is true. Being based on form rather than content, logic is not empirically based. Thus it does not matter what P means; to use the example of Pinker (1997), P could be 'my car has been eaten by rats'.

Why do so many tests show that people are bad at problems involving logic? One factor concerns the ambiguity of certain logical words. For example, the word 'or' can either mean 'and/or', as in A or B or both, or it can mean 'exclusive or', as in 'A or B, but not both'. The correct or intended meaning can only be inferred from the context, so our knowledge of the empirical world becomes relevant. For example, when we see a restaurant advertising 'a free soda or hot beverage with your meal', we immediately understand the 'or' in this context to mean 'exclusive or'; we can have either a soda or hot beverage, but not both.

The psychologist Peter Wason was particularly interested in Popper's criterion of scientific hypotheses, that they should be falsifiable. He wondered whether everyday learning was

▶

---

in fact hypothesis testing, in terms of looking for evidence that contradicts a hypothesis. In 1966 he devised a test that was designed to see how people perform when it comes to falsifying hypotheses. This well-known test can be described as follows. A set of four cards has letters on one side and numbers on the other. The objective is to test the rule 'if a card has D on one side, it has a 3 on the other side', in other words a simple P-implies-Q statement. Subjects are shown four cards, as in Figure 10.3, and are asked which ones they would have to turn over to see if the rule is true.

**Figure 10.3    Wason test**

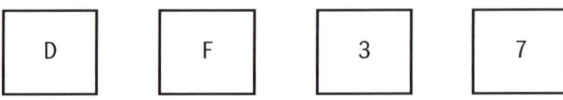

A hypothesis of the form 'If P then Q' is violated only when P is true and Q is false. This means that the first and the fourth cards must be turned over. However, in numerous tests over the last 40 years only about 10% of subjects select the right cards. Most subjects pick either just the first card or the first and third cards. It should be seen that picking the third card cannot falsify the hypothesis; if the reverse side is not-D, this does not constitute a falsification, since the hypothesis does not say that only D cards have a 3 on the other side. Furthermore, the ambiguity factor mentioned above cannot account for the observed findings. If people interpreted the hypothesis as 'if D then 3 *and vice versa*', they would have to turn over all four cards.

According to Cosmides and Tooby (1992) the results can be explained in terms of EP: humans have not evolved to solve abstract logical problems, but rather to respond to problems structured as social exchanges when they are presented in terms of costs and benefits. More specifically, we have evolved to detect cheaters in social contract situations. A cheater can be defined as a person who receives a benefit without paying a cost (i.e. a free-rider). They supported this hypothesis by performing several Wason-like tests with subtly designed variations. The basic variation was to pose the situation where the subject was a bouncer in a bar: their job is to eject under-age drinkers (cheaters). The problem can be posed logically as 'if a person is drinking alcohol, they must be over 18'. In general terms this is again an 'if P then Q' statement, where P refers to drinking alcohol and Q refers to being of a legal age. The four cards in this case appear as shown in Figure 10.4.

**Figure 10.4    Wason test in terms of a social contract**

Given the test in this form the vast majority of subjects (about 75%) picked the correct first and third cards, even though the logic is identical with the original problem. However, it should be noted that the Cosmides and Tooby hypothesis regarding social contracts is not the only explanation of these findings. There are two main alternative theories: availability and facilitation theories.

**1**    *Availability theory*

Although this theory comes in different forms, they all essentially argue that framing the logic of the problem in terms of a familiar real-world situation rather than in abstract terms accounts for the difference in performance. Therefore Cosmides and Tooby performed various other experiments to test this alternative hypothesis.

The first kind of experiment involved using familiar real-world situations that did not involve social contracts. For example, subjects were asked to test the statement 'if a person travels to Boston, then he takes a subway'. Performance on such descriptive/causal tests was better than on the abstract form of the problem, with 48% of subjects responding correctly, but it was still well below the level of performance on the social contract version of the test. Furthermore, even when the social contract was expressed in unfamiliar terms, such as 'if a man eats cassava root, he must have a tattoo on his face', performance was still higher than in descriptive situations.

**2**  *Facilitation theory*

This essentially states that social contracts facilitate logical reasoning. The results of the experiments described above could still be explained by the fact that the correct answer in terms of evolutionary adaptation also happens to be the logically correct answer. In order to test this theory Cosmides and Tooby devised an experiment with a 'switched' form of social contract. In the standard form, a social contract can be expressed as 'if the other party takes the benefit, then it pays the cost'; in switched form the contract becomes 'if the other party pays the cost, then it takes the benefit'. For example, the same social contract is expressed in the following two statements:

- If you give me your watch, I'll give you $20 (standard form).
- If I give you $20, you give me your watch (switched form).

In the first statement, from your point of view, taking the benefit (me receiving the watch) constitutes the logical category P, whereas in the second statement it relates to Q. However, in either case cheating (from your point of view) means that I receive the watch without paying you the $20. This experiment is represented in Figure 10.5.

**Figure 10.5**  **Wason test in terms of a switched social contract**

| | Taking benefit | Not taking benefit | Paying cost | Not paying cost |
|---|---|---|---|---|
| Standard form | P | not-P | Q | not-Q |
| Switched form | Q | not-Q | P | not-P |

In the standard social contract the first and fourth cards should again be selected, since they are required in order to detect cheating, and they also happen to be the logically correct answer. However, in the switched form of the contract, the logically correct answer involving P and not-Q means selecting the second and third cards. Thus there is a difference between the solution for cheater detection (first and fourth cards) and the logically correct solution, and it is this factor that allows the facilitation theory to be tested. It should be noted that EP supports the cheater detection hypothesis, since consistently altruistic persons who pay the cost without receiving a benefit would not have been likely to survive in our evolutionary past; there would thus have been no selection pressure for 'altruist detection', unlike the strong pressure for cheater detection.

Cosmides and Tooby found that, when presented with the switched form of social contract, about 70% of subjects gave the valid solution for cheater detection but logically incorrect answer. This result validates the prediction arising from EP, that we are not attuned to detect altruistic, or foolish, acts such as people paying costs and not receiving benefits in the same way that we are attuned to detecting cheaters. Other experiments by the same authors have confirmed these findings.

It is clear from the above example that the concept of cheating depends on whose perspective is taken, mine or yours. Gigerenzer and Hug (1992) utilized this difference in perspective to conduct further tests of facilitation theory against the cheater detection theory of Cosmides and Tooby. They asked subjects to test the statement 'if an employee gets a pension, then that employee must have worked for the firm for at least 10 years'. The subjects were divided into two groups, one being told they were the employer and the other being told that they were the employee. For employers providing a pension is a cost, whereas getting the pension is a benefit to the employee. Likewise, working for at least ten years is a benefit to the employer but a cost to the employee. The situation is shown in Figure 10.6, assuming a standard form of contract where the logical construct P corresponds to the other party receiving the benefit.

**Figure 10.6**  Wason test in terms of different perspectives

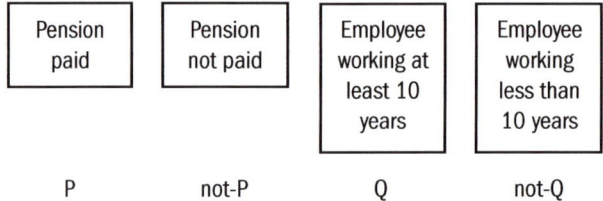

Thus each group defined cheating in a different way: for employers cheating constituted paying a pension without the employee working for ten years (P and not-Q). However, for employees cheating relates to working for at least ten years and not being paid a pension (Q and not-P). The logically correct answer for either group is 'P and not-Q', as always, since this is independent of content or perspective. Facilitation theory predicts no difference between the two groups regarding the proportion of correct responses, while the cheater detection hypothesis predicts a higher correct response rate from the employer group. Gigerenzer and Hug found that for the employer group about 75% gave the correct 'P and not-Q' response, with a negligible proportion responding with 'not-P and Q'. However, for the employee group, only about 15% gave the logically correct response, with about 60% giving the incorrect, but cheater-detecting, response 'not-P and Q'. These results provide another strong vindication of the cheater detection hypothesis.

## Questions

1   Give examples of familiar and unfamiliar social contracts. What does the cheater detection hypothesis predict regarding responses testing the breaking of such contracts?

2   Explain why using the switched form of social contract is a useful way of testing facilitation theory against the cheater detection hypothesis.

3   Explain why the use of different perspectives is a useful tool in testing the cheater detection hypothesis.

4   Explain why evolutionary psychology (EP) predicts cheater detection much better than altruist detection.

## Case 10.2  Public goods and free-riding

We have already seen that the provision of public goods presents problems in the standard model, both because people are unwilling to contribute and because they are unwilling to punish other non-contributors due to the cost involved. This case study examines the results of a series of public goods experiments by Fehr and Gächter (2000), showing how reciprocity, both positive and negative, affects the situation.

The basic form of the experiment involves a group of four members, each of whom is given 20 tokens. All four people decide simultaneously how many tokens to keep for themselves and how many tokens to invest in a common public good. For each token that is privately kept there is a return of the same amount. For each token that is invested in the public good each of the subjects earns 0.4 tokens, regardless of whether they have contributed or not. Thus the private return for investing a token is 0.4 tokens, while the social return is 1.6 tokens (since there are four players). According to the standard model nobody will want to invest in the public good in this situation, since it is more profitable to keep the tokens privately (i.e. defect), and therefore each individual player will earn 20 tokens altogether. However, we can see that this is in effect a multiplayer PD situation. If all the players cooperate, with each one contributing all their tokens to the public good, they will each end up with a return of 32 tokens (it is assumed in the simple model that there are constant returns to investment). This optimal solution cannot ever be an equilibrium in the standard model.

If we now introduce positive reciprocity into the model, this means that players are willing to contribute if others are also willing to contribute. However, in order to sustain such contributions there has to be a high proportion of players with such a motivation. In reality we know that there is a significant proportion of people who are motivated by pure self-interest, and this makes it difficult to achieve an equilibrium with positive contributions.

How does introducing negative reciprocity affect the situation? In this case negative reciprocity means retaliating against defectors or non-contributors who are free-riding. In the simplest version of the game the only form retaliation can take is to free-ride also. This punishes everyone else, whether they are free-riding or not. Thus people may free-ride either out of pure self-interest or because they are demonstrating negative reciprocity. The result is that negative reciprocity is even more likely to lead to a solution where there are no positive contributions, since 'selfish' players are inducing reciprocal players to defect.

This situation changes radically if players can observe the contributions of others, and punish specifically those who do not contribute. The experiment can be modified so that players can reduce the number of tokens of any other player, at a cost of 1/3 token for every token reduced. It is important to impose a cost here, not only for realism, but also because this allows a distinction to be made between 'selfish' players and reciprocal players. Selfish players will never be willing to punish others because of the cost involved, and the punishment opportunity will not affect the outcome of the game. However, those players with negative reciprocity may be willing to punish free-riders, and this in turn may induce selfish players to cooperate and contribute. Thus the end result may be the opposite of that achieved without the punishment opportunity, with reciprocal types ensuring general cooperation rather than selfish types ensuring general defection.

In the experiments performed by Fehr and Gächter (2000) the various forms of the game described above were used, using two versions. One version was called the 'Perfect Stranger' version; this involved 24 subjects formed into six groups of four players each, with the game

▶

being repeated six times. Every time the game was repeated the groups were shuffled, so that no player ended up playing with any other more than once. This ensures that people treat the game as essentially a 'one-shot' game, so that their actions have no consequences for later games. In the 'Partner' version, on the other hand, the same four players played ten times; thus this was a 'repeated' game, where actions in one time period could have consequences in later periods. Both versions of the game were implemented with and without the punishment opportunity, and all interactions were anonymous. Where applicable, the punishment in each period occurred after observing the contributions in that period.

The results of the experiments are illustrated in Figure 10.7. NP refers to the 'no punishment' version, while WP refers to the version with punishment.

**Figure 10.7**    Evolution of cooperation in public goods game

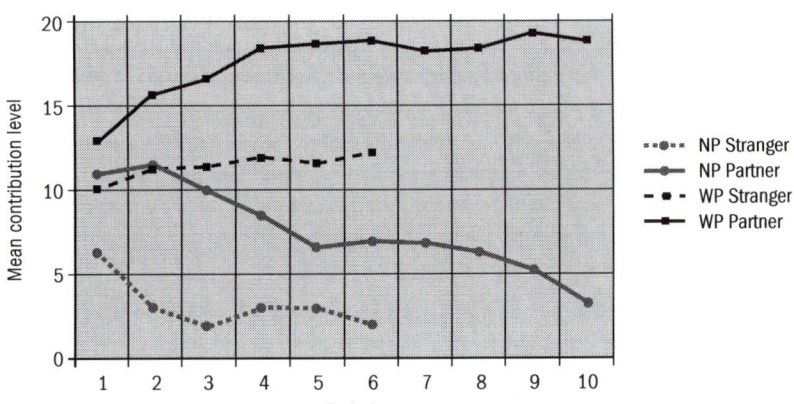

*Source: Fehr, E., and Gächter, S. Fairness and retaliation: The Economics of Reciprocity. Journal of Economic Perspectives, 14(3), 2001, 159–181, Figure 2, with permission from the American Economic Association.*

### Questions

1    Interpret the graph in terms of cooperation in the absence of a punishment opportunity.

2    Explain how the opportunity for punishment affects the development of cooperation.

3    What are the implications of the above findings as far as public policy is concerned?

4    Explain how public goods games are affected when free-riders punish cooperators.

## Case 10.3  Sales force compensation

The issue of determining the optimal structure for sales force compensation essentially involves a sequential game between manager and salesperson. It is an example of the principal-agent problem. The essential problem for the manager (as principal) is that, if the effort of the salesperson (as agent) cannot be contracted on or is not fully observable, a self-interested salesperson will always shirk, assuming that effort is costly (Klaes,

2015b). Therefore the manager has to design a contract that prevents moral hazard, or post-contract opportunism by the salesperson. The situation is complicated by IA and reciprocity, which allows us to test the standard model against a behavioral model incorporating social preferences. If salespeople feel guilty about shirking, or repay kindness with reciprocal effort, they will not shirk as often as pure self-interest and the standard model would predict.

Fehr, Klein and Schmidt (2004) therefore propose a contract involving a bonus scheme (BC) as being more effective than a standard incentive contract that imposes a penalty for shirking (IC). The parameters of the situation are modeled as follows:

$c(e) = f(e)$   cost of salesperson's effort is a function of the level of effort, with rising marginal cost from 1 to 4 in the permissible range of $e$ (1 to 10). This is shown in Table 10.6.

**Table 10.6**   Effort costs for salesperson

| e | 1 | 2 | 3 | 4 | 5 | 6 | 7 | 8 | 9 | 10 |
|---|---|---|---|---|---|---|---|---|---|----|
| c(e) | 0 | 1 | 2 | 4 | 6 | 8 | 10 | 13 | 16 | 20 |

In the first stage the manager offers contract; in the second stage the salesperson decides whether to accept or reject. If they accept they receive $w$ immediately, and choose effort $e$ in the third stage. In the fourth and final stage the manager observes effort $e$ accurately, and may impose a penalty in the IC or award a bonus in the BC.

Under the IC: effort can be monitored at the cost of $K$

$w = g(e^*, f)$ where $w$ = wage offered, $e^*$ is effort demanded, and
$f$ = penalty for being caught shirking, meaning that $e < e^*$
Probability of monitoring technology working = $1/3$

Under the BC: $w = h(e^*, b^*)$ where $w$ = wage offered, $e^*$ is effort demanded, and
$b^*$ = promised bonus for salesperson
neither $e^*$ nor $b^*$ are binding; the manager may award a bonus either greater or less than $b^*$.

The expected payoffs for both manager and salesperson can now be calculated for each contract.

With IC:  if $e \geq e^*$,  $\pi_M = 10 \times e - w - K$      $\pi_S = w - c(e)$
If $e < e^*$,  $\pi_M = 10 \times e - w - K + 0.33f$   $\pi_S = w - c(e) - 0.33f$

With BC:  $\pi_M = 10 \times e - w - b$      $\pi_S = w - c(e) + b$

Note that the bonus here is not necessarily the promised bonus of $b^*$.

There is a large gain from exchange here if the salesperson gives high effort, because the marginal gain to the manager of a unit of effort is 10, while the marginal cost to the salesperson is only 1 to 4 units. Therefore the optimal outcome is for the manager not to invest in the monitoring technology and for the salesperson to choose $e = 10$, giving a combined surplus of $10 \times e - c(e) = 80$, since the cost of $e = 10$ is 20. However, this is not an equilibrium outcome.

Under the IC the optimal contract would be ($w$ = 4, $e^*$ = 4, $f$ = 13), resulting in $\pi_M$ = 26 and $\pi_S$ = 0.

Under the BC the purely selfish manager will never pay a bonus in the last stage, and the salesperson, knowing this, will only supply the minimum work effort, $e$ = 1. Thus the optimal contract will be ($w$ = 0, $e^*$ = 1, $b^*$ = 0), resulting in $\pi_M$ = 10 and $\pi_S$ = 0.

Under the above conditions managers will always choose the IC over the BC, according to the standard model. This is basically saying that, if managers realize that salespeople do not expect to get bonuses and are therefore likely to shirk, it is better to use an IC and set the demanded level of work at a moderate level, enforced by a probabilistic fine.

However, when Fehr, Klein and Schmidt tested this model empirically in an experiment, the results did not support the standard model. The investigators asked a group of subjects to act as managers and choose either a BC or IC. They then had to make offers to another group of subjects acting as salespeople, who then chose their level of effort. Managers chose the BC 88% of the time, and salespeople reciprocated by supplying a greater effort than necessary. Managers in turn reciprocated by paying higher bonus payments. As a result of the greater effort, payoffs to both manager and salesperson were higher under the BC than under the IC. The study concluded that the empirical findings supported the FS IA model described earlier.

### Questions

1   Explain how the empirical results could be interpreted as supporting the IA model as far the behavior of the subjects was concerned.

2   The IA model predicts that there will be a pooling equilibrium for managers under the BC, with both purely selfish and fair-minded managers offering the same wage. Why would this happen?

3   The IA model predicts that fair-minded salespersons will put in less effort than purely selfish ones under a BC. Why would this happen?

4   What tends to happen when incentive contracts are combined with bonus contracts?

## Case 10.4  Obesity, diet and health

Obesity is currently estimated to be one of the top three social burdens in the world as a whole, ranking just behind smoking and armed violence, war and terrorism. The global cost is estimated at around $2 trillion, or 2.8% of world GDP (MGI, 2014). About 2.1 billion people, about 30% of the world population, are estimated to be overweight or obese; that is about two and a half times the number of people estimated to be undernourished according to the McKinsey Global Institute (MGI).

The costs of obesity are difficult to estimate, for two main reasons. First, it is related to many different medical conditions and adverse health effects, notably heart disease and type-2 diabetes, but also conditions such as hypertension, liver disease and joint problems. The second reason is that obesity incurs both direct costs on health and medical services, often funded by governments, and indirect costs, such as increased absenteeism from work, disabilities and lower productivity, incurred by individuals and employers. In the UK the direct costs were estimated to be about £16 billion in 2014, with indirect costs amounting to a further £31 billion (MGI, 2014). The indirect costs are also sometimes measured in terms of disability-adjusted life years (DALYs). It has also been argued that there are other costs for individuals in terms of loss of self-esteem and feelings of ostracism within certain communities.

So what is obesity? The most common metric is body-mass index (BMI), which is calculated by dividing a person's weight in kilograms by the square of their height in meters. A BMI over 25 is considered overweight, while a measure over 30 is considered obese. Medical authorities generally admit that this is a very crude measure of obesity, and many health professionals consider waist measurement or visceral (abdominal fat) to be more appropriate, but BMI is still the most widely used measure, mainly because statistics relating to it are most readily available. In the UK for example 25% of adults are obese, while a further 37% are overweight (MGI, 2014).

There are various aspects of behavioral economics that are relevant in the discussion of the obesity problem, and these aspects help us to understand some of the glaring paradoxes that are found. The following are some of the most obvious:

**1** Most obesity is preventable by appropriate lifestyle and nutrition policies, as much as 90% according to one study (Yusuf et al., 2004). So why do we have the problem?

**2** In developing countries obesity is more common among the more affluent, while in developed countries it is more common among the less affluent. The countries which have the greatest obesity problem are those which have only become prosperous in the last few decades, like Kuwait, Saudi Arabia and the UAE, or those which are still low or middle income, like Mexico, Syria and Venezuela.

**3** In developed countries there is a strong positive correlation between obesity and social deprivation. Yet deprivation normally involves income and food deprivation which should, other things being equal, cause lower calorie intake and less obesity.

**4** While obesity has been a steadily rising trend in many developed countries, there have also been concerns that a negative body image, especially among young people, is unhealthy and leads to mental problems. Thus some health care professionals advocate a policy whereby physical shape and condition are regarded as unimportant, in direct contrast to policies focusing on weight and lifestyle management.

It is clear from these observations that obesity is a complex problem, operating at both an individual level and a societal level, and there is an interaction of a wide variety of different factors that are relevant: individual psychology, biology and genetics; sociological and cultural factors; geography, including access to social and physical facilities, and urban/environmental planning; marketing practices of food suppliers, such as advertising and labeling; and the policies of governments and health organizations. Thus there are no simple solutions. In a recent global survey the MGI (2014) examined the effectiveness of 44 different policies conducted in 16 different areas. As we will see many of these have proved ineffective, or even counter-productive. Before examining these policies it is useful to consider the areas within behavioral economics that have been discussed in previous chapters, which are all relevant to the obesity issue.

▶

- Methodology – Research into causes of obesity, and particularly cardiovascular disease (CVD), has involved much controversy. Most medical studies are either epidemiological in nature, involving a multifactorial observational analysis, or are controlled experiments, normally involving randomized controlled trials (RCTs). RCTs are generally regarded as the superior method, but are limited to relatively small samples. Two areas of controversy have arisen. The first concerns the reigning paradigm among health care professionals, sometimes referred to as the diet-heart hypothesis or lipid hypothesis. This hypothesis was originally suggested by Ancel Keys in 1953 and fundamentally consists of two aspects: excessive fat intake, in particular of saturated fats, causes high cholesterol in the blood; and high cholesterol in turn causes CVD. For over 50 years this hypothesis became virtually universally accepted in the medical profession, and is still repeated by organizations such as the American Heart Association and the NHS in the UK. However, increasing evidence over the last ten years has cast doubt over both components of the hypothesis. Some commentators have even suggested that the emphasis on low-fat diets has been counter-productive, reducing the health of millions of people, since fats, and particularly saturated fats, provide essential nutrients (Kendrick, 2007). These investigators have shifted the blame for obesity and CVD to excessive carbohydrate intake, especially of refined carbohydrates and sugar, and unhealthy fats such as trans-fats. The second area of controversy concerns the influence of pharmaceutical companies, in particular producers of statins, which have been touted as a 'miracle' cure for CVD. Statins are currently the best-selling drug in the USA, and are a multibillion-dollar business. These firms have funded a large number of research studies, which has led to a lively discussion on the influence they may wield as a result. Some medical researchers are now advocating universal use of statins for anyone over 50, regardless of whether they have a history of heart disease, in spite of various side effects that have been reported.

- Reference points – People tend to judge themselves with reference to their peers. Thus in a culture or subculture where many others are overweight or obese people may regard this as normal. The flip side of this is that reference points, particularly for young people, are often determined by the social media and celebrities. This serves to create unrealistic social norms, especially when images are easily distorted by the use of Photoshop facilities and airbrushing techniques. A recent study in the UK found that an increasing proportion of girls between 10 and 15 were unhappy with their lives and were worried about their looks (Children's Society, 2016). In the four years up to 2013–14 the proportion who were unhappy increased from 11% to 14%, while the proportion worried about their looks increased from 30% to 34%. It is also notable that this increasing trend was only found among girls, not among boys, where the proportions were considerably lower.

- Beliefs – There are various aspects of our belief systems that are relevant to the obesity issue. First, as already mentioned in relation to methodology, certain beliefs can become established in a community, for example a medical community, and they then become a paradigm which is difficult to shift. From the perspective of the community as a whole, reputations can depend on upholding a certain theory or hypothesis, and it can become dangerous for others to question these, since it may be difficult to achieve publication, promotion, or further a career. From an individual perspective, self-serving bias and confirmatory bias are both relevant, so that new findings and evidence that conflicts with existing beliefs are ignored. This is also relevant for consumers. A recent study by the Behavioural Insights Team, an advisory body to the UK government, found that consumers tend to significantly under-report their calorie intake, by as much as 30%. This underestimation was found in particular among those who were obese or who were watching their diet (Behavioural Insights Team, 2016). Cognitive dissonance is also relevant here, so that under-reporting of calorie intake may be combined with an under-reporting of body weight to preserve a consistent self-image.

- Discounting – This is one factor that is frequently ignored in analysis of the obesity problem, but is extremely important in long-term weight management. Eating more quantity and tastier food generally yields short-term hedonic benefits, but both the additional quantity and the additional tastiness tend to involve additional calories, and this in turn causes long-term costs in terms of weight gain and obesity. A rational person, assuming they have perfect information and are discounting exponentially, would be able to achieve an optimal trade-off in this situation. However, if the person is discounting hyperbolically, or has an instantaneous utility function modified by visceral factors, they would not be able to do this. Thus we may forever be making promises to ourselves about following better dieting behavior, but then consistently yield to temptation.

- Social norms – We have already seen that social norms are important when it comes to reference points, but they also have another implication, in that they vary from country to country and also between different cultures. In certain cultures being obese is regarded as a sign of affluence and is therefore socially desirable, in particular when it comes to attracting mates/partners. In some countries, notably in Africa, 'fat camps' exist that have the explicit aim of increasing the bodyweight of prospective brides.

After this brief survey of behavioral factors we can now consider policy implications. Many of these have been heavily influenced by political rather than purely economic factors. For example, the government in Iran has experimented with direct food handouts. Other agencies have also used these, but mainly to relieve food security problems in emergencies. Food banks, like those that have started up in the UK in the last few years, share some similarities with this policy, but are less centralized in organization. Generally such programs are expensive to operate because of distribution costs, and are aimed at providing food security rather than improving the obesity problem. The US government has operated the Supplemental Nutrition Assistance Program (SNAP), better known as Food Stamps, for decades, but, while this reduces distribution costs and improves food security, the program is generally recognized to increase obesity among the poorer sector of the population. The pathways here are quite complex, and include the creation of a feast-famine cycle driven by the periodic system of payments, and income effects causing a greater expenditure on food than would otherwise occur, with expenditure concentrated on energy-dense foods (Economist Intelligence Unit, 2014).

Other governments, like Malaysia, have experimented with cash payouts, but these lead to many of the same problems as direct food supplementation in terms of increasing obesity. Egypt has tried a more targeted approach, using food subsidies for what are regarded as essential foods like bread and grains. These have also been counter-productive, resulting in a large increase in obesity. Other countries, like Denmark, have taken a contrasting approach, taxing foods high in fats. This is also counter-productive, since fats contain essential nutrients. Foods and drinks high in sugars and other refined products make a more appropriate target.

Many governments have introduced new policies relating to food labeling. These policies have also been problematic. In this case the main problem is information overload, and the additional time it takes to read labels while supermarket shopping. Furthermore, many people are not knowledgeable enough to understand the information and its implications. More recently some food experts have suggested policies to overcome this problem, for example by having some kind of star system for calorie content, or exercise equivalents, like one serving equals 15 minutes of light exercise like jogging. These are both easier and quicker to understand than labels giving loads of information on nutrients, preservatives, flavorings and so on.

Let us now consider policy in the UK in more detail. The MGI has described this as fragmented and inadequate. While the total social costs of obesity have been estimated at £47 billion, the government only spends little over 1% of this, £638 million, on obesity reduction and prevention. The MGI advocates a comprehensive and coordinated approach, involving central government, government agencies, local government, media, schools, retailers, restaurants, food and drink manufacturers, employers, parents and community leaders. It estimates that the 44 interventions it has studied would bring 20% of overweight or obese people back to normal weight within five or ten years. These interventions include: portion control in packaged foods; parental education programs; changes in school meal design; food labeling regulations; media restrictions; taxes on sugary drinks; and improvements in transportation infrastructure, particularly to aid cyclists. What is notable here is that some interventions are much more effective than others, and also there is a large variation in cost effectiveness. For example, the most effective program in terms of increasing DALYs is portion control, estimated to be over 20 times as effective as public health campaigns. By far the most cost-effective intervention is media restrictions, at $50 per year saved, compared with $31,000 per year saved for an active transport program.

It would then appear that, at a time when deeply unpopular cuts in NHS services are being implemented by the UK government, a more effective long-term policy of obesity reduction would make such cuts unnecessary because of the cost savings involved. Already some health authorities have announced that they intend to postpone surgeries for obese persons, since their budgets are forcing them to prioritize treatments. A more radical and controversial policy would involve replacing the current national insurance system, where payments are based on income, with an insurance system found in free markets, where premiums are based on risk. This would entail obese persons paying higher premiums for health insurance, in the same way that drivers with bad driving records pay higher premiums. This kind of system is more efficient from a purely economic perspective, since it avoids the problem of moral hazard, where people do not pay the consequences of the risks they take. It would, however, be highly regressive as a tax, and be viewed as discriminatory. Others would argue that discrimination is not a bad thing per se, since after all we are currently discriminating against bad drivers. It all depends on whether people are able to change their identity or behavior; thus racial discrimination is bad because one cannot change one's race. It is highly unlikely that this argument will ever be resolved on purely economic grounds.

## Questions

1 Explain why obesity is more of a problem with poorer people in developed countries, while being more of a problem for more affluent people in developing countries.

2 Explain why it is particularly difficult to design programs that address obesity among young people, in particular teenagers.

3 One study claims that 90% of obesity is preventable, yet the MGI estimates that even comprehensive policies can bring only 20% of overweight or obese people back to normal weight over the long term. Discuss the reasons for this discrepancy.

4 Explain the behavioral factors underlying calorie under-reporting.

5 What is the role of nudge policies in tackling obesity?

PART · V

# Conclusion

# CHAPTER 11

# Behavioral Economics: Summary and Outlook

## 11.1    The agenda of behavioral economics

In this concluding chapter we will review some of the most important issues with which behavioral economics is concerned. In order to do this it is sensible to start with a summary of how behavioral economics is related to 'standard economics', and what its objectives are.

### *Good theories*

The purpose of any science is to develop theories that can accurately explain and predict phenomena. Perhaps the most prevalent criticism of economics is that it fails to do this very well in many cases. Of course, economists are often put in the spotlight, making public forecasts regarding the state of the economy, growth, inflation and unemployment rates, stock market indices, currency values and so on. When these forecasts go awry, as they often do, the status of economics as a valid science is called into question. If the forecasts are wrong, then the underlying theory must be wrong too, no matter how complex it may be.

All theories are based on assumptions, or axioms. If a theory is wrong it is often an indication that these assumptions are misplaced. We have also seen that assumptions are made, not because they are necessarily believed to be realistic, but because they simplify the analysis.

Economic theories should not be criticized simply because they make unrealistic assumptions. Theorizing relies on abstracting key explanatory features from the rich complexity of the phenomena under investigation. Some theories can make some surprisingly accurate predictions even when they are based on rather abstract and prima facie unrealistic assumptions. This is the argument economists use when justifying the 'as-if' approach. However, when a theory fails to explain and predict well because of misplaced assumptions, then it is time to reject or revise the theory by constructing it on a sounder base of assumptions. In behavioral economics, this base has been drawn from other sciences, such as psychology, sociology, and biology, including neuroscience. These sciences can provide economics with 'process theories', and are essential in achieving the unifying and integrative approach advocated throughout this text.

Let us recall at this point the main criteria, discussed in the first chapter, that are generally agreed to be important in establishing any scientific theory as being good and useful:

1  *Congruence with reality*

This relates to explaining existing empirical observations, and thus having good fit. The effect of this should be to explain anomalies and produce more accurate predictions (although we have seen that goodness of fit and prediction do not necessarily go together).

2  *Generality*

Theories are more useful when they have a greater range of application. Sometimes this attribute is referred to as fruitfulness.

3  *Tractability*

This characteristic refers to how easily a theory can be applied to different specific situations in terms of making predictions. Mathematical complexity is often an issue in this regard.

4  *Parsimony*

We have now seen that some theories are more parsimonious than others, meaning that they are based on fewer assumptions or parameters. However, excessive parsimony may adversely affect both congruence with reality and generality.

Behavioral economics criticizes neoclassical economic models for being excessively parsimonious, resulting in a lack of congruence with reality or empirical fit. We saw in the first chapter that Ho, Lim and Camerer (2006) have proposed the addition of two more criteria: precision and psychological plausibility. They, and other behavioral economists, perceive their task as involving the revision of the basic assumptions underlying the neoclassical model (NM) and placing them on a sounder psychological foundation. This should, and does, improve congruence with reality, at the cost of reduced parsimony and sometimes analytical tractability. However, another benefit of the addition of more complex assumptions and parameters is that this often leads to more precise, as well as more accurate, predictions than those of the NM. It is helpful at this stage if we illustrate the agenda of behavioral economics by using some of the examples discussed throughout the book.

## Examples of behavioral revisions to the neoclassical model

The examples given below illustrate that in some cases modeling a situation in behavioral terms, and using the model to make predictions is relatively easy, while in other cases the relevant behavioral factors are much more difficult to incorporate into a model capable of precise prediction. We will start with those examples where the use of additional parameters is more obvious and straightforward.

- *Game theory*

  This example is taken first, since it relates to the point in the previous paragraph regarding predictions. The standard model often predicts multiple equilibria, like in the market entry situation discussed in Case 9.3. Learning theory, thinking steps and other behavioral concepts of equilibrium like the quantal response equilibrium (QRE), can be introduced into the analysis by adding new parameters into the relevant models. Behavioral game theory can then provide more precise predictions about what will happen.

- *Loss-aversion*

  We have seen that this is a widespread phenomenon. It appears to provide the best explanation for the equity premium puzzle, along with choice bracketing. Loss-aversion can be modeled using a loss-aversion coefficient.

- *Conformity bias*

  This results in a herding phenomenon, widely observed in many markets, particularly financial ones. It is more difficult to model than loss aversion since it can involve both other-conferred utility and revised probability estimates.

- *Confirmation bias*

  This bias, where people pay more attention to news supporting existing beliefs and ignore or discount conflicting evidence, has received increasing attention in recent years, because of its prominence in both the financial crisis of 2007 and in the Trump/Brexit phenomena. The situation can be modeled by modifying the Bayesian updating of probabilities to allow for the misperception of signals.

- *Impatience and time-inconsistent preferences*

  These factors are often modeled using hyperbolic discounting models. These models add the parameter $\beta$ to the standard discounting model, where $\beta$ represents a preference for immediacy. A more complex model can take bounded rationality into account, by introducing a further parameter, $b$, which measures a consumer's beliefs regarding their value of $\beta$. Dual-self models can also be modeled using a game-theoretic framework.

- *Inequity-aversion and reciprocity models*

  By taking into account social preferences, these models can explain many seemingly irrational or unselfish actions, like refusing small offers in ultimatum bargaining games or cooperating in public goods games. For example, the inequality-aversion model of Fehr and Schmidt (1999) uses the coefficients $\alpha$ and $\beta$ as envy and guilt coefficients respectively. Reciprocity models tend to be more complex.

* *Choice bracketing*

  This aspect of mental accounting means that people select certain accounting periods over which they measure gains and losses. The choice of shorter periods results in a greater chance of making a loss in any given period.

* *Lack of fungibility*

  This factor explains why people may simultaneously borrow at high rates of interest, such as on a credit card, when they have current assets earning a much lower interest rate.

* *The representativeness heuristic*

  This and other heuristics have a profound effect on people's judgments of probability, causing severe errors.

* *Anchoring effects*

  These affect both judgment and choice. Purely random influences, like social security numbers, have been shown to affect people's valuation of items.

* *Endowment effects*

  Owners, or sellers, often place a higher value on items than buyers, reducing frequency of transactions. Again loss-aversion coefficients may be relevant.

* *Framing effects*

  We have seen that different ways of presenting identical information can cause preference reversals, like in the 'Asian disease' situation.

* *Decision weighting*

  This can be used to translate objective probabilities into the subjective probabilities that are used to make decisions under risk.

Obviously this list is not exhaustive, but it does review a wide variety of situations where behavioral theories can improve on the NM in terms of congruence with reality.

However, there are claimed to be two problems with the behavioral approach that we have come across in relation to accounting for the above factors, and these have led to some criticisms of behavioral economics.

## 11.2   Criticisms of behavioral economics

*A profusion of models*

One alleged problem, described by Fudenberg (2006), is that there are too many behavioral models, many of which have few applications. Fudenberg gives the example of modeling mistakes in inference, quoting various different models:

1   The confirmation bias models of Rabin and Schrag (1999) and Yariv (2002), which propose that agents miscode evidence that their prior beliefs indicate is unlikely.

2   The model of Rabin (2002a), which proposes that agents update as Bayesians in terms of modifying prior probabilities in the light of new evidence, but that they treat independent draws as draws with replacement. For example, if a lottery number has just come up, people would regard it as unlikely to come up again next week, even though lottery draws are independent from one week to the next.

3   The model of Barberis, Shleifer and Vishny (1998), which proposes that agents mistakenly see trends in independent and identically distributed data, such as spins of a roulette wheel or daily stock market fluctuations.

There are four points that can be made in response to the above criticisms:

1  *Different models are appropriate in different decision situations*

This point has been made a number of times in previous chapters: in Chapter 5 in relation to decision-making under risk and uncertainty; in Chapter 8 in relation to inter-temporal decisions; and in Chapter 10 in relation to decision-making when social preferences are relevant. Camerer and Loewenstein (2004) admit that the discipline is not a unified theory, but is rather 'a collection of tools or ideas'. They also claim that the same is true of neoclassical economics. They repeat the claim of Arrow (1986), that economic models do not derive much predictive power from the single general tool of utility maximization. They then claim that behavioral economics is more like a power drill, which uses a wide variety of drill bits to perform different jobs. Thus the concepts of other-regarding preferences and social norms may be the appropriate analytical tools when examining public goods provision and bargaining games; the concept of time-additive separable utility may be relevant in asset pricing; remembered utility (or disutility) may be relevant in the decision to have a colonoscopy; anticipatory utility may be relevant in considering the decision to postpone a pleasurable experience; and loss-aversion may be relevant in explaining asymmetrical price elasticities.

2  *Populations are heterogeneous*

Modeling heterogeneous populations is a complex task, and we have seen an aspect of this problem in the inequality-aversion model of Fehr–Schmidt (1999). Not only do different people have different values of the parameters in a model, such as envy and guilt coefficients, but also different models may apply to different people or different cultures.

3  *Conflicting theories are a feature of many sciences*

In some cases, as in the example given by Fudenberg (2006) above, there are conflicting theories relating to the same phenomenon. Thus we cannot use as a response here the 'power drill' analogy of Camerer and Loewenstein (2004) discussed in the first point, where different tools are appropriate for different jobs. However, behavioral economics is hardly unique in terms of being a science where there are many conflicting theories regarding the explanation of a given set of phenomena. One example from psychology relates to the phenomenon where emotional reactions to life-changing events are surprisingly short-lived. There is now a substantial body of research in this area, but there are still five main competing theories relating to it. Even in mainstream economics we find that there are often areas where there are conflicting theories, and these conflicts can continue for decades. This is particularly true in macroeconomics, where definitive evidence is difficult to find given the complex interrelationships involved; the Keynesianism vs. Monetarism debate is likely to continue for some time to come. We agree with Fudenberg and grant that this is not an ideal situation from a scientific point of view. However, to some extent this is inevitable given the status of behavioral economics as explained in the next point.

4  *Behavioral economics is a relatively new science*

It is going through what may be termed the growth phase of its product life cycle (PLC). Using the PLC analogy, the growth phase is characterized by a profusion of product variations and firms, and then, as the maturity phase is reached, these products and firms are winnowed down by the market forces of competition. A similar process can be applied to the development of models in behavioral economics. As further research is carried out, some models are likely to be winnowed out as lacking support, while others have their status confirmed.

*Lack of normative status*

We discussed this criticism in Chapter 5 in comparing prospect theory with expected utility theory (EUT). It is alleged that, by attempting to describe reality better, behavioral economics has lost its normative status. This is important because normative status is necessary in order for individuals, firms and governments to make good policy decisions.

As we have seen, the term normative is ambiguous when it is used in an economic context. The ambiguity arises from the interpretation of the word 'should', as for example in the expression 'people should contribute toward public goods'. For our purposes here, no moral or value judgment is implied by the term 'should'. The normative aspect implies a prescriptive status: what is necessary in order to achieve optimization. Therefore the statement involves a conditional, and can be interpreted as meaning 'people should contribute toward public goods *if they want to maximize their utilities*'. Obviously a utility function incorporating social preferences is required here. In this example behavioral economics is able to provide a normative statement in the prescriptive sense.

The area of behavioral economics where such prescriptive status is most inclined to break down is where individuals are making judgments and choices, and was discussed in Chapters 3, 4 and 5. We saw for example that preferences and choices are not necessarily based simply on attitudes and judgments, and they are frequently not well-formed or stable. This complication arises from the violation of certain assumptions in the NM relating to description invariance, procedural invariance, and extensionality. There are also different concepts of utility: decision utility; experienced utility, which may be either remembered utility or real-time utility; anticipatory utility, which is based on predicted utility; residual utility, arising from reminiscence; and diagnostic utility, which people infer from their actions. The NM only considers decision utility, which it assumes is based on attitudes and preferences, which in turn are assumed to be consistent.

Once these demonstrated anomalies in the NM are taken into account, the simple utility maximization model involving indifference curve analysis is no longer applicable. We have also seen that under conditions of risk a similar situation occurs, in that we can no longer use a simple EUT preference function that is to be maximized. However, in spite of the problems raised by the violation of basic assumptions, this does not mean that the behavioral model cannot be prescriptive in principle. Although the analysis is more complicated, and often difficult to achieve in practical terms, it was shown in Chapters 4 and 5 that prescriptive statements can still be possible. If we use the concepts of real-time, or moment-based, utility, and psychological utility, in order to provide an all-inclusive measure of utility, then we can draw some conclusions about maximizing welfare. For example, we can attempt to resolve the paradox that people may value more highly a job with a higher relative salary but lower absolute salary, because they think it will make them happier, but actually choose a job with lower relative salary and higher absolute salary. Thus behavioral economics is still useful as a guide to policy decisions, but only by becoming aware of such paradoxes and complications to which behavioral economics draws attention can better policy decisions be made.

## 11.3    Methodology

For example, reductionism is often opposed in the social sciences, since practitioners find that their authority is being usurped by disciplines lower down the hierarchy or causal chain. It is not proposed here to revisit all the methodological issues described in the second chapter, relating for example to experimental design, but to focus instead on the most fundamental issues. In particular, the methodology advocated here involves using some of the 'best practice' from the various behavioral sciences that are currently in conflict with each other, in order to unify these sciences. When economists use the approaches and models commonly associated with psychology, sociology and biology, in addition to their usual methods, in an appropriate combination, then the behavioral sciences will make the most progress in terms of explaining and predicting decision-making. At a normative level, this will also help people to make better decisions, in terms of improving welfare. This aspect is discussed in Section 11.5. In order to facilitate this unification the following issues need to be clarified and resolved: (1) relationships between assumptions and conclusions; (2) the role of gene-culture coevolution; (3) the role of game theory; and (4) the relationship between parsimony and universality.

### Assumptions and conclusions

Students frequently misinterpret and misuse these two terms. It is a basic tenet of the scientific method that in any science one starts off with certain assumptions, and based on theory and empirical evidence, one proceeds to form certain conclusions. These conclusions may involve a rejection of some original theory or hypothesis, a confirmation of it, or a modification and refinement of it. Where matters become confusing is that in the causal sequence of events, and this involves the relationships between different sciences, conclusions in one area become assumptions in another. We have seen some examples of this in the first two chapters, but more specific examples are needed here to illustrate this phenomenon in terms of how it relates to behavioral economics.

The NM assumes that people are purely self-interested. As we have seen, this is an example of an assumption that is made for convenience, to simplify analysis, rather than because it is believed to be universally true. It is obviously a useful assumption, enabling a wide variety of predictions to be made, many of which are reasonably accurate. Behavioral economics attempts to find a sounder psychological foundation for economic theorizing, and therefore takes into account social preferences when trying to explain behavior. In attempting to build this better foundation the behavioral approach aims to search for **psychological regularity**. For example, it may find psychological regularity in the empirical evidence that people tend to reject low offers in ultimatum bargaining games, and that people also tend not to make such offers. This finding, a contradiction to the NM, then provides a basis for a behavioral theory incorporating social preferences. In this context this aspect of psychological regularity becomes an 'assumption' on which the development of different behavioral theories, like inequality-aversion and reciprocity, can be based.

However, this analysis only goes one level down the causal sequence. We can then ask: what causes people to have both positive and negative reciprocity? Behavioral economics leaves many questions with this status, for example:

- Why are people influenced by framing effects?
- Why do people exhibit loss-aversion?
- Why do people show self-serving bias?
- Why do people have endowment effects?
- Why do people make choices that do not appear to make them happy?

It is not usually regarded as part of the agenda of behavioral economics to answer these questions. These effects, or psychological regularities, are taken as being the building blocks, or 'assumptions' on which alternative theories to the standard model must be constructed. The task of answering these questions is 'delegated' to psychology, where these regularities are treated as being 'conclusions' that must be explained by underlying psychological theories. Psychologists in turn make certain assumptions regarding neuroscience, in terms of how the brain works at a physiological level, and in terms of how the brain has evolved. Thus we move one further level down the causal sequence into the realms of neuroscience and evolutionary biology. As explained in the second chapter, this is the nature of hierarchical reductionism, which has proven to be extremely effective over the last few centuries in terms of developing theories with wide and deep explanatory and predictive powers.

## The role of gene-culture coevolution

The discussion of reductionism, assumptions and conclusions leads us once more to the equally controversial role of evolutionary psychology (EP), which has been touched on several times throughout the book. In order to obtain a proper perspective the role of EP has to be viewed as being a component of the larger role of gene-culture coevolution. Not even the most extreme evolutionary psychologist would claim that *all* human behavior can be explained by examining, and guessing, what our ancestral lives and environments were like and theorizing about how human brains adapted to this. Unfortunately this is a straw man that has become popular in much of the social science literature critiquing the discipline. More realistically, the problem of EP is summarized by Camerer and Loewenstein (2004, p. 40) as follows:

> it is easy to figure out whether an evolutionary story identifies causes sufficient to bring about particular behavior, but it is almost impossible to know if those causes were the ones that actually did bring it about.

This problem leads to the main criticism of EP as a science: that it fails to make testable, meaning falsifiable, predictions. It is useful to illustrate this problem by taking one particular example, concerning the tendency to cooperate rather than defect in 'one-shot' situations like prisoner's dilemma (PD) games. The claim in EP is that subjects in these 'one-shot' games are unable to switch off their inbuilt cooperation mechanisms. Thus even when they are told explicitly that they are playing a one-shot game, and acknowledge this, in psychological terms they are still playing a repeated game. As Camerer and Loewenstein point out, this makes the EP hypothesis unfalsifiable if one is trying to predict comparative behavior in one-shot games with behavior in repeated games. However, as we have seen in the previous chapter, some predictions of behavior in one-shot games are possible; Kanazawa and Fontaine (2013) find experimental evidence that there is a significant negative relationship between intelligence and the tendency to cooperate in one-shot PD games. The authors relate this to the **Savanna Principle**, which maintains that behavior adapted to our ancestral environment may no longer be optimal in our current post-industrial society.

Certainly there is a need to be aware of the problem of making predictions. Indeed, evolutionary psychologists will always face the problem that concrete evidence from our ancestral Pleistocene past is flimsy. The archaeological and biological record is sparse and is likely to remain so, although progress in molecular biology and genetics may make some progress in the latter area. Therefore conjecture and speculation, despised by 'hard' scientists in particular, is inevitable. Much theory in EP proceeds on the basis of examining modern observations and making the following comparison:

Prob (theory X from EP | observed values) > or < Prob (other theory Y | observed values)

The EP theory is regarded as being vindicated if the EP theory has greater probability of generating the observed data than any other theory. In many situations there is no other recognized theory. For example, we have seen from Kahneman and Tversky (1973) that people are much better at solving problems when given data involving frequencies rather than probabilities. Single event probabilities are often nonsensical in practical terms. For example, it may make little sense to say that there is a 35% chance that a woman is pregnant: either she is or she isn't pregnant. Similarly, in evolutionary terms it may seem strange to say that there is a probability of 0.375 of finding berries in a particular valley. On the other hand people understand more readily the statement that, in the last eight visits to the valley, one found berries three times. This may be regarded as another 'just-so' story, but the author is not aware of any other comparable theory in cognitive psychology which can explain this phenomenon.

In addition, it should also be pointed out that EP predictions are falsifiable in a number of areas. If experiments were to observe a widespread general tendency to defect in one-shot games, this would falsify the hypothesis. We have also given an example in Case 10.1 related to the Wason test, where EP can make some sharp and falsifiable predictions. Let us take a final example from a different area, regarded as being the domain of cultural influences. Parasites are known to degrade physical appearance. Evolutionary psychologists Gangestad and Buss (1993) therefore made a prediction that people living in ecologies with a high prevalence of parasites should place a greater value on physical attractiveness in a mate than people living in ecologies with a low prevalence of parasites. This hypothesis was tested by collecting data from 29 cultures relating to the prevalence of parasites and the importance that people in those cultures attached to physical attractiveness in a marriage partner. The results confirmed the hypothesis, finding significant positive correlation between the two variables. This example is taken because it illustrates how cultural differences, often assumed to be non-evolutionary in nature, can be explained by universal evolved psychological mechanisms that are differentially activated across cultures. Of course, other theories may be developed to explain the same observed relationship, but the essential point is that EP, when used carefully and thoughtfully, can provide testable hypotheses.

## The role of game theory

We have seen, particularly in Chapters 2, 9 and 10, that game theory plays a fundamental role in understanding decision-making, simply because so many decisions we make involve some kind of social interaction. However, we have also seen that standard game theory is inadequate for modeling many situations, since it is either silent, for example indicating multiple equilibria, or it produces anomalies, as in bargaining games. In order to gain a better understanding of decision-making we need to take account of other-regarding preferences and bounded rationality in particular, and recognize the failure of backward induction. This means that other approaches to game theory, meaning behavioral game theory and evolutionary game theory need to be used in conjunction with the standard approach. The inevitable result is more complexity in terms of the analysis, and this is related to the next issue. It is also worth recalling from our discussion of game theory that most applications of game theory to behavioral issues remain wedded much more closely to key aspects of the NM than other approaches in behavioral economics, which has implications for how we can more deeply integrate substantively behavioral principles in economic analysis.

## Parsimony and universality

Another criticism leveled at EP is that the explanations that it provides lack universality, and appear to have an ad hoc nature about them. We have come across these terms before in connection with the evaluation of theories. The term ad hoc means 'for a particular purpose', and scientists tend to use the term disapprovingly, since it often implies that a theory is being twisted or convoluted in an unnatural way to explain away undesirable observations that cannot be explained by any standard form of the theory. The result is a loss of parsimony, as the theory becomes more cumbersome. A good example from the field of astronomy is the invention in medieval times of the concept of 'epicycles' (circular orbits centered on other circular orbits). The purpose was to explain aberrations in the observed movements of the planets that could not be explained by the standard Ptolemaic theory of the geocentric universe. Copernicus's theory of the heliocentric universe, combined with Kepler's notion of elliptical planetary orbits, turned out to be a much more parsimonious theory, as well as being more accurate.

However desirable parsimony and universality may be to our structure-loving minds, the irony is that the human mind appears to be good at some things, but is surprisingly incapable of performing other functions. Evolutionary psychologists explain this behavior in terms of the modularity of the brain; it is not a universal problem-solving device. In order for the brain to develop such a broad capacity enormous resources would be required, and this would be very wasteful, since many of the capabilities of such a brain would never be required in real life. The EP model, expressed most clearly in various contributions from Cosmides and Tooby (see, for example, Cosmides and Tooby, 1987, 1992, 1996, 2000), is that the brain did indeed develop in an ad hoc fashion, as it adapted to deal with the problems that it actually had to face in reality. They liken the mind to a Swiss army knife, with many blades designed for specific tasks. Furthermore, evolution always operates by building on structures that are already present, even if those structures are no longer necessary or useful; the human body is full of such mechanisms, such as the appendix and the spleen.

EP, by proposing that the mind is a device with ad hoc functions, is not alone in terms of appearing to involve ad hoc explanations. The same accusation is often leveled at behavioral economics; this is essentially the criticism of Fudenberg (2006) that was discussed earlier.

This discussion may seem to lead to a messy, even contradictory, conclusion regarding the desirability of parsimony and generality. There are two points that may clarify this:

1   If we accept that the mind is modular (and certainly more evidence is needed regarding the nature of this modularity), then it should come as no surprise that a variety of tools is necessary to study its functions and operations, as they are manifested in human attitudes and behavior.

2   This variety of tools may still have some commonality, just as all the various drill bits can be used with the same drill. In behavioral economics there are various commonalities; in particular the concepts discussed in prospect theory and mental accounting have a very general application to a wide variety of human behavior.

This discussion relating to EP will now help us to draw some conclusions relating to rationality, a recurring theme throughout this book.

## 11.4   Are we really irrational?

As more studies claiming and documenting the violations of rationality described above have been published, there have also been several attempts to re-establish the status of rationality by defending the notion that people do generally behave rationally. These defenses make various objections to the claims of irrationality. Shafir and LeBoeuf (2002) have classified these objections into three main categories: trivializations, misinterpretations and inappropriate tests. We will follow this useful classification in the following discussion.

### Trivializations

This category of objection relates to the claim that the alleged violations of rationality are unsystematic and unreliable. There are five main aspects that can be considered here: randomness, incentives, justification, expertise and need for cognition (NC).

**1**   *Randomness*

Sometimes it is claimed that deviations from the norms prescribed by the standard model of rationality are purely random errors, commonly observed in statistical distributions. This claim is easily refuted however, since a closer look at the evidence in a large number of studies shows systematic errors of overwhelming statistical significance. We have seen that systematic errors are in a predictable direction, for example many preference reversals.

**2**   *Incentives*

A common claim is the participants in studies often lack the required motivation to provide true or reliable results. In general, however, it has been observed that incentives do not reduce, let alone eliminate, the observed violations of rationality. This is not to say that incentives do not affect behavior in experiments. For example, we have seen that, by using earned as opposed to unearned rewards in a dictator game, many subjects do behave purely selfishly, as the standard model predicts (Cherry, Frykblom and Shogren, 2002). However, in the extensive review by Camerer and Hogarth (1999) of 74 studies that manipulated incentives, the authors concluded that 'there is no replicated study in which a theory of rational choice was rejected at low stakes … and accepted at high stakes'. Most violations persist in the face of even large incentives, for example the amount of one month's salary in a study involving Chinese workers (Kachelmeier and Shehata, 1992). Furthermore, incentives do not prevent a large proportion of small businesses failing. Neither do incentives help to reduce the incidence of optical illusions. It should also be noted that, even if incentives are successful in increasing motivation, people still need to apply the correct insights in order to improve their performance; mere enthusiasm does not suffice for good decision-making.

**3**   *Justification*

Another method that can be used to increase the involvement of participants is to ask them to justify their responses. Although this sometimes reduces inconsistencies like framing effects (Takemura, 1994; Sieck and Yates, 1997), such effects often persist even when justification is provided (Fagley and Miller, 1987; Levin and Chapman, 1990; Miller and Fagley, 1991; Takemura, 1993). As with incentives, greater involvement does not ensure better performance; insight is still required.

**4**   *Expertise*

It is sometimes claimed that more expert subjects are more likely to exhibit rational choice, having more relevant knowledge and familiarity with the tasks involved. A variation of this objection is that people learn from their mistakes, and thus become more expert. An example of a study reporting this finding is List (2004), who found that experience in the market eliminated the endowment effect. The problem with this 'learning effect' objection is that learning relies on feedback. In real life this feedback is problematical because many situations are unique, outcomes are often delayed, and they often influenced by multiple factors. People do not frequently sell their houses, for example, and even when they do repeat this process, it is often under quite different circumstances from previously. Even when people do learn from experience there is much evidence that experts make the same sort of violations that non-experts do. For example, physicians and nurses have been found to make preferences and choices violating the first two criteria for rationality, involving the laws of probability and consistency (Casscells, Schoenberger and Graboys, 1978; Redelmeier and Shafir, 1995; Redelmeier, Shafir and Aujla, 2001). Financial experts have been prone to making judgments and choices involving preference reversal and framing effects (Benartzi and Thaler, 1995; Siegel and Thaler, 1997; Tversky and Kahneman, 1992). Professional gamblers have also been observed to exhibit preference reversal

(Lichtenstein and Slovic, 1973). It appears that experts are subject to certain judgmental biases discussed earlier, like overconfidence (Faust, Hart, and Guilmette, 1988) and hindsight bias (Arkes et al., 1981). It is therefore highly improbable that such violations can be attributed to lack of motivation or understanding.

5    *Need for cognition*

This factor relates to the notion that people differ in their tendency to engage in and enjoy thinking. It has been proposed that people with a greater NC are more motivated to make better decisions, and are more likely to give proper consideration to the relevant aspects. There is indeed some evidence that certain violations may be reduced with high-NC participants, for example framing effects, with improved judgments in conditional probability situations, and less consideration of irrelevant factors like sunk costs (Smith and Levin, 1996; Stanovich and West, 1999). However, in spite of these results, there is no evidence that high-NC participants have better insight in judgments involving hypothesis testing and PD situations (Stanovich and West, 1999).

There are some studies that combine several of the above objections. For example, the **discovered preference hypothesis (DPH)** developed by Plott (1996) proposes that people's preferences are not necessarily revealed in their decisions, as we saw in discussing criticisms of prospect theory in Chapter 5. According to this theory, preferences have to be discovered through a process of information gathering, deliberation and trial-and-error learning. Subjects must therefore have adequate opportunities and incentives for discovery, and it is claimed that studies lacking these factors are unreliable. It has been argued that the best type of experimental design to ensure that the requirements of the DPH are met is a **single-task individual-choice** design (Cubitt, Starmer and Sugden, 2001). Such a design can ensure that subjects get an opportunity to practice a single task repeatedly, with the requisite learning effect, and it can also ensure simplicity and transparency, which are difficult to achieve in market-based studies, where tasks are more complex and involve interactions with others. However, when Cubitt, Starmer and Sugden reviewed the results of nine different experiments involving such a design, they found that the results still violated the criteria for rationality, specifically in terms of the independence axiom for consistent choices in Allais-type situations.

In summary it seems fair to say that violations of rationality cannot be dismissed as trivial errors in performance. Such violations persist even with highly motivated experts who give serious consideration to the problems involved.

## Misinterpretations

A second objection to the rationality violations is that the irrationality perceived by researchers arises because participants tend to adopt a different understanding of the tasks from that intended, and that in the light of the participants' understanding their responses are rational (Hertwig and Gigerenzer, 1999; Hilton, 1995; Levinson, 1995; Macdonald, 1986; Schwarz, 1996; Slugoski and Wilson, 1998). We will discuss four main aspects of this objection.

1    *The conjunction error*

It is sometimes claimed that subjects may infer that the researcher only gives relevant and non-redundant information. This is particularly important in tasks relating to the representativeness heuristic, like the Linda problem discussed earlier, involving conjuncts and conjunctives. When comparing the statements 'Linda is a bank teller' and 'Linda is a bank teller and is active in the feminist movement', subjects may infer that in the first statement Linda is *not* active in the feminist movement, and therefore rate the statement as less probable than the second statement. In more general terms, subjects may, after seeing the statement with the conjunctive A and B, infer that the conjunct statement involving just A refers to 'A and not B'. Indeed, some studies have found that rewording the construct and giving some logical clues, like saying 'Linda is a bank teller whether or not she is active in the feminist movement' does tend to reduce the conjunction error (Dulany and Hilton, 1991; Politzer and Noveck, 1991). Another study has found that the tendency to make the error was correlated with a person's conversational skill (Slugoski and Wilson, 1998). However, other studies have found that the conjunction error occurs across a wide variety of problems, and persists in a majority of subjects even when reinterpretations of the conjuncts are given to aid subjects in understanding the logic (Morier and Borgida, 1984; Tversky and Kahneman, 1983).

**2**   *Under-reliance on base rates*

Another kind of error relating to representativeness concerns the insufficient reliance on base rates in likelihood judgments. A good example is the AIDS diagnosis situation (Tversky and Kahneman, 1982), where a base rate of one in a thousand people have the disease, but people, even medical experts, are over-influenced by the representativeness description that the positive test is 95% accurate. The critique here is that conversational inferences are again important. When the base rate is stated *after* the representativeness description, rather than before, this increases the reliance on base rates and improves the normativeness of responses, meaning that they conform more closely to the rationality model (Krosnick, Li and Lehman, 1990). When descriptions are said to be randomly sampled and unreliable reliance on base rates increases significantly (Ginossar and Trope, 1987; Schwarz et al., 1991). Also, when base rates are varied in the experiment, reliance on base rates improves (Fischhoff, Slovic and Lichtenstein, 1979). In spite of these improvements in performance, however, the evidence suggests that an under-reliance on base rates persists (Fischhoff, Slovic and Lichtenstein, 1979; Schwarz et al., 1991).

**3**   *Framing effects*

It has also been claimed that conversational factors may be involved in framing effects, like the Asian disease situation discussed earlier. Some researchers have suggested that the frames in options A and C, supposedly identical, may not be seen as such by some subjects (Berkeley and Humphreys, 1982; Macdonald, 1986). For example, option A, 'saving 200 lives with certainty', may be construed as meaning 'saving *at least* 200 lives', while option C, '400 dying with certainty', may be construed as '*at least* 400 people dying'. Obviously, under this construal option A is preferable to option C, and the apparent preference reversal disappears. However, evidence also suggests that the majority of subjects do not interpret the options in this manner, and do in fact interpret the options as identical (Stanovich and West, 1998).

**4**   *Interpretations of probability*

A further area where different interpretations of terms may be involved concerns the general concept of probability. There are three main interpretations of the term probability:

(i)   Classical – probabilities are determined a priori; typical situations involve gambling, like tossing a coin, rolling a die, or drawing a playing card from a pack.

(ii)  Empirical – probabilities are determined a posteriori; past similar situations are observed and relative frequencies are used to calculate probabilities. A typical example is the probability of rain in September in London.

(iii) Subjective – probabilities are estimated based on intuition and experience. An example is the probability that firm A will increase its price next month.

However, it should be stressed that in all three cases the general mathematical maxims of probability hold true, for example the probability of any event must be between 0 and 1, 0 referring to impossible and 1 referring to certain.

It has been objected that some subjects do not interpret probability in mathematical terms, and this causes them to make certain errors, like the conjunction fallacy (Hertwig and Gigerenzer, 1999). This study showed that this error could be reduced by adding further information in the tasks involved. However, other studies have shown that subjects do not have different interpretations of probability than researchers, and that the conjunction fallacy persists even when further information is given to aid judgments (Tversky and Kahneman, 1983; Kahneman and Tversky, 1996; Stanovich and West, 1998).

It should also be stated in summary that we have to be careful not to legitimize all misinterpretations by subjects, for this tends to beg the issue. We must ask *why* subjects tend to misinterpret certain terms in certain ways.

## Inappropriate tests

The last, and most fundamental, group of objections to violations of rationality are based on the appropriateness of tests for rationality. Shafir and LeBoeuf (2002) classify these objections into three main categories: computational limitations, inappropriate problem formats and inappropriate norms.

**1**  *Computational limitations*

Some researchers have objected that computational limitations are the source of many violations, and that it is not useful to define rationality in such a way that it is out of reach for the majority of people. This is really the easiest objection to counter. Most of the tasks involved in the experiments described earlier are computationally very simple. It appears to be the conceptual aspects that cause problems and errors (Agnoli and Krantz, 1989; Fong and Nisbett, 1991; Frank, Gilovich and Regan, 1993). Furthermore, when the source of the errors is pointed out, subjects quickly learn to avoid them (Fiedler, 1988; Tversky and Kahneman, 1986; Tversky and Shafir, 1992). It seems therefore that the problem lies in the heuristic procedures used.

**2**  *Inappropriate problem formats*

It has been suggested, in particular by evolutionary psychologists, that the type of problem used in many experiments has been the cause of many problems, and that if the nature of the problems set is changed to coincide more with the types of problem encountered during our Pleistocene past, then the errors will tend to disappear (Cosmides and Tooby, 1996; Gigerenzer, 1996b). This point is discussed further in the next two subsections; at this stage it is sufficient to point out that, indeed, general performance on many tasks, like the Wason test discussed in Case 10.1, is improved when the terms of the problem are restated to resemble realistic situations in our past, like enforcing social contracts (Cosmides and Tooby, 1992; Gigerenzer and Hug, 1992). However, this objection is really only valid if the problems set in experiments do not resemble current everyday problems, and this is not the case. Most of the tasks and problems are not entirely abstract, and the interesting point is that, while people may be proficient at solving problems related to our evolutionary past, they are not nearly as proficient at solving current problems. In this situation it appears to make sense to define rationality as relating to current problems, not those of our past. However, this does not invalidate the most important point of the evolutionary psychologists, which is that our minds evolved to solve past, not current, problems.

**3**    *Inappropriate norms*

The most fundamental of all objections to the rationality violations is that inappropriate normative standards of rationality are imposed (Binmore, 1999; Gigerenzer, 1996a; Gigerenzer, Hoffrage, and Kleinbolting, 1991; Lopes and Oden, 1991; Plott, 1996; Smith, 1990; Wetherick, 1971). This objection relates to the definition of rationality and the discussion in the first chapter, which was furthered in Chapter 3 in the section on broadening rationality. In essence this objection proposes a relaxation of some of the normative rules in the standard model to accommodate certain aspects of choice and behavior that violate principles such as independence and transitivity.

The essential problem with this approach is that the suggestions as to which principles to relax are often somewhat arbitrary. Furthermore, if rationality is redefined in order to allow such a relaxation, rational choice may then involve violations of simple laws of probability, with the result that 'rational' individuals will engage in gambles that in general they are bound to lose (Osherson, 1995; Resnik, 1987; Stein, 1996).

It can be argued that there are at least three approaches here that are not arbitrary. A first approach essentially limits the application of EUT to situations involving risk, and excludes situations involving uncertainty (Binmore, 1999; Plott, 1996). This therefore excludes all new situations decision-makers might encounter, like buying a house. In principle there is nothing incorrect about this approach, but in practice it imposes severe limits on the application of EUT. Furthermore, it can still be claimed that violations of rationality will occur even in the more limited scenario.

A second approach is that of Vernon Smith (1990, 1991), described briefly earlier in the chapter. Smith's views have much in common with the work of a founding father of behavioral economics, Simon (1956, 1957, 1959, 1978). Both reject the norms of the standard model as far as rationality is concerned. Smith claims that the appropriate norms for judging rationality are the end results of decision-making, in terms of long-run market efficiency. He also stresses that short-run errors and biases may be corrected in the long run by experience and learning.

The most obvious problem here is that short-run errors and biases are often not corrected by learning, as mentioned earlier. Furthermore, there are some glaring systematic and long-run inefficiencies in the market; a prominent example is a phenomenon referred to as the 'equity premium puzzle', discussed at length in Case 6.1. Equities in the USA have over the long run (since 1926) yielded an annual return about 6% higher than bonds, which is a much greater difference than can be explained by any reasonable degree of risk aversion. Other examples, such as the tendency to bet on long shots in the last race of the day, were also discussed in Chapter 5.

A third approach is the one advocated in Chapter 3, in the section related to broadening rationality. This takes into account Smith's considerations of experience and learning, Simon's concept of bounded rationality, and the notion of compatibility with empirical observations, related to rational expectations. This approach therefore does shift the norms of 'conventional models' somewhat, but, as the concept of conventional models is not a static one, some of these factors, like bounded rationality, are already being incorporated into mainstream models. Given bounded rationality, one may concur with the conclusion of Gigerenzer, and propose that some heuristics may be rational in the broad sense, even if they are not optimal according to the NM. It is fair to say that the majority of people would claim to generally adhere to these 'broadened' norms, although they are still widely violated in practice.

By way of summary we can say that in general the above objections relating to trivializations, misinterpretations, and inappropriate tests cannot explain the large body of systematic evidence documenting a wide variety of violations of the NM of rationality.

However, it does not make sense to redefine rationality in a drastic way in order to allow for a large number of violations; instead we should aim to understand them in order to make better predictions.

## 11.5    Welfare and happiness

*Measuring happiness*

Although happiness, and the search for happiness, is the most fundamental part of our lives, economists are not 'happy' with examining the concept. The term 'happiness' is not frequently found in the economics literature, unlike the concept of welfare, which is found in abundance. This is partly because welfare can be measured in objective terms, usually in terms of GDP per head. Since the 1990s both economists and politicians have taken a greater interest in measuring welfare, and there is some controversy over this issue, with an increasing number of variables now being taken into account. These include not just real income, but also factors such as life expectancy, health levels, environmental quality, job satisfaction and stress levels. However, when these other variables are taken into consideration, some of them (like the last two) have to be measured subjectively, and a subjective weighting system must be used. The consequence of this is that economists tend to refer to such measures as relating to **subjective well-being (SWB)** as opposed to economic welfare. Nevertheless, it is this concept of SWB that corresponds with happiness, and that people are concerned with in terms of maximization; GDP per head, consumption and other economic variables are simply means to that end.

Another frequently used method of measuring happiness is simply to ask people. Perhaps the most prominent example of this is the World Values Survey. This has been carried out by a network of social scientists on an ongoing basis since 1981, and encompasses nearly 100 countries. Representative samples of 1,000 people from each country are asked to report their satisfaction with 'life as a whole these days', on a scale from 1 (dissatisfied) to 10 (satisfied). Early findings from this survey included a correlation of 0.62 between mean LS and mean purchasing power income across all countries (World Values Study Group, 1994; see Diener, 2000, p. 37).

These surveys have found that that there are important cultural factors affecting reports of LS. In general cultural factors vary across two dimensions: (1) traditional versus secular-rational values; and (2) survival versus self-expression values. In cultures where traditional values are important (for example Asia, Africa and the USA) people judge their LS by comparing their individual situations with social norms, such as employment and marital status, while in secular-rational cultures (for example North-Western Europe) people introspect as far as their emotions are concerned in order to judge their happiness. In cultures where survival values, meaning physical and economic security, are important (for example Eastern Europe), reports of LS tend to be lower than in countries where self-expression values (like democracy, civil rights and environmental protection) are more important.

Because (1) happiness can only be measured subjectively, and (2) cultural factors have an important influence, it is difficult to make meaningful comparisons between different countries. Neuroscience is now beginning to allow us to estimate objective measures of happiness, through the use of positron emission tomography (PET) and functional magnetic resonance imaging (fMRI) scans, but there is still much more to be achieved in this respect. Even if objective measures of happiness are attainable, we have already seen both in this chapter and in Chapter 3 that the relationship between economic welfare and happiness is a complex and controversial one. The main controversy concerns whether happiness depends more on absolute level of income or on relative income.

In order to address this issue it is necessary to begin by stating that the variables are most commonly measured in terms of real GDP per capita and LS. LS is usually measured on a ten-point ladder scale, while real GDP per capita is measured on a log scale to take into account diminishing returns. There are three main forms of data that can be used to test the nature of this relationship: (1) the cross-person relationship between well-being and income within a country; (2) the cross-country relationship; and (3) the time series relationship between growth in well-being and economic growth. Easterlin (1974, 1995, 2010) was the first economist to research these relationships, concluding that, as far as (1) is concerned, richer people in a country are happier than poorer people within the same country, but that as far as (2) and (3) are concerned there was no relationship between income and happiness. This conclusion became known as the 'Easterlin paradox', which Easterlin interpreted as meaning that relative income rather than absolute income was the prime determinant of happiness.

Over time, the conclusions have been somewhat watered down. In 1995 the second conclusion regarding cross-section comparisons was dropped. Another study by Sacks, Stevenson and Wolfers (SSW) (2012) also contradicted this conclusion. SSW examine the cross-country relationship using data from the Gallup World Poll relating to 122 countries in 2010. They find a strong relationship between log of income and LS, where income explains over half of the variation in LS. Furthermore, they find that there is no evidence of satiation, so that richer countries follow the same log-linear relationship as for other countries. They also find that the gradient of the relationship for cross-country data is the same as for cross-person data, supporting an argument that absolute levels of income are relevant in determining LS.

The relationship becomes more problematical with the third type of comparison, examining time-series data for different countries. The data for many European countries fits the same general pattern as the first two comparisons above, with economic growth being associated with higher LS, according to Eurobarometer survey data from 1973 to 2009 (SSW). There appear to be two main exceptions outside Europe: Japan and the USA. SSW explain the Japanese exception as being caused by changes in definitions used to record LS during the period 1958–1991; they claim that when these changes are allowed for the data indicate that economic growth does increase LS.

The US situation is also problematical. If we examine the data for the USA in the period 1973–2004, it appears that increasing income over time does not improve happiness, supporting the Easterlin paradox. However, SSW point out that the USA is different from both European countries and Japan in terms of increasing inequality. Income inequality increased at least twice as much in the USA during the relevant period as in Europe. Since the above relationship is based on General Social Survey data it is relevant that the average income of the households in the sample increased by a far lower proportion than the average income of the population as a whole. Thus SSW speculate that the sample responding to the Survey did not report significant increases in LS because they were not experiencing significant increases in real income. In fact the lowest 20% of households experienced a fall in real income in the period 1979–2010, with the next two quintiles experiencing only very small increases, at annual rates of 0.1% and 0.3% respectively (Rietveld et al., 2013).

Other recent studies do not appear to support the third of Easterlin's conclusions. Diener, Tay and Oishi (2013) also report that the time-series conclusions were not justified over the short run, based on data from 158 countries. Moreover, Veenhoven and Vergunst (2014) find that the conclusions are not justified over the long run either. Their study involves 67 countries with 199 time-series over 10 to over 40 years. The report that happiness increased in 62% of the countries in the study, with no significant difference between rich and poor countries.

The above findings therefore appear to support the hypothesis that in general absolute income does determine LS, and this is very important in terms of policy implications.

The evidence of increasing income inequality, particularly in the USA, is also important in this respect. These policy implications are discussed in a later section.

## Psychological models

Psychologists have proposed several theories of happiness to account for these empirical findings:

1   Happiness is a dispositional trait rather than a reaction to external events (Costa and McCrae, 1984; Lykken and Tellegen, 1996). There is also some genetic evidence for this, related to the influence of the 5-HTT gene (De Neve et al., 2012).

2   People adapt to repeated experiences of the same event, as that experience becomes a reference point to which new experiences are compared (Brickman and Campbell, 1971; Kahneman and Tversky, 1979; Parducci, 1995).

3   Happiness results more from pursuing a goal rather than attaining a goal (Davidson, 1994; Diener, 2000).

4   People possess a psychological immune system that speeds recovery from negative emotional events (Freud, 1937; Festinger, 1957; Taylor, 1991; Gilbert et al., 1998; Vaillant, 2000).

5   Conflicts exist between human agency and the evaluation of that agency (Deaton and Stone, 2013).

6   People reduce the emotional power of events by 'making sense' of them; this is also referred to as **ordinization**, meaning making events ordinary, predictable and explainable (Wilson et al., 2000).

Although each theory may explain some aspects of the empirical data observed, the first four all tend to leave certain aspects unexplained. The first theory does not explain why external events do affect happiness or why this effect is short-lived. The second theory does not explain why single occurrences of an event cause adaptation or a return to the original emotional state. The third theory does not explain why people recover rapidly from negative events, and is therefore asymmetrical. The fourth theory is asymmetrical in the other direction: it cannot explain why people recover quickly from positive events. The fifth theory is definitely paradoxical. People may say that parenthood is the most important and satisfying thing in their lives, but also report less LS when they have children. The psychological phenomenon underlying this paradox appears to be **focalism**. The implication of this is that when people are focusing on an aspect of their lives, such as parenthood or autonomy, they rate it highly, but outside this context, when they are not focusing on that aspect, they do not rate it highly. This issue is discussed further in the next section, since it is an illustration of a problem in pursuing happiness.

The sixth theory is in many ways the most satisfactory in terms of explaining the different findings. In order to understand it further the concepts of homeostasis and allostasis need to be explained. **Homeostasis** is a well-known biological principle, whereby various systems in the body have an optimal set point, and deviations from this point trigger negative feedback processes that attempt to restore it. Examples are body temperature, the level of blood sugar and electrolyte balance. The term **allostasis** was introduced by Sterling and Eyer (1988) to refer to a different type of feedback system whereby a variable is maintained within a healthy range, but at the same time is allowed to vary in response to environmental demands. Heart rate, blood pressure and hormone levels are variables in this category. Thus when we exercise both heart rate and blood pressure are allowed to rise in order to optimize performance. Wilson, Gilbert and Centerbar (2003) suggest that happiness is also a variable in this category. There is some empirical evidence for this in econometric models of happiness, showing that it is autoregressive. Bottan and

Perez Truglia (2011) use dynamic regression models on individual-level panel data for four countries, Japan, Germany, the UK and Switzerland, and find that in each case the coefficient for lagged happiness is positive and significant.

Wilson and colleagues also give an explanation regarding why an allostatic system represents a functional adaptation as far as happiness is concerned; in fact they give three reasons. First, they claim that it is dysfunctional for people to remain in an extreme emotional state, since they cannot adjust to new emotional events. Second, people in extreme emotional states tend to make less rational decisions, resulting in self-harming results, as already discussed. Third, extreme emotional states are physiologically debilitating when they continue for sustained periods; a good example of such situations occurs in wartime, when soldiers may be under extreme stress for prolonged periods, resulting in neurasthenia, 'shellshock' and post-traumatic stress disorder (PTSD).

The theory also maintains that the ordinization process evolved as a cognitive mechanism in order to maintain affective or emotional stability. This aspect involves the **uncertainty aversion principle**, a fundamental factor in many psychological theories. The principle is described by Gilovich (1991):

> We are predisposed to see order, pattern, and meaning in the world, and we find randomness, chaos, and meaninglessness unsatisfying. Human nature abhors a lack of predictability and the absence of meaning.

Again it is easy to see evolutionary advantages in uncertainty aversion. It drives people to take steps to reduce uncertainty, by trying to explain and predict their environment, thus furthering their chances of survival and reproduction. Reducing uncertainty also plays a large part in increasing pleasure and decreasing pain, relating the principle to the standard model. The implications of the uncertainty aversion principle for the standard model were discussed further in Chapter 5.

The implications of the principle are very general. It has been argued that the main function of religion and art is to help people make sense out of a confusing, unpredictable world (e.g. Jobes, 1974; Pfeiffer, 1982; Dennett, 1995; Pinker, 1997). We now need to consider more specifically how ordinization involves uncertainty aversion, how the ordinization process operates, and finally what its implications are for decision-making.

Ordinization is the process of assimilation, accommodation and 'sense making' (Wilson et al., 2001), and it is a process that occurs automatically, without any conscious awareness. As time goes on painful events become part of our life story, making them seem less novel and surprising. The events cause us less sadness, both because we think about them less and because when we do, the emotional reaction is less strong. In this situation ordinization and uncertainty aversion result in positive hedonic consequences, as pain is reduced. A similar process occurs for positive effects, but in this case there is a paradox, since the hedonic consequences are negative: we seek positive experiences that increase pleasure, but by doing so we rob these experiences of their future hedonic power. This paradox will be discussed further at the end of the section, in connection with EUT, but we can give an example here for illustration. We may have a goal of seeking promotion, which, when achieved, gives intense satisfaction in the immediate aftermath. As time progresses we think about the event less, and it becomes an accepted and normal part of our life history. It may even come to appear inevitable in retrospect, a phenomenon known as **hindsight bias**. More generally this bias means that events become more predictable in retrospect than in prospect, and this is an important feature of ordinization, again being a result of non-conscious, automatic mental processes (Pohl and Hell, 1996). However, the paradox is that sometime after gaining the promotion we are essentially in the same emotional state as before the promotion, and in order to increase pleasure and happiness we now have to progress to the next rung. Of course, if and when that is achieved, the same phenomenon will occur again. We are in the situation of the Red

Queen from Alice in Wonderland, who has to run faster and faster just to stay still. As Matt Ridley (1993) has noted in his book of the same title, this phenomenon is ubiquitous in biological systems, because of homeostasis and 'arms races'.

The discussion of ordinization explains why emotional reactions tend to be short-lived. But why do we consistently tend to underestimate the effects? One reason for this durability bias is that the relevant mental processes are automatic and non-conscious. A second reason is that we may fail to generalize from our experiences; we may come to believe that there was a specific factor involved (we bought a bad TV set, or we were not really that angry), rather than a general process. A final reason involves the phenomenon of **retrospective durability bias**. For example, we may forget that the product did not make us happy for as long as we had originally anticipated. Both prospective and retrospective durability bias may be caused by **focalism**, meaning that people think too much about the event in question and fail to consider the consequences of the many other events that are either likely to be going on, or were going on, in their lives (Schkade and Kahneman, 1998; Wilson et al., 2000).

There is another empirical finding that requires a psychological explanation. Studies have found that the age profile for happiness tends to be U-shaped in many countries, with a dip in the middle years of life. Some researchers have been skeptical of this result, since it has been largely based on self-report surveys. However, a recent study by Blanchflower and Oswald (2016) evades this problem by examining the use of antidepressant drugs in 27 European countries, using this as a proxy for measuring happiness. They find supporting evidence for the U-shaped profile, with people using the most antidepressants, and presumably being least happy, in their late 40s. One psychological explanation for this involves unmet expectations (Schwandt, 2016), which again involves reference dependence. This study uses LS data from Germany and finds that younger people systematically overestimate their happiness in later adulthood, while older people systematically underestimate their later happiness. The 'mid-life crisis' occurs when people have to face up to unmet expectations and come to grips with the fact that their long-held aspirations will now never be met. Once people come to terms with this, based on homeostasis theory, their mental states can recover and things turn out to be not as bad as originally feared.

### Economic models

Only recently have economists started to develop models of happiness. A good example is the model of Graham and Oswald (2010), which illustrates a unification of various sciences. Their model is based on evolutionary biology, and the assumption that happy individuals are more likely to breed successfully. Unhappy people tend to have higher stress levels, and therefore compromised immune systems, and also are more likely to take greater risks, resulting in death. The variables and structure of the model take into account psychological factors such as dispositional traits and a decaying memory of past experiences, but it is analogous in a number of ways to a standard economic capital investment model involving a production function. The capital in this case is referred to as '**hedonic capital**' rather than physical capital, and this naturally decreases over time unless people invest in it.

The production function in Equation (11.1) shows that hedonic energy ($y$) in any time period is a function of dispositional traits towards happiness ($z$), hedonic capital ($k$), and the parameter $\alpha$, which is positive but less than one, to reflect diminishing returns to hedonic capital. The variable $v_t$ is a measure of the effect of random life events in the relevant period:

$$y_t = zk_t^{\alpha} + v_t \tag{11.1}$$

Hedonic energy can then be used to either produce happiness or to invest in hedonic capital:

$$y_t = h_t + i_t \qquad (11.2)$$

The stock of hedonic capital depreciates over time, but can be increased by investment:

$$k_{t+1} = (1 - \delta)k_t + i_t \qquad (11.3)$$

where $\delta$ is the rate at which hedonic capital depreciates. Thus if people have a bad shock they can draw on their hedonic capital, that is, disinvest, in order to smooth out this life event. Similarly a fortunate life event, like a promotion, could result in an investment in hedonic capital.

Like other economic models based on evolutionary biology, the situation is viewed as a principal-agent problem, with Nature being the principal and the individual being the agent. The virtue of this game-theoretic approach is that it incorporates the principle of natural selection as far as Nature is concerned, but does not allow Nature to program individuals' brains completely for making every possible lifetime decision, since this would require a huge brain capacity, which would be very wasteful in terms of using precious energy resources. Thus in the principal-agent model Nature wishes to maximize biological fitness, meaning expected happiness, and determines a set of decision rules or policies in terms of hardwiring the brain; the individual, who is more informed about the specifics of a situation, then has some flexibility in making decisions according to these rules.

Graham and Oswald claim that this model both captures essential psychological traits and successfully predicts the tendency toward mean-reversion of happiness observed in many empirical studies, because of the model's 'smoothing' characteristics.

## 11.6    Problems in pursuing happiness

The assumption that people act in such a way as to maximize their expected utility is the most fundamental neoclassical pillar underlying the standard model. However, because of the various problems already discussed relating to rationality, substantial doubts are cast regarding the validity of this model. Even if we extend the standard economic measure of welfare to include the hedonic aspects of happiness, there still remain problems with EUT as a normative theory. Schooler, Ariely and Loewenstein (2001) classify these problems into three categories:

1    Limits to hedonic introspection
2    The adverse effects of hedonic introspection on well-being
3    The self-defeating nature of happiness-seeking

These problems will now be discussed in turn.

*Limits to hedonic introspection*

**Hedonic introspection** refers to the subjective measurement of one's own happiness or utility by the individual. It might initially seem self-evident that the individual is in the best position to report their own state of happiness, and relying on self-reports is certainly the easiest way to measure happiness. Furthermore, studies indicate that such measurements have relatively stable qualities of **validity** and **reliability**. In order for a measure to possess validity it has to measure the variable that it is supposed to measure. Lyubomirsky and Lepper (1999) have shown that individuals' self-reports of their overall happiness are reasonably well correlated with assessments made by friends and spouses. The quality of reliability means that repeated tests yield similar results. Again, correlations were quite high.

However, there are various problems related to measuring happiness by relying on self-reports, some of which have already been discussed in previous sections. The first point to note here is that there is a fundamental distinction between individuals' continuous hedonic experience and their intermittent reflective appraisal (sometimes referred to as meta-awareness or meta-consciousness). Thus, although every waking moment involves a hedonic experience, registered as visceral feelings, we only consciously assess these experiences intermittently. We cannot spend our whole lives consciously asking ourselves how happy we feel; sometimes we only realize after the event that we were happy, or unhappy, during that period of time.

When we do intermittently reflect on our happiness state there is then the issue of how we infer it. This is not as simple as it may sound, for it is not like taking a pulse; as we have already seen, there is no single scale we can use here, for we can experience both happiness and sadness simultaneously. There appear to be two main influences here which may not be intuitively obvious. One, which again has already been discussed, relates to the self-perception theory attributed to Bem (1972). Bem's central premise is that people often lack meta-awareness of their own internal states, with the result that they tend to infer these states, attitudes and preferences from their behavior. This process is subject to considerable error, in terms of misattribution. Not only do people make inferences from their behavior that may be in error, but they may also misattribute sources of visceral arousal. For example, a study by Zillman (1978) showed that arousal induced by exercise could be misattributed to anger, and a study by Dutton and Aron (1974) showed that arousal induced by fear could be misattributed to sexual attraction.

The second influence on our self-report of happiness is the situational context. Research indicates that people's valuation of experiences is strongly affected by prior questions they are asked. Such effects are known as anchoring effects, as we have seen. For example, a study by Strack, Martin and Stepper (1988) asked college students how many times they had gone out on a date in the last month, and then asked how happy they had been overall. Other students were asked the same questions but in the reverse order. For the first group who were asked about dates first, the correlation between the two responses was 0.66; for the second group who were asked about happiness first, the correlation was close to zero. Thus the happiness response for the first group was anchored to the question about dating, indicating that the students were inferring the dating question was a cue to their happiness.

Related to the problem of anchoring is a problem of focalism, mentioned in the previous section. When people are asked to focus on a particular issue, such as having children, they are likely to rate this aspect of their lives highly, but people with children generally report less LS (Hansen, 2011). Similarly, Stevenson and Wolfers (2009) find that women rate autonomy highly, but greater autonomy is associated with a decline in LS.

In summary, it can be seen that the results of the hedonic introspection research in general shed considerable doubt on our abilities to measure our subjective happiness at all accurately.

### The adverse effects of hedonic introspection on well-being

'Ask yourself whether you are happy and you cease to be so' is a famous quotation by John Stuart Mill (1873). There are a variety of studies that indicate that hedonic introspection reduces the experience of happiness compared with situations where such introspection is absent. Some of these studies relate to specific hedonic experiences, some relate to happiness in general.

Taking the specific studies first, one body of research has exposed subjects to a series of painful stimuli of varying intensities, profiles and durations, comparing the reports of those subjects who gave frequent online appraisals with those who simply evaluated the whole experience in retrospect (Ariely, 1998; Ariely and Zauberman, 2000). The result was that the first group was less sensitive in general to various aspects of the experience.

Another study with similar implications was discussed earlier, in connection with self-deception, and relates to preferences for different strawberry jams (Wilson and Schooler, 1991). It appears that the requirement to reflect on judgment reduced the ability of the participants to evaluate the jams, by 'muffling' their hedonic experience. Wilson and colleagues (2000) found a similar result in a study examining the evaluation of the quality of relationships with a significant other. Rapid judgments, without time for reflection, gave more reliable results, showing the importance of 'gut feeling'.

A final area of well-being worth mentioning in this context concerns humor. One study has shown that, when people were asked to reflect on why they found certain cartoons funny, they actually found them less funny (Cupchik and Leventhal, 1974). Thus there appear to be a variety of hedonic experiences where reflection spoils enjoyment.

Various reasons have been proposed to explain the above findings. First, introspection, by focusing on the self, automatically detracts from attention to the experience. Subtle features of the experience may therefore be overlooked, detracting from the hedonic appraisal. A second reason is that increased reflection and evaluation may cause the subject to consider features of the experience that were lacking in some way, thus also detracting from enjoyment.

Another group of studies has examined the overall happiness levels of different types of people. The general finding is that happy people tend to be less introspective (e.g. Veenhoven, 1988; Lyubomirsky and Lepper, 1999). Furthermore, unhappy people tend to be more self-conscious and ruminative (Musson and Alloy, 1988; Ingram, 1990). However, there is one main problem in interpreting these results; the relationships are correlational, which gives no indication of causation. It may well be that, rather than introspection causing unhappiness, unhappiness may cause introspection. Likewise, happy people may have no motive for introspection.

It is therefore difficult to come to a general conclusion regarding the effects of introspection on happiness. Indeed, recent research by Goldsmith and colleagues (2013) reports that daily monitoring of happiness can increase self-reported happiness. This research also explores the next problem.

### The self-defeating nature of happiness-seeking

Several philosophers and writers have claimed that the pursuit of happiness is self-defeating. Again, an example can be found in John Stuart Mill (1873, p. 100):

> Those only are happy who have their minds fixed on some object other than their own happiness; on the happiness of others, on the improvement of mankind, even on some art or pursuit, followed not as a means, but as itself an ideal end. Aiming thus at something else, they find happiness by the way.

Schooler, Ariely and Loewenstein (2001) propose three reasons for the self-defeating nature of seeking happiness:

**1**   *People have faulty theories of happiness*

In particular this relates to the phenomenon already discussed in connection with homeostasis and allostasis. People who are motivated by increasing their material wealth tend to underestimate the short-term nature of the increased happiness that results. Studies have shown that such people tend to be less happy than people with other goals, such as achieving psychological growth, having satisfying personal relationships, and improving the world (Kasser and Ryan 1993, 1996). Once again it should be realized that these studies are correlational, and do not prove causation. It may well be that unhappiness may motivate people to increase material wealth, and Kasser and Ryan (1996) have found that people experiencing troubled childhoods are more likely to pursue wealth as a primary goal than people with normal childhoods.

2    *Loss of intrinsic value of activities*

Considerable research indicates that when people perform activities for external reward, for example money, the activities lose their intrinsic appeal. It is therefore plausible that if people perform activities, like going to a concert, with the primary goal of achieving happiness, they may obtain less enjoyment than if they performed the same activities for their intrinsic value, meaning in this example enjoying the music.

3    *Increased monitoring of happiness*

It is likely that people pursuing happiness will monitor their happiness more frequently, and we have already seen that increased monitoring may well reduce happiness.

One approach to the empirical investigation of the issue of the self-defeating nature of happiness-seeking is to examine the relationship between selfishness and happiness, using selfishness as a proxy variable for intensity of happiness-seeking. A study by Konow (2000) revealed that people who were more selfish in a dictator game showed markedly lower levels of happiness than people who were more generous to team-mates.

Another empirical approach has been used by Schooler, Ariely and Loewenstein (2001). They performed an extensive study with 475 participants to examine their goals, plans and the realization of these goals for New Year's Eve 2000. This study has particular value since it was not an experiment, and therefore the goals and plans of the participants were self-determined, not determined by an experimenter. One main conclusion of the study was that those who had made the most ambitious plans and devoted the most energy to their celebrations, presumably meaning those most concerned with the pursuit of happiness, were most likely to be disappointed.

The conclusion from all the studies on the pursuit of happiness therefore appears to be a paradox: if we explicitly pursue happiness and monitor the results we are not likely to achieve our goal. Yet if we never evaluate our experiences, we can have no idea what kind of activities to pursue at all, and are also unlikely to achieve happiness. Thus it seems that we are damned if we do and damned if we don't. Schooler, Ariely and Loewenstein, however, are reasonably optimistic. They point to evidence that our unconscious automatic psychological mechanisms may be highly effective at both pursuing goals and monitoring our effectiveness in achieving them (Wegner, 1994; Bargh and Chartrand, 1999). In practice we may be like pilots who can fly most of the time on automatic pilot and only occasionally have to engage in manual control. As Schooler, Ariely and Loewenstein conclude: 'the challenge is determining when it is best to man the controls, and when it is better to simply enjoy the ride' (p. 66).

More recent research by Goldsmith and colleagues (2013) mentioned earlier in the section challenges some of the findings above. Not only were subjects asked to monitor their happiness, but, unlike other experiments, they were given the freedom to pursue activities of their own choosing, while being urged on a daily basis to do their best to be happy. The authors report that subjects did indeed self-report a greater level of happiness. Two other points are noteworthy about this study. First, it was conducted over a fairly protracted time period, with subjects making self-reports over several weeks. Second, subjects focused more on positive events in their lives and having positive interactions with others; they did not report greater consumption. This finding supports conclusions in other research that people derive more satisfaction in the long term from experiences, not from goods; in fact Yang, Carmon, and Dhar (2012) report that greater consumption of goods can lead to reduced happiness. Goldsmith and colleagues (2013) conclude that people may need practice over some time to learn how to maximize happiness by increasing its salience in their lives, and then learning how to address the relevant trade-offs between activities.

What is the significance of these three problems discussed above? It is possible to take the view that we can be rational from the point of view of the four criteria discussed in Chapter 3, in terms of attitudes and preferences adhering to logic and probability theory, being coherent, not being based on irrelevant factors, and not being incompatible with known empirical observations, but we may still not follow the norms of EUT. However, there is one final important point to make at the end of this section, which was also made in Chapter 5 in relation to prospect theory. Criteria for normativeness are not the same, or should not be the same, as criteria for descriptiveness. The fact that there are various problems associated with the pursuit of happiness does not mean that EUT is necessarily flawed from the point of view of predicting behavior, at either the individual level or the aggregate level. It may not be a good model to follow in terms of its policy implications, but it may in principle still be a good predictor of actual behavior, which is what of course economists are largely concerned with. However, as we have seen in practice throughout the previous chapters, EUT often fails as a good descriptive model also.

## 11.7    Policy implications

This aspect has been discussed in many chapters, in connection with specific behavioral areas. Now that we have discussed rationality and happiness, it is useful to summarize some of the most important implications, as far as individuals, firms, and governments are concerned.

### *Individuals*

Four main aspects of importance will be summarized here, relating to (1) happiness, (2) emotions and memory, (3) inter-temporal conflicts in decision-making, and (4) game theory.

**1**    *Happiness*

We have seen that happiness is both difficult to define and measure and difficult, if not self-defeating, to pursue. There are many different factors involved, and the implications of Pinker's 'three-act tragedy' are of fundamental importance. In evolutionary terms we must remember that we did not evolve as happiness-maximizing beings, but rather instead use happiness for a proxy of how good our chances of survival and reproduction are at any point in time. So, in short, food and sex make us happy, and in that order according to some recent research. The fundamental problem that we find is that this proxy mechanism is easily hijacked and sent off the rails. This can be caused by three main factors: (1) our evolved mechanisms may no longer be suited to our current environment (causing us to like fatty and sugary foods for example); (2) bounded rationality (causing us to use easily fooled heuristics); and (3) inter-temporal conflicts, discussed next. Evidence suggests that introverted and introspecting people tend to be less happy than extraverts. Another finding is the paradox that the pursuit of happiness may be self-defeating, and it may be that we are at our happiest in retrospect when we are not thinking about our happiness. The problem with both observations lies in establishing causation: are we happier because we are not thinking about being happy, or are we not thinking about being happy because we are too busy actually being happy?

Another paradoxical conclusion is that we may be happier if we cease to act purely rationally. For example, we may be happier if we choose to ignore certain information that causes us anxiety, or if we choose to not seek such information. Of course, this kind of action may not be in our long-term self-interest, such as when we choose not to visit a doctor when we have a worrying medical symptom.

### 2    Emotions and memory

Again there are a number of implications here. The first involves durability bias. Currently experienced emotional or visceral states tend to influence decisions relating to the future, even when those states will not persist for long into the future. For example, we buy consumer durables like TV sets and furniture because we anticipate that these goods will bring us lasting pleasure. Durability bias suggests therefore that we tend to pay too much for such goods, since the resulting pleasure will not last as long as we anticipated. Similarly, negative states may influence behavior, so that when we are angry we may make elaborate plans on taking revenge, which turn out to be a waste of time after our anger has cooled off.

A second implication is that people underestimate the effect of future emotional or visceral states on future behavior. Thus if we fail to predict tomorrow's pain of awakening we may fail to anticipate the need to place the alarm clock on the other side of the room, to prevent our switching it off immediately in the morning and going back to sleep. Even if we can predict the intensity of a visceral state, like the desire to smoke or eat chocolate, we may not be able to anticipate the effect on behavior (driving for an hour to find an open shop). This factor is also of importance in understanding the relapse behavior of addicts, who, after a period of abstinence, believe that they can indulge in low level consumption (of alcohol, drugs, gambling) without relapsing.

Another implication is that people forget the influence that emotional or visceral states had on their past behavior. This can mean that they find past behavior influenced by such states to be increasingly perplexing as time goes on. For example pregnant women can get food cravings very different from their normal tastes, and find it very difficult months later to understand such past cravings. People also tend to remember pain and fear badly, probably because it is difficult to re-experience, as opposed to merely recall, these states. Again, pregnant women tend to forget the pain of previous childbirth; they may initially decide to forgo anesthesia, but when labor starts they often reverse this decision (Christensen-Szalanski, 1984). An important policy implication of this phenomenon is that the kind of scare tactics which are sometimes used in promotional programs to deter people from smoking, taking drugs or committing crimes, often prove ineffective over a sustained period, and sometimes even prove counter-productive (Finkenauer, 1982; Lewis, 1983).

### 3    Inter-temporal conflicts

These conflicts were discussed in Chapter 8, as an important anomaly in the discounted utility model. According to the DUM there will usually be a time-consistency in preferences, but in reality time-inconsistent preferences are often observed, even when benefits are fixed in future time. Continuing with our food example above, we may decide now that we will not have a tasty dessert after dinner at the restaurant tomorrow, but when the dessert trolley comes around we succumb to temptation. The problem is exacerbated by two other related tendencies that we have discussed: we tend to underestimate the strength of future temptations, and overestimate our ability to overcome these temptations.

There may be many possible explanations for this behavior, and various alternative models to the DUM have been discussed, but where does this leave the individual in terms of optimizing their behavior or happiness? We have seen that the main policy implication here is that we need to make credible commitments. In the above example this may mean eating something healthy before going to the restaurant, designing specific rewards for 'good' behavior, only taking enough money for a main course, or even wearing tight clothes that make it uncomfortable to eat too much. The reader may suspect that the author has had plentiful experience of this particular problem!

Another area where inter-temporal conflicts frequently arise is saving habits (money and wealth can be viewed as a means of acquiring food and sex). Many people do not save enough during their working lives to afford a comfortable retirement. Again credible commitments are important in overcoming this problem. We have seen that the use of automatic savings devices (having amounts deducted from our salaries), and the use of illiquid savings accounts that are costly and inconvenient to withdraw from, may serve as effective commitments. This aspect of behavior is also a problem for public policy, as will be discussed in the final section on policy implications.

The other fundamental area where inter-temporal conflicts occur relates to sexual behavior. A high proportion of people have indulged in sexual relations that they have later regretted. Again, commitment devices are important. Marriage does not appear to be one of them, in terms of effectiveness, at least in many present societies; in the USA about 44% of marriages currently end in divorce. One important point here is that sexual appetite is like appetite for food in at least one respect: it tends to build over time, until it is satisfied; it then falls to a low level and gradually builds again in a series of cycles. We have also seen that, as far as food is concerned, commitment often involves satiating the appetite before temptation takes hold; hence it may be best to go to the supermarket just after eating, not when one is hungry. A similar logic can be applied to developing ways of pre-empting sexual temptation. The main problem in this case is that sexual temptation is often less predictable in timing compared with food temptation.

**4**   *Game theory*

There have been numerous examples in Chapters 9 and 10 where an understanding of game theory can help people make better decisions. This is particularly true when our understanding is enriched by the incorporation of behavioral and psychological game theory. It is important to remember that many of the decisions we have to make in social situations are where we are interacting with the same people on a regular and repeated basis. The considerations here are different from those situations when we are interacting with strangers whom we may never interact with again.

*Firms*

Some of the behavioral aspects discussed above also have policy implications for firms. Three main factors are discussed here: inter-temporal conflicts, loss-aversion and game theory.

**1**   *Inter-temporal conflicts*

If firms know that people succumb easily to temptations in terms of inter-temporal preferences, they may take advantage of this in a number of ways. We have already mentioned the wheeling around of dessert trolleys in restaurants, which plays on the urgency of visceral factors. The distinction between investment goods and leisure goods has also been seen to be important in terms of contract design. It is better for firms to charge below marginal cost for investment goods like health club memberships, and above marginal cost for leisure goods like mobile phone usage. As far as saving and spending is concerned, financial organizations can make attractive offers of loans, sometimes framing these in particular ways: 'no money down'; 'no payments for eighteen months'; 'pay all your debts with one low monthly payment'; and flexible repayment schemes that allow lower repayments when a borrower's income falls, balanced by higher repayments when income rises. Some of these practices may be regarded as ethically questionable of course, since they take advantage of human frailties and may cause unhappiness later. However, they are certainly frequently used.

**2**   *Loss-aversion*

This is another important behavioral concept that firms can profitably employ, especially when coupled with framing effects. We have seen, for example, that it may be better for firms to reduce prices by framing the reduction in terms of a discount or a rebate. This means that if a firm later wants to raise prices, it can then frame this rise as an ending of the discount, causing less loss-aversion and adverse consumer reaction than a standard price rise. Another method of raising prices in a latent way and avoiding loss-aversion is to reduce the quantity offered for a given price. Consumers are less likely to notice that their cereal box is now 350 grams instead of 375 grams than if the price goes up from £1.99 to £2.13, although the effect is exactly the same in terms of price per unit weight.

**3**   *Game theory*

There are a number of lessons to be learned here, particularly as far as bargaining and negotiation is concerned. These situations can arise with employees, customers, and competitors. One example we have discussed is the use of a most-favored-customer-clause (MFCC), which has the twin advantages to the firm of reassuring customers regarding prices, and paradoxically serving as a signaling device to other firms that the firm intends to maintain higher prices. The appropriate use and interpretation of signaling devices is particularly important for firms in both competitive and cooperative environments. As another example, a firm may expand its capacity as a signal that it intends to produce more output in the future, discouraging entry into the market. In oligopolistic markets, direct communication between firms that may imply cooperation is illegal in many countries; for example, several private schools in the UK have been prosecuted for sharing information regarding costs, because it was suspected that this led to higher fees being charged. In this kind of situation firms can effectively use signals regarding price-setting, without needing any direct communications. Many economists suspect that the tobacco and airline industries use such signals effectively.

As far as relationships with employees are concerned, firms need to understand concepts of fairness in determining salaries and salary differentials. In many financial firms, where salaries can be extremely high, it is strictly against company policy for employees to reveal their individually negotiated salaries to other employees, for fear of causing resentment and envy. As we have seen, an employee may be delighted to learn that they have just been given a 10% raise, until they learn that a colleague has been given a 20% raise. Not only is the level of pay important, but also the structure of pay. We have seen in Chapter 10 that bonus contracts tend to be more efficient and result in greater welfare of both parties than either trust or incentive contracts. An understanding of social preferences, reference points and focal points, along with self-serving bias, is necessary for a firm to have satisfactory negotiations with employees.

A broader issue with regard to pay concerns the increasing differentials between the pay of senior managers and the pay of lower-level workers, particularly in the USA. The Hay Group (2014) reports that this differential increased by 2.2% in Europe as a whole, but by 10.6% in the USA. This has been caused by global economic forces, with many lower level jobs being automated or off-shored, while improvements in IT have increased productivity of managers. The result has been a feeling of resentment and alienation among many in the USA, a widely reported phenomenon in the wake of the 2016 election. This issue is discussed further in the context of government policy.

## Governments

The behavioral concepts and principles applied in the situations above are also applicable as far as government policy is concerned. We will start this time with perhaps the most obvious example, loss-aversion.

**1**  *Loss-aversion*

If a government wants to stay in power and retain votes, having a vital and growing economy is extremely helpful. In a recession people are losing jobs and income, and even a stagnant or slowing economy can have adverse electoral implications if conditions are worse than people had expected. Certainly, worsening economic conditions for many working-class people, particularly in relative terms, have been blamed for both the Trump victory in the USA and the Brexit vote in the UK in 2016. The importance of economic fundamentals has been important in many countries since 2007, when the global financial crisis threatened many countries. Governments have faced recession, collapsing banking systems, and record budget deficits, making policy decisions extremely difficult in view of the trade-offs involved. Many of these trade-offs are inter-temporal in nature, for example the issue whether to employ more expansionary fiscal policy now, to boost the economy and reduce employment, at the cost of greater deficits, risk of loss of confidence in the financial markets, and the necessity of harsher cutbacks in spending in the future. These inter-temporal conflicts are discussed further below.

**2**  *Inter-temporal conflicts*

Time-inconsistent preferences are important for governments for a number of reasons. First of all many people would charge the government with the duty of helping to increase their state of happiness. How far a government should interfere with the freedom of individuals in order to further their own interests is of course a controversial topic. We are not going to consider the arguments of parochial government versus 'nanny' state here. However, there are some areas of policy where governments can help people overcome their tendencies to succumb to temptation resulting in regrets later that are relatively uncontroversial. One broad area concerns pensions and saving for retirement. In view of the well-established tendency for people to save insufficient funds for a comfortable retirement, there are various routes that governments can take to reduce this problem. One method, used in more socialist countries, is simply to collect higher tax revenues in order to pay a moderate government pension to everyone. This creates a problem of moral hazard, in that people lose the incentive to save, relying solely on government-provided pensions. Many countries with developed economies and aging populations are finding it increasingly difficult to fund pensions in this way. Some of the more market-oriented of these economies, like the UK, are trying to provide incentives for people to take out sufficient private pensions on a voluntary basis. In order to encourage participation it is better to frame such participation as the default option, rather than having people have to actively opt into such a scheme. Another means of encouraging saving for retirement is to use the tax system, by offering tax breaks on retirement accounts like individual retirement accounts (IRAs) in the USA.

As far as the effects of paying pensions on government budgets are concerned, one possible way of reducing the burden is to offer people the option of receiving a lump sum rather than an ongoing payment. We have seen evidence that, in the case of public employees, this may save a considerable sum for the state, as people tend to opt for lump sum payments in spite of the high implicit discount rate. Of course, if this practice were to be implemented on a large scale for all government-provided pensions, the savings involved would have to be balanced against the likelihood of hardship later for those people with time-inconsistent preferences, who fritter away their lump sums without planning for the future.

Health care is another policy area where there are inter-temporal conflicts. In the USA the Affordable Care Act, better known as Obamacare, was enacted in 2010 in order to extend health care coverage to many poorer households that were not covered by Medicaid. By making health insurance obligatory by law the act has succeeded in increasing coverage, but it is costing many people significantly more in terms of premiums. Many healthier people are opting out of health insurance, since the fines involved are not as large as the increased premiums they would have to pay, and this is causing adverse selection, so that people in poorer health have to pay higher premiums than they would have to pay if everyone was covered. It is therefore a complex problem, involving many aspects, not just myopic preferences.

Another area of government policy where time-inconsistent preferences are of importance concerns addiction. The term addiction in this context is applied in the broadest sense to include not just recreational drugs, with which it is most commonly associated, but also alcohol, tobacco, gambling and even food. We have seen that visceral influences play a large role here. Addiction not only causes unhappiness and suffering for addicts themselves, but also imposes heavy externalities. These relate to the effects on the families of addicts, the resulting increase in crime, and additional costs imposed on the state in terms of care and rehabilitation. Tackling the causes of addiction is a formidable task. In particular it involves a unified approach involving all the behavioral sciences. First, there is a sociocultural approach: for example, examining the causes of the drug culture among the young, which appears particularly prevalent in the UK. It also involves a psychological approach: researching the factors that cause particular individuals to be vulnerable to different types of addiction is important here. Finally, it involves a neurophysiological approach: this may also help to identify those people most vulnerable, but it should also lead to the development of medical treatments and drugs which counter the effects of addiction.

An important policy implication here, discussed in Chapter 8, is that making the production and distribution of addictive substances illegal may be counterproductive. This is because it increases transactions costs for suppliers, encouraging larger transactions and greater consumption. High excise taxes may be a more effective method of discouraging consumption.

Both of the problem issues above, health care and addiction, are related to a broader issue of individual health. As discussed in the case study in the previous chapter on obesity, poor life style and resulting poor health imposes huge costs on both individuals and the country as a whole. Furthermore, there is a considerable body of evidence that poor health and poor psychological functioning (e.g. anxiety, depression and hostility) are correlated. A study of Trump voters in the recent US election may shed some light on this relationship. Using county level statistics compiled by the Institute for Health Metrics and Evaluation, it has been reported that being a white person without a college education was a good predictor of being a Trump voter, explaining 41% of the variation in voting swing to Republican from 2012 to 2016 (Economist, 2016c). However, the Economist reports that an even better predictor was poor health, based on a composite index involving life expectancy, obesity, diabetes, heavy drinking and lack of exercise; these factors explained 43% of the voting swing, keeping other factors constant. These findings again suggest that poor health is related to both demographic factors and psychological factors.

Of course, correlation is no indicator of causation, so this does not necessarily imply that voting preference is determined by good physical health or that health is determined by good psychological functioning. Some recent studies have indicated this positive relationship does exist (Diener and Chan, 2011; Boehm and Kubzansky, 2012). However, in this situation it is difficult to unravel cause and effect, and it may be that the relationship is circular.

What is the lesson for government policy here? It would appear that the most important one for getting into power and staying there is not to neglect lower-level workers, either in economic terms or in social terms. It has already been seen that market forces relating to globalization have not been kind to such workers, but governments in many countries, not just the USA, have not been doing enough to alleviate the effects of these market forces. This has led to the rise of extreme political parties favoring racist, xenophobic, anti-immigration policies. Reforming education policies, offering more extensive training and apprentice schemes, and similar work-based incentives would help here. As we have seen in connection with nudging, people need guidance but also want autonomy. Thus a delicate balance is called for in various aspects of policy – education, health and employment.

3    *Game theory*

Once again we see that game theory is a universal factor in decision-making. Again also the incorporation of behavioral game theory elements is important for government policy. There are a number of policy areas that have possible applications; five of these are discussed here, but this is not intended as an exhaustive list:

**a)**   *Auctions*

Governments and government agencies are sometimes in a position to sell business operations or licenses to businesses to operate in certain areas. Large sums of money are usually involved, so it is important for governments to raise a maximum amount. The amount raised is highly sensitive to the method used for the sale. The various privatizations by the UK government in the 1980s and 1990s did not manage this efficiently. The general method was to invite the public to tender for a number of shares at a fixed price. In some cases the share offer was oversubscribed by a factor of four, indicating that the government, and its investment bank advisers, had considerably underestimated the market value of the operations being sold. When shares were later sold on the secondary market at much higher prices than the par value, often within days of the original issue, huge profits were made by speculators at the expense of the government.

An alternative approach is to auction operations to the highest bidder or bidders. An example of a successful auction relates to the sale of radio licenses by the Federal Communications Commission (FCC) in the USA, in 1994. The FCC took the advice of game theorists, notably Binmore, in establishing the rules for the auction's structure. These were complicated, following a simultaneous, multiple-round format. The end result was that, after 46 rounds of bidding over a five-day period, ten nationwide licences were sold for a total of over $600 million. This sum was over ten times the highest estimates that had appeared in the press.

**b)**   *International trade*

Governments frequently have to negotiate trade deals on a bilateral or multilateral basis. They also often unilaterally determine import tariffs and export subsidies, as well as other less obvious trade barriers. They may even appear to take actions that harm their own country, like imposing voluntary export restraints (VERs). The effects of all of these actions are generally counter-intuitive: tariffs and subsidies often reduce overall welfare within the country imposing them, while VERs may improve welfare (at least compared with the likely alternatives). This is not the context to explore the effects of these policy measures in detail, but frequently a major problem is a lack of game-theoretic analysis: how are other governments and other firms likely to react?

This failure is particularly evident in the imposition of trade sanctions. As we have seen, when these are imposed on poor countries ruled by dictators, they often backfire, causing unnecessary hardship and bolstering the regime at which they are aimed. The problem is again a lack of iterative thought.

c)  *Environmental protection*

This is essentially an aspect of the tragedy of the commons problem, which is increasingly affecting the world economy as a whole. Overfishing is a prime example. However, environmental protection, related to reducing greenhouse gases and global warming, has become a major, some would say the major, issue in the world economy. This is not just because of the catastrophic consequences that could follow current trends in greenhouse emissions, but also because of the huge political problems in dealing with the situation. These problems relate largely to the temporal and spatial aspects involved. Temporally, the current behavior of economic agents has no significant effect on their welfare because of the long time lags, extending into decades. This aspect is aggravated by the spatial aspects, that, because of winds and currents, one agent's pollution often turns out to be their neighbors' problem. National governments, even if they are concerned with environmental issues, are keen to ensure that their country is not overburdened with the costs of protection, while other countries get a free ride. However, unlike other public goods games, it is difficult to ensure cooperation because of problems in monitoring behavior and enforcing punishment.

d)  *Counter-terrorism*

Another major international issue relates to the so-called 'war on terror'. Over the last decade various western governments have reduced liberties in a number of ways in order to combat terrorism. The costs of this involve not only reduced liberties, but also increased transactions costs for individuals and firms (for example, going through airport security), and of course administration costs. The benefits include not only reduced terrorist activity, but also the perception of greater safety. Evidence suggests that there is a non-linear relationship between counter-terrorism spending and terrorist activity, featuring diminishing returns (Arin et al., 2011), at least in the UK. However, whether counter-terrorism spending reduces the efforts of terrorists, or whether it just makes these efforts easier to detect is still an open issue.

e)  *Mediation*

Bargaining impasses are often caused by self-serving bias and multiple focal points. However, we have seen that one way to resolve these problems is to have some form of mediation where the bargaining parties can have the weaknesses of their positions explained. Governments, or their agencies, can serve as independent arbiters in industrial relations or employment disputes in particular. An example of such an agency is the Advisory, Conciliation and Arbitration Service (ACAS) in the UK. There is some evidence that the existence of this organization has helped to reduce the number and length of industrial disputes over the last two decades.

Thus we can see that in some situations the government is acting as a player that is trying either to cooperate with or to compete with other players. In other cases the government may be acting as a mediator, which resembles the role of the 'choreographer', in trying to achieve a correlated equilibrium that is superior to other outcomes in terms of the welfare of the other players.

## 11.8    Future directions for behavioral economics

There have been various indications throughout the book where either areas of research or types of research are necessary in order to take the discipline forward. Appropriate topics to discuss at this stage are: decision-making heuristics; the formation of social preferences; learning processes; the theory of mental representations; the role of the emotions in decision-making; and the role of neurobiology.

### *Decision-making heuristics*

We have seen, particularly in the early chapters, that people frequently use heuristics or simplifying rules, when they make decisions, and we have seen that the root cause of this is the existence of bounded rationality. These heuristic devices are of wide variety, including the representativeness heuristic, the availability heuristic, the $1/n$ principle, fuzzy trace theory and the procedural approach. It is not intended here to review all the heuristics discussed, and their shortcomings. However, there is one area of heuristics that has not been discussed so far. This relates to the case-based decision-making approach. Whereas the NM examines future outcomes and their associated probabilities, the case-based approach is based on assessing the similarity of the current situation with various past decision situations, evaluating average outcomes from particular actions in these past situations, and weighting them by the similarity of previous cases to the current one (Gilboa and Schmeidler, 1995, 2001). The approach is therefore based on the common observation that we all use past experience in some way as a guide to future experience. However, the choice of relevant criteria for judging similarity, and assessment using these criteria, obviously involves a heuristic process. This is best illustrated by an example. Say that we are offered a new job and are deciding whether to take it. We may have been in a similar situation in the past on several occasions. What outcomes were important? These may include salary, or salary relative to one's reference group; working hours; amount of time traveling; working conditions; type of boss; quality of working environment; and so on. If we took a job based just on salary in the past, and this proved to be a bad experience, we may discount this criterion in our current decision.

### *The formation of social preferences*

We have reviewed various models incorporating social preferences in Chapter 10, and have also seen that these can explain behavior in both real-life situations and experimental studies better than the simplistic 'pure' self-interest model of the standard model. However, more research needs to be carried out on the underlying psychology involved and also the development of social norms. For example, it would be useful to know the relative importance of negative and positive reciprocity, and the relative importance of both of these compared with inequality-aversion. The importance of intentions also needs to be studied further, which means taking into account foregone payoffs. These can be studied by various methods of experimental psychology, and the results incorporated into modified social preference models. These can be tested by using further game-theoretical experiments in an ongoing process of refinement and increased understanding. We have also seen that the development of social norms is a complex phenomenon, relying on the process of 'team reasoning', but this area needs much further research, in particular to understand why social norms vary between different social groups and over time.

This increased understanding of social preferences may have significant benefits for public policy, as will be discussed shortly.

## Learning processes

These processes were examined in Chapter 9. As with social preference models (and many other economic models), better models, in terms of goodness-of-fit and prediction, are likely to be more complex, taking into account all of the elements of information that people seem to use in the learning process. Once again, foregone payoffs, both one's own and those of other players, are likely to be of importance here in improving our understanding. Learning strategies and processes such as randomization is another area where further research is needed. This research also has important implications for equilibrium analysis. Most conventional and non-conventional approaches assume some kind of equilibrium in their analysis, but, if learning takes a long time, a non-equilibrium type of analysis may be more appropriate. A wider range of experimental situation may also help understanding. Most of the game theory models used to test learning have involved competitive or competitive situations in a highly stylized manner. Different types of experiment may be required if we are to understand better how children learn language, for example, and also how child learning is different from adult learning. This last aspect is considered further in the last area of direction, neurobiology.

## The theory of mental representations

This is a relatively new area in psychology, and is concerned with how people form mental models or perceptions of a situation, in particular the elements in a game situation. In the words of Camerer (2003, p. 475):

> The theory of mental representations maps raw descriptions of social situations into the kinds of familiar games theorists study and the kinds of rules people use to decide what to choose.

This theory is currently not well-developed, but it has certain elements in common with the equally new area of case-based decision-making, discussed earlier.

The relevance and importance of developing theory in this area can be illustrated by an example from Camerer (2003). One of his student subjects commented after an experimental session playing the stag hunt game: 'I can't believe you guys are still studying the prisoners' dilemma!' The confusion of these two games is interesting. The common element is that rationality can lead to inefficiency, in terms of not resulting in a Pareto-dominant outcome. However, the 'uppity, trigger-happy' student had ignored that in stag hunt, unlike PD, there are two Nash equilibria, and one of them is Pareto-dominant, while in PD, unlike stag hunt, there is a single dominant strategy equilibrium. His confusion led him to 'defect' in each round of play, a rational solution in PD, but not in stag hunt. The student had failed to undertake an essential basic task in any game situation: examine payoffs to see if there are any dominated strategies. The performance of this task would have differentiated between the two types of game.

There is insufficient evidence at present to draw any general conclusions regarding the extent of the type of confusion above, or other types of error in mental representation. It would be interesting to see whether subjects make the same errors when such games are presented in more realistic situations rather than abstract ones. A prediction of EP would be that errors would be substantially reduced in situations that resembled real life, in the same manner as the Wason test variations. This would make a good topic for a PhD dissertation for any enterprising reader!

*The role of the emotions in decision-making*

This subject was discussed in Chapters 3 and 8 in relation to preferences and in particular time-inconsistent preferences. We also saw in Chapter 4 that emotions may also play a role in determining our beliefs and how we update them in accordance with new information. Thus the role of emotions is a topic that is related to the more general area of decision-making heuristics discussed earlier, and to the role of neurobiology, discussed next. As far as the issue of whether the emotions have a beneficial or detrimental effect on decision-making, the evidence is mixed. Traditionally, since at least the days of Descartes, rationality, in the sense of the absence of emotion, has been regarded as being optimal. However, since the late 1980s, various researchers in economics, notably Frank (1985) and Hirshleifer (1987), have suggested that emotions are an evolutionary adaptation and serve an important beneficial role, in that they serve as credible commitments. This theory is also supported by evidence in neurobiology, in particular the work of Damasio (1994). The issue is discussed in more detail in the first case study at the end of the chapter, in the context of patients suffering brain damage.

*The role of neurobiology*

No discussion of future directions for behavioral economics would be complete without a reference to the role of neurobiology. This aspect has been touched on at various points in the book, with the importance of neuroscientific evidence being discussed in the contexts of mental accounting, intertemporal choice and social preferences. Many social scientists are wary of the encroachment of neurobiology on their disciplines, being suspicious of a reductionist agenda. However, as was made clear in the first chapter, there have been a number of recent technological developments, particularly in terms of brain scanning and imaging techniques like PET, fMRI, electroencephalography (EEG) and regional cerebral blood flow (rCBF). These can shed considerable light on various topics of interest in behavioral economics, and are especially relevant in decision-making heuristics, learning processes and the role of the emotions. We are finding that different types of thinking or mental process are performed in different parts of the brain, indicating the importance of brain structure or anatomy. We are also finding that different chemicals and hormones have dramatic effects on behavior, although of course the effects of alcohol on behavior and decision-making have been known in general terms for thousands of years. The proportion of the populations in developed countries who are now taking regular prescription drugs, for example Prozac and Ritalin, to improve mental performance has increased enormously over the last two decades. This has in fact become an important public policy issue, in view of recent evidence that such drugs can have long-term harmful effects. Thus the importance of brain physiology is becoming better recognized.

Another controversial area, relating to the nature of 'free will', concerns the role of genetic factors. Ongoing research in this area is continually finding links between genetic makeup and behavior. Examples include the tendency to commit various criminal acts, tendencies to addictive behavior, tendencies for thrill-seeking, tendencies to certain diseases, various personality traits and disorders like autism, and of course intelligence. The anti-reductionist lobby regards this trend towards genetic explanations as distasteful, or politically incorrect, labeling the findings as 'genetic determinism', but there is no doubt that the trend is gathering scientific momentum. As with EP, one has to ward against the 'straw man' accusations. The label 'genetic determinism' is such a straw man, since it implies an extreme view that behavior is completely controlled by genetic factors, with no environmental influences (and this is ignoring the interactions between genetics and environment, such as developments in the womb). What the scientific findings are usually implying is that genetic factors have a predisposing influence, making certain behavioral effects more likely.

## 11.9    Applications

### Case 11.1  The effects of brain damage on decision-making

The following story might be called 'the curious case of Phineas Gage'. The year was 1848. Gage, 25 years old, was a construction foreman involved in building a railway in Vermont. It was customary in the course of construction to use explosives to blast and clear away rock, in order to build a straighter and more level track. Gage was an expert in such a task, and was described by his bosses as 'the most efficient and capable' man in their employ. However, in the course of tamping an explosive charge, there was an accident, and the ensuing explosion caused the iron rod used to tamp the charge to be blown right through Gage's head. The rod entered through his left cheek, pierced the base of his skull, traversed the front of his brain and exited through the top of his head. The rod measured just over a meter in length, had a diameter just over three centimeters, and weighed about six kilograms. It was tapered, and it was the pointed end that entered first, or the story may well have been different.

We do not need to dwell on the gory details, but some description of the incident is necessary in order to understand its implications. First of all, Gage not only survived the accident, but made a remarkable recovery, returning in terms of outward appearances to close to his previous self. Indeed, he was talking within a few minutes of the accident, and, having been carried in an ox cart about a kilometer to get medical assistance, he was able to get out of the cart himself, with only a little help from his men. He was then able to explain 'perfectly rationally' to the doctor the nature and circumstances of the accident. Gage was pronounced cured in less than two months. According to his doctor, Gage's physical recovery was complete. He could touch, hear, and see, and was not paralyzed 'of limb or tongue'. He had lost the sight in his left eye, but his vision was perfect in the right. He walked firmly, used his hands with dexterity, and had no noticeable difficulty with speech or language.

However, Gage's unfortunate story was only just beginning. According to his doctor 'the equilibrium or balance, so to speak, between his intellectual faculty and animal propensities' had been destroyed. He was now:

> fitful, irreverent, indulging at times in the grossest profanity which was not previously his custom, manifesting but little deference for his fellows, impatient of restraint or advice when it conflicts with his desires, at times pertinaciously obstinate, yet capricious and vacillating, devising many plans of future operation, which are no sooner arranged than they are abandoned ... A child in his intellectual capacity and manifestations, he has the animal passions of a strong man.

This description marks a dramatic change in Gage's personality. Before the accident he was reported to have 'temperate habits' and 'considerable energy of character'. He had possessed 'a well balanced mind and was looked upon by those who knew him as a shrewd, smart businessman, very energetic and persistent in executing all his plans of action'. In short, as his friends and acquaintances noted, 'Gage is no longer Gage'. After the accident his employers were not willing to take him back because of the changes in him, and he drifted from job to job, unable to secure and maintain the type of steady, remunerative job that he had once held. He died at the age of 38, after a series of epileptic fits.

▶

The reason for telling this harrowing tale is that it illustrates a vital point. In the words of Damasio (1994), there are:

> systems in the human brain dedicated more to reasoning than to anything else, and in particular to the personal and social dimensions of reasoning.

After exhuming Gage's body, his skull has been examined using the latest neuroimaging techniques, and it is now possible to draw certain conclusions regarding the extent of his brain damage. It was concentrated in the prefrontal cortices, mainly in the ventromedial sector. According to Damasio, this damage 'compromised his ability to plan for the future, to conduct himself according to the social rules he previously had learned, and to decide on the course of action that ultimately would be most advantageous to his survival'.

One can only draw limited conclusions from a single medical case study. It was obvious that certain parts of the brain had specialized functions, and could function independently of others, but more detailed conclusions are only possible by examining other similar cases. Damasio, as a professor of neurology and a practitioner, has been in an ideal environment in which to encounter such cases. He describes a modern equivalent, whom he refers to as 'Elliot', who suffered similar damage after a surgical operation to remove a brain tumor. The damage was again largely in the ventromedial sector of the prefrontal cortices, the main difference from Gage being that the damage was more on the right side. Like Gage, Elliot's physical capacities were not affected, nor were most of his intellectual faculties, including language and memory. His IQ was tested and showed no impairment, being in the superior range. He appeared charming, knowledgeable and with a laconic sense of humor. However, after the operation, his personality and judgment were severely affected. He became easily distracted, engrossing himself in the detail of trivial or irrelevant tasks, and became incapable of maintaining a normal schedule, time management or forward planning. He lost his job, and various others. Simple and basic decisions, like whether to take an umbrella when going out, would take ages to make, as he would tediously weigh up all the pros and cons. He made a string of consistently bad business, financial and personal decisions, and proved incapable of learning from his past mistakes. Most important of all, from Damasio's point of view as a diagnostic, Elliot appeared emotionally flat, describing his fall from grace and disastrous personal experiences with a wry and detached tone.

It was this last characteristic that provided Damasio with the material from which he developed a new theory, which he refers to as the '**somatic marker hypothesis**'. Essentially, this states that the emotions are necessary in order for us to make good decisions, not just in a social environment, but in any real-life setting. The somatic markers act as a decision-making heuristic, enabling is to narrow down possible strategies from an initially huge range of possibilities. Without this heuristic we tend, like Elliot, to waste a lot of time evaluating courses of action that are simply not worthy of consideration. For example, if we are faced with a decision whether to take a new and highly paid job in a different country, we may immediately be overcome by the emotion that we cannot leave our friends or relatives behind. This somatic marker prevents us from considering and evaluating all the other factors related to the decision, and we immediately make the decision to refuse the position.

This hypothesis is in direct contrast to the belief of Descartes, that we need to use reason alone, and not the emotions, if we are to make the best decisions. Hence the title of Damasio's book: *Descartes' Error*.

▼

**Questions**

**1**  What do the cases of Gage and Elliot tell us about the nature of rationality?

**2**  What does this case study reveal regarding the relationship between the brain and the mind?

**3**  Behavioral economics seeks a sound psychological foundation; what then is the relevance of neuroscience?

## Case 11.2  The bioeconomic causes of war

The title of this case comes from an article by Hirshleifer (1998). His article relates to many of the concepts discussed in the book, although we have rarely mentioned the phenomenon of warfare. The case study is included here to indicate the broad range of phenomena that the tools of behavioral economics are able to analyze. Thus we will be able to see the relevance of bargaining, game theory, self-serving bias and focal points, social preferences, reciprocity, and EP.

Hirshleifer states that the premise of bioeconomics is that:

> Our preferences have themselves evolved to serve economic functions in a very broad sense: those preferences were selected that promoted survival in a world of scarcity and competition.

The most fundamental drives in both non-human animals and humans concern food and sex. Most conflict between animals is on an individual basis, and is directly related to these objectives. When male animals fight over territory, territory represents resources of food, and also females are often only attracted to males who possess a territory. Territory always represents more access to females. Chimpanzees are the only non-human animals known to fight in groups (although dolphins may also do so), and the objective of the kinds of raid that they carry out into other territories is always to gain access to females.

It may be claimed that humans have the dubious distinction of being the only species that conducts organized warfare. However, in human warfare between primitive tribes the objectives in fighting are usually again food and sex. Chagnon (1983) studied the warlike Yanomamo tribe at length and concluded that female capture was the primary motive. He also noted that Yanomamo men who have killed more enemies in battle also produce more offspring. Keeley (1996) noted that wars were often caused by multiple factors, and estimated that, among American Indian societies, material motives (land, booty, poaching and slaves) contributed to 70% of wars, while women contributed to 58%.

In much of human history the same appears to have been true. Genghis Khan was certainly more concerned with access to women than with access to material resources. It is a tribute to his phenomenal success in this regard that it has been estimated that one in twenty Asians can now claim descent from him. In many ancient wars the vanquished males were universally slaughtered, while females became slaves/concubines/wives.

Food and sex may have been the dominant issues, but why does war break out? War represents the ultimate breakdown of a bargaining process. An individual or group of individuals

▶

wants something (food or sex) possessed by another individual or group, and they cannot agree to the terms of a transaction. Of course, in this impasse situation one party can just walk away dissatisfied, and this frequently occurs in the animal kingdom when one animal backs down from a confrontation. So why do animals and humans fight? For physical combat to occur both parties must evaluate the benefits from fighting to be greater than the costs. If only one party does so but the other does not, then the second party will back down, and combat is avoided. One method animals have of avoiding costly combat is to have some display of arms first; the purpose, unconscious though it may be, is to increase both parties' information regarding the strengths and weaknesses of the opponent. If both parties have perfect information, and encode it correctly, no combat can occur. Combat therefore tends to occur when the two combatants are pretty evenly matched, as well as the stakes being high in order to justify the potential high costs.

A factor that is therefore clearly relevant in the outbreak of human warfare is overconfidence, or self-serving bias, which in this case may not be so self-serving, since it may lead to costly defeat or death. Many wars have been fought and lost through underestimating either the strength of the enemy or the costs involved in fighting in terms of resources. Certainly this accusation can be leveled at both Germany and Japan in World War II.

Historically, most wars were fought between groups of people who were related in terms of kinship. The same is still true of tribal wars today. As civilizations grew in size, often due to returns to scale from industrialized production and increased productivity, kinship was greatly diluted and the related concept of affiliation became important. Many social scientists have noted that, even when assignment to different groups is purely arbitrary, bonds of affiliation are soon formed (Sherif and Sherif, 1964). Experiments dividing subjects into 'prisoners' and 'guards' have had frightening consequences, as the 'guards' come to regard the prisoners as inferior beings to be punished and humiliated. An essential part of our human psychological makeup is an 'us and them' mentality, which evolved from kinship ties.

Affiliation can occur on the basis of many kinds of tie: class, interest, age and location are common. Nationality, ethnicity and religion are particularly important in causing strong bonds – bonds strong enough to kill and risk being killed for. Diamond (1997) argues that a key factor in the formation of large warlike groups has been religion. He defines religion as an ideology that manipulates group members to become peaceful and obedient internally, and suicidally brave when it comes to external warfare. It is also notable that in societies where affiliation is particularly strong, the members often use kinship terms, like 'brother' and 'sister', in referring to other members; the leader of the group may be referred to as 'father' or 'mother'.

As affiliation has become more important and kinship less so, the issues of food and sex appear to have disappeared into the background. Material welfare is still important, although this is often referred to in abstract terms. For example, in 1914 German war aims were linked to finding its 'place in the sun'. In the 1930s, the war movement was linked to a similar concept, *lebensraum*, but by this time there was a strong feeling of aggrievement, particularly related to racial hatred. As the importance of food and sex has declined in explicit terms, the concepts of dominance, prestige and honor appear to have taken their place.

In the twentieth century in particular, it seemed that biological motives were no longer relevant in warfare. The historian Ferguson (1998) has claimed that in World War I the main motive for ordinary men fighting was that war was regarded as sport, as fun. Certainly there is a primitive, visceral thrill of the hunt involved, often evoked by soldiers' writings of the time. However, it might well be that this was a minority view, considering the massive slaughter, appalling conditions and futility of the fighting. Writers and poets like Graves, Sassoon and Owen were certainly more affected by the latter factors.

Ferguson (Ch. 12, 'The joy of war?') further contends:

> Today's neo-Darwinian genetic determinism may be more scientifically respectable than Freud's mixture of psychoanalysis and amateur anthropology, but the latter seems better able to explain the readiness of millions of men to spend four and a quarter years killing and being killed. (It is certainly hard to see how the deaths of so many men who had not married and fathered children could possibly have served the interests of Dawkins's 'selfish genes'.)

This passage displays a misunderstanding of 'genetic determinism' and the operations of 'selfish genes'. As explained in the previous chapter, genes do not operate in the teleological manner suggested by Ferguson, but in a purely mechanistic way. We have seen that this is the main reason why they can so easily be fooled or hijacked to serve irrational and self-destructive ends.

Hirshleifer (1998) on the other hand claims that one main factor why sex has become less important as an issue in war is that war leaders have far greater internal opportunities than before; they do not need to invade other countries in order to obtain access to females. Maybe this is why President Clinton never declared war.

### Questions

1 Explain the fundamental flaw in the argument by Ferguson: 'It is certainly hard to see how the deaths of so many men who had not married and fathered children could possibly have served the interests of Dawkins's "selfish genes".'

2 Explain why self-serving bias is important in causing war.

3 How have the aims of war changed over time?

## Case 11.3 Getting children to eat vegetables

Obesity and health-related problems like heart disease and diabetes are increasing in many high-income countries. Furthermore the incidence of these problems appears to be increasing fastest among school-age children. The costs to national economies are substantial in terms of decreased productivity and increased health care costs. Health experts are fairly unanimous in laying the blame on bad diet and lack of exercise. The problem appears to be greatest among low-income households, either because of lack of knowledge or because of the high perceived cost of buying healthy foods such as fruit and vegetables.

▶

A couple of experiments have been carried out in a study by Just and Price (2013) in order to examine the effects of incentives on the consumption of fruit and vegetables.

## Objectives of the study

There were three main objectives involved:

1 To examine and compare the effects of different types of incentive.
2 To examine and compare the effects on children with different parental incomes.
3 To examine the cost-effectiveness of an incentive program.

## Experimental design

These experiments involved providing a variety of different incentives in 15 different schools (in the first experiment) in order to see how the consumption of fruit and vegetables at school lunches would respond. At some of these schools as many as 77% of the pupils received free or reduced price lunches because of low parental income, while in other schools the proportion was only 17%. Thus it was possible to see how parental income affected increased consumption. Three different variations of types of incentive were used: amount of cash reward (5 cents and 25 cents per day); cash and prize; and immediate reward and delayed reward. This allowed the researchers to use six different treatments: (1) large immediate cash reward, (2) large delayed cash reward, (3) immediate prize, (4) delayed prize, (5) immediate small cash reward, and (6) no incentive (as a control). The delay in each case was that the reward was received at the end of the month.

The prize involved participation in a raffle, where the total value of the prizes was equal to the number of kids who ate their fruits or vegetables for that day multiplied by 25 cents. Many of the prizes were related to some form of active recreation such as rip-sticks, tennis rackets, soccer balls and swim goggles.

The treatment days occurred over five lunch periods spanning 2–3 weeks. On each treatment day there was a message in the morning announcements about the reward students could receive by eating a serving of fruits or vegetables that day. Prizes were displayed near where data was collected, visible to all students.

## Results

1 Overall, the proportion of children consuming at least one serving of fruit and vegetables increased from a baseline of 33% before the experiment to 60% (an increase of 80%). The incentive resulting in the largest increase was the larger immediate cash reward, which increased the proportion to 71%, whereas the delayed cash reward of the same amount increased the proportion to 63%. Surprisingly, the delayed prize increased the proportion more (to 60%) than the immediate prize (53%). The researchers propose that this difference is explained by the fact that, when the prize was delayed, all the prizes for the five-day period were displayed as opposed to just the prizes for one day.

2 The experiment revealed a substantial difference in effect between the schools with the highest-income children and those with the lowest-income children. For the richest children the increase in consumption was only 18%, whereas for the poorest the increase was 38%.

**3** The program was found to be highly cost-effective compared to other programs designed to increase consumption of fruit and vegetables. The main aspect of this was that wastage, in terms of items thrown in the trash, was reduced by 43% compared with the baseline situation. Administrative costs, involving the cost of the rewards and the labor costs of distributing the rewards, were also low.

Two other findings emerged from the study:

**1** There was no evidence of the incentive program reducing the number of servings consumed by children who normally ate more than one serving a day. The researchers originally feared that the program might create a social norm of consuming exactly one serving of fruit/vegetables per day, but this did not appear to be the case.

**2** In a second experiment, involving a further eight schools, the after-effects of the incentive program were monitored in order to examine the long-run effects of such a program. Although the proportion of children consuming fruit and vegetables remained higher than the original level for the two weeks immediately following the program, in the next two weeks (two to four weeks after the incentive program ended) consumption returned to the baseline level before the program started.

## Questions

**1** What aspects of behavioral economics are relevant in this study?

**2** Explain the significance of the difference in behavior between low-income and high-income children.

**3** Comment on the long-run effects of the incentive program.

**4** What other incentives do you think might be effective in increasing children's consumption of fruit and vegetables, apart from the ones used in the study?

# Bibliography

Abbink, K., Irlenbusch, B., Renner, E. (2000). The moonlighting game: An experimental study on reciprocity and retribution. *Journal of Economic Behavior and Organization*, *42*(2), 265–277.

Abdellaoui, M. (2000). Parameter-free eliciting of utilities and probability weighting functions. *Management Science*, *46*(11), 1497–1512.

Abdellaoui, M., Bleichrodt, H., Paraschiv, C. (2007). Loss aversion under prospect theory: A parameter-free measurement. *Management Science*, *53*, 1659–1674.

Abeler, J., Falk, A., Goette, L., Huffman, D. (2011). Reference points and effort provision. *American Economic Review*, *101*(2), 470–492.

Abramson, L. Y., Metalsky, G. I., Alloy, L. B. (1979). Judgment of contingency in depressed and nondepressed students: Sadder but wiser? *Journal of Experimental Psychology*, *108*(4), 441–485.

Acar-Burkay, S., Fennis, B., Warlop, L. (2014). Trusting others: The polarization effect of need for closure. *Journal of Personality and Social Psychology*, *107*(4), 719–735.

Achtziger, A., Alós-Ferrer, C., Wagner, A. K. (2015). Money, depletion, and prosociality in the dictator game. *Journal of Neuroscience, Psychology, and Economics*, *8*(1), 1–14.

Adam, M., Kroll, E. (2012). Physiological evidence of attraction to chance. *Journal of Neuroscience, Psychology, And Economics*, *5*(3), 152–165.

Adams, J. S. (1963). Toward an understanding of inequity. *Journal of Abnormal and Social Psychology*, *67*, 422–436.

Agarwal, S., Skiba, P. M., Tobacman, J. (2009). Payday loans and credit cards: New liquidity and credit scoring puzzles. *American Economic Review*, *99*(2), 412–417.

Agell, J., Lundborg, P. (1995). Theories of pay and unemployment: Survey evidence from Swedish manufacturing firms. *Scandinavian Journal of Economics*, *97*(2), 295–308.

Agnoli, F., Krantz, D. H. (1989). Suppressing natural heuristics by formal instruction: the case of the conjunction fallacy. *Cognitive Psychology*, *21*(4), 515–550.

Ahmed, A. M., Salas, O. (2011). Implicit influences of Christian religious representations on dictator and prisoner's dilemma game decisions. *Journal of Socio-Economics*, *40*(3), 242–246.

Ainslie, G. W. (1975). Specious reward: A behavioral theory of impulsiveness and impulsive control. *Psychological Bulletin*, *82*(4), 463–496.

———. (1986). Beyond microeconomics: Conflict among interest in a multiple self as a determinant of value. In J. Elster (Ed.), *The Multiple Self* (pp. 133–175). Cambridge: Cambridge University Press.

———. (1991). Derivation of 'rational' economic behavior from hyperbolic discount curves. *American Economic Review*, *81*(2), 334–340.

———. (1992). *Picoeconomics: The Strategic Interaction of Successive Motivational States within the Person*. Cambridge: Cambridge University Press.

———. (2001). *Breakdown of Will*. Cambridge: Cambridge University Press.

Ainslie, G. W., Haendel, V. (1983). The motives of the will. In E. Gottheil, K. Durley, T. Skodola, H. Waxman (Eds), *Etiologic Aspects of Alcohol and Drug Abuse* (pp. 119–140). Springfield, IL: Charles C. Thomas.

Ainslie, G. W., Haslam, N. (1992). Hyperbolic discounting. In G. Loewenstein, J. Elster (Eds), *Choice Over Time* (pp. 57–92). New York: Russell Sage.

Akerlof, G. A. (1982). Labor contracts as partial gift exchange. *Quarterly Journal of Economics*, *97*(4), 543–569.

Albrecht, A., Weber., M. (1997). An empirical study on intertemporal decision making under risk. *Management Science*, *43*, 813–826.

Aldrovandi, S., Brown, G. D. A., Wood, A. M. (2015). Social norms and rank-based nudging: Changing willingness to pay for healthy food. *Journal of Experimental Psychology: Applied*, *21*(3), 242–254.

Ali, M. (1977). Probability and utility estimates for racetrack bettors. *Journal of Political Economy*, *85*(4), 803–815.

Allais, M. (1953). Le comportement de l'homme rationnel devant le risque: Critique des postulats et axioms de l'école américaine. *Econometrica*, *21*(4), 503–546.

Aloysius, J. A. (2005). Ambiguity aversion and the equity premium puzzle: A re-examination of experimental data on repeated gambles. *Journal of Socio-Economics*, *34*(5), 635–655.

Alpert, M., Raiffa, H. (1982). A progress report on the training of probability assessors. In D. Kahneman, P. Slovic, A. Tversky (Eds), *Judgment Under Uncertainty: Heuristics and Biases* (pp. 294–305). Cambridge: Cambridge University Press.

Andersen, S., Harrison, G. W., Lau, M. I., Rutström, E. E. (2008). Elicitation using multiple price list formats. *Experimental Economics*, *12*(3), 365–366.

Anderson, C., Brion, S., Moore, D. A., Kennedy, J. A. (2012). A status-enhancement account of overconfidence. *Journal of Personality and Social Psychology*, *103*(4), 718–735.

Anderson, E. W., Hansen, L. P., Sargent, T. J. (2003). A quartet of semigroups for model specification, robustness, prices of risk, and model detection. *Journal of the European Economic Association*, *1*(1), 68–123.

Andreoni, J., Miller, J. H. (1993). Rational cooperation in the finitely repeated prisoner's dilemma: Experimental evidence. *Economic Journal*, *103*(418), 570–585.

Andreoni, J., Sprenger, C. (2012). Estimating time preferences from convex budgets. *American Economic Review*, *102*(7), 3333–3356.

Ang, A., Bekaert, G., Liu, J. (2005). Why stocks may disappoint. *Journal of Financial Economics,* *76*(3), 471–508.

Angner, E. (2016). *A Course in Behavioral Economics* (2nd ed.). London: Palgrave.

Apicella, C. D., Dreber, A., Campbell, B., Grasy, P. B., Hoffman. M., Little, A. C. (2008). Testosterone and financial risk preferences. *Evolution and Human Behavior*, *29*(6), 384–390.

Arena, R., Dow, S., Klaes, M. (Eds). (2009). *Open Economics: Economics in Relation to Other Disciplines*. London: Routledge.

Argyle, M. (1999). Causes and correlates of happiness. In D. Kahneman, E. Diener, N. Schwarz (Eds), *Well-being: The Foundation of Hedonic Psychology* (pp. 353–373). New York: Russell Sage.

Ariely, D. (1998). Combining experiences over time: The effects of duration, intensity changes and on-papers line measurements on retrospective pain evaluations. *Journal of Behavioral Decision Making*, *11*(1), 19–45.

———. (2008). *Predictably Irrational: The Hidden Forces That Shape Our Decisions*. London: HarperCollins.

———. (2010). *The Upside of Irrationality*. London: Harper.

Ariely, D. (2013). *The (Honest) Truth about Dishonesty*. New York: HarperCollins.

Ariely, D., Huber, J., Wertenbroch, K. (2005). When do losses loom larger than gains? *Journal of Marketing Research*, *42*(2), 134–138.

Ariely, D., Loewenstein, G., Prelec, D. (2000). Coherent arbitrariness: Duration-sensitive pricing of hedonic stimuli around an arbitrary anchor. Working Paper. Pittsburgh: Department of Social and Decision Sciences, Carnegie Mellon University.

———. (2003). "Coherent arbitrariness": Stable demand curves without stable preferences. *Quarterly Journal of Economics*, *118*(1), 73–105.

———. (2006). Tom Sawyer and the construction of value. *Journal of Economic Behavior and Organisation, 60*(1), 1–10.

Ariely, D., Wertenbroch, K. (2002). Procrastination, deadline, and performance: Self-control by precommitment. *Psychological Science*, *13*(3), 219–224.

Ariely, D., Zauberman, G. (2000). On the making of an experience: The effects of breaking and combining experiences on their overall evaluation. *Journal of Behavioral Decision Making*, *13*(2), 219–232.

Arin, K. P., Lorz, O., Reich, O. F. M., Spagnolo, N. (2011). Exploring the dynamic between terror and anti-terror spending: Theory and UK-evidence. *Journal of Economic Behavior and Organization*, *77*(2), 189–202.

Arkes, H. R. (1991). Costs and benefits of judgment errors: Implications for debiasing. *Psychological Bulletin*, *110*(3), 486–498.

Arkes, H. R., Blumer, C. (1985). The psychology of sunk cost. *Organizational Behavior and Human Decision Processes*, *35*(1), 124–140.

Arkes, H. R., Wortmann, R. L., Saville, P. D., Harkness, A. R. (1981). Hindsight bias among physicians weighing the likelihood of diagnoses. *Journal of Applied Psychology*, *66*(2), 252–254.

Arnsten, A. F. T. (2015). Stress weakens prefrontal networks: Molecular insults to higher cognition. *Nature Neuroscience*, *18*(10), 1376–1385.

Arrow, K. J. (1986). Rationality of self and others in an economic system. *Journal of Business*, *59*(4), S385–S399.

Asch, M. J. (1951). Nondirective teaching in psychology: An experimental study. *Psychological Monographs*, *65*(4), Washington, DC: American Psychological Association.

Asch, S. E. (1955). Opinions and Social Pressure. *Scientific American*, November, *193*(5), 31–35.

Ashraf, N., Karlan, D., Yin, W. (2006). Tying Odysseus to the mast: Evidence from a commitment savings product in the Philippines. *Quarterly Journal of Economics*, *121*(2), 673–697.

Augenblick, N., Niederle, M., Sprenger, C. (2015). Working over time: Dynamic inconsistency in real effort tasks. *The Quarterly Journal of Economics*, *130*(3), 1067–1115.

Aumann, R. J. (1987). Correlated equilibrium as an extension of Bayesian rationality. *Econometrica*, *55*(1), 1–18.

Ausubel, L. M. (1999). *Adverse Selection in the Credit Card Market*. College Park: University of Maryland.

Axelrod, R. (1985). *The Evolution of Cooperation*. New York: Basic Books.

Aydinli, A., Bertini, M. (2012). Consumer reactance to conditional price promotions. In Z. Gürhan-Canli, C. Otnes, R. Zhu (Eds): NA - *Advances in Consumer Research* (Vol. 40, pp. 195–197). Duluth, MN: Association for Consumer Research.

Aydinli, A., Bertini, M. Lambrecht, A. (2014). Price promotion for emotional impact. *Journal of Marketing*, *78*(4), 80–96.

Ayduk, O., Mendoza-Denton, R., Mischel, W., Downey, G., Peake, P. K., Rodriguez, M. (2000). Regulating the interpersonal self: Strategic self-regulation for coping with rejection sensitivity. *Journal of Personality & Social Psychology*, *79*(5), 776–792.

Ayton, P., Fischer, I. (2004). The Hot Hand Fallacy and the Gambler's Fallacy: Two faces of subjective randomness? *Memory & Cognition*, *32*(8), 1369–1378.

Babcock, L., Loewenstein, G. (1997). Explaining bargaining impasse: The role of self-serving bias. *Journal of Economic Perspectives*, *11*(1), 109–126.

Babcock, L., Loewenstein, G., Issacharoff, I. (1997). Creating convergence: Debiasing biased litigants. *Law and Social Inquiry*, *22*(4), 913–925.

Babcock, L., Loewenstein, G., Issacharoff, I., Camerer, C. (1995). Biased judgments of fairness in bargaining. *American Economic Review*, *85*(5), 1337–1343.

Baca-Motes, K., Brown, A., Gneezy, A., Keenan, E. A., Nelson, L. D. (2013). Commitment and behavior change: Evidence from the field. *Journal of Consumer Research*, *39*(5), 1070–1084.

Backhouse, R. E., Klaes, M. (2009). Applying Economics, using Evidence. *Journal of Economic Methodology*, *16*(2), 139–144.

Bahry, D. L., Wilson, R. K. (2006). Confusion or fairness in the field? Rejections in the ultimatum game under the strategy method. *Journal of Economic Behavior and Organization*, *60*(1), 37–54.

Ballinger, T. P., Wilcox, N. T. (1997). Decisions, error and heterogeneity. *Economic Journal*, *107*(443), 1090–1105.

Bambauer-Sachse, S., Dupuy, A. (2012). Do price promotions lead to a reduction of the internal reference price and if so, under which conditions is this effect less strong? In Z. Gürhan-Canli, C. Otnes, R. Zhu (Eds), *NA - Advances in Consumer Research* (Vol. 40, pp. 334–341).

Bansal, R., Yaron, A. (2004). Risks for the long run: A potential resolution of asset pricing puzzles. *Journal of Finance*, *59*(4), 1481–1509.

Barber, B. M., Odean, T. (2001). Boys will be boys: Gender, overconfidence, and common stock investment. *Quarterly Journal of Economics*, *116*(1), 261–292.

———. (2008). All that glitters: The effect of attention and news on the buying behavior of individual and institutional investors. *Review of Financial Studies*, *21*(2), 785–818.

Barberis, N., Huang, M. (2001). Mental accounting, loss-aversion, and individual stock returns. *Journal of Finance*, *56*(4), 1247–1292.

Barberis, N., Huang, M., Santos, T. (2001). Prospect theory and asset prices. *Quarterly Journal of Economics*, *116*(1), 1–53.

Barberis, N., Shleifer, A., Vishny, R. (1998). A model of investor sentiment. *Journal of Financial Economics*, *49*(3), 307–343.

Barberis, N., Xiong, W. (2009). What drives the disposition effect? An analysis of a long-standing preference-based explanation. *Journal of Finance*, *64*(2), 751–784.

Bardsley, N., Mehta, J., Starmer, C., Sugden, R. (2010). Explaining focal points: Cognitive hierarchy theory versus team reasoning. *Economic Journal*, *120*(543), 40–79.

Bargh, J. A., Chartand, T. L. (1999). The unbearable automaticity of being. *American Psychologist*, *54*(7), 462–479.

Bargh, J. A., Chen, M., Burrows, L. (1996). Automaticity of social behavior: Direct effects of trait construct and stereotype activation on action. *Journal of Personality and Social Psychology*, *71*(2), 230–244.

Bartels, D. M., Rips, L. J. (2010). Psychological connectedness and intertemporal choice. *Journal of Experimental Psychology: General*, *139*(1), 49–69.

Bateman, H., Dobrescu, L. I., Newell, B. R., Ortmann, A., Thorp, S. (2016). As easy as pie: How retirement savers use prescribed investment disclosures. *Journal of Economic Behavior and Organization*, *121*(1), 60–76.

Batson, C. D. (1991). *The Altruism Question*. Chicago: Chicago University Press.

Batson, C. D., Fultz, J., Schoenrade, P. (1987). Distress and empathy: Two qualitatively distinct vicarious emotions with different motivational consequences. *Journal of Personality*, *55*(1), 19–39.

Battigalli, P., Dufwenberg, M. (2007). Guilt in games. *American Economic Review*, *97*(2), 170–176.

———. (2009). Dynamic psychological games. *Journal of Economic Theory*, *144*(1), 1–35.

Baumeister, R. F. (2001). The psychology of irrationality: why people make foolish, self-defeating choices. In I. Brocas, J. D. Carillo (Eds), *The Psychology of Economic Decisions* (pp. 3–16). Oxford: Oxford University Press.

Baumeister, R. F., Bratslavsky, E., Muraven, M., Tice, D. M. (1998). Ego depletion: Is the active self a limited resource? *Journal of Personality and Social Psychology*, *74*(5), 1252–1265.

Baumeister, R. F., Heatherton, T. F. (1996). Self-regulation failure: An overview. *Psychological Inquiry*, *7*(1), 1–15.

Baumeister, R. F., Heatherton, T. F., Tice, D. M. (1993). When ego threats lead to self-regulation failure: Negative consequences of high self-esteem. *Journal of Personality and Social Psychology*, *64*(1), 141–156.

Baumhart, R. (1968). *An Honest Profit*. New York: Prentice-Hall.

Beard, T. R., Beil, R. (1994). Do people rely on the self-interested maximization of others? An experimental test. *Management Science*, *40*(2), 252–262.

Bechara, A. (2005). Decision-making, impulse control and loss of willpower to resist drugs: a neurocognitive perspective. *Nature Neuroscience*, *8*(11), 1458–1463.

Bechara, A., Damasio, H., Damasio, A., Lee, G. (1999). Different contributions of the human amygdala and ventromedial prefrontal cortex to decision making. *Journal of Neuroscience*, *19*(13), 5473–5481.

Becker, G. S. (1976). Altruism, egoism, and genetic fitness: Economics and sociobiology. *Journal of Economic Literature*, *14*(3), 817–826.

Becker, G. S., Murphy, K. M. (1988). A theory of rational addiction. *Journal of Political Economy*, *96*(4), 675–701.

Becker, J. L., Sarin, R. K. (1987). Lottery dependent utility. *Management Science*, *33*(11), 1367–1382.

Bell, D. E. (1985). Disappointment in decision making under uncertainty. *Operations Research*, *33*(1), 1–27.

Bellemare, C., Kröger, S., van Soest, A. (2008). Measuring inequity aversion in a heterogeneous population using experimental decisions and subjective probabilities. *Econometrica*, *76*(4), 815–839.

Bem, D. J. (1972). Self-perception theory. In L. Berkowitz (Ed.), *Advances in Experimental Social Psychology* (Vol. 6, pp. 1–62). New York: Academic Press.

Benartzi, S. (2001). Excessive extrapolation and the allocation of 401(k) accounts to company stock. *Journal of Finance*, *56*(5), 1747–1764.

Benartzi, S., Thaler, R. H. (1995). Myopic loss aversion and the equity premium puzzle. *Quarterly Journal of Economics*, *110*(1), 73–92.

———. (1998). *Illusory Diversification and Retirement Savings*, Working Paper, University of Chicago and UCLA.

———. (1999). Risk aversion or myopia? Choices in repeated gambles and retirement investments. *Management Science*, *45*(3), 364–381.

———. (2001). Naïve diversification strategies in defined contribution savings plans. *American Economic Review*, *91*(1), 79–98.

Benjamin, J., Li, L., Patterson, C., Greenberg, B. D. (1996). Population and familial association between the D4 dopamine receptor gene and measures of novelty seeking. *Nature Genetics*, *12*(1), 81–84.

Bentham, J. [1789](1948). *An Introduction to the Principle of Morals and Legislations*. Oxford: Blackwell.

Benzion, U., Rapoport, A., Yagil, J. (1989). Discount rates inferred from decisions: An experimental study. *Management Science*, *35*(3), 270–284.

Berg, J., Dickhaut, J., McCabe, K. (1995). Trust, reciprocity, and social history. *Games and Economic Behavior*, *10*(1), 122–142.

Berger, J., Fitzsimons, G. (2008). Dogs on the street, Pumas on your feet: How cues in the environment influence product evaluation and choice. *Journal of Marketing Research*, *45*(1), 1–14.

Berkeley, D., Humphreys, P. (1982). Structuring decision problems and the 'bias' heuristic. *Acta Psychologica*, *50*, 201–252.

Berkman, E. T., Burklund, L., Lieberman, M. D. (2009). Inhibitory spillover: Intentional motor inhibition produces incidental limbic inhibition via right inferior frontal cortex. *NeuroImage*, *47*(2), 705–712.

Bernheim, B. D. (2009). The psychology and neurobiology of judgement and decision making: what's in it for economics? In P. W. Glimcher, C. F. Camerer, E. Fehr, R. A. Poldrack (Eds), *Neuroeconomics: Decision-Making and the Brain* (pp. 115–126). London: Academic Press.

Bernheim, B. D., Rangel, A. (2007). Toward choice-theoretic foundations for behavioral welfare economics. *American Economic Review*, *97*(2), 464–470.

———. (2009). Beyond revealed preference: Choice-theoretic foundations for behavioral welfare economics. *Quarterly Journal of Economics*, *124*(1), 51–104.

Bernheim, B. D., Rangel, A. (2004). Addiction and cue-triggered decision processes. *American Economic Review*, *94*(5), 1558–1590.

Bernheim, B. D., Scholz, J. K. (1993). Do Americans save too little? *Federal Reserve Bank of Philadelphia Business Review*, Sep/Oct, 3–20.

Bernoulli, D. [1738] (1954). Exposition of a new theory on the measurement of risk. *Econometrica*, *22*(1), 23–36.

Berns, G. S., Capra, C. M., Chappelow, J. (2007). Nonlinear neurological weighting functions for aversive outcomes. *NeuroImage*, *39*(4), 2047–2057.

Berridge, K. C. (2001). Irrational pursuits: Hyperincentives from a visceral brain. In I. Brocas, J. D. Carillo (Eds), *The Psychology of Economic Decisions* (pp. 17–40). Oxford: Oxford University Press.

———. (2007). The debate over dopamine's role in reward: The case for incentive salience. *Psychopharmacology*, *191*(3), 391–431.

Berridge, K. C., Robinson, T. E. (1998). What is the role of dopamine in reward: Hedonic impact, reward learning, or incentive salience? *Brain Research Reviews*, *28*(3), 309–369.

Beshears, J., Choi, J. J., Laibson, D., Madrian, B. C. (2008). How are preferences revealed? *Journal of Public Economics*, *92*(8–9), 1787–1794.

———. (2013). Simplification and saving. *Journal of Economic Behavior and Organization*, *95*(November), 130–145.

Bewley, T. F. (1998). Why not cut pay? *European Economic Review*, *42*, 459–490.

Bi, L., Montalto, C. (2005). Is there a credit card puzzle? An exploratory study. *Consumer Interests Annual*, *51*, 72.

Biais, B., Weber, M. (2009). Hindsight bias, risk perception, and investment performance. *Management Science*, *55*(6), 1018–1029.

Bilgin, B., LeBoeuf, R. (2010). Looming losses in future time perception. *Journal of Marketing Research*, *47*(3), 520–530.

Binmore, K. (1999). Why experiment in economics? *Economic Journal*, *109*(453), 16–24.

Binmore, K., Shaked, A. (2010a). Experimental economics: Where next? *Journal of Economic Behavior and Organization*, *73*(1), 87–100.

———. (2010b). Experimental economics: Where next? A Brief Rejoinder. *Journal of Economic Behavior and Organization*, *73*(1), 120–121.

Binmore, K., Shaked, A., Sutton, J. (1985). Testing noncooperative bargaining theory: A preliminary study. *American Economic Review*, *75*(5), 1178–1180.

———. (1989). An outside option experiment. *Quarterly Journal of Economics*, *104*(4), 753–770.

Birbaumer, N., Veit, R., Lotze, M., Erb, M., Hermann, C., Grodd, W., Flor, H. (2005). Deficient fear conditioning in psychopathy: A functional magnetic resonance imaging study. *Archives of General Psychiatry*, *62*(7), 799–805.

Birks, J. B. (1962). *Rutherford at Manchester*. New York: W.A. Benjamin.

Birnbaum, M. H. (1997). Violations of monotonicity in judgment and decision making. In A. A. J. Marley (Ed.), *Choice, Decision and Measurement: Essays in Honor of R. Duncan Luce* (pp. 73–100). Mahwah, NJ: Erlbaum.

———. (1999). Paradoxes of Allais, stochastic dominance, and decision weights. In J. C. Shanteau, B. A. Mellers, D. Schum (Eds), *Decision Science and Technology: Reflections on the Contributions of Ward Edwards* (pp. 27–52). Norwell, MA: Kluwer Academic.

———. (2004). Causes of Allais common consequence paradoxes: An experimental dissection. *Journal of Mathematical Psychology*, *48*, 87–106.

———. (2006). Evidence against prospect theories in gambles with positive, negative, and mixed consequences. *Journal of Economic Psychology*, *27*, 737–761.

———. (2007). Tests of branch splitting and branch-splitting independence in Allais paradoxes with positive and mixed consequences. *Organizational Behavior and Human Decision Processes*, *102*(2), 154–173.

———. (2008). New paradoxes of risky decision making. *Psychological Review*, *115*(2), 463–501.

Birnbaum, M. H., Bahra, J. (2007). Gain-loss separability and coalescing in risky decision making. *Management Science*, *53*(6), 1016–1028.

Birnbaum, M. H., Navarrete, J. B. (1998). Testing descriptive utility theories: Violations of stochastic dominance and cumulative independence. *Journal of Risk and Uncertainty*, *17*(1), 49–78.

Birnbaum, M. H., Patton, J. N., Lott, M. K. (1999). Evidence against rank-dependent utility theories: Tests of cumulative independence, interval independence, stochastic dominance, and transitivity. *Organizational Behavior and Human Decision Processes*, *77*(1), 44–83.

Birnbaum, M. H., Stegner, S. E. (1979). Source credibility in social judgment: Bias, expertise, and the judge's point of view. *Journal of Personality and Social Psychology*, *37*(1), 48–74.

Birnbaum, M. H., Zimmermann, J. M. (1998). Buying and selling prices of investments: Configural weight model of interactions predicts violations of joint independence. *Organizational Behavior and Human Decision Processes*, *74*(2), 145–187.

Blanchflower, D. G., Oswald, A. J. (2016). Antidepressants and age: A new form of evidence for U-shaped well-being through life. *Journal of Economic Behavior and Organization*, *127*, 46–58.

Blaug, M. (1992). *The Methodology of Economics. Or, How Economists Explain* (2nd ed.). Cambridge: Cambridge University Press.

———. (2001). No history of ideas, please, we're economists. *Journal of Economic Perspectives*, *15*(1), 145–164.

Bloomfield, R. (1994). Learning a mixed strategy equilibrium in the laboratory. *Journal of Economic Behavior and Organization*, *25*(3), 411–436.

Blount, S. (1995). When social outcomes aren't fair: The effect of causal attributions on preferences. *Organizational Behavior and Human Decision Processes*, *63*(2), 131–144.

Bó, P. D., Fréchette, G. R. (2011). The evolution of cooperation in infinitely repeated games: Experimental evidence. *American Economic Review*, *101*(1), 411–429.

Bodner, R., Prelec, D. (1997). *The diagnostic value of actions in a self-signaling model*, MIT mimeo.

———. (2001). Self-signaling and diagnostic utility in everyday decision making. In I. Brocas, J. D. Carillo (Eds), *The Psychology of Economic Decisions* (pp. 105–123). New York: Oxford University Press.

Boehm, J. K., Kubzansky, L. D. (2012). The heart's content: The association between positive psychological well-being and cardiovascular health. *Psychological Bulletin, 138*(4), 655–691.

Böhm-Bawerk, E. (1889). *Capital and Interest* (1970th ed.). South Holland, IL: Libertarian Press.

Bohnet, I., Frey, B. (1999). The sound of silence in prisoner's dilemma and dictator games. *Journal of Economic Behavior and Organization*, *38*(1), 43–57.

Boles, T. L., Messick, D. M. (1995). A reverse outcome bias: The influence of multiple reference points on the evaluation of outcomes and decisions. *Organizational Behavior and Human Decision Processes*, *61*(3), 262–275.

Bolles, R. C. (1975). *The Theory of Motivation* (2nd ed). New York: Harper and Row.

Bolton, G. E. (1991). A comparative model of bargaining: Theory and evidence. *American Economic Review*, *81*(5), 1096–1136.

Bolton, G. E., Katok, E., Zwick, R. (1998). Dictator game giving: Rules of fairness versus acts of kindness. *International Journal of Game Theory*, *27*(2), 269–299.

Bolton, G. E., Ockenfels, A. (2000). ERC: A theory of equity, reciprocity, and competition. *American Economic Review*, *90*(1), 166–193.

Bolton, G. E., Zwick, R. (1995). Anonymity versus punishment in ultimatum bargaining. *Games and Economic Behavior*, *10*(1), 95–121.

Bonatti, A., Hörner, J. (2011). Collaborating. *American Economic Review*, *101*(2), 632–663.

Bonau, S. (2017). A case for behavioural game theory. *Journal of Game Theory*, *6*(1), 7–14.

Boone, J. L. (1998). The evolution of magnanimity: When is it better to give than to receive? *Human Nature*, *9*(1), 1–21.

Bordalo, P., Gennaioli, N., Shleifer, A. (2012). Salience theory of choice under risk. *Quarterly Journal of Economics. 127*(3) 1243–1285.

Bose, S., Ladley, D., Li, X. (2016), The Role of Hormones in Financial Markets (March 7). Available at SSRN: https://ssrn.com/abstract=2743087 or http://dx.doi.org/10.2139/ssrn.2743087.

Bostedt, G., Brännlund, R. (2012). Rationality, fairness and the cost of distrust. *Journal of Socio-Economics*, *41*(4), 345–349.

Bostic, R., Gabriel, S, Painter, G. (2006). *Housing wealth, financial wealth, and consumption: New evidence from microdata*. Lusk Center for Real Estate, University of Southern California.

Bottan, N. L., Perez Truglia, R. (2011). Deconstructing the hedonic treadmill: Is happiness autoregressive? *Journal of Socio-Economics*, *40*(3), 224–236.

Bowles, S., Gintis, H. (2004). The evolution of strong reciprocity: cooperation in heterogeneous populations. *Theoretical Population Biology*, *65*(1), 17–28.

———. (2013). *A Cooperative Species*. Princeton: Princeton University Press.

Bowman, D., Minehart, D., Rabin, M. (1999). Loss-aversion in a savings model. *Journal of Economic Behavior and Organization*, *38*(2), 155–178.

Brandstätter, E., Gigerenzer, G., Hertwig, R. (2006). The priority heuristic: Making choices without trade-offs. *Psychological Review*, *113*(2), 409–432.

———. (2008). Risky choice with heuristics: Reply to Birnbaum. *Psychological Review*, *115*(1), 281–290.

Brehm, J. W. (1966). *A theory of psychological reactance*. New York: Academic Press.

Brickman, P., Campbell, D. T. (1971). Hedonic relativism and planning the good society. In M. H. Appley (Ed.) (pp. 287–305). New York: Academic Press.

Brickman, P., Coates, D., Janoff-Bulman, R. (1978). Lottery winners and accident victims: Is happiness relative? *Journal of Personality and Social Psychology*, *36*(8), 917–927.

Brigden, N., Häubl, M. (2012). Slow sinkers are the real stinkers: Why a plummeting stock price can be better for investors than a gradual decline. In. In Z. Gürhan-Canli, C. Otnes, R. Zhu (Eds), *NA – Advances in Consumer Research* (Vol. 40, pp. 743–744). Duluth, MN: Association for Consumer Research.

Brocas, I., Carrillo, J. D. (2004). Entrepreneurial boldness and excessive investment. *Journal of Economics and Management Strategy*, *13*(2), 321–350.

———. (2008a). The brain as a hierarchical organization. *American Economic Review*, *98*(4), 1312–1346.

———. (2008b). Theories of the mind. *American Economic Review*, *98*(2), 175–180.

Brookshire, D., Coursey, D. (1987). Measuring the value of a public good: An empirical comparison of elicitation procedures. *American Economic Review*, *77*(4), 554–566.

Brosnan, S. F. (2008). Inequity and prosocial behavior in chimpanzees. In E. V. Lonsdorf, S. R. Ross, T. Matsuzawa (Eds), *The Mind of the Chimpanzee* (pp. 282–295). Chicago: University of Chicago Press.

Brosnan, S. F., de Waal, F. B. M. (2003). Monkeys reject unequal pay. *Nature*, *425*, 297–299.

Brough, A. R., Chernev, A. (2012). When opposites detract: Categorical reasoning and subtractive valuations of product combinations. *Journal of Consumer Research*, *39*(2), 399–414.

Brown, A. L., Camerer, C. F., Lovallo, D. (2012). To review or not review? Limited strategic thinking at the box office. *American Economic Review*, *4*(2), 1–28.

Brown, G. D. A., Wood, A. M., Ogden, R. S., Maltby, J. (2014). Do student evaluations of university reflect inaccurate beliefs or actual experience? A relative rank model. *Journal of Behavioral Decision Making*, *28*(1), 14–26.

Brown, G. W. (1951). Iterative solution of games by fictitious play. In T. C. Koopmans (Ed.), *Activity Analysis of Production and Allocation* (pp. 374–376). New York: Wiley.

Browning, M., Behrens, T. E., Jocham, G., O'Reilly, J. X., Bishop, S. J. (2015). Anxious individuals have difficulty learning the causal statistics of aversive environments. *Nature Neuroscience*, *18*(4), 590–596.

Bruno, P., Melnyk, V., Völckner, F. (2017). Temperature and emotions: Effects of physical temperature on responses to emotional advertising. *International Journal of Research in Marketing*, 34(1), 302–320.

Bucciol, A., Houser, D., Piovesan, M. (2010). Willpower in children and adults: A survey of results and economic implications. *International Review of Economics*, 57(3), 259–267.

Bucciol, A., Landini, F., Piovesan, M. (2013). Unethical behavior in the field: Demographic characteristics and beliefs of the cheater. *Journal of Economic Behavior and Organization*, 93, 248–257.

Bucciol, A., Piovesan, M. (2011). Luck or cheating? A field experiment on honesty with children. *Journal of Economic Psychology,* 32(1), 73–78.

Buchan, N. R., Croson, R. T. A., Johnson, E. J. (2004). When do fair beliefs influence bargaining behavior? Experimental bargaining in Japan and the United States. *Journal of Consumer Research*, *31*(1), 181–190.

Buehler, R., Griffin, D., Ross, M. (1994). Exploring the planning fallacy: Why people underestimate their task completion times. *Journal of Personality and Social Psychology*, *67*(3), 366–381.

Bunting, D. (2009). The saving decline: Macro-facts, micro-behavior. *Journal of Economic Behavior and Organization*, *70*(1/2), 282–295.

Burger, N., Charness, G., Lynham, J. (2011). Field and online experiments in self-control. *Journal of Economic Behavior and Organization*, 77(3), 393–404.

Burgstahler, D., Dichev, I. (1997). Earnings management to avoid earnings decreases and losses. *Journal of Accounting and Economics*, *24*(1), 99–126.

Burnham, T. C. (2007). High-testosterone men reject low ultimatum game offers. *Proceedings of the Royal Society B: Biological Sciences*, *274*(1623), 2327–2330.

Burnham, T. C., Phelan, J. (2001). *Mean Genes: Can We Tame Our Primal Instincts?* London: Simon and Schuster.

Burson, K. A., Larrick, R. P., Klayman, J. (2005). Judgments of performance: The relative, the absolute, and the in-between. *Working Paper*, No. 1015, Ross School of Business, University of Michigan.

Burton, Marie (2010). *Keeping the Plates Spinning: Perceptions of Payday Loans in Great Britain*. London: Consumer Focus.

Bushman, B. J., Moeller, S. J., Konrath, S., Crocker, J. (2012). Investigating the link between liking versus wanting self-esteem and depression in a nationally representative sample of American adults. *Journal of Personality*, *80*(5), 1453–1469.

Buss, D. M. (1999). *Evolutionary Psychology: The New Science of the Mind*. Needham Heights, MA: Allyn and Bacon.

Busse, M. R., Pope, D. G., Pope, J. C., Silva-Risso, J. (2015). The psychological effect of weather on car purchases. *The Quarterly Journal of Economics*, *130*(1), 371–414.

Butler, D. J., Loomes, G. C. (2007). Imprecision as an account of the preference reversal phenomenon. *American Economic Review*, *97*(1), 277–297.

Cai, F., Bagchi, R., Gauri, D. K. (2016). Boomerang effects of low price discounts: How low price discounts affect purchase propensity. *Journal of Consumer Research*, *42*(5), 804–816.

Camerer, C. F. (1989). An experimental test of several generalised utility theories. *Journal of Risk and Uncertainty*, *2*(1), 61–104.

———. (1992). Recent tests of generalizations of expected utility theories. In W. Edwards (Ed.) *Utility Theories: Measurement and Applications* (pp. 207–251), Dordrecht: Kluwer Academic, 207–251.

———. (1997). Progress in behavioral game theory. *Journal of Economic Perspectives*, *11*(4), 167–188.

———. (2000). Prospect theory in the wild: Evidence from the field. In D. Kahneman, A. Tversky (Eds), *Choices, Values, and Frames* (pp. 288–300). New York: Cambridge University Press and Russell Sage.

———. (2003). *Behavioral Game Theory: Experiments in Strategic Interaction*. New York: Russell Sage Foundation.

———. (2005). Three cheers – psychological, theoretical, empirical – for loss-aversion. *Journal of Marketing Research*, *42*(2), 129–133.

———. (2009). Behavioral game theory and the neural basis of strategic choice. In P. W. Glimcher, C. F. Camerer, E. Fehr, R. A. Poldrack (Eds), *Neuroeconomics: Decision-Making and the Brain* (pp. 193–206). London: Academic Press.

Camerer, C. F., Babcock, L., Loewenstein, G., Thaler, R. H. (1997). Labor supply of New York city cabdrivers: One day at a time. *Quarterly Journal of Economics*, *112*(2), 407–441.

Camerer, C. F., Dreber, A., Forsell, E., Ho, T., Huber, J., Johanneson, M., Kirchler, M., Almenberg, J., Altmejd, A., Chan, T., Heikensten, E., Holzmeister, F., Imai, T., Isaksson, S., Nave, G., Pfeiffer, T., Razen, M., Wu, H. (2016). Evaluating replicability of laboratory experiments in economics. *Science, 351*(6280), 1433–1436.

Camerer, C. F., Ho, T. (1994). Violations of the betweenness axiom and nonlinearity in probability. *Journal of Risk and Uncertainty*, *8*, 167–196.

———. (1999a). Experience-weighted attraction learning in games: Estimates from weak-link games. In D. Budescu, I. Erev, R. Zwick (Eds), *Games and Human Behavior: Essays in Honor of Amnon Rapaport* (pp. 31–52). Mahwah, NJ: Erlbaum.

———. (1999b). Experience-weighted attraction learning in normal-form games. *Econometrica*, *67*, 827–874.

Camerer, C. F., Ho, T., Chong, K. (2004). A cognitive hierarchy model of games. *Quarterly Journal of Economics*, *119*(3), 861–898.

———. (2002). Sophisticated experience-weighted attraction learning and strategic teaching in repeated games. *Journal of Economic Theory*, *104*(1), 137–188.

Camerer, C. F., Hogarth, R. M. (1999). The effects of financial incentives in experiments: a review and capital-labor-production framework. *Journal of Risk and Uncertainty*, *19*(1–3), 7–42.

Camerer, C. F., Johnson, E., Rymon, T., Sen, S. (1994). Cognition and framing in sequential bargaining for gains and losses. In K. Binmore, A. Kirman, P. Tani (Eds), *Frontiers of Game Theory* (pp. 27–47). Cambridge, MA: MIT Press.

Camerer, C. F., Kahneman, D., Tversky, A. (2000). Prospect theory in the wild: Evidence from the field. In D. Kahneman, A. Tversky (Eds), *Choices, Values, and Frames* (pp. 288–300). New York: Cambridge University Press.

Camerer, C. F., Loewenstein, G. (1993). Information, fairness, and efficiency in bargaining. In B. Mellers, J. Baron (Eds) *Psychological Perspectives on Justice: Theory and Applications* (pp. 155–179). Cambridge: Cambridge University Press.

———. (2004). Behavioral Economics: Past, Present and Future. In C. F. Camerer, G. Loewenstein, M. Rabin (Eds), *Advances in Behavioral Economics* (pp. 3–51). Princeton: Princeton University Press.

Camerer, C. F., Loewenstein, G., Prelec, D. (2005). Neuroeconomics: How neuroscience can inform economics. *Journal of Economic Literature*, *43*(1), 9–64.

Camerer, C. F., Lovallo, D. (1999). Overconfidence and excess entry: an experimental approach. *American Economic Review*, *89*(1), 306–318.

Camerer, C. F., Weigelt, K. (1988). Experimental tests of a sequential equilibrium reputation model. *Econometrica*, *56*(1), 1–36.

Cameron, L. A. (1999). Raising the stakes in the ultimatum game: Experimental evidence from Indonesia. *Economic Inquiry*, *37*(1), 47–59.

Campbell, R., Sawden, L. (Eds). (1985). *Paradoxes of Rationality and Cooperation*. Vancouver: University of British Columbia Press.

Canova, F., De Nicoló, G. (2003). The properties of the equity premium and the risk-free rate: an investigation across time and countries. *International Monetary Fund Staff Papers*, *50*(2), 222–249.

Caplin, A., Dean, M. (2008). Economic insights from 'neuroeconomic' data. *American Economic Review*, *98*(2), 169–174.

———. (2009). Axiomatic neuroeconomics. In P. W. Glimcher, C. F. Camerer, E. Fehr, R. A. Poldrack (Eds), *Neuroeconomics: Decision-Making and the Brain* (pp. 21–31). London: Academic Press.

Caplin, A., Dean, M., Glimcher, P. W., Rutledge, R. B. (2010). Measuring beliefs and rewards: A neuroeconomic approach. *Quarterly Journal of Economics*, *125*(3), 923–960.

Cappelen, A. W., Konow, J., Sørensen, E. Ø., Tungodden, B. (2013). Just luck: An experimental study of risk-taking and fairness. *American Economic Review*, *103*(4), 1398–1413.

Carrillo, J. D. (2004). To be consumed with moderation. *European Economic Review*, *49*(1), 99–111.

Caroll, G. D., Choi, J. J., Laibson, D., Madrian, B. C., Metrick, A. (2009). Optimal defaults and active decisions. *Quarterly Journal of Economics*, *12*(4), 1639–1674.

Carpenter, J. P. (2003). Bargaining outcomes as the result of coordinated expectations. *Journal of Conflict Resolution*, *47*(2), 119–139.

Carpenter, J. P., Bowles, S., Gintis, H., Hwang, S.-H. (2009). Strong reciprocity and team production: Theory and evidence. *Journal of Economic Behavior and Organization*, *71*(2), 221–232.

Carré, J. M., McCormick, C. M., Mondloch, C. J. (2009). Facial structure is a reliable cue of aggressive behavior. *Psychological Science*, *20*(10), 1194–1198.

Carter, J. R., Irons, M. D. (1991). Are economists different, and if so, why? *Journal of Economic Perspectives*, *5*, 171–177.

Caruso, E. M., Waytz, A., Epley, N. (2010). The intentional mind and the hot hand: Perceiving intentions makes streaks seem likely to continue. *Cognition*, *116*(1), 149–153.

Casari, M., Luini, L. (2009). Cooperation under alternative punishment institutions: An experiment. *Journal of Economic Behavior and Organization*, *71*(2), 273–282.

Cason, T. N., Mui, V.-L. (1998). Social influence and the strategy method in the sequential dictator game. *Journal of Mathematical Psychology*, *42*(2-3), 248–265.

Casscells, W., Schoenberger, A., Graboys, T. (1978). Interpretation by physicians of clinical laboratory results. *New England Journal of Medicine*, *299*(18), 999–1001.

Cavalli-Sforza, L. L., Feldman, M. W. (1981). *Cultural Transmission and Evolution*. Princeton: Princeton University Press.

Cavalli-Sforza, L. L., and Feldman, M. W. (1982). Theory and observation in cultural transmission. *Science*, *218*(4567), 19–27.

Cawley, J., Meyerhoefer, C. (2012). The medical care costs of obesity: An instrumental variables approach. *Journal of Health Economics*, *31*(1), 219–230.

CFA (Consumer Finance Association). (2015). *A Modern Credit Revolution: An Analysis of the Short-term Credit Market*. London: CFA. Retrieved from www.cfa-uk.co.uk/wp-content/uploads/2016/11/SMF-Report-AKT10796.pdf.

Chabris, C. F., Laibson, D., Morris, C. L., Schuldt, J. P., Taubinsky, D. (2008). Individual laboratory-measured discount rates predict field behavior. *Journal of Risk and Uncertainty*, *37*(2–3), 237–269.

Chagnon, N. A. (1983). *Yanomamo: The Fierce People* (3rd ed). New York: Holt, Rinehart and Winston.

———. (1988). Life histories, blood revenge, and warfare in a tribal population. *Science*, *239*(4843), 985–992.

———. (1990). Reproductive and somatic conflicts of interest in the genesis of violence and warfare among tribesmen. In J. Haas (Ed.), *The Anthropology of War* (pp. 77–104). Cambridge: Cambridge University Press.

Chakravarti, D., Krish, R., Pallab, P., Srivastava, J. (2002). Partitioned presentation of multicomponent bundle prices: Evaluation, choice and underlying processing effects. *Journal of Consumer Psychology*, *12*(3), 215–229.

Chan, E. Y., Saqib, N. (2010). Justification of hedonic consumption pre- vs. post-consuming. Paper presented at the Southern Ontario Behavioural Decision Research Conference, Schulich School of Business, York University, Toronto: SSRN. Retrieved from http://dx.doi.org/10.2139/ssrn.1570325.

Chang, C. J., Yen, S.-H., Duh, R.-R. (2002). An empirical examination of competing theories to explain the framing effect in accounting-related decisions. *Behavioral Research in Accounting*, *14*(1), 35–64.

Chang, S. W. C., Gariépy, J.-F., Platt, M. L. (2013). Neuronal reference frames for social decisions in primate frontal cortex. *Nature Neuroscience*, *16*(2), 243–250.

Chang, T. Y., Solomon, D. H., Westerfield, M. M. (2016). Looking for Someone to Blame: Delegation, Cognitive Dissonance, and the Disposition Effect. *Journal of Finance*, *71*(1), 267–302.

Chapman, D. A. (2002). Does intrinsic habit formation actually resolve the equity premium puzzle. *Review of Economic Dynamics*, *5*(3), 618–645.

Chapman, G. B. (1996). Temporal discounting and utility for health and money. *Journal of Experimental Psychology: Learning, Memory, Cognition*, *22*(3), 771–791.

———. (2000). Preferences for improving and declining sequences of health outcomes. *Journal of Behavioral Decision Making*, *13*(2), 203–218.

Chapman, G. B., Elstein, A. S. (1995). Valuing the future: Temporal discounting of health and money. *Medical Decision Making*, *15*(4), 373–386.

Chapman, G. B., Nelson, R., Hier, D. B. (1999). Familiarity and time preferences: Decision making about treatments for migraine headaches and Crohn's disease. *Journal of Experimental Psychology: Applied*, *5*(1), 17–34.

Charness, G., Gneezy, U. (2008). What's in a name? Anonymity and social distance in dictator and ultimatum games. *Journal of Economic Behavior and Organization*, *68*(1), 29–35.

Charness, G., Gneezy, U., Kuhn, M. A. (2013). Experimental methods: Extra-laboratory experiments-extending the reach of experimental economics. *Journal of Economic Behavior and Organization*, *91*(July), 93–100.

Charness, G., Haruvy, E., Sonsino, D. (2007). Social distance and reciprocity: An internet experiment. *Journal of Economic Behavior and Organization*, *63*(1), 88–103.

Charness, G., Rabin, M. (2002). Understanding social preferences with simple tests. *Quarterly Journal of Economics*, *117*(3), 817–869.

Chatterjee, P., Irmak, C., Rose, R. L. (2013). The endowment effect as self-enhancement in response to threat. *Journal of Consumer Research*, *40*(3), 460–476.

Chaudhuri, A. (1998). The ratchet principle in a principal agent problem with unknown costs: An experimental analysis. *Journal of Economic Behavior and Organization*, *37*(3), 291–304.

Cheema, A., Soman, D. (2002). Consumer responses to unexpected price changes: Affective reactions and mental accounting effects. *Advances in Consumer Research*, *29*, 342.

———. (2006). Malleable mental accounting: The effect of flexibility on the justification of attractive spending and consumption decisions. *Journal of Consumer Psychology*, *16*(1), 33–44.

———. (2008). The effects of partitions on controlling consumption. *Journal of Marketing Research*, *45*(6), 665–675.

Chen, C., Burton, M., Greenberger, E., Dmitrevea, J. (1999). Population migration and the variation of dopamine D4 receptor (DRD4) allele frequencies around the globe. *Evolution and Human Behavior*, *20*(5), 309–324.

Chen, H., Marmorstein, H., Tsiros, M., Rao, A. R. (2012). When more is less: The impact of base value neglect on consumer preferences for bonus packs over price discounts. *Journal of Marketing*, *76*(4), 64–77.

Chen, H., Rao, A. R. (2007). When two plus two is not equal to four: Errors in processing multiple percentage changes. *Journal of Consumer Research*, *34*(3), 327–340.

Chen, M. K. (2013). The effect of language on economic behavior: Evidence from savings rates, health behaviors, and retirement assets. *American Economic Review*, *103*(2), 690–731.

Chen, P., Myers, C. G., Kopelman, S., Garcia, S. M. (2012). The hierarchical face: Higher rankings lead to less cooperative looks. *Journal of Applied Psychology*, *97*(2), 479–486.

Cherry, T. L., Frykblom, P., Shogren, J. F. (2002). Hardnose the dictator. *American Economic Review*, *92*(4), 1218–1221.

Chetty, R., Friedman, J. N., Leth-Petersen, S., Nielsen, T. H., Olsen, T. (2014). Active vs. passive decisions and crowd-out in retirement savings accounts: Evidence from Denmark. *The Quarterly Journal of Economics*, *129*(3), 1141–1219.

Chew, S. H. (1983). A generalization of the quasilinear mean with applications to the measurement of income inequality and decision theory resolving the Allais paradox. *Econometrica*, *51*(4), 1065–1092.

Chew, S. H., Epstein, L. G., Segal, U. (1991). Mixture symmetry and quadratic utility. *Econometrica*, *59*(1), 139–163.

Chew, S. H., MacCrimmon, K. (1979). Alpha-nu choice theory: A generalisation of expected utility theory. *Working Paper*, No. 669, Faculty of Commerce and Business Administration, University of British Columbia.

Chiappori, P.-A., Levitt, S., Groseclose, T. (2003). Testing mixed strategy equilibria when players are heterogeneous: The case of penalty kicks. *American Economic Review*, *92*(4), 1138–1151.

The Children's Society (2016). *The Good Childhood Report*. London: The Children's Society.

Choi, J. J., Laibson, D., Madrian, B. (2009a). Mental accounting in portfolio choice: Evidence from a flypaper effect. *American Economic Review*, *99*(5), 2085–2095.

———. (2009b). Reducing the complexity costs of 401(k) participation through Quick Enrollmentt™. In D. A. Wise (Ed.), *Developments in the Economics of Aging* (pp. 57–82). Chicago: University of Chicago Press.

Choi, J., Li, Y. (2014). When paying $92 plus $5 shipping is acceptable but paying $97 is not: The role of justification on the effectiveness of partitioned pricing. In J. Cotte, S. Wood (Eds), *NA – Advances in Consumer Research* (Vol. 42, pp. 432–433). Duluth, MN: Association for Consumer Research.

Choi, S. (2012). A cognitive hierarchy model of learning in networks. *Review of Economic Design, 16*(2), 215–250.

Christensen-Szalanski, J. J. (1984). Discount functions and the measurement of patients' values: Women's decisions during child birth. *Medical Decision Making, 4*(1), 47–58.

Chu, C. Y. C., Chien, H.-K., Lee, R. D. (2010). The evolutionary theory of time preferences and intergenerational transfers. *Journal of Economic Behavior and Organization, 76*(3), 451–464.

Chung, D., Christopoulos, G. I., King-Casas, B., Ball, S. B., Chiu, P. H. (2015). Social signals of safety and risk confer utility and have asymmetric effects on observers' choices. *Nature Neuroscience, 18*(6), 912–916.

Chung, S. H., Herrnstein, R. J. (1967). Choice and delay of reinforcement. *Journal of the Experimental Analysis of Behavior, 10*(1), 67–74.

Cialdini, R. B. (1984). *Influence*. New York: Morrow.

Clark, A. E., Frijters, P., Shields, M. A. (2008). Relative income, happiness, and utility: An explanation for the Easterlin paradox and other puzzles. *Journal of Economic Literature, 46*(1), 95–144.

Clark, A. E., Oswald, A. J. (1996). Satisfaction and comparison income. *Journal of Public Economics, 61*(3), 359–381.

Clithero, J. A., Tankersley, D., Huettel, S. A. (2008). Foundations of neuroeconomics: From philosophy to practice. *PLoS Biology, 6*(11), 2348–2353.

Clotfelter, C. T., Cook, P. J. (1993). The gambler's fallacy in lottery play. *Management Science, 39*(12), 1521–1525.

Coates, J. M., Herbert, J. (2008). Endogenous steroids and financial risk taking on a London trading floor. *Proceedings of the National Academy of Sciences*, 105(16), 6167–6172.

Coats, A. W. (1976). Economics and psychology: A resurrection Story. In P. E. Earl (Ed.), *Psychological Economics* (pp. 211–225). Springer: Dordrecht.

Coelho do Vale, R., Pieters, R., Zeelenberg, M. (2016). The benefits of behaving badly on occasion: Successful regulation by planned hedonic deviations. *Journal of Consumer Psychology, 26*(1), 17–28.

Colby, H., Li, M., Chapman, G. (2014). Carrots by default: Are healthy defaults a blessing or a curse? In S. Wood, J. Cotte (Eds), *NA - Advances in Consumer Research* (Vol. 42, pp. 439–442). Duluth, MN: Association for Consumer Research. Retrieved from www.acrwebsite.org/volumes/1018031/volumes/v42/NA-42.

Coller, M., Williams, M. B. (1999). Eliciting individual discount rates. *Experimental Economy, 2*(2), 107–127.

Comerford, D. A., Ubel, P. A. (2013). Effort aversion: Job choice and compensation decisions overweight effort. *Journal of Economic Behavior and Organization, 92*, 152–162.

Conlin, M., O'Donoghue, T., Vogelsang, T. J. (2007). Projection bias in catalog orders. *American Economic Review, 97*(4), 1217–1249.

Conlisk, J. (1989). Three variants on the Allais example. *American Economic Review, 79*, 392–407.

Constantinides, G. M. (1990). Habit formation: A resolution of the equity premium puzzle, term premium, and risk-free rate puzzles. *Journal of Political Economy*, *98*(3), 519–543.

Cooper, D., Garvin, S., Kagel, J. (1997a). Adaptive learning versus equilibrium refinements in an entry limit pricing game. *Economic Journal*, *107*(442), 553–575.

———. (1997b). Signalling and adaptive learning in an entry limit pricing game. *RAND Journal of Economics*, *28*(4), 662–683.

Cooper, R. W., DeJong, D., Forsythe, R., Ross, T. (1990). Selection criteria in coordination games: Some experimental results. *American Economic Review*, *80*(1), 218–33.

———. (1994). Alternative institutions for resolving coordination problems: Experimental evidence on forward induction and preplay communication. In J. Friedman (Ed.), *Problems of Coordination in Economic Activity*. Dordrecht: Kluwer.

Cosmides, L., Tooby, J. (1987). From evolution to behavior: Evolutionary psychology as the missing link. In J. Dupre (Ed.), *The latest on the best: Essays on evolution and optimality*. Cambridge, MA: The MIT Press.

———. (1992). Cognitive adaptations for social exchange. In J. Barkow, L. Cosmides, J. Tooby (Eds), *The Adapted Mind: Evolutionary Psychology and the Generation of Culture* (pp. 163–228). New York: Oxford University Press.

———. (1996). Are humans good intuitive statisticians after all? Rethinking some conclusions from the literature in judgment under uncertainty. *Cognition*, *58*(1), 1–73.

Costa, P. T., Jr., McCrae, R. R. (1984). Personality is a lifelong determinant of well-being. In C. Malatesta, C. Izard (Eds), *Affective Processes in Adult Development and Aging* (pp. 141–156). Beverly Hills, CA: Sage.

Costa-Gomes, M., Crawford, V., Broseta, B. (2001). Cognition and behavior in normal-form games: An experimental study. *Econometrica*, *69*(5), 1193–1235.

Costello, F., Watts, P. (2014). Surprisingly rational: Probability theory plus noise explains biases in judgment. *Psychological Review*, *121*(3), 463–480.

Coursey, D., Hovis, J., Schulze, W. (1987). The disparity between willingness to accept and willingness to pay measures of value. *Quarterly Journal of Economics*, *102*(3), 679–690.

Cowley, E. (2008). The perils of hedonic editing. *Journal of Consumer Research*, *35*(1), 71–84.

Cox, J. (2004). How to identify trust and reciprocity. *Games and Economic Behavior*, *46*(2), 260–281.

Cramton, P. (1992). Strategic delay in bargaining with two-sided uncertainty. *Review of Economic Studies*, *59*, 205–225.

Crawford, V. P., Gneezy, U., Rottenstreich, Y. (2008). The power of focal points is limited: Even minute payoff asymmetry may yield large coordination failures. *American Economic Review*, *98*(4), 1443–1458.

Crawford, V. P., Meng, J. (2011). New York City cabdrivers' labor supply revisited: Reference-dependent preferences with rational-expectations targets for hours and income. *American Economic Review*, *101*(5), 1912–1932.

Cronqvist, H., Thaler, R. H. (2004). Design choices in privatized social-security systems: Learning from the Swedish experience. *American Economic Review*, *94*(2), 424-428.

Croson, R. T. A. (1996). Information in ultimatum games: An experimental study. *Journal of Economic Behavior and Organization*, *30*(2), 197–212.

Croson, R. T. A., Konow, J. (2009). Social preferences and moral biases. *Journal of Economic Behavior and Organization*, *69*(3), 201–212.

Cross, K. P. (1977). Not can, but will college teaching be improved? *New Directions for Higher Education*, *17*, 1–15.

Cryder, C., Xiao, L. (2014). Spending credit like a windfall gain. In S. Wood, J. Cotte (Eds), *NA – Advances in Consumer Research Volume* (Vol. 42, pp. 32–35). Duluth, MN: Association for Consumer Research.

Cubitt, R. C., Starmer, C., Sugden, R. (2001). Discovered preferences and the experimental evidence of violations of expected utility theory. *Journal of Economic Methodology*, *3*(8), 385–414.

Cupchik, G. C., Leventhal, H. (1974). Consistency between expressive behavior and the evaluation of humorous stimuli: The role of sex and self-observation. *Journal of Personality and Social Psychology*, *30*, 429–442.

Daly, M., Wilson, M. (1988). *Homicide*. Hawthorne, NY: Aldine de Gruyter.

Damasio, A. R. (1994). *Descartes' Error: Emotion, Reason, and the Human Brain*. New York: Putnam Berkley.

———. (2009). Neuroscience and the emergence of neuroeconomics. In P. W. Glimcher, C. F. Camerer, E. Fehr, R. A. Poldrack (Eds), *Neuroeconomics: Decision-Making and the Brain* (pp. 207–214). London: Academic Press.

Damon, W. (1980). Patterns of change in children's social reasoning: A two-year longitudinal study. *Child Development*, *51*(4), 1010–1017.

Daniel, T. E., Seale, D. A., Rapoport, A. (1998). Strategic play and adaptive learning in the sealed-bid bargaining mechanism. *Journal of Mathematical Psychology*, *42*(2-3), 133–166.

Davidson, R. J. (1994). Asymmetric brain function, affective style, and psychopathology: The role of early experience and plasticity. *Development and Psychopathology*, *6*(04), 741–758.

Davis, D. F., Bagchi, R., Block, L. G. (2012). Alliteration alters: Phonetic overlap in promotional messages influences evaluations and choice. *Journal of Retailing*, *92*(1), 1–12.

Daw, N. D., Kakade, S., Dayan, P. (2002). Opponent reactions between serotonin and dopamine. *Neural Networks*, *15*(4-6), 603–616.

Dawber, T. R., Moore, F. E., Mann, G. V. (1957). II. Coronary heart disease in the Framingham Study. *American Journal of Public Health and the Nations Health*, *47*(4, Pt. 2), 4–24.

Dawkins, R. (1976). *The Selfish Gene*. Oxford: Oxford University Press.

———. (1986). *The Blind Watchmaker*. London: Longman.

De Bondt, W. F. M., Thaler, R. H. (1985). Does the stock market overreact? *Journal of Finance*, *40*(3), 793–805.

de Long, J., Shleifer, A., Summers, L., Waldmann, R. (1991). The survival of noise traders in financial markets. *The Journal of Business*, *64*(1), 1–19.

De Martino, B., Kumaran, D., Seymour, B., Dolan, R. J. (2006). Frames, biases and rational decision making in the human brain. *Science*, *313*(5787), 684–687.

de Mello, L., Kongsrud, P. M., Price, R. (2004). Saving behavior and the effectiveness of fiscal policy. OECD: Economics Department Working Papers, 397.

De Neve, J.-E., Christakis, N. A., Fowler, J. H., Frey, B. S. (2012). Genes, economics, and happiness. *Journal of Neuroscience, Psychology, and Economics*, *5*(4), 193–211.

de Quervain. D., Fischbacher, U., Treyer, V., Schellhammer, M., Schyder, U., Buck, A., Fehr, E. (2004). The neural basis of altruistic punishment. *Science, 305*(5688), 1254–1258.

de Vany, A. (2011). *The New Evolution Diet: The Smart Way to Lose Weight, Feel Great and Live Longer*. London: Vermillion.

Deacon, M. (2016). In a world of post-truth politics, Andrea Leadsom will make the perfect PM. *The Daily Telegraph*. July 9. Retrieved from www.telegraph.co.uk/news/2016/07/09/in-a-world-of-post-truth-politics-andrea-leadsom-will-make-the-p/.

Deaton, A., Stone, A. A. (2013). Two happiness puzzles. *American Economic Review, 103*(3), 591–597.

Deci, E. L., Koestner, R., Ryan, R. M. (1999). A meta-analytic review of experiments examining the effects of extrinsic rewards on intrinsic motivation. *Psychological Bulletin, 125*(6), 627–668.

Deck, C., Kimbrough, E. O. (2013). Do market incentives crowd out charitable giving? *Journal of Socio-Economics, 47*, 16–24.

Dehaene, S. (1992). Cross-linguistic regularities in the frequency of number words. *Cognition, 43*(1), 1–29.

Dekel, E., Ely, J. C., Yilankaya, O. (2007). Evolution of preferences. *Review of Economic Studies, 74*(3), 685–704.

DellaVigna, S. (2009). Psychology and economics: Evidence from the field. *Journal of Economic Literature, 47*(2), 315–72.

DellaVigna, S., Malmendier, U. (2004). Contract design and self-control: Theory and evidence. *Quarterly Journal of Economics, 119*(2), 353–402.

———. (2006). Paying not to go to the gym. *American Economic Review, 96*(3), 694–719.

Dennett, D. (1984). Cognitive wheels: The frame problem of AI. In C. Hookway (Ed.). Minds, Machines and Evolution (pp. 129–151). Cambridge: Cambridge University Press.

———. (1995). *Darwin's Dangerous Idea*. London: Penguin.

Dewitte, S., Bruyneel, S., Geyskens, K. (2009). Self-regulating enhances self-regulation in subsequent consumer decisions involving similar response conflicts. *Journal of Consumer Research, 36*(3), 394–405.

Dhar, R., Huber, J., Khan, U. (2007). The shopping momentum effect. *Journal of Marketing Research, 44*(4), 370–378.

Dhar, R., Wertenbroch, K. (2012). Self-signaling and the costs and benefits of temptation in consumer choice. *Journal of Marketing Research, 49*(1), 15–25.

Di Muro, F., Noseworthy, T. J. (2013). Money isn't everything, but it helps if it doesn't look used: How the physical appearance of money influences spending. *Journal of Consumer Research, 39*(6), 1330–1342.

Diamond, J. (1991). *The Third Chimpanzee: The Evolution and Future of the Human Animal*. New York: Harper Perennial.

———. (1997). *Guns, Germs, and Steel*. New York: Norton.

———. (2005). *Collapse: How Civilizations Choose to Fail or Succeed*. London: Penguin.

Diamond, P., Köszegi, B. (2003). Quasi-hyperbolic discounting and retirement. *Journal of Public Economics, 87*(9/10), 1839–1872.

Diener, E. (2000). Subjective well-being: The science of happiness and a proposal for a national index. *American Psychologist, 55*(1), 34–43.

Diener, E., Tay, L., Oishi, S. (2013). Rising income and the subjective well-being of nations. *Journal of Personality and Social Psychology*, *104*(2), 267–276.

Dixit, A., Nalebuff, B. (1991). *Thinking Strategically*. New York: Norton.

Dixon, N. F. (1976). *On the Psychology of Military Incompetence*. London: Jonathan Cape.

Do, A. M., Rupert, A. V., Wolford, G. (2008). Evaluations of pleasurable experiences: The peak–end rule. *Psychonomic Bulletin and Review*, *15*(1), 96–98.

Dobzhansky, T. (1973). Nothing in biology makes sense except in the light of evolution. *The American Biology Teacher*, *35*(3), 125–129.

Dogerlioglu-Demir, K., Koçaş, C. (2014). Seemingly incidental anchoring: The effect of incidental environmental anchors on consumers' willingness to pay. *Marketing Letters*, *26*(4), 607–618.

Dommer, S. L., Swaminathan, V. (2013). Explaining the endowment effect through ownership: The role of identity, gender, and self-threat. *Journal of Consumer Research*, *39*(5), 1034–1050.

Dougherty, M. R., Franco-Watkins, A. M., Thomas, R. (2008). Psychological plausibility of the theory of probabilistic mental models and the fast and frugal heuristics. *Psychological Review*, *115*(1), 199–213.

Drakopoulos, S. A., Katselidis, I. (2017). The relationship between psychology and economics: Insights from the history of economic thought. *MPRA Working Paper*, No. 77485. March.

Dreber, A., Hoffman, M., (2010). Biological basis of sex differences in risk aversion and competitiveness. Mimeo.

Drechsel-Grau, M., Schmid, K. D. (2014). Consumption-savings decisions under upward-looking comparisons. *Journal of Economic Behavior and Organization*, *106*(October), 254–268.

Drezner, D. W. (2016). Why the post-truth political era might be around for a while. *Washington Post*. June 16. Retrieved from www.washingtonpost.com/posteverything/wp/2016/06/16/why-the-post-truth-political-era-might-be-around-for-a-while/.

Drichoutis, A. C., Nayga, R. M. (2013). Eliciting risk and time preferences under induced mood states. *Journal of Socio-Economics*, *45*(August), 18–27.

Drumwright, M. E. (1992). A demonstration of anomalies in evaluations of bundling. *Marketing Letters*, *3*(4), 311–321.

Duesenberry, J. (1949). *Income, Saving, and the Theory of Consumer Behavior*. Cambridge, MA: Harvard University Press.

Duflo, E., Kremer, M., Robinson, J. (2011). Nudging farmers to use fertilizer: Theory and experimental evidence from Kenya. *American Economic Review*, *101*(6), 2350–2390.

Dufwenberg, M. (2002). Marital investment, time consistency and emotions. *Journal of Economic Behavior and Organization*, *48*(1), 57–69.

Dufwenberg, M., Gneezy, U. (2000). Price competition and market concentration: An experimental study. *International Journal of Industrial Organization*, *18*(2000), 7–22.

Dufwenberg, M., Kirchsteiger, G. (2004). A theory of sequential reciprocity. *Games and Economic Behavior*, *47*(2), 268–298.

Dugatkin, L. A. (1991). Dynamics of the tit for tat strategy during predator inspection in guppies. *Behavioral Ecology and Sociobiology*, *29*(2), 127–132.

Duh, H. I., Grubliauskiene, A., Dewitte, S. (2016). Pre-exposure to food temptation reduces subsequent consumption: A test of the procedure with a South-African sample. *Appetite*, *96*, 636–641.

Dulany, D. E., Hilton, D. J. (1991). Conversational implicature, conscious representation, and the conjunction fallacy. *Social Cognition*, *9*(1), 85–110.

Dunning, D. (2007). Self-image motives and consumer behaviour: how sacrosanct self-beliefs sway preferences in the marketplace. *Journal of Consumer Psychology*, *17*(4), 237–249.

Dunning, D., Anderson, J. E., Schlösser, T., Ehlebracht, D., Fetchenhauer, D. (2014). Trust at zero acquaintance: More a matter of respect than expectation of reward. *Journal of Personality and Social Psychology*, *107*(1), 122–141.

Dunning, D., Meyerowitz, J. A., Holzberg, A. D. (1989). Ambiguity and self-evaluation: The role of idiosyncratic trait definitions in self-serving assessments of ability. *Journal of Personality and Social Psychology*, *57*(6), 1082–1090.

Dutton, D. G., Aron, A. P. (1974). Some evidence for heightened sexual attraction under conditions of high anxiety. *Journal of Personality and Social Psychology*, *30*(4), 510–517.

Duxbury, D., Keasey, K., Zhang, H., Chow, S. L. (2005). Mental accounting and decision making: Evidence under reverse conditions where money is spent for time saved. *Journal of Economic Psychology*, *26*(4), 567–580.

Eagly, A., Chaiken, S. (1996). Attitude structure and function. In D. Gilbert, S. Fiske, G. Lindzey (Eds), *The Handbook of Social Psychology* (4th ed). New York: McGraw-Hill.

Earl, P. E. (1990). Economics and psychology: A survey. *Economic Journal*, *100*(402), 718–755.

Easterlin, R. A. (1974). Does economic growth improve the human lot? In P. A. David, W. R. Melvin (Eds), *Nations and Households in Economic Growth* (pp. 89–125). New York: Academic Press.

———. (1995). Will raising the incomes of all increase the happiness of all? *Journal of Economic Behavior and Organization*, *29*(1), 35–47.

———. (2001). Income and happiness: Towards a unified theory. *Economic Journal*, *111*(473), 464–484.

———. (2009). Lost in transition: Life satisfaction on the road to capitalism. *Journal of Economic Behavior and Organization*, *71*(2), 130–145.

Easterlin, R. A., McVey, L. A., Switek, M., Sawangfa, O., Zweig, J. S. (2010). The happiness-income paradox revisited. *Proceedings of the National Academy of Sciences*, *107*(52), 22463–22468.

Ebert, J. E. J., Prelec, D. (2007). The fragility of time: Time-insensitivity and valuation of the near and far future. *Management Science*, *53*(9), 1423–1438.

Eckel, C. C., El-Gamal, M. A., Wilson, R. K. (2009). Risk loving after the storm: A Bayesian-Network study of Hurricane Katrina evacuees. *Journal of Economic Behavior and Organization*, *69*(2), 110–124.

Eckel, C. C., Gintis, H. (2010). Blaming the messenger: Notes on the current state of experimental economics. *Journal of Economic Behavior and Organization*, *73*(1), 109–119.

Eckel, C. C., Grossman, P. (1996a). Altruism in anonymous dictator games. *Games and Economic Behavior*, *16*(2), 181–191.

———. (1996b). The relative price of fairness: Gender differences in a punishment game. *Journal of Economic Behavior and Organization*, *30*(2), 143–158.

———. (2001). Chivalry and solidarity in ultimatum games. *Economic Inquiry*, *39*(2), 171–188.

Economist. (2016a). Comradely capitalism: How America accidentally nationalised its mortgage market. *The Economist*. August 20. Retrieved from www.economist.

com/news/briefing/21705316-how-america-accidentally-nationalised-its-mortgage-market-comradely-capitalism.

———. (2016b). Post-truth politics: Art of the lie. *The Economist*. September 10. Retrieved from www.economist.com/news/leaders/21706525-politicians-have-always-lied-does-it-matter-if-they-leave-truth-behind-entirely-art.

———. (2016c). Illness as indicator: Local health outcomes predict Trumpward swings. *The Economist*. November 19. Retrieved from www.economist.com/news/united-states/21710265-local-health-outcomes-predict-trumpward-swings-illness-indicator.

Economist Intelligence Unit. (2014). *The Burden of Obesity: Its Relationship With Food Security*. London: The Economist. Retrieved from www.eiu.com/public/topical_report.aspx?campaignid=burdenobesity2014.

Edgeworth, F. Y. (1881). *Mathematical Psychics*. London: Kegan Paul.

Edmans, A., Garcia, D., Norli, O. (2007). Sports sentiment and stock returns. *Journal of Finance*, *62*(4), 1967–1998.

Edwards, W. (1954). The theory of decision making. *Psychological Bulletin*, *51*(4), 380–417.

———. (1955). The prediction of decisions among bets. *Journal of Experimental Psychology*, *50*(3), 201–214.

———. (1961). Behavioral decision theory. *Annual Review of Psychology*, *12*, 473–498.

———. (1962). Subjective probabilities inferred from decisions. *Psychological Review*, *69*(2), 109–135.

Egan Brad, L. C., Lakshminarayanan, V. R., Jordan, M. R., Phillips, W. C., Santos, L. R. (2016). The evolution and development of peak-end effects for past and prospective experiences. *Journal of Neuroscience, Psychology, and Economics*, *9*(1), 1–13.

Egan, D., Merkle, C., Weber, M. (2014). Second-order beliefs and the individual investor. *Journal of Economic Behavior and Organization*, *107*(November, Part B), 652–666.

Ehrlinger, J., Dunning, D. (2003). How chronic self-views influence (and potentially mislead) estimates of performance. *Journal of Personality and Social Psychology*, *84*(1), 5–17.

Eklund, A., Nichols, T. E., Knutsson, H. (2016). Cluster failure: Why fMRI inferences for spatial extent have inflated false-positive rates. *Proceedings of the National Academy of Sciences*, *113*(28), 7900–7905.

Ellsberg, D. (1961). Risk, ambiguity and the Savage axioms. *Quarterly Journal of Economics*, *75*(4), 643–669.

Elster, J. (1979). *Ulysses and the Sirens: Studies in Rationality and Irrationality*. Cambridge: Cambridge University Press.

———. (1985a). Rationality, morality, and collective action. *Ethics*, *96*(1), 136–55.

———. (1985b). Weakness of will and the free-rider problem. *Economics and Philosophy*, 1(2), 231–265.

———. (1989). When rationality fails. In K. Cook, M. Levi (Eds), *Limits of Rationality*. Chicago: University of Chicago Press.

———. (1998). Emotions and economic theory. *Journal of Economic Literature*, *36*(1), 47–74.

Emanuele, E., Brondino, N., Bertona, M., Re, S., Geroldi, D. (2008). Relationship between platelet serotonin content and rejections of unfair offers in the ultimatum game. *Neuroscience Letters*, *437*(2), 158–161.

Engel, C., Zhurakhovska, L. (2014). Conditional cooperation with negative externalities - An experiment. *Journal of Economic Behavior and Organization*, *108*(December, Part A), 252–260.

Engen, E. M., Gale, W. G., Uccello, C. E. (1999). The adequacy of household saving. *Brookings Papers on Economic Activity*, 2, 65–187.

Epley, N., Gneezy, A. (2007). The framing of financial windfalls and implications for public policy. *Journal of Socio-Economics*, *36*(1), 36–47.

Epley, N., Mak, D., Idson, L. (2006). Bonus or rebate? The impact of income framing on spending and saving. *Journal of Behavioral Decision Making*, *19*(3), 213–227.

Epstein, L. G., Zin, S. E. (1989). Substitution risk aversion, and the temporal behavior of consumption growth and asset returns: A theoretical framework. *Econometrica*, *57*(4), 937–969.

Epstein, L. H., Paluch, R., Smith, J. D., Sayette, M. (1997). Allocation of attentional resources during habituation to food cues. *Psychophysiology*, 34, 59–64.

Epstein, L. H., Saad, F. G., Giacomelli, A. M., Roemmich, J. N. (2005). Effects of allocation of attention on habituation to olfactory and visual food stimuli in children. *Physiology and Behavior*, *84*(2), 313–331.

Epstein, L. H., Temple, J. L., Roemmich, J. N., Bouton, M. E. (2009). Habituation as a determinant of food intake. *Psychological Review*, *116*(2), 384–407.

Epstein, S. (1994). Integration of the cognitive and the psychodynamic unconscious. *American Psychologist*, *49*(8), 709–724.

Ermisch, J., Gambetta, D. (2010). Do strong family ties inhibit trust? *Journal of Economic Behavior and Organization*, *75*(3), 365–376.

Estle, S. J., Green, L., Myerson, J., Holt, D. D. (2007). Discounting of monetary and directly consumable rewards. *Psychological Science*, *18*(1), 58–63.

Evangelidis, I., Levav, J. (2013). Prominence versus dominance: How relationships between alternatives drive decision strategy and choice. *Journal of Marketing Research*, *50*(6), 753–766.

Evans, D. J., Sezer, H. (2004). Social discount rates for six major countries. *Applied Economics Letters*, *11*, 557–560.

Evans, J., Over, D. E. (1996). *Rationality and Reasoning*. Hove: Psychology Press.

Evans, J. S. B. T. (2011). Dual-process theories of reasoning: Contemporary issues and developmental applications. *Developmental Review*, *31*(2–3), 86–102.

Evans, J. S. B. T., Stanovich, K. E. (2013). Dual-process theories of higher cognition. *Perspectives on Psychological Science*, *8*(3), 223–241.

Eyster, E., Rabin, M. (2014). Extensive imitation is irrational and harmful. *Quarterly Journal of Economics*, *129*(4), 1861–1898.

Fagley, N. S., Miller, P. M. (1987). The effects of decision framing on choice of risky versus certain options. *Organizational Behavior and Human Decision Processes*, *39*(2), 264–277.

———. (1997). Framing effects and arenas of choice: Your money or your life? *Organizational Behavior and Human Decision Processes*, *71*(3), 355–373.

Falk, A., Fehr, E., Fischbacher, U. (2001). Driving forces of informal sanctions. *Working Paper*, Institute for Empirical Research in Economics, University of Zürich.

———. (2008). Testing theories of fairness – Intentions matter. *Games and Economic Behavior*, *62*(1), 287–303.

Falk, A., Fischbacher, U. (2005). Modeling strong reciprocity. In H. Gintis, S. Bowles, R. Boyd, E. Fehr (Eds), *Moral Sentiments and Material Interests: The Foundations of Cooperation in Economic Life* (pp. 193–214). Cambridge, MA: MIT Press.

———. (2006). A theory of reciprocity. *Games and Economic Behavior*, *54*(2), 293–315.

Farber, H. S. (2005). Is tomorrow another day? The labor supply of New York City cab drivers. *Journal of Political Economy*, *113*(1), 46–82.

———. (2008). Reference-dependent preferences and labor supply: The case of New York City taxi drivers. *American Economic Review*, *98*(3), 1069–1082.

Farrell, H. (2012). The consequences of the internet for politics. *Annual Review of Political Science*, *15*(1), 35–52.

Faust, D., Hart, K. J., Guilmette, T. J. (1988). Pediatric malingering: The capacity of children to fake believable deficits on neuropsychological testing. *Journal of Consulting and Clinical Psychology*, *56*(4), 578–582.

Fedorikhin, A., Patrick, V. M. (2010). Positive mood and resistance to temptation: The interfering influence of elevated arousal. *Journal of Consumer Research*, *37*(4), 698–711.

Feenberg, J., Skinner, J. (1989). Sources of IRA saving. In L. Summers (Ed.), *Tax Policy and the Economy* (Vol. 3, pp. 25–46). Cambridge, MA: MIT Press.

Fehr, E. (2009). Social preferences and the brain. In P. W. Glimcher, C. F. Camerer, E. Fehr, R. A. Poldrack (Eds), *Neuroeconomics: Decision-Making and the Brain* (pp. 215–232). London: Academic Press.

Fehr, E., Falk, A. (1999). Wage rigidity in a competitive incomplete contract market. *Journal of Political Economy*, *107*(1), 106–134.

Fehr, E., Fischbacher, U. (2004). Third-party punishment and social norms. *Evolution and Human Behavior*, *25*(2), 63–87.

———. (2005). The economics of strong reciprocity. In H. Gintis, S. Bowles, R. Boyd, E. Fehr (Eds), *Moral Sentiments and Material Interests: The Foundations of Cooperation in Economic Life* (pp. 151–192). Cambridge, MA: MIT Press.

Fehr, E., Fischbacher, U., Kosfeld, M. (2005). Neuroeconomic foundations of trust and social preferences: Initial evidence. *American Economic Review, 95*(2), 346–351.

Fehr, E., Gächter, S. (2000). Cooperation and punishment in public goods experiments. *American Economic Review*, *90*(4), 980–994.

———. (2001). Fairness and retaliation. *Journal of Economic Perspectives*, *14*(3), 159–181.

Fehr, E., Goette, L. (2007). Do workers work more if wages are high? Evidence from a randomized field experiment. *American Economic Review*, *97*(1), 298–317.

Fehr, E., Hoff, K., Kshetramade, M. (2008). Spite and development. *American Economic Review*, *98*(2), 494–499.

Fehr, E., Hoff, K. (2011). Introduction: tastes, castes and culture: The influence of society on preferences. *Economic Journal*, *121*(556), F396–F412.

Fehr, E., Klein, A., Schmidt, K. M. (2004). Contracts, fairness and incentives. *Discussion Paper* No. 2004-07, Department of Economics, University of Munich.

———. (2007). Fairness and contract design. *Econometrica*, *75*(1), 121–154.

Fehr, E., Schmidt, K. M. (1999). A theory of fairness, competition and cooperation. *Quarterly Journal of Economics*, *114*(3), 817–868.

———. (2007). Adding a stick to the carrot? The interaction of bonuses and fines. *American Economic Review*, *97*(2), 177–181.

———. (2010). On inequity aversion: A reply to Binmore and Shaked. *Journal of Economic Behavior and Organization*, *73*(1), 101–108.

Fehr, E., Tyran, J.-R. (2003). What causes nominal inertia? Insights from experimental economics. In I. Brocas, Juan D. Carillo (Eds), *The Psychology of Economic Decisions* (pp. 299–314). Oxford: Oxford University Press.

Fehr-Duda, H., Epper, T., Bruhin, A., Schubert, R. (2011). Risk and rationality: The effects of mood and decision rules on probability weighting. *Journal of Economic Behavior and Organization*, *78*(1), 14–24.

Ferguson, N. (1998). *The Pity of War*. London: Allen Lane.

Fernandez, K. V., Lastovicka, J. L. (2011). Making magic: Fetishes in contemporary consumption. *Journal of Consumer Research*, *38*(2), 278–299.

Ferson, W. E., Constantinides, G. M. (1991). Habit persistence and durability in aggregate consumption: Empirical tests. *Journal of Financial Economics*, *29*(2), 199–240.

Festinger, L. (1954). A theory of social comparison processes. *Human Relations*, *7*(2), 117–140.

———. (1957). *A Theory of Cognitive Dissonance*. Stanford, CA: Stanford University Press.

Festinger, L., Riecken, H. W., Schachter, S. (1956). *When Prophesy Fails*. Minneapolis: University of Minnesota Press.

Fiedler, K. (1988). The dependence of the conjunction fallacy on subtle linguistic factors. *Psychological Research*, *50*(2), 123–129.

Fielding, D., Stracca, L. (2007). Myopic loss aversion, disappointment aversion, and the equity premium puzzle. *Journal of Economic Behavior and Organization*, *64*(2), 250–268.

Finkelstein, S. R., Fishbach, A. (2010). When healthy food makes you hungry. *Journal of Consumer Research*, *37*(3), 357–367.

Finkenauer, J. (1982). *Scared Straight! And the Panacea Phenomenon*. Englewood Cliffs, NJ: Prentice Hall.

Finlayson, A. C., McCay, B. J. (1998). Crossing the threshold of ecosystem resilience: The commercial extinction of northern cod. In F. Berkes, C. Folke (Eds), *Linking Social and Ecological Systems: Management Practices and Social mechanisms for Building Resilience* (pp. 311–337). Cambridge: Cambridge University Press.

Fischbacher, U., Gächter, S. (2010). Social preferences, beliefs, and the dynamics of free-riding in public goods experiments. *American Economic Review*, *100*(1), 541–556.

Fischhoff, B., Slovic, P., Lichtenstein, S. (1979). Subjective sensitivity analysis. *Organizational Behavior and Human Performance*, *23*(3), 339–359.

Fishburn, P. C. (1970). *Utility Theory and Decision Making*. New York: Wiley.

———. (1983). Transitive measurable utility. *Journal of Economic Theory*, *31*(2), 293–317.

Fisher, I. (1930). *The Theory of Interest*. New York: Macmillan.

Fiske, A. P., Tetlock, P. (1997). Taboo trade-offs: reactions to transactions that transgress the domain of relationships. *Political Psychology*, *18*(2), 255–297.

Fliessbach, K., Weber, B., Trautner, P., Dohmen, T., Sunde, U., Elger, C. E., Falk, A. (2007). Social comparison affects reward-related brain activity in the human ventral striatum. *Science*, *318*(5854), 1305–1308.

Fodor, J. (1975). *The Language of Thought*. New York: Crowell.

Fong, G. T., Nisbett, R. E. (1991). Immediate and delayed transfer of training effects in statistical reasoning. *Journal of Experimental Psychology*, *120*(1), 34–45.

Forsythe, R., Horowitz, J. L., Savin, N. E., Sefton, M. (1994). Fairness in simple bargaining experiments. *Games and Economic Behavior*, *6*(3), 347–369.

Forsythe, R., Kennan, J., Sopher, B. (1991). Dividing a shrinking pie: An experimental study of strikes in bargaining games with complete information. In R. M. Isaac (Ed.), *Research in Experimental Economics* (Vol. 4, pp. 223–267). Greenwich, CN: JAI Press.

Foubert, B., Gijsbrechts, E. (2007). Shopper response to bundle promotions for packaged goods. *Journal of Marketing Research*, *44*, 647–62.

Fox, C. R., Poldrack, R. A. (2008). Prospect theory and the brain. In P. W. Glimcher, C. F. Camerer, E. Fehr, R. A. Poldrack (Eds), *Neuroeconomics: Decision-Making and the Brain* (pp. 145–174). London: Academic Press.

Fox, J. (2015). From 'economic man' to behavioral economics. *Harvard Business Review*, *93*(May), 78–85.

Frank, R. H. (1985). *Choosing the Right Pond – Human Behavior and the Quest for Status*. Oxford: Oxford University Press.

———. (1988). *Passions within Reason: The Strategic Role of the Emotions*. New York: Norton.

Frank, R. H., Gilovich, T., Regan, D. T. (1993). Does studying economics inhibit cooperation? *Journal of Economic Perspectives*, *7*, 159–171.

Frank, R. H., Hutchens, R. M. (1993). Wages, seniority, and the demand for rising consumption profiles. *Journal of Economic Behavior and Organization*, *21*(3), 251–76.

Frederick, S. (2012). Overestimating others' willingness to pay. *Journal of Consumer Research*, *39*(1), 1–21.

Frederick, S., Lee, L., Baskin, E. (2014). The limits of attraction. *Journal of Marketing Research*, *51*(4), 487–507.

Frederick, S., Loewenstein, G. (1999). Hedonic adaptation. In D. Kahneman, E. Diener, N. Schwarz (Eds), *Well-Being: The Foundations of Hedonic Psychology* (pp. 302–329). New York: Russell Sage.

Frederick, S., Loewenstein, G., O'Donoghue, T. (2002). Time discounting and time preference: A critical review. *Journal of Economic Literature*, XL, June, 351–401.

Frederick, S., Novemsky, N., Wang, J., Dhar, R., Nowlis, S. (2009). Opportunity cost neglect. *Journal of Consumer Research*, *36*(4), 553–561.

Fredrickson, B. L. (2000). Extracting meaning from past affective experiences: The importance of peaks, ends, and specific emotions. *Cognition and Emotion*, *14*(4), 577–606.

Freling, T., Saini, R., Yang, Z. (2012). Do higher stakes lead to better choices? In Z. Gürhan-Canli, C. Otnes, R. Zhu (Eds) *NA - Advances in Consumer Research Volume* (Vol. 40, pp. 926–927), Duluth, MN: Association for Consumer Research, 926–927.

Freud, A. (1937). *The Ego and the Mechanisms of Defense*. London: Hogarth Press.

Frey, B., Bohnet, I. (1995). Institutions affect fairness: Experimental investigations. *Journal of Institutional and Theoretical Economics*, *151*(2), 286–303.

———. (1997). Identification in democratic society. *Journal of Socio-Economics*, *26*(1), 25–38.

Frey, B., Oberholzer-Gee, F. (1997). The cost of price incentives: An empirical analysis of motivation crowding-out. *American Economic Review*, *87*(4), 746–755.

Friedman, M. (1953). The methodology of positive economics. In *Essays in Positive Economics* (pp. 3–43). Chicago: University of Chicago Press.

Friedman, M. (1957). *A Theory of the Consumption Function*. Princeton: Princeton University Press.

Friedman, M., Savage, L. J. (1948). The utility analysis of choices involving risks. *Journal of Political Economy*, *56*(4), 279–304.

Friese, M., Wänke, M. (2014). Personal prayer buffers self-control depletion. *Journal of Experimental Social Psychology*, *51*(2014), 56–59.

Frimer, J. A., Schaefer, N. K., Oakes, H. (2014). Moral actor, selfish agent. *Journal of Personality and Social Psychology*, *106*(5), 790–802.

Frydman, C., Rangel, A. (2014). Debiasing the disposition effect by reducing the saliency of information about a stock's purchase price. *Journal of Economic Behavior and Organization*, *107*(November, Part B), 541–552.

Fu, T., Koutstaal, W., Fu, C. H. Y., Poon, L., Cleare, A. J. (2005). Depression, confidence, and decision: Evidence against depressive realism. *Journal of Psychopathology and Behavioral Assessment*, *27*(4), 243–252.

Fuchs, V. (1982). Time preferences and health: An exploratory study. In V. Fuchs (Ed.), *Economic Aspects of Health* (pp. 93–120). Chicago: University of Chicago Press.

Fudenberg, D. (2006). Advancing beyond 'Advances in Behavioral Economics'. *Journal of Economic Literature*, *44*(3), 694–711.

Fudenberg, D., Levine, D. K. (1998). *The Theory of Learning in Games*. Cambridge, MA: MIT Press.

———. (2006). A dual self model of impulse control. *American Economic Review*, *96*(5), 1449–1476.

Gabaix, X., Laibson, D. (2001). The 6D bias and the equity premium puzzle. *NBER/Macroeconomics Annual*, *16*(1), 257–312.

Gächter, S., Falk, A. (2002). Reputation and reciprocity: Consequences for the labour relation. *Scandinavian Journal of Economics*, *104*(1), 1–26.

Gächter, S., Hermann, B. (2011). The limits of self-governance when cooperators get punished: Experimental evidence from urban and rural Russia. *European Economic Review*, *55*(2), 193–210.

Gächter, S., Orzen, H., Renner, E., Starmer, C. (2009). Are experimental economists prone to framing effects? A natural field experiment. *Journal of Economic Behavior and Organization*, *70*(3), 443–446.

Gailliot, M. T., Baumeister, R., DeWall, C. N., Maner, J. K., Plant, E. A., Tice, D. M., Brewer, L. E., Schmeichel, B. J. (2007). Self-control relies on glucose as a limited energy source: Willpower is more than a metaphor. *Journal of Personality and Social Psychology*, *92*(2), 325–336.

Galanter, E., Pliner, P. (1974). Cross-modality matching of money against other continua. In H. R. Moskowitz (Ed.), *Sensation and Measurement* (pp. 65–76). Dordrecht: Reidel.

Gallistel, C. R. (2009). The neural mechanisms that underlie decision making. In P. W. Glimcher, C. F. Camerer, E. Fehr, R. A. Poldrack (Eds), *Neuroeconomics: Decision-Making and the Brain* (pp. 419–424). London: Academic Press.

Gangestad, S. W., Buss, D. M. (1993). Pathogen prevalence and human mate preferences. *Ethology and Sociobiology 14*(2), 89–96.

Garbarino, E., Slonim, R., Sydnor, J. (2011): Digit ratios (2D:4D) as predictors of risky decision making. *Journal of Risk and Uncertainty*, *42*, 1–26.

García, D. (2013). Sentiment during recessions. *Journal of Finance*, *68*(3), 1267–1300.

Garcia, S. M., Tor, A., Gonzalez, R. (2006). Ranks and rivals: A theory of competition. *Personality and Social Psychology Bulletin*, *32*(7), 970–982.

Garvey, A. M., Germann, F., Bolton, L. E. (2015). Performance brand placebos: How brands improve performance and consumers take the credit. *Journal of Consumer Research*, *42*(6), 931–951.

Gathergood, J., Weber, J. (2014). Self-control, financial literacy and the co-holding puzzle. *Journal of Economic Behavior and Organization*, *107*(November, Part B), 455–469.

Geanakoplos, J., Pearce, D., Stacchetti, E. (1989). Psychological games and sequential rationality. *Games and Economic Behavior*, *1*(1), 60–79.

Genesove, D., Mayer, C. (2001). Loss-aversion and seller behavior: Evidence from the housing market. *Quarterly Journal of Economics*, *116*(4), 1233–1260.

Gennaioli, N., Shleifer, A., Vishny, R. (2015). Neglected risks: The psychology of financial crises. *American Economic Review*, *105*(5), 310–314.

Gerber, A., Rohde, K. I. M. (2010). Risk and preference reversals in intertemporal choice. *Journal of Economic Behavior and Organization*, *76*(3), 654–668.

Gertner, R. (1993). Game shows and economic behavior: risk taking on 'Card Sharks'. *Quarterly Journal of Economics*, *108*(2), 507–521.

Gibbons, R. (1997). Incentives and careers in organizations. In D. Kreps, K. Wallis (Eds), *Advances in Economics and Econometrics: Theory and Applications* (Vol. 2, pp. 1–37). Cambridge: Cambridge University Press.

Gigerenzer, G. (1996a). On narrow norms and vague heuristics: A reply to Kahneman and Tversky. *Psychological Review*, *103*(3), 592–596.

———. (1996b). Rationality: Why social context matters. In P. B. Baltes, U. Staudinger (Eds), *Interactive Minds: Life-Span Perspectives on the Social Foundation of Cognition* (pp. 319–346). Cambridge: Cambridge University Press.

———. (2004). Fast and frugal heuristics: The tools of bounded rationality. In D. J. Koehler, N. Harvey (Eds), *Handbook of Judgment and Decision Making* (pp. 62–88). Oxford: Blackwell.

Gigerenzer, G., Goldstein, D. G. (1996). Reasoning the fast and frugal way: Models of bounded rationality. *Psychological Review*, *103*(4), 650–69.

Gigerenzer, G., Hoffrage, U., Kleinbolting, H. (1991). Probabilistic mental models: A Brunswikian theory of confidence. *Psychological Review*, *98*(4), 506–528.

Gigerenzer, G., Hug, K. (1992). Domain-specific reasoning: Social contracts, cheating and perspective change. *Cognition*, *43*(2), 127–171.

Gigerenzer, G., Todd, P. M., ABC Research Group. (1999). *Simple Heuristics That Make Us Smart*. New York: Oxford University Press.

Gigliotti, G., Sopher, B. (1993). A test of generalized expected utility theory. *Theory and Decision*, *35*(1), 75–106.

Gilbert, B., Graff Zivin, J. (2014). Dynamic salience with intermittent billing: Evidence from smart electricity meters. *Journal of Economic Behavior and Organization*, *107*(November, Part A), 176–190.

Gilbert, D. F., Pinel, E. C., Wilson, T. D., Blumberg, S. J., Wheatley, J. P. (1998). Immune neglect: A source of durability bias in affective forecasting. *Journal of Personality and Social Psychology*, *75*(3), 617–638.

Gilboa, I., Schmeidler, D. (1995). Case-based decision theory. *Quarterly Journal of Economics*, *110*(3), 605–639.

———. (2001). *A Theory of Case-Based Decisions*. Cambridge: Cambridge University Press.

Gilovich, T. (1991). *How We Know What Isn't So: The Fallibility of Human Reason in Everyday Life*. New York: The Free Press.

Gilovich, T., Vallone, R., Tversky, A. (1985). The hot hand in basketball: On the misperception of random sequences. *Cognitive Psychology*, *17*(3), 295–314.

Ginossar, Z., Trope, Y. (1987). Problem solving in judgment under uncertainty. *Journal of Personality and Social Psychology*, *52*(3), 464–474.

Gintis, H. (2009). *The Bounds of Reason: Game Theory and the Unification of the Behavioral Sciences*. Princeton: Princeton University Press.

Gintis, H., Smith, E. A., Bowles, S. (2001). Cooperation and costly signalling. *Journal of Theoretical Biology*, *213*(1), 103–119.

Glaeser, E. L. (2004). Psychology and the market. *American Economic Review*, *94*(2), 408–413.

Glassner, B. (1999). *The Culture of Fear: Why Americans are Afraid of the Wrong Things*. New York: Basic Books.

Glätzle-Rützler, D., Sutter, M., Zeileis, A. (2015). No myopic loss aversion in adolescents? An experimental note. *Journal of Economic Behavior and Organization*, *111*(March), 169–176.

Glimcher, P. W. (2003). *Decisions, Uncertainty, and the Brain: The Science of Neuroeconomics*. Cambridge, MA: MIT Press.

———. (2009). Choice: towards a standard back-pocket model. In P. W. Glimcher, C. F. Camerer, E. Fehr, R. A. Poldrack (Eds), *Neuroeconomics: Decision-Making and the Brain* (pp. 503–522). London: Academic Press.

Glimcher, P. W., Kable, J., Louie, K. (2007). Neuroeconomic studies of impulsivity: Now or just as soon as possible? *American Economic Review*, *97*(2), 142–147.

Gneezy, A., Gneezy, U., Nelson, L. D., Brown, A. (2010). Shared social responsibility: A field experiment in pay-what-you-want pricing and charitable giving. *Science*, *329*(5989), 325–327.

Gneezy, U., Kapteyn, A., Potters, J. (2003). Evaluation periods and asset prices in a market experiment. *Journal of Finance*, *58*(2), 821–838.

Gneezy, U., Potters, J. (1997). An experiment on risk taking and evaluating periods. *Quarterly Journal of Economics*, *112*(2), 631–646.

Gneezy, U., Rustichini, A. (2000). A fine is a price. *Journal of Legal Studies*, *29*(1), 1–17.

Goeree, J. K., Holt, C. A. (2001). Ten little treasures of game theory and ten intuitive contradictions. *American Economic Review*, *91*(5), 1402–1422.

Goeree, J. K., Yariv, L. (2015). Conformity in the lab. *Journal of the Economic Science Association*, *1*(1), 15–28.

Goldsmith, K., Gal, D., Raghunathan, R., Cheatham, L. (2013). The pursuit of happiness: Can it make you happy? In S. Botti, A. Labroo (Eds), *NA – Advances in Consumer Research* (Vol. 41, pp. 444–445). Duluth, MN: Association for Consumer Research.

Gollwitzer, P. M., Heckhausen, H., Ratajczak, H. (1990). From weighing to willing: Approaching a change decision through pre- or postdecisional implementation. *Organizational Behavior and Human Decision Processes*, *45*(1), 41–46.

Gonzalez, R., Wu, G. (1999). On the shape of the probability weighting function. *Cognitive Psychology*, *38*(1), 129–166.

Gosline, R., Banker, R., Lee, J. (2013). Brands status and reverse placebo effects: High status products inhibit performance despite being preferred. In S. Botti, A. Labroo (Eds) *NA - Advances in Consumer Research* (Vol. 41, pp. 688–689), Duluth, MN: Association for Consumer Research.

Goswami, I., Urminsky, O. (2015). The 'mere-reminder' effect of salient calorie labeling. *Chicago Booth Research Paper*, *15*(19).

Gourville, J. T. (1998). Pennies-a-day: The effect of temporal reframing on transaction evaluation. *Journal of Consumer Research*, *24*(4), 395–403.

Gourville, J. T., Soman, D. (1998). Payment depreciation: The effects of temporally separating payments from consumption. *Journal of Consumer Research*, *25*(2), 160–174.

Graeff, F. G., Guimarães, F. S., DeAndrade, T. G. C. S., Deakin, J. F. W. (1996). Role of 5-HT in stress, anxiety, and depression. *Pharmacology Biochemistry and Behavior*, *54*(1), 129–141.

Graham, L., Oswald, A. J. (2010). Hedonic capital, adaptation and resilience. *Journal of Economic Behavior and Organization*, *76*(2), 372–384.

Green, J., Jullien, B. (1988). Ordinal independence in nonlinear utility theory. *Journal of Risk and Uncertainty*, *1*(4), 355–387.

Green, L., Fry, A., Myerson, J. (1994). Temporal discounting and preference reversals in choice between delayed outcomes. *Psychonomic Bulletin and Review*, *1*(3), 383–389.

Greenberg, A. E. (2014). On the complementarity of prosocial norms: The case of restaurant tipping during the holidays. *Journal of Economic Behavior and Organization*, *97*(January), 103–112.

Greenspan, A., Kennedy, J. (2005). Estimates of home mortgage originations, repayments, and debt on one-to-four family residences. *Working Paper*, No. 2005–41, Federal Reserve, Washington, DC.

Grether, D. M, Plott, C. P. (1979). Economic Theory of Choice and the Preference Reversal Phenomenon. *American Economic Review, 69*(4), 623–648.

Grimm, V., Mengel, F. (2011). Let me sleep on it: Delay reduces rejection rates in ultimatum games. *Economics Letters*, *111*(2), 113–115.

Gross, J. J. (1998). Sharpening the focus: Emotion regulation, arousal, and social competence. *Psychological Inquiry*, *9*(4), 287–290.

———. (2002). Emotion regulation: Affective, cognitive, and social consequences. *Psychophysiology*, *39*(3), 281–291.

Gross, J. J., John, O. P. (2003). Individual differences in two emotion regulation processes: Implications for affect, relationships, and well-being. *Journal of Personality and Social Psychology*, *85*(2), 348–362.

Grubb, M. (2009). Selling to overconfident consumers. *American Economic Review*, *99*(5), 1770–1807.

Gruber, J., Köszegi, B. (2001). Is addiction rational? Theory and evidence. *Quarterly Journal of Economics*, *116*(4), 1261–1303.

Grubliauskiene, A., Dewitte, S. (2014). Temptation in the background: Non-consummatory exposure to food temptation enhances self-regulation in boys but not in girls. *Frontiers in Psychology*, *5*(Article 788).

Guéguen, N., Jacob, C. (2013). Behavioral consequences of money: When the automated teller machine reduces helping behavior. *Journal of Socio-Economics*, *47*, 103–104.

Gul, F. (1991). A theory of disappointment in decision making under uncertainty. *Econometrica*, *59*(3), 667–686.

Gul, F., Pesendorfer, W. (2001). Temptation and self-control. *Econometrica*, *69*(6), 1403–1436.

———. (2007). Welfare without happiness. *American Economic Review*, *97*(2), 471–476.

———. (2008). The case for 'mindless economics'. In A. Caplin, A. Schotter (Eds), *The Foundations of Positive and Normative Economics* (pp. 3–39). Oxford: Oxford University Press.

Guryan, J., Kearney, M. S. (2008). Gambling at lucky stores: Empirical evidence from state lottery sales. *American Economic Review*, *98*(1), 458–473.

Güth, W., Marchand, N., Rullière, J. L. (1997). On the reliability of reciprocal fairness - An experimental study. *Discussion paper*, Humboldt University Berlin.

Güth, W., Schmidt, C., Sutter, M. (2003). Fairness in the mail and opportunism in the internet: A newspaper experiment on ultimatum bargaining. *German Economic Review*, *4*(2), 243–265.

Güth, W., Schmittberger, R., Schwarze, B. (1987). An experimental analysis of ultimatum bargaining. *Journal of Economic Behavior and Organization*, *3*(4), 367–388.

Güth, W., Tietz, R. (1985). Strategic power versus distributive justice: An experimental analysis of ultimatum bargaining. In H. Brandstätter, E. Kirchler (Eds), *Economic Psychology* (pp. 129–137). Linz: Trauner.

———. (1986). Auctioning ultimatum bargaining positions: How to act if rational decisions are unacceptable? In R. W. Scholz (Ed.), *Current Issues in West German Decision Research* (pp. 173–185). New York: P. Lang.

Güth, W., Van Damme, E. (1998). Information, strategic behavior and fairness in ultimatum bargaining: An experimental study. *Journal of Mathematical Psychology*, *42*(2-3), 227–247.

Haigh, M. S., List, J. A. (2005). Do professional traders exhibit myopic loss-version? An experimental analysis. *Journal of Finance*, *60*(1), 523–534.

Halevy, Y. (2008). Strotz meets Allais: Diminishing impatience and the certainty effect. *American Economic Review*, *98*(3), 1145–1162.

Halfmann, K., Hedgcock, W., Denburg, N. L. (2013). Age-related differences in discounting future gains and losses. *Journal of Neuroscience, Psychology, and Economics*, *6*(1), 42–54.

Hamer, D. (1998). *Living with our Genes*. New York: Doubleday.

Han, D., Duhachek, A., Agrawal, N. (2014). Emotions shape decisions through construal level: The case of guilt and shame. *Journal of Consumer Research*, *41*(4), 1047–1064.

Han, S., Lerner, J. S., Keltner, D. (2007). Feelings and consumer decision making: The Appraisal-Tendency Framework. *Journal of Consumer Psychology*, *17*(3), 158–168.

Handa, J. (1977). Risk, probability, and a new theory of cardinal utility. *Journal of Political Economy*, *85*(1), 97–122.

Handel, B. R. (2013). Adverse selection and inertia in health insurance markets: When nudging hurts. *American Economic Review*, *103*(7), 2643–2682.

Hansen, T. (2011). Parenthood and happiness: A review of folk theories versus empirical evidence. *Social Indicators Research*, *108*(1), 29–64.

Hao, L., Houser, D. (2017). Perceptions, intentions, and cheating. *Journal of Economic Behavior and Organization*, *133*, 52–73.

Hardie, B. G. S., Johnson, E. J., Fader, P. S. (1993). Modeling loss-aversion and reference dependence effects on brand choice. *Marketing Science*, *12*(4), 378–394.

Hardisty, D. J., Appelt, K. C., Weber, E. U. (2012). Good or bad, we want it now: Fixed-cost present bias for gains and losses explains magnitude asymmetries in intertemporal choice. *Journal of Behavioral Decision Making*, *26*(4), 348–361.

Hariharan, A., Adam, M. T. P., Astor, P. J., Weinhardt, C. (2015). Emotion regulation and behavior in an individual decision trading experiment: Insights from psychophysiology. *Journal of Neuroscience, Psychology, and Economics*, *8*(3), 186–202.

Harle, K. M., Sanfey, A. G. (2007). Incidental sadness biases social economic decisions in the Ultimatum Game. *Emotion*, *7*(4), 876–881.

Harless, D. W. (1992). Predictions about indifference curves inside the unit triangle: A test of variants of expected utility. *Journal of Economic Behavior and Organization*, *18*(3), 391–414.

Harrison, G., Lau, M. I., Williams, M. B. (2002). Estimating individual discount rates in Denmark: A field experiment. *American Economic Review*, *92*(5), 1606–1617.

Harrison, G., McCabe, K. (1992). Testing noncooperative bargaining theory in experiments. In R. M. Isaac (Ed.), *Research in Experimental Economics* (Vol. 5, pp. 137–169). Greenwich, CN: JAI Press.

———. (1996). Expectations and fairness in a simple bargaining experiment. *International Journal of Game Theory*, *25*(3), 303–327.

Harsanyi, J. C., Selten, R. (1988). *A General Theory of Equilibrium in Games*. Cambridge, MA: MIT Press.

Harvey, C. M. (1986). Value functions for infinite-period planning. *Management Science*, *32*(9), 1123–1139.

Hastings, J. S., Shapiro, J. M. (2013). Fungibility and consumer choice: Evidence from commodity price shocks. *The Quarterly Journal of Economics*, *128*(4), 1449–1498.

Hausch, D. B., Ziemba, W. T. (1995). Efficiency of sports and betting markets. In R. A. Jarrow, V. Maksimovic, W. T. Ziemba (Eds), *Handbooks in Operations Research and Management Science: Finance* (pp. 545–580). Amsterdam: North-Holland.

He, H., Modest, D. M. (1995). Market frictions and consumption-based asset pricing. *Journal of Political Economy*, *103*(1), 94–117.

Heath, C., Fennema, M. G. (1996). Mental depreciation and marginal decision making. *Organizational Behavior and Human Decision Processes*, *68*(2), 95–108.

Heath, C., Soll, J. B. (1996). Mental budgeting and consumer decisions. *Journal of Consumer Research*, *23*(1), 40–52.

Heatherton, T. F., Wagner, D. D. (2011). Cognitive neuroscience of self-regulation failure. *Trends in Cognitive Sciences*, *15*(3), 132–139.

Heberlein, T. A., Bishop, R. C. (1986). Assessing the validity of contingent valuation: Three field experiments. *Science of the Total Environment*, *56*(1986), 99–107.

Hedesström, T. M., Svedsäter, H., Gärlin, T. (2004). Identifying heuristic choice rules in the Swedish premium pension scheme. *Journal of Behavioral Finance*, *5*(1), 32–42.

Hedgcock, W., Rao, A. R. (2009). Trade-off aversion as an explanation for the attraction effect: A functional magnetic resonance imaging study. *Journal of Marketing Research*, *46*(1), 1–13.

Heidhues, P., Köszegi, B. (2010). Exploiting naivete about self control in the credit market. *American Economic Review*, *100*(5), 2279–2303.

Heilman, C., Nakamoto, K., Rao, A. (2002). Pleasant surprises: Consumer response to unexpected in-store coupons. *Journal of Marketing Research*, *39*(2), 242–252.

Hein, G., Morishima, Y., Leiberg, S., Sul, S., Fehr, E. (2016). The brain's functional network architecture reveals human motives. *Science*, *351*(6277), 1074–1078.

Heinz, M., Juranek, S., Rau, H. A. (2012). Do women behave more reciprocally than men? Gender differences in real effort dictator games. *Journal of Economic Behavior and Orgainzation*, *83*(1), 105–110.

Helion, C., Gilovich, T. (2014). Gift cards and mental accounting: Green-lighting hedonic spending. *Journal of Behavioral Decision Making*, *27*(4), 386–393.

Helson, H. (1964). *Adaptation Level Theory: An Experimental and Systematic Approach to Behavior*. New York: Harper.

Henrich, J., Boyd, R., Bowles, S., Camerer, C., Fehr, E., Gintis, H., McElreath, R. (2001). In search of homo economicus: Behavioral experiments in 15 small-scale societies. *American Economic Review*, *91*(2), 73–78.

Henrich, J., Boyd, R., Bowles, S., Camerer, C., Fehr, E., Gintis, H., Alvard, M., Barr, A., Ensminger, J., Hill, K., Gil-White, F., Gurven, M., Marlowe, F., Patton, J. Q., Smith, N., Tracer, D. (2005). 'Economic man' in cross-cultural perspective: Behavioral experiments in 15 small-scale societies. *Behavioral and Brain Sciences*, *28*(6), 795–855.

Henrich, J. P., Ensminger, J. (2014). *Experimenting with Social Norms*. New York: Russell Sage.

Henry, R., Terraneo, S. (2010). Ciao, British shoplifter, I see you from 'ere. *Sunday Times*. November 21. Retrieved from www.thetimes.co.uk/article/ciao-british-shoplifter-i-see-you-from-ere-p06g2wkt6dr.

Herold, F. (2012). Carrot or stick? The evolution of reciprocal preferences in a haystack model. *American Economic Review*, *102*(2), 914–940.

Herrman, B., Thöni, C., Gächter, S. (2008). Antisocial punishment across societies. *Science*, *319*(5868), 1362–1367.

Hershfield, H. E., Cohen, T. R., Thompson, L. (2012). Short horizons and tempting situations: Lack of continuity to our future selves leads to unethical decision making and behavior. *Organizational Behavior and Human Decision Processes*, *117*(2), 298–310.

Hertwig, R., Gigerenzer, G. (1999). The 'conjunction fallacy' revisited: How intelligent inferences look like reasoning errors. *Journal of Behavioral Decision Making*, *12*(4), 275–305.

Hertwig, R., Ortmann, A. (2001). Experimental practices in economics: A methodological challenge for psychologists. *Behavioral and Brain Sciences*, *24*(3), 383–403.

Heukelom, F. (2014). *Behavioral Economics: A History*. New York: Cambridge University Press.

Hey, J. D., Orme, C. (1994). Investigating generalizations of expected utility theory using experimental data. *Econometrica*, *62*(6), 1291–1326.

Higgins, E. T., Cesario, J., Hagiwara, N., Spiegel, S., Pittman, T. (2010). Increasing or decreasing interest in activities: The role of regulatory fit. *Journal of Personality and Social Psychology*, *98*(4), 559–572.

Hilton, D. J. (1995). The social context of reasoning: Conversational inference and rational judgment. *Psychological Bulletin*, *118*(2), 248–271.

Hirshleifer, D., Shumway, T. (2003). Good day sunshine: Stock returns and the weather. *Journal of Finance*, *58*(3), 1009–1032.

Hirshleifer, J. (1987). On the emotions as guarantors of threats and promises. In J. Dupré (Ed.), *The Latest on the Best* (pp. 307–326). Cambridge, MA: MIT Press.

———. (1998). The bioeconomic causes of war. *Managerial and Decision Economics*, *19*(7-8), 457–466.

Ho, D. E., Imai, K. (2008). Estimating causal effects of ballot order from a randomized natural experiment: The California alphabet lottery, 1978–2002. *Public Opinion Quarterly*, *72*(2), 216–240.

Ho, T., Camerer, C., Weigelt, K. (1998). Iterated dominance and iterated best-response in experimental p-beauty contests. *American Economic Review*, *88*(4), 947–969.

Ho, T., Lim, N., Camerer, C. (2006). Modeling the psychology of consumer and firm behavior with behavioral economics. *Journal of Marketing Research*, *43*, 307–331.

Hochman, G., Ayal, S., Ariely, D. (2014). Keeping your gains close but your money closer: The prepayment effect in riskless choices. *Journal of Economic Behavior and Organization*, *107*(November, Part B), 582–594.

Hodgson, D. (1999). Hume's mistake. *Journal of Consciousness Studies*, *6*(8-9), 201–224.

Hodgson, G. M. (1998). The approach of institutional economics. *Journal of Economic Literature*, *36*, 166–192.

Hodgson, T. L., Guala, F., Miller, T., Summers, I. (2012). Limbic and prefrontal activity during conformity and violation of norms in a coordination game. *Journal of Neuroscience, Psychology, and Economics*, *5*(1), 1–17.

Hoelzl, E., Rustichini, A. (2005). Overconfident: Do you put your money on it? *Economic Journal*, *115*(503), 305–318.

Hoffman, E., McCabe, K., Shachat, K., Smith, V. (1994). Preferences, property rights and anonymity in bargaining games. *Games and Economic Behavior*, *7*(3), 346–380.

Hoffman, E., McCabe, K., Smith, V. (1996). On expectations and monetary stakes in ultimatum games. *International Journal of Game Theory*, *25*, 289–301.

———. (1998). Behavioral foundations of reciprocity: Experimental economics and evolutionary psychology. *Economic Inquiry*, *36*(3), 335–52.

Holcomb, J. S., Nelson, P. S. (1992). Another experimental look at individual time preference. *Rationality and Society*, *4*(2), 199–220.

Holladay, J. S., Price, M. K., Wanamaker, M. (2015). The perverse impact of calling for energy conservation. *Journal of Economic Behavior and Organization*, *110*, 1–18.

Holt, C. A. (2006). *Markets, Games, and Strategic Behavior*. London: Pearson.

Homans, G. C. (1961). *Social Behavior: Its Elementary Forms*. New York: Harcourt, Brace and World.

Hood, B. (2010). *The Science of Superstition*. New York: HarperCollins.

Hossain, M., Saini, R. (2013). The hedonic-shift for freebies: How preference for hedonic options disproportionately enhanced when their price falls to zero. In S. Botti, A. Labroo (Eds), *NA - Advances in Consumer Research* (Vol. 41, pp. 637–639). Duluth, MN: Association for Consumer Research. Retrieved from http://acrwebsite.org/volumes/1015416/volumes/v41/NA-41.

Hsee, C. K. (1996). The evaluability hypothesis: An explanation of preference reversals between joint and separate evaluations of alternatives. *Organizational Behavior and Human Decision Processes*, *67*(3), 247–257.

Hsee, C. K., Abelson, R. P., Salovey, P. (1991). The relative weighting of position and velocity in satisfaction. *Psychological Science*, *2*(4), 263–266.

Hsee, C. K., Loewenstein, G., Blount, S., Bazerman, M. H. (1999). Preference reversals between joint and separate evaluations: A review and theoretical analysis. *Psychological Bulletin*, *125*(5), 576–590.

Hsu, M., Bhatt, M., Adolphs, R., Tranel, D., Camerer, C. F. (2005). Neural systems responding to degrees of uncertainty in human decision-making. *Science*, *310*(5754), 1680–1683.

Hsu, M., Zhao, C., Krajbich, I., Camerer, C. F. (2009). Neural correlates of nonlinear weighting of probability. *Journal of Neuroscience*, *29*(7), 2231–2237.

Huber, J., Payne, J. W., Puto, C. (1982). Adding asymmetrically dominated alternatives: Violations of regularity and the similarity hypothesis. *Journal of Consumer Research*, *9*, 90–98.

Huber, J., Payne, J. W., Puto, C. P. (2014). Let's be honest about the attraction effect. *Journal of Marketing Research*, *51*(4), 520–525.

Huber, J., Puto, C. (1983). Market boundaries and product choice: Illustrating attraction and substitution effects. *Journal of Consumer Research*, *10*, 31–44.

Hudson, E. (2013). Does relative material wealth matter for child and adolescent life satisfaction? *Journal of Socio-Economics*, *46*, 38–47.

Humphrey, S. J. (1998). More mixed results on boundary effects. *Economics Letters*, *61*(1), 79–84.

———. (2000). The common consequence effect: Testing a unified explanation of some recent mixed evidence. *Journal of Economic Behavior and Organization*, *41*(3), 239–262.

———. (2001a). Are event-splitting effects actually boundary effects? *Journal of Risk and Uncertainty, 22*(1), 79–93.

———. (2001b). Non-transitive choice: Event-splitting effects or framing effects? *Economica, 68*(269), 77–96.

Humphreys, D. K., Gasparrini, A., Wiebe, D. J. (2017). Evaluating the impact of Florida's 'Stand your ground' self-defense law on homicide and suicide by firearm: An interrupted time series study. *JAMA Internal Medicine, 177*(1), 44–50.

Hung, M.-W., Wang, J.-Y. (2005). Asset prices under prospect theory and habit formation. *Review of Pacific Basin Financial Markets and Policies, 8*(1), 1–29.

Huys, Q., Dayan, P. (2009). A Bayesian formulation of behavioral control. *Cognition, 113*(3), 314–328.

Hytönen, K. (2014). Neuroscientific evidence for contextual effects in decision making. *Behavioral and Brain Sciences, 37*(1), 33–34.

Ibbotson, R. G., Chen, P. (2003). Long-run stock returns: Participating in the real economy. *Financial Analysts Journal, 59*(1), 88–98.

Ikeda, S., Kang, M.-I., Ohtake, F. (2010). Hyperbolic discounting, the sign effect, and the body mass index. *Journal of Health Economics, 29*(2), 268–284.

Ingram, R. E. (1990). Self-focused attention in clinical disorders: Review and a conceptual model. *Psychological Bulletin, 107*(2), 156–76.

Iorio, A. (2005). Your vehicle's trade-in value: The real truth! [Blog]. November 19. Retrieved from www.insidercarsecrets.com/car-trade-in-value.html.

Is, G. (2010). Do we follow others when we should? A simple test of rational expectations. *American Economic Review, 100*(5), 2340–2360.

Isaac, M. S., Brough, A. R. (2014). Judging a part by the size of its whole: The category size bias in probability judgments. *Journal of Consumer Research, 41*(2), 310–325.

Isoni, A. Brooks, P., Loomes, G., Sugden, R. (2016). Do markets reveal preferences or shape them? *Journal of Economic Behavior and Organization, 122*, 1–16.

Iyengar, S. S., Lepper, M. R. (2000). When choice is demotivating: Can one desire too much of a good thing? *Journal of Personality and Social Psychology, 79*(6), 995–1006.

Jakiela, P. (2011). Social preferences and fairness norms as informal institutions: Experimental evidence. *American Economic Review, 101*(3), 509–13.

Janakiraman, N., Meyer, R., Morales, A. (2002). The mental accounting of price shocks: The effects of unexpected price changes on cross-category purchase patterns. *Advances in Consumer Research, 29*(4), 342–343.

Janis, I. (1967). Effects of fear arousal on attitude change. In L. Berkowitz (Ed.), *Advances in Experimental Social Psychology* (pp. 166–224). New York: Academic Press.

Jensen, K., Call, J., Tomasello, M. (2007). Chimpanzees are rational maximizers in an ultimatum game. *Science, 318*(5847), 107–109.

Jetter, M., Walker, J. K. (2015). Game, set, and match: Do women and men perform differently in competitive situations? *Journal of Economic Behavior and Organization, 119*(November), 96–108.

Jevons, H. S. (1905). *Essays on Economics*. London: Macmillan.

Jevons, W. S. (1888). *The Theory of Political Economy*. London: Macmillan.

Jha-Dang, P., Banerjee, A. (2005). A theory based explanation of differential consumer response to different promotions. *Advances in Consumer Research, 32*, 235–236.

Job, V., Dweck, C. S., Walton, G. M. (2010). Ego depletion – Is it all in your head? Implicit theories about willpower affect self-regulation. *Psychological Science*, *21*(11), 1686–1693.

Jobes, J. (1974). A revelatory function of art. *British Journal of Aesthetics*, *14*(2), 124–133.

Johansson, P., Hall, L., Tärning, B., Sikström, S., Chater, N. (2013). Choice blindness and preference change: You will like this paper better if you (believe you) chose to read it! *Journal of Behavioral Decision Making*, *27*(3), 281–289.

Johnson, E. J., Camerer, C., Sen, S., Rymon, T. (2002). Detecting failures of backward induction: Monitoring information search in sequential bargaining experiments. *Journal of Economic Theory*, *104*(1), 16–47.

Johnson, E. J., Hershey, J., Meszaros, J., Kunreuther, H. (1992). Framing, probability distortions, and insurance decisions. *Journal of Risk and Uncertainty*, *7*(1), 35–51.

Johnson, M. D., Herrmann, A., Bauer, H. H. (1999). The effects of price bundling on consumer evaluations of product offerings. *International Journal of Research in Marketing*, *16*(2), 129–142.

Johnson, M. D., Ilies, R., Boles, T. L. (2012). Alternative reference points and outcome evaluation: The influence of affect. *Journal of Applied Psychology*, *97*(1), 33–45.

Johnson-Laird, P. N., Byrne, R. M. J., Schaeken, R. S. (1992). Propositional reasoning by model. *Psychological Review*, *99*(3), 418–439.

Johnson-Laird, P. N., Legrenzi, P., Girotto, V., Legrenzi, M.S. (2000). Illusions in reasoning about consistency. *Science*, *288*(5465), 531–532.

Jones, C. P., Wilson, J. W. (2005). The equity risk premium controversy. *Journal of Investing*, *14*(2), 37–43.

Jones-Lee, M. W., Loomes, G., Philips, P. R. (1995). Valuing the prevention of non-fatal road injuries: Contingent valuation versus standard gambles. *Oxford Economic Papers*, *47*(4), 675–695.

Jordan, J. S. (1991). Bayesian learning in normal-form games. *Games and Economic Behavior*, *3*(1), 60–81.

Jullien, B., Salanié, B. (2000). Estimating preferences under risk: The case of racetrack bettors. *Journal of Political Economy*, *108*(3), 503–530.

Just, D. R., Price, J. (2013). Using incentives to encourage healthy eating in children. *Journal of Human Resources*, *48*(4), 855–872.

Kacelnik, A. (1997). Normative and descriptive models of decision making: time discounting and risk sensitivity. In G. R. Bock, G. Cardew (Eds), *Characterizing Human Psychological Adaptations: Ciba Foundation Symposium 208* (pp. 51–70). Chichester: Wiley.

Kachelmeier, S. J., Shehata, M. (1992). Examining risk preferences under high monetary incentives: Experimental evidence from the People's Republic of China. *American Economic Review*, *82*(5), 1120–1141.

Kadous, K., Tayler, W. B., Thayer, J. M., Young, D. (2014). Individual Characteristics and the Disposition Effect: The Opposing Effects of Confidence and Self-Regard. *Journal of Behavioral Finance*, *15*(3), 235–250.

Kagel, J., Kim, C., Moser, D. (1996). Fairness in ultimatum games with asymmetric information and asymmetric payoffs. *Games and Economic Behavior*, *13*(1), 100–110.

Kahneman, D. (1986). Comments on the contingent valuation method. In R. G. Cummings, D. S. Brookshire, W. D. Schulze (Eds), *Valuing Environmental Goods: An Assessment of the Contingent Valuation Method* (pp. 185–194). Totowa, NJ: Rowman and Allanheld.

———. (1994). New challenges to the rationality assumption. *Journal of Institutional and Theoretical Economics*, *150*(1), 18–36.

———. (2000). Experienced utility and objective happiness: A moment-based approach. In D. Kahneman, A. Tversky (Eds), *Choices, Values, and Frames* (pp. 673–692). New York: Cambridge University Press.

———. (2011). *Thinking, Fast and Slow*. London: Macmillan.

Kahneman, D., Diener, E., Schwartz, N. (Eds). (1999). *Well-Being: The Foundations of Hedonic Psychology*. New York: Russell Sage.

Kahneman, D., Frederick, S. (2002). Representativeness revisited: Attribute substitution in intuitive judgment. In T. Gilovich, D. Griffin, D. Kahneman (Eds), *Heuristics and Biases: The Psychology of Intuitive Judgment* (pp. 49–81). New York: Cambridge University Press.

———. (2005). A model of heuristic judgment. In K. J. Holyoak, R. G. Morrison (Eds), *The Cambridge Handbook of Thinking and Reasoning* (pp. 267–293). Cambridge: Cambridge University Press.

Kahneman, D., Knetsch, J. L., Thaler, R. H. (1986). Fairness as a constraint on profit seeking: Entitlements in the market. *American Economic Review*, *76*(4), 728–741.

———. (1990). Experimental tests of the endowment effect and the Coase theorem. *Journal of Political Economy*, *98*(6), 1352–1375.

Kahneman, D., Lovallo, D. (1993). Timid choices and bold forecasts: A cognitive perspective on risk taking. *Management Science*, *39*(1), 17–31.

Kahneman, D., Ritov, I. (1994). Determinants of stated willingness to pay for public goods – A study in the headline method. *Journal of Risk and Uncertainty*, *9*(1), 5–38.

Kahneman, D., Ritov, I., Schkade, D. A. (2000). Economic preferences or attitude expressions? An analysis of dollar responses to public issues. *Journal of Risk and Uncertainty*, *19*(1), 223–235.

Kahneman, D., Schkade, D. A., Sunstein, C. R. (1998). Shared outrage and erratic awards: The psychology of punitive damages. *Journal of Risk and Uncertainty*, *16*, 49–86.

Kahneman, D., Slovic, P., Tversky, A. (1982). *Judgement Under Uncertainty: Heuristics and Biases*. Cambridge: Cambridge University Press.

Kahneman, D., Snell, J. (1992). Predicting a changing taste: Do people know what they will like? *Journal of Behavioral Decision Making*, *5*(3), 187–200.

Kahneman, D., Sugden, R. (2005). Experienced utility as a standard of policy evaluation. *Environmental and Resource Economics*, *32*(1), 161–181.

Kahneman, D., Tversky, A. (1972). Subjective probability: A judgement of representativeness. *Cognitive Psychology*, *3*(1972), 430–454.

———. (1973). On the psychology of prediction. *Psychological Review*, *80*(4), 237–251.

———. (1979). Prospect theory: An analysis of decision under risk. *Econometrica*, *47*(2), 263–291.

———. (1982). Judgement of and by representativeness. In D. Kahneman, P. Slovic, A. Tversky (Eds), *Judgement under Uncertainty: Heuristics and Biases* (pp. 84–100). New York: Cambridge University Press.

———. (1984). Choices, values, and frames. *The American Psychologist*, *39*(4), 341–350.

———. (1992). Advances in prospect theory: Cumulative representation of uncertainty. *Journal of Risk and Uncertainty*, *5*(4), 297–324.

———. (1996). On the reality of cognitive illusions. *Psychological Review*, *103*, 582–91.

Kahneman, D., Wakker, P. P., Sarin, R. (1997). Back to Bentham? Explorations of experienced utility. *Quarterly Journal of Economics*, *112*(2), 375–405.

Kamas, L., Preston, A. (2012). The importance of being confident; gender, career choice and willingness to compete. *Journal of Economic Behavior and Organization*, *83*(1), 82–97.

Kamins, M. A., Folkes, V. S., Fedorikhin, A. (2009). Promotional bundles and consumers' price judgments: When the best things in life are not free. *Journal of Consumer Research*, *36*(4), 660–670.

Kanazawa, S., Fontaine, L. (2013). Intelligent people defect more in a one-shot prisoner's dilemma game. *Journal of Neuroscience, Psychology, and Economics*, *6*(3), 201–213.

Kane, R. (1996). *The Significance of Free Will*. Oxford: Oxford University Press.

Kaplan, H. R. (1978). *Lottery Winners: How They Won and How Winning Changed Their Lives*. New York: Harper and Row.

Kasser, T., Ryan, R.M. (1993). A dark side of the American dream: Correlates of financial success as a central life aspiration. *Journal of Personality and Social Psychology*, *65*(2), 41–42.

———. (1996). Further examining the American dream: Differential correlates of intrinsic and extrinsic goals. *Journal of Personality and Social Psychology*, *22*(3), 280–287.

Keeley, L. H. (1996). *War Before Civilization*. New York: Oxford University Press.

Keltner, D., Van Kleef, G. A., Chen, S., Kraus, M. W. (2008). A reciprocal influence model of social power: Emerging principles and lines of inquiry. In M. A. Zanna (Ed.), *Advances in Experimental Social Psychology* (Vol. 40, pp. 151–192). London: Academic Press.

Kendrick, M. (2007). *The Great Cholesterol Con*. London: John Blake.

Kennan, J., Wilson, R. (1990). Theories of bargaining delays. *Science*, *249*(4973), 1124–1128.

Keren, G., Roelofsma, P. (1995). Immediacy and certainty in intertemporal choice. *Organizational Behavior and Human Decision Processes*, *63*(3), 287–297.

Keynes, J. M. (1936). *The General Theory of Employment, Interest, and Money*. London: Macmillan.

Keys, A. (1957). Epidemiologic aspects of coronary artery disease. *Journal of Chronic Diseases*, *6*(4–5), 552–559.

Khadjavi, M., Lange, A. (2013). Prisoners and their dilemma. *Journal of Economic Behavior and Organization*, *92*(August), 163–175.

Khalil, E. L. (2011). The mirror neuron paradox: How far is understanding from mimicking? *Journal of Economic Behavior and Organization*, *77*(1), 86–96.

Kida, T., Moreno, K., Smith, J. (2010). Investment decision making: Do experienced decision makers fall prey to the paradox of choice? *Journal of Behavioral Finance*, *11*(1), 21–30.

Kim, B. K., Zauberman, G. (2009). Perception of anticipatory time in temporal discounting. *Journal of Neuroscience, Psychology, and Economics*, *2*(2), 91–101.

King, A., King, J. (2011). Golden eggs and plastic eggs: Hyperbolic preferences and the persistence of debit. *Journal of Economics and Finance*, *35*(1), 93–103.

Kirby, K. N., Marakovic, N. N. (1995). Modeling myopic decisions: Evidence for hyperbolic delay-discounting with subjects and amounts. *Organizational Behavior and Human Decision Processes*, *64*(1), 22–30.

Kirby, K. N., Petry, N. M., Bickel, W. (1999). Heroin addicts have higher discount rates for delayed rewards than non-drug-using controls. *Journal of Experimental Psychology: General*, *128*(1), 78–87.

Kirchler, E., Maciejovsky, B. (2002). Simultaneous over- and under-confidence: Evidence from experimental asset markets. *Journal of Risk and Uncertainty*, *25*(1), 65–85.

Kirschner, M. W., Gerhart, J. C. (2006). *The Plausibility of Life: Resolving Darwin's Dilemma*. New Haven, CT: Yale University Press.

Kiyonari, T., Barclay, P. (2008). Cooperation in social dilemmas: Free-riding may be thwarted by second-order reward rather than by punishment. *Journal of Personality and Social Psychology*, *95*(4), 826–842.

Klaes, M. (2002). Some remarks on the place of psychological and social elements in a theory of custom. *American Journal of Economics and Sociology*, *61*(2), 519–530.

———. (2003). Residual categories and the evolution of economic knowledge. In H. S. Jensen, L. M. Richter, M. T. Vendelø (Eds), *The Evolution of Scientific Knowledge* (pp. 37–56). Cheltenham: Elgar.

———. (2004). Evolutionary economics: In defence of 'vagueness'. *Journal of Economic Methodology*, *11*(3), 359–376.

———. (2008). Rationality at work: Reframing social framing. In M. C. Galavotti, R. Scazzieri, P. Suppes (Eds), *Reasoning, Rationality and Probability* (pp. 211–231). Stanford, CA: CSLI.

———. (2015a). Greenwald-Stiglitz theorem and behavioral economics. In M. Altman (Ed.), *Real-World Decision Making: An Encyclopedia of Behavioral Economics* (pp. 181–183). Santa Barbara, CA: Greenwood.

———. (2015b). Principal-agent theory and behavioral economics. In M. Altman (Ed.), *Real-World Decision Making: An Encyclopedia of Behavioral Economics* (pp. 339–341). Santa Barbara, CA: Greenwood.

———. (2015c). Prospect theory. In M. Altman (Ed.), *Real-World Decision Making: An Encyclopedia of Behavioral Economics* (pp. 345–347). Santa Barbara, CA: Greenwood.

———. (2015d). Self-fulfilling prophecies. In M. Altman (Ed.), *Real-World Decision Making: An Encyclopedia of Behavioral Economics* (pp. 379–380). Santa Barbara, CA: Greenwood.

———. (2015e). Transaction costs and behavioral economics. In M. Altman (Ed.), *Real-World Decision Making: An Encyclopedia of Behavioral Economics* (pp. 440–442). Santa barbara, CA: Greenwood.

Klaes, M., Lightfoot, G., Lilley, S. (2011). Market masculinities and electronic trading. In S. Long, B. Sievers (Eds), *Towards a Socioanalysis of Money, Finance and Capitalism* (pp. 349–362). London: Routledge.

Klaes, M., Sent, E.-M. (2005). A conceptual history of bounded rationality. *History of Political Economy*, *37*(1), 27–60.

Klayman, J., Soll, J. B., Gonzalez-Vallejo, C., Barlas, S. (1999). Overconfidence:It depends on how, what, and whom you ask. *Organizational Behavior and Human Decision Processes*, *79*(3), 216–47.

Kliger, D., Levit, B. (2009). Evaluation periods and asset prices: Myopic loss aversion at the financial marketplace. *Journal of Economic Behavior and Organization*, *71*(2), 361–371.

Kliger, D., Tsur, I. (2011). Prospect theory and risk-seeking behavior by troubled firms. *Journal of Behavioral Finance*, *12*(1), 29–40.

Knack, S., Keefer, P. (1997). Does social capital have an economic payoff? A cross-country investigation. *Quarterly Journal of Economics*, *112*(4), 1251–88.

Knetsch, J. L. (1989). The endowment effect and evidence of nonreversible indifference curves. *American Economic Review*, *79*(5), 1277–1284.

Knetsch, J. L., Sinden, J. A. (1984). Willingness to pay and compensation demanded: Experimental evidence of an unexpected disparity in measures of value. *Quarterly Journal of Economics, 99*(3), 507–521.

Knetsch, J. L., Wong, W.-K. (2009). The endowment effect and the reference state: Evidence and manipulations. *Journal of Economic Behavior and Organization, 71*(2), 407–413.

Knez, M. J., Camerer, C. (1995). Social comparison and outside options in 3-person ultimatum games. *Games and Economic Behavior, 10*(1), 65–94.

Knez, P., Smith, V. L., Williams, A. (1985). Individual rationality, market rationality, and value estimation. *American Economic Review, 75*, 397–402.

Knoch, D., Gianotti, L., Pascual-Leone, A., Treyer, V., Regard, M., Hohmann, M., Brugger, P. (2006). Disruption of right prefrontal cortex by low-frequency repetitive transcranial magnetic stimulation induces risk-taking behavior. *Journal of Neuroscience, 26*(24), 6469–6472.

Knoch, D., Nitsche, M. A., Fischbacher, U., Eisenegger, C., Pascual-Leone, A., Fehr, E. (2008). Studying the neurobiology of social interaction with transcranial direct current stimulation – The example of punishing unfairness. *Cerebral Cortex, 18*(9), 1987–1990.

Knutson, B., Adams, C. M., Fong, G. W., Hommer, D. (2001a). Anticipation of increasing monetary reward selectively recruits nucleus accumbens. *Journal of Neuroscience, 21*(16), RC159.

Knutson, B., Delgado, M. R., Phillips, P. E. M. (2009). Representation of subjective value in the striatum. In P. W. Glimcher, C. F. Camerer, E. Fehr, R. A. Poldrack (Eds), *Neuroeconomics: Decision-Making and the Brain* (pp. 389–406). London: Academic Press.

Knutson, B., Fong, G. W., Adams, C. W. (2001b). Dissociation of reward anticipation and outcome with event-related fMRI. *NeuroReport, 12*(17), 3683–3687.

Knutson, B., Fong, G. W., Bennett, S. M., Adams, C. W., Hommer, D. (2003). A region of mesial prefrontal cortex tracks monetarily rewarding outcomes: Characterization with rapid event-related fMRI. *NeuroImage, 18*(2), 263–272.

Knutson, B., Rick, S., Wimmer, G. E., Prelec, D., Loewenstein, G. (2007). Neural predictors of purchases. *Neuron, 53*(1), 147–156.

Kocher, M. G., Krawczyk, M., van Winden, F. (2014). 'Let me dream on!' Anticipatory emotions and preference for timing in lotteries. *Journal of Economic Behavior and Organization, 98*(February), 29–40.

Kocherlakota, N. R. (1996). The equity premium: It's still a puzzle. *Journal of Economic Literature, 34*(1), 42–71.

Komlos, J., Smith, P. K., Bogin, B. (2004). Obesity and the rate of time preference: Is there a connection? *Journal of Biosocial Science, 36*(2), 209–219.

Konow, J. (2000). Fair shares: Accountability and cognitive dissonance in allocation decisions. *American Economic Review, 90*(4), 1072–1091.

Koopmans, T. C. (1960). Stationary ordinal utility and impatience. *Econometrica, 28*(2), 287–309.

Kooreman, P. (1997). The labeling effect of a child benefit system. *American Economic Review, 90*(3), 571–583.

Kosfeld, M., Heinrichs, M., Zak, P. J., Fischbacher, U., Fehr, E. (2005). Oxytocin increases trust in humans. *Nature, 435*(7042), 673–676.

Köszegi, B., Rabin, M. (2006). A model of reference-dependent preferences. *Quarterly Journal of Economics, 121*(4), 1133–1165.

Krosnick, J. A., Li, F., Lehman, D. R. (1990). Conversational conventions, order of information acquisition, and the effect of base rates and individuating information on social judgments. *Journal of Personality and Social Psychology*, *59*(6), 1140–1152.

Kruger, J., Dunning, D. (1999). Unskilled and unaware of it: How difficulties in recognizing one's own incompetence lead to inflated self-assessments. *Journal of Personality and Social Psychology*, *77*(6), 1121–1134.

Kubinska, E., Markiewicz, L., Tyszka, T. (2012). Disposition effect among contrarian and momentum investors. *Journal of Behavioral Finance*, *13*(3), 214–225.

Kühberger, A. (1995). The framing of decisions: A new look at old problems. *Organizational Behavior and Human Decision Processes*, *62*, 230–240.

Kuhn, T. S. (1970). *The Structure of Scientific Revolutions* (2nd ed.). Chicago: University of Chicago Press.

Kuhnen, C. (2015). Asymmetric learning from financial information. *Journal of Finance*, *70*(5), 2029–2062.

Kuhnen, C., Knutson, B. (2005). The neural basis of financial risk-taking. *Neuron*, *47*, 763–770.

Kumar, A., Lim, S. S. (2008). How do decision frames influence the stock investment choices of individual investors? *Management Science*, *54*(6), 1052–1064.

Kunreuther, H., Ginsberg, R., Miller, L., Slovic, P., Bradley, B., Katz, N. (1978). *Disaster Insurance Protection: Public Policy Lessons*. New York: Wiley.

Kuziemko, I., Buell, R. W., Reich, T., Norton, M. I. (2014). 'Last-place aversion': Evidence and redistributive implications. *Quarterly Journal of Economics*, *129*(1), 105–149.

Kuzmics, C., Rodriguez-Sickert, C. (2009). The evolution of moral codes of behavior. *Available at http://dx.doi.org/10.2139/ssrn.910292*.

Laibson, D. L. (1997). Golden eggs and hyperbolic discounting. *Quarterly Journal of Economics*, *112*, 443–477.

———. (1998). Life-cycle consumption and hyperbolic discount functions. *European Economic Review*, *42*(3–5), 861–871.

Laibson, D. L., Maxted, P., Repetto, A., Tobacman, J. (2017). Estimating discounting functions with consumption choices over the lifecycle. Unpublished. Retrieved from http://assets.wharton.upenn.edu/~tobacman/papers.html.

Lancaster, K. J. (1963). An axiomatic theory of consumer time preference. *International Economic Review*, *4*, 221–231.

Lang, P. (1995). The emotion probe: Studies of emotion and attention. *American Psychologist*, *50*, 372–385.

Langer, E. J. (1975). The illusion of control. *Journal of Personality and Social Psychology*, *32*(2), 311–328.

Langer, T., Weber, M. (2001). Prospect theory, mental accounting, and differences in aggregated and segregated evaluation of lottery portfolios. *Management Science*, *47*(5), 716–733.

———. (2005). Myopic prospect theory versus myopic loss-aversion: How general is the phenomenon? *Journal of Economic Behavior and Organization*, *56*(1), 25–38.

———. (2008). Does commitment or feedback influence myopic loss aversion? An experimental analysis. *Journal of Economic Behavior and Organization*, *64*(3/4), 810–819.

Larrick, R. P., Blount, S. (1997). The claiming effect: Why players are more generous in social dilemmas than in ultimatum games. *Journal of Personality and Social Psychology*, *72*, 810–825.

Larrick, R. P., Boles, T. L. (1995). Avoiding regret in decisions with feedback: A negotiation example. *Organizational Behavior and Human Decision Processes*, *63*(1), 87–97.

Larwood, L., Whitaker, W. (1977). Managerial myopia: Self-serving biases in organizational planning. *Journal of Applied Psychology*, *62*, 194–198.

Lattimore, P. K., Baker, J. R., Witte, A. D. (1992). The influence of probability on risky choice: A parametric examination. *Journal of Economic Behavior and Organization*, *17*, 377–400.

Lazear, E. P. (2000). Performance pay and productivity. *American Economic Review*, *90*(5), 1346–1361.

LeBoeuf, R. A. (2006). Discount rates for time versus dates: The sensitivity of discounting to time-interval description. *Journal of Marketing Research*, *43*, 59–72.

Leclerc, F., Schmidt, B., Dube, L. (1995). Decision making and waiting time: Is time like money? *Journal of Consumer Research*, *22*, 110–119.

LeDoux, J. E. (1996). *The Emotional Brain: The Mysterious Underpinnings of Emotional Life*. New York: Simon and Schuster.

Ledyard, J. (1995). Public goods: A survey of experimental research. In J. Kagel, A. E. Roth (Eds), *Handbook of Experimental Economics* (pp. 111–118). Princeton: Princeton University Press.

Lee, N. C., de Groot, R. H. M., Boschloo, A., Dekker, S., Krabbendam, L., Jolles, J. (2013). Age and educational track influence adolescent discounting of delayed rewards. *Frontiers in Psychology*, *4*, Article 993.

Leith, K. P., Baumeister, R. F. (1996). Why do bad moods increase self-defeating behavior? Emotion, risk-taking, and self-regulation. *Journal of Personality and Social Psychology*, *71*, 1250–1267.

Lerner, J. S., Keltner, D. (2001). Fear, anger, and risk. *Journal of Personality and Social Psychology*, *81*, 146–159.

Lerner, J. S., Li, Y., Weber, E. U. (2013). The financial costs of sadness. *Psychological Science*, *24*(1), 72–79.

Levav, J., McGraw, P. (2009). Emotional accounting: How feelings about money influence consumer choice. *Journal of Marketing Research*, *46*, 66–80.

Levin, I. P., Chapman, D. P. (1990). Risk taking, frame of reference, and characterization of victim groups in AIDS treatment decisions. *Journal of Experimental and Social Psychology*, *26*, 421–434.

Levin, I. P., Schneider, S. L., Gaeth, G. J. (1998). All frames are not created equal: A typology and critical analysis of framing effects. *Organizational Behavior and Human Decision Processes*, *76*, 149–188.

Levinson, S. C. (1995). Interactional biases in human thinking. In E. Goody (Ed.), *Social Intelligence and Interaction* (pp. 221–260). Cambridge: Cambridge University Press.

Levitt, S. C., List, J. A. (2007). What do laboratory experiments measuring social preferences reveal about the real world? *Journal of Economic Perspectives*, *21*(2), 153–174.

Levitt, S. D., Dubner, S. J. (2005). *Freakonomics*. London: Allen Lane.

Levy, M., Levy, H. (2002). Prospect theory: Much ado about nothing? *Management Science*, *48*(10), 1334–1349.

Lewis, R. J. (1983). Scared straight – California style. *Criminal Justice and Behavior*, *10*, 209–226.

Libet, B. (1985). Unconscious cerebral initiative and the role of conscious will in voluntary action. *Behavioral and Brain Sciences*, *8*(4), 529–566.

———. (1993). The neural time factor in conscious and unconscious events. *Experimental and Theoretical Studies of Consciousness*, *174*, 123–146.

Libet, B., Gleason, C. A., Wright, E. W., Jr., Pearl, D. K. (1983). Time of conscious intention to act in relation to onset of cerebral activity (readiness-potential). *Brain*, *106*, 623–642.

Lichtenstein, S., Fischoff, B. (1977). Do those who know more also know more about how much they know? The calibration of probability judgments. *Organizational Behavior and Human Performance*, *16*, 1–12.

Lichtenstein, S., Slovic, P. (1973). Response-induced reversals of preference in gambling: An extended replication in Las Vegas. *Journal of Experimental Psychology*, *101*, 16–20.

Lima, S. (1984). Downy woodpecker foraging behavior: Efficient sampling in simple stochastic environments. *Ecology*, *67*, 377–385.

Lin, L., McFerran, B. (2012). The (ironic) Dove Effect: How normalizing overweight body types increases unhealthy food consumption and lowers motivation to engage in healthy behaviors. In Z. Gürhan-Canli, C. Otnes, R. Zhu (Eds), *NA - Advances in Consumer Research* (Vol. 40, pp. 37–41). Duluth, MN: Association for Consumer Research. Retrieved from www.acrwebsite.org/volumes/1011741/volumes/v40/NA-40.

Lindquist, K. A., Siegel, E. H., Quigley, K. S., Barrett, L. F. (2013). The hundred-year emotion war: Are emotions natural kinds or psychological constructions? Comment on Lench, Flores, and Bench (2011). *Psychological Bulletin*, *139*(1), 255–263.

List, J. A. (2004). Neoclassical theory versus prospect theory: Evidence from the marketplace. *Econometrica*, *72*(2), 615–625.

———. (2011). Does market experience eliminate market anomalies? The case of exogenous market experience. *American Economic Review*, *101*(3), 313–317.

List, J. A., Cherry, T. L. (2000). Learning to accept in ultimatum games: Evidence from an experimental design that generates low offers. *Experimental Economics*, *3*, 11–31.

———. (2008). Examining the role of fairness in high stakes allocation decisions. *Journal of Economic Behavior and Organization*, *65*(1), 1–8.

Littlewood, J. E. (1953). *A Mathematician's Miscellany*. London: Methuen.

Liu, M. W. (2014). Utility blindness: Why do we fall for deals? *Journal of Consumer Behaviour*, *13*(1), 42–49.

Liu, P., Fitzsimons, G. (2013). Avoiding behavioral resistance to diet and exercise messages. In S. Botti, A. Labroo (Eds), *NA – Advances in Consumer Research* (Vol. 41, pp. 142–146). Duluth, MN: Association for Consumer Research. Retrieved from http://acrwebsite.org/volumes/1014947/volumes/v41/NA-41.

Livnat, A., Pippenger, N. (2006). An optimal brain can be composed of conflicting agents. In *Proceedings of the National Academy of Sciences* (Vol. 103, pp. 3198–3202).

Loewenstein, G. (1987). Anticipation and the valuation of delayed consumption. *Economic Journal*, *87*, 666–684.

———. (1988). Frames of mind in intertemporal choice. *Management Science*, *34*, 200–214.

———. (1996). Out of control: Visceral influences on behavior. *Organizational Behavior and Human Decision Processes*, *65*(3), 272–292.

———. (2000). Emotions in economic theory and economic behavior. *American Economic Review*, *90(2)*, 426–432.

Loewenstein, G., Issacharoff, S., Camerer, C., Babcock, L. (1993). Self-serving assessments of fairness and pretrial bargaining. *Journal of Legal Studies*, *22*, 135–159.

Loewenstein, G., O'Donoghue, T., Rabin, M. (2003). Projection bias in predicting future utility. *Quarterly Journal of Economics*, *118*(4), 1209–1248.

Loewenstein, G., Prelec, D. (1992). Anomalies in intertemporal choice: Evidence and interpretation. *Quarterly Journal of Economics*, *107*(2), 573–597.

———. (1993). Preferences for sequences of outcomes. *Psychological Review*, *100*(1), 91–108.

Loewenstein, G., Sicherman, N. (1991). Do workers prefer increasing wage profiles? *Journal of Labor Economics*, *9*(1), 67–84.

Loewenstein, G., Thompson, L., Bazerman, M. H. (1989). Social utility and decision making in interpersonal contexts. *Journal of Personality and Social Psychology*, *62*(3), 426–441.

Long, J. B. D., Shleifer, A., Summers, L. H., Waldmann, R. J. (1991). The survival of noise traders in financial markets. *Journal of Business*, *64*(1), 1–19.

Loomes, G., Starmer, C., Sugden, R. (2003). Do anomalies disappear in repeated markets? *Economic Journal*, *113*, 153–166.

Loomes, G., Sugden, R. (1982). Regret theory: An alternative theory of rational choice under uncertainty. *Economic Journal*, *92*, 805–824.

———. (1986). Disappointment and dynamic consistency in choice under uncertainty. *Review of Economic Studies*, *53*(2), 271–282.

———. (1987). Some implications of a more general form of regret theory. *Journal of Economic Theory*, *41*(2), 270–287.

———. (1995). Incorporating a stochastic element into decision theories. *European Economic Review*, *39*, 641–648.

———. (1998). Testing different stochastic specifications of risky choice. *Economica*, *65*, 581–598.

Lopes, L. L., Oden, G. C. (1991). The rationality of intelligence. In E. Eells, T. Maruszewski (Eds), *Probability and Rationality: Studies on L. Jonathan Cohen's Philosophy of Science* (Vol. 21, pp. 199–223). Amsterdam: Rodopi.

Lopez, R. B., Hofmann, W., Wagner, D. D., Kelley, W. M., Heatherton, T. F. (2014). Neural predictors of giving in to temptation in daily life. *Psychological Science*, *25*(7), 1337–1344.

Lu, J., Xie, X., Wang, M., Tang, X. (2015). Double reference points: The effects of social and financial reference points on decisions under risk. *Journal of Behavioral Decision Making*, *28*(5), 451–463.

Luce, R. D., Fishburn, P. C. (1991). Rank- and sign-dependent linear utility models for finite first-order gambles. *Journal of Risk and Uncertainty*, *4*, 29–59.

———. (1995). A note on deriving rank-dependent utility using additive joint receipts. *Journal of Risk and Uncertainty*, *11*, 5–16.

Lund, D. A., Caserta, M. S., Diamond, M. F. (1989). Impact of spousal bereavement on the subjective well-being of older adults. In D. A. Lund (Ed.), *Older Bereaved Spouses: Research with Practical Implications* (pp. 3–15). New York: Hemisphere.

Luttmer, E. F. P., Singhal, M. (2011). Culture, context and the taste for redistribution. *American Economic Journal: Economic Policy*, *3*(1), 157–179.

Luttmer, E. G. J. (1996). Asset pricing in economies with frictions. *Econometrica*, *64*, 1439–1467.

Lykken, D., Tellegen, A. (1996). Happiness is a stochastic phenomenon. *Psychological Science*, *7*, 186–189.

Lyubomirsky, S., Lepper, H. S. (1999). A measure of subjective happiness: Preliminary reliability and construct validation. *Social Indicators Research*, *46*, 137–155.

MacCrimmon, K. R., Smith, M. (1986). Imprecise equivalences: Preference reversals in money and probability. *Working Paper*, No. 1211, University of British Columbia, Vancouver.

MacDonald, R. R. (1986). Credible conceptions and implausible probabilities. *British Journal of Mathematical and Statistical Psychology*, *39*, 15–27.

MacDonald, T. K., Ross, M. (1999). Assessing the accuracy of predictions about dating relationships: How and why do lovers' predictions differ from those made by observers? *Personality and Social Psychology Bulletin*, *25*, 1417–1429.

McFerran, B., Dahl, D. W., Fitzsimons, G. J., Morales, A. C. (2010). I'll have what she's having: Effects of social influence and body type on the food choices of others. *Journal of Consumer Research*, *36*(6), 915–929.

McGlothlin, W. H. (1956). Stability of choices among uncertain alternatives. *American Journal of Psychology*, *69*, 604–15.

McGuire, J. T., Kable, J. W. (2013). Rational temporal predictions can underlie apparent failures to delay gratification. *Psychological Review*, *120*(2), 395–410.

McKelvey, R. D., Palfrey, T. R. (1992). An experimental study of the centipede game. *Econometrica*, *58*, 1321–1339.

McKenzie, C. R. M., Sher, S., Müller-Trede, J., Lin, C., Liersch, M. J., Rawstron, A. G. (2015). Are longshots only for losers? A new look at the last race effect. *Journal of Behavioral Decision Making*, *29*(1), 25–36.

McKernan, S.-M., Ratcliffe, C., Kuehn, D. (2013). Prohibitions, price caps, and disclosures: A look at state policies and alternative financial product use. *Journal of Economic Behavior and Organization*, *95*, 207–223.

MGI (McKinsey Global Institute) (2005). *The Coming Demographic Deficit: How Aging Populations Will Reduce Global Savings*. McKinsey & Co. Available at https://www.mckinsey.com/industries/financial-services/our-insights/the-coming-demographic-deficit

MGI (McKinsey Global Institute) (2014). *Overcoming Obesity: An initial Economic Analysis*. McKinsey & Co.Available at https://www.mckinsey.com/industries/healthcare-systems-and-services/our-insights/how-the-world-could-better-fight-obesity

Machina, M. J. (1982). 'Expected utility' theory without the independence axiom. *Econometrica*, *50*, 277–323.

———. (1983). *The Economic Theory of Individual Behavior Toward Risk: Theory, Evidence, and New Directions*. Technical Report, No. 433, Department of Economics, Stanford University.

MacKeigan, L. D., Larson, L. N., Draugalis, J. R., Bootman, J. L., Burns, L. R. (1993). Time preference for health gains versus health losses. *Pharmacoeconomics*, *3*(5), 374–386.

Mackiewicz, R., Falkowski, A. (2015). Sensitivity to price changes according to the Weber fraction: Implications for the general price elasticity. In K. Diehl, C. Yoon (Eds), *NA – Advances in Consumer Research* (Vol. 43). Duluth, MN: Association for Consumer Research. Retrieved from http://acrwebsite.org/volumes/1019332/volumes/v43/NA-43

Madrian, B. C., Shea, D. F. (2001). The power of suggestion: Inertia in 401(k) participation and savings behavior. *Quarterly Journal of Economics*, *116*(4), 1149–1187.

Maenhout, P. J. (2004). Robust portfolio rules and asset pricing. *Review of Financial Studies*, *17*(4), 951–983.

Maier-Rigaud, F. P., Martinsson, P., Staffiero, G. (2010). Ostracism and the provision of a public good: Experimental evidence. *Journal of Economic Behavior and Organization*, *73*(3), 387–395.

Mäki, U. (Ed.). (2009). *The Methodology of Positive Economics: Reflections on the Milton Friedman Legacy*. Cambridge: Cambridge University Press.

Mallpress, D., Fawcett, T., Houston, A., McNamara, J. (2015). Risk attitudes in a changing environment: An evolutionary model of the fourfold pattern of risk preferences. *Psychological Review*, *122*(2), 364–375.

Malmendier, U., Lee, Y. H. (2011). The bidder's curse. *American Economic Review*, *101*(2), 749–787.

Malmendier, U., Tate, G. (2005). CEO overconfidence and corporate investment. *Journal of Finance*, *60*, 2661–2700.

———. (2008). Who makes acquisitions? CEO overconfidence and the market's reaction. *Journal of Financial Economics*, *89*(1), 20–43.

Maniadis, Z., Tufano, F., List, J. A. (2014). One swallow doesn't make a summer: New evidence on anchoring effects. *American Economic Review*, *104*(1), 277–290.

Mankiw, N. G., Zeldes, S. (1991). The consumption of stockholders and nonstockholders. *Journal of Financial Economics*, *29*(1), 97–112.

Margolis, H. (1982). *Selfishness, Altruism and Rationality: A Theory of Social Choice*. Cambridge: Cambridge University Press.

*Marketing Magazine* (2011). Domino's Pizza turns to behavioural economics. May 5.

Markowitz, H. (1952). The utility of wealth. *Journal of Political Economy*, *60*, 151–58.

Marsh, A. A., Finger, E. C., Mitchell, D. G. V., Reid, M.E., Sims, C., Kosson, D. S., Towbin, K. E., Leibenluft, E., Pine, D. S., Blair, R. J. R. (2008). Reduced amygdala response to fearful expressions in children and adolescents with callous-unemotional traits and disruptive behavior disorders. *American Journal of Psychiatry, 165*, 712–720.

Marsh, A. A., Stoycos, S. A., Brethel-Hauritz, K. M., Robinson, P., VanMeter, J. W., Cardinale, E. M. (2014). Neural and cognitive characteristics of extraordinary altruists. *PNAS, 111*(42), 15036–15041.

Mayer, T., Russell, T. (2005). Income smoothing and self-control: The case of school teachers. *Economic Enquiry*, *43*(4), 823–30.

Maynard Smith, J. (1976). Evolution and the theory of games. *American Scientist*, *64*, 41–45.

———. (1982). *Evolution and the Theory of Games*. Cambridge: Cambridge University Press.

Maynard Smith, J., Price, G. R. (1973). The logic of animal conflict. *Nature, 246*, 15–18.

Mead, N. L., Patrick, V. M. (2016). The taming of desire: Unspecific postponement reduces desire for and consumption of postponed temptations. *Journal of Personality and Social Psychology*, *110*(1), 20–35.

Mehra, R. (2003). The equity premium: Why is it a puzzle? *Financial Analysts Journal*, *59*(1), 54–69.

Mehra, R., Prescott, E. C. (1985). The equity premium: A puzzle. *Journal of Monetary Economics*, *15*, 145–161.

Mehta, J., Starmer, C., Sugden, R. (1992). An experimental investigation of focal points in coordination and bargaining: Some preliminary results. In J. Geweke (Ed.), *Decision Making under Risk and Uncertainty: New Models and Findings* (pp. 211–220). Norwell, MA: Kluwer.

———. (1994a). Focal points in pure coordination games: An experimental investigation. *Theory and Decision*, *36*(2), 163–185.

———. (1994b). The nature of salience: An experimental investigation of pure coordination games. *American Economic Review*, *84*(3), 658–673.

Meier, S., Sprenger, C. D. (2013). Discounting financial literacy: Time preferences and participation in financial education programs. *Journal of Economic Behavior and Organization*, *95*, 159–174.

Meyer, D. J., Meyer, J. (2005). Risk preferences in multi-period consumption models, the equity premium puzzle, and habit formation utility. *Journal of Monetary Economics*, *52*(8), 1497–1515.

Meyer, R. F. (1976). Preferences over time. In R. L. Keeney, H. Raiffa (Eds), *Decisions with Multiple Objectives* (pp. 473–514). New York: Wiley.

Meyvis, T., Ratner, R. K., Levav, J. (2010). Why we don't learn to accurately forecast our feelings: How the misremembering of our predictions blinds us to our past forecasting errors. *Journal of Experimental Psychology: General*, *139*(4), 579–589.

Milgram, S. (1963). Behavioral study of obedience. *The Journal of Abnormal and Social Psychology*, *67*(4), 371–378.

Milinski, M. (1987). Tit for tat and the evolution of cooperation in sticklebacks. *Nature*, *325*, 433–435.

Milkman, K. and Beshears, J. (2009). Mental accounting and small windfalls: Evidence from an online grocer. *Journal of Economic Behavior and Organization*, *71*(2), 384–394.

Mill, J. S. (1873). *Autobiography*. London: Penguin.

Miller, D. T., Taylor, B. R. (1995). Counterfactual thought, regret and superstition: How to avoid kicking yourself. In N. J. R., J. M. Olson (Eds), *What Might Have Been: The Social Psychology of Counterfactual Thinking* (pp. 305–332). Mahwah, NJ: Erlbaum.

Miller, P. M., Fagley, N. S. (1991). The effects of framing, problem variations, and providing rationale on choice. *Personality and Social Psychology Bulletin*, *17*, 517–522.

Milyavskaya, M., Inzlicht, M., Hope, N., Koestner, R. (2015). Saying 'no' to temptation: Want-to motivation improves self-regulation by reducing temptation rather than by increasing self-control. *Journal of Personality and Social Psychology*, *109*(4), 677–693.

Miravete, E. (2003). Choosing the wrong calling plan? Ignorance and learning. *American Economic Review*, *93*, 297–310.

Mischel, W. (1974). Process in delay of gratification. In L. Berkowitz (Ed.), *Advances in Experimental Social Psychology* (Vol. 7, pp. 249–292). New York: Academic Press.

Mischel, W., Ebbesen, E. B. (1970). Attention in delay of gratification. *Journal of Personality and Social Psychology*, *16*(2), 329–337.

Mischel, W., Grusec, J., Masters, J. C. (1969). Effects of expected delay time on subjective value of rewards and punishments. *Journal of Personality and Social Psychology*, *11*(4), 363–373.

Mischel, W., Metzner, R. (1962). Preference for delayed reward as a function of age, intelligence, and length of delay interval. *Journal of Abnormal Psychology*, *64*(6), 425–431.

Mischel, W., Shoda, Y., Peake, P. K. (1988). The nature of adolescent competencies predicted by preschool delay of gratification. *Journal of Personality and Social Psychology*, *54*(4), 687–696.

Mischel, W., Shoda, Y., Rodriguez, M. L. (1992). Delay of gratification in children. In G. Loewenstein, J. Elster (Eds), *Choice Over Time* (pp. 147–164). New York: Russell Sage.

Mishra, A., Mishra, H. (2011). The influence of price discount versus bonus pack on the preference for virtue and vice foods. *Journal of Marketing Research*, *48*(1), 196–206.

Mitzkewitz, M., Nagel, R. (1993). Experimental results on ultimatum games with incomplete information. *International Journal of Game Theory*, *22*, 171–98.

Mochon, D. (2013). Single-option aversion. *Journal of Consumer Research*, *40*(3), 555–566.

Modigliani, F., Brumberg, R. (1954). Utility analysis and the consumption function: An interpretation of cross-section data. In K. K. Kurihara (Ed.), *Post Keynesian Economics* (pp. 383–436). New Brunswick, NJ: Rutgers University Press.

Molden, D. C., Hui, C. M., Scholer, A. A., Meier, B. P., Noreen, E. E., D'Agostino, P. R., Martin, V. (2012). Motivational versus metabolic effects of carbohydrates on self-control. *Psychological Science*, *23*(10), 1137–1144.

Moll, J., Krueger, F., Zahn, R., Pardini, M., de Oliveira-Souza, R., Grafman, J. (2006). Human fronto-mesolimbic networks guide decisions about charitable donation. In *Proceedings of the National Academy of Science, USA* (Vol. 103, pp. 15623–8).

Moore, D. A., Healy, P. J. (2008). The trouble with overconfidence. *Psychological Review*, *115*(2), 502–517.

Morales, A. C., Fitzsimons, G. J. (2007). Product contagion: Changing consumer evaluations through physical contact with disgusting products. *Journal of Marketing Research*, *44*, 272–283.

Morales, A. C., Wu, E. C., Fitzsimons, G. J. (2012). How disgust enhances the effectiveness of fear appeals. *Journal of Marketing Research*, *49*(3), 383–393.

Morier, D. M., Borgida, E. (1984). The conjunction fallacy: A task specific phenomenon? *Personal and Social Psychology Bulletin*, *10*, 243–252.

Morrin, M., Inman, J. J., Broniarczyk, S. M., Nenkov, G. Y., Reuter, J. (2012). Investing for retirement: The moderating effect of fund assortment size on the 1/N heuristic. *Journal of Marketing Research*, *49*(4), 537–550.

Mukherjee, A., Dubé, L. (2012). Mixing emotions: The use of humor in fear advertising. *Journal of Consumer Behaviour*, *11*(2), 147–161.

Mukhopadhyay, A., Sengupta, J., Ramanathan, S. (2008). Recalling past temptations: An information-processing perspective on the dynamics of self-control. *Journal of Consumer Research*, *35*, 586–598.

Munasinghe, L., Sicherman, N. (2006). Why do dancers smoke? Smoking, time preference, and wage dynamics. *Eastern Economic Journal*, *32*(4), 595–616.

Muraven, M. (2008). Autonomous self-control is less depleting. *Journal of Research in Personality*, *42*(3), 763–770.

Muraven, M., Baumeister, R. F. (2000). Self-regulation and depletion of limited resources: Does self-control resemble a muscle? *Psychological Bulletin*, *126*, 227–259.

Muraven, M., Baumeister, R. F., Tice, D. M. (1999). Longitudinal improvement of self-regulation through practice: Building self-control through repeated exercise. *Journal of Social Psychology*, *139*, 446–457.

Muraven, M., Shmueli, D., Burkley, E. (2006). Conserving self-control strength. *Journal of Personality and Social Psychology*, *91*(3), 524–537.

Muraven, M., Slessareva, E. (2003). Mechanisms of self-control failure: Motivation and limited resources. *Personality and Social Psychology Bulletin*, *29*(7), 894–906.

Muraven, M., Tice, D. M., Baumeister, R. F. (1998). Self-control as a limited resource: Regulatory depletion patterns. *Journal of Personality and Social Psychology*, *74*(3), 774–789.

Murnighan, J. K., Saxon, M. S. (1998). Ultimatum bargaining by children and adults. *Journal of Economic Psychology*, *19*, 415–445.

Musson, F. F., Alloy, L. B. (1988). Depression and self-directed attention. In L. B. Alloy (Ed.), *Cognitive Processes in Depression* (pp. 193–220). New York: Guilford Press.

Myers, D. G., Diener, E. (1995). Who is happy? *Psychological Science*, *6*, 10–19.

Myrseth, K. O. R., Fishbach, A., Trope, Y. (2009). Counteractive self-control. *Psychological Science*, *20*(2), 159–163.

Nagel, R. (1995). Unravelling in guessing games: An experimental study. *American Economic Review*, *85*, 1313–1326.

Nakazono, Y. (2013). Strategic behavior of Federal Open Market Committee board members: Evidence from members' forecasts. *Journal of Economic Behavior and Organization*, *93*, 62–70.

Nash, J. (1950). The bargaining problem. *Econometrica*, *18*, 155–162.

———. (1951). Non-cooperative games. *Annals of Mathematics*, *54*, 286–295.

NcClure, S. M., Laibson, D. L., Loewenstein, G., Cohen, J. D. (2004). Separate neural systems value immediate and delayed monetary rewards. *Science*, *306*(5695), 503–507.

Neale, M. A., Bazerman, M. H. (1985). The effects of framing and negotiator overconfidence on bargaining behaviors and outcomes. *Academy of Management Journal*, *28*(1), 34–49.

Neelin, J., Sonnenschein, H., Spiegel, M. (1988). A further test of noncooperative bargaining theory: Comment. *American Economic Review*, *78*, 824–836.

Neilson, W. S. (1992). A mixed fan hypothesis and its implications for behavior toward risk. *Journal of Economic Behavior and Organisation*, *19*, 197–211.

Netzer, N. (2009). Evolution of time preferences and attitudes toward risk. *American Economic Review*, *99*, 937–95.

Newell, A., Simon, H. A. (1972). *Human Problem Solving*. Englewood Cliffs, NJ: Prentice-Hall.

Newell, R. G., Pizer, W. A. (2003). Discounting the distant future: How much do uncertain rates increase valuations? *Journal of Environmental Economics and Management*, *46*(1), 52–71.

Newman, G. E., Diesendruck, G., Bloom, P. (2011). Celebrity contagion and the value of objects. *Journal of Consumer Research*, *38*(2), 215–228.

Niv, Y., Montague, P. R. (2008). Theoretical and empirical studies of learning. In P. W. Glimcher, C. F. Camerer, E. Fehr, R. A. Poldrack (Eds), *Neuroeconomics: Decision-Making and the Brain* (pp. 331–52). London: Academic Press.

Nordgren, L. F., Dijksterhuis, A. P. (2009). The devil is in the deliberation: Thinking too much reduces preference consistency. *Journal of Consumer Research*, *36*(1), 39–46.

Novemsky, N., Kahneman, D. (2005a). How do intentions affect loss-aversion? *Journal of Marketing Research*, *42*, 139–140.

———. (2005b). The boundaries of loss-aversion. *Journal of Marketing Research*, *42*, 119–128.

Nowak, M. A., May, R. M., Sigmund, K. (1995). The arithmetics of mutual help. *Scientific American*, *272*, 50–55.

Nussbaum, M. C., Sen, A. K. (Eds). (1993). *The Quality of Life*. Oxford: Clarendon Press.

Nyarko, Y., Schotter, A. (2002). An experimental study of belief learning using elicited beliefs. *Econometrica*, *70*, 971–1005.

Nyhan, B., Reifler, J. (2010). When corrections fail: The persistence of political misperceptions. *Political Behavior*, *32*(2), 303–330.

Ochs, J. (1995). Games with unique, mixed strategy equilibria: An experimental study. *Games and Economic Behavior*, *10*, 202–217.

Ochs, J., Roth, A. E. (1989). An experimental study of sequential bargaining. *American Economic Review*, *79*, 355–384.

O'Curry, S. (1997). Income source effects. *Working Paper*, Department of Marketing, DePaul University, Chicago.

O'Curry, S., Strahilevitz, M. (2001). Probability and mode of acquisition effects on choices between hedonic and utilitarian options. *Marketing Letters*, *12*(1), 37–49.

Odean, T. (1998). Are investors reluctant to realize their losses? *Journal of Finance, 53*, 1775–1798.

———. (1999). Do investors trade too much? *American Economic Review, 89*(5), 1279–98.

O'Doherty, J. P. (2004). Reward representations and reward-related learning in the human brain: Insights from neuroimaging. *Current Opinion in Neurobiology 14*(6), 769–776.

O'Doherty, J. P., Kringelbach, M. L., Rolls, E. T., Hornak, J., Andrews, C. (2001). Reward and punishment representations in the human orbitofrontal cortex. *Nature Neuroscience, 4*(1), 95–102.

O'Donoghue, T., Rabin, M. (2001). Choice and procrastination. *Quarterly Journal of Economics, 116*(1), 121–160.

———. (2008). Procrastination on long-term projects. *Journal of Economic Behavior and Organization, 66*(2), 161–175.

Oehler, A., Heilmann, K., Läger, V., Oberländer, M. (2003). Coexistence of disposition investors and momentum traders in stock markets: Experimental evidence. *Journal of International Financial Markets, Institutions and Money, 13*(5), 503–524.

Offerman, T. (2002). Hurting hurts more than helping helps: The role of the self-serving bias. *European Economic Review, 46*(8), 1423–1437.

Okada, E. M. (2001). Trade-ins, mental accounting, and product replacement decisions. *Journal of Consumer Research, 27*(4), 433–446.

Olds, J., Miller, P. (1954). Positive reinforcement caused by electrical stimulation of septal area and other regions of rat brain. *Journal of Comparative and Physiological Psychology, 47*, 419–427.

Olmstead, A. L., Rhode, P. (1985). Rationing without government: The West Coast gas famine of 1920. *American Economic Review, 75*(5), 1044–1055.

Olsen, R. A., Troughton, G. H. (2000). Are risk premium anomalies caused by ambiguity? *Financial Analysts Journal, 56*(2), 24–31.

Ortoleva, P., Snowberg, E. (2015). Overconfidence in political behavior. *American Economic Review, 105*(2), 504–535.

Osherson, D. N. (1995). Probability judgment. In E. E. Smith, D.N. Osherson (Eds), *Thinking: An Invitation to Cognitive Science* (2nd ed, Vol. 3, pp. 35–75). Cambridge, MA: MIT Press.

Östling, R., Wang, J. T., Chou, E., Camerer, C. F. (2011). Testing game theory in the field: Swedish LUPI lottery games. *American Economic Journal: Microeconomics, 3*(3), 1–33.

Ostrom, E. (1998). A behavioral approach to the rational choice theory of collective action. *American Political Science Review, 92*, 1–22.

———. (2000). Collective action and the evolution of social norms. *Journal of Economic Perspectives, 14*, 137–158.

Oyefeso, O. (2006). Would there ever be consensus value and source of the equity risk premium? A review of the extant literature. *International Journal of Theoretical and Applied Finance, 9*(2), 199–215.

Pachur, T., Hertwig, R., Steinmann, F. (2012). How do people judge risks: Availability heuristic, affect heuristic, or both? *Journal of Experimental Psychology: Applied, 18*(3), 314–330.

Palacios-Huerta, I. (2003). Professionals play minimax. *Review of Economic Studies, 70*, 395–415.

Palm, R., M., H., Blanchard, D., Lyons, D. (1990). *Earthquake Insurance in California*. Boulder, CO: Westview: Press.

Palmeira, M. M., Srivastava, J. (2013). Free offer ? Cheap product: A selective accessibility account on the valuation of free offers. *Journal of Consumer Research*, *40*(4), 644–656.

Papies, E. K., Pronk, T. M., Keesman, M., Barsalou, L. W. (2015). The benefits of simply observing: Mindful attention modulates the link between motivation and behavior. *Journal of Personality and Social Psychology*, *108*(1), 148–170.

Parducci, A. (1995). *Happiness, Pleasure, and Judgment: The Contextual Theory and Its Applications*. Mahway, NJ: Erlbaum.

Parks, C. D., Stone, A. B. (2010). The desire to expel unselfish members from the group. *The Journal of Personality and Social Psychology*, *99*(2), 303–310.

Paserman, M. D. (2008). Job search and hyperbolic discounting: Structural estimation and policy evaluation. *Economic Journal*, *118*(531), 1418–1452.

Paulus, M. P., Frank, L. R. (2006). Anterior cingulate activity modulates non-linear decision weight function of uncertain prospects. *Neuroimage*, *30*, 668–677.

Payne, J. W., Schkade, D. A., Desvousges, W., Aultman, C. (2000). Valuation of multiple environmental programs. *Journal of Risk and Uncertainty*, *21*, 95–115.

Peachey, K. (2015). Loan shark fear amid payday lending crackdown. *BBC News*. July 21. Retrieved from www.bbc.co.uk/news/business-33592180.

Peters, A., Schweiger, U., Pellerin, L., Hubold, C., Oltmanns, K. M., Conrad, M, Schultes, B., Born, J., Fehm, H. L., Born, J. (2004). The selfish brain: Competition for energy resources. Neuroscience and Behavioral Reviews, 28(2), 143–180.

Pfattheicher, S., Landhäußer, A., Keller, J. (2014). Individual differences in antisocial punishment in public goods situations: The interplay of cortisol with testosterone and dominance. *Journal of Behavioral Decision Making*, *27*(4), 340–348.

Pfeiffer, J. E. (1982). *Explosion: An Enquiry into the Origins of Art and Religion*. New York: Harper and Row.

Phelps, E. S., Pollak, R. A. (1968). On second-best national saving and game-equilibrium growth. *Review of Economic Studies*, *35*, 185–199.

Phillips, D. P., Liu, G. C., Kwok, K., Jarvinen, J. R., Zhang, W., Abramson, I. S. (2001). The Hound of the Baskervilles effect: Natural experiment on the influence of psychological stress on timing of death. *British Medical Journal*, *323*(7327), 1443–1446.

Pidgeon, N., Hood, C., Jones, D., Turner, B., Gibson, R. (1992). Risk perception. In *Risk Analysis, Perceptions and Management* (pp. 89–134). London: Royal Society.

Pigou, A. C. (1920). *The Economics of Welfare*. 4th ed. London: Macmillan.

Pillutla, M. M., Chen, X.-P. (1999). Social norms and cooperation in social dilemmas: The effects of context and feedback. *Organizational Behavior and Human Decision Processes*, *78*(2), 81–103.

Pinger, P., Ruhmer-Krell, I., Schumacher, H. (2016). The compromise effect in action: Lessons from a restaurant's menu. *Journal of Economic Behavior and Organization*, *128*, 14–34.

Pinker, S. (1997). *How the Mind Works*. New York: Norton.

Plassman, H., O'Doherty, J., Rangel, A. (2007). Orbitofrontal cortex encodes willingness to pay in everyday economic transactions. *Journal of Neuroscience*, *27*, 9984–9988.

Plat, M. I., Padoa-Schioppa, C. (2009). Neuronal representations of value. In P. W. Glimcher, C. F. Camerer, E. Fehr, R. A. Poldrack (Eds), *Neuroeconomics: Decision-Making and the Brain* (pp. 441–459). London: Academic Press.

Platt, M. L., McCoy. (2005). Risk-sensitive neurons in macaque posterior cingulate cortex. *Nature Neuroscience*, *8*(9), 1220–1227.

Plott, C. R. (1996). Rational individual behavior in markets and social choice processes: The discovered preference hypothesis. In K. J. Arrow, E. Colombatto, M. Perlman, C. Schmidt (Eds), *The Rational Foundations of Economic Behavior* (pp. 225–250). New York: St Martin's Press.

Plott, C. R., Zeiler, K. (2005). The willingness to pay – willingness to accept gap, the 'endowment effect', subject misconceptions, and experimental procedures for eliciting evaluations. *American Economic Review*, *95*(3), 530–545.

———. (2007). Exchange asymmetries incorrectly interpreted as evidence of endowment effect theory and prospect theory? *American Economic Review*, *97*(4), 1449–1466.

Plous, S. (1993). *The Psychology of Judgment and Decision Making*. New York: McGraw-Hill.

Plutchik, R., Conte, H. R. (Eds). (1997). *Circumplex Models of Personality and Emotions*. Washington, DC: American Psychological Association.

Pocheptsova, A., Espinoza Petersen, F., Etkin, J. (2015). Two birds, one stone? Positive mood makes products seem less useful for multiple-goal pursuit. *Journal of Consumer Psychology*, *25*(2), 296–303.

Pohl, R. F., Hell, W. (1996). No reduction in hindsight bias after complete information and repeated testing. *Organizational Behavior and Human Decision Processes*, *67*, 49–58.

Poldrack, R. A. (2006). Can cognitive processes be inferred from neuroimaging data? *Trends in Cognitive Sciences*, *10*, 59–63.

Politzer, G., Noveck, I. A. (1991). Are conjunctional rule violations the result of conversational rule violations? *Journal of Psycholinguistic Research*, *20*, 83–103.

Poortvliet, P. M., Janssen, O., Van Yperen, N. W., Van de Vliert, E. (2009). Low ranks make the difference: How achievement goals and ranking information affect cooperation intentions. *Journal of Experimental Social Psychology*, *45*(5), 1144–1147.

Pope, D. G., Schweitzer, M. E. (2011). Is Tiger Woods loss averse? Persistent bias in the face of experience, competition, and high stakes. *American Economic Review*, *101*(1), 129–157.

Prelec, D. (1989). Decreasing impatience: Definition and consequences. *Working Paper*, No. 90-015, Harvard Business School, Cambridge, MA.

———. (2004). Decreasing impatience: A criterion for non-stationary time preference and 'hyperbolic' discounting. *Scandinavian Journal of Economics*, *106*(3), 511–532.

Prelec, D., Loewenstein, G. (1998). The red and the black: Mental accounting of savings and debt. *Marketing Science*, *17*(1), 4–27.

Prelec, D., Simester, D. (2001). Always leave home without it: A further investigation of the credit-card effect on willingness to pay. *Marketing Letters*, *12*(1), 5–12.

Prendergast, C. (1999). The provision of incentives in firms. *Journal of Economic Literature*, *37*(1), 7–63.

Pronin, E. (2008). How we see ourselves and how we see others. *Science*, *320*, 1177–1180.

Pronin, E., Kugler, M. B. (2007). Valuing thoughts, ignoring behavior: The introspection illusion as a source of the bias blind spot. *Journal of Experimental Social Psychology*, *43*(4), 565–578.

Putler, D. (1992). Incorporating reference price effects into a theory of consumer choice. *Marketing Science*, *11*, 287–309.

Quattrone, G. A., Tversky, A. (1984). Causal versus diagnostic contingencies: On self-deception and on the voter's illusion. *Journal of Personality and Social Psychology*, *46*, 237–248.

Quiggin, J. (1982). A theory of anticipated utility. *Journal of Economic Behavior and Organization*, *3*(4), 324–345.

———. (1993). *Generalized Expected Utility Theory: The Rank-dependent Model*. Boston: Kluwer Academic.

Quinn, M. (2016). Jeremy Bentham, 'The Psychology of Economic Man', and Behavioural Economics. *Œconomia. History, Methodology, Philosophy*, *6*(1), 3–32.

Raab, M., Gula, B., Gigerenzer, G. (2012). The hot hand exists in volleyball and is used for allocation decisions. *Journal of Experimental Psychology: Applied*, *18*(1), 81–94.

Rabin, M. (1993). Incorporating fairness into game theory and economics. *American Economic Review*, *83*(5), 1281–1302.

———. (2002a). A perspective on psychology and economics. *European Economic Review*, *46*, 657–685.

———. (2002b). Inference by believers in the law of small numbers. *Quarterly Journal of Economics*, *117*, 775–816.

Rabin, M., Schrag, J. C. (1999). First impressions matter: A model of confirmatory bias. *Quarterly Journal of Economics*, *114*, 37–82.

Rachlin, H. (2000). *The Science of Self-control*. Cambridge, MA: Harvard University Press.

Rae, J. (1834/1905). *The Sociological Theory of Capital*. London: Macmillan.

Raffaelli, T. (2003). *Marshall's Evolutionary Economics*. London: Routledge.

Raghubir, P., Srivastava, J. (2009). The denomination effect. *Journal of Consumer Research*, *36*(4), 701–13.

Ramanathan, S., Williams, P. (2007). Immediate and delayed emotional consequences of indulgence: The moderating influence of personality type on mixed emotions. *Journal of Consumer Research*, *34*, 212–223.

Ramnani, N., Owen, A. M. (2004). Anterior prefrontal cortex insights into function from anatomy and neuromimaging. *Nature Reviews Neuroscience*, *5*, 184–194.

Ramsden, C. E., Zamora, D., Majchrzak-Hong, S., Faurot, K. R., Broste, S. K., Frantz, R. P., Davis, J. M., Ringel, A., Suchindran, C.M., Hibbeln, J. R. (2016). Re-evaluation of the traditional diet-heart hypothesis: analysis of recovered data from Minnesota Coronary Experiment (1968–73). *BMJ*, i1246.

Rangel, A. (2009). The computation and comparison of value in goal-directed choice. In P. W. Glimcher, C. F. Camerer, E. Fehr, R. A. Poldrack (Eds), *Neuroeconomics: Decision-Making and the Brain* (pp. 425–440). London: Academic Press.

Rangel, A. (2013). Regulation of dietary choice by the decision-making circuitry. *Nature Neuroscience*, *16*(12), 1717–1724.

Rapoport, A., Budescu, D. V. (1997). Randomization in individual choice behavior. *Psychological Review*, *104*, 603–617.

Rapoport, A., Sundali, J. A., Potter, R. E. (1996). Ultimatums in two-person bargaining with one-sided uncertainty: Offer games. *International Journal of Game Theory*, *25*, 475–494.

Rapoport, A., Weg, E., Felsenthal, D. S. (1990). Effects of fixed costs in two-person sequential bargaining. *Theory and Decision*, *28*, 47–71.

Rashes, M. S. (2001). Massively confused investors making conspicuously ignorant choices (MCI-MCIC). *Journal of Finance*, *56*(5), 1911–27.

Read, D., Frederick, S., Orsel, B., Rahman, J. (2005). Four score and seven years from now: The date/delay effect in temporal discounting. *Management Science*, *51*(9), 1326–35.

Read, D., Loewenstein, G. (1995). Diversification bias: Explaining the discrepancy in variety seeking between combined and separated choices. *Journal of Experimental Psychology: Applied*, *1*, 34–49.

Read, D., Read, N. L. (2004). Time discounting over the lifespan. *Organizational Behavior and Human Decision Processes*, *94*(1), 22–32.

Read, D., Roelofsma, P. (2003). Subadditive discounting versus hyperbolic discounting: A comparison of choice and matching. *Organizational Behavior and Human Decision Processes*, *91*(2), 140–53.

Read, D., van Leeuwen, B. (1998). Predicting hunger: The effects of appetite and delay on choice. *Organizational Behavior and Human Decision Processes*, *76*(2), 189–205.

Redelmeier, D. A., Heller, D. N. (1993). Time preference in medical decision making and cost-effectiveness analysis. *Medical Decision Making*, *13*(3), 212–217.

Redelmeier, D. A., Kahneman, D. (1996). Patients' memories of painful medical treatments: Real-time and retrospective evaluations of two minimally invasive procedures. *Pain*, *66*, 3–8.

Redelmeier, D. A., Shafir, E. (1995). Medical decision making in situations that offer multiple alternatives. *Journal of the American Marketing Association*, *273*, 302–305.

Redelmeier, D. A., Shafir, E., Aujla, P. (2001). The beguiling pursuit of more information. *Medical Decision Making*, *21*(5), 376–387.

Redelmeier, D. A., Tversky, A. (1992). On the framing of multiple prospects. *Psychological Science*, *3*(3), 191–193.

Regner, T. (2015). Why consumers pay voluntarily: Evidence from online music. *Journal of Behavioral and Experimental Economics*, *57*, 205–214.

Regner, T., Barria, J. A. (2009). Do consumers pay voluntarily? The case of online music. *Journal of Economic Behavior and Organization*, *71*(2), 395–406.

Reinholtz, N., Bartels, D. M., Parker, J. R. (2015). On the mental accounting of restricted-use funds: How gift cards change what people purchase. *Journal of Consumer Research*, *42*(4), 596–614.

Resnik, M. D. (1987). *Choices: An Introduction to Decision Theory*. Minneapolis: University of Minnesota Press.

Restak, R. (1984). *The Brain*. New York: Bantam.

Rettie, R., Burchell, K., Barnham, C. (2014). Social normalisation: Using marketing to make green normal. *Journal of Consumer Behaviour*, *13*(1), 9–17.

Reyna, V. F., Brainerd, C. J. (1991). Fuzzy-trace theory and framing effects in choice: gist extraction, truncation, and conversion. *Journal of Behavioral Decision Making*, *4*, 249–262.

Rha, J.-Y., Rajagopal, P. (2001). Is time like money? Consumers' mental accounting of time. *Consumer Interest Annual*, *47*, 1–2.

Richins, M. L. (2013). When wanting is better than having: Materialism, transformation expectations, and product-evoked emotions in the purchase process. *Journal of Consumer Research*, *40*(1), 1–18.

Ridley, M. (1993). *The Red Queen: Sex and the Evolution of Human Nature*. London: Viking.

———. (1996). *The Origins of Virtue*. London: Penguin.

———. (2004). *Nature via Nurture*. London: Harper Perennial.

Riener, G., Traxler, C. (2012). Norms, moods, and free lunch: Longitudinal evidence on payments from a Pay-What-You-Want restaurant. *Journal of Socio-Economics*, *41*(4), 476–483.

Rietveld, C. A., Cesarini, D., Benjamin, D. J., Koellinger, P. D., De Neve, J.-E., Tiemeier, H., Johannesson, M., Magnusson, P. K. E., Pedersen, N. L., Krueger, R. F., Bartels, M. (2013). Molecular genetics and subjective well-being. *Proceedings of the National Academy of Sciences, 110*(24), 9692–9697.

Rilling, J. K., Gutman, D. A., Zeh, T. R., Pagnoni, G., Berus, G. S., Kilts, C. D. (2002). A neural basis for social cooperation. *Neuron*, *35*(2), 395–405.

Rilling, J. K., Sanfey, A. G., Aronson, J. A., Nystrom, L. E., Cohen, J. D. (2004). Opposing bold responses to reciprocated and unreciprocated altruism in putative reward pathways. *Neuroreport*, *15*(16), 2539–2543.

Rind, B. (1996). Effects of beliefs about weather conditions on tipping. *Journal of Applied Social Psychology*, *26*(2), 137–147.

Risen, J., Critcher, C. R. (2011). Visceral fit: While in a visceral state, associated states of the world seem more likely. *Journal of Personality and Social Psychology*, *100*, 777–793.

Risen, J., Gilovich, T. (2007). Another look at why people are reluctant to exchange lottery tickets. *Journal of Personality and Social Psychology*, *93*(1), 12–22.

Risen, J. L. (2016). Believing what we do not believe: Acquiescence to superstitious beliefs and other powerful intuitions. *Psychological Review*, *123*(2), 182–207.

Rizzo, J. A., Zeckhauser, R. J. (2007). Pushing incomes to reference points: Why do male doctors earn more? *Journal of Economic Behavior and Organization*, *63*(3), 514–536.

Robbins, J. M., Ford, M. T., Tetrick, L. E. (2012). Perceived unfairness and employee health: A meta-analytic integration. *Journal of Applied Psychology*, *97*(2), 235–272.

Roberts, D. (2010). Post-truth politics. April 1. [Blog] Retrieved from http://grist.org/article/2010-03-30-post-truth-politics/.

Robinson, J. (1951). An iterative method of solving a game. *Annals of Mathematics*, *54*, 296–301.

Robson, A. (2002). Evolution and human nature. *Journal of Economic Perspectives*, *16*(2), 89–106.

Robson, A., Samuelson, L. (2007). The Evolution of intertemporal preferences. *American Economic Review. 97*(2), 496–500.

———. (2009). The Evolution of time preference under aggregate uncertainty. *American Economic Review*, *99*(5), 1925–1953.

Robson, A., Szentes, B. (2008). Evolution of time preference by natural selection: comment. *American Economic Review*, *98*(3), 1178–1188.

Rockenbach, B. (2004). The behavioral relevance of mental accounting for the pricing of option contracts. *Journal of Economic Behavior and Organization*, *53*, 513–527.

Roelofsma, P. (1994). *Intertemporal Choice*. Amsterdam: Free University.

Rogers, A. R. (1994). Evolution of time preference by natural selection. *American Economic Review*, *84*(3), 460–481.

Rohr, M., Kamm, F., Koenigstorfer, J., Groeppel-Klein, A., Wentura, D. (2015). The color red supports avoidance reactions to unhealthy food. *Experimental Psychology*, *62*(5), 335–345.

Romero, M., Biswas, D. (2016). Healthy-left, unhealthy-right: Can displaying healthy items to the left (versus right) of unhealthy items nudge healthier choices? *Journal of Consumer Research*, *43*(1), 103–112.

Rosenqvist, O., Skans, O. N. (2015). Confidence enhanced performance? – The causal effects of success on future performance in professional golf tournaments. *Journal of Economic Behavior and Organization*, *117*, 281–295.

Rosenzweig, E., Gilovich, T. (2012). Buyer's remorse or missed opportunity? Differential regrets for material and experiential purchases. *Journal of Personality and Social Psychology*, *102*(2), 215–223.

Ross, M., Sicoly, F. (1979). Egocentric biases in availability and attribution. *Journal of Personality and Social Psychology*, *37*, 322–336.

Roth, A. E., Malouf, M. (1979). Game-theoretic models and the role of information in bargaining. *Psychological Review*, *86*, 574–594.

Roth, A. E., Murnighan, J. K. (1982). The role of information in bargaining: An experimental study. *Econometrica*, *50*, 1123–1142.

Roth, A. E., Prasnikar, V., Okuno-Fujiwara, M., Zamir, S. (1991). Bargaining and market behavior in Jerusalem, Ljubljana, Pittsburgh and Tokyo: An experimental study. *American Economic Review*, *81*(5), 1068–1095.

Roth, A. E., Schoumaker, F. (1983). Expectations and reputations in bargaining: An experimental study. *American Economic Review*, *73*(3), 362–372.

Rousu, M.C., Corrigan, J.R., Harris, D., Hayter, J. K., Houser, S., Lafrancois, B. A., Onafowora, O., Colson, G., Hoffer, A. (2014). Do monetary incentives matter in classroom experiments? Effects on course performance. *The Journal of Economic Education,* *46*(4), 341–349.

Rozin, P., Fallon, A. E. (1987). A perspective on disgust. *Psychological Review*, *94*(1), 23–41.

Rozin, P., Millman, L., Nemeroff, C. (1986). Operation of the laws of sympathetic magic in disgust and other domains. *Journal of Personality and Social Psychology*, *40*(4), 703–712.

Rubinstein, A. (1988). Similarity and decision making under risk (Is there a utility solution to the Allais paradox?). *Journal of Economic Theory*, *46*, 145–153.

———. (1989). The electronic mail game: Strategic behavior under 'almost common knowledge'. *American Economic Review*, *79*(3), 385–391.

———. (2003). 'Economics and Psychology'? The case of hyperbolic discounting. *International Economic Review*, *44*(4), 1207–1216.

Rule, N. O., Krendl, A. C., Ivcevic, Z., Ambady, N. (2013). Accuracy and consensus in judgments of trustworthiness from faces: Behavioral and neural correlates. *Journal of Personality and Social Psychology*, *104*(3), 409–426.

Russell, J. A. (1980). A circumplex model of affect. *Journal of Personality and Social Psychology*, *39*, 1161–1178.

Russell, J. A., Carroll, J. M. (1999). On the bipolarity of positive and negative affect. *Psychological Bulletin*, *125*, 3–30.

Ryle, G. (1949). *The Concept of Mind*. Chicago: University of Chicago Press.

Sacks, D. W., Stevenson, B., Wolfers, J. (2012). The new stylized facts about income and subjective well-being. *Emotion*, *12*(6), 1181–1187.

Sagi, A., Friedland, N. (2007). The cost of richness: The effect of the size and diversity of decision sets on post-decision regret. *Journal of Personality and Social Psychology*, *93*(4), 515–524.

Saini, R., Monga, A. (2008). How I decide depends on what I spend: Use of heuristics is greater with time than for money. *Journal of Consumer Research*, *34*, 914–19.

Samper, A., Schwartz, J. A. (2013). Price inferences for sacred versus secular goods: Changing the price of medicine influences perceived health risk. *Journal of Consumer Research*, *39*(6), 1343–1358.

Samuelson, P. A. (1937). A note on measurement of utility. *Review of Economic Studies*, *4*, 155–161.

———. (1963). Risk and uncertainty: A fallacy of large numbers. In J. Stiglitz (Ed.), *Collected Scientific Papers of P. A. Samuelson* (Vol. 1, pp. 153–158). Cambridge MA: MIT Press.

Samuelson, W., Zeckhauser, R. (1988). Status quo bias in decision making. *Journal of Risk and Uncertainty, 1*, 7–59.

Sanfey, A. G., Rilling, J. K., Aronson, J. A., Nystrom, L. E., Cohen, J. D. (2003). The neural basis of economic decision-making in the ultimatum game. *Science*, *300*, 1755–1758.

Saunders, E. M., Jr. (1993). Stock prices and Wall Street weather. *American Economic Review*, *83*(5), 1337–1345.

Sausgruber, R., Tyran, J.-R. (2014). Discriminatory taxes are unpopular – Even when they are efficient and distributionally fair. *Journal of Economic Behavior and Organization*, *108*, 463–476.

Savary, J., Kleiman, T., Hassin, R. R., Dhar, R. (2015). Positive consequences of conflict on decision making: When a conflict mindset facilitates choice. *Journal of Experimental Psychology: General*, *144*(1), 1–6.

Sayman, S., Öncüler, A. (2009). An investigation of time inconsistency. *Management Science*, *55*(3), 470–482.

Scheibehenne, B., Greifeneder, R., Todd, P. M. (2010). Can there ever be too many options? A meta-analytic review of choice overload. *Journal of Consumer Research*, *37*, 409–425.

Schelling, T. C. (1960). *The Strategy of Conflict*. Cambridge, MA: Harvard University Press.

———. (1984). Self-command in practice, in policy, and in a theory of rational choice. *American Economic Review*, *74*(2), 1–11.

Schkade, D., Kahneman, D. (1998). Does living in California make people happy? A focusing illusion in judgements of life satisfaction. *Psychological Science*, *9*, 340–346.

Schley, D. (2013). When 15% off plus 10% off is more than 30% Off: Multiple-discount promotions are preferred to larger single-discount promotions. In S. Botti, A. Labroo (Eds), *NA Advances in Consumer Research* (Vol. 41). Duluth, MN: Association for Consumer Research. Retrieved from http://acrwebsite.org/volumes/1015657/volumes/v41/NA-41.

Schmidt, U., Starmer, C., Sugden, R. (2008). Third-generation prospect theory. *Journal of Risk and Uncertainty*, *36*(3), 203–223.

Schmidt, U., Zank, H. (2005). What is loss aversion? *Journal of Risk and Uncertainty*, *30*(2), 157–167.

Scholer, A. A., Zou, X., Fujita, K., Stroessner, S. J., Higgins, E. T. (2010). When risk seeking becomes a motivational necessity. *Journal of Personality and Social Psychology*, *99*(2), 215–231.

Scholten, M., Read, D. (2010). The psychology of intertermporal tradeoffs. *Psychological Review, 117*(3), 925–944.

Scholz, J. K., Seshadri, A., Khitatrakun, S. (2006). Are Americans saving 'optimally' for retirement? *Journal of Political Economy*, *114*(4), 607–643.

Schooler, J. W., Ariely, D., Loewenstein, G. (2001). The pursuit and assessment of happiness can be self-defeating. In I. Brocas, J. D. Carillo (Eds), *The Psychology of Economic Decisions* (pp. 41–70). New York: Oxford University Press.

Schultz, W., Apicella, P., Ljungberg, T. (1993). Responses of monkey dopamine neurons to reward and conditioned stimuli during successive steps of learning a delayed response task. *Journal of Neuroscience, 13*, 900–913.

Schulze, W., Maertens, A., Wansink, B. (2013). Eating dogfood: Examining the relative roles of reason and emotion. *Journal of Economic Behavior and Organization, 92*, 202–213.

Schwandt, H. (2016). Unmet aspirations as an explanation for the age U-shape in wellbeing. *Journal of Economic Behavior and Organization, 122*, 75–87.

Schwartz, J. M. (1999). A role for volition and attention in the generation of new brain circuitry: Toward a neurobiology of mental force. *Journal of Consciousness Studies, 6*, 115–142.

Schwarz, N. (1996). *Cognition and Communication: Judgmental Biases, Research Methods, and the Logic of Conversation.* Mahwah, NJ: Erlbaum.

Schwarz, N., Strack, F., Hilton, D., Naderer, G. (1991). Base rates, representativeness, and the logic of conversation: The contextual relevance of 'irrelevant' information. *Social Cognition, 9*, 67–84.

Schwarz, N., Strack, F., Kommer, D., Wagner, D. (1987). Soccer, rooms, and the quality of your life: Mood effects on judgments of satisfaction with life in general and with specific domains. *European Journal of Social Psychology, 17*, 69–79.

Schweitzer, M., Solnick, S. (1999). The influence of physical attractiveness and gender on ultimatum game decisions. *Organizational Behavior and Human Decision Processes, 79*, 199–215.

Scopelliti, I., Botti, S., Donato, C. (2013). Vicarious control: Exposure to mastery and perceived self-efficacy. In G. Cornelissen, E. Reutskaja, A. Valenzuela (Eds), *E - European Advances in Consumer Research* (Vol. 10, pp. 302–303). Duluth, MN: Association for Consumer Research, Pages. Retrieved from http://acrwebsite.org/volumes/1014161/volumes/v10e/E-10.

Seeyave, D. M., Coleman, S., Appugliese, D., Corwyn, R. F., Bradley, R. H., Davidson, N. S., Kaciroti N., Lumeng, J. C. (2009). Ability to delay gratification at age 4 years and risk of overweight at age 11 years. *Archives of Pediatrics and Adolescent Medicine, 163*(4), 303–308.

Sela, A., Simonson, I., Kivetz, R. (2013). Beating the market: The allure of unintended value. *Journal of Marketing, 50*(6), 691–705.

Selten, R. (1980). A note on evolutionarily stable strategies in asymmetric animal conflicts. *Journal of Theoretical Biology, 84*, 93–101.

Sen, A. K. (1977). Rational fools: A critique of the behavioral foundations of economic theory. *Philosophy and Public Affairs, 6*, 317–344.

———. (1987). *On Ethics and Economics.* Oxford: Blackwell.

———. (1990). Rational behavior. In J. Eatwell, M. Milgate, P. Newman (Eds), *The New Palgrave: Utility and Probability* (pp. 198–216). New York: Norton.

Senior, N. W. (1836). *An Outline of the Science of Political Economy.* London: Clowes and Sons.

Sevilla, J., Bagchi, R. (2014). The effect of numeric roundness on probability perceptions and choice. In J. Cotte, S. Wood (Eds), *NA – Advances in Consumer Research* (Vol. 42, pp. 672–676). Duluth, MN: Association for Consumer Research. Retrieved from http://acrwebsite.org/volumes/1018072/volumes/v42/NA-42.

Shachat, J. M. (2002). Mixed strategy play and the minimax hypothesis. *Journal of Economic Theory, 104*, 189–226.

Shaddy, F., Lee, L. (2012). A penny saved is another penny spurned: The effect of promotions on consumer impatience. In Z. Gürhan-Canli, C. Otnes, R. Zhu (Eds),

*NA – Advances in Consumer Research* (Vol. 40, pp. 911–912). Duluth, MN: Association for Consumer Research.

Shafir, E., LeBoeuf, R. (2002). Rationality. *Annual Review of Psychology*, *53*, 491–517.

Shafir, E., Diamond, P., Tversky, A. (1997). Money illusion. *Quarterly Journal of Economics*, *112*(2), 341–74.

Shah, A. K., Oppenheimer, D. M. (2008). Heuristics made easy: An effort-reduction framework. *Psychological Bulletin*, *134*(2), 207–222.

Shah, A. M., Eisenkraft, N., Bettman, J. R., Chartrand, T. L. (2013). 'Paper or plastic?': How we pay influences post-transaction connection. *Journal of Consumer Research*, *42*(5), 688–708.

Shah, J. Y., Kruglanski, A. W. (2002). Priming against your will: How accessible alternatives affect goal pursuit. *Journal of Experimental Social Psychology*, *38*(4), 368–383.

Shapiro, J. M. (2005). Is there a daily discount rate? Evidence from the food stamp nutrition cycle. *Journal of Public Economics*, *89*(2/3), 303–325.

Shapiro, M. D., Slemrod, J. (2003). Consumer response to tax rebates. *American Economic Review*, *93*, 381–396.

Shea, J. (1995a). Myopia, liquidity constraints, and aggregate consumption. *Journal of Money, Credit, Banking*, *27*(3), 798–805.

———. (1995b). Union contracts and the life cycle/permanent income hypothesis. *American Economic Review*, *85*(1), 186–200.

Shefrin, H. M., Statman, M. (1984). Explaining investor preference for cash dividends. *Journal of Financial Economics*, *13*, 253–282.

———. (1985). The disposition to sell winners too early and ride losers too long. *Journal of Financial Economics*, *40*, 777–790.

Shefrin, H. M., Thaler, R. H. (1992). Mental accounting, saving, and self-control. In G. Loewenstein, J. Elster (Eds), *Choice Over Time* (pp. 287–330). New York: Russell Sage.

Sherif, M., Sherif, C. W. (1964). *Reference Groups: Exploration into Conformity and Deviation of Adolescents*. New York: Harper and Row.

Shiv, B., Carmon, Z., Ariely, D. (2005). Placebo effects of marketing actions: Consumers may get what they pay for. *Journal of Marketing Research*, *42*(4), 383–393.

Shiv, B. and Fedorikhin, A. (1999). Heart and mind in conflict: The interplay of affect and cognition in consumer decision making. *Journal of Consumer Research, 26* (3), 278–292.

Shivakoti, G. P., Ostrom, E. (Eds). (2002). *Improving Irrigation Governance and Management in Nepal*. Oakland, CA: ICS Press.

Shoda, Y., Mischel, W., Peake, P. K. (1990). Predicting adolescent cognitive and self-regulatory competencies from preschool delay of gratification. *Developmental Psychology*, *26*(6), 978–986.

Shogren, J. F., Shin, S. Y., Hayes, D. J., Kliebenstein, J., B. (1994). Resolving differences in willingness to pay and willingness to accept. *American Economic Review*, *84*(1), 255–270.

Shue, K., Luttmer, E. F. P. (2009). Who misvotes? The effect of differential cognition costs on election outcomes. *American Economic Journal: Economic Policy*, *1*(1), 229–257.

Sieck, W., Yates, J. F. (1997). Exposition effects on decision making: Choice and confidence in choice. *Organizational Behavior and Human Decision Processes*, *70*, 207–219.

Siegel, J., Thaler, R. H. (1997). Anomalies: The equity premium puzzle. *Journal of Economic Perspectives*, *11*, 191–200.

Siemens, J. C. (2007). When consumption benefits precede costs: Towards an understanding of 'buy now, pay later' transactions. *Journal of Behavioral Decision Making*, *20*, 521–531.

Siganos, A., Vagenas-Nanos, E., Verwijmeren, P. (2014). Facebook's daily sentiment and international stock markets. *Journal of Economic Behavior and Organization*, *107*, 730–743.

Simon, H. A. (1955). A behavioral model of rational choice. *Quarterly Journal of Economics*, *69*, 99–118.

———. (1956). Rational choice and the structure of the environment. *Psychological Review*, *63*, 129–138.

———. (1957). *Models of Man: Social and Rational*. New York: Wiley.

———. (1959). Theories of decision making in economics and behavioral science. *American Economic Review*, *49*(3), 252–283.

———. (1978). Rationality as process and as product of thought. *American Economic Review, 68(2)*, 1–16.

———. (1990). Invariants of human behavior. *Annual Review of Psychology*, *41*, 1–19.

Simonsohn, U. (2010). Weather to go to college. *Economic Journal*, *120*(543), 270–280.

Simonson, I. (1990). The effect of purchase quantity and timing on variety-seeking behavior. *Journal of Marketing Research*, *17*, 150–162.

Simonson, I., Tversky, A. (1992). Choice in context: Tradeoff contrast and extremeness aversion. *Journal of Marketing Research*, *29*(3), 281–295.

Singer, T., Seymour, B., O'Doherty, J. P., Stephan, K. E., Dolan, R. J., Frith, C. D. (2006). Empathic neural responses are modulated by the perceived fairness of others. *Nature*, *439*(7075), 466–469.

Skiba, P. M., Tobacman, J. (2008). Payday loans, uncertainty, and discounting: Explaining patterns of borrowing, repayment and default. *Vanderbilt Law and Economics Research Paper*, No. 08-33. Retrieved from https://ssrn.com/abstract=1319751.

Sliwka, D. (2007). Trust as a signal of a social norm and the hidden costs of incentive schemes. *American Economic Review*, *97*(3), 999–1012.

Sloman, S. A. (1996). The empirical case for two systems of reasoning. *Psychological Bulletin*, *119*, 3–22.

Slonim, R. L. and Guillen, P. (2010). Gender selection discrimination: Evidence from a trust game. *Journal of Economic Behavior and Organization*, *76*(2), 385–405.

Slonim, R. L., Roth, A. E. (1998). Learning in high-stakes ultimatum games: An experiment in the Slovak republic. *Econometrica*, *66*, 569–596.

Slovic, P., Fischhoff, B., Lichtenstein, S. (1982). Response mode, framing, and information-processing effects in risk management. In R. Hogarth (Ed.), *New Directions for Methodology of Social and Behavioral Science* (pp. 21–36). San Francisco: Jossey-Bass.

Slovic, P., Lichtenstein, S. (1983). Preference reversals: A broader perspective. *American Economic Review*, *73*, 596–605.

Slugoski, B. R., Wilson, A. E. (1998). Contribution of conversation skills to the production of judgmental errors. *European Journal of Social Psychology*, *28*, 575–601.

Smaldino, P. E., McElreath, R. (2016). The natural selection of bad science. *Royal Society Open Science*, *3*(9), 160384.

Smith, A. [1759] (2000). *The Theory of Moral Sentiments*. Amherst, NY: Prometheus.

Smith, E. A., Bird, R. B. (2005). Costly signaling and cooperative behavior. In H. Gintis, S. Bowles, R. Boyd, E. Fehr (Eds), *Moral Sentiments and Material Interests: The Foundations of Cooperation in Economic Life* (pp. 115–148). Cambridge, MA: MIT Press.

Smith, G., Levere, M., Kurtzman, R. (2009). Poker player behavior after big wins and big losses. *Management Science*, *55*(9), 1547–1555.

Smith, P. K., Bogin, B., Bishai, D. (2005). Are time preference and body mass index associated? *Economics and Human Biology*, *3*(2), 259–270.

Smith, S. M., Levin, I. P. (1996). Need for cognition and choice framing effects. *Journal of Behavioral Decision Making*, *9*, 283–290.

Smith, V. L. (1990). *Schools of Economic Thought: Experimental Economics*. Aldershot: Edward Elgar.

———. (1991). Rational choice: The contrast between economics and psychology. *Journal of Political Economy*, *99*, 877–897.

Soll, J. B., Klayman, J. (2004). Overconfidence in interval estimates. *Journal of Experimental Psychology: Learning, Memory, and Cognition*, *30*, 299–314.

Solnick, S. J. (2001). Gender differences in the ultimatum game. *Economic Inquiry*, *39*, 189–200.

Solomon, R. L. (1980). The opponent-process theory of acquired motivation. *American Psychologist*, *35*, 691–712.

Soman, D. (1997). Contextual effects of payment mechanism on purchase intention: Check or charge? Unpublished Working Paper, University of Colorado.

———. (2004). The effect of time delay on multi-attribute choice. *Journal of Economic Psychology*, *25*(2), 153–175.

Soman, D., Cheema, A. (2002). The effect of credit on spending decisions: The role of the credit limit and credibility. *Marketing Science*, *21*(1), 32–53.

Soman, D., Gourville, J. T. (2001). Transaction decoupling: How price bundling affects the decision to consume. *Journal of Marketing Research*, *38*(1), 30–44.

Soster, R. L., Monga, A., Bearden, W. O. (2010). Tracking costs of time and money: How accounting periods affect mental accounting. *Journal of Consumer Research*, *37*(4), 712–721.

Spitzer, M., Fischbacher, U., Herrnberger, B., Grön, G., Fehr, E. (2007). The neural signature of social norm compliance. *Neuron*, *56*, 185–196.

Stahl, D. O. (1996). Boundedly rational rule learning in a guessing game. *Games and Economic Behavior*, *16*, 303–30.

———. (1999a). Evidence based rules and learning in symmetric normal-form games. *International Journal of Game Theory*, *28*, 111–30.

———. (1999b). Sophisticated learning and learning sophistication. Working Paper, No. 99002, Center for Applied Research in Economics, University of Texas. Retrieved from https://papers.ssrn.com/sol3/papers.cfm?abstract_id=410921.

———. (2000). Rule learning in symmetric normal-form games. *Games and Economic Behavior*, *32*, 105–38.

———. (2001). Population rule learning in normal-form games: Theory and evidence. *Journal of Economic Behavior and Organization*, *45*, 19–35.

———. (2004). Action-reinforcement learning versus rule learning. In D. J. Zizzo (Ed.), *Transfer of Knowledge in Economic Decision Making* (pp. 44–72). London: Palgrave Macmillan.

Stahl, D. O., Wilson, P. (1995). On players' models of other players: Theory and experimental evidence. *Games and Economic Behavior*, *10*, 218–254.

Stanovich, K. E. (1999). *Who is Rational? Studies of Individual Differences in Reasoning*. Mahwah, NJ: Erlbaum.

Stanovich, K. E., West, R.F. (1999). Discrepancies between normative and descriptive models of decision making and the understanding/acceptance principle. *Cognitive Psychology*, *38*, 349–385.

———. (1998). Individual differences in framing and conjunction effects. *Thinking and Reasoning, 4*, 289–317.

Starmer, C. (1999). Cycling with rules of thumb: An experimental test for a new form of non-transitive behaviour. *Theory and Decision, 46*, 141–158.

———. (2000). Developments in non-expected utility theory: The hunt for a descriptive theory of choice under risk. *Journal of Economic Literature, 38*, 332–382.

———. (2005). Normative notions in descriptive dialogues. *Journal of Economic Methodology, 12*(2), 277–289.

Starmer, C., Sugden, R. (1989). Violations of the independence axiom in common ratio problems: An experimental test of some competing hypotheses. *Annals of Operations Research, 19*, 79–102.

———. (1993). Testing for juxtaposition and event-splitting effects. *Journal of Risk and Uncertainty, 6*, 235–54.

———. (1998). Testing alternative explanations of cyclical choices. *Economica, 65*(259), 347–361.

Stavrova, O., Ehlebracht, D. (2016). Cynical beliefs about human nature and income: Longitudinal and cross-cultural analyses. *Journal of Personality and Social Psychology, 110*(1), 116–132.

Steel, P. (2007). The nature of procrastination: A meta-analytic and theoretical review of quintessential self-regulatory failure. *Psychological Bulletin, 133*(1), 65–94.

Stein, E. (1996). *Without Good Reason: The Rationality Debate in Philosophy and Cognitive Science*. New York: Oxford University Press.

Stein, R., Ackerman, J., Bargh, J. (2012). Rebels without a clue: Nonconscious motivation for autonomy preservation moderates social decision biases. In Z. Gürhan-Canli, C. Otnes, R. Zhu (Eds), *NA – Advances in Consumer Research* (Vol. 40, pp. 701–702). Duluth, MN: Association for Consumer Research. Retrieved from http://acrwebsite.org/volumes/1011751/volumes/v40/NA-40.

Steiner, A. P., Redish, A. D. (2014). Behavioral and neurophysiological correlates of regret in rat decision-making on a neuroeconomic task. *Nature Neuroscience, 17*(7), 995–1002.

Sterling, P., Eyer, J. (1988). Allostasis: A new paradigm to explain arousal pathology. In S. Fisher, J. Reason (Eds), *Handbook of Life Stress, Cognition and Health* (pp. 629–648). Chichester: Wiley.

Stevenson, B., Wolfers, J. (2009). The paradox of declining female happiness. *American Economic Journal: Economic Policy, 1*(2), 190–225.

Stewart, J., Wise, R. A. (1992). Reinstatement of heroin self-administration habits: Morphine prompts and naltrexone discourages renewed responding after extinction. *Psychopharmacology, 108*, 779–784.

Stigler, G. J. (1950). The development of utility theory. II. *Journal of Political Economy, 58*(5), 373–396.

———. (1981). Economics or ethics? In S. M. McMurrin (Ed.), *The Tanner Lectures on Human Values* (Vol. 2, pp. 145–191). Salt Lake City: University of Utah Press.

Stirrat, M., Perrett, D. I. (2010). Valid facial cues to cooperation and trust. *Psychological Science, 21*(3), 349–354.

Stone, A. A. (1995). Measures of affective response. In S. Cohen, R. Kessler, L. Gordon (Eds), *Measuring Stress: A Guide for Social and Health Scientists* (pp. 148–171). New York: Cambridge University Press.

Stone, E. R., Yates, F., Parker, A. M. (1994). Risk communication: Absolute versus relative expressions of low-probability risks. *Organizational Behavior and Human Decision Processes, 60*, 387–408.

Stouffer, S. A., Lumsdaine, A. A., Lumsdaine, M. H., Williams, R. M., Jr., Smith, I. L., Cottrell, L. S., Jr. (1949). *The American Soldier*. Princeton: Princeton University Press.

Strack, F., Martin, L. L., Stepper, S. (1988). Inhibiting and facilitating conditions of the human smile: A nonobtrusive test of the facial feedback hypothesis. *Journal of Personality and Social Psychology*, *54*(5), 768–777.

Straub, P., Murnighan, K. (1995). An experimental investigation of ultimatum games: Information, fairness, expectations, and lowest acceptable offers. *Journal of Economic Behavior and Organization*, *27*, 345–364.

Strotz, R. H. (1955). Myopia and inconsistency in dynamic utility maximization. *Review of Economic Studies*, *23*, 165–180.

Strough, J., Schlosnagle, L., Karns, T., Lemaster, P., Pichayayothin, N. (2013). No time to waste: Restricting life-span temporal horizons decreases the sunk-cost fallacy. *Journal of Behavioral Decision Making*, *27*(1), 78–94.

Suh, E., Diener, E., Fujita, F. (1996). Events and subjective well-being: Only recent events matter. *Journal of Personality and Social Psychology*, *70*, 1091–1102.

Suk, K., Lee, J., Lichtenstein, D. R. (2012). The influence of price presentation order on consumer choice. *Journal of Marketing Research*, *49*(5), 708–717.

Sunstein, C. R. (2002). Probability neglect: Emotions, worst cases, and law. *Yale Law Journal*, *112*(1), 61.

Sunstein, C. R., Kahneman, D., Schkade, D. A. (1998). Assessing punitive damages. *Yale Law Journal*, *107(7)*, 2071–2153.

Suri, G., Sheppes, G., Leslie, S., Gross, J. J. (2014). Stairs or escalator? Using theories of persuasion and motivation to facilitate healthy decision making. *Journal of Experimental Psychology: Applied*, *20*(4), 295–302.

Sutter, M., Kocher, M. G., Glätzle-Rützler, D., Trautmann, S. T. (2013). Impatience and uncertainty: Experimental decisions predict adolescents' field behavior. *American Economic Review*, *103*(1), 510–531.

Sutton, S. K., Davidson, R. J. (1997). Prefrontal brain asymmetry: A biological substrate of behavioral approach and inhibition systems. *Psychological Science*, *8*, 204–210.

Svenson, O. (1981). Are we all less risky and more skilful than our fellow drivers? *Acta Psychologica*, *47*(2), 143–148.

Svirsky, D. (2014). Money is no object: Testing the endowment effect in exchange goods. *Journal of Economic Behavior and Organization*, *106*, 227–234.

Swann, J., William B., Gill, M. J. (1997). Confidence and accuracy in person perception: Do we know what we think we know about our relationship partners? *Journal of Personality and Social Psychology*, *73*(4), 747–757.

Tabibnia, G., Satpute, A. B., Lieberman, M. D. (2008). The sunny side of fairness: Preference for fairness activates reward circuitry (and disregarding unfairness activates self-control circuitry). *Psychological Science*, *19*(4), 339–347.

Takemura, K. (1993). The effect of decision frame and decision justification on risky choice. *Japanese Psychological Research*, *35*, 36–40.

———. (1994). Influence of elaboration on the framing of decisions. *Journal of Psychology*, *128*, 33–39.

Taleb, N. N. (2007). *The Black Swan*. New York: Random House.

Tang, W., Bearden, J. N., Tsetlin, I. (2009). Ultimatum deadlines. *Management Science*, *55*(8), 1423–1437.

Taylor, S. E. (1991). Asymmetrical effects of positive and negative events: The mobilization-minimization hypothesis. *Psychological Bulletin*, *110*, 67–85.

Temple, J. L., Giacomelli, A. M., Kent, K. M., Roemmich, J. N., Epstein, L. H. (2007). Television watching increases motivated responding for food and energy intake in children. *American Journal of Clinical Nutrition*, *85*, 355–361.

Terrell, D. (1994). A test of the gambler's fallacy: Evidence from pari-mutuel games. *Journal of Risk and Uncertainty*, *8*(3), 309–317.

Tetlock, P. E. (1999). Theory-driven reasoning about plausible pasts and probable futures in world politics: Are we prisoners of our preconceptions? *American Journal of Political Science*, *43*(2), 335–366.

———. (2002). Social functionalist frameworks for judgment and choice: Intuitive politicians, theologians, and prosecutors. *Psychological Review*, *109*, 451–471.

———. (2005). Gauging the heuristic value of heuristics. *Behavioral and Brain Sciences*, *28*(4), 562–563.

Tetlock, P., Kristel, O. V., Elson, B., Green, M., Lerner, J. (2000). The psychology of the unthinkable: Taboo trade-offs, forbidden base rates, and heretical counterfactuals. *Journal of Personality and Social Psychology*, *78*, 853–870.

Thaler, R. H. (1980). Toward a positive theory of consumer choice. *Journal of Economic Behavior and Organization*, *1*, 39–60.

———. (1981). Some empirical evidence on dynamic inconsistency. *Economic Letters*, *8*, 201–207.

———. (1985). Mental accounting and consumer choice. *Marketing Science*, *4*, 199–214.

———. (1999). Mental accounting matters. *Journal of Behavioral Decision Making*, *12*, 183–206.

———. (2015). *Misbehaving*. New York: Norton.

Thaler, R. H., Johnson, E. J. (1990). Gambling with the house money and trying to break even: The effects of prior outcomes on risky choice. *Management Science*, *36*(6), 643–60.

Thaler, R. H., Shefrin. (1981). An economic theory of self-control. *Journal of Political Economy*, *89*(2), 392–406.

Thaler, R. H., Sunstein , C. R. (2009). *Nudge*. London: Penguin.

Thaler, R. H., Tversky, A., Kahneman, D., Schwartz, A. (1997). The effect of myopia and loss-aversion on risk taking: An experimental test. *Quarterly Journal of Economics*, *112*, 647–661.

Thaler, R. H., Ziemba, W. (1988). Parimutuel betting markets: Racetracks and lotteries. *Journal of Economic Perspectives*, *2*, 161–174.

Thomas, M., Park, J. (2012). Do emotions decrease or increase present bias in monetary decisions? In Z. Gürhan-Canli, C. Otnes, R. Zhu (Eds), *NA - Advances in Consumer Research* (Vol. 40, pp. 293–297). Duluth, MN: Association for Consumer Research. Retrieved from www.acrwebsite.org/volumes/1012950/volumes/v40/NA-40.

Tice, D. M., Baumeister, R. F. (1997). Longitudinal study of procrastination, performance, stress, and health: The costs and benefits of dawdling. *Psychological Science*, *8*, 454–458.

Tice, D. M., Baumeister, R. F., Shmueli, D., Muraven, M. (2007). Restoring the self: Positive affect helps improve self-regulation following ego depletion. *Journal of Experimental Social Psychology*, *43*(3), 379–384.

Tierney, J. (2011). Urge to own that Clapton guitar is contagious, scientists find. *New York Times*, 9 March, p. A16.

Titmuss, R. M. (1971). The gift of blood. In B. Abel-Smith, K. Titmuss (Eds), *The Philosophy of Welfare: Selected Writings by R.M. Titmuss*. London: Allen and Unwin, 1987.

Tobin, J. (1972). Inflation and unemployment. *American Economic Review*, *62*(1), 1–18.

Tom, S. M., Fox, C. R., Trepel, C., Poldrack, R. A. (2007). The neural basis of loss aversion in decision making under risk. *Science*, *315*, 515–518.

Tooby, J., Cosmides, L. (1984). The psychological foundations of culture. In J. H. Barkow, L. Cosmides, J. Tooby (Eds), *The Adapted Mind* (pp. 19–136). Oxford: Oxford University Press.

Tooby, J., Cosmides, L. (2000). *Evolutionary Psychology: Foundational Papers*. Cambridge, MA: MIT Press.

Townsend, C., Liu, W. (2012). Is planning good for you? The differential impact of planning on self-regulation. *Journal of Consumer Research*, *39*(4), 688–703.

Train, K. (1985). Discount rates in consumers' energy-related decisions: A review of the literature. *Energy*, *10*(12), 1243–1253.

———. (1991). *Optimal Regulation*. Cambridge, MA: MIT Press.

Tricomi, E., Rangel, A., Camerer, C. F., O'Doherty, J. (2010). Neural evidence for inequality-averse social preferences. *Nature*, *463*, 1089–1092.

Trivers, R. (1971). The evolution of reciprocal altruism. *Quarterly Review of Biology*, *46*, 35–57.

———. (1985). *Social Evolution*. Menlo Park, CA: Cummings.

———. (2013). *Deceit and Self-deception*. London: Penguin.

Tuk, M. A., Zhang, K., Sweldens, S. (2015). The propagation of self-control: Self-control in one domain simultaneously improves self-control in other domains. *Journal of Experimental Psychology: General*, *144*(3), 639–654.

Tversky, A., Griffin, D. (2000). Endowments and contrast in judgments of well-being. In D. Kahneman, A. Tversky (Eds), *Choices, Values and Frames* (pp. 709–725). New York: Cambridge University Press.

Tversky, A., Kahneman, D. (1971). Belief in the law of small numbers. *Psychological Bulletin*, *76*, 105–110.

———. (1973). Availability: A heuristic for judging frequency and probability. *Cognitive Psychology*, *5*, 207–232.

———. (1981). The framing of decisions and the psychology of choice. *Science*, *211*, 453–458.

———. (1982). Evidential impact of base rates. In D. Kahneman, P. Slovic, A. Tversky (Eds), *Judgement under Uncertainty: Heuristics and Biases* (pp. 153–160). New York: Cambridge University Press.

———. (1983). Extensional versus intuitive reasoning: The conjunction fallacy in probability judgement. *Psychological Review*, *90*, 293–315.

———. (1986). Rational choice and the framing of decisions. *Journal of Business*, *59*, 251–278.

———. (1992). Advances in prospect theory: Cumulative representation of uncertainty. *Journal of Risk and Uncertainty*, *5*, 297–323.

Tversky, A., Koehler, D. K. (1994). Support theory: A nonextensional representation of subjective probability. *Psychological Review*, *101*(4), 547–567.

Tversky, A., Sattath, S., Slovic, P. (1988). Contingent weighting in judgment and choice. *Psychological Review*, *93*(3), 371–384.

Tversky, A., Shafir, E. (1992). Choice under conflict. The dynamics of deferred decision. *Psychological Science*, *3*(6), 358–361.

Tversky, A., Slovic, P., Kahneman, D. (1990). The causes of preference reversal. *American Economic Review*, *80*, 204–217.

Ülkümen, G., Thomas, M., Morwitz, V. G. (2008). Will I spend more in 12 months or a year? The effect of ease of estimation and confidence on budget estimates. *Journal of Consumer Research*, *35*, 245–256.

Usta, M., Häubl, G. (2011). Self-regulatory strength and consumers' relinquishment of decision control: When less effortful decisions are more resource depleting. *Journal of Marketing Research*, *48*(2), 403–412.

Vaillant, G. (2000). Adaptive mental mechanisms: Their role in positive psychology. *American Psychologist*, *55*, 89–98.

Valley, K., Thompson, L., Gibbons, R., Bazerman, M. H. (2002). How communication improves efficiency in bargaining games. *Games and Economic Behavior*, *38*, 127–155.

Van Boven, L., White, K., Huber, M. (2009). Immediacy bias in emotion perception: Current emotions seem more intense that previous emotions. *Journal of Experimental Psychology: General*, *138*(3), 368–382.

Van der Pol, M. (2010). Health, education and time preference. *Health Economics*, *20*(8), 917–929.

Van Dillen, L. F., Papies, E. K., Hofmann, W. (2013). Turning a blind eye to temptation: How cognitive load can facilitate self-regulation. *Journal of Personality and Social Psychology*, *104*(3), 427–443.

Van Ittersum, K., Wansink, B. (2012). Plate size and color suggestibility: The Delboeuf Illusion's bias on serving and eating behavior. *Journal of Consumer Research*, *39*(2), 215–228.

———. (2013). Extraverted children are more biased by bowl sizes than introverts. *PLoS ONE*, *8*(10), e78224.

Varey, C. A., Kahneman, D. (1992). Experiences extended across time: Evaluation of moments and episodes. *Journal of Behavioral Decision Making*, *5*(3), 169–185.

Veblen, T. (1898). Why is economics not an evolutionary science? *Quarterly Journal of Economics*, *12*(4), 373–397.

Veenhoven, R. (1988). Utility of happiness. *Social Indicators Research*, *20*, 333–354.

Veenhoven, R., Vergunst, F. (2014). The Easterlin Illusion: Economic growth does go with greater happiness. *International Journal of Happiness and Development*, *1*(4), 311–343.

Veit, R., Flor, H., Erb, M., Hermann, C., Lotze, M., Grodd, W., Birbaumer, N. (2002). Brain circuits involved in emotional learning in antisocial behavior and social phobia in humans. *Neuroscience Letters*, *328*(3), 233–236.

Venti, S. F., Wise, D. A. (1989). Aging, moving, and housing wealth. In D. A. Wise (Ed.), *Economics of Aging* (pp. 9–48). Chicago: University of Chicago Press.

Vohs, K. D., Baumeister, R. F., Schmeichel, B. J., Twenge, J. M., Nelson, N. M., Tice, D. M. (2008). Making choices impairs subsequent self-control: A limited-resource account of decision making, self-regulation, and active initiative. *Journal of Personality and Social Psychology*, *94*(5), 883–898.

Vollaard, B. (2012). Preventing crime through selective incapacitation. *Economic Journal*, *123*(567), 262–284.

Von Mises, L. (1949). *Human Action: A Treatise on Economics*. London: Hodge

Von Neumann, J., Morgenstern, O. (1944). *The Theory of Games and Economic Behavior*. Princeton: Princeton University Press.

Vosgerau, J. (2010). How prevalent is wishful thinking? Misattribution of arousal causes optimism and pessimism in subjective probabilities. *Journal of Experimental Psychology*, *139*(1), 32–48.

Waber, R. L., Shiv, B., Carmon, Z., Ariely, D. (2008). Commercial features of placebo and therapeutic efficacy. *JAMA*, *299*(9), 1016–1017.

Wadhwa, M., Zhang, K. (2015). This number just feels right: The impact of roundedness of price numbers on product evaluations. *Journal of Consumer Research*, *41*(5), 1172–1185.

Wager, T. D., Rilling, J. K., Smith, E. E., Sokolik, A., Casey, K. L., Davidson, R. J., Kosslyn, S. M., Rose, R. M., Cohen, J. D. (2004). Placebo-induced changes in fMRI in the anticipation and experience of pain. *Science*, *303*, 1162–1167.

Wakker, P. P. (2003). The data of Levy and Levy. *Management Science*, *49*(7), 979–981.

Wakker, P. P., Thaler, R. H., Tversky, A. (1997). Probabilistic insurance. *Journal of Risk and Uncertainty*, *15*, 5–26.

Walker, M., Wooders, J. (2001). Minimax play at Wimbledon. *American Economic Review*, *91*(5), 1528–1538.

Wan, E. W., Sternthal, B. (2008). Regulating the effects of depletion through monitoring. *Personality and Social Psychology Bulletin*, *34*(1), 32–46.

Wang, P., Mariman, E. C. (2008). Insulin resistance in an energy-centered perspective. *Physiology and Behavior*, *94*(2), 198–205.

Wang, X. T. (1996). Framing effects: Dynamics and task domains. *Organizational Behavior and Human Decision Processes*, *68*, 145–157.

Wang, X. T., Johnston, V. S. (1995). Perceived social context and risk preference: A reexamination of framing effects in a life-death decision problem. *Journal of Behavioral Decision Making*, *8*, 279–293.

Wansink, B. (2006). *Mindless Eating – Why We Eat More Than We Think*. New York: Bantam-Dell.

Wansink, B., Cheney, M. M. (2005). Super bowls: Serving bowl size and food consumption. *Journal of the American Medical Association*, *293*(14), 1727–1728.

Wansink, B., Hanks, A. S., Just, D. R. (2012). From Coke to Coors: A field study of a fat tax and its unintended consequences (May 26). Available at SSRN: https://ssrn.com/abstract=2079840 or http://dx.doi.org/10.2139/ssrn.2079840.

Wansink, B., Just, D. R., Payne, C. R. (2009). Mindless eating and healthy heuristics for the irrational. *American Economic Review*, *99*(2), 165–169.

Wansink, B., van Ittersum, K., Payne, C. R. (2014). Larger bowl size increases the amount of cereal children request, consume, and waste. *Journal of Pediatrics*, *164*(2), 323–326.

Warr, P. (1999). Well-being and the workplace. In D. Kahneman, E. Diener, N. Schwarz (Eds), *Well-being: The Foundations of Hedonic Psychology* (pp. 392–412). New York: Cambridge University Press.

Wason, P. C. (1966). Reasoning. In B. M. Foss (Ed.), *New Horizons in Psychology* (pp. 135–151). Harmondsworth: Penguin.

Weber, J. M., Murnighan, J. K. (2008). Suckers or saviors? Consistent contributors in social dilemmas. *Journal of Personality and Social Psychology*, *95*(6), 1340–1353.

Weber, R. (2001). Behavior and learning in the 'dirty faces' game. *Experimental Economics*, *4*, 229–242.

Wegner, D. M. (1994). Ironic processes of mental control. *Psychological Review*, *101*, 34–52.

———. (2002). *The Illusion of Conscious Will*. Cambridge, MA: MIT Press.

Weil, P. (1989). The equity premium puzzle and the risk-free rate puzzle. *Journal of Monetary Economics*, *15*, 145–161.

Weinberg, S. L. (2004). The diet-heart hypothesis: A critique. *Journal of the American College of Cardiology, 43*(5), 731–733.

Weinstein, N. D. (1980). Unrealistic optimism about future life events. *Journal of Personality and Social Psychology, 39*, 806–820.

Weller, R. E., Cook, E. W., Avsar, K. B., Cox, J. E. (2008). Obese women show greater delay discounting than healthy-weight women. *Appetite, 51*(3), 563–569.

Wertenbroch, K. (1998). Consumption self-control by rationing purchase quantities of virtue and vice. *Marketing Science, 17*(4), 317–337.

———. (1999). Firm profits and consumer psychology: Consumers pay more for less of what they like too much. *U.S. Industry Today, 21* December.

Wetherick, N. E. (1971). Representativeness in a reasoning problem: A reply to Shapiro. *Bulletin of the British Psychological Society, 24*, 213–214.

Wilcox, K., Vallen, B., Block, L., Fitzsimons, G. (2009). Vicarious goal fulfilment: When the mere presence of a healthy option leads to an ironically indulgent decision. *Journal of Consumer Research, 36*(3), 380–393.

Wilkinson, G. S. (1984). Reciprocal food sharing in the vampire bat. *Nature, 308*, 181–184.

Wilkinson, J. N. (1996). Marketing in the health club industry. Ph.D. dissertation, City University, London.

———. (2003). Frequency of price promotion: A consumer deadline model. *Working Paper*, Department of Business and Economics, Richmond the American International University in London.

———. (2004). Utility theory and evolutionary psychology: Some implications and empirical evidence. *Working Paper*, Department of Business and Economics, Richmond the American International University in London.

Williams, C. A. Jr. (1966a). Attitudes toward speculative risks as an indicator of attitudes toward pure risks. *Journal of Risk and Insurance, 33*, 577–586.

Williams, E. F., Dunning, D., Kruger, J. (2013). The hobgoblin of consistency: Algorithmic judgment strategies underlie inflated self-assessments of performance. *Journal of Personality and Social Psychology, 104*(6), 976–994.

Williams, G. C. (1966b). *Adaptation and Natural Selection: A Critique of Some Current Evolutionary Thought*. Princeton: Princeton University Press.

Wilson, E. O. (1998). *Consilience*. London: Little, Brown.

Wilson, T. D., Lindsay, S., Schooler, T. Y. (2000). A model of dual attitudes. *Psychological Review, 107*(1), 101–126.

Wilson, T. D., Schooler, T. Y. (1991). Thinking too much: Introspection can reduce the quality of preferences and decisions. *Journal of Personality and Social Psychology, 60*(2), 181–192.

Wilson, T. D., Wheatley, T., Meyers, J. M., Gilbert, D. T., Axsom, D. (2000). Focalism: A source of durability bias in affective forecasting. *Journal of Personality and Social Psychology, 78*, 821–836.

Windmann, S., Kirsch, P., Mier, D. (2006). On framing effects in decision making: Linking lateral versus medial orbitofrontal cortex activation to choice outcome processing. *Journal of Cognitive Neuroscience, 18*, 1198–1211.

Winkler, R. (2006). Does 'better' discounting lead to 'worse' outcomes in long-run decisions? The dilemma of hyperbolic discounting. *Ecological Economics, 57*(4), 573–582.

Winston, G. C. (1980). Addiction and backsliding: A theory of compulsive consumption. *Journal of Economic Behavior and Organization, 1*, 295–324.

Witt, U. (2011). Economic behavior: Evolutionary versus behavioral perspectives. *Biological Theory*, *6*(4), 388–398.

Wong, W. K. (2008). How much time-inconsistency is there and does it matter? Evidence on self-awareness, size, and effects. *Journal of Economic Behavior and Organization*, *68*, 645–656.

Woodford, M. (2012). Prospect theory as efficient perceptual distortion. *American Economic Review*, *102*(3), 41–46.

World Values Study Group. (1994). *World Values Survey, 1981–1984 and 1990–1993* [data]. Ann Arbor, MI: Institute for Social Research and Inter-university Consortium for Political and Social Research.

Wortman, C. B., Silver, R. C., Kessler, R. C. (1993). The meaning of loss and adjustment to bereavement. In M. S. Stroebe, W. Stroebe, R. O. Hansson (Eds), *Handbook of Bereavement: Theory, Research, and Intervention* (pp. 349–366). New York: Cambridge University Press.

Wozniak, D. (2012). Gender differences in a market with relative performance feedback: Professional tennis players. *Journal of Economic Behavior and Organization*, *83*, 158–171.

Wu, G., Gonzalez, R. (1996). Curvature of the probability weighting function. *Management Science, 42*, 1676–1690.

Wu, G., Markle, A. B. (2008). An empirical test of gain-loss separability in prospect theory. *Management Science*, *54*(7), 1322–1335.

Wunsch, J. S., Olowu, D. (Eds). (1995). *The Failure of the Centralized State: Institutions and Self-Governance in Africa* (2nd ed). Oakland, CA: ICS Press.

Xiao, E., Houser, D. (2005). Emotion expression in human punishment behavior. *PNAS - Proceedings of the National Academy of Sciences*, *102*(20), 7398–7401.

Yang, H., Carmon, Z., Dhar, R. (2012). More possessions can make you less happy. In Z. Gürhan-Canli, C. Otnes, R. Zhu (Eds), *NA – Advances in Consumer Research* (Vol. 40, pp. 106–111). Duluth, MN: Association for Consumer Research.

Yang, S., Lynn, M. (2014). More evidence challenging the robustness and usefulness of the attraction effect. *Journal of Marketing Research*, *51*(4), 508–513.

Yang, X., Mao, H., Jia, L., Bublitz, M. (2014). How exposure to romantic stimuli affects consumer preference for sweet food. In J. Cotte, S. Wood (Eds), *NA – Advances in Consumer Research Volume 42* (pp. 748–749). Duluth, MN: Association for Consumer Research. Retrieved from http://acrwebsite.org/volumes/1018055/volumes/v42/NA-42.

Yariv, L. (2002). I'll see it when I believe it: A simple model of cognitive consistency. *Cowles Foundation Discussion Paper*, (No. 1352). Retrieved from http://cowles.yale.edu/cfdp-1352.

Yates, J. F., Watts, R. A. (1975). Preferences for deferred losses. *Organizational Behavior and Human Performance*, *13*(2), 294–306.

Yilmaz, M. (2013). Repeated moral hazard with a time-inconsistent agent. *Journal of Economic Behavior and Organization*, *95*, 70–89.

Yoo, K.-Y., de Serres, A. (2004). Tax treatment of private pension savings in OECD countries and the net tax cost per unit of contribution to tax-favoured schemes. Working Paper, No. 406, OECD Economics Department, Paris. Retrieved from http://dx.doi.org/10.1787/387535760801.

Yuan, J., Sun, G.-Z., Siu, R. (2014). The lure of illusory luck: How much are people willing to pay for random shocks. *Journal of Economic Behavior and Organization*, *106*, 269–280.

Yusuf, S., Hawken, S., Ounpuu, S., Dans, T., Avezum ,A., Lanas, F., McQueen, M., Budaj, A., Pais, P., Varigos, J., Lisheng, L. (2004). Effect of potentially modifiable risk factors associated with myocardial infarction in 52 countries (the INTERHEART study): case-control study. *Lancet*, *364*(9438), 937–952.

Zahavi, A. (1975). Mate selection: A selection for a handicap. *Journal of Theoretical Biology*, *53*, 205–214.

Zak, P. J. (2011). The physiology of moral sentiments. *Journal of Economic Behavior and Organization*, *77*(1), 53–65.

Zak, P. J., Kurzban, R., Ahmadi, S., Swerdloff, R. S., Park, J., Efremidze, L., Redwine, K., Morgan, K., Matzner, W. T. (2009). Testosterone Administration Decreases Generosity in the Ultimatum Game. *PLoS ONE*, *4*(12), e8330.

Zak, P. J., Kurzban, R., Matzner, W. T. (2004). The neurobiology of trust. *Annals of the New York Academy of Sciences*, *1032*, 224–227.

Zak, P. J., Stanton, A. A., Ahmadi, S. (2007). Oxytocin increases generosity in humans. *PLoS ONE*, *2*(11), e 1128.

Zhang, L., Rashad, I. (2007). Obesity and time preference: The health consequences of discounting the future. *Journal of Biosocial Science*, *40*(1), 97–113.

Zhang, Y., Shrum, L. J. (2009). The influence of self-construal on impulsive consumption. *Journal of Consumer Research*, *35*(5), 838–850.

Zhong, C.-B., Bohns, V. K., Gino, F. (2010). Good lamps are the best police. *Psychological Science*, *21*(3), 311–314.

Zhou, C. (1999). Informational asymmetry and market imperfections: Another solution to the equity premium puzzle. *Journal of Financial and Quantitative Analysis*, *34*(4), 445–469.

Zhu, R., Chen, X., Dasgupta, S. (2008). Can trade-ins hurt you? Exploring the effect of a trade-in on consumers' willingness to pay for a new product. *Journal of Marketing Research*, *45*, 159–170.

Zillman, D. (1978). Attribution and misattribution of excitatory reactions. In J. H. Harvey, W. J. Ickes, R. F. Kidd (Eds), *New Directions in Attribution Research* (Vol. 2, pp. 335–368). Hillsdale, NJ: Erlbaum.

Zimbardo, P. G. (1972). Comment: Pathology of imprisonment. *Society*, *9*(6), 4–8.

Zink, C. F., Pagnoni, G., Martin, M. E. (2003). Human striatal response to salient nonrewarding stimuli. *Journal of Neuroscience*, *23*, 8092–8097.

Zuckerman, M. (1979). Attributions of success and failure revisited, or: The motivational bias is alive and well in attribution theory. *Journal of Personality*, *47*, 245–287.

# Index